OpenMP Application Programming Interface Specification Version 5.0

OpenMP Architecture Review Board
Edited by Michael Klemm and Bronis R. de Supinski

OpenMP Application Programming Interface Specification Version 5.0
ISBN: 978-1-7311996-0-7

OpenMP Architecture Review Board
 OpenMP Application Programming Interface Specification Version 5.0

1. Parallel programming (Computer science). 2. Parallel processing (Electronic computers)
Library of Congress: QA76.642 .O61 2018   Dewey: 005.2

Copyright © 2018 OpenMP Architecture Review Board
First Printing: December 2018

Permission to copy without fee all or part of this material is granted, provided the OpenMP Architecture Review Board copyright notice and the title of this document appear. Notice is given that copying is by permission of the OpenMP Architecture Review Board. Please address requests for additional information to info@openmp.org.

OpenMP Architecture Review Board
www.openmp.org

Foreword

Version 5.0 of the OpenMP® Application Programming Interface (API) Specification marks a major milestone in 21 years of OpenMP history. OpenMP API Version 5.0 makes many significant additions to the specification and represents the largest increase in its total page count in its history. While many of these additional pages cover new first-party and third-party tool interfaces, they also document major additions to the portion of the API that directly targets users.

The OpenMP API is used as the programming model of choice in a variety of domains, including physics, automotive and aeronautic simulations, biotechnology, automation and robotics, financial analysis, and much more. The OpenMP API is the de facto standard for shared-memory on-node programming of systems from embedded systems to the largest supercomputers that are equipped with accelerator devices.

With Version 5.0, the OpenMP API extends the functionality of many existing constructs. The device constructs have been extended to simplify the use of accelerators such as GPUs. Improvements include reduced verbosity and improved support for applications with many functions or procedures such as object-oriented C++ code. Other major enhancements provide reverse offload back to the host device and deep copy of complex data structures.

Enhancements to other existing functionality support reductions across explicit tasks and extend the set of loops to which OpenMP constructs may be applied. Perhaps most importantly, the set of normative references for OpenMP base languages has been expanded to include every currently adopted C, C++, and Fortran standard.

This new version also introduces many new and powerful features to enable new classes of applications to use OpenMP for parallelization. OpenMP now provides a mechanism to describe OpenMP contexts and to tailor an application to them. This support not only allows the selection of an OpenMP directive based on the context with metadirectives, but also allows a function that provides improved performance in a specific context to be substituted for another through the declare variant directive. Further, a descriptive loop construct now provides more information to the compiler without enforcing a particular parallel execution order.

Finally, as mentioned above, the OpenMP API specification now defines interfaces that performance and correctness tools can use to improve the productivity of OpenMP programmers. The new interfaces enable tool vendors to create third-party tools such as debuggers that attach to an OpenMP application or otherwise run outside of it, as well as first-party, low-overhead tools that directly correlate performance data or faults with the OpenMP constructs used in the code. While many such tools already existed, the new interfaces greatly simplify portable implementations of them.

These are just a few examples of the features that have been added to the OpenMP API specification with the latest version. For a more detailed list, the reader should consult Appendix B at the end of the specification.

We guide the reader to the OpenMP website (https://www.openmp.org), which is a primary source of information about the OpenMP specification as well as a free PDF of the document. It also provides links to detailed examples, auxiliary specification documents, recorded tutorials, workshop presentations, the Q&A forum, and OpenMP-related workshops and conferences.

Finally, we thank the many Language Committee representatives of members of the OpenMP Architecture Review Board as well as researchers who participated as members of cOMPunity for their countless and invaluable contributions to this document.

Sincerely,

Michael Klemm
Chief Executive Officer
OpenMP Architecture Review Board

Bronis R. de Supinski
OpenMP Language Committee Chair
Lawrence Livermore National Labs

Contents

1 Introduction   1
     1.1 Scope 1
     1.2 Glossary 2
         1.2.1 Threading Concepts 2
         1.2.2 OpenMP Language Terminology 2
         1.2.3 Loop Terminology 8
         1.2.4 Synchronization Terminology 9
         1.2.5 Tasking Terminology 10
         1.2.6 Data Terminology 12
         1.2.7 Implementation Terminology 17
         1.2.8 Tool Terminology 17
     1.3 Execution Model 20
     1.4 Memory Model 23
         1.4.1 Structure of the OpenMP Memory Model 23
         1.4.2 Device Data Environments 24
         1.4.3 Memory Management 25
         1.4.4 The Flush Operation 25
         1.4.5 Flush Synchronization and *Happens Before* 27
         1.4.6 OpenMP Memory Consistency 28
     1.5 Tool Interfaces 29
         1.5.1 OMPT 29
         1.5.2 OMPD 30

1.6	OpenMP Compliance	31
1.7	Normative References	31
1.8	Organization of this Document	34

2 Directives 37

2.1	Directive Format		38
	2.1.1	Fixed Source Form Directives	41
	2.1.2	Free Source Form Directives	41
	2.1.3	Stand-Alone Directives	42
	2.1.4	Array Shaping	43
	2.1.5	Array Sections	44
	2.1.6	Iterators	47
2.2	Conditional Compilation		49
	2.2.1	Fixed Source Form Conditional Compilation Sentinels	50
	2.2.2	Free Source Form Conditional Compilation Sentinel	50
2.3	Variant Directives		51
	2.3.1	OpenMP Context	51
	2.3.2	Context Selectors	53
	2.3.3	Matching and Scoring Context Selectors	55
	2.3.4	Metadirectives	56
	2.3.5	`declare variant` Directive	58
2.4	`requires` Directive		60
2.5	Internal Control Variables		63
	2.5.1	ICV Descriptions	64
	2.5.2	ICV Initialization	66
	2.5.3	Modifying and Retrieving ICV Values	68
	2.5.4	How ICVs are Scoped	70
		2.5.4.1 How the Per-Data Environment ICVs Work	72
	2.5.5	ICV Override Relationships	72
2.6	`parallel` Construct		74
	2.6.1	Determining the Number of Threads for a `parallel` Region	78
	2.6.2	Controlling OpenMP Thread Affinity	80
2.7	`teams` Construct		82

- 2.8 Worksharing Constructs 86
  - 2.8.1 `sections` Construct 86
  - 2.8.2 `single` Construct 89
  - 2.8.3 `workshare` Construct 92
- 2.9 Loop-Related Directives 95
  - 2.9.1 Canonical Loop Form 95
  - 2.9.2 Worksharing-Loop Construct 101
    - 2.9.2.1 Determining the Schedule of a Worksharing-Loop 109
  - 2.9.3 SIMD Directives 110
    - 2.9.3.1 `simd` Construct 110
    - 2.9.3.2 Worksharing-Loop SIMD Construct 114
    - 2.9.3.3 `declare simd` Directive 116
  - 2.9.4 `distribute` Loop Constructs 120
    - 2.9.4.1 `distribute` Construct 120
    - 2.9.4.2 `distribute simd` Construct 123
    - 2.9.4.3 Distribute Parallel Worksharing-Loop Construct 125
    - 2.9.4.4 Distribute Parallel Worksharing-Loop SIMD Construct 126
  - 2.9.5 `loop` Construct 128
  - 2.9.6 `scan` Directive 132
- 2.10 Tasking Constructs 135
  - 2.10.1 `task` Construct 135
  - 2.10.2 `taskloop` Construct 140
  - 2.10.3 `taskloop simd` Construct 146
  - 2.10.4 `taskyield` Construct 147
  - 2.10.5 Initial Task 148
  - 2.10.6 Task Scheduling 149
- 2.11 Memory Management Directives 152
  - 2.11.1 Memory Spaces 152
  - 2.11.2 Memory Allocators 152
  - 2.11.3 `allocate` Directive 156
  - 2.11.4 `allocate` Clause 158
- 2.12 Device Directives 160
  - 2.12.1 Device Initialization 160

2.12.2	`target data` Construct	161
2.12.3	`target enter data` Construct	164
2.12.4	`target exit data` Construct	166
2.12.5	`target` Construct	170
2.12.6	`target update` Construct	176
2.12.7	`declare target` Directive	180
2.13	Combined Constructs	185
2.13.1	Parallel Worksharing-Loop Construct	185
2.13.2	`parallel loop` Construct	186
2.13.3	`parallel sections` Construct	188
2.13.4	`parallel workshare` Construct	189
2.13.5	Parallel Worksharing-Loop SIMD Construct	190
2.13.6	`parallel master` Construct	191
2.13.7	`master taskloop` Construct	192
2.13.8	`master taskloop simd` Construct	194
2.13.9	`parallel master taskloop` Construct	195
2.13.10	`parallel master taskloop simd` Construct	196
2.13.11	`teams distribute` Construct	197
2.13.12	`teams distribute simd` Construct	198
2.13.13	Teams Distribute Parallel Worksharing-Loop Construct	200
2.13.14	Teams Distribute Parallel Worksharing-Loop SIMD Construct	201
2.13.15	`teams loop` Construct	202
2.13.16	`target parallel` Construct	203
2.13.17	Target Parallel Worksharing-Loop Construct	205
2.13.18	Target Parallel Worksharing-Loop SIMD Construct	206
2.13.19	`target parallel loop` Construct	208
2.13.20	`target simd` Construct	209
2.13.21	`target teams` Construct	210
2.13.22	`target teams distribute` Construct	211
2.13.23	`target teams distribute simd` Construct	213
2.13.24	`target teams loop` Construct	214
2.13.25	Target Teams Distribute Parallel Worksharing-Loop Construct	215
2.13.26	Target Teams Distribute Parallel Worksharing-Loop SIMD Construct	216

2.14 Clauses on Combined and Composite Constructs	218
2.15 `if` Clause	220
2.16 `master` Construct	221
2.17 Synchronization Constructs and Clauses	223
2.17.1 `critical` Construct	223
2.17.2 `barrier` Construct	226
2.17.3 Implicit Barriers	228
2.17.4 Implementation-Specific Barriers	230
2.17.5 `taskwait` Construct	230
2.17.6 `taskgroup` Construct	232
2.17.7 `atomic` Construct	234
2.17.8 `flush` Construct	242
2.17.8.1 Implicit Flushes	246
2.17.9 `ordered` Construct	250
2.17.10 Depend Objects	254
2.17.10.1 `depobj` Construct	254
2.17.11 `depend` Clause	255
2.17.12 Synchronization Hints	260
2.18 Cancellation Constructs	263
2.18.1 `cancel` Construct	263
2.18.2 `cancellation point` Construct	267
2.19 Data Environment	269
2.19.1 Data-Sharing Attribute Rules	269
2.19.1.1 Variables Referenced in a Construct	270
2.19.1.2 Variables Referenced in a Region but not in a Construct	273
2.19.2 `threadprivate` Directive	274
2.19.3 List Item Privatization	279
2.19.4 Data-Sharing Attribute Clauses	282
2.19.4.1 `default` Clause	282
2.19.4.2 `shared` Clause	283
2.19.4.3 `private` Clause	285
2.19.4.4 `firstprivate` Clause	286
2.19.4.5 `lastprivate` Clause	288

	2.19.4.6	`linear` Clause	290
2.19.5		Reduction Clauses and Directives	293
	2.19.5.1	Properties Common To All Reduction Clauses	294
	2.19.5.2	Reduction Scoping Clauses	299
	2.19.5.3	Reduction Participating Clauses	300
	2.19.5.4	`reduction` Clause	300
	2.19.5.5	`task_reduction` Clause	303
	2.19.5.6	`in_reduction` Clause	303
	2.19.5.7	`declare reduction` Directive	304
2.19.6		Data Copying Clauses	309
	2.19.6.1	`copyin` Clause	310
	2.19.6.2	`copyprivate` Clause	312
2.19.7		Data-Mapping Attribute Rules, Clauses, and Directives	314
	2.19.7.1	`map` Clause	315
	2.19.7.2	`defaultmap` Clause	324
	2.19.7.3	`declare mapper` Directive	326
2.20		Nesting of Regions	328

3 Runtime Library Routines — 331

3.1	Runtime Library Definitions		332
3.2	Execution Environment Routines		334
	3.2.1	`omp_set_num_threads`	334
	3.2.2	`omp_get_num_threads`	335
	3.2.3	`omp_get_max_threads`	336
	3.2.4	`omp_get_thread_num`	337
	3.2.5	`omp_get_num_procs`	338
	3.2.6	`omp_in_parallel`	339
	3.2.7	`omp_set_dynamic`	340
	3.2.8	`omp_get_dynamic`	341
	3.2.9	`omp_get_cancellation`	342
	3.2.10	`omp_set_nested`	343
	3.2.11	`omp_get_nested`	344
	3.2.12	`omp_set_schedule`	345
	3.2.13	`omp_get_schedule`	347

3.2.14	`omp_get_thread_limit`	348
3.2.15	`omp_get_supported_active_levels`	349
3.2.16	`omp_set_max_active_levels`	350
3.2.17	`omp_get_max_active_levels`	351
3.2.18	`omp_get_level`	352
3.2.19	`omp_get_ancestor_thread_num`	353
3.2.20	`omp_get_team_size`	354
3.2.21	`omp_get_active_level`	355
3.2.22	`omp_in_final`	356
3.2.23	`omp_get_proc_bind`	357
3.2.24	`omp_get_num_places`	358
3.2.25	`omp_get_place_num_procs`	359
3.2.26	`omp_get_place_proc_ids`	360
3.2.27	`omp_get_place_num`	362
3.2.28	`omp_get_partition_num_places`	362
3.2.29	`omp_get_partition_place_nums`	363
3.2.30	`omp_set_affinity_format`	364
3.2.31	`omp_get_affinity_format`	366
3.2.32	`omp_display_affinity`	367
3.2.33	`omp_capture_affinity`	368
3.2.34	`omp_set_default_device`	369
3.2.35	`omp_get_default_device`	370
3.2.36	`omp_get_num_devices`	371
3.2.37	`omp_get_device_num`	372
3.2.38	`omp_get_num_teams`	373
3.2.39	`omp_get_team_num`	374
3.2.40	`omp_is_initial_device`	375
3.2.41	`omp_get_initial_device`	376
3.2.42	`omp_get_max_task_priority`	377
3.2.43	`omp_pause_resource`	378
3.2.44	`omp_pause_resource_all`	380
3.3 Lock Routines		381
3.3.1	`omp_init_lock` and `omp_init_nest_lock`	384

- 3.3.2 `omp_init_lock_with_hint` and `omp_init_nest_lock_with_hint` 385
- 3.3.3 `omp_destroy_lock` and `omp_destroy_nest_lock` 387
- 3.3.4 `omp_set_lock` and `omp_set_nest_lock` 388
- 3.3.5 `omp_unset_lock` and `omp_unset_nest_lock` 390
- 3.3.6 `omp_test_lock` and `omp_test_nest_lock` 392
- 3.4 Timing Routines 394
  - 3.4.1 `omp_get_wtime` 394
  - 3.4.2 `omp_get_wtick` 395
- 3.5 Event Routine 396
  - 3.5.1 `omp_fulfill_event` 396
- 3.6 Device Memory Routines 397
  - 3.6.1 `omp_target_alloc` 397
  - 3.6.2 `omp_target_free` 399
  - 3.6.3 `omp_target_is_present` 400
  - 3.6.4 `omp_target_memcpy` 400
  - 3.6.5 `omp_target_memcpy_rect` 402
  - 3.6.6 `omp_target_associate_ptr` 403
  - 3.6.7 `omp_target_disassociate_ptr` 405
- 3.7 Memory Management Routines 406
  - 3.7.1 Memory Management Types 406
  - 3.7.2 `omp_init_allocator` 409
  - 3.7.3 `omp_destroy_allocator` 410
  - 3.7.4 `omp_set_default_allocator` 411
  - 3.7.5 `omp_get_default_allocator` 412
  - 3.7.6 `omp_alloc` 413
  - 3.7.7 `omp_free` 414
- 3.8 Tool Control Routine 415

4 OMPT Interface 419

- 4.1 OMPT Interfaces Definitions 419
- 4.2 Activating a First-Party Tool 420
  - 4.2.1 `ompt_start_tool` 420
  - 4.2.2 Determining Whether a First-Party Tool Should be Initialized 421

- 4.2.3 Initializing a First-Party Tool 423
  - 4.2.3.1 Binding Entry Points in the OMPT Callback Interface 424
- 4.2.4 Monitoring Activity on the Host with OMPT 425
- 4.2.5 Tracing Activity on Target Devices with OMPT 427
- 4.3 Finalizing a First-Party Tool 432
- 4.4 OMPT Data Types 433
  - 4.4.1 Tool Initialization and Finalization 433
  - 4.4.2 Callbacks 434
  - 4.4.3 Tracing 435
    - 4.4.3.1 Record Type 435
    - 4.4.3.2 Native Record Kind 435
    - 4.4.3.3 Native Record Abstract Type 436
    - 4.4.3.4 Record Type 436
  - 4.4.4 Miscellaneous Type Definitions 438
    - 4.4.4.1 `ompt_callback_t` 438
    - 4.4.4.2 `ompt_set_result_t` 438
    - 4.4.4.3 `ompt_id_t` 439
    - 4.4.4.4 `ompt_data_t` 440
    - 4.4.4.5 `ompt_device_t` 441
    - 4.4.4.6 `ompt_device_time_t` 441
    - 4.4.4.7 `ompt_buffer_t` 441
    - 4.4.4.8 `ompt_buffer_cursor_t` 442
    - 4.4.4.9 `ompt_dependence_t` 442
    - 4.4.4.10 `ompt_thread_t` 443
    - 4.4.4.11 `ompt_scope_endpoint_t` 443
    - 4.4.4.12 `ompt_dispatch_t` 444
    - 4.4.4.13 `ompt_sync_region_t` 444
    - 4.4.4.14 `ompt_target_data_op_t` 444
    - 4.4.4.15 `ompt_work_t` 445
    - 4.4.4.16 `ompt_mutex_t` 445
    - 4.4.4.17 `ompt_native_mon_flag_t` 446
    - 4.4.4.18 `ompt_task_flag_t` 446
    - 4.4.4.19 `ompt_task_status_t` 447

4.4.4.20	`ompt_target_t`	448
4.4.4.21	`ompt_parallel_flag_t`	448
4.4.4.22	`ompt_target_map_flag_t`	449
4.4.4.23	`ompt_dependence_type_t`	450
4.4.4.24	`ompt_cancel_flag_t`	450
4.4.4.25	`ompt_hwid_t`	451
4.4.4.26	`ompt_state_t`	452
4.4.4.27	`ompt_frame_t`	454
4.4.4.28	`ompt_frame_flag_t`	455
4.4.4.29	`ompt_wait_id_t`	456
4.5	OMPT Tool Callback Signatures and Trace Records	457
4.5.1	Initialization and Finalization Callback Signature	457
4.5.1.1	`ompt_initialize_t`	457
4.5.1.2	`ompt_finalize_t`	458
4.5.2	Event Callback Signatures and Trace Records	459
4.5.2.1	`ompt_callback_thread_begin_t`	459
4.5.2.2	`ompt_callback_thread_end_t`	460
4.5.2.3	`ompt_callback_parallel_begin_t`	461
4.5.2.4	`ompt_callback_parallel_end_t`	463
4.5.2.5	`ompt_callback_work_t`	464
4.5.2.6	`ompt_callback_dispatch_t`	465
4.5.2.7	`ompt_callback_task_create_t`	467
4.5.2.8	`ompt_callback_dependences_t`	468
4.5.2.9	`ompt_callback_task_dependence_t`	470
4.5.2.10	`ompt_callback_task_schedule_t`	470
4.5.2.11	`ompt_callback_implicit_task_t`	471
4.5.2.12	`ompt_callback_master_t`	473
4.5.2.13	`ompt_callback_sync_region_t`	474
4.5.2.14	`ompt_callback_mutex_acquire_t`	476
4.5.2.15	`ompt_callback_mutex_t`	477
4.5.2.16	`ompt_callback_nest_lock_t`	479
4.5.2.17	`ompt_callback_flush_t`	480
4.5.2.18	`ompt_callback_cancel_t`	481

4.5.2.19	`ompt_callback_device_initialize_t`	482
4.5.2.20	`ompt_callback_device_finalize_t`	484
4.5.2.21	`ompt_callback_device_load_t`	484
4.5.2.22	`ompt_callback_device_unload_t`	486
4.5.2.23	`ompt_callback_buffer_request_t`	486
4.5.2.24	`ompt_callback_buffer_complete_t`	487
4.5.2.25	`ompt_callback_target_data_op_t`	488
4.5.2.26	`ompt_callback_target_t`	490
4.5.2.27	`ompt_callback_target_map_t`	492
4.5.2.28	`ompt_callback_target_submit_t`	494
4.5.2.29	`ompt_callback_control_tool_t`	495

4.6 OMPT Runtime Entry Points for Tools 497
    4.6.1 Entry Points in the OMPT Callback Interface 497

4.6.1.1	`ompt_enumerate_states_t`	498
4.6.1.2	`ompt_enumerate_mutex_impls_t`	499
4.6.1.3	`ompt_set_callback_t`	500
4.6.1.4	`ompt_get_callback_t`	502
4.6.1.5	`ompt_get_thread_data_t`	503
4.6.1.6	`ompt_get_num_procs_t`	503
4.6.1.7	`ompt_get_num_places_t`	504
4.6.1.8	`ompt_get_place_proc_ids_t`	505
4.6.1.9	`ompt_get_place_num_t`	506
4.6.1.10	`ompt_get_partition_place_nums_t`	507
4.6.1.11	`ompt_get_proc_id_t`	508
4.6.1.12	`ompt_get_state_t`	508
4.6.1.13	`ompt_get_parallel_info_t`	510
4.6.1.14	`ompt_get_task_info_t`	512
4.6.1.15	`ompt_get_task_memory_t`	514
4.6.1.16	`ompt_get_target_info_t`	515
4.6.1.17	`ompt_get_num_devices_t`	516
4.6.1.18	`ompt_get_unique_id_t`	517
4.6.1.19	`ompt_finalize_tool_t`	517

4.6.2	Entry Points in the OMPT Device Tracing Interface	518
	4.6.2.1 `ompt_get_device_num_procs_t`	518
	4.6.2.2 `ompt_get_device_time_t`	519
	4.6.2.3 `ompt_translate_time_t`	520
	4.6.2.4 `ompt_set_trace_ompt_t`	521
	4.6.2.5 `ompt_set_trace_native_t`	522
	4.6.2.6 `ompt_start_trace_t`	523
	4.6.2.7 `ompt_pause_trace_t`	524
	4.6.2.8 `ompt_flush_trace_t`	525
	4.6.2.9 `ompt_stop_trace_t`	526
	4.6.2.10 `ompt_advance_buffer_cursor_t`	527
	4.6.2.11 `ompt_get_record_type_t`	528
	4.6.2.12 `ompt_get_record_ompt_t`	529
	4.6.2.13 `ompt_get_record_native_t`	530
	4.6.2.14 `ompt_get_record_abstract_t`	531
4.6.3	Lookup Entry Points: `ompt_function_lookup_t`	531

5 OMPD Interface 533

5.1 OMPD Interfaces Definitions 534
5.2 Activating an OMPD Tool 534
    5.2.1 Enabling the Runtime for OMPD 534
    5.2.2 `ompd_dll_locations` 535
    5.2.3 `ompd_dll_locations_valid` 536
5.3 OMPD Data Types 536
    5.3.1 Size Type 536
    5.3.2 Wait ID Type 537
    5.3.3 Basic Value Types 537
    5.3.4 Address Type 538
    5.3.5 Frame Information Type 538
    5.3.6 System Device Identifiers 539
    5.3.7 Native Thread Identifiers 539
    5.3.8 OMPD Handle Types 540
    5.3.9 OMPD Scope Types 541
    5.3.10 ICV ID Type 542

5.3.11	Tool Context Types		542
5.3.12	Return Code Types		543
5.3.13	Primitive Type Sizes		544

5.4 OMPD Tool Callback Interface 545
    5.4.1 Memory Management of OMPD Library 545
        5.4.1.1 `ompd_callback_memory_alloc_fn_t` 546
        5.4.1.2 `ompd_callback_memory_free_fn_t` 546
    5.4.2 Context Management and Navigation 547
        5.4.2.1 `ompd_callback_get_thread_context_for_thread_id_fn_t` 547
        5.4.2.2 `ompd_callback_sizeof_fn_t` 549
    5.4.3 Accessing Memory in the OpenMP Program or Runtime 549
        5.4.3.1 `ompd_callback_symbol_addr_fn_t` 550
        5.4.3.2 `ompd_callback_memory_read_fn_t` 551
        5.4.3.3 `ompd_callback_memory_write_fn_t` 553
    5.4.4 Data Format Conversion: `ompd_callback_device_host_fn_t` ... 554
    5.4.5 Output: `ompd_callback_print_string_fn_t` 556
    5.4.6 The Callback Interface 556

5.5 OMPD Tool Interface Routines 558
    5.5.1 Per OMPD Library Initialization and Finalization 558
        5.5.1.1 `ompd_initialize` 558
        5.5.1.2 `ompd_get_api_version` 559
        5.5.1.3 `ompd_get_version_string` 560
        5.5.1.4 `ompd_finalize` 561
    5.5.2 Per OpenMP Process Initialization and Finalization 562
        5.5.2.1 `ompd_process_initialize` 562
        5.5.2.2 `ompd_device_initialize` 563
        5.5.2.3 `ompd_rel_address_space_handle` 564
    5.5.3 Thread and Signal Safety 565
    5.5.4 Address Space Information 565
        5.5.4.1 `ompd_get_omp_version` 565
        5.5.4.2 `ompd_get_omp_version_string` 566

5.5.5	Thread Handles	567
5.5.5.1	`ompd_get_thread_in_parallel`	567
5.5.5.2	`ompd_get_thread_handle`	568
5.5.5.3	`ompd_rel_thread_handle`	569
5.5.5.4	`ompd_thread_handle_compare`	570
5.5.5.5	`ompd_get_thread_id`	570
5.5.6	Parallel Region Handles	571
5.5.6.1	`ompd_get_curr_parallel_handle`	571
5.5.6.2	`ompd_get_enclosing_parallel_handle`	572
5.5.6.3	`ompd_get_task_parallel_handle`	573
5.5.6.4	`ompd_rel_parallel_handle`	574
5.5.6.5	`ompd_parallel_handle_compare`	575
5.5.7	Task Handles	576
5.5.7.1	`ompd_get_curr_task_handle`	576
5.5.7.2	`ompd_get_generating_task_handle`	577
5.5.7.3	`ompd_get_scheduling_task_handle`	578
5.5.7.4	`ompd_get_task_in_parallel`	579
5.5.7.5	`ompd_rel_task_handle`	580
5.5.7.6	`ompd_task_handle_compare`	580
5.5.7.7	`ompd_get_task_function`	581
5.5.7.8	`ompd_get_task_frame`	582
5.5.7.9	`ompd_enumerate_states`	583
5.5.7.10	`ompd_get_state`	585
5.5.8	Display Control Variables	586
5.5.8.1	`ompd_get_display_control_vars`	586
5.5.8.2	`ompd_rel_display_control_vars`	587
5.5.9	Accessing Scope-Specific Information	588
5.5.9.1	`ompd_enumerate_icvs`	588
5.5.9.2	`ompd_get_icv_from_scope`	590
5.5.9.3	`ompd_get_icv_string_from_scope`	591
5.5.9.4	`ompd_get_tool_data`	592
5.6	Runtime Entry Points for OMPD	594
5.6.1	Beginning Parallel Regions	594

	5.6.2	Ending Parallel Regions	595
	5.6.3	Beginning Task Regions	595
	5.6.4	Ending Task Regions	596
	5.6.5	Beginning OpenMP Threads	597
	5.6.6	Ending OpenMP Threads	597
	5.6.7	Initializing OpenMP Devices	598
	5.6.8	Finalizing OpenMP Devices	599

6 Environment Variables — 601

- 6.1 `OMP_SCHEDULE` 601
- 6.2 `OMP_NUM_THREADS` 602
- 6.3 `OMP_DYNAMIC` 603
- 6.4 `OMP_PROC_BIND` 604
- 6.5 `OMP_PLACES` 605
- 6.6 `OMP_STACKSIZE` 607
- 6.7 `OMP_WAIT_POLICY` 608
- 6.8 `OMP_MAX_ACTIVE_LEVELS` 608
- 6.9 `OMP_NESTED` 609
- 6.10 `OMP_THREAD_LIMIT` 610
- 6.11 `OMP_CANCELLATION` 610
- 6.12 `OMP_DISPLAY_ENV` 611
- 6.13 `OMP_DISPLAY_AFFINITY` 612
- 6.14 `OMP_AFFINITY_FORMAT` 613
- 6.15 `OMP_DEFAULT_DEVICE` 615
- 6.16 `OMP_MAX_TASK_PRIORITY` 615
- 6.17 `OMP_TARGET_OFFLOAD` 615
- 6.18 `OMP_TOOL` 616
- 6.19 `OMP_TOOL_LIBRARIES` 617
- 6.20 `OMP_DEBUG` 617
- 6.21 `OMP_ALLOCATOR` 618

A OpenMP Implementation-Defined Behaviors — 619

B Features History — 627

- B.1 Deprecated Features 627

B.2	Version 4.5 to 5.0 Differences	627
B.3	Version 4.0 to 4.5 Differences	631
B.4	Version 3.1 to 4.0 Differences	633
B.5	Version 3.0 to 3.1 Differences	634
B.6	Version 2.5 to 3.0 Differences	635

Index   **639**

List of Figures

2.1 Determining the **schedule** for a Worksharing-Loop 109

4.1 First-Party Tool Activation Flow Chart 422

List of Tables

1.1	Map-Type Decay of Map Type Combinations	16
2.1	ICV Initial Values	66
2.2	Ways to Modify and to Retrieve ICV Values	68
2.3	Scopes of ICVs	70
2.4	ICV Override Relationships	72
2.5	`schedule` Clause *kind* Values	104
2.6	`schedule` Clause *modifier* Values	106
2.7	`ompt_callback_task_create` callback flags evaluation	139
2.8	Predefined Memory Spaces	152
2.9	Allocator Traits	153
2.10	Predefined Allocators	155
2.11	Implicitly Declared C/C++ *reduction-identifiers*	294
2.12	Implicitly Declared Fortran *reduction-identifiers*	295
3.1	Standard Tool Control Commands	417
4.1	OMPT Callback Interface Runtime Entry Point Names and Their Type Signatures	426
4.2	Valid Return Codes of `ompt_set_callback` for Each Callback	428
4.3	OMPT Tracing Interface Runtime Entry Point Names and Their Type Signatures	430
5.1	Mapping of Scope Type and OMPD Handles	542
5.2	OMPD-specific ICVs	589
6.1	Defined Abstract Names for `OMP_PLACES`	605
6.2	Available Field Types for Formatting OpenMP Thread Affinity Information	613

CHAPTER 1

Introduction

The collection of compiler directives, library routines, and environment variables described in this document collectively define the specification of the OpenMP Application Program Interface (OpenMP API) for parallelism in C, C++ and Fortran programs.

This specification provides a model for parallel programming that is portable across architectures from different vendors. Compilers from numerous vendors support the OpenMP API. More information about the OpenMP API can be found at the following web site

`http://www.openmp.org`

The directives, library routines, environment variables, and tool support defined in this document allow users to create, to manage, to debug and to analyze parallel programs while permitting portability. The directives extend the C, C++ and Fortran base languages with single program multiple data (SPMD) constructs, tasking constructs, device constructs, worksharing constructs, and synchronization constructs, and they provide support for sharing, mapping and privatizing data. The functionality to control the runtime environment is provided by library routines and environment variables. Compilers that support the OpenMP API often include a command line option to the compiler that activates and allows interpretation of all OpenMP directives.

1.1 Scope

The OpenMP API covers only user-directed parallelization, wherein the programmer explicitly specifies the actions to be taken by the compiler and runtime system in order to execute the program in parallel. OpenMP-compliant implementations are not required to check for data dependencies, data conflicts, race conditions, or deadlocks, any of which may occur in conforming programs. In addition, compliant implementations are not required to check for code sequences that cause a program to be classified as non-conforming. Application developers are responsible for correctly using the OpenMP API to produce a conforming program. The OpenMP API does not cover compiler-generated automatic parallelization.

1.2 Glossary

1.2.1 Threading Concepts

thread	An execution entity with a stack and associated static memory, called *threadprivate memory*.
OpenMP thread	A *thread* that is managed by the OpenMP implementation.
thread number	A number that the OpenMP implementation assigns to an OpenMP thread. For threads within the same team, zero identifies the master thread and consecutive numbers identify the other threads of this team.
idle thread	An *OpenMP thread* that is not currently part of any `parallel` region.
thread-safe routine	A routine that performs the intended function even when executed concurrently (by more than one *thread*).
processor	Implementation-defined hardware unit on which one or more *OpenMP threads* can execute.
device	An implementation-defined logical execution engine.
	COMMENT: A *device* could have one or more *processors*.
host device	The *device* on which the *OpenMP program* begins execution.
target device	A device onto which code and data may be offloaded from the *host device*.
parent device	For a given `target` region, the device on which the corresponding `target` construct was encountered.

1.2.2 OpenMP Language Terminology

base language	A programming language that serves as the foundation of the OpenMP specification.
	COMMENT: See Section 1.7 on page 31 for a listing of current *base languages* for the OpenMP API.

	base program	A program written in a *base language*.
	program order	An ordering of operations performed by the same thread as determined by the execution sequence of operations specified by the *base language*.
		COMMENT: For C11 and C++11, *program order* corresponds to the *sequenced before* relation between operations performed by the same thread.
	structured block	For C/C++, an executable statement, possibly compound, with a single entry at the top and a single exit at the bottom, or an OpenMP *construct*.
		For Fortran, a block of executable statements with a single entry at the top and a single exit at the bottom, or an OpenMP *construct*.
		COMMENT: See Section 2.1 on page 38 for restrictions on *structured blocks*.
	compilation unit	For C/C++, a translation unit.
		For Fortran, a program unit.
	enclosing context	For C/C++, the innermost scope enclosing an OpenMP *directive*.
		For Fortran, the innermost scoping unit enclosing an OpenMP *directive*.
	directive	For C/C++, a `#pragma`, and for Fortran, a comment, that specifies *OpenMP program* behavior.
		COMMENT: See Section 2.1 on page 38 for a description of OpenMP *directive* syntax.
	metadirective	A *directive* that conditionally resolves to another *directive* at compile time.
	white space	A non-empty sequence of space and/or horizontal tab characters.
	OpenMP program	A program that consists of a *base program* that is annotated with OpenMP *directives* or that calls OpenMP API runtime library routines
	conforming program	An *OpenMP program* that follows all rules and restrictions of the OpenMP specification.
	declarative directive	An OpenMP *directive* that may only be placed in a declarative context. A *declarative directive* results in one or more declarations only; it is not associated with the immediate execution of any user code.
	executable directive	An OpenMP *directive* that is not declarative. That is, it may be placed in an executable context.
	stand-alone directive	An OpenMP *executable directive* that has no associated user code except for that which appears in clauses in the directive.

construct		An OpenMP *executable directive* (and for Fortran, the paired **end** *directive*, if any) and the associated statement, loop or *structured block*, if any, not including the code in any called routines. That is, the lexical extent of an *executable directive*.
combined construct		A construct that is a shortcut for specifying one construct immediately nested inside another construct. A combined construct is semantically identical to that of explicitly specifying the first construct containing one instance of the second construct and no other statements.
composite construct		A construct that is composed of two constructs but does not have identical semantics to specifying one of the constructs immediately nested inside the other. A composite construct either adds semantics not included in the constructs from which it is composed or the nesting of the one construct inside the other is not conforming.
combined target construct		A *combined construct* that is composed of a **target** construct along with another construct.
region		All code encountered during a specific instance of the execution of a given *construct* or of an OpenMP library routine. A *region* includes any code in called routines as well as any implicit code introduced by the OpenMP implementation. The generation of a *task* at the point where a *task generating construct* is encountered is a part of the *region* of the *encountering thread*. However, an *explicit task region* corresponding to a *task generating construct* is not part of the *region* of the *encountering thread* unless it is an *included task region*. The point where a **target** or **teams** directive is encountered is a part of the *region* of the *encountering thread*, but the *region* corresponding to the **target** or **teams** directive is not.

COMMENTS:

A *region* may also be thought of as the dynamic or runtime extent of a *construct* or of an OpenMP library routine.

During the execution of an *OpenMP program*, a *construct* may give rise to many *regions*.

active parallel region	A **parallel** *region* that is executed by a *team* consisting of more than one *thread*.
inactive parallel region	A **parallel** *region* that is executed by a *team* of only one *thread*.
active target region	A **target** *region* that is executed on a *device* other than the *device* that encountered the **target** *construct*.
inactive target region	A **target** *region* that is executed on the same *device* that encountered the **target** *construct*.

sequential part	All code encountered during the execution of an *initial task region* that is not part of a **parallel** *region* corresponding to a **parallel** *construct* or a **task** *region* corresponding to a **task** *construct*.	

COMMENTS:

A *sequential part* is enclosed by an *implicit parallel region*.

Executable statements in called routines may be in both a *sequential part* and any number of explicit **parallel** *regions* at different points in the program execution.

master thread	An *OpenMP thread* that has *thread* number 0. A *master thread* may be an *initial thread* or the *thread* that encounters a **parallel** *construct*, creates a *team*, generates a set of *implicit tasks*, and then executes one of those *tasks* as *thread* number 0.
parent thread	The *thread* that encountered the **parallel** *construct* and generated a **parallel** *region* is the *parent thread* of each of the *threads* in the *team* of that **parallel** *region*. The *master thread* of a **parallel** *region* is the same *thread* as its *parent thread* with respect to any resources associated with an *OpenMP thread*.
child thread	When a thread encounters a **parallel** construct, each of the threads in the generated **parallel** region's team are *child threads* of the encountering *thread*. The **target** or **teams** region's *initial thread* is not a *child thread* of the thread that encountered the **target** or **teams** construct.
ancestor thread	For a given *thread*, its *parent thread* or one of its *parent thread's ancestor threads*.
descendent thread	For a given *thread*, one of its *child threads* or one of its *child threads' descendent threads*.
team	A set of one or more *threads* participating in the execution of a **parallel** *region*.

COMMENTS:

For an *active parallel region*, the team comprises the *master thread* and at least one additional *thread*.

For an *inactive parallel region*, the *team* comprises only the *master thread*.

league	The set of *teams* created by a **teams** construct.
contention group	An initial *thread* and its *descendent threads*.
implicit parallel region	An *inactive parallel region* that is not generated from a **parallel** *construct*. *Implicit parallel regions* surround the whole *OpenMP program*, all **target** *regions*, and all **teams** *regions*.
initial thread	The *thread* that executes an *implicit parallel region*.

initial team		The *team* that comprises an *initial thread* executing an *implicit parallel region*.
nested construct		A *construct* (lexically) enclosed by another *construct*.
closely nested construct		A *construct* nested inside another *construct* with no other *construct* nested between them.
nested region		A *region* (dynamically) enclosed by another *region*. That is, a *region* generated from the execution of another *region* or one of its *nested regions*.
		COMMENT: Some nestings are *conforming* and some are not. See Section 2.20 on page 328 for the restrictions on nesting.
closely nested region		A *region nested* inside another *region* with no **parallel** *region nested* between them.
strictly nested region		A *region nested* inside another *region* with no other *region nested* between them.
all threads		All OpenMP *threads* participating in the *OpenMP program*.
current team		All *threads* in the *team* executing the innermost enclosing **parallel** *region*.
encountering thread		For a given *region*, the *thread* that encounters the corresponding *construct*.
all tasks		All *tasks* participating in the *OpenMP program*.
current team tasks		All *tasks* encountered by the corresponding *team*. The *implicit tasks* constituting the **parallel** *region* and any *descendent tasks* encountered during the execution of these *implicit tasks* are included in this set of tasks.
generating task		For a given *region*, the task for which execution by a *thread* generated the *region*.
binding thread set		The set of *threads* that are affected by, or provide the context for, the execution of a *region*.
		The *binding thread* set for a given *region* can be *all threads* on a *device*, *all threads* in a *contention group*, all *master threads* executing an enclosing **teams** *region*, the *current team*, or the *encountering thread*.
		COMMENT: The *binding thread set* for a particular *region* is described in its corresponding subsection of this specification.
binding task set		The set of *tasks* that are affected by, or provide the context for, the execution of a *region*.
		The *binding task* set for a given *region* can be *all tasks*, the *current team tasks*, all *tasks of the current team that are generated in the region*, the *binding implicit task*, or the *generating task*.
		COMMENT: The *binding task* set for a particular *region* (if applicable) is described in its corresponding subsection of this specification.

binding region The enclosing *region* that determines the execution context and limits the scope of the effects of the bound *region* is called the *binding region*.

Binding region is not defined for *regions* for which the *binding thread set* is *all threads* or the *encountering thread*, nor is it defined for *regions* for which the *binding task set* is *all tasks*.

COMMENTS:

The *binding region* for an `ordered` *region* is the innermost enclosing *loop region*.

The *binding region* for a `taskwait` *region* is the innermost enclosing *task region*.

The *binding region* for a `cancel` *region* is the innermost enclosing *region* corresponding to the *construct-type-clause* of the `cancel` construct.

The *binding region* for a `cancellation point` *region* is the innermost enclosing *region* corresponding to the *construct-type-clause* of the `cancellation point` construct.

For all other *regions* for which the *binding thread set* is the *current team* or the *binding task set* is the *current team tasks*, the *binding region* is the innermost enclosing `parallel` *region*.

For *regions* for which the *binding task set* is the *generating task*, the *binding region* is the *region* of the *generating task*.

A `parallel` *region* need not be *active* nor explicit to be a *binding region*.

A *task region* need not be explicit to be a *binding region*.

A *region* never binds to any *region* outside of the innermost enclosing `parallel` *region*.

orphaned construct A *construct* that gives rise to a *region* for which the *binding thread set* is the *current team*, but is not nested within another *construct* giving rise to the *binding region*.

worksharing construct A *construct* that defines units of work, each of which is executed exactly once by one of the *threads* in the *team* executing the *construct*.

For C/C++, *worksharing constructs* are `for`, `sections`, and `single`.

For Fortran, *worksharing constructs* are `do`, `sections`, `single` and `workshare`.

device construct An OpenMP *construct* that accepts the `device` clause.

device routine		A function (for C/C+ and Fortran) or subroutine (for Fortran) that can be executed on a *target device*, as part of a `target` region.
place		An unordered set of *processors* on a device.
place list		The ordered list that describes all OpenMP *places* available to the execution environment.
place partition		An ordered list that corresponds to a contiguous interval in the OpenMP *place list*. It describes the *places* currently available to the execution environment for a given parallel *region*.
place number		A number that uniquely identifies a *place* in the *place list*, with zero identifying the first *place* in the *place list*, and each consecutive whole number identifying the next *place* in the *place list*.
thread affinity		A binding of *threads* to *places* within the current *place partition*.
SIMD instruction		A single machine instruction that can operate on multiple data elements.
SIMD lane		A software or hardware mechanism capable of processing one data element from a *SIMD instruction*.
SIMD chunk		A set of iterations executed concurrently, each by a *SIMD lane*, by a single *thread* by means of *SIMD instructions*.
memory		A storage resource to store and to retrieve variables accessible by OpenMP threads.
memory space		A representation of storage resources from which *memory* can be allocated or deallocated. More than one memory space may exist.
memory allocator		An OpenMP object that fulfills requests to allocate and to deallocate *memory* for program variables from the storage resources of its associated *memory space*.
handle		An opaque reference that uniquely identifies an abstraction.

1.2.3 Loop Terminology

loop-associated directive		An OpenMP *executable* directive for which the associated user code must be a loop nest that is a *structured block*.
associated loop(s)		The loop(s) controlled by a *loop-associated directive*.
		COMMENT: If the *loop-associated directive* contains a `collapse` or an `ordered(n)` clause then it may have more than one *associated loop*.
sequential loop		A loop that is not associated with any OpenMP *loop-associated directive*.

SIMD loop		A loop that includes at least one *SIMD chunk*.
non-rectangular loop nest		A loop nest for which the iteration count of a loop inside the loop nest is the not same for all occurrences of the loop in the loop nest.
doacross loop nest		A loop nest that has cross-iteration dependence. An iteration is dependent on one or more lexicographically earlier iterations.
	COMMENT:	The `ordered` clause parameter on a worksharing-loop directive identifies the loop(s) associated with the *doacross loop nest*.

1.2.4 Synchronization Terminology

barrier — A point in the execution of a program encountered by a *team* of *threads*, beyond which no *thread* in the team may execute until all *threads* in the *team* have reached the barrier and all *explicit tasks* generated by the *team* have executed to completion. If *cancellation* has been requested, threads may proceed to the end of the canceled *region* even if some threads in the team have not reached the *barrier*.

cancellation — An action that cancels (that is, aborts) an OpenMP *region* and causes executing *implicit* or *explicit* tasks to proceed to the end of the canceled *region*.

cancellation point — A point at which implicit and explicit tasks check if cancellation has been requested. If cancellation has been observed, they perform the *cancellation*.

> COMMENT: For a list of cancellation points, see Section 2.18.1 on page 263.

flush — An operation that a *thread* performs to enforce consistency between its view and other *threads'* view of memory.

flush property — Properties that determine the manner in which a *flush* operation enforces memory consistency. These properties are:

- *strong*: flushes a set of variables from the current thread's temporary view of the memory to the memory;
- *release*: orders memory operations that precede the flush before memory operations performed by a different thread with which it synchronizes;
- *acquire*: orders memory operations that follow the flush after memory operations performed by a different thread that synchronizes with it.

> COMMENT: Any *flush* operation has one or more *flush properties*.

strong flush — A *flush* operation that has the *strong flush property*.

release flush		A *flush* operation that has the *release flush property*.
acquire flush		A *flush* operation that has the *acquire flush property*.
atomic operation		An operation that is specified by an `atomic` construct and atomically accesses and/or modifies a specific storage location.
atomic read		An *atomic operation* that is specified by an `atomic` construct on which the `read` clause is present.
atomic write		An *atomic operation* that is specified by an `atomic` construct on which the `write` clause is present.
atomic update		An *atomic operation* that is specified by an `atomic` construct on which the `update` clause is present.
atomic captured update		An *atomic operation* that is specified by an `atomic` construct on which the `capture` clause is present.
read-modify-write		An *atomic operation* that reads and writes to a given storage location.
		COMMENT: All *atomic update* and *atomic captured update* operations are *read-modify-write* operations.
sequentially consistent atomic construct		An `atomic` construct for which the `seq_cst` clause is specified.
non-sequentially consistent atomic construct		An `atomic` construct for which the `seq_cst` clause is not specified
sequentially consistent atomic operation		An *atomic operation* that is specified by a *sequentially consistent atomic construct*.

1.2.5 Tasking Terminology

task		A specific instance of executable code and its data environment that the OpenMP implementation can schedule for execution by threads.
task region		A *region* consisting of all code encountered during the execution of a *task*.
		COMMENT: A `parallel` *region* consists of one or more implicit *task regions*.
implicit task		A *task* generated by an *implicit parallel region* or generated when a `parallel` *construct* is encountered during execution.

binding implicit task	The *implicit task* of the current thread team assigned to the encountering thread.
explicit task	A *task* that is not an *implicit task*.
initial task	An *implicit task* associated with an *implicit parallel region*.
current task	For a given *thread*, the *task* corresponding to the *task region* in which it is executing.
child task	A *task* is a *child task* of its generating *task region*. A *child task region* is not part of its generating *task region*.
sibling tasks	*Tasks* that are *child tasks* of the same *task region*.
descendent task	A *task* that is the *child task* of a *task region* or of one of its *descendent task regions*.
task completion	*Task completion* occurs when the end of the *structured block* associated with the *construct* that generated the *task* is reached.
	COMMENT: Completion of the *initial task* that is generated when the program begins occurs at program exit.
task scheduling point	A point during the execution of the current *task region* at which it can be suspended to be resumed later; or the point of *task completion*, after which the executing thread may switch to a different *task region*.
	COMMENT: For a list of *task scheduling points*, see Section 2.10.6 on page 149.
task switching	The act of a *thread* switching from the execution of one *task* to another *task*.
tied task	A *task* that, when its *task region* is suspended, can be resumed only by the same *thread* that suspended it. That is, the *task* is tied to that *thread*.
untied task	A *task* that, when its *task region* is suspended, can be resumed by any *thread* in the team. That is, the *task* is not tied to any *thread*.
undeferred task	A *task* for which execution is not deferred with respect to its generating *task region*. That is, its generating *task region* is suspended until execution of the structured block associated with the *undeferred task* is completed.
included task	A *task* for which execution is sequentially included in the generating *task region*. That is, an *included task* is *undeferred* and executed by the *encountering thread*.
merged task	A *task* for which the *data environment*, inclusive of ICVs, is the same as that of its generating *task region*.
mergeable task	A *task* that may be a *merged task* if it is an *undeferred task* or an *included task*.
final task	A *task* that forces all of its *child tasks* to become *final* and *included tasks*.

	task dependence	An ordering relation between two *sibling tasks*: the *dependent task* and a previously generated *predecessor task*. The *task dependence* is fulfilled when the *predecessor task* has completed.
	dependent task	A *task* that because of a *task dependence* cannot be executed until its *predecessor tasks* have completed.
	mutually exclusive tasks	*Tasks* that may be executed in any order, but not at the same time.
	predecessor task	A *task* that must complete before its *dependent tasks* can be executed.
	task synchronization construct	A **taskwait**, **taskgroup**, or a **barrier** *construct*.
	task generating construct	A *construct* that generates one or more *explicit tasks*.
	target task	A *mergeable* and *untied task* that is generated by a **target**, **target enter data**, **target exit data**, or **target update** *construct*.
	taskgroup set	A set of tasks that are logically grouped by a **taskgroup** *region*.

1.2.6 Data Terminology

	variable	A named data storage block, for which the value can be defined and redefined during the execution of a program.
		COMMENT: An array element or structure element is a variable that is part of another variable.
	scalar variable	For C/C++, a scalar variable, as defined by the base language.
		For Fortran, a scalar variable with intrinsic type, as defined by the base language, excluding character type.
	aggregate variable	A variable, such as an array or structure, composed of other variables.
	array section	A designated subset of the elements of an array that is specified using a subscript notation that can select more than one element.
	array item	An array, an array section, or an array element.
	shape-operator	For C/C++, an array shaping operator that reinterprets a pointer expression as an array with one or more specified dimensions.

implicit array For C/C++, the set of array elements of non-array type T that may be accessed by applying a sequence of [] operators to a given pointer that is either a pointer to type T or a pointer to a multidimensional array of elements of type T.

For Fortran, the set of array elements for a given array pointer.

COMMENT: For C/C++, the implicit array for pointer p with type T (*)[10] consists of all accessible elements p[i][j], for all i and j=0..9.

base pointer For C/C++, an lvalue pointer expression that is used by a given lvalue expression or array section to refer indirectly to its storage, where the lvalue expression or array section is part of the implicit array for that lvalue pointer expression.

For Fortran, a data pointer that appears last in the designator for a given variable or array section, where the variable or array section is part of the pointer target for that data pointer.

COMMENT: For the array section (*p0).x0[k1].p1->p2[k2].x1[k3].x2[4][0:n], where identifiers pi have a pointer type declaration and identifiers xi have an array type declaration, the *base pointer* is: (*p0).x0[k1].p1->p2.

named pointer For C/C++, the *base pointer* of a given lvalue expression or array section, or the *base pointer* of one of its *named pointers*.

For Fortran, the *base pointer* of a given variable or array section, or the *base pointer* of one of its *named pointers*.

COMMENT: For the array section (*p0).x0[k1].p1->p2[k2].x1[k3].x2[4][0:n], where identifiers pi have a pointer type declaration and identifiers xi have an array type declaration, the *named pointers* are: p0, (*p0).x0[k1].p1, and (*p0).x0[k1].p1->p2.

containing array For C/C++, a non-subscripted array (a *containing array*) that appears in a given lvalue expression or array section, where the lvalue expression or array section is part of that *containing array*.

For Fortran, an array (a *containing array*) without the **POINTER** attribute and without a subscript list that appears in the designator of a given variable or array section, where the variable or array section is part of that *containing array*.

COMMENT: For the array section (*p0).x0[k1].p1->p2[k2].x1[k3].x2[4][0:n], where identifiers pi have a pointer type declaration and identifiers xi have an array type declaration, the *containing arrays* are: (*p0).x0[k1].p1->p2[k2].x1 and (*p0).x0[k1].p1->p2[k2].x1[k3].x2.

| | **base array** | For C/C++, a *containing array* of a given lvalue expression or array section that does not appear in the expression of any of its other *containing arrays*. |

For Fortran, a *containing array* of a given variable or array section that does not appear in the designator of any of its other *containing arrays*.

> COMMENT: For the array section (*p0).x0[k1].p1->p2[k2].x1[k3].x2[4][0:n], where identifiers p*i* have a pointer type declaration and identifiers x*i* have an array type declaration, the *base array* is: (*p0).x0[k1].p1->p2[k2].x1[k3].x2.

named array For C/C++, a *containing array* of a given lvalue expression or array section, or a *containing array* of one of its *named pointers*.

For Fortran, a *containing array* of a given variable or array section, or a *containing array* of one of its *named pointers*.

> COMMENT: For the array section (*p0).x0[k1].p1->p2[k2].x1[k3].x2[4][0:n], where identifiers p*i* have a pointer type declaration and identifiers x*i* have an array type declaration, the *named arrays* are: (*p0).x0, (*p0).x0[k1].p1->p2[k2].x1, and (*p0).x0[k1].p1->p2[k2].x1[k3].x2.

base expression The *base array* of a given array section or array element, if it exists; otherwise, the *base pointer* of the array section or array element.

> COMMENT: For the array section (*p0).x0[k1].p1->p2[k2].x1[k3].x2[4][0:n], where identifiers p*i* have a pointer type declaration and identifiers x*i* have an array type declaration, the *base expression* is: (*p0).x0[k1].p1->p2[k2].x1[k3].x2.

More examples for C/C++:

- The *base expression* for x[i] and for x[i:n] is x, if x is an array or pointer.
- The *base expression* for x[5][i] and for x[5][i:n] is x, if x is a pointer to an array or x is 2-dimensional array.
- The *base expression* for y[5][i] and for y[5][i:n] is y[5], if y is an array of pointers or y is a pointer to a pointer.

Examples for Fortran:

- The *base expression* for x(i) and for x(i:j) is x.

attached pointer A pointer variable in a device data environment to which the effect of a **map** clause assigns the address of an object, minus some offset, that is created in the device data environment. The pointer is an attached pointer for the remainder of its lifetime in the device data environment.

simply contiguous array section		An array section that statically can be determined to have contiguous storage or that, in Fortran, has the `CONTIGUOUS` attribute.
structure		A structure is a variable that contains one or more variables.
		For C/C++: Implemented using struct types.
		For C++: Implemented using class types.
		For Fortran: Implemented using derived types.
private variable		With respect to a given set of *task regions* or *SIMD lanes* that bind to the same `parallel` *region*, a *variable* for which the name provides access to a different block of storage for each *task region* or *SIMD lane*.
		A *variable* that is part of another variable (as an array or structure element) cannot be made private independently of other components.
shared variable		With respect to a given set of *task regions* that bind to the same `parallel` *region*, a *variable* for which the name provides access to the same block of storage for each *task region*.
		A *variable* that is part of another variable (as an array or structure element) cannot be *shared* independently of the other components, except for static data members of C++ classes.
threadprivate variable		A *variable* that is replicated, one instance per *thread*, by the OpenMP implementation. Its name then provides access to a different block of storage for each *thread*.
		A *variable* that is part of another variable (as an array or structure element) cannot be made *threadprivate* independently of the other components, except for static data members of C++ classes.
threadprivate memory		The set of *threadprivate variables* associated with each *thread*.
data environment		The *variables* associated with the execution of a given *region*.
device data environment		The initial *data environment* associated with a device.
device address		An *implementation-defined* reference to an address in a *device data environment*.
device pointer		A *variable* that contains a *device address*.
mapped variable		An original *variable* in a *data environment* with a corresponding *variable* in a device *data environment*.
		COMMENT: The original and corresponding *variables* may share storage.

TABLE 1.1: Map-Type Decay of Map Type Combinations

	alloc	to	from	tofrom	release	delete
alloc	alloc	alloc	alloc	alloc	release	delete
to	alloc	to	alloc	to	release	delete
from	alloc	alloc	from	from	release	delete
tofrom	alloc	to	from	tofrom	release	delete

map-type decay   The process used to determine the final map type when mapping a variable with a user defined mapper. Table 1.1 shows the final map type that the combination of the two map types determines.

mappable type   A type that is valid for a *mapped variable*. If a type is composed from other types (such as the type of an array or structure element) and any of the other types are not mappable then the type is not mappable.

> COMMENT: Pointer types are *mappable* but the memory block to which the pointer refers is not *mapped*.

For C, the type must be a complete type.

For C++, the type must be a complete type.

In addition, for class types:

- All member functions accessed in any `target` region must appear in a `declare target` directive.

For Fortran, no restrictions on the type except that for derived types:

- All type-bound procedures accessed in any target region must appear in a `declare target` directive.

defined   For *variables*, the property of having a valid value.

For C, for the contents of *variables*, the property of having a valid value.

For C++, for the contents of *variables* of POD (plain old data) type, the property of having a valid value.

For *variables* of non-POD class type, the property of having been constructed but not subsequently destructed.

For Fortran, for the contents of *variables*, the property of having a valid value. For the allocation or association status of *variables*, the property of having a valid status.

> COMMENT: Programs that rely upon *variables* that are not *defined* are *non-conforming programs*.

class type   For C++, *variables* declared with one of the `class`, `struct`, or `union` keywords.

1.2.7 Implementation Terminology

supporting *n* active levels of parallelism Implies allowing an *active parallel region* to be enclosed by *n-1 active parallel regions*.

supporting the OpenMP API Supporting at least one active level of parallelism.

supporting nested parallelism Supporting more than one active level of parallelism.

internal control variable A conceptual variable that specifies runtime behavior of a set of *threads* or *tasks* in an *OpenMP program*.

> COMMENT: The acronym ICV is used interchangeably with the term *internal control variable* in the remainder of this specification.

compliant implementation An implementation of the OpenMP specification that compiles and executes any *conforming program* as defined by the specification.

> COMMENT: A *compliant implementation* may exhibit *unspecified behavior* when compiling or executing a *non-conforming program*.

unspecified behavior A behavior or result that is not specified by the OpenMP specification or not known prior to the compilation or execution of an *OpenMP program*.

Such *unspecified behavior* may result from:

- Issues documented by the OpenMP specification as having *unspecified behavior*.
- A *non-conforming program*.
- A *conforming program* exhibiting an *implementation-defined* behavior.

implementation defined Behavior that must be documented by the implementation, and is allowed to vary among different *compliant implementations*. An implementation is allowed to define this behavior as *unspecified*.

> COMMENT: All features that have *implementation-defined* behavior are documented in Appendix A.

deprecated For a construct, clause, or other feature, the property that it is normative in the current specification but is considered obsolescent and will be removed in the future.

1.2.8 Tool Terminology

tool Executable code, distinct from application or runtime code, that can observe and/or modify the execution of an application.

first-party tool		A tool that executes in the address space of the program that it is monitoring.
third-party tool		A tool that executes as a separate process from the process that it is monitoring and potentially controlling.
activated tool		A *first-party tool* that successfully completed its initialization.
event		A point of interest in the execution of a thread.
native thread		A thread defined by an underlying thread implementation.
tool callback		A function that a tool provides to an OpenMP implementation to invoke when an associated event occurs.
registering a callback		Providing a *tool callback* to an OpenMP implementation.
dispatching a callback at an event		Processing a callback when an associated *event* occurs in a manner consistent with the return code provided when a *first-party tool* registered the callback.
thread state		An enumeration type that describes the current OpenMP activity of a *thread*. A *thread* can be in only one state at any time.
wait identifier		A unique opaque handle associated with each data object (for example, a lock) used by the OpenMP runtime to enforce mutual exclusion that may cause a thread to wait actively or passively.
frame		A storage area on a thread's stack associated with a procedure invocation. A frame includes space for one or more saved registers and often also includes space for saved arguments, local variables, and padding for alignment.
canonical frame address		An address associated with a procedure *frame* on a call stack that was the value of the stack pointer immediately prior to calling the procedure for which the invocation is represented by the frame.
runtime entry point		A function interface provided by an OpenMP runtime for use by a tool. A runtime entry point is typically not associated with a global function symbol.
trace record		A data structure in which to store information associated with an occurrence of an *event*.
native trace record		A *trace record* for an OpenMP device that is in a device-specific format.
signal		A software interrupt delivered to a *thread*.
signal handler		A function called asynchronously when a *signal* is delivered to a *thread*.
async signal safe		The guarantee that interruption by *signal* delivery will not interfere with a set of operations. An async signal safe *runtime entry point* is safe to call from a *signal handler*.

code block		A contiguous region of memory that contains code of an OpenMP program to be executed on a device.
OMPT		An interface that helps a *first-party tool* monitor the execution of an OpenMP program.
OMPT interface state		A state that indicates the permitted interactions between a first-party tool and the OpenMP implementation.
OMPT active		An *OMPT interface state* in which the OpenMP implementation is prepared to accept runtime calls from a *first party tool* and it dispatches any registered callbacks and in which a first-party tool can invoke *runtime entry points* if not otherwise restricted.
OMPT pending		An *OMPT interface state* in which the OpenMP implementation can only call functions to initialize a *first party tool* and in which a *first-party tool* cannot invoke *runtime entry points*.
OMPT inactive		An *OMPT interface state* in which the OpenMP implementation will not make any callbacks and in which a *first-party tool* cannot invoke *runtime entry points*.
OMPD		An interface that helps a *third-party tool* inspect the OpenMP state of a program that has begun execution.
OMPD library		A dynamically loadable library that implements the *OMPD* interface.
image file		An executable or shared library.
address space		A collection of logical, virtual, or physical memory address ranges that contain code, stack, and/or data. Address ranges within an address space need not be contiguous. An address space consists of one or more *segments*.
segment		A portion of an address space associated with a set of address ranges.
OpenMP architecture		The architecture on which an OpenMP *region* executes.
tool architecture		The architecture on which an *OMPD* tool executes.
OpenMP process		A collection of one or more *threads* and *address spaces*. A process may contain *threads* and *address spaces* for multiple *OpenMP architectures*. At least one thread in an OpenMP process is an OpenMP *thread*. A process may be live or a core file.
address space handle		A *handle* that refers to an *address space* within an OpenMP process.
thread handle		A *handle* that refers to an OpenMP *thread*.
parallel handle		A *handle* that refers to an OpenMP parallel *region*.
task handle		A *handle* that refers to an OpenMP task *region*.
descendent handle		An output *handle* that is returned from the *OMPD* library in a function that accepts an input *handle*: the output *handle* is a descendent of the input *handle*.

	ancestor handle	An input *handle* that is passed to the *OMPD* library in a function that returns an output *handle*: the input *handle* is an ancestor of the output *handle*. For a given *handle*, the ancestors of the *handle* are also the ancestors of the handle's descendent.
		COMMENT: A *handle* cannot be used by the tool in an *OMPD* call if any ancestor of the *handle* has been released, except for *OMPD* calls that release the *handle*.
	tool context	An opaque reference provided by a tool to an *OMPD* library. A *tool context* uniquely identifies an abstraction.
	address space context	A *tool context* that refers to an *address space* within a process.
	thread context	A *tool context* that refers to a *native thread*.
	native thread identifier	An identifier for a native thread defined by a thread implementation.

1.3 Execution Model

The OpenMP API uses the fork-join model of parallel execution. Multiple threads of execution perform tasks defined implicitly or explicitly by OpenMP directives. The OpenMP API is intended to support programs that will execute correctly both as parallel programs (multiple threads of execution and a full OpenMP support library) and as sequential programs (directives ignored and a simple OpenMP stubs library). However, it is possible and permitted to develop a program that executes correctly as a parallel program but not as a sequential program, or that produces different results when executed as a parallel program compared to when it is executed as a sequential program. Furthermore, using different numbers of threads may result in different numeric results because of changes in the association of numeric operations. For example, a serial addition reduction may have a different pattern of addition associations than a parallel reduction. These different associations may change the results of floating-point addition.

An OpenMP program begins as a single thread of execution, called an initial thread. An initial thread executes sequentially, as if the code encountered is part of an implicit task region, called an initial task region, that is generated by the implicit parallel region surrounding the whole program.

The thread that executes the implicit parallel region that surrounds the whole program executes on the *host device*. An implementation may support other *target devices*. If supported, one or more devices are available to the host device for offloading code and data. Each device has its own threads that are distinct from threads that execute on another device. Threads cannot migrate from one device to another device. The execution model is host-centric such that the host device offloads `target` regions to target devices.

When a **target** construct is encountered, a new *target task* is generated. The *target task* region encloses the **target** region. The *target task* is complete after the execution of the **target** region is complete.

When a *target task* executes, the enclosed **target** region is executed by an initial thread. The initial thread may execute on a *target device*. The initial thread executes sequentially, as if the target region is part of an initial task region that is generated by an implicit parallel region. If the target device does not exist or the implementation does not support the target device, all **target** regions associated with that device execute on the host device.

The implementation must ensure that the **target** region executes as if it were executed in the data environment of the target device unless an **if** clause is present and the **if** clause expression evaluates to *false*.

The **teams** construct creates a *league of teams*, where each team is an initial team that comprises an initial thread that executes the **teams** region. Each initial thread executes sequentially, as if the code encountered is part of an initial task region that is generated by an implicit parallel region associated with each team.

If a construct creates a data environment, the data environment is created at the time the construct is encountered. The description of a construct defines whether it creates a data environment.

When any thread encounters a **parallel** construct, the thread creates a team of itself and zero or more additional threads and becomes the master of the new team. A set of implicit tasks, one per thread, is generated. The code for each task is defined by the code inside the **parallel** construct. Each task is assigned to a different thread in the team and becomes tied; that is, it is always executed by the thread to which it is initially assigned. The task region of the task being executed by the encountering thread is suspended, and each member of the new team executes its implicit task. There is an implicit barrier at the end of the **parallel** construct. Only the master thread resumes execution beyond the end of the **parallel** construct, resuming the task region that was suspended upon encountering the **parallel** construct. Any number of **parallel** constructs can be specified in a single program.

parallel regions may be arbitrarily nested inside each other. If nested parallelism is disabled, or is not supported by the OpenMP implementation, then the new team that is created by a thread encountering a **parallel** construct inside a **parallel** region will consist only of the encountering thread. However, if nested parallelism is supported and enabled, then the new team can consist of more than one thread. A **parallel** construct may include a **proc_bind** clause to specify the places to use for the threads in the team within the **parallel** region.

When any team encounters a worksharing construct, the work inside the construct is divided among the members of the team, and executed cooperatively instead of being executed by every thread. There is a default barrier at the end of each worksharing construct unless the **nowait** clause is present. Redundant execution of code by every thread in the team resumes after the end of the worksharing construct.

When any thread encounters a *task generating construct*, one or more explicit tasks are generated. Execution of explicitly generated tasks is assigned to one of the threads in the current team, subject to the thread's availability to execute work. Thus, execution of the new task could be immediate, or deferred until later according to task scheduling constraints and thread availability. Threads are allowed to suspend the current task region at a task scheduling point in order to execute a different task. If the suspended task region is for a tied task, the initially assigned thread later resumes execution of the suspended task region. If the suspended task region is for an untied task, then any thread may resume its execution. Completion of all explicit tasks bound to a given parallel region is guaranteed before the master thread leaves the implicit barrier at the end of the region. Completion of a subset of all explicit tasks bound to a given parallel region may be specified through the use of task synchronization constructs. Completion of all explicit tasks bound to the implicit parallel region is guaranteed by the time the program exits.

When any thread encounters a **simd** construct, the iterations of the loop associated with the construct may be executed concurrently using the SIMD lanes that are available to the thread.

When a **loop** construct is encountered, the iterations of the loop associated with the construct are executed in the context of its encountering thread(s), as determined according to its binding region. If the **loop** region binds to a **teams** region, the region is encountered by the set of master threads that execute the **teams** region. If the **loop** region binds to a **parallel** region, the region is encountered by the team of threads executing the **parallel** region. Otherwise, the region is encountered by a single thread.

If the **loop** region binds to a **teams** region, the encountering threads may continue execution after the **loop** region without waiting for all iterations to complete; the iterations are guaranteed to complete before the end of the **teams** region. Otherwise, all iterations must complete before the encountering thread(s) continue execution after the **loop** region. All threads that encounter the **loop** construct may participate in the execution of the iterations. Only one of these threads may execute any given iteration.

The **cancel** construct can alter the previously described flow of execution in an OpenMP region. The effect of the **cancel** construct depends on its *construct-type-clause*. If a task encounters a **cancel** construct with a **taskgroup** *construct-type-clause*, then the task activates cancellation and continues execution at the end of its **task** region, which implies completion of that task. Any other task in that **taskgroup** that has begun executing completes execution unless it encounters a **cancellation point** construct, in which case it continues execution at the end of its **task** region, which implies its completion. Other tasks in that **taskgroup** region that have not begun execution are aborted, which implies their completion.

For all other *construct-type-clause* values, if a thread encounters a **cancel** construct, it activates cancellation of the innermost enclosing region of the type specified and the thread continues execution at the end of that region. Threads check if cancellation has been activated for their region at cancellation points and, if so, also resume execution at the end of the canceled region.

If cancellation has been activated regardless of *construct-type-clause*, threads that are waiting inside a barrier other than an implicit barrier at the end of the canceled region exit the barrier and resume execution at the end of the canceled region. This action can occur before the other threads reach that barrier.

Synchronization constructs and library routines are available in the OpenMP API to coordinate tasks and data access in `parallel` regions. In addition, library routines and environment variables are available to control or to query the runtime environment of OpenMP programs.

The OpenMP specification makes no guarantee that input or output to the same file is synchronous when executed in parallel. In this case, the programmer is responsible for synchronizing input and output processing with the assistance of OpenMP synchronization constructs or library routines. For the case where each thread accesses a different file, no synchronization by the programmer is necessary.

1.4 Memory Model

1.4.1 Structure of the OpenMP Memory Model

The OpenMP API provides a relaxed-consistency, shared-memory model. All OpenMP threads have access to a place to store and to retrieve variables, called the *memory*. In addition, each thread is allowed to have its own *temporary view* of the memory. The temporary view of memory for each thread is not a required part of the OpenMP memory model, but can represent any kind of intervening structure, such as machine registers, cache, or other local storage, between the thread and the memory. The temporary view of memory allows the thread to cache variables and thereby to avoid going to memory for every reference to a variable. Each thread also has access to another type of memory that must not be accessed by other threads, called *threadprivate memory*.

A directive that accepts data-sharing attribute clauses determines two kinds of access to variables used in the directive's associated structured block: shared and private. Each variable referenced in the structured block has an original variable, which is the variable by the same name that exists in the program immediately outside the construct. Each reference to a shared variable in the structured block becomes a reference to the original variable. For each private variable referenced in the structured block, a new version of the original variable (of the same type and size) is created in memory for each task or SIMD lane that contains code associated with the directive. Creation of the new version does not alter the value of the original variable. However, the impact of attempts to access the original variable during the region corresponding to the directive is unspecified; see Section 2.19.4.3 on page 285 for additional details. References to a private variable in the structured block refer to the private version of the original variable for the current task or SIMD lane. The relationship between the value of the original variable and the initial or final value of the private version depends on the exact clause that specifies it. Details of this issue, as well as other issues with privatization, are provided in Section 2.19 on page 269.

The minimum size at which a memory update may also read and write back adjacent variables that are part of another variable (as array or structure elements) is implementation defined but is no larger than required by the base language.

A single access to a variable may be implemented with multiple load or store instructions and, thus, is not guaranteed to be atomic with respect to other accesses to the same variable. Accesses to variables smaller than the implementation defined minimum size or to C or C++ bit-fields may be implemented by reading, modifying, and rewriting a larger unit of memory, and may thus interfere with updates of variables or fields in the same unit of memory.

If multiple threads write without synchronization to the same memory unit, including cases due to atomicity considerations as described above, then a data race occurs. Similarly, if at least one thread reads from a memory unit and at least one thread writes without synchronization to that same memory unit, including cases due to atomicity considerations as described above, then a data race occurs. If a data race occurs then the result of the program is unspecified.

A private variable in a task region that subsequently generates an inner nested **parallel** region is permitted to be made shared by implicit tasks in the inner **parallel** region. A private variable in a task region can also be shared by an explicit task region generated during its execution. However, it is the programmer's responsibility to ensure through synchronization that the lifetime of the variable does not end before completion of the explicit task region sharing it. Any other access by one task to the private variables of another task results in unspecified behavior.

1.4.2 Device Data Environments

When an OpenMP program begins, an implicit **target data** region for each device surrounds the whole program. Each device has a device data environment that is defined by its implicit **target data** region. Any **declare target** directives and the directives that accept data-mapping attribute clauses determine how an original variable in a data environment is mapped to a corresponding variable in a device data environment.

When an original variable is mapped to a device data environment and a corresponding variable is not present in the device data environment, a new corresponding variable (of the same type and size as the original variable) is created in the device data environment. Conversely, the original variable becomes the new variable's corresponding variable in the device data environment of the device that performs the mapping operation.

The corresponding variable in the device data environment may share storage with the original variable. Writes to the corresponding variable may alter the value of the original variable. The impact of this possibility on memory consistency is discussed in Section 1.4.6 on page 28. When a task executes in the context of a device data environment, references to the original variable refer to the corresponding variable in the device data environment. If an original variable is not currently mapped and a corresponding variable does not exist in the device data environment then accesses to the original variable result in unspecified behavior unless the **unified_shared_memory** clause is specified on a **requires** directive for the compilation unit.

The relationship between the value of the original variable and the initial or final value of the corresponding variable depends on the *map-type*. Details of this issue, as well as other issues with mapping a variable, are provided in Section 2.19.7.1 on page 315.

The original variable in a data environment and the corresponding variable(s) in one or more device data environments may share storage. Without intervening synchronization data races can occur.

1.4.3 Memory Management

The host device, and target devices that an implementation may support, have attached storage resources where program variables are stored. These resources can have different traits. A memory space in an OpenMP program represents a set of these storage resources. Memory spaces are defined according to a set of traits, and a single resource may be exposed as multiple memory spaces with different traits or may be part of multiple memory spaces. In any device, at least one memory space is guaranteed to exist.

An OpenMP program can use a *memory allocator* to allocate *memory* in which to store variables. This *memory* will be allocated from the storage resources of the *memory space* associated with the memory allocator. Memory allocators are also used to deallocate previously allocated *memory*. When an OpenMP memory allocator is not used to allocate memory, OpenMP does not prescribe the storage resource for the allocation; the memory for the variables may be allocated in any storage resource.

1.4.4 The Flush Operation

The memory model has relaxed-consistency because a thread's temporary view of memory is not required to be consistent with memory at all times. A value written to a variable can remain in the thread's temporary view until it is forced to memory at a later time. Likewise, a read from a variable may retrieve the value from the thread's temporary view, unless it is forced to read from memory. OpenMP flush operations are used to enforce consistency between a thread's temporary view of memory and memory, or between multiple threads' view of memory.

If a flush operation is a strong flush, it enforces consistency between a thread's temporary view and memory. A strong flush operation is applied to a set of variables called the *flush-set*. A strong flush restricts reordering of memory operations that an implementation might otherwise do. Implementations must not reorder the code for a memory operation for a given variable, or the code for a flush operation for the variable, with respect to a strong flush operation that refers to the same variable.

If a thread has performed a write to its temporary view of a shared variable since its last strong flush of that variable, then when it executes another strong flush of the variable, the strong flush does not complete until the value of the variable has been written to the variable in memory. If a thread performs multiple writes to the same variable between two strong flushes of that variable, the strong flush ensures that the value of the last write is written to the variable in memory. A strong flush of a variable executed by a thread also causes its temporary view of the variable to be discarded, so that if its next memory operation for that variable is a read, then the thread will read from memory and capture the value in its temporary view. When a thread executes a strong flush, no later memory operation by that thread for a variable involved in that strong flush is allowed to start until the strong flush completes. The completion of a strong flush executed by a thread is defined as the point at which all writes to the flush-set performed by the thread before the strong flush are visible in memory to all other threads, and at which that thread's temporary view of the flush-set is discarded.

A strong flush operation provides a guarantee of consistency between a thread's temporary view and memory. Therefore, a strong flush can be used to guarantee that a value written to a variable by one thread may be read by a second thread. To accomplish this, the programmer must ensure that the second thread has not written to the variable since its last strong flush of the variable, and that the following sequence of events are completed in this specific order:

1. The value is written to the variable by the first thread;

2. The variable is flushed, with a strong flush, by the first thread;

3. The variable is flushed, with a strong flush, by the second thread; and

4. The value is read from the variable by the second thread.

If a flush operation is a release flush or acquire flush, it can enforce consistency between the views of memory of two synchronizing threads. A release flush guarantees that any prior operation that writes or reads a shared variable will appear to be completed before any operation that writes or reads the same shared variable and follows an acquire flush with which the release flush synchronizes (see Section 1.4.5 on page 27 for more details on flush synchronization). A release flush will propagate the values of all shared variables in its temporary view to memory prior to the thread performing any subsequent atomic operation that may establish a synchronization. An acquire flush will discard any value of a shared variable in its temporary view to which the thread has not written since last performing a release flush, so that it may subsequently read a value propagated by a release flush that synchronizes with it. Therefore, release and acquire flushes may also be used to guarantee that a value written to a variable by one thread may be read by a second thread. To accomplish this, the programmer must ensure that the second thread has not written to the variable since its last acquire flush, and that the following sequence of events happen in this specific order:

1. The value is written to the variable by the first thread;

2. The first thread performs a release flush;

3. The second thread performs an acquire flush; and

4. The value is read from the variable by the second thread.

> Note – OpenMP synchronization operations, described in Section 2.17 on page 223 and in Section 3.3 on page 381, are recommended for enforcing this order. Synchronization through variables is possible but is not recommended because the proper timing of flushes is difficult.

The flush properties that define whether a flush operation is a strong flush, a release flush, or an acquire flush are not mutually disjoint. A flush operation may be a strong flush and a release flush; it may be a strong flush and an acquire flush; it may be a release flush and an acquire flush; or it may be all three.

1.4.5 Flush Synchronization and *Happens Before*

OpenMP supports thread synchronization with the use of release flushes and acquire flushes. For any such synchronization, a release flush is the source of the synchronization and an acquire flush is the sink of the synchronization, such that the release flush *synchronizes with* the acquire flush.

A release flush has one or more associated *release sequences* that define the set of modifications that may be used to establish a synchronization. A release sequence starts with an atomic operation that follows the release flush and modifies a shared variable and additionally includes any read-modify-write atomic operations that read a value taken from some modification in the release sequence. The following rules determine the atomic operation that starts an associated release sequence.

- If a release flush is performed on entry to an atomic operation, that atomic operation starts its release sequence.

- If a release flush is performed in an implicit **flush** region, an atomic operation that is provided by the implementation and that modifies an internal synchronization variable, starts its release sequence.

- If a release flush is performed by an explicit **flush** region, any atomic operation that modifies a shared variable and follows the **flush** region in its thread's program order starts an associated release sequence.

An acquire flush is associated with one or more prior atomic operations that read a shared variable and that may be used to establish a synchronization. The following rules determine the associated atomic operation that may establish a synchronization.

- If an acquire flush is performed on exit from an atomic operation, that atomic operation is its associated atomic operation.

- If an acquire flush is performed in an implicit **flush** region, an atomic operation that is provided by the implementation and that reads an internal synchronization variable is its associated atomic operation.

- If an acquire flush is performed by an explicit **flush** region, any atomic operation that reads a shared variable and precedes the **flush** region in its thread's program order is an associated atomic operation.

A release flush synchronizes with an acquire flush if an atomic operation associated with the acquire flush reads a value written by a modification from a release sequence associated with the release flush.

An operation X *simply happens before* an operation Y if any of the following conditions are satisfied:

1. X and Y are performed by the same thread, and X precedes Y in the thread's program order;
2. X synchronizes with Y according to the flush synchronization conditions explained above or according to the base language's definition of *synchronizes with*, if such a definition exists; or
3. There exists another operation Z, such that X simply happens before Z and Z simply happens before Y.

An operation X *happens before* an operation Y if any of the following conditions are satisfied:

1. X happens before Y according to the base language's definition of *happens before*, if such a definition exists; or
2. X simply happens before Y.

A variable with an initial value is treated as if the value is stored to the variable by an operation that happens before all operations that access or modify the variable in the program.

1.4.6 OpenMP Memory Consistency

The following rules guarantee the observable completion order of memory operations, as seen by all threads.

- If two operations performed by different threads are sequentially consistent atomic operations or they are strong flushes that flush the same variable, then they must be completed as if in some sequential order, seen by all threads.

- If two operations performed by the same thread are sequentially consistent atomic operations or they access, modify, or, with a strong flush, flush the same variable, then they must be completed as if in that thread's program order, as seen by all threads.

- If two operations are performed by different threads and one happens before the other, then they must be completed as if in that *happens before* order, as seen by all threads, if:

- both operations access or modify the same variable;
- both operations are strong flushes that flush the same variable; or
- both operations are sequentially consistent atomic operations.

- Any two atomic memory operations from different **atomic** regions must be completed as if in the same order as the strong flushes implied in their respective regions, as seen by all threads.

The flush operation can be specified using the **flush** directive, and is also implied at various locations in an OpenMP program: see Section 2.17.8 on page 242 for details.

▼───▼

Note – Since flush operations by themselves cannot prevent data races, explicit flush operations are only useful in combination with non-sequentially consistent atomic directives.

▲───▲

OpenMP programs that:

- Do not use non-sequentially consistent atomic directives;
- Do not rely on the accuracy of a *false* result from **omp_test_lock** and **omp_test_nest_lock**; and
- Correctly avoid data races as required in Section 1.4.1 on page 23,

behave as though operations on shared variables were simply interleaved in an order consistent with the order in which they are performed by each thread. The relaxed consistency model is invisible for such programs, and any explicit flush operations in such programs are redundant.

1.5 Tool Interfaces

The OpenMP API includes two tool interfaces, OMPT and OMPD, to enable development of high-quality, portable, tools that support monitoring, performance, or correctness analysis and debugging of OpenMP programs developed using any implementation of the OpenMP API,

1.5.1 OMPT

The OMPT interface, which is intended for *first-party* tools, provides the following:

- A mechanism to initialize a first-party tool;

- Routines that enable a tool to determine the capabilities of an OpenMP implementation;
- Routines that enable a tool to examine OpenMP state information associated with a thread;
- Mechanisms that enable a tool to map implementation-level calling contexts back to their source-level representations;
- A callback interface that enables a tool to receive notification of OpenMP *events*;
- A tracing interface that enables a tool to trace activity on OpenMP target devices; and
- A runtime library routine that an application can use to control a tool.

OpenMP implementations may differ with respect to the *thread states* that they support, the mutual exclusion implementations that they employ, and the OpenMP events for which tool callbacks are invoked. For some OpenMP events, OpenMP implementations must guarantee that a registered callback will be invoked for each occurrence of the event. For other OpenMP events, OpenMP implementations are permitted to invoke a registered callback for some or no occurrences of the event; for such OpenMP events, however, OpenMP implementations are encouraged to invoke tool callbacks on as many occurrences of the event as is practical. Section 4.2.4 specifies the subset of OMPT callbacks that an OpenMP implementation must support for a minimal implementation of the OMPT interface.

An implementation of the OpenMP API may differ from the abstract execution model described by its specification. The ability of tools that use the OMPT interface to observe such differences does not constrain implementations of the OpenMP API in any way.

With the exception of the `omp_control_tool` runtime library routine for tool control, all other routines in the OMPT interface are intended for use only by tools and are not visible to applications. For that reason, a Fortran binding is provided only for `omp_control_tool`; all other OMPT functionality is described with C syntax only.

1.5.2 OMPD

The OMPD interface is intended for *third-party* tools, which run as separate processes. An OpenMP implementation must provide an OMPD library that can be dynamically loaded and used by a third-party tool. A third-party tool, such as a debugger, uses the OMPD library to access OpenMP state of a program that has begun execution. OMPD defines the following:

- An interface that an OMPD library exports, which a tool can use to access OpenMP state of a program that has begun execution;
- A callback interface that a tool provides to the OMPD library so that the library can use it to access the OpenMP state of a program that has begun execution; and

- A small number of symbols that must be defined by an OpenMP implementation to help the tool find the correct OMPD library to use for that OpenMP implementation and to facilitate notification of events.

Section 5 describes OMPD in detail.

1.6 OpenMP Compliance

The OpenMP API defines constructs that operate in the context of the base language that is supported by an implementation. If the implementation of the base language does not support a language construct that appears in this document, a compliant OpenMP implementation is not required to support it, with the exception that for Fortran, the implementation must allow case insensitivity for directive and API routines names, and must allow identifiers of more than six characters. An implementation of the OpenMP API is compliant if and only if it compiles and executes all other conforming programs, and supports the tool interface, according to the syntax and semantics laid out in Chapters 1, 2, 3, 4 and 5. Appendices A, B, C, and D, as well as sections designated as Notes (see Section 1.8 on page 34) are for information purposes only and are not part of the specification.

All library, intrinsic and built-in routines provided by the base language must be thread-safe in a compliant implementation. In addition, the implementation of the base language must also be thread-safe. For example, **ALLOCATE** and **DEALLOCATE** statements must be thread-safe in Fortran. Unsynchronized concurrent use of such routines by different threads must produce correct results (although not necessarily the same as serial execution results, as in the case of random number generation routines).

Starting with Fortran 90, variables with explicit initialization have the **SAVE** attribute implicitly. This is not the case in Fortran 77. However, a compliant OpenMP Fortran implementation must give such a variable the **SAVE** attribute, regardless of the underlying base language version.

Appendix A lists certain aspects of the OpenMP API that are implementation defined. A compliant implementation must define and document its behavior for each of the items in Appendix A.

1.7 Normative References

- ISO/IEC 9899:1990, *Information Technology - Programming Languages - C*.

    This OpenMP API specification refers to ISO/IEC 9899:1990 as C90.

- ISO/IEC 9899:1999, *Information Technology - Programming Languages - C*.

    This OpenMP API specification refers to ISO/IEC 9899:1999 as C99.

- ISO/IEC 9899:2011, *Information Technology - Programming Languages - C*.

    This OpenMP API specification refers to ISO/IEC 9899:2011 as C11. While future versions of the OpenMP specification are expected to address the following features, currently their use may result in unspecified behavior.

    – Supporting the noreturn property

    – Adding alignment support

    – Creation of complex value

    – Threads for the C standard library

    – Thread-local storage

    – Parallel memory sequencing model

    – Atomic

- ISO/IEC 14882:1998, *Information Technology - Programming Languages - C++*.

    This OpenMP API specification refers to ISO/IEC 14882:1998 as C++98.

- ISO/IEC 14882:2011, *Information Technology - Programming Languages - C++*.

    This OpenMP API specification refers to ISO/IEC 14882:2011 as C++11. While future versions of the OpenMP specification are expected to address the following features, currently their use may result in unspecified behavior.

    – Alignment support

    – Standard layout types

    – Allowing move constructs to throw

    – Defining move special member functions

    – Concurrency

    – Data-dependency ordering: atomics and memory model

    – Additions to the standard library

    – Thread-local storage

    – Dynamic initialization and destruction with concurrency

    – C++11 library

- ISO/IEC 14882:2014, *Information Technology - Programming Languages - C++*.

  This OpenMP API specification refers to ISO/IEC 14882:2014 as C++14. While future versions of the OpenMP specification are expected to address the following features, currently their use may result in unspecified behavior.

  – Sized deallocation
  – What signal handlers can do

- ISO/IEC 14882:2017, *Information Technology - Programming Languages - C++*.

  This OpenMP API specification refers to ISO/IEC 14882:2017 as C++17.

- ISO/IEC 1539:1980, *Information Technology - Programming Languages - Fortran*.

  This OpenMP API specification refers to ISO/IEC 1539:1980 as Fortran 77.

- ISO/IEC 1539:1991, *Information Technology - Programming Languages - Fortran*.

  This OpenMP API specification refers to ISO/IEC 1539:1991 as Fortran 90.

- ISO/IEC 1539-1:1997, *Information Technology - Programming Languages - Fortran*.

  This OpenMP API specification refers to ISO/IEC 1539-1:1997 as Fortran 95.

- ISO/IEC 1539-1:2004, *Information Technology - Programming Languages - Fortran*.

  This OpenMP API specification refers to ISO/IEC 1539-1:2004 as Fortran 2003.

- ISO/IEC 1539-1:2010, *Information Technology - Programming Languages - Fortran*.

  This OpenMP API specification refers to ISO/IEC 1539-1:2010 as Fortran 2008. While future versions of the OpenMP specification are expected to address the following features, currently their use may result in unspecified behavior.

  – Submodules
  – Coarrays
  – DO CONCURRENT
  – Allocatable components of recursive type
  – Pointer initialization
  – Value attribute is permitted for any nonallocatable nonpointer nonarray
    Simply contiguous arrays rank remapping to rank>1 target
  – Polymorphic assignment
  – Accessing real and imaginary parts
  – Pointer function reference is a variable

- Recursive I/O
- The BLOCK construct
- EXIT statement (to terminate a non-DO construct)
- ERROR STOP
- Internal procedure as an actual argument
- Generic resolution by procedureness
- Generic resolution by pointer vs. allocatable
- Impure elemental procedures

Where this OpenMP API specification refers to C, C++ or Fortran, reference is made to the base language supported by the implementation.

1.8 Organization of this Document

The remainder of this document is structured as follows:

- Chapter 2 "Directives"
- Chapter 3 "Runtime Library Routines"
- Chapter 4 "OMPT Interface"
- Chapter 5 "OMPD Interface"
- Chapter 6 "Environment Variables"
- Appendix A "OpenMP Implementation-Defined Behaviors"
- Appendix B "Features History"

Some sections of this document only apply to programs written in a certain base language. Text that applies only to programs for which the base language is C or C++ is shown as follows:

———————————————— C / C++ ————————————————

C/C++ specific text...

———————————————— C / C++ ————————————————

Text that applies only to programs for which the base language is C only is shown as follows:

———————————————— C ————————————————

C specific text...

———————————————— C ————————————————

Text that applies only to programs for which the base language is C90 only is shown as follows:

―――――――――――――――― C90 ――――――――――――――――

C90 specific text...

―――――――――――――――― C90 ――――――――――――――――

Text that applies only to programs for which the base language is C99 only is shown as follows:

―――――――――――――――― C99 ――――――――――――――――

C99 specific text...

―――――――――――――――― C99 ――――――――――――――――

Text that applies only to programs for which the base language is C++ only is shown as follows:

―――――――――――――――― C++ ――――――――――――――――

C++ specific text...

―――――――――――――――― C++ ――――――――――――――――

Text that applies only to programs for which the base language is Fortran is shown as follows:

―――――――――――――――― Fortran ――――――――――――――――

Fortran specific text......

―――――――――――――――― Fortran ――――――――――――――――

Where an entire page consists of base language specific text, a marker is shown at the top of the page. For Fortran-specific text, the marker is:

- - - - - - - - - - - - - - - - Fortran (cont.) - - - - - - - - - - - - - - - -

For C/C++-specific text, the marker is:

- - - - - - - - - - - - - - - - C/C++ (cont.) - - - - - - - - - - - - - - - -

Some text is for information only, and is not part of the normative specification. Such text is designated as a note, like this:

▼――――――――――――――――――――――――――――――――▼

Note – Non-normative text...

▲――――――――――――――――――――――――――――――――▲

This page intentionally left blank

CHAPTER 2

Directives

This chapter describes the syntax and behavior of OpenMP directives.

---- C / C++ ----

In C/C++, OpenMP directives are specified by using the **#pragma** mechanism provided by the C and C++ standards.

---- C / C++ ----

---- Fortran ----

In Fortran, OpenMP directives are specified by using special comments that are identified by unique sentinels. Also, a special comment form is available for conditional compilation.

---- Fortran ----

Compilers can therefore ignore OpenMP directives and conditionally compiled code if support of the OpenMP API is not provided or enabled. A compliant implementation must provide an option or interface that ensures that underlying support of all OpenMP directives and OpenMP conditional compilation mechanisms is enabled. In the remainder of this document, the phrase *OpenMP compilation* is used to mean a compilation with these OpenMP features enabled.

---- Fortran ----

Restrictions

The following restriction applies to all OpenMP directives:

- OpenMP directives, except **simd** and any declarative directive, may not appear in pure procedures.

- OpenMP directives may not appear in the WHERE and FORALL constructs.

---- Fortran ----

2.1 Directive Format

───────────────── C / C++ ─────────────────

OpenMP directives for C/C++ are specified with **#pragma** directives. The syntax of an OpenMP directive is as follows:

#pragma omp *directive-name [clause[[,] clause] ...] new-line*

Each directive starts with **#pragma omp**. The remainder of the directive follows the conventions of the C and C++ standards for compiler directives. In particular, white space can be used before and after the **#**, and sometimes white space must be used to separate the words in a directive. Preprocessing tokens following **#pragma omp** are subject to macro replacement.

Some OpenMP directives may be composed of consecutive **#pragma** directives if specified in their syntax.

Directives are case-sensitive.

Each of the expressions used in the OpenMP syntax inside of the clauses must be a valid *assignment-expression* of the base language unless otherwise specified.

───────────────── C / C++ ─────────────────
───────────────── C++ ─────────────────

Directives may not appear in **constexpr** functions or in constant expressions. Variadic parameter packs cannot be expanded into a directive or its clauses except as part of an expression argument to be evaluated by the base language, such as into a function call inside an **if** clause.

───────────────── C++ ─────────────────
───────────────── Fortran ─────────────────

OpenMP directives for Fortran are specified as follows:

sentinel directive-name [clause[[,] clause]...]

All OpenMP compiler directives must begin with a directive *sentinel*. The format of a sentinel differs between fixed form and free form source files, as described in Section 2.1.1 on page 41 and Section 2.1.2 on page 41.

Directives are case insensitive. Directives cannot be embedded within continued statements, and statements cannot be embedded within directives.

Each of the expressions used in the OpenMP syntax inside of the clauses must be a valid *expression* of the base language unless otherwise specified.

In order to simplify the presentation, free form is used for the syntax of OpenMP directives for Fortran in the remainder of this document, except as noted.

───────────────── Fortran ─────────────────

Only one *directive-name* can be specified per directive (note that this includes combined directives, see Section 2.13 on page 185). The order in which clauses appear on directives is not significant. Clauses on directives may be repeated as needed, subject to the restrictions listed in the description of each clause.

Some clauses accept a *list*, an *extended-list*, or a *locator-list*. A *list* consists of a comma-separated collection of one or more *list items*. An *extended-list* consists of a comma-separated collection of one or more *extended list items*. A *locator-list* consists of a comma-separated collection of one or more *locator list items*.

―――――――――――――――――― C / C++ ――――――――――――――――――

A *list item* is a variable or an array section. An *extended list item* is a *list item* or a function name. A *locator list item* is any lvalue expression, including variables, or an array section.

―――――――――――――――――― C / C++ ――――――――――――――――――

―――――――――――――――――― Fortran ――――――――――――――――――

A *list item* is a variable, array section or common block name (enclosed in slashes). An *extended list item* is a *list item* or a procedure name. A *locator list item* is a *list item*.

When a named common block appears in a *list*, it has the same meaning as if every explicit member of the common block appeared in the list. An explicit member of a common block is a variable that is named in a **COMMON** statement that specifies the common block name and is declared in the same scoping unit in which the clause appears.

Although variables in common blocks can be accessed by use association or host association, common block names cannot. As a result, a common block name specified in a data-sharing attribute, a data copying or a data-mapping attribute clause must be declared to be a common block in the same scoping unit in which the clause appears.

If a list item that appears in a directive or clause is an optional dummy argument that is not present, the directive or clause for that list item is ignored.

If the variable referenced inside a construct is an optional dummy argument that is not present, any explicitly determined, implicitly determined, or predetermined data-sharing and data-mapping attribute rules for that variable are ignored. Otherwise, if the variable is an optional dummy argument that is present, it is present inside the construct.

―――――――――――――――――― Fortran ――――――――――――――――――

For all base languages, a *list item*, an *extended list item*, or a *locator list item* is subject to the restrictions specified in Section 2.1.5 on page 44 and in each of the sections describing clauses and directives for which the *list*, the *extended-list*, or the *locator-list* appears.

Some executable directives include a structured block. A structured block:

- may contain infinite loops where the point of exit is never reached;
- may halt due to an IEEE exception;

C / C++

- may contain calls to **exit()**, **_Exit()**, **quick_exit()**, **abort()** or functions with a **_Noreturn** specifier (in C) or a **noreturn** attribute (in C/C++);
- may be an expression statement, iteration statement, selection statement, or try block, provided that the corresponding compound statement obtained by enclosing it in **{** and **}** would be a structured block; and

C / C++

Fortran

- may contain **STOP** statements.

Fortran

Restrictions

Restrictions to structured blocks are as follows:

- Entry to a structured block must not be the result of a branch.
- The point of exit cannot be a branch out of the structured block.

C / C++

- The point of entry to a structured block must not be a call to **setjmp()**.
- **longjmp()** and **throw()** must not violate the entry/exit criteria.

C / C++

--- Fortran ---

2.1.1 Fixed Source Form Directives

The following sentinels are recognized in fixed form source files:

```
!$omp | c$omp | *$omp
```

Sentinels must start in column 1 and appear as a single word with no intervening characters. Fortran fixed form line length, white space, continuation, and column rules apply to the directive line. Initial directive lines must have a space or a zero in column 6, and continuation directive lines must have a character other than a space or a zero in column 6.

Comments may appear on the same line as a directive. The exclamation point initiates a comment when it appears after column 6. The comment extends to the end of the source line and is ignored. If the first non-blank character after the directive sentinel of an initial or continuation directive line is an exclamation point, the line is ignored.

Note – In the following example, the three formats for specifying the directive are equivalent (the first line represents the position of the first 9 columns):

```
c23456789
!$omp parallel do shared(a,b,c)

c$omp parallel do
c$omp+shared(a,b,c)

c$omp paralleldoshared(a,b,c)
```

2.1.2 Free Source Form Directives

The following sentinel is recognized in free form source files:

```
!$omp
```

The sentinel can appear in any column as long as it is preceded only by white space. It must appear as a single word with no intervening white space. Fortran free form line length, white space, and continuation rules apply to the directive line. Initial directive lines must have a space after the sentinel. Continued directive lines must have an ampersand (&) as the last non-blank character on the line, prior to any comment placed inside the directive. Continuation directive lines can have an ampersand after the directive sentinel with optional white space before and after the ampersand.

Comments may appear on the same line as a directive. The exclamation point (!) initiates a
comment. The comment extends to the end of the source line and is ignored. If the first non-blank
character after the directive sentinel is an exclamation point, the line is ignored.

One or more blanks or horizontal tabs are optional to separate adjacent keywords in
directive-names unless otherwise specified.

Note – In the following example the three formats for specifying the directive are equivalent (the
first line represents the position of the first 9 columns):

```
!23456789
      !$omp parallel do &
               !$omp shared(a,b,c)

      !$omp parallel &
    !$omp&do shared(a,b,c)

!$omp paralleldo shared(a,b,c)
```

Fortran

2.1.3 Stand-Alone Directives

Summary

Stand-alone directives are executable directives that have no associated user code.

Description

Stand-alone directives do not have any associated executable user code. Instead, they represent
executable statements that typically do not have succinct equivalent statements in the base
language. There are some restrictions on the placement of a stand-alone directive within a program.
A stand-alone directive may be placed only at a point where a base language executable statement is
allowed.

Restrictions

---------- C / C++ ----------

- A stand-alone directive may not be used in place of the statement following an `if`, `while`, `do`, `switch`, or `label`.

---------- C / C++ ----------

---------- Fortran ----------

- A stand-alone directive may not be used as the action statement in an `if` statement or as the executable statement following a label if the label is referenced in the program.

---------- Fortran ----------

---------- C / C++ ----------

2.1.4 Array Shaping

If an expression has a type of pointer to T, then a shape-operator can be used to specify the extent of that pointer. In other words, the shape-operator is used to reinterpret, as an n-dimensional array, the region of memory to which that expression points.

Formally, the syntax of the shape-operator is as follows:

> *shaped-expression* := ([s_1] [s_2] ... [s_n]) *cast-expression*

The result of applying the shape-operator to an expression is an lvalue expression with an n-dimensional array type with dimensions $s_1 \times s_2 \ldots \times s_n$ and element type T.

The precedence of the shape-operator is the same as a type cast.

Each s_i is an integral type expression that must evaluate to a positive integer.

Restrictions

Restrictions to the shape-operator are as follows:

- The type T must be a complete type.
- The shape-operator can appear only in clauses where it is explicitly allowed.
- The result of a shape-operator must be a named array of a list item.
- The type of the expression upon which a shape-operator is applied must be a pointer type.

---------- C++ ----------

- If the type T is a reference to a type T', then the type will be considered to be T' for all purposes of the designated array.

---------- C++ ----------

---------- C / C++ ----------

2.1.5 Array Sections

An array section designates a subset of the elements in an array.

─────────────── C / C++ ───────────────

To specify an array section in an OpenMP construct, array subscript expressions are extended with the following syntax:

> [*lower-bound* : *length* : *stride*] or
> [*lower-bound* : *length* :] or
> [*lower-bound* : *length*] or
> [*lower-bound* : : *stride*] or
> [*lower-bound* : :] or
> [*lower-bound* :] or
> [: *length* : *stride*] or
> [: *length* :] or
> [: *length*] or
> [: : *stride*]
> [: :]
> [:]

The array section must be a subset of the original array.

Array sections are allowed on multidimensional arrays. Base language array subscript expressions can be used to specify length-one dimensions of multidimensional array sections.

Each of the *lower-bound*, *length*, and *stride* expressions if specified must be an integral type *expression* of the base language. When evaluated they represent a set of integer values as follows:

{ *lower-bound*, *lower-bound* + *stride*, *lower-bound* + 2 * *stride*,... , *lower-bound* + ((*length* - 1) * *stride*) }

The *length* must evaluate to a non-negative integer.

The *stride* must evaluate to a positive integer.

When the size of the array dimension is not known, the *length* must be specified explicitly.

When the *stride* is absent it defaults to 1.

When the *length* is absent it defaults to $\lceil (size - lower\text{-}bound)/stride \rceil$, where *size* is the size of the array dimension.

When the *lower-bound* is absent it defaults to 0.

---------------------------- C/C++ (cont.) ----------------------------

The precedence of a subscript operator that uses the array section syntax is the same as the precedence of a subscript operator that does not use the array section syntax.

Note – The following are examples of array sections:

```
a[0:6]
a[0:6:1]
a[1:10]
a[1:]
a[:10:2]
b[10][:][:]
b[10][:][:0]
c[42][0:6][:]
c[42][0:6:2][:]
c[1:10][42][0:6]
S.c[:100]
p->y[:10]
this->a[:N]
(p+10)[:N]
```

Assume **a** is declared to be a 1-dimensional array with dimension size 11. The first two examples are equivalent, and the third and fourth examples are equivalent. The fifth example specifies a stride of 2 and therefore is not contiguous.

Assume **b** is declared to be a pointer to a 2-dimensional array with dimension sizes 10 and 10. The sixth example refers to all elements of the 2-dimensional array given by **b[10]**. The seventh example is a zero-length array section.

Assume **c** is declared to be a 3-dimensional array with dimension sizes 50, 50, and 50. The eighth example is contiguous, while the ninth and tenth examples are not contiguous.

The final four examples show array sections that are formed from more general base expressions.

The following are examples that are non-conforming array sections:

```
s[:10].x
p[:10]->y
*(xp[:10])
```

For all three examples, a base language operator is applied in an undefined manner to an array section. The only operator that may be applied to an array section is a subscript operator for which the array section appears as the postfix expression.

C / C++

Fortran

Fortran has built-in support for array sections although some restrictions apply to their use, as enumerated in the following section.

Fortran

Restrictions

Restrictions to array sections are as follows:

- An array section can appear only in clauses where it is explicitly allowed.
- A *stride* expression may not be specified unless otherwise stated.

C / C++

- An element of an array section with a non-zero size must have a complete type.
- The base expression of an array section must have an array or pointer type.
- If a consecutive sequence of array subscript expressions appears in an array section, and the first subscript expression in the sequence uses the extended array section syntax defined in this section, then only the last subscript expression in the sequence may select array elements that have a pointer type.

C / C++

C++

- If the type of the base expression of an array section is a reference to a type T, then the type will be considered to be T for all purposes of the array section.
- An array section cannot be used in an overloaded [] operator.

C++

Fortran

- If a stride expression is specified, it must be positive.
- The upper bound for the last dimension of an assumed-size dummy array must be specified.
- If a list item is an array section with vector subscripts, the first array element must be the lowest in the array element order of the array section.
- If a list item is an array section, the last *part-ref* of the list item must have a section subscript list.

Fortran

2.1.6 Iterators

Iterators are identifiers that expand to multiple values in the clause on which they appear.

The syntax of the **iterator** modifier is as follows:

iterator(*iterators-definition*)

where *iterators-definition* is one of the following:

iterator-specifier [, *iterators-definition*]

where *iterator-specifier* is one of the following:

[*iterator-type*] *identifier* = *range-specification*

where:

- *identifier* is a base language identifier.

―――――――――――――――――― C / C++ ――――――――――――――――――

- *iterator-type* is a type name.

―――――――――――――――――― C / C++ ――――――――――――――――――

―――――――――――――――――― Fortran ――――――――――――――――――

- *iterator-type* is a type specifier.

―――――――――――――――――― Fortran ――――――――――――――――――

- *range-specification* is of the form *begin* : *end*[: *step*], where *begin* and *end* are expressions for which their types can be converted to *iterator-type* and *step* is an integral expression.

―――――――――――――――――― C / C++ ――――――――――――――――――

In an *iterator-specifier*, if the *iterator-type* is not specified then the type of that iterator is of **int** type.

―――――――――――――――――― C / C++ ――――――――――――――――――

―――――――――――――――――― Fortran ――――――――――――――――――

In an *iterator-specifier*, if the *iterator-type* is not specified then the type of that iterator is default integer.

―――――――――――――――――― Fortran ――――――――――――――――――

In a *range-specification*, if the *step* is not specified its value is implicitly defined to be 1.

An iterator only exists in the context of the clause in which it appears. An iterator also hides all accessible symbols with the same name in the context of the clause.

The use of a variable in an expression that appears in the *range-specification* causes an implicit reference to the variable in all enclosing constructs.

C / C++

The values of the iterator are the set of values $i_0, \ldots, i_{N-1}$ where:

- $i_0 = $ (*iterator-type*) *begin*,
- $i_j = $ (*iterator-type*) $(i_{j-1} + step)$, and
- if $step > 0$,
  - $i_0 < $ (*iterator-type*) *end*,
  - $i_{N-1} < $ (*iterator-type*) *end*, and
  - (*iterator-type*) $(i_{N-1} + step) \geq $ (*iterator-type*) *end*;
- if $step < 0$,
  - $i_0 > $ (*iterator-type*) *end*,
  - $i_{N-1} > $ (*iterator-type*) *end*, and
  - (*iterator-type*) $(i_{N-1} + step) \leq $ (*iterator-type*) *end*.

C / C++

Fortran

The values of the iterator are the set of values $i_1, \ldots, i_N$ where:

- $i_1 = begin$,
- $i_j = i_{j-1} + step$, and
- if $step > 0$,
  - $i_1 \leq end$,
  - $i_N \leq end$, and
  - $i_N + step > end$;
- if $step < 0$,
  - $i_1 \geq end$,
  - $i_N \geq end$, and
  - $i_N + step < end$.

Fortran

The set of values will be empty if no possible value complies with the conditions above.

For those clauses that contain expressions that contain iterator identifiers, the effect is as if the list item is instantiated within the clause for each value of the iterator in the set defined above, substituting each occurrence of the iterator identifier in the expression with the iterator value. If the set of values of the iterator is empty then the effect is as if the clause was not specified.

The behavior is unspecified if $i_j + step$ cannot be represented in *iterator-type* in any of the $i_j + step$ computations for any $0 \leq j < N$ in C/C++ or $0 < j \leq N$ in Fortran.

Restrictions

- An expression that contains an iterator identifier can only appear in clauses that explicitly allow expressions that contain iterators.
- The *iterator-type* must not declare a new type.

―――――――――――――――――― C / C++ ――――――――――――――――――

- The *iterator-type* must be an integral or pointer type.
- The *iterator-type* must not be **const** qualified.

―――――――――――――――――― C / C++ ――――――――――――――――――
―――――――――――――――――― Fortran ――――――――――――――――――

- The *iterator-type* must be an integer type.

―――――――――――――――――― Fortran ――――――――――――――――――

- If the *step* expression of a *range-specification* equals zero, the behavior is unspecified.
- Each iterator identifier can only be defined once in an *iterators-definition*.
- Iterators cannot appear in the *range-specification*.

2.2 Conditional Compilation

In implementations that support a preprocessor, the **_OPENMP** macro name is defined to have the decimal value *yyyymm* where *yyyy* and *mm* are the year and month designations of the version of the OpenMP API that the implementation supports.

If a **#define** or a **#undef** preprocessing directive in user code defines or undefines the **_OPENMP** macro name, the behavior is unspecified.

―――――――――――――――――― Fortran ――――――――――――――――――

The OpenMP API requires Fortran lines to be compiled conditionally, as described in the following sections.

------- Fortran (cont.) -------

2.2.1 Fixed Source Form Conditional Compilation Sentinels

The following conditional compilation sentinels are recognized in fixed form source files:

```
!$ | *$ | c$
```

To enable conditional compilation, a line with a conditional compilation sentinel must satisfy the following criteria:

- The sentinel must start in column 1 and appear as a single word with no intervening white space;
- After the sentinel is replaced with two spaces, initial lines must have a space or zero in column 6 and only white space and numbers in columns 1 through 5;
- After the sentinel is replaced with two spaces, continuation lines must have a character other than a space or zero in column 6 and only white space in columns 1 through 5.

If these criteria are met, the sentinel is replaced by two spaces. If these criteria are not met, the line is left unchanged.

Note – In the following example, the two forms for specifying conditional compilation in fixed source form are equivalent (the first line represents the position of the first 9 columns):

```
c23456789
!$ 10 iam = omp_get_thread_num() +
!$   &           index

#ifdef _OPENMP
   10 iam = omp_get_thread_num() +
      &           index
#endif
```

2.2.2 Free Source Form Conditional Compilation Sentinel

The following conditional compilation sentinel is recognized in free form source files:

```
!$
```

To enable conditional compilation, a line with a conditional compilation sentinel must satisfy the following criteria:

- The sentinel can appear in any column but must be preceded only by white space;
- The sentinel must appear as a single word with no intervening white space;

- Initial lines must have a space after the sentinel;
- Continued lines must have an ampersand as the last non-blank character on the line, prior to any comment appearing on the conditionally compiled line.

Continuation lines can have an ampersand after the sentinel, with optional white space before and after the ampersand. If these criteria are met, the sentinel is replaced by two spaces. If these criteria are not met, the line is left unchanged.

Note – In the following example, the two forms for specifying conditional compilation in free source form are equivalent (the first line represents the position of the first 9 columns):

```
c23456789
  !$ iam = omp_get_thread_num() +      &
  !$&    index

#ifdef _OPENMP
    iam = omp_get_thread_num() +       &
          index
#endif
```

Fortran

2.3 Variant Directives

2.3.1 OpenMP Context

At any point in a program, an OpenMP context exists that defines traits that describe the active OpenMP constructs, the execution devices, and functionality supported by the implementation. The traits are grouped into trait sets. The following trait sets exist: *construct*, *device* and *implementation*.

The *construct* set is composed of the directive names, each being a trait, of all enclosing constructs at that point in the program up to a **target** construct. Combined and composite constructs are added to the set as distinct constructs in the same nesting order specified by the original construct. The set is ordered by nesting level in ascending order. Specifically, the ordering of the set of constructs is $c_1, \ldots, c_N$, where c_1 is the construct at the outermost nesting level and c_N is the construct at the innermost nesting level. In addition, if the point in the program is not enclosed by a **target** construct, the following rules are applied in order:

1. For functions with a **declare simd** directive, the *simd* trait is added to the beginning of the set as c_1 for any generated SIMD versions so the total size of the set is increased by 1.

2. For functions that are determined to be function variants by a **declare variant** directive, the selectors $c_1, \ldots, c_M$ of the **construct** selector set are added in the same order to the beginning of the set as $c_1, \ldots, c_M$ so the total size of the set is increased by M.

3. For functions within a **declare target** block, the *target* trait is added to the beginning of the set as c_1 for any versions of the function that are generated for **target** regions so the total size of the set is increased by 1.

The *simd* trait can be further defined with properties that match the clauses accepted by the **declare simd** directive with the same name and semantics. The *simd* trait must define at least the *simdlen* property and one of the *inbranch* or *notinbranch* properties.

The *device* set includes traits that define the characteristics of the device being targeted by the compiler at that point in the program. At least the following traits must be defined:

- The *kind(kind-name-list)* trait specifies the general kind of the device. The following *kind-name* values are defined:
  - *host*, which specifies that the device is the host device;
  - *nohost*, which specifies that the devices is not the host device; and
  - the values defined in the "OpenMP Context Definitions" document, which is available at http://www.openmp.org/.
- The *isa(isa-name-list)* trait specifies the Instruction Set Architectures supported by the device. The accepted *isa-name* values are implementation defined.
- The *arch(arch-name-list)* trait specifies the architectures supported by the device. The accepted *arch-name* values are implementation defined.

The *implementation* set includes traits that describe the functionality supported by the OpenMP implementation at that point in the program. At least the following traits can be defined:

- The *vendor(vendor-name-list)* trait, which specifies the vendor identifiers of the implementation. OpenMP defined values for *vendor-name* are defined in the "OpenMP Context Definitions" document, which is available at http://www.openmp.org/.
- The *extension(extension-name-list)* trait, which specifies vendor specific extensions to the OpenMP specification. The accepted *extension-name* values are implementation defined.
- A trait with a name that is identical to the name of any clause that can be supplied to the **requires** directive.

Implementations can define further traits in the *device* and *implementation* sets. All implementation defined traits must follow the following syntax:

identifier[(context-element[, context-element[, ...]])]

context-element:
  identifier[(context-element[, context-element[, ...]])]
  or
  context-value

context-value:
  constant string
  or
  constant integer expression

where *identifier* is a base language identifier.

2.3.2 Context Selectors

Context selectors are used to define the properties of an OpenMP context that a directive or clause can match. OpenMP defines different sets of selectors, each containing different selectors.

The syntax to define a *context-selector-specification* is the following:

trait-set-selector[, trait-set-selector[, ...]]

trait-set-selector:
  trait-set-selector-name={*trait-selector[, trait-selector[, ...]]*}

trait-selector:
  trait-selector-name[([trait-score:] trait-property[, trait-property[, ...]])]

trait-score:
  score(*score-expression*)

The **construct** selector set defines the *construct* traits that should be active in the OpenMP context. The following selectors can be defined in the **construct** set: **target**; **teams**; **parallel**; **for** (in C/C++); **do** (in Fortran); and **simd**. The properties of each selector are the same properties that are defined for the corresponding trait. The **construct** selector is an ordered list $c_1, \ldots, c_N$.

The **device** and **implementation** selector sets define the traits that should be active in the corresponding trait set of the OpenMP context. The same traits defined in the corresponding traits sets can be used as selectors with the same properties. The **kind** selector of the **device** selector set can also be set to the value **any**, which is as if no **kind** selector was specified.

The **user** selector set defines the **condition** selector that provides additional user-defined conditions.

─────────────────────────── C ───────────────────────────

The **condition**(*boolean-expr*) selector defines a *constant expression* that must evaluate to true for the selector to be true.

─────────────────────────── C ───────────────────────────

─────────────────────────── C++ ───────────────────────────

The **condition**(*boolean-expr*) selector defines a **constexpr** expression that must evaluate to true for the selector to be true.

─────────────────────────── C++ ───────────────────────────

─────────────────────────── Fortran ───────────────────────────

The **condition**(*logical-expr*) selector defines a *constant expression* that must evaluate to true for the selector to be true.

─────────────────────────── Fortran ───────────────────────────

A *score-expression* must be an constant integer expression.

Implementations can allow further selectors to be specified. Implementations can ignore specified selectors that are not those described in this section.

Restrictions

- Each *trait-set-selector-name* can only be specified once.
- Each *trait-selector-name* can only be specified once.
- A *trait-score* cannot be specified in traits from the **construct** or **device** *trait-selector-sets*.

2.3.3 Matching and Scoring Context Selectors

A given context selector is compatible with a given OpenMP context if the following conditions are satisfied:

- All selectors in the **user** set of the context selector are true;

- All selectors in the **construct**, **device**, and **implementation** sets of the context selector appear in the corresponding trait set of the OpenMP context;

- For each selector in the context selector, its properties are a subset of the properties of the corresponding trait of the OpenMP context; and

- Selectors in the **construct** set of the context selector appear in the same relative order as their corresponding traits in the *construct* trait set of the OpenMP context.

Some properties of the **simd** selector have special rules to match the properties of the *simd* trait:

- The **simdlen(**N**)** property of the selector matches the *simdlen(M)* trait of the OpenMP context if $M\%N$ equals zero; and

- The **aligned(**$list{:}N$**)** property of the selector matches the *aligned(list:M)* trait of the OpenMP context if $N\%M$ equals zero.

Among compatible context selectors, a score is computed using the following algorithm:

1. Each trait that appears in the *construct* trait set in the OpenMP context is given the value 2^{p-1} where p is the position of the construct trait, c_p, in the set;

2. The **kind**, **arch**, and **isa** selectors are given the values 2^l, 2^{l+1} and 2^{l+2}, respectively, where l is the number of traits in the *construct* set;

3. Traits for which a *trait-score* is specified are given the value specified by the *trait-score score-expression*;

4. The values given to any additional selectors allowed by the implementation are implemented defined;

5. Other selectors are given a value of zero; and

6. A context selector that is a strict subset of another context selector has a score of zero. For other context selectors, the final score is the sum of the values of all specified selectors plus 1. If the traits that correspond to the **construct** selectors appear multiple times in the OpenMP context, the highest valued subset of traits that contains all selectors in the same order are used.

2.3.4 Metadirectives

Summary

A metadirective is a directive that can specify multiple directive variants of which one may be conditionally selected to replace the metadirective based on the enclosing OpenMP context.

Syntax

───────────── C / C++ ─────────────

The syntax of a metadirective takes one of the following forms:

```
#pragma omp metadirective [clause[ [,] clause] ... ] new-line
```

or

```
#pragma omp begin metadirective [clause[ [,] clause] ... ] new-line
    stmt(s)
#pragma omp end metadirective
```

where *clause* is one of the following:

> **when** (*context-selector-specification* : [*directive-variant*])
> **default** (*directive-variant*)

───────────── C / C++ ─────────────

───────────── Fortran ─────────────

The syntax of a metadirective takes one of the following forms:

```
!$omp metadirective [clause[ [,] clause] ... ]
```

or

```
!$omp begin metadirective [clause[ [,] clause] ... ]
    stmt(s)
!$omp end metadirective
```

where *clause* is one of the following:

> **when** (*context-selector-specification* : [*directive-variant*])
> **default** (*directive-variant*)

───────────── Fortran ─────────────

In the **when** clause, *context-selector-specification* specifies a context selector (see Section 2.3.2).

In the **when** and **default** clauses, *directive-variant* has the following form and specifies a directive variant that specifies an OpenMP directive with clauses that apply to it.

> *directive-name* [*clause*[[,] *clause*] ...]

Description

A metadirective is a directive that behaves as if it is either ignored or replaced by the directive variant specified in one of the **when** or **default** clauses that appears on the metadirective.

The OpenMP context for a given metadirective is defined according to Section 2.3.1. For each **when** clause that appears on a metadirective, the specified directive variant, if present, is a candidate to replace the metadirective if the corresponding context selector is compatible with the OpenMP context according to the matching rules defined in Section 2.3.3. If only one compatible context selector specified by a **when** clause has the highest score and it specifies a directive variant, the directive variant will replace the metadirective. If more than one **when** clause specifies a compatible context selector that has the highest computed score and at least one specifies a directive variant, the first directive variant specified in the lexical order of those **when** clauses will replace the metadirective.

If no context selector from any **when** clause is compatible with the OpenMP context and a **default** clause is present, the directive variant specified in the **default** clause will replace the metadirective.

If a directive variant is not selected to replace a metadirective according to the above rules, the metadirective has no effect on the execution of the program.

The **begin metadirective** directive behaves identically to the **metadirective** directive, except that the directive syntax for the specified directive variants must accept a paired **end** *directive*. For any directive variant that is selected to replace the **begin metadirective** directive, the **end metadirective** directive will be implicitly replaced by its paired **end** *directive* to demarcate the statements that are affected by or are associated with the directive variant. If no directive variant is selected to replace the **begin metadirective** directive, its paired **end metadirective** directive is ignored.

Restrictions

Restrictions to metadirectives are as follows:

- The directive variant appearing in a **when** or **default** clause must not specify a **metadirective**, **begin metadirective**, or **end metadirective** directive.

- The context selector that appears in a **when** clause must not specify any properties for the **simd** selector.

- Any replacement that occurs for a metadirective must not result in a non-conforming OpenMP program.

- Any directive variant that is specified by a **when** or **default** clause on a **begin metadirective** directive must be an OpenMP directive that has a paired **end** *directive*, and the **begin metadirective** directive must have a paired **end metadirective** directive.

- The **default** clause may appear at most once on a metadirective.

2.3.5 `declare variant` Directive

Summary

The `declare variant` directive declares a specialized variant of a base function and specifies the context in which that specialized variant is used. The `declare variant` directive is a declarative directive.

Syntax

───── C / C++ ─────

The syntax of the `declare variant` directive is as follows:

```
#pragma omp declare variant (variant-func-id) clause new-line
[#pragma omp declare variant (variant-func-id) clause new-line]
[ ... ]
   function definition or declaration
```

where *clause* is one of the following:

> `match` (*context-selector-specification*)

and where *variant-func-id* is the name of a function variant that is either a base language identifier or, for C++, a *template-id*.

───── C / C++ ─────
───── Fortran ─────

The syntax of the `declare variant` directive is as follows:

```
!$omp declare variant ([base-proc-name:]variant-proc-name) clause
```

where *clause* is one of the following:

> `match` (*context-selector-specification*)

and where *variant-proc-name* is the name of a function variant that is a base language identifier.

───── Fortran ─────

Description

The `declare variant` directive declares the *base function* to have the specified function variant. The context selector in the `match` clause is associated with the variant.

The OpenMP context for a call to a given base function is defined according to Section 2.3.1. If the context selector that is associated with a declared function variant is compatible with the OpenMP context of a call to a base function according to the matching rules defined in Section 2.3.3 then a call to the variant is a candidate to replace the base function call. For any call to the base function for which candidate variants exist, the variant with the highest score is selected from all compatible variants. If multiple variants have the highest score, the selected variant is implementation defined. If a compatible variant exists, the call to the base function is replaced with a call to the selected variant. If no compatible variants exist then the call to the base function is not changed.

Different **declare variant** directives may be specified for different declarations of the same base function.

Any differences that the specific OpenMP context requires in the prototype of the variant from the base function prototype are implementation defined.

─────────────── C++ ───────────────

The function variant is determined by base language standard name lookup rules ([basic.lookup]) of *variant-func-id* with arguments that correspond to the argument types in the base function declaration.

The *variant-func-id* and any expressions inside of the **match** clause are interpreted as if they appeared at the scope of the trailing return type of the base function.

─────────────── C++ ───────────────

Restrictions

Restrictions to the **declare variant** directive are as follows:

- Calling functions that a **declare variant** directive determined to be a function variant directly in an OpenMP context that is different from the one that the **construct** selector set of the context selector specifies is non-conforming.

- If a function is determined to be a function variant through more than one **declare variant** directive then the **construct** selector set of their context selectors must be the same.

─────────────── C / C++ ───────────────

- If the function has any declarations, then the **declare variant** directives for any declarations that have one must be equivalent. If the function definition has a **declare variant**, it must also be equivalent. Otherwise, the result is unspecified.

─────────────── C / C++ ───────────────

─────────────── C++ ───────────────

- The **declare variant** directive cannot be specified for a virtual function.

- The type of the function variant must be compatible with the type of the base function after the implementation-defined transformation for its OpenMP context.

─────────────── C++ ───────────────

---------- Fortran ----------

- *base-proc-name* must not be a generic name, procedure pointer, or entry name.
- If *base-proc-name* is omitted then the **declare variant** directive must appear in the specification part of a subroutine subprogram or a function subprogram.
- Any **declare variant** directive must appear in the specification part of a subroutine, subprogram, function subprogram, or interface body to which it applies.
- If a **declare variant** directive is specified in an interface block for a procedure then it must match a **declare variant** directive in the definition of the procedure.
- If a procedure is declared via a procedure declaration statement then the procedure *base-proc-name* should appear in the same specification.
- If a **declare variant** directive is specified for a procedure name with an explicit interface and a **declare variant** directive is also specified for the definition of the procedure, the two **declare variant** directives must match. Otherwise the result is unspecified.

---------- Fortran ----------

Cross References

- OpenMP Context Specification, see Section 2.3.1 on page 51.
- Context Selectors, see Section 2.3.2 on page 53.

2.4 requires Directive

Summary

The **requires** directive specifies the features that an implementation must provide in order for the code to compile and to execute correctly. The **requires** directive is a declarative directive.

Syntax

---------- C / C++ ----------

The syntax of the **requires** directive is as follows:

    #pragma omp requires clause[[[,] clause] ...] new-line

---------- C / C++ ----------

---------- Fortran ----------

The syntax of the **requires** directive is as follows:

```
!$omp requires clause[ [ [,] clause] ... ]
```
---------- Fortran ----------

Where *clause* is either one of the requirement clauses listed below or a clause of the form
ext_*implementation-defined-requirement* for an implementation defined requirement clause.

> **reverse_offload**
> **unified_address**
> **unified_shared_memory**
> **atomic_default_mem_order(seq_cst | acq_rel | relaxed)**
> **dynamic_allocators**

Description

The **requires** directive specifies features that an implementation must support for correct execution. The behavior that a requirement clause specifies may override the normal behavior specified elsewhere in this document. Whether an implementation supports the feature that a given requirement clause specifies is implementation defined.

The **requires** directive specifies requirements for the execution of all code in the current compilation unit.

Note – Use of this directive makes your code less portable. Users should be aware that not all devices or implementations support all requirements.

When the **reverse_offload** clause appears on a **requires** directive, the implementation guarantees that a **target** region, for which the **target** construct specifies a **device** clause in which the **ancestor** modifier appears, can execute on the parent device of an enclosing **target** region.

When the **unified_address** clause appears on a **requires** directive, the implementation guarantees that all devices accessible through OpenMP API routines and directives use a unified address space. In this address space, a pointer will always refer to the same location in memory from all devices accessible through OpenMP. The pointers returned by **omp_target_alloc** and accessed through **use_device_ptr** are guaranteed to be pointer values that can support pointer arithmetic while still being native device pointers. The **is_device_ptr** clause is not necessary for device pointers to be translated in **target** regions, and pointers found not present are not set to null but keep their original value. Memory local to a specific execution context may be exempt from this requirement, following the restrictions of locality to a given execution context, thread, or contention group. Target devices may still have discrete memories and dereferencing a device pointer on the host device or host pointer on a target device remains unspecified behavior.

The **unified_shared_memory** clause implies the **unified_address** requirement, inheriting all of its behaviors. Additionally, memory in the device data environment of any device visible to OpenMP, including but not limited to the host, is considered part of the device data environment of all devices accessible through OpenMP except as noted below. Every device address allocated through OpenMP device memory routines is a valid host pointer. Memory local to an execution context as defined in **unified_address** above may remain part of distinct device data environments as long as the execution context is local to the device containing that environment.

The **unified_shared_memory** clause makes the **map** clause optional on **target** constructs and the **declare target** directive optional for static lifetime variables accessed inside **declare target** functions. Scalar variables are still firstprivate by default when referenced inside **target** constructs. Values stored into memory by one device may not be visible to another device until those two devices synchronize with each other or both devices synchronize with the host.

The **atomic_default_mem_order** clause specifies the default memory ordering behavior for **atomic** constructs that must be provided by an implementation. If the default memory ordering is specified as **seq_cst**, all **atomic** constructs on which *memory-order-clause* is not specified behave as if the **seq_cst** clause appears. If the default memory ordering is specified as **relaxed**, all **atomic** constructs on which *memory-order-clause* is not specified behave as if the **relaxed** clause appears.

If the default memory ordering is specified as **acq_rel**, **atomic** constructs on which *memory-order-clause* is not specified behave as if the **release** clause appears if the atomic write or atomic update operation is specified, as if the **acquire** clause appears if the atomic read operation is specified, and as if the **acq_rel** clause appears if the atomic captured update operation is specified.

The **dynamic_allocators** clause removes certain restrictions on the use of memory allocators in **target** regions. It makes the **uses_allocators** clause optional on **target** constructs for the purpose of using allocators in the corresponding **target** regions. It allows calls to the **omp_init_allocator** and **omp_destroy_allocator** API routines in **target** regions. Finally, it allows default allocators to be used by **allocate** directives, **allocate** clauses, and **omp_alloc** API routines in **target** regions.

Implementers are allowed to include additional implementation defined requirement clauses. All implementation defined requirements should begin with **ext_**. Requirement names that do not start with **ext_** are reserved.

Restrictions

The restrictions for the **requires** directive are as follows:

- Each of the clauses can appear at most once on the directive.

- At most one **requires** directive with **atomic_default_mem_order** clause can appear in a single compilation unit.
- A **requires** directive with a **unified_address**, **unified_shared_memory**, or **reverse_offload** clause must appear lexically before any device constructs or device routines.
- A **requires** directive with any of the following clauses must appear in all *compilation units* of a program that contain device constructs or device routines or in none of them:
    - **reverse_offload**
    - **unified_address**
    - **unified_shared_memory**
- The **requires** directive with **atomic_default_mem_order** clause may not appear lexically after any **atomic** construct on which *memory-order-clause* is not specified.

---------- C ----------

- The **requires** directive may only appear at file scope.

---------- C ----------

---------- C++ ----------

- The **requires** directive may only appear at file or namespace scope.

---------- C++ ----------

2.5 Internal Control Variables

An OpenMP implementation must act as if there are internal control variables (ICVs) that control the behavior of an OpenMP program. These ICVs store information such as the number of threads to use for future **parallel** regions, the schedule to use for worksharing loops and whether nested parallelism is enabled or not. The ICVs are given values at various times (described below) during the execution of the program. They are initialized by the implementation itself and may be given values through OpenMP environment variables and through calls to OpenMP API routines. The program can retrieve the values of these ICVs only through OpenMP API routines.

For purposes of exposition, this document refers to the ICVs by certain names, but an implementation is not required to use these names or to offer any way to access the variables other than through the ways shown in Section 2.5.2 on page 66.

2.5.1 ICV Descriptions

The following ICVs store values that affect the operation of `parallel` regions.

- *dyn-var* - controls whether dynamic adjustment of the number of threads is enabled for encountered `parallel` regions. There is one copy of this ICV per data environment.
- *nthreads-var* - controls the number of threads requested for encountered `parallel` regions. There is one copy of this ICV per data environment.
- *thread-limit-var* - controls the maximum number of threads participating in the contention group. There is one copy of this ICV per data environment.
- *max-active-levels-var* - controls the maximum number of nested active `parallel` regions. There is one copy of this ICV per device.
- *place-partition-var* - controls the place partition available to the execution environment for encountered `parallel` regions. There is one copy of this ICV per implicit task.
- *active-levels-var* - the number of nested active `parallel` regions that enclose the current task such that all of the `parallel` regions are enclosed by the outermost initial task region on the current device. There is one copy of this ICV per data environment.
- *levels-var* - the number of nested parallel regions that enclose the current task such that all of the `parallel` regions are enclosed by the outermost initial task region on the current device. There is one copy of this ICV per data environment.
- *bind-var* - controls the binding of OpenMP threads to places. When binding is requested, the variable indicates that the execution environment is advised not to move threads between places. The variable can also provide default thread affinity policies. There is one copy of this ICV per data environment.

The following ICVs store values that affect the operation of worksharing-loop regions.

- *run-sched-var* - controls the schedule that is used for worksharing-loop regions when the `runtime` schedule kind is specified. There is one copy of this ICV per data environment.
- *def-sched-var* - controls the implementation defined default scheduling of worksharing-loop regions. There is one copy of this ICV per device.

The following ICVs store values that affect program execution.

- *stacksize-var* - controls the stack size for threads that the OpenMP implementation creates. There is one copy of this ICV per device.
- *wait-policy-var* - controls the desired behavior of waiting threads. There is one copy of this ICV per device.
- *display-affinity-var* - controls whether to display thread affinity. There is one copy of this ICV for the whole program.

- *affinity-format-var* - controls the thread affinity format when displaying thread affinity. There is one copy of this ICV per device.
- *cancel-var* - controls the desired behavior of the `cancel` construct and cancellation points. There is one copy of this ICV for the whole program.
- *default-device-var* - controls the default target device. There is one copy of this ICV per data environment.
- *target-offload-var* - controls the offloading behavior. There is one copy of this ICV for the whole program.
- *max-task-priority-var* - controls the maximum priority value that can be specified in the `priority` clause of the `task` construct. There is one copy of this ICV for the whole program.

The following ICVs store values that affect the operation of the OMPT tool interface.

- *tool-var* - controls whether an OpenMP implementation will try to register a tool. There is one copy of this ICV for the whole program.
- *tool-libraries-var* - specifies a list of absolute paths to tool libraries for OpenMP devices. There is one copy of this ICV for the whole program.

The following ICVs store values that affect the operation of the OMPD tool interface.

- *debug-var* - controls whether an OpenMP implementation will collect information that an OMPD library can access to satisfy requests from a tool. There is one copy of this ICV for the whole program.

The following ICVs store values that affect default memory allocation.

- *def-allocator-var* - controls the memory allocator to be used by memory allocation routines, directives and clauses when a memory allocator is not specified by the user. There is one copy of this ICV per implicit task.

2.5.2 ICV Initialization

TABLE 2.1: ICV Initial Values

ICV	Environment Variable	Initial value
dyn-var	`OMP_DYNAMIC`	See description below
nthreads-var	`OMP_NUM_THREADS`	Implementation defined
run-sched-var	`OMP_SCHEDULE`	Implementation defined
def-sched-var	(none)	Implementation defined
bind-var	`OMP_PROC_BIND`	Implementation defined
stacksize-var	`OMP_STACKSIZE`	Implementation defined
wait-policy-var	`OMP_WAIT_POLICY`	Implementation defined
thread-limit-var	`OMP_THREAD_LIMIT`	Implementation defined
max-active-levels-var	`OMP_MAX_ACTIVE_LEVELS`, `OMP_NESTED`	See description below
active-levels-var	(none)	*zero*
levels-var	(none)	*zero*
place-partition-var	`OMP_PLACES`	Implementation defined
cancel-var	`OMP_CANCELLATION`	*false*
display-affinity-var	`OMP_DISPLAY_AFFINITY`	*false*
affinity-format-var	`OMP_AFFINITY_FORMAT`	Implementation defined
default-device-var	`OMP_DEFAULT_DEVICE`	Implementation defined
target-offload-var	`OMP_TARGET_OFFLOAD`	`DEFAULT`
max-task-priority-var	`OMP_MAX_TASK_PRIORITY`	*zero*
tool-var	`OMP_TOOL`	*enabled*
tool-libraries-var	`OMP_TOOL_LIBRARIES`	*empty string*
debug-var	`OMP_DEBUG`	*disabled*
def-allocator-var	`OMP_ALLOCATOR`	Implementation defined

Table 2.1 shows the ICVs, associated environment variables, and initial values.

Description

- Each device has its own ICVs.
- The initial value of *dyn-var* is implementation defined if the implementation supports dynamic adjustment of the number of threads; otherwise, the initial value is *false*.
- The value of the *nthreads-var* ICV is a list.
- The value of the *bind-var* ICV is a list.
- The initial value of *max-active-levels-var* is the number of active levels of parallelism that the implementation supports if **OMP_NUM_THREADS** or **OMP_PROC_BIND** is set to a comma-separated list of more than one value. Otherwise, the initial value of *max-active-levels-var* is implementation defined.

The host and target device ICVs are initialized before any OpenMP API construct or OpenMP API routine executes. After the initial values are assigned, the values of any OpenMP environment variables that were set by the user are read and the associated ICVs for the host device are modified accordingly. The method for initializing a target device's ICVs is implementation defined.

Cross References

- **OMP_SCHEDULE** environment variable, see Section 6.1 on page 601.
- **OMP_NUM_THREADS** environment variable, see Section 6.2 on page 602.
- **OMP_DYNAMIC** environment variable, see Section 6.3 on page 603.
- **OMP_PROC_BIND** environment variable, see Section 6.4 on page 604.
- **OMP_PLACES** environment variable, see Section 6.5 on page 605.
- **OMP_STACKSIZE** environment variable, see Section 6.6 on page 607.
- **OMP_WAIT_POLICY** environment variable, see Section 6.7 on page 608.
- **OMP_MAX_ACTIVE_LEVELS** environment variable, see Section 6.8 on page 608.
- **OMP_NESTED** environment variable, see Section 6.9 on page 609.
- **OMP_THREAD_LIMIT** environment variable, see Section 6.10 on page 610.
- **OMP_CANCELLATION** environment variable, see Section 6.11 on page 610.
- **OMP_DISPLAY_AFFINITY** environment variable, see Section 6.13 on page 612.
- **OMP_AFFINITY_FORMAT** environment variable, see Section 6.14 on page 613.
- **OMP_DEFAULT_DEVICE** environment variable, see Section 6.15 on page 615.
- **OMP_MAX_TASK_PRIORITY** environment variable, see Section 6.16 on page 615.
- **OMP_TARGET_OFFLOAD** environment variable, see Section 6.17 on page 615.

- **OMP_TOOL** environment variable, see Section 6.18 on page 616.
- **OMP_TOOL_LIBRARIES** environment variable, see Section 6.19 on page 617.
- **OMP_DEBUG** environment variable, see Section 6.20 on page 617.
- **OMP_ALLOCATOR** environment variable, see Section 6.21 on page 618.

2.5.3 Modifying and Retrieving ICV Values

Table 2.2 shows the method for modifying and retrieving the values of ICVs through OpenMP API routines.

TABLE 2.2: Ways to Modify and to Retrieve ICV Values

ICV	Ways to Modify Value	Ways to Retrieve Value
dyn-var	`omp_set_dynamic()`	`omp_get_dynamic()`
nthreads-var	`omp_set_num_threads()`	`omp_get_max_threads()`
run-sched-var	`omp_set_schedule()`	`omp_get_schedule()`
def-sched-var	(none)	(none)
bind-var	(none)	`omp_get_proc_bind()`
stacksize-var	(none)	(none)
wait-policy-var	(none)	(none)
thread-limit-var	`thread_limit` clause	`omp_get_thread_limit()`
max-active-levels-var	`omp_set_max_active_levels()`, `omp_set_nested()`	`omp_get_max_active_levels()`
active-levels-var	(none)	`omp_get_active_level()`
levels-var	(none)	`omp_get_level()`
place-partition-var	(none)	See description below
cancel-var	(none)	`omp_get_cancellation()`
display-affinity-var	(none)	(none)
affinity-format-var	`omp_set_affinity_format()`	`omp_get_affinity_format()`

table continued on next page

table continued from previous page

ICV	Ways to Modify Value	Ways to Retrieve Value
default-device-var	`omp_set_default_device()`	`omp_get_default_device()`
target-offload-var	(none)	(none)
max-task-priority-var	(none)	`omp_get_max_task_priority()`
tool-var	(none)	(none)
tool-libraries-var	(none)	(none)
debug-var	(none)	(none)
def-allocator-var	`omp_set_default_allocator()`	`omp_get_default_allocator()`

Description

- The value of the *nthreads-var* ICV is a list. The runtime call `omp_set_num_threads` sets the value of the first element of this list, and `omp_get_max_threads` retrieves the value of the first element of this list.

- The value of the *bind-var* ICV is a list. The runtime call `omp_get_proc_bind` retrieves the value of the first element of this list.

- Detailed values in the *place-partition-var* ICV are retrieved using the runtime calls `omp_get_partition_num_places`, `omp_get_partition_place_nums`, `omp_get_place_num_procs`, and `omp_get_place_proc_ids`.

Cross References

- `thread_limit` clause of the `teams` construct, see Section 2.7 on page 82.
- `omp_set_num_threads` routine, see Section 3.2.1 on page 334.
- `omp_get_max_threads` routine, see Section 3.2.3 on page 336.
- `omp_set_dynamic` routine, see Section 3.2.7 on page 340.
- `omp_get_dynamic` routine, see Section 3.2.8 on page 341.
- `omp_get_cancellation` routine, see Section 3.2.9 on page 342.
- `omp_set_nested` routine, see Section 3.2.10 on page 343.
- `omp_get_nested` routine, see Section 3.2.11 on page 344.
- `omp_set_schedule` routine, see Section 3.2.12 on page 345.
- `omp_get_schedule` routine, see Section 3.2.13 on page 347.

- **omp_get_thread_limit** routine, see Section 3.2.14 on page 348.
- **omp_get_supported_active_levels**, see Section 3.2.15 on page 349.
- **omp_set_max_active_levels** routine, see Section 3.2.16 on page 350.
- **omp_get_max_active_levels** routine, see Section 3.2.17 on page 351.
- **omp_get_level** routine, see Section 3.2.18 on page 352.
- **omp_get_active_level** routine, see Section 3.2.21 on page 355.
- **omp_get_proc_bind** routine, see Section 3.2.23 on page 357.
- **omp_get_place_num_procs** routine, see Section 3.2.25 on page 359.
- **omp_get_place_proc_ids** routine, see Section 3.2.26 on page 360.
- **omp_get_partition_num_places** routine, see Section 3.2.28 on page 362.
- **omp_get_partition_place_nums** routine, see Section 3.2.29 on page 363.
- **omp_set_affinity_format** routine, see Section 3.2.30 on page 364.
- **omp_get_affinity_format** routine, see Section 3.2.31 on page 366.
- **omp_set_default_device** routine, see Section 3.2.34 on page 369.
- **omp_get_default_device** routine, see Section 3.2.35 on page 370.
- **omp_get_max_task_priority** routine, see Section 3.2.42 on page 377.
- **omp_set_default_allocator** routine, see Section 3.7.4 on page 411.
- **omp_get_default_allocator** routine, see Section 3.7.5 on page 412.

2.5.4 How ICVs are Scoped

Table 2.3 shows the ICVs and their scope.

TABLE 2.3: Scopes of ICVs

ICV	Scope
dyn-var	data environment
nthreads-var	data environment

table continued on next page

table continued from previous page

ICV	Scope
run-sched-var	data environment
def-sched-var	device
bind-var	data environment
stacksize-var	device
wait-policy-var	device
thread-limit-var	data environment
max-active-levels-var	device
active-levels-var	data environment
levels-var	data environment
place-partition-var	implicit task
cancel-var	global
display-affinity-var	global
affinity-format-var	device
default-device-var	data environment
target-offload-var	global
max-task-priority-var	global
tool-var	global
tool-libraries-var	global
debug-var	global
def-allocator-var	implicit task

Description

- There is one copy per device of each ICV with device scope.
- Each data environment has its own copies of ICVs with data environment scope.
- Each implicit task has its own copy of ICVs with implicit task scope.

Calls to OpenMP API routines retrieve or modify data environment scoped ICVs in the data environment of their binding tasks.

2.5.4.1 How the Per-Data Environment ICVs Work

When a `task` construct or `parallel` construct is encountered, the generated task(s) inherit the values of the data environment scoped ICVs from the generating task's ICV values.

When a `parallel` construct is encountered, the value of each ICV with implicit task scope is inherited, unless otherwise specified, from the implicit binding task of the generating task unless otherwise specified.

When a `task` construct is encountered, the generated task inherits the value of *nthreads-var* from the generating task's *nthreads-var* value. When a `parallel` construct is encountered, and the generating task's *nthreads-var* list contains a single element, the generated task(s) inherit that list as the value of *nthreads-var*. When a `parallel` construct is encountered, and the generating task's *nthreads-var* list contains multiple elements, the generated task(s) inherit the value of *nthreads-var* as the list obtained by deletion of the first element from the generating task's *nthreads-var* value. The *bind-var* ICV is handled in the same way as the *nthreads-var* ICV.

When a *target task* executes a `target` region, the generated initial task uses the values of the data environment scoped ICVs from the device data environment ICV values of the device that will execute the region.

If a `teams` construct with a `thread_limit` clause is encountered, the *thread-limit-var* ICV from the data environment of the initial task for each team is instead set to a value that is less than or equal to the value specified in the clause.

When encountering a worksharing-loop region for which the `runtime` schedule kind is specified, all implicit task regions that constitute the binding parallel region must have the same value for *run-sched-var* in their data environments. Otherwise, the behavior is unspecified.

2.5.5 ICV Override Relationships

Table 2.4 shows the override relationships among construct clauses and ICVs.

TABLE 2.4: ICV Override Relationships

ICV	construct clause, if used
dyn-var	(none)
nthreads-var	`num_threads`
run-sched-var	`schedule`

table continued on next page

table continued from previous page

ICV	construct clause, if used
def-sched-var	**schedule**
bind-var	**proc_bind**
stacksize-var	(none)
wait-policy-var	(none)
thread-limit-var	(none)
max-active-levels-var	(none)
active-levels-var	(none)
levels-var	(none)
place-partition-var	(none)
cancel-var	(none)
display-affinity-var	(none)
affinity-format-var	(none)
default-device-var	(none)
target-offload-var	(none)
max-task-priority-var	(none)
tool-var	(none)
tool-libraries-var	(none)
debug-var	(none)
def-allocator-var	**allocator**

Description

- The **num_threads** clause overrides the value of the first element of the *nthreads-var* ICV.
- If a **schedule** clause specifies a modifier then that modifier overrides any modifier that is specified in the *run-sched-var* ICV.
- If *bind-var* is not set to *false* then the **proc_bind** clause overrides the value of the first element of the *bind-var* ICV; otherwise, the **proc_bind** clause has no effect.

Cross References

- **parallel** construct, see Section 2.6 on page 74.
- **proc_bind** clause, Section 2.6 on page 74.
- **num_threads** clause, see Section 2.6.1 on page 78.

- Worksharing-Loop construct, see Section 2.9.2 on page 101.
- **schedule** clause, see Section 2.9.2.1 on page 109.

2.6 `parallel` Construct

Summary

The parallel construct creates a team of OpenMP threads that execute the region.

Syntax

─────────────── C / C++ ───────────────

The syntax of the `parallel` construct is as follows:

```
#pragma omp parallel [clause[ [, ] clause] ... ] new-line
    structured-block
```

where *clause* is one of the following:

```
if ([parallel :] scalar-expression)
num_threads (integer-expression)
default (shared | none)
private (list)
firstprivate (list)
shared (list)
copyin (list)
reduction ([reduction-modifier ,] reduction-identifier : list)
proc_bind (master | close | spread)
allocate ([allocator :] list)
```

─────────────── C / C++ ───────────────

---------- Fortran ----------

The syntax of the **parallel** construct is as follows:

```
!$omp parallel [clause[ [,] clause] ... ]
    structured-block
!$omp end parallel
```

where *clause* is one of the following:

    if (*[parallel :] scalar-logical-expression*)
    num_threads (*scalar-integer-expression*)
    default(**private** | **firstprivate** | **shared** | **none**)
    private(*list*)
    firstprivate(*list*)
    shared(*list*)
    copyin(*list*)
    reduction(*[reduction-modifier ,] reduction-identifier : list*)
    proc_bind(**master** | **close** | **spread**)
    allocate(*[allocator :] list*)

---------- Fortran ----------

Binding

The binding thread set for a **parallel** region is the encountering thread. The encountering thread becomes the master thread of the new team.

Description

When a thread encounters a **parallel** construct, a team of threads is created to execute the **parallel** region (see Section 2.6.1 on page 78 for more information about how the number of threads in the team is determined, including the evaluation of the **if** and **num_threads** clauses). The thread that encountered the **parallel** construct becomes the master thread of the new team, with a thread number of zero for the duration of the new **parallel** region. All threads in the new team, including the master thread, execute the region. Once the team is created, the number of threads in the team remains constant for the duration of that **parallel** region.

The optional **proc_bind** clause, described in Section 2.6.2 on page 80, specifies the mapping of OpenMP threads to places within the current place partition, that is, within the places listed in the *place-partition-var* ICV for the implicit task of the encountering thread.

Within a **parallel** region, thread numbers uniquely identify each thread. Thread numbers are consecutive whole numbers ranging from zero for the master thread up to one less than the number

of threads in the team. A thread may obtain its own thread number by a call to the
omp_get_thread_num library routine.

A set of implicit tasks, equal in number to the number of threads in the team, is generated by the encountering thread. The structured block of the **parallel** construct determines the code that will be executed in each implicit task. Each task is assigned to a different thread in the team and becomes tied. The task region of the task being executed by the encountering thread is suspended and each thread in the team executes its implicit task. Each thread can execute a path of statements that is different from that of the other threads.

The implementation may cause any thread to suspend execution of its implicit task at a task scheduling point, and to switch to execution of any explicit task generated by any of the threads in the team, before eventually resuming execution of the implicit task (for more details see Section 2.10 on page 135).

There is an implied barrier at the end of a **parallel** region. After the end of a **parallel** region, only the master thread of the team resumes execution of the enclosing task region.

If a thread in a team executing a **parallel** region encounters another **parallel** directive, it creates a new team, according to the rules in Section 2.6.1 on page 78, and it becomes the master of that new team.

If execution of a thread terminates while inside a **parallel** region, execution of all threads in all teams terminates. The order of termination of threads is unspecified. All work done by a team prior to any barrier that the team has passed in the program is guaranteed to be complete. The amount of work done by each thread after the last barrier that it passed and before it terminates is unspecified.

Execution Model Events

The *parallel-begin* event occurs in a thread that encounters a **parallel** construct before any implicit task is created for the corresponding **parallel** region.

Upon creation of each implicit task, an *implicit-task-begin* event occurs in the thread that executes the implicit task after the implicit task is fully initialized but before the thread begins to execute the structured block of the **parallel** construct.

If the **parallel** region creates a native thread, a *native-thread-begin* event occurs as the first event in the context of the new thread prior to the *implicit-task-begin* event.

Events associated with implicit barriers occur at the end of a **parallel** region. Section 2.17.3 describes events associated with implicit barriers.

When a thread finishes an implicit task, an *implicit-task-end* event occurs in the thread after events associated with implicit barrier synchronization in the implicit task.

The *parallel-end* event occurs in the thread that encounters the **parallel** construct after the thread executes its *implicit-task-end* event but before the thread resumes execution of the encountering task.

If a native thread is destroyed at the end of a **parallel** region, a *native thread-end* event occurs in the thread as the last event prior to destruction of the thread.

Tool Callbacks

A thread dispatches a registered **ompt_callback_parallel_begin** callback for each occurrence of a *parallel-begin* event in that thread. The callback occurs in the task that encounters the **parallel** construct. This callback has the type signature **ompt_callback_parallel_begin_t**. In the dispatched callback, (*flags* **& ompt_parallel_team**) evaluates to *true*.

A thread dispatches a registered **ompt_callback_implicit_task** callback with **ompt_scope_begin** as its *endpoint* argument for each occurrence of an *implicit-task-begin* event in that thread. Similarly, a thread dispatches a registered **ompt_callback_implicit_task** callback with **ompt_scope_end** as its *endpoint* argument for each occurrence of an *implicit-task-end* event in that thread. The callbacks occur in the context of the implicit task and have type signature **ompt_callback_implicit_task_t**. In the dispatched callback, (*flags* **& ompt_task_implicit**) evaluates to *true*.

A thread dispatches a registered **ompt_callback_parallel_end** callback for each occurrence of a *parallel-end* event in that thread. The callback occurs in the task that encounters the **parallel** construct. This callback has the type signature **ompt_callback_parallel_end_t**.

A thread dispatches a registered **ompt_callback_thread_begin** callback for the *native-thread-begin* event in that thread. The callback occurs in the context of the thread. The callback has type signature **ompt_callback_thread_begin_t**.

A thread dispatches a registered **ompt_callback_thread_end** callback for the *native-thread-end* event in that thread. The callback occurs in the context of the thread. The callback has type signature **ompt_callback_thread_end_t**.

Restrictions

Restrictions to the **parallel** construct are as follows:

- A program that branches into or out of a **parallel** region is non-conforming.
- A program must not depend on any ordering of the evaluations of the clauses of the **parallel** directive, or on any side effects of the evaluations of the clauses.
- At most one **if** clause can appear on the directive.
- At most one **proc_bind** clause can appear on the directive.
- At most one **num_threads** clause can appear on the directive. The **num_threads** expression must evaluate to a positive integer value.

———————————————————— C++ ————————————————————
- A **throw** executed inside a **parallel** region must cause execution to resume within the same **parallel** region, and the same thread that threw the exception must catch it.
———————————————————— C++ ————————————————————

Cross References

- OpenMP execution model, see Section 1.3 on page 20.
- **num_threads** clause, see Section 2.6 on page 74.
- **proc_bind** clause, see Section 2.6.2 on page 80.
- **allocate** clause, see Section 2.11.4 on page 158.
- **if** clause, see Section 2.15 on page 220.
- **default**, **shared**, **private**, **firstprivate**, and **reduction** clauses, see Section 2.19.4 on page 282.
- **copyin** clause, see Section 2.19.6 on page 309.
- **omp_get_thread_num** routine, see Section 3.2.4 on page 337.
- **ompt_scope_begin** and **ompt_scope_end**, see Section 4.4.4.11 on page 443.
- **ompt_callback_thread_begin_t**, see Section 4.5.2.1 on page 459.
- **ompt_callback_thread_end_t**, see Section 4.5.2.2 on page 460.
- **ompt_callback_parallel_begin_t**, see Section 4.5.2.3 on page 461.
- **ompt_callback_parallel_end_t**, see Section 4.5.2.4 on page 463.
- **ompt_callback_implicit_task_t**, see Section 4.5.2.11 on page 471.

2.6.1 Determining the Number of Threads for a **parallel** Region

When execution encounters a **parallel** directive, the value of the **if** clause or **num_threads** clause (if any) on the directive, the current parallel context, and the values of the *nthreads-var*, *dyn-var*, *thread-limit-var*, and *max-active-levels-var* ICVs are used to determine the number of threads to use in the region.

Using a variable in an **if** or **num_threads** clause expression of a **parallel** construct causes an implicit reference to the variable in all enclosing constructs. The **if** clause expression and the **num_threads** clause expression are evaluated in the context outside of the **parallel** construct, and no ordering of those evaluations is specified. In what order or how many times any side effects of the evaluation of the `num_threads` or `if` clause expressions occur is also unspecified.

When a thread encounters a `parallel` construct, the number of threads is determined according to Algorithm 2.1.

Algorithm 2.1

let *ThreadsBusy* be the number of OpenMP threads currently executing in this contention group;

let *ActiveParRegions* be the number of enclosing active parallel regions;

if an `if` clause exists

then let *IfClauseValue* be the value of the `if` clause expression;

else let *IfClauseValue* = *true*;

if a `num_threads` clause exists

then let *ThreadsRequested* be the value of the `num_threads` clause expression;

else let *ThreadsRequested* = value of the first element of *nthreads-var*;

let *ThreadsAvailable* = (*thread-limit-var* - *ThreadsBusy* + 1);

if (*IfClauseValue* = *false*)

then number of threads = 1;

else if (*ActiveParRegions* = *max-active-levels-var*)

then number of threads = 1;

else if (*dyn-var* = *true*) **and** (*ThreadsRequested* $\leq$ *ThreadsAvailable*)

then $1 \leq$ number of threads $\leq$ *ThreadsRequested*;

else if (*dyn-var* = *true*) **and** (*ThreadsRequested* > *ThreadsAvailable*)

then $1 \leq$ number of threads $\leq$ *ThreadsAvailable*;

else if (*dyn-var* = *false*) **and** (*ThreadsRequested* $\leq$ *ThreadsAvailable*)

then number of threads = *ThreadsRequested*;

else if (*dyn-var* = *false*) **and** (*ThreadsRequested* > *ThreadsAvailable*)

then behavior is implementation defined;

> Note – Since the initial value of the *dyn-var* ICV is implementation defined, programs that depend on a specific number of threads for correct execution should explicitly disable dynamic adjustment of the number of threads.

Cross References

- *nthreads-var*, *dyn-var*, *thread-limit-var*, and *max-active-levels-var* ICVs, see Section 2.5 on page 63.
- **parallel** construct, see Section 2.6 on page 74.
- **num_threads** clause, see Section 2.6 on page 74.
- **if** clause, see Section 2.15 on page 220.

2.6.2 Controlling OpenMP Thread Affinity

When a thread encounters a **parallel** directive without a **proc_bind** clause, the *bind-var* ICV is used to determine the policy for assigning OpenMP threads to places within the current place partition, that is, within the places listed in the *place-partition-var* ICV for the implicit task of the encountering thread. If the **parallel** directive has a **proc_bind** clause then the binding policy specified by the **proc_bind** clause overrides the policy specified by the first element of the *bind-var* ICV. Once a thread in the team is assigned to a place, the OpenMP implementation should not move it to another place.

The **master** thread affinity policy instructs the execution environment to assign every thread in the team to the same place as the master thread. The place partition is not changed by this policy, and each implicit task inherits the *place-partition-var* ICV of the parent implicit task.

The **close** thread affinity policy instructs the execution environment to assign the threads in the team to places close to the place of the parent thread. The place partition is not changed by this policy, and each implicit task inherits the *place-partition-var* ICV of the parent implicit task. If T is the number of threads in the team, and P is the number of places in the parent's place partition, then the assignment of threads in the team to places is as follows:

- $T \leq P$: The master thread executes on the place of the parent thread. The thread with the next smallest thread number executes on the next place in the place partition, and so on, with wrap around with respect to the place partition of the master thread.

- $T > P$: Each place p will contain S_p threads with consecutive thread numbers where $\lfloor T/P \rfloor \leq S_p \leq \lceil T/P \rceil$. The first S_0 threads (including the master thread) are assigned to the place of the parent thread. The next S_1 threads are assigned to the next place in the place partition, and so on, with wrap around with respect to the place partition of the master thread. When P does not divide T evenly, the exact number of threads in a particular place is implementation defined.

The purpose of the **spread** thread affinity policy is to create a sparse distribution for a team of T threads among the P places of the parent's place partition. A sparse distribution is achieved by first subdividing the parent partition into T subpartitions if $T \leq P$, or P subpartitions if $T > P$. Then one thread ($T \leq P$) or a set of threads ($T > P$) is assigned to each subpartition. The *place-partition-var* ICV of each implicit task is set to its subpartition. The subpartitioning is not only a mechanism for achieving a sparse distribution, it also defines a subset of places for a thread to use when creating a nested **parallel** region. The assignment of threads to places is as follows:

- $T \leq P$: The parent thread's place partition is split into T subpartitions, where each subpartition contains $\lfloor P/T \rfloor$ or $\lceil P/T \rceil$ consecutive places. A single thread is assigned to each subpartition. The master thread executes on the place of the parent thread and is assigned to the subpartition that includes that place. The thread with the next smallest thread number is assigned to the first place in the next subpartition, and so on, with wrap around with respect to the original place partition of the master thread.

- $T > P$: The parent thread's place partition is split into P subpartitions, each consisting of a single place. Each subpartition is assigned S_p threads with consecutive thread numbers, where $\lfloor T/P \rfloor \leq S_p \leq \lceil T/P \rceil$. The first S_0 threads (including the master thread) are assigned to the subpartition containing the place of the parent thread. The next S_1 threads are assigned to the next subpartition, and so on, with wrap around with respect to the original place partition of the master thread. When P does not divide T evenly, the exact number of threads in a particular subpartition is implementation defined.

The determination of whether the affinity request can be fulfilled is implementation defined. If the affinity request cannot be fulfilled, then the affinity of threads in the team is implementation defined.

Note – Wrap around is needed if the end of a place partition is reached before all thread assignments are done. For example, wrap around may be needed in the case of **close** and $T \leq P$, if the master thread is assigned to a place other than the first place in the place partition. In this case, thread 1 is assigned to the place after the place of the master place, thread 2 is assigned to the place after that, and so on. The end of the place partition may be reached before all threads are assigned. In this case, assignment of threads is resumed with the first place in the place partition.

2.7 `teams` Construct

Summary

The `teams` construct creates a league of initial teams and the initial thread in each team executes the region.

Syntax

─────────── C / C++ ───────────

The syntax of the `teams` construct is as follows:

```
#pragma omp teams [clause[ [,] clause] ... ] new-line
    structured-block
```

where *clause* is one of the following:

```
num_teams(integer-expression)
thread_limit(integer-expression)
default(shared | none)
private(list)
firstprivate(list)
shared(list)
reduction([default ,] reduction-identifier : list)
allocate([allocator :] list)
```

─────────── C / C++ ───────────
─────────── Fortran ───────────

The syntax of the `teams` construct is as follows:

```
!$omp teams [clause[ [,] clause] ... ]
    structured-block
!$omp end teams
```

where *clause* is one of the following:

> **num_teams** (*scalar-integer-expression*)
> **thread_limit** (*scalar-integer-expression*)
> **default**(shared | firstprivate | private | none)
> **private**(*list*)
> **firstprivate**(*list*)
> **shared**(*list*)
> **reduction**(*[default ,] reduction-identifier : list*)
> **allocate**(*[allocator :] list*)

──────────────── Fortran ────────────────

Binding

The binding thread set for a **teams** region is the encountering thread.

Description

When a thread encounters a **teams** construct, a league of teams is created. Each team is an initial team, and the initial thread in each team executes the **teams** region.

The number of teams created is implementation defined, but is less than or equal to the value specified in the **num_teams** clause. A thread may obtain the number of initial teams created by the construct by a call to the **omp_get_num_teams** routine.

The maximum number of threads participating in the contention group that each team initiates is implementation defined, but is less than or equal to the value specified in the **thread_limit** clause.

On a combined or composite construct that includes **target** and **teams** constructs, the expressions in **num_teams** and **thread_limit** clauses are evaluated on the host device on entry to the **target** construct.

Once the teams are created, the number of initial teams remains constant for the duration of the **teams** region.

Within a **teams** region, initial team numbers uniquely identify each initial team. Initial team numbers are consecutive whole numbers ranging from zero to one less than the number of initial teams. A thread may obtain its own initial team number by a call to the **omp_get_team_num** library routine. The policy for assigning the initial threads to places is implementation defined. The **teams** construct sets the *place-partition-var* and *default-device-var* ICVs for each initial thread to an implementation-defined value.

After the teams have completed execution of the **teams** region, the encountering task resumes execution of the enclosing task region.

Execution Model Events

The *teams-begin* event occurs in a thread that encounters a **teams** construct before any initial task is created for the corresponding **teams** region.

Upon creation of each initial task, an *initial-task-begin* event occurs in the thread that executes the initial task after the initial task is fully initialized but before the thread begins to execute the structured block of the **teams** construct.

If the **teams** region creates a native thread, a *native-thread-begin* event occurs as the first event in the context of the new thread prior to the *initial-task-begin* event.

When a thread finishes an initial task, an *initial-task-end* event occurs in the thread.

The *teams-end* event occurs in the thread that encounters the **teams** construct after the thread executes its *initial-task-end* event but before it resumes execution of the encountering task.

If a native thread is destroyed at the end of a **teams** region, a *native-thread-end* event occurs in the thread as the last event prior to destruction of the thread.

Tool Callbacks

A thread dispatches a registered **ompt_callback_parallel_begin** callback for each occurrence of a *teams-begin* event in that thread. The callback occurs in the task that encounters the **teams** construct. This callback has the type signature **ompt_callback_parallel_begin_t**. In the dispatched callback, (*flags* **& ompt_parallel_league**) evaluates to *true*.

A thread dispatches a registered **ompt_callback_implicit_task** callback with **ompt_scope_begin** as its *endpoint* argument for each occurrence of an *initial-task-begin* in that thread. Similarly, a thread dispatches a registered **ompt_callback_implicit_task** callback with **ompt_scope_end** as its *endpoint* argument for each occurrence of an *initial-task-end* event in that thread. The callbacks occur in the context of the initial task and have type signature **ompt_callback_implicit_task_t**. In the dispatched callback, (*flags* **& ompt_task_initial**) evaluates to *true*.

A thread dispatches a registered **ompt_callback_parallel_end** callback for each occurrence of a *teams-end* event in that thread. The callback occurs in the task that encounters the **teams** construct. This callback has the type signature **ompt_callback_parallel_end_t**.

A thread dispatches a registered **ompt_callback_thread_begin** callback for the *native-thread-begin* event in that thread. The callback occurs in the context of the thread. The callback has type signature **ompt_callback_thread_begin_t**.

A thread dispatches a registered **ompt_callback_thread_end** callback for the *native-thread-end* event in that thread. The callback occurs in the context of the thread. The callback has type signature **ompt_callback_thread_end_t**.

Restrictions

Restrictions to the **teams** construct are as follows:

- A program that branches into or out of a **teams** region is non-conforming.
- A program must not depend on any ordering of the evaluations of the clauses of the **teams** directive, or on any side effects of the evaluation of the clauses.
- At most one **thread_limit** clause can appear on the directive. The **thread_limit** expression must evaluate to a positive integer value.
- At most one **num_teams** clause can appear on the directive. The **num_teams** expression must evaluate to a positive integer value.
- A **teams** region can only be strictly nested within the implicit parallel region or a **target** region. If a **teams** construct is nested within a **target** construct, that **target** construct must contain no statements, declarations or directives outside of the **teams** construct.
- **distribute**, **distribute simd**, distribute parallel worksharing-loop, distribute parallel worksharing-loop SIMD, **parallel** regions, including any **parallel** regions arising from combined constructs, **omp_get_num_teams()** regions, and **omp_get_team_num()** regions are the only OpenMP regions that may be strictly nested inside the **teams** region.

Cross References

- **parallel** construct, see Section 2.6 on page 74.
- **distribute** construct, see Section 2.9.4.1 on page 120.
- **distribute simd** construct, see Section 2.9.4.2 on page 123.
- **allocate** clause, see Section 2.11.4 on page 158.
- **target** construct, see Section 2.12.5 on page 170.
- **default**, **shared**, **private**, **firstprivate**, and **reduction** clauses, see Section 2.19.4 on page 282.
- **omp_get_num_teams** routine, see Section 3.2.38 on page 373.
- **omp_get_team_num** routine, see Section 3.2.39 on page 374.
- **ompt_callback_thread_begin_t**, see Section 4.5.2.1 on page 459.
- **ompt_callback_thread_end_t**, see Section 4.5.2.2 on page 460.
- **ompt_callback_parallel_begin_t**, see Section 4.5.2.3 on page 461.
- **ompt_callback_parallel_end_t**, see Section 4.5.2.4 on page 463.
- **ompt_callback_implicit_task_t**, see Section 4.5.2.11 on page 471.

2.8 Worksharing Constructs

A worksharing construct distributes the execution of the corresponding region among the members of the team that encounters it. Threads execute portions of the region in the context of the implicit tasks that each one is executing. If the team consists of only one thread then the worksharing region is not executed in parallel.

A worksharing region has no barrier on entry; however, an implied barrier exists at the end of the worksharing region, unless a **nowait** clause is specified. If a **nowait** clause is present, an implementation may omit the barrier at the end of the worksharing region. In this case, threads that finish early may proceed straight to the instructions that follow the worksharing region without waiting for the other members of the team to finish the worksharing region, and without performing a flush operation.

The OpenMP API defines the worksharing constructs that are described in this section as well as the worksharing-loop construct, which is described in Section 2.9.2 on page 101.

Restrictions

The following restrictions apply to worksharing constructs:

- Each worksharing region must be encountered by all threads in a team or by none at all, unless cancellation has been requested for the innermost enclosing parallel region.

- The sequence of worksharing regions and **barrier** regions encountered must be the same for every thread in a team.

2.8.1 sections Construct

Summary

The **sections** construct is a non-iterative worksharing construct that contains a set of structured blocks that are to be distributed among and executed by the threads in a team. Each structured block is executed once by one of the threads in the team in the context of its implicit task.

Syntax

---------- C / C++ ----------

The syntax of the `sections` construct is as follows:

```
#pragma omp sections [clause[ [, ] clause] ... ] new-line
    {
    [#pragma omp section new-line]
        structured-block
    [#pragma omp section new-line
        structured-block]
    ...
    }
```

where *clause* is one of the following:

> **private**(*list*)
> **firstprivate**(*list*)
> **lastprivate**([*lastprivate-modifier*:] *list*)
> **reduction**([*reduction-modifier* ,] *reduction-identifier* : *list*)
> **allocate**([*allocator* :] *list*)
> **nowait**

---------- C / C++ ----------

---------- Fortran ----------

The syntax of the `sections` construct is as follows:

```
!$omp sections [clause[ [, ] clause] ... ]
    [!$omp section]
        structured-block
    [!$omp section
        structured-block]
    ...
!$omp end sections [nowait]
```

where *clause* is one of the following:

> **private**(*list*)
> **firstprivate**(*list*)
> **lastprivate**([*lastprivate-modifier*:] *list*)
> **reduction**([*reduction-modifier* ,] *reduction-identifier* : *list*)
> **allocate**([*allocator* :] *list*)

---------- Fortran ----------

Binding

The binding thread set for a `sections` region is the current team. A `sections` region binds to the innermost enclosing `parallel` region. Only the threads of the team that executes the binding `parallel` region participate in the execution of the structured blocks and the implied barrier of the `sections` region if the barrier is not eliminated by a `nowait` clause.

Description

Each structured block in the `sections` construct is preceded by a `section` directive except possibly the first block, for which a preceding `section` directive is optional.

The method of scheduling the structured blocks among the threads in the team is implementation defined.

There is an implicit barrier at the end of a `sections` construct unless a `nowait` clause is specified.

Execution Model Events

The *section-begin* event occurs after an implicit task encounters a `sections` construct but before the task executes any structured block of the `sections` region.

The *sections-end* event occurs after an implicit task finishes execution of a `sections` region but before it resumes execution of the enclosing context.

The *section-begin* event occurs before an implicit task starts to execute a structured block in the `sections` construct for each of those structured blocks that the task executes.

Tool Callbacks

A thread dispatches a registered `ompt_callback_work` callback with `ompt_scope_begin` as its *endpoint* argument and `ompt_work_sections` as its *wstype* argument for each occurrence of a *section-begin* event in that thread. Similarly, a thread dispatches a registered `ompt_callback_work` callback with `ompt_scope_end` as its *endpoint* argument and `ompt_work_sections` as its *wstype* argument for each occurrence of a *sections-end* event in that thread. The callbacks occur in the context of the implicit task. The callbacks have type signature `ompt_callback_work_t`.

A thread dispatches a registered `ompt_callback_dispatch` callback for each occurrence of a *section-begin* event in that thread. The callback occurs in the context of the implicit task. The callback has type signature `ompt_callback_dispatch_t`.

Restrictions

Restrictions to the `sections` construct are as follows:

- Orphaned `section` directives are prohibited. That is, the `section` directives must appear within the `sections` construct and must not be encountered elsewhere in the `sections` region.
- The code enclosed in a `sections` construct must be a structured block.
- Only a single `nowait` clause can appear on a `sections` directive.

──────────────────────────── C++ ────────────────────────────

- A throw executed inside a `sections` region must cause execution to resume within the same section of the `sections` region, and the same thread that threw the exception must catch it.

──────────────────────────── C++ ────────────────────────────

Cross References

- `allocate` clause, see Section 2.11.4 on page 158.
- `private`, `firstprivate`, `lastprivate`, and `reduction` clauses, see Section 2.19.4 on page 282.
- `ompt_scope_begin` and `ompt_scope_end`, see Section 4.4.4.11 on page 443.
- `ompt_work_sections`, see Section 4.4.4.15 on page 445.
- `ompt_callback_work_t`, see Section 4.5.2.5 on page 464.
- `ompt_callback_dispatch_t`, see Section 4.5.2.6 on page 465.

2.8.2 `single` Construct

Summary

The `single` construct specifies that the associated structured block is executed by only one of the threads in the team (not necessarily the master thread), in the context of its implicit task. The other threads in the team, which do not execute the block, wait at an implicit barrier at the end of the `single` construct unless a `nowait` clause is specified.

Syntax

---------- C / C++ ----------

The syntax of the single construct is as follows:

```
#pragma omp single [clause[ [, ] clause] ... ] new-line
    structured-block
```

where *clause* is one of the following:

> `private`(*list*)
> `firstprivate`(*list*)
> `copyprivate`(*list*)
> `allocate`(*[allocator :] list*)
> `nowait`

---------- C / C++ ----------

---------- Fortran ----------

The syntax of the **single** construct is as follows:

```
!$omp single [clause[ [, ] clause] ... ]
    structured-block
!$omp end single [end_clause[ [, ] end_clause] ... ]
```

where *clause* is one of the following:

> `private`(*list*)
> `firstprivate`(*list*)
> `allocate`(*[allocator :] list*)

and *end_clause* is one of the following:

> `copyprivate`(*list*)
> `nowait`

---------- Fortran ----------

Binding

The binding thread set for a **single** region is the current team. A **single** region binds to the innermost enclosing **parallel** region. Only the threads of the team that executes the binding **parallel** region participate in the execution of the structured block and the implied barrier of the **single** region if the barrier is not eliminated by a **nowait** clause.

Description

Only one of the encountering threads will execute the structured block associated with the **single** construct. The method of choosing a thread to execute the structured block each time the team encounters the construct is implementation defined. There is an implicit barrier at the end of the **single** construct unless a **nowait** clause is specified.

Execution Model Events

The *single-begin* event occurs after an **implicit task** encounters a **single** construct but before the task starts to execute the structured block of the **single** region.

The *single-end* event occurs after an implicit task finishes execution of a **single** region but before it resumes execution of the enclosing region.

Tool Callbacks

A thread dispatches a registered **ompt_callback_work** callback with **ompt_scope_begin** as its *endpoint* argument for each occurrence of a *single-begin* event in that thread. Similarly, a thread dispatches a registered **ompt_callback_work** callback with **ompt_scope_begin** as its *endpoint* argument for each occurrence of a *single-end* event in that thread. For each of these callbacks, the *wstype* argument is **ompt_work_single_executor** if the thread executes the structured block associated with the **single** region; otherwise, the *wstype* argument is **ompt_work_single_other**. The callback has type signature **ompt_callback_work_t**.

Restrictions

Restrictions to the **single** construct are as follows:

- The **copyprivate** clause must not be used with the **nowait** clause.
- At most one **nowait** clause can appear on a **single** construct.

―――――――――――――――――――― C++ ――――――――――――――――――――

- A throw executed inside a **single** region must cause execution to resume within the same **single** region, and the same thread that threw the exception must catch it.

―――――――――――――――――――― C++ ――――――――――――――――――――

Cross References

- `allocate` clause, see Section 2.11.4 on page 158.
- `private` and `firstprivate` clauses, see Section 2.19.4 on page 282.
- `copyprivate` clause, see Section 2.19.6.2 on page 312.
- `ompt_scope_begin` and `ompt_scope_end`, see Section 4.4.4.11 on page 443.
- `ompt_work_single_executor` and `ompt_work_single_other`, see Section 4.4.4.15 on page 445.
- `ompt_callback_work_t`, Section 4.5.2.5 on page 464.

---------- Fortran ----------

2.8.3 workshare Construct

Summary

The `workshare` construct divides the execution of the enclosed structured block into separate units of work, and causes the threads of the team to share the work such that each unit is executed only once by one thread, in the context of its implicit task.

Syntax

The syntax of the `workshare` construct is as follows:

```
!$omp workshare
     structured-block
!$omp end workshare [nowait]
```

Binding

The binding thread set for a `workshare` region is the current team. A `workshare` region binds to the innermost enclosing `parallel` region. Only the threads of the team that executes the binding `parallel` region participate in the execution of the units of work and the implied barrier of the `workshare` region if the barrier is not eliminated by a `nowait` clause.

------ Fortran (cont.) ------

Description

There is an implicit barrier at the end of a **workshare** construct unless a **nowait** clause is specified.

An implementation of the **workshare** construct must insert any synchronization that is required to maintain standard Fortran semantics. For example, the effects of one statement within the structured block must appear to occur before the execution of succeeding statements, and the evaluation of the right hand side of an assignment must appear to complete prior to the effects of assigning to the left hand side.

The statements in the **workshare** construct are divided into units of work as follows:

- For array expressions within each statement, including transformational array intrinsic functions that compute scalar values from arrays:
  - Evaluation of each element of the array expression, including any references to **ELEMENTAL** functions, is a unit of work.
  - Evaluation of transformational array intrinsic functions may be freely subdivided into any number of units of work.
- For an array assignment statement, the assignment of each element is a unit of work.
- For a scalar assignment statement, the assignment operation is a unit of work.
- For a **WHERE** statement or construct, the evaluation of the mask expression and the masked assignments are each a unit of work.
- For a **FORALL** statement or construct, the evaluation of the mask expression, expressions occurring in the specification of the iteration space, and the masked assignments are each a unit of work.
- For an **atomic** construct, the atomic operation on the storage location designated as x is a unit of work.
- For a **critical** construct, the construct is a single unit of work.
- For a **parallel** construct, the construct is a unit of work with respect to the **workshare** construct. The statements contained in the **parallel** construct are executed by a new thread team.
- If none of the rules above apply to a portion of a statement in the structured block, then that portion is a unit of work.

The transformational array intrinsic functions are **MATMUL, DOT_PRODUCT, SUM, PRODUCT, MAXVAL, MINVAL, COUNT, ANY, ALL, SPREAD, PACK, UNPACK, RESHAPE, TRANSPOSE, EOSHIFT, CSHIFT, MINLOC**, and **MAXLOC**.

It is unspecified how the units of work are assigned to the threads executing a **workshare** region.

---------- Fortran (cont.) ----------

If an array expression in the block references the value, association status, or allocation status of private variables, the value of the expression is undefined, unless the same value would be computed by every thread.

If an array assignment, a scalar assignment, a masked array assignment, or a **FORALL** assignment assigns to a private variable in the block, the result is unspecified.

The **workshare** directive causes the sharing of work to occur only in the **workshare** construct, and not in the remainder of the **workshare** region.

Execution Model Events

The *workshare-begin* event occurs after an implicit task encounters a **workshare** construct but before the task starts to execute the structured block of the **workshare** region.

The *workshare-end* event occurs after an implicit task finishes execution of a **workshare** region but before it resumes execution of the enclosing context.

Tool Callbacks

A thread dispatches a registered **ompt_callback_work** callback with **ompt_scope_begin** as its *endpoint* argument and **ompt_work_workshare** as its *wstype* argument for each occurrence of a *workshare-begin* event in that thread. Similarly, a thread dispatches a registered **ompt_callback_work** callback with **ompt_scope_end** as its *endpoint* argument and **ompt_work_workshare** as its *wstype* argument for each occurrence of a *workshare-end* event in that thread. The callbacks occur in the context of the implicit task. The callbacks have type signature **ompt_callback_work_t**.

Restrictions

The following restrictions apply to the **workshare** construct:

- The only OpenMP constructs that may be closely nested inside a **workshare** construct are the **atomic**, **critical**, and **parallel** constructs.
- Base language statements that are encountered inside a **workshare** construct but that are not enclosed within a **parallel** construct that is nested inside the **workshare** construct must consist of only the following:
  - array assignments
  - scalar assignments
  - **FORALL** statements
  - **FORALL** constructs
  - **WHERE** statements

– **WHERE** constructs

- All array assignments, scalar assignments, and masked array assignments that are encountered inside a **workshare** construct but are not nested inside a **parallel** construct that is nested inside the **workshare** construct must be intrinsic assignments.

- The construct must not contain any user defined function calls unless the function is **ELEMENTAL** or the function call is contained inside a **parallel** construct that is nested inside the **workshare** construct.

Cross References

- **parallel** construct, see Section 2.6 on page 74.
- **critical** construct, see Section 2.17.1 on page 223.
- **atomic** construct, see Section 2.17.7 on page 234.
- **ompt_scope_begin** and **ompt_scope_end**, see Section 4.4.4.11 on page 443.
- **ompt_work_workshare**, see Section 4.4.4.15 on page 445.
- **ompt_callback_work_t**, see Section 4.5.2.5 on page 464.

─────────────── Fortran ───────────────

2.9 Loop-Related Directives

2.9.1 Canonical Loop Form

─────────────── C / C++ ───────────────

The loops associated with a loop-associated directive have *canonical loop form* if they conform to the following:

for (*init-expr*; *test-expr*; *incr-expr*) *structured-block*	
init-expr	One of the following: *var = lb* *integer-type var = lb* *random-access-iterator-type var = lb* *pointer-type var = lb*

continued on next page

---------- C/C++ (cont.) ----------

continued from previous page

test-expr	One of the following: *var relational-op b* *b relational-op var*
incr-expr	One of the following: ++*var* *var*++ - - *var* *var* - - *var* += *incr* *var* - = *incr* *var* = *var* + *incr* *var* = *incr* + *var* *var* = *var* - *incr*

var	One of the following:
	    A variable of a signed or unsigned integer type.
	    For C++, a variable of a random access iterator type.
	    For C, a variable of a pointer type.
	This variable must not be modified during the execution of the *for-loop* other than in *incr-expr*.

relational-op	One of the following: < <= > >= !=
lb and *b*	Expressions of a type compatible with the type of *var* that are loop invariant with respect to the outermost associated loop or are one of the following (where *var-outer*, *a1*, and *a2* have a type compatible with the type of *var*, *var-outer* is *var* from an outer associated loop, and *a1* and *a2* are loop invariant integer expressions with respect to the outermost loop):

continued on next page

continued from previous page

	var-outer
	var-outer + a2
	a2 + var-outer
	var-outer - a2
	a2 - var-outer
	*a1 * var-outer*
	*a1 * var-outer + a2*
	*a2 + a1 * var-outer*
	*a1 * var-outer - a2*
	*a2 - a1 * var-outer*
	*var-outer * a1*
	*var-outer * a1 + a2*
	*a2 + var-outer * a1*
	*var-outer * a1 - a2*
	*a2 - var-outer * a1*
incr	An integer expression that is loop invariant with respect to the outermost associated loop.

―――― C / C++ ――――

―――― Fortran ――――

The loops associated with a loop-associated directive have *canonical loop form* if each of them is a *do-loop* that is a *do-construct* or an *inner-shared-do-construct* as defined by the Fortran standard. If an **end do** directive follows a *do-construct* in which several loop statements share a **DO** termination statement, then the directive can only be specified for the outermost of these **DO** statements.

The *do-stmt* for any *do-loop* must conform to the following:

DO [label] var = lb , b [, incr]	
var	A variable of integer type.
lb and *b*	Expressions of a type compatible with the type of *var* that are loop invariant with respect to the outermost associated loop or are one of the following (where *var-outer*, *a1*, and *a2* have a type compatible with the type of *var*, *var-outer* is *var* from an outer associated loop, and *a1* and *a2* are loop invariant integer expressions with respect to the outermost loop): *var-outer* *var-outer* + *a2* *a2* + *var-outer* *var-outer* - *a2* *a2* - *var-outer* *a1* * *var-outer* *a1* * *var-outer* + *a2* *a2* + *a1* * *var-outer* *a1* * *var-outer* - *a2* *a2* - *a1* * *var-outer* *var-outer* * *a1* *var-outer* * *a1* + *a2* *a2* + *var-outer* * *a1* *var-outer* * *a1* - *a2* *a2* - *var-outer* * *a1*
incr	An integer expression that is loop invariant with respect to the outermost associated loop. If it is not explicitly specified, its value is assumed to be 1.

─────────────────────────── Fortran ───────────────────────────

The canonical form allows the iteration count of all associated loops to be computed before executing the outermost loop. The *incr* and *range-expr* are evaluated before executing the loop-associated construct. If *b* or *lb* is loop invariant with respect to the outermost associated loop, it is evaluated before executing the loop-associated construct. If *b* or *lb* is not loop invariant with respect to the outermost associated loop, *a1* and/or *a2* are evaluated before executing the loop-associated construct. The computation is performed for each loop in an integer type. This type is derived from the type of *var* as follows:

- If *var* is of an integer type, then the type is the type of *var*.

---- C++ ----

- If *var* is of a random access iterator type, then the type is the type that would be used by *std::distance* applied to variables of the type of *var*.

---- C++ ----

---- C ----

- If *var* is of a pointer type, then the type is **ptrdiff_t**.

---- C ----

The behavior is unspecified if any intermediate result required to compute the iteration count cannot be represented in the type determined above.

There is no implied synchronization during the evaluation of the *lb*, *b*, or *incr* expressions. It is unspecified whether, in what order, or how many times any side effects within the *lb*, *b*, or *incr* expressions occur.

Note – Random access iterators are required to support random access to elements in constant time. Other iterators are precluded by the restrictions since they can take linear time or offer limited functionality. The use of tasks to parallelize those cases is therefore advisable.

---- C++ ----

A range-based for loop that is valid in the base language and has a begin value that satisfies the random access iterator requirement has *canonical loop form*. Range-based for loops are of the following form:

for (*range-decl*: *range-expr*) *structured-block*

The *begin-expr* and *end-expr* expressions are derived from *range-expr* by the base language and assigned to variables to which this specification refers as **__begin** and **__end** respectively. Both **__begin** and **__end** are privatized. For the purpose of the rest of the standard **__begin** is the iteration variable of the range-for loop.

---- C++ ----

Restrictions

The following restrictions also apply:

C / C++

- If *test-expr* is of the form *var relational-op b* and *relational-op* is < or <= then *incr-expr* must cause *var* to increase on each iteration of the loop. If *test-expr* is of the form *var relational-op b* and *relational-op* is > or >= then *incr-expr* must cause *var* to decrease on each iteration of the loop.

- If *test-expr* is of the form *b relational-op var* and *relational-op* is < or <= then *incr-expr* must cause *var* to decrease on each iteration of the loop. If *test-expr* is of the form *b relational-op var* and *relational-op* is > or >= then *incr-expr* must cause *var* to increase on each iteration of the loop.

- If *test-expr* is of the form *b != var* or *var != b* then *incr-expr* must cause *var* either to increase on each iteration of the loop or to decrease on each iteration of the loop.

- If *relational-op* is != and *incr-expr* is of the form that has *incr* then *incr* must be a constant expression and evaluate to -1 or 1.

C / C++

C++

- In the **simd** construct the only random access iterator types that are allowed for *var* are pointer types.

- The *range-expr* of a range-for loop must be loop invariant with respect to the outermost associated loop, and must not reference iteration variables of any associated loops.

- The loops associated with an ordered clause with a parameter may not include range-for loops.

C++

- The *b*, *lb*, *incr*, and *range-expr* expressions may not reference any *var* or member of the *range-decl* of any enclosed associated loop.

- For any associated loop where the *b* or *lb* expression is not loop invariant with respect to the outermost loop, the *var-outer* that appears in the expression may not have a random access iterator type.

- For any associated loop where *b* or *lb* is not loop invariant with respect to the outermost loop, the expression $b - lb$ will have the form $c * var\text{-}outer + d$, where c and d are loop invariant integer expressions. Let *incr-outer* be the *incr* expression of the outer loop referred to by *var-outer*. The value of $c * incr\text{-}outer \mod incr$ must be 0.

Cross References

- **simd** construct, see Section 2.9.3.1 on page 110.
- **lastprivate** clause, see Section 2.19.4.5 on page 288.
- **linear** clause, see Section 2.19.4.6 on page 290.

2.9.2 Worksharing-Loop Construct

Summary

The worksharing-loop construct specifies that the iterations of one or more associated loops will be executed in parallel by threads in the team in the context of their implicit tasks. The iterations are distributed across threads that already exist in the team that is executing the **parallel** region to which the worksharing-loop region binds.

Syntax

―――――――――――――― C / C++ ――――――――――――――

The syntax of the worksharing-loop construct is as follows:

#pragma omp for *[clause[[,] clause] ...] new-line*
    for-loops

where clause is one of the following:

    private (*list*)
    firstprivate (*list*)
    lastprivate ([*lastprivate-modifier* :] *list*)
    linear (*list[: linear-step]*)
    reduction ([*reduction-modifier*,]*reduction-identifier* : *list*)
    schedule ([*modifier* [, *modifier*] :]*kind*[, *chunk_size*])
    collapse (*n*)
    ordered[(*n*)]
    nowait
    allocate ([*allocator* :]*list*)
    order(concurrent)

The **for** directive places restrictions on the structure of all associated *for-loops*. Specifically, all associated *for-loops* must have *canonical loop form* (see Section 2.9.1 on page 95).

―――――――――――――― C / C++ ――――――――――――――

---- Fortran ----

The syntax of the worksharing-loop construct is as follows:

```
!$omp do [clause[ [,] clause] ... ]
    do-loops
[!$omp end do [nowait]]
```

where *clause* is one of the following:

    `private`(*list*)
    `firstprivate`(*list*)
    `lastprivate`([*lastprivate-modifier*:] *list*)
    `linear`(*list*[: *linear-step*])
    `reduction`([*reduction-modifier*,]*reduction-identifier* : *list*)
    `schedule`([*modifier* [, modifier]:]*kind*[, *chunk_size*])
    `collapse`(*n*)
    `ordered`[(*n*)]
    `allocate`([*allocator* :]*list*)
    `order(concurrent)`

If an **end do** directive is not specified, an **end do** directive is assumed at the end of the *do-loops*.

The **do** directive places restrictions on the structure of all associated *do-loops*. Specifically, all associated *do-loops* must have *canonical loop form* (see Section 2.9.1 on page 95).

---- Fortran ----

Binding

The binding thread set for a worksharing-loop region is the current team. A worksharing-loop region binds to the innermost enclosing **parallel** region. Only the threads of the team executing the binding **parallel** region participate in the execution of the loop iterations and the implied barrier of the worksharing-loop region if the barrier is not eliminated by a **nowait** clause.

Description

The worksharing-loop construct is associated with a loop nest that consists of one or more loops that follow the directive.

There is an implicit barrier at the end of a worksharing-loop construct unless a **nowait** clause is specified.

The **collapse** clause may be used to specify how many loops are associated with the worksharing-loop construct. The parameter of the **collapse** clause must be a constant positive integer expression. If a **collapse** clause is specified with a parameter value greater than 1, then the iterations of the associated loops to which the clause applies are collapsed into one larger iteration space that is then divided according to the **schedule** clause. The sequential execution of the iterations in these associated loops determines the order of the iterations in the collapsed iteration space. If no **collapse** clause is present or its parameter is 1, the only loop that is associated with the worksharing-loop construct for the purposes of determining how the iteration space is divided according to the **schedule** clause is the one that immediately follows the worksharing-loop directive.

If more than one loop is associated with the worksharing-loop construct then the number of times that any intervening code between any two associated loops will be executed is unspecified but will be at least once per iteration of the loop enclosing the intervening code and at most once per iteration of the innermost loop associated with the construct. If the iteration count of any loop that is associated with the worksharing-loop construct is zero and that loop does not enclose the intervening code, the behavior is unspecified.

The integer type (or kind, for Fortran) used to compute the iteration count for the collapsed loop is implementation defined.

A worksharing-loop has logical iterations numbered 0,1,...,N-1 where N is the number of loop iterations, and the logical numbering denotes the sequence in which the iterations would be executed if a set of associated loop(s) were executed sequentially. At the beginning of each logical iteration, the loop iteration variable of each associated loop has the value that it would have if the set of the associated loop(s) were executed sequentially. The **schedule** clause specifies how iterations of these associated loops are divided into contiguous non-empty subsets, called chunks, and how these chunks are distributed among threads of the team. Each thread executes its assigned chunk(s) in the context of its implicit task. The iterations of a given chunk are executed in sequential order by the assigned thread. The *chunk_size* expression is evaluated using the original list items of any variables that are made private in the worksharing-loop construct. It is unspecified whether, in what order, or how many times, any side effects of the evaluation of this expression occur. The use of a variable in a **schedule** clause expression of a worksharing-loop construct causes an implicit reference to the variable in all enclosing constructs.

Different worksharing-loop regions with the same schedule and iteration count, even if they occur in the same parallel region, can distribute iterations among threads differently. The only exception is for the **static** schedule as specified in Table 2.5. Programs that depend on which thread executes a particular iteration under any other circumstances are non-conforming.

See Section 2.9.2.1 on page 109 for details of how the schedule for a worksharing-loop region is determined.

The schedule *kind* can be one of those specified in Table 2.5.

The schedule *modifier* can be one of those specified in Table 2.6. If the **static** schedule kind is specified or if the **ordered** clause is specified, and if the **nonmonotonic** modifier is not specified, the effect is as if the **monotonic** modifier is specified. Otherwise, unless the **monotonic** modifier is specified, the effect is as if the **nonmonotonic** modifier is specified. If a **schedule** clause specifies a modifier then that modifier overrides any modifier that is specified in the *run-sched-var* ICV.

The **ordered** clause with the parameter may also be used to specify how many loops are associated with the worksharing-loop construct. The parameter of the **ordered** clause must be a constant positive integer expression if specified. The parameter of the **ordered** clause does not affect how the logical iteration space is then divided. If an **ordered** clause with the parameter is specified for the worksharing-loop construct, then those associated loops form a *doacross loop nest*.

If the value of the parameter in the **collapse** or **ordered** clause is larger than the number of nested loops following the construct, the behavior is unspecified.

If an **order(concurrent)** clause is present, then after assigning the iterations of the associated loops to their respective threads, as specified in Table 2.5, the iterations may be executed in any order, including concurrently.

TABLE 2.5: schedule Clause *kind* Values

static	When *kind* is **static**, iterations are divided into chunks of size *chunk_size*, and the chunks are assigned to the threads in the team in a round-robin fashion in the order of the thread number. Each chunk contains *chunk_size* iterations, except for the chunk that contains the sequentially last iteration, which may have fewer iterations.
	When no *chunk_size* is specified, the iteration space is divided into chunks that are approximately equal in size, and at most one chunk is distributed to each thread. The size of the chunks is unspecified in this case.
	A compliant implementation of the **static** schedule must ensure that the same assignment of logical iteration numbers to threads will be used in two worksharing-loop regions if the following conditions are satisfied: 1) both worksharing-loop regions have the same number of loop iterations, 2) both worksharing-loop regions have the same value of *chunk_size* specified, or both worksharing-loop regions have no *chunk_size* specified, 3) both worksharing-loop regions bind to the same parallel region, and 4) neither loop is associated with a SIMD construct. A data dependence between the same logical iterations in two such loops is guaranteed to be satisfied allowing safe use of the **nowait** clause.

table continued on next page

table continued from previous page

dynamic	When *kind* is **dynamic**, the iterations are distributed to threads in the team in chunks. Each thread executes a chunk of iterations, then requests another chunk, until no chunks remain to be distributed. Each chunk contains *chunk_size* iterations, except for the chunk that contains the sequentially last iteration, which may have fewer iterations. When no *chunk_size* is specified, it defaults to 1.
guided	When *kind* is **guided**, the iterations are assigned to threads in the team in chunks. Each thread executes a chunk of iterations, then requests another chunk, until no chunks remain to be assigned. For a *chunk_size* of 1, the size of each chunk is proportional to the number of unassigned iterations divided by the number of threads in the team, decreasing to 1. For a *chunk_size* with value k (greater than 1), the size of each chunk is determined in the same way, with the restriction that the chunks do not contain fewer than k iterations (except for the chunk that contains the sequentially last iteration, which may have fewer than k iterations). When no *chunk_size* is specified, it defaults to 1.
auto	When *kind* is **auto**, the decision regarding scheduling is delegated to the compiler and/or runtime system. The programmer gives the implementation the freedom to choose any possible mapping of iterations to threads in the team.
runtime	When *kind* is **runtime**, the decision regarding scheduling is deferred until run time, and the schedule and chunk size are taken from the *run-sched-var* ICV. If the ICV is set to **auto**, the schedule is implementation defined.

Note – For a team of p threads and a loop of n iterations, let $\lceil n/p \rceil$ be the integer q that satisfies $n = p * q - r$, with $0 <= r < p$. One compliant implementation of the **static** schedule (with no specified *chunk_size*) would behave as though *chunk_size* had been specified with value q. Another compliant implementation would assign q iterations to the first $p - r$ threads, and $q - 1$ iterations to the remaining r threads. This illustrates why a conforming program must not rely on the details of a particular implementation.

A compliant implementation of the **guided** schedule with a *chunk_size* value of k would assign $q = \lceil n/p \rceil$ iterations to the first available thread and set n to the larger of $n - q$ and $p * k$. It would then repeat this process until q is greater than or equal to the number of remaining iterations, at which time the remaining iterations form the final chunk. Another compliant implementation could use the same method, except with $q = \lceil n/(2p) \rceil$, and set n to the larger of $n - q$ and $2 * p * k$.

TABLE 2.6: **schedule** Clause *modifier* Values

monotonic	When the **monotonic** modifier is specified then each thread executes the chunks that it is assigned in increasing logical iteration order.
nonmonotonic	When the **nonmonotonic** modifier is specified then chunks are assigned to threads in any order and the behavior of an application that depends on any execution order of the chunks is unspecified.
simd	When the **simd** modifier is specified and the loop is associated with a SIMD construct, the *chunk_size* for all chunks except the first and last chunks is $new\_chunk\_size = \lceil chunk\_size/simd\_width \rceil * simd\_width$ where *simd_width* is an implementation-defined value. The first chunk will have at least *new_chunk_size* iterations except if it is also the last chunk. The last chunk may have fewer iterations than *new_chunk_size*. If the **simd** modifier is specified and the loop is not associated with a SIMD construct, the modifier is ignored.

Execution Model Events

The *ws-loop-begin* event occurs after an implicit task encounters a worksharing-loop construct but before the task starts execution of the structured block of the worksharing-loop region.

The *ws-loop-end* event occurs after a worksharing-loop region finishes execution but before resuming execution of the encountering task.

The *ws-loop-iteration-begin* event occurs once for each iteration of a worksharing-loop before the iteration is executed by an implicit task.

Tool Callbacks

A thread dispatches a registered **ompt_callback_work** callback with **ompt_scope_begin** as its *endpoint* argument and **work_loop** as its *wstype* argument for each occurrence of a *ws-loop-begin* event in that thread. Similarly, a thread dispatches a registered **ompt_callback_work** callback with **ompt_scope_end** as its *endpoint* argument and **work_loop** as its *wstype* argument for each occurrence of a *ws-loop-end* event in that thread. The callbacks occur in the context of the implicit task. The callbacks have type signature **ompt_callback_work_t**.

A thread dispatches a registered **ompt_callback_dispatch** callback for each occurrence of a *ws-loop-iteration-begin* event in that thread. The callback occurs in the context of the implicit task. The callback has type signature **ompt_callback_dispatch_t**.

Restrictions

Restrictions to the worksharing-loop construct are as follows:

- No OpenMP directive may appear in the region between any associated loops.
- If a `collapse` clause is specified, exactly one loop must occur in the region at each nesting level up to the number of loops specified by the parameter of the `collapse` clause.
- If the `ordered` clause is present, all loops associated with the construct must be perfectly nested; that is there must be no intervening code between any two loops.
- If a `reduction` clause with the `inscan` modifier is specified, neither the `ordered` nor `schedule` clause may appear on the worksharing-loop directive.
- The values of the loop control expressions of the loops associated with the worksharing-loop construct must be the same for all threads in the team.
- Only one `schedule` clause can appear on a worksharing-loop directive.
- The `schedule` clause must not appear on the worksharing-loop directive if the associated loop(s) form a non-rectangular loop nest.
- The `ordered` clause must not appear on the worksharing-loop directive if the associated loop(s) form a non-rectangular loop nest.
- Only one `collapse` clause can appear on a worksharing-loop directive.
- *chunk_size* must be a loop invariant integer expression with a positive value.
- The value of the *chunk_size* expression must be the same for all threads in the team.
- The value of the *run-sched-var* ICV must be the same for all threads in the team.
- When `schedule(runtime)` or `schedule(auto)` is specified, *chunk_size* must not be specified.
- A *modifier* may not be specified on a `linear` clause.
- Only one `ordered` clause can appear on a worksharing-loop directive.
- The `ordered` clause must be present on the worksharing-loop construct if any `ordered` region ever binds to a worksharing-loop region arising from the worksharing-loop construct.
- The `nonmonotonic` modifier cannot be specified if an `ordered` clause is specified.
- Either the `monotonic` modifier or the `nonmonotonic` modifier can be specified but not both.
- The loop iteration variable may not appear in a `threadprivate` directive.
- If both the `collapse` and `ordered` clause with a parameter are specified, the parameter of the `ordered` clause must be greater than or equal to the parameter of the `collapse` clause.

- A **linear** clause or an **ordered** clause with a parameter can be specified on a worksharing-loop directive but not both.
- If an **order(concurrent)** clause is present, all restrictions from the **loop** construct with an **order(concurrent)** clause also apply.
- If an **order(concurrent)** clause is present, an **ordered** clause may not appear on the same directive.

―――――――――――――――――― C / C++ ――――――――――――――――――

- The associated *for-loops* must be structured blocks.
- Only an iteration of the innermost associated loop may be curtailed by a **continue** statement.
- No statement can branch to any associated **for** statement.
- Only one **nowait** clause can appear on a **for** directive.
- A throw executed inside a worksharing-loop region must cause execution to resume within the same iteration of the worksharing-loop region, and the same thread that threw the exception must catch it.

―――――――――――――――――― C / C++ ――――――――――――――――――
―――――――――――――――――― Fortran ――――――――――――――――――

- The associated *do-loops* must be structured blocks.
- Only an iteration of the innermost associated loop may be curtailed by a **CYCLE** statement.
- No statement in the associated loops other than the **DO** statements can cause a branch out of the loops.
- The *do-loop* iteration variable must be of type integer.
- The *do-loop* cannot be a **DO WHILE** or a **DO** loop without loop control.

―――――――――――――――――― Fortran ――――――――――――――――――

Cross References

- **order(concurrent)** clause, see Section 2.9.5 on page 128.
- **ordered** construct, see Section 2.17.9 on page 250.
- **depend** clause, see Section 2.17.11 on page 255.
- **private**, **firstprivate**, **lastprivate**, **linear**, and **reduction** clauses, see Section 2.19.4 on page 282.
- **ompt_scope_begin** and **ompt_scope_end**, see Section 4.4.4.11 on page 443.
- **ompt_work_loop**, see Section 4.4.4.15 on page 445.
- **ompt_callback_work_t**, see Section 4.5.2.5 on page 464.
- **OMP_SCHEDULE** environment variable, see Section 6.1 on page 601.

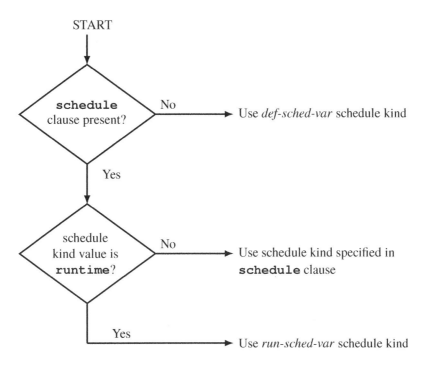

FIGURE 2.1: Determining the **schedule** for a Worksharing-Loop

2.9.2.1 Determining the Schedule of a Worksharing-Loop

When execution encounters a worksharing-loop directive, the **schedule** clause (if any) on the directive, and the *run-sched-var* and *def-sched-var* ICVs are used to determine how loop iterations are assigned to threads. See Section 2.5 on page 63 for details of how the values of the ICVs are determined. If the worksharing-loop directive does not have a **schedule** clause then the current value of the *def-sched-var* ICV determines the schedule. If the worksharing-loop directive has a **schedule** clause that specifies the **runtime** schedule kind then the current value of the *run-sched-var* ICV determines the schedule. Otherwise, the value of the **schedule** clause determines the schedule. Figure 2.1 describes how the schedule for a worksharing-loop is determined.

Cross References

- ICVs, see Section 2.5 on page 63.

2.9.3 SIMD Directives

2.9.3.1 `simd` Construct

Summary

The `simd` construct can be applied to a loop to indicate that the loop can be transformed into a SIMD loop (that is, multiple iterations of the loop can be executed concurrently using SIMD instructions).

Syntax

The syntax of the `simd` construct is as follows:

──────────── C / C++ ────────────

```
#pragma omp simd [clause[ [, ] clause] ... ] new-line
    for-loops
```

where *clause* is one of the following:

> `if ([simd :] scalar-expression)`
> `safelen (length)`
> `simdlen (length)`
> `linear (list[ : linear-step])`
> `aligned (list[ : alignment])`
> `nontemporal (list)`
> `private (list)`
> `lastprivate ([ lastprivate-modifier: ] list)`
> `reduction ([ reduction-modifier, ]reduction-identifier : list)`
> `collapse (n)`
> `order (concurrent)`

The `simd` directive places restrictions on the structure of the associated *for-loops*. Specifically, all associated *for-loops* must have *canonical loop form* (Section 2.9.1 on page 95).

──────────── C / C++ ────────────

―――――――――――――――――――――――― Fortran ――――――――――――――――――――――――

```
!$omp simd [clause[ [,] clause ... ]
    do-loops
[!$omp end simd]
```

where *clause* is one of the following:

> **if** ([**simd** :] *scalar-logical-expression*)
> **safelen** (*length*)
> **simdlen** (*length*)
> **linear** (*list*[: *linear-step*])
> **aligned** (*list*[: *alignment*])
> **nontemporal** (*list*)
> **private** (*list*)
> **lastprivate** ([*lastprivate-modifier*:] *list*)
> **reduction** ([*reduction-modifier*,]*reduction-identifier* : *list*)
> **collapse** (*n*)
> **order** (**concurrent**)

If an **end simd** directive is not specified, an **end simd** directive is assumed at the end of the *do-loops*.

The **simd** directive places restrictions on the structure of all associated *do-loops*. Specifically, all associated *do-loops* must have *canonical loop form* (see Section 2.9.1 on page 95).

―――――――――――――――――――――――― Fortran ――――――――――――――――――――――――

Binding

A **simd** region binds to the current task region. The binding thread set of the **simd** region is the current team.

Description

The **simd** construct enables the execution of multiple iterations of the associated loops concurrently by means of SIMD instructions.

The **collapse** clause may be used to specify how many loops are associated with the construct. The parameter of the **collapse** clause must be a constant positive integer expression. If no **collapse** clause is present, the only loop that is associated with the **simd** construct is the one that immediately follows the directive.

If more than one loop is associated with the `simd` construct, then the iterations of all associated loops are collapsed into one larger iteration space that is then executed with SIMD instructions. The sequential execution of the iterations in all associated loops determines the order of the iterations in the collapsed iteration space.

If more than one loop is associated with the `simd` construct then the number of times that any intervening code between any two associated loops will be executed is unspecified but will be at least once per iteration of the loop enclosing the intervening code and at most once per iteration of the innermost loop associated with the construct. If the iteration count of any loop that is associated with the `simd` construct is zero and that loop does not enclose the intervening code, the behavior is unspecified.

The integer type (or kind, for Fortran) used to compute the iteration count for the collapsed loop is implementation defined.

A SIMD loop has logical iterations numbered 0,1,...,N-1 where N is the number of loop iterations, and the logical numbering denotes the sequence in which the iterations would be executed if the associated loop(s) were executed with no SIMD instructions. At the beginning of each logical iteration, the loop iteration variable of each associated loop has the value that it would have if the set of the associated loop(s) were executed sequentially. The number of iterations that are executed concurrently at any given time is implementation defined. Each concurrent iteration will be executed by a different SIMD lane. Each set of concurrent iterations is a SIMD chunk. Lexical forward dependencies in the iterations of the original loop must be preserved within each SIMD chunk.

The `safelen` clause specifies that no two concurrent iterations within a SIMD chunk can have a distance in the logical iteration space that is greater than or equal to the value given in the clause. The parameter of the `safelen` clause must be a constant positive integer expression. The `simdlen` clause specifies the preferred number of iterations to be executed concurrently unless an `if` clause is present and evaluates to *false*, in which case the preferred number of iterations to be executed concurrently is one. The parameter of the `simdlen` clause must be a constant positive integer expression.

────────────────────────── C / C++ ──────────────────────────

The `aligned` clause declares that the object to which each list item points is aligned to the number of bytes expressed in the optional parameter of the `aligned` clause.

────────────────────────── C / C++ ──────────────────────────

────────────────────────── Fortran ──────────────────────────

The `aligned` clause declares that the location of each list item is aligned to the number of bytes expressed in the optional parameter of the `aligned` clause.

────────────────────────── Fortran ──────────────────────────

The optional parameter of the **aligned** clause, *alignment*, must be a constant positive integer expression. If no optional parameter is specified, implementation-defined default alignments for SIMD instructions on the target platforms are assumed.

The **nontemporal** clause specifies that accesses to the storage locations to which the list items refer have low temporal locality across the iterations in which those storage locations are accessed.

Restrictions

- No OpenMP directive may appear in the region between any associated loops.
- If a **collapse** clause is specified, exactly one loop must occur in the region at each nesting level up to the number of loops specified by the parameter of the **collapse** clause.
- The associated loops must be structured blocks.
- A program that branches into or out of a **simd** region is non-conforming.
- Only one **collapse** clause can appear on a **simd** directive.
- A *list-item* cannot appear in more than one **aligned** clause.
- A *list-item* cannot appear in more than one **nontemporal** clause.
- Only one **safelen** clause can appear on a **simd** directive.
- Only one **simdlen** clause can appear on a **simd** directive.
- If both **simdlen** and **safelen** clauses are specified, the value of the **simdlen** parameter must be less than or equal to the value of the **safelen** parameter.
- A *modifier* may not be specified on a **linear** clause.
- The only OpenMP constructs that can be encountered during execution of a **simd** region are the **atomic** construct, the **loop** construct, the **simd** construct and the **ordered** construct with the **simd** clause.
- If an **order(concurrent)** clause is present, all restrictions from the **loop** construct with an **order(concurrent)** clause also apply.

─────────── C / C++ ───────────

- The **simd** region cannot contain calls to the **longjmp** or **setjmp** functions.

─────────── C / C++ ───────────

─────────── C ───────────

- The type of list items appearing in the **aligned** clause must be array or pointer.

─────────── C ───────────

―――――――――――――――――― C++ ――――――――――――――――――

- The type of list items appearing in the `aligned` clause must be array, pointer, reference to array, or reference to pointer.

- No exception can be raised in the `simd` region.

―――――――――――――――――― C++ ――――――――――――――――――

―――――――――――――――――― Fortran ――――――――――――――――――

- The *do-loop* iteration variable must be of type `integer`.

- The *do-loop* cannot be a `DO WHILE` or a `DO` loop without loop control.

- If a list item on the `aligned` clause has the `ALLOCATABLE` attribute, the allocation status must be allocated.

- If a list item on the `aligned` clause has the `POINTER` attribute, the association status must be associated.

- If the type of a list item on the `aligned` clause is either `C_PTR` or Cray pointer, the list item must be defined.

―――――――――――――――――― Fortran ――――――――――――――――――

Cross References

- `order(concurrent)` clause, see Section 2.9.5 on page 128.
- `if` Clause, see Section 2.15 on page 220.
- `private`, `lastprivate`, `linear` and `reduction` clauses, see Section 2.19.4 on page 282.

2.9.3.2 Worksharing-Loop SIMD Construct

Summary

The worksharing-loop SIMD construct specifies that the iterations of one or more associated loops will be distributed across threads that already exist in the team and that the iterations executed by each thread can also be executed concurrently using SIMD instructions. The worksharing-loop SIMD construct is a composite construct.

Syntax

---C / C++---

#pragma omp for simd *[clause[[,] clause] ...] new-line*
    for-loops

where *clause* can be any of the clauses accepted by the **for** or **simd** directives with identical meanings and restrictions.

---C / C++---

---Fortran---

!$omp do simd *[clause[[,] clause] ...]*
    do-loops
[**!$omp end do simd** *[nowait]]*

where *clause* can be any of the clauses accepted by the **simd** or **do** directives, with identical meanings and restrictions.

If an **end do simd** directive is not specified, an **end do simd** directive is assumed at the end of the *do-loops*.

---Fortran---

Description

The worksharing-loop SIMD construct will first distribute the iterations of the associated loop(s) across the implicit tasks of the parallel region in a manner consistent with any clauses that apply to the worksharing-loop construct. The resulting chunks of iterations will then be converted to a SIMD loop in a manner consistent with any clauses that apply to the **simd** construct.

Execution Model Events

This composite construct generates the same events as the worksharing-loop construct.

Tool Callbacks

This composite construct dispatches the same callbacks as the worksharing-loop construct.

Restrictions

All restrictions to the worksharing-loop construct and the `simd` construct apply to the worksharing-loop SIMD construct. In addition, the following restrictions apply:

- No `ordered` clause with a parameter can be specified.
- A list item may appear in a `linear` or `firstprivate` clause but not both.

Cross References

- worksharing-loop construct, see Section 2.9.2 on page 101.
- `simd` construct, see Section 2.9.3.1 on page 110.
- Data attribute clauses, see Section 2.19.4 on page 282.

2.9.3.3 `declare simd` Directive

Summary

The `declare simd` directive can be applied to a function (C, C++ and Fortran) or a subroutine (Fortran) to enable the creation of one or more versions that can process multiple arguments using SIMD instructions from a single invocation in a SIMD loop. The `declare simd` directive is a declarative directive. There may be multiple `declare simd` directives for a function (C, C++, Fortran) or subroutine (Fortran).

Syntax

The syntax of the `declare simd` directive is as follows:

─────────────────── C / C++ ───────────────────

```
#pragma omp declare simd [clause[ [,] clause] ... ] new-line
[#pragma omp declare simd [clause[ [,] clause] ... ] new-line
[ ... ]
    function definition or declaration
```

where *clause* is one of the following:

```
simdlen(length)
linear(linear-list[ : linear-step])
aligned(argument-list[ : alignment])
uniform(argument-list)
inbranch
notinbranch
```

─────────────────── C / C++ ───────────────────

Fortran

```
!$omp declare simd [ (proc-name) ] [clause[ [, ] clause] ... ]
```

where *clause* is one of the following:

> **simdlen** (*length*)
> **linear** (*linear-list*[: *linear-step*])
> **aligned** (*argument-list*[: *alignment*])
> **uniform** (*argument-list*)
> **inbranch**
> **notinbranch**

Fortran

Description

C / C++

The use of one or more **declare simd** directives immediately prior to a function declaration or definition enables the creation of corresponding SIMD versions of the associated function that can be used to process multiple arguments from a single invocation in a SIMD loop concurrently.

The expressions appearing in the clauses of each directive are evaluated in the scope of the arguments of the function declaration or definition.

C / C++

Fortran

The use of one or more **declare simd** directives for a specified subroutine or function enables the creation of corresponding SIMD versions of the subroutine or function that can be used to process multiple arguments from a single invocation in a SIMD loop concurrently.

Fortran

If a SIMD version is created, the number of concurrent arguments for the function is determined by the **simdlen** clause. If the **simdlen** clause is used its value corresponds to the number of concurrent arguments of the function. The parameter of the **simdlen** clause must be a constant positive integer expression. Otherwise, the number of concurrent arguments for the function is implementation defined.

C++

The special *this* pointer can be used as if it was one of the arguments to the function in any of the **linear**, **aligned**, or **uniform** clauses.

C++

The **uniform** clause declares one or more arguments to have an invariant value for all concurrent invocations of the function in the execution of a single SIMD loop.

―――――――――――――――― C / C++ ――――――――――――――――

The **aligned** clause declares that the object to which each list item points is aligned to the number of bytes expressed in the optional parameter of the **aligned** clause.

―――――――――――――――― C / C++ ――――――――――――――――
―――――――――――――――― Fortran ――――――――――――――――

The **aligned** clause declares that the target of each list item is aligned to the number of bytes expressed in the optional parameter of the **aligned** clause.

―――――――――――――――― Fortran ――――――――――――――――

The optional parameter of the **aligned** clause, *alignment*, must be a constant positive integer expression. If no optional parameter is specified, implementation-defined default alignments for SIMD instructions on the target platforms are assumed.

The **inbranch** clause specifies that the SIMD version of the function will always be called from inside a conditional statement of a SIMD loop. The **notinbranch** clause specifies that the SIMD version of the function will never be called from inside a conditional statement of a SIMD loop. If neither clause is specified, then the SIMD version of the function may or may not be called from inside a conditional statement of a SIMD loop.

Restrictions

- Each argument can appear in at most one **uniform** or **linear** clause.
- At most one **simdlen** clause can appear in a **declare simd** directive.
- Either **inbranch** or **notinbranch** may be specified, but not both.
- When a *linear-step* expression is specified in a **linear** clause it must be either a constant integer expression or an integer-typed parameter that is specified in a **uniform** clause on the directive.
- The function or subroutine body must be a structured block.
- The execution of the function or subroutine, when called from a SIMD loop, cannot result in the execution of an OpenMP construct except for an **ordered** construct with the **simd** clause or an **atomic** construct.
- The execution of the function or subroutine cannot have any side effects that would alter its execution for concurrent iterations of a SIMD chunk.
- A program that branches into or out of the function is non-conforming.

―――――――――――――――― C / C++ ――――――――――――――――

- If the function has any declarations, then the **declare simd** construct for any declaration that has one must be equivalent to the one specified for the definition. Otherwise, the result is unspecified.
- The function cannot contain calls to the **longjmp** or **setjmp** functions.

―――――――――――――――― C / C++ ――――――――――――――――

C

- The type of list items appearing in the `aligned` clause must be array or pointer.

C

C++

- The function cannot contain any calls to `throw`.
- The type of list items appearing in the `aligned` clause must be array, pointer, reference to array, or reference to pointer.

C++

Fortran

- *proc-name* must not be a generic name, procedure pointer or entry name.
- If *proc-name* is omitted, the `declare simd` directive must appear in the specification part of a subroutine subprogram or a function subprogram for which creation of the SIMD versions is enabled.
- Any `declare simd` directive must appear in the specification part of a subroutine subprogram, function subprogram or interface body to which it applies.
- If a `declare simd` directive is specified in an interface block for a procedure, it must match a `declare simd` directive in the definition of the procedure.
- If a procedure is declared via a procedure declaration statement, the procedure *proc-name* should appear in the same specification.
- If a `declare simd` directive is specified for a procedure name with explicit interface and a `declare simd` directive is also specified for the definition of the procedure then the two `declare simd` directives must match. Otherwise the result is unspecified.
- Procedure pointers may not be used to access versions created by the `declare simd` directive.
- The type of list items appearing in the `aligned` clause must be `C_PTR` or Cray pointer, or the list item must have the `POINTER` or `ALLOCATABLE` attribute.

Fortran

Cross References

- `linear` clause, see Section 2.19.4.6 on page 290.
- `reduction` clause, see Section 2.19.5.4 on page 300.

2.9.4 `distribute` Loop Constructs

2.9.4.1 `distribute` Construct

Summary

The `distribute` construct specifies that the iterations of one or more loops will be executed by the initial teams in the context of their implicit tasks. The iterations are distributed across the initial threads of all initial teams that execute the `teams` region to which the `distribute` region binds.

Syntax

─────────── C / C++ ───────────

The syntax of the `distribute` construct is as follows:

```
#pragma omp distribute [clause[ [,] clause] ... ] new-line
    for-loops
```

Where *clause* is one of the following:

> `private`(*list*)
> `firstprivate`(*list*)
> `lastprivate`(*list*)
> `collapse`(*n*)
> `dist_schedule`(*kind*[, *chunk_size*])
> `allocate`([*allocator* :]*list*)

The `distribute` directive places restrictions on the structure of all associated *for-loops*. Specifically, all associated *for-loops* must have *canonical loop form* (see Section 2.9.1 on page 95).

─────────── C / C++ ───────────
─────────── Fortran ───────────

The syntax of the `distribute` construct is as follows:

```
!$omp distribute [clause[ [,] clause] ... ]
    do-loops
[!$omp end distribute]
```

Where *clause* is one of the following:

> **private**(*list*)
> **firstprivate**(*list*)
> **lastprivate**(*list*)
> **collapse**(*n*)
> **dist_schedule**(*kind*[, *chunk_size*])
> **allocate**([*allocator* :]*list*)

If an **end distribute** directive is not specified, an **end distribute** directive is assumed at the end of the *do-loops*.

The **distribute** directive places restrictions on the structure of all associated *do-loops*. Specifically, all associated *do-loops* must have *canonical loop form* (see Section 2.9.1 on page 95).

―――――――――――――― Fortran ――――――――――――――

Binding

The binding thread set for a **distribute** region is the set of initial threads executing an enclosing **teams** region. A **distribute** region binds to this **teams** region.

Description

The **distribute** construct is associated with a loop nest consisting of one or more loops that follow the directive.

There is no implicit barrier at the end of a **distribute** construct. To avoid data races the original list items modified due to **lastprivate** or **linear** clauses should not be accessed between the end of the **distribute** construct and the end of the **teams** region to which the **distribute** binds.

The **collapse** clause may be used to specify how many loops are associated with the **distribute** construct. The parameter of the **collapse** clause must be a constant positive integer expression. If no **collapse** clause is present or its parameter is 1, the only loop that is associated with the **distribute** construct is the one that immediately follows the **distribute** construct. If a **collapse** clause is specified with a parameter value greater than 1 and more than one loop is associated with the **distribute** construct, then the iteration of all associated loops are collapsed into one larger iteration space. The sequential execution of the iterations in all associated loops determines the order of the iterations in the collapsed iteration space.

A distribute loop has logical iterations numbered 0,1,...,N-1 where N is the number of loop iterations, and the logical numbering denotes the sequence in which the iterations would be executed if the set of associated loop(s) were executed sequentially. At the beginning of each logical iteration, the loop iteration variable of each associated loop has the value that it would have if the set of the associated loop(s) were executed sequentially.

If more than one loop is associated with the **distribute** construct then the number of times that any intervening code between any two associated loops will be executed is unspecified but will be at least once per iteration of the loop enclosing the intervening code and at most once per iteration of the innermost loop associated with the construct. If the iteration count of any loop that is associated with the **distribute** construct is zero and that loop does not enclose the intervening code, the behavior is unspecified.

The integer type (or kind, for Fortran) used to compute the iteration count for the collapsed loop is implementation defined.

If **dist_schedule** is specified, *kind* must be **static**. If specified, iterations are divided into chunks of size *chunk_size*, chunks are assigned to the initial teams of the league in a round-robin fashion in the order of the initial team number. When no *chunk_size* is specified, the iteration space is divided into chunks that are approximately equal in size, and at most one chunk is distributed to each initial team of the league. The size of the chunks is unspecified in this case.

When no **dist_schedule** clause is specified, the schedule is implementation defined.

Execution Model Events

The *distribute-begin* event occurs after an implicit task encounters a **distribute** construct but before the task starts to execute the structured block of the **distribute** region.

The *distribute-end* event occurs after an implicit task finishes execution of a **distribute** region but before it resumes execution of the enclosing context.

Tool Callbacks

A thread dispatches a registered **ompt_callback_work** callback with **ompt_scope_begin** as its *endpoint* argument and **ompt_work_distribute** as its *wstype* argument for each occurrence of a *distribute-begin* event in that thread. Similarly, a thread dispatches a registered **ompt_callback_work** callback with **ompt_scope_end** as its *endpoint* argument and **ompt_work_distribute** as its *wstype* argument for each occurrence of a *distribute-end* event in that thread. The callbacks occur in the context of the implicit task. The callbacks have type signature **ompt_callback_work_t**.

Restrictions

Restrictions to the **distribute** construct are as follows:

- The **distribute** construct inherits the restrictions of the worksharing-loop construct.
- Each **distribute** region must be encountered by the initial threads of all initial teams in a league or by none at all.

- The sequence of the **distribute** regions encountered must be the same for every initial thread of every initial team in a league.
- The region corresponding to the **distribute** construct must be strictly nested inside a **teams** region.
- A list item may appear in a **firstprivate** or **lastprivate** clause but not both.
- The **dist_schedule** clause must not appear on the **distribute** directive if the associated loop(s) form a non-rectangular loop nest.

Cross References

- **teams** construct, see Section 2.7 on page 82
- worksharing-loop construct, see Section 2.9.2 on page 101.
- **ompt_work_distribute**, see Section 4.4.4.15 on page 445.
- **ompt_callback_work_t**, see Section 4.5.2.5 on page 464.

2.9.4.2 distribute simd Construct

Summary

The **distribute simd** construct specifies a loop that will be distributed across the master threads of the **teams** region and executed concurrently using SIMD instructions. The **distribute simd** construct is a composite construct.

Syntax

The syntax of the **distribute simd** construct is as follows:

─────────────── C / C++ ───────────────

| **#pragma omp distribute simd** *[clause[[,] clause] ...] newline*
| *for-loops*

where *clause* can be any of the clauses accepted by the **distribute** or **simd** directives with identical meanings and restrictions.

─────────────── C / C++ ───────────────

―――――― Fortran ――――――
```
!$omp distribute simd [clause[ [,] clause] ... ]
    do-loops
[!$omp end distribute simd]
```

where *clause* can be any of the clauses accepted by the **distribute** or **simd** directives with identical meanings and restrictions.

If an **end distribute simd** directive is not specified, an **end distribute simd** directive is assumed at the end of the *do-loops*.

―――――― Fortran ――――――

Description

The **distribute simd** construct will first distribute the iterations of the associated loop(s) according to the semantics of the **distribute** construct and any clauses that apply to the distribute construct. The resulting chunks of iterations will then be converted to a SIMD loop in a manner consistent with any clauses that apply to the **simd** construct.

Execution Model Events

This composite construct generates the same events as the **distribute** construct.

Tool Callbacks

This composite construct dispatches the same callbacks as the **distribute** construct.

Restrictions

- The restrictions for the **distribute** and **simd** constructs apply.
- A list item may not appear in a **linear** clause unless it is the loop iteration variable of a loop that is associated with the construct.
- The **conditional** modifier may not appear in a **lastprivate** clause.

Cross References

- **simd** construct, see Section 2.9.3.1 on page 110.
- **distribute** construct, see Section 2.9.4.1 on page 120.
- Data attribute clauses, see Section 2.19.4 on page 282.

2.9.4.3 Distribute Parallel Worksharing-Loop Construct

Summary

The distribute parallel worksharing-loop construct specifies a loop that can be executed in parallel by multiple threads that are members of multiple teams. The distribute parallel worksharing-loop construct is a composite construct.

Syntax

The syntax of the distribute parallel worksharing-loop construct is as follows:

―――――――――――――――――― C / C++ ――――――――――――――――――
```
#pragma omp distribute parallel for [clause[ [, ] clause] ... ] newline
    for-loops
```

where *clause* can be any of the clauses accepted by the **distribute** or parallel worksharing-loop directives with identical meanings and restrictions.

―――――――――――――――――― C / C++ ――――――――――――――――――
―――――――――――――――――― Fortran ―――――――――――――――――――
```
!$omp distribute parallel do [clause[ [, ] clause] ... ]
    do-loops
[!$omp end distribute parallel do]
```

where *clause* can be any of the clauses accepted by the **distribute** or parallel worksharing-loop directives with identical meanings and restrictions.

If an **end distribute parallel do** directive is not specified, an **end distribute parallel do** directive is assumed at the end of the *do-loops*.

―――――――――――――――――― Fortran ―――――――――――――――――――

Description

The distribute parallel worksharing-loop construct will first distribute the iterations of the associated loop(s) into chunks according to the semantics of the **distribute** construct and any clauses that apply to the **distribute** construct. Each of these chunks will form a loop. Each resulting loop will then be distributed across the threads within the **teams** region to which the **distribute** construct binds in a manner consistent with any clauses that apply to the parallel worksharing-loop construct.

Execution Model Events

This composite construct generates the same events as the **distribute** and parallel worksharing-loop constructs.

Tool Callbacks

This composite construct dispatches the same callbacks as the `distribute` and parallel worksharing-loop constructs.

Restrictions

- The restrictions for the `distribute` and parallel worksharing-loop constructs apply.
- No `ordered` clause can be specified.
- No `linear` clause can be specified.
- The `conditional` modifier may not appear in a `lastprivate` clause.

Cross References

- `distribute` construct, see Section 2.9.4.1 on page 120.
- Parallel worksharing-loop construct, see Section 2.13.1 on page 185.
- Data attribute clauses, see Section 2.19.4 on page 282.

2.9.4.4 Distribute Parallel Worksharing-Loop SIMD Construct

Summary

The distribute parallel worksharing-loop SIMD construct specifies a loop that can be executed concurrently using SIMD instructions in parallel by multiple threads that are members of multiple teams. The distribute parallel worksharing-loop SIMD construct is a composite construct.

Syntax

───────────────── C / C++ ─────────────────

The syntax of the distribute parallel worksharing-loop SIMD construct is as follows:

```
#pragma omp distribute parallel for simd \
        [clause[ [,] clause] ... ] newline
    for-loops
```

where *clause* can be any of the clauses accepted by the `distribute` or parallel worksharing-loop SIMD directives with identical meanings and restrictions.

───────────────── C / C++ ─────────────────

―――――― Fortran ――――――

The syntax of the distribute parallel worksharing-loop SIMD construct is as follows:

```
!$omp distribute parallel do simd [clause[ [,] clause] ... ]
    do-loops
[!$omp end distribute parallel do simd]
```

where *clause* can be any of the clauses accepted by the **distribute** or parallel worksharing-loop SIMD directives with identical meanings and restrictions.

If an **end distribute parallel do simd** directive is not specified, an **end distribute parallel do simd** directive is assumed at the end of the *do-loops*.

―――――― Fortran ――――――

Description

The distribute parallel worksharing-loop SIMD construct will first distribute the iterations of the associated loop(s) according to the semantics of the **distribute** construct and any clauses that apply to the **distribute** construct. The resulting loops will then be distributed across the threads contained within the **teams** region to which the **distribute** construct binds in a manner consistent with any clauses that apply to the parallel worksharing-loop construct. The resulting chunks of iterations will then be converted to a SIMD loop in a manner consistent with any clauses that apply to the **simd** construct.

Execution Model Events

This composite construct generates the same events as the **distribute** and parallel worksharing-loop SIMD constructs.

Tool Callbacks

This composite construct dispatches the same callbacks as the **distribute** and parallel worksharing-loop SIMD constructs.

Restrictions

- The restrictions for the **distribute** and parallel worksharing-loop SIMD constructs apply.
- No **ordered** clause can be specified.
- A list item may not appear in a **linear** clause unless it is the loop iteration variable of a loop that is associated with the construct.
- The *conditional* modifier may not appear in a **lastprivate** clause.

Cross References

- **distribute** construct, see Section 2.9.4.1 on page 120.
- Parallel worksharing-loop SIMD construct, see Section 2.13.5 on page 190.
- Data attribute clauses, see Section 2.19.4 on page 282.

2.9.5 loop Construct

Summary

A **loop** construct specifies that the iterations of the associated loops may execute concurrently and permits the encountering thread(s) to execute the loop accordingly.

Syntax

──────── C / C++ ────────

The syntax of the **loop** construct is as follows:

> **#pragma omp loop** *[clause[[,] clause] ...] new-line*
>   *for-loops*

where *clause* is one of the following:

> **bind**(*binding*)
> **collapse**(*n*)
> **order(concurrent)**
> **private**(*list*)
> **lastprivate**(*list*)
> **reduction**([**default** ,]*reduction-identifier* : *list*)

where *binding* is one of the following:

> **teams**
> **parallel**
> **thread**

The **loop** directive places restrictions on the structure of all associated *for-loops*. Specifically, all associated *for-loops* must have *canonical loop form* (see Section 2.9.1 on page 95).

──────── C / C++ ────────

---------- Fortran ----------

The syntax of the **loop** construct is as follows:

```
!$omp loop [clause[ [,] clause] ... ]
    do-loops
[!$omp end loop]
```

where *clause* is one of the following:

> **bind**(*binding*)
> **collapse**(*n*)
> **order**(**concurrent**)
> **private**(*list*)
> **lastprivate**(*list*)
> **reduction**([*default* ,]*reduction-identifier* : *list*)

where *binding* is one of the following:

> **teams**
> **parallel**
> **thread**

If an **end loop** directive is not specified, an **end loop** directive is assumed at the end of the *do-loops*.

The **loop** directive places restrictions on the structure of all associated *do-loops*. Specifically, all associated *do-loops* must have *canonical loop form* (see Section 2.9.1 on page 95).

---------- Fortran ----------

Binding

If the **bind** clause is present on the construct, the binding region is determined by *binding*. Specifically, if *binding* is **teams** and there exists an innermost enclosing **teams** region then the binding region is that **teams** region; if *binding* is **parallel** then the binding region is the innermost enclosing parallel region, which may be an implicit parallel region; and if *binding* is **thread** then the binding region is not defined. If the **bind** clause is not present on the construct and the **loop** construct is closely nested inside a **teams** or **parallel** construct, the binding region is the corresponding **teams** or **parallel** region. If none of those conditions hold, the binding region is not defined.

If the binding region is a **teams** region, then the binding thread set is the set of master threads that are executing that region. If the binding region is a parallel region, then the binding thread set is the team of threads that are executing that region. If the binding region is not defined, then the binding thread set is the encountering thread.

Description

The `loop` construct is associated with a loop nest that consists of one or more loops that follow the directive. The directive asserts that the iterations may execute in any order, including concurrently.

The `collapse` clause may be used to specify how many loops are associated with the `loop` construct. The parameter of the `collapse` clause must be a constant positive integer expression. If a `collapse` clause is specified with a parameter value greater than 1, then the iterations of the associated loops to which the clause applies are collapsed into one larger iteration space with unspecified ordering. If no `collapse` clause is present or its parameter is 1, the only loop that is associated with the `loop` construct is the one that immediately follows the `loop` directive.

If more than one loop is associated with the `loop` construct then the number of times that any intervening code between any two associated loops will be executed is unspecified but will be at least once per iteration of the loop enclosing the intervening code and at most once per iteration of the innermost loop associated with the construct. If the iteration count of any loop that is associated with the `loop` construct is zero and that loop does not enclose the intervening code, the behavior is unspecified.

The iteration space of the associated loops correspond to logical iterations numbered 0,1,...,N-1 where N is the number of loop iterations, and the logical numbering denotes the sequence in which the iterations would be executed if a set of associated loop(s) were executed sequentially. At the beginning of each logical iteration, the loop iteration variable of each associated loop has the value that it would have if the set of the associated loop(s) were executed sequentially.

Each logical iteration is executed once per instance of the `loop` region that is encountered by the binding thread set.

If the `order(concurrent)` clause appears on the `loop` construct, the iterations of the associated loops may execute in any order, including concurrently. If the `order` clause is not present, the behavior is as if the `order(concurrent)` clause appeared on the construct.

The set of threads that may execute the iterations of the `loop` region is the binding thread set. Each iteration is executed by one thread from this set.

If the `loop` region binds to a `teams` region, the threads in the binding thread set may continue execution after the `loop` region without waiting for all iterations of the associated loop(s) to complete. The iterations are guaranteed to complete before the end of the `teams` region.

If the `loop` region does not bind to a `teams` region, all iterations of the associated loop(s) must complete before the encountering thread(s) continue execution after the `loop` region.

Restrictions

Restrictions to the `loop` construct are as follows:

- If the `collapse` clause is specified then there may be no intervening OpenMP directives between the associated loops.

- At most one `collapse` clause can appear on a `loop` directive.
- A list item may not appear in a `lastprivate` clause unless it is the loop iteration variable of a loop that is associated with the construct.
- If a `loop` construct is not nested inside another OpenMP construct and it appears in a procedure, the `bind` clause must be present.
- If a `loop` region binds to a `teams` or parallel region, it must be encountered by all threads in the binding thread set or by none of them.
- If the `bind` clause is present and *binding* is `teams`, the `loop` region corresponding to the `loop` construct must be strictly nested inside a `teams` region.
- If the `bind` clause is present and *binding* is `parallel`, the behavior is unspecified if the `loop` region corresponding to a `loop` construct is closely nested inside a `simd` region.
- The only constructs that may be nested inside a `loop` region are the `loop` construct, the `parallel` construct, the `simd` construct, and combined constructs for which the first construct is a `parallel` construct.
- A `loop` region corresponding to a `loop` construct may not contain calls to procedures that contain OpenMP directives.
- A `loop` region corresponding to a `loop` construct may not contain calls to the OpenMP Runtime API.
- If a threadprivate variable is referenced inside a `loop` region, the behavior is unspecified.

---------------- C / C++ ----------------

- The associated *for-loops* must be structured blocks.
- No statement can branch to any associated `for` statement.

---------------- C / C++ ----------------

---------------- Fortran ----------------

- The associated *do-loops* must be structured blocks.
- No statement in the associated loops other than the DO statements can cause a branch out of the loops.

---------------- Fortran ----------------

Cross References

- The `single` construct, see Section 2.8.2 on page 89.
- The Worksharing-Loop construct, see Section 2.9.2 on page 101.
- SIMD directives, see Section 2.9.3 on page 110.
- `distribute` construct, see Section 2.9.4.1 on page 120.

2.9.6 `scan` Directive

Summary

The `scan` directive specifies that scan computations update the list items on each iteration.

Syntax

─────────────────────────── C / C++ ───────────────────────────

The syntax of the `scan` directive is as follows:

loop-associated-directive
for-loop-headers
{
    structured-block
    `#pragma omp scan` *clause new-line*
    structured-block
}

where *clause* is one of the following:

> `inclusive` (*list*)
> `exclusive` (*list*)

and where *loop-associated-directive* is a `for`, `for simd`, or `simd` directive.

─────────────────────────── C / C++ ───────────────────────────
─────────────────────────── Fortran ───────────────────────────

The syntax of the `scan` directive is as follows:

loop-associated-directive
do-loop-headers
    structured-block
    `!$omp scan` *clause*
    structured-block
do-termination-stmts(s)
[end-loop-associated-directive]

where *clause* is one of the following:

> `inclusive` (*list*)
> `exclusive` (*list*)

and where *loop-associated-directive* (*end-loop-associated-directive*) is a `do` (`end do`), `do simd` (`end do simd`), or `simd` (`end simd`) directive.

─────────────────────────── Fortran ───────────────────────────

Description

The **scan** directive may appear in the body of a loop or loop nest associated with an enclosing worksharing-loop, worksharing-loop SIMD, or **simd** construct, to specify that a scan computation updates each list item on each loop iteration. The directive specifies that either an inclusive scan computation is to be performed for each list item that appears in an **inclusive** clause on the directive, or an exclusive scan computation is to be performed for each list item that appears in an **exclusive** clause on the directive. For each list item for which a scan computation is specified, statements that lexically precede or follow the directive constitute one of two phases for a given logical iteration of the loop – an *input phase* or a *scan phase*.

If the list item appears in an **inclusive** clause, all statements in the structured block that lexically precede the directive constitute the *input phase* and all statements in the structured block that lexically follow the directive constitute the *scan phase*. If the list item appears in an **exclusive** clause and the iteration is not the last iteration, all statements in the structured block that lexically precede the directive constitute the *scan phase* and all statements in the structured block that lexically follow the directive constitute the *input phase*. If the list item appears in an **exclusive** clause and the iteration is the last iteration, the iteration does not have an *input phase* and all statements that lexically precede or follow the directive constitute the *scan phase* for the iteration. The *input phase* contains all computations that update the list item in the iteration, and the *scan phase* ensures that any statement that reads the list item uses the result of the scan computation for that iteration.

The result of a scan computation for a given iteration is calculated according to the last *generalized prefix sum* ($PRESUM_{last}$) applied over the sequence of values given by the original value of the list item prior to the loop and all preceding updates to the list item in the logical iteration space of the loop. The operation $PRESUM_{last}(op, a_1, \ldots, a_N)$ is defined for a given binary operator *op* and a sequence of N values $a_1, \ldots, a_N$ as follows:

- if $N = 1$, a_1

- if $N > 1$, $op(\ PRESUM_{last}(op, a_1, \ldots, a_K), PRESUM_{last}(op, a_L, \ldots, a_N)\ )$, where $1 \leq K + 1 = L \leq N$.

At the beginning of the *input phase* of each iteration, the list item is initialized with the initializer value of the *reduction-identifier* specified by the **reduction** clause on the innermost enclosing construct. The *update value* of a list item is, for a given iteration, the value of the list item on completion of its *input phase*.

Let *orig-val* be the value of the original list item on entry to the enclosing worksharing-loop, worksharing-loop SIMD, or **simd** construct. Let *combiner* be the combiner for the *reduction-identifier* specified by the **reduction** clause on the construct. And let u_I be the update value of a list item for iteration *I*. For list items appearing in an **inclusive** clause on the **scan** directive, at the beginning of the *scan phase* for iteration *I* the list item is assigned the result of the operation $PRESUM_{last}(\ combiner, orig\text{-}val, u_0, \ldots, u_I)$. For list items appearing in an **exclusive** clause on the **scan** directive, at the beginning of the *scan phase* for iteration $I = 0$

the list item is assigned the value *orig-val*, and at the beginning of the *scan phase* for iteration $I > 0$ the list item is assigned the result of the operation $\text{PRESUM}_{\text{last}}($ *combiner*, *orig-val*, $u_0, \ldots, u_{I-1})$.

Restrictions

Restrictions to the **scan** directive are as follows:

- Exactly one **scan** directive must appear in the loop body of an enclosing worksharing-loop, worksharing-loop SIMD, or **simd** construct on which a **reduction** clause with the **inscan** modifier is present.

- A list item that appears in the **inclusive** or **exclusive** clause must appear in a **reduction** clause with the **inscan** modifier on the enclosing worksharing-loop, worksharing-loop SIMD, or **simd** construct.

- Cross-iteration dependences across different logical iterations must not exist, except for dependences for the list items specified in an **inclusive** or **exclusive** clause.

- Intra-iteration dependences from a statement in the structured block preceding a **scan** directive to a statement in the structured block following a **scan** directive must not exist, except for dependences for the list items specified in an **inclusive** or **exclusive** clause.

Cross References

- worksharing-loop construct, see Section 2.9.2 on page 101.
- **simd** construct, see Section 2.9.3.1 on page 110.
- worksharing-loop SIMD construct, see Section 2.9.3.2 on page 114.
- **reduction** clause, see Section 2.19.5.4 on page 300.

2.10 Tasking Constructs

2.10.1 `task` Construct

Summary

The `task` construct defines an explicit task.

Syntax

――――――――――――― C / C++ ―――――――――――――

The syntax of the `task` construct is as follows:

```
#pragma omp task [clause[ [,] clause] ... ] new-line
    structured-block
```

where *clause* is one of the following:

> `if([ task :] ` *scalar-expression*`)`
> `final(`*scalar-expression*`)`
> `untied`
> `default(shared | none)`
> `mergeable`
> `private(`*list*`)`
> `firstprivate(`*list*`)`
> `shared(`*list*`)`
> `in_reduction(`*reduction-identifier* : *list*`)`
> `depend(`*[depend-modifier,] dependence-type* : *locator-list*`)`
> `priority(`*priority-value*`)`
> `allocate([`*allocator* :`] `*list*`)`
> `affinity([`*aff-modifier* :`] `*locator-list*`)`
> `detach(`*event-handle*`)`

where *aff-modifier* is one of the following:

> `iterator(`*iterators-definition*`)`

where *event-handle* is a variable of the `omp_event_handle_t` type.

――――――――――――― C / C++ ―――――――――――――

CHAPTER 2. DIRECTIVES   135

───────────────── Fortran ─────────────────

The syntax of the **task** construct is as follows:

```
!$omp task [clause[ [,] clause] ... ]
    structured-block
!$omp end task
```

where *clause* is one of the following:

    if (*[* **task** *:]* *scalar-logical-expression*)
    final (*scalar-logical-expression*)
    untied
    default (**private** | **firstprivate** | **shared** | **none**)
    mergeable
    private (*list*)
    firstprivate (*list*)
    shared (*list*)
    in_reduction (*reduction-identifier* : *list*)
    depend (*[depend-modifier,]* *dependence-type* : *locator-list*)
    priority (*priority-value*)
    allocate (*[allocator :]* *list*)
    affinity (*[aff-modifier :]* *locator-list*)
    detach (*event-handle*)

where *aff-modifier* is one of the following:

    iterator (*iterators-definition*)

where *event-handle* is an integer variable of **omp_event_handle_kind** *kind*.

───────────────── Fortran ─────────────────

Binding

The binding thread set of the **task** region is the current team. A **task** region binds to the innermost enclosing **parallel** region.

Description

The **task** construct is a *task generating construct*. When a thread encounters a **task** construct, an explicit task is generated from the code for the associated *structured-block*. The data environment of the task is created according to the data-sharing attribute clauses on the **task** construct, per-data environment ICVs, and any defaults that apply. The data environment of the task is destroyed when the execution code of the associated *structured-block* is completed.

The encountering thread may immediately execute the task, or defer its execution. In the latter case, any thread in the team may be assigned the task. Completion of the task can be guaranteed using task synchronization constructs. If a **task** construct is encountered during execution of an outer task, the generated **task** region corresponding to this construct is not a part of the outer task region unless the generated task is an included task.

If a **detach** clause is present on a **task** construct a new event *allow-completion-event* is created. The *allow-completion-event* is connected to the completion of the associated **task** region. The original *event-handle* will be updated to represent the *allow-completion-event* event before the task data environment is created. The *event-handle* will be considered as if it was specified on a `firstprivate` clause. The use of a variable in a **detach** clause expression of a **task** construct causes an implicit reference to the variable in all enclosing constructs.

If no **detach** clause is present on a **task** construct the generated **task** is completed when the execution of its associated *structured-block* is completed. If a **detach** clause is present on a **task** construct the task is completed when the execution of its associated *structured-block* is completed and the *allow-completion-event* is fulfilled.

When an **if** clause is present on a **task** construct, and the **if** clause expression evaluates to *false*, an undeferred task is generated, and the encountering thread must suspend the current task region, for which execution cannot be resumed until execution of the *structured block* that is associated with the generated task is completed. The use of a variable in an **if** clause expression of a **task** construct causes an implicit reference to the variable in all enclosing constructs.

When a **final** clause is present on a **task** construct and the **final** clause expression evaluates to *true*, the generated task will be a final task. All **task** constructs encountered during execution of a final task will generate final and included tasks. The use of a variable in a **final** clause expression of a **task** construct causes an implicit reference to the variable in all enclosing constructs. Encountering a **task** construct with the **detach** clause during the execution of a final task results in unspecified behavior.

The **if** clause expression and the **final** clause expression are evaluated in the context outside of the **task** construct, and no ordering of those evaluations is specified..

A thread that encounters a task scheduling point within the **task** region may temporarily suspend the **task** region. By default, a task is tied and its suspended **task** region can only be resumed by the thread that started its execution. If the **untied** clause is present on a **task** construct, any thread in the team can resume the **task** region after a suspension. The **untied** clause is ignored if a `final` clause is present on the same `task` construct and the `final` clause expression evaluates to *true*, or if a task is an included task.

The `task` construct includes a task scheduling point in the task region of its generating task, immediately following the generation of the explicit task. Each explicit `task` region includes a task scheduling point at the end of its associated *structured-block*.

When the `mergeable` clause is present on a `task` construct, the generated task is a *mergeable task*.

The `priority` clause is a hint for the priority of the generated task. The *priority-value* is a non-negative integer expression that provides a hint for task execution order. Among all tasks ready to be executed, higher priority tasks (those with a higher numerical value in the `priority` clause expression) are recommended to execute before lower priority ones. The default *priority-value* when no `priority` clause is specified is zero (the lowest priority). If a value is specified in the `priority` clause that is higher than the *max-task-priority-var* ICV then the implementation will use the value of that ICV. A program that relies on task execution order being determined by this *priority-value* may have unspecified behavior.

The `affinity` clause is a hint to indicate data affinity of the generated task. The task is recommended to execute closely to the location of the list items. A program that relies on the task execution location being determined by this list may have unspecified behavior.

The list items that appear in the `affinity` clause may reference iterators defined by an *iterators-definition* appearing in the same clause. The list items that appear in the `affinity` clause may include array sections.

───────────────── C / C++ ─────────────────

The list items that appear in the `affinity` clause may use shape-operators.

───────────────── C / C++ ─────────────────

If a list item appears in an `affinity` clause then data affinity refers to the original list item.

Note – When storage is shared by an explicit `task` region, the programmer must ensure, by adding proper synchronization, that the storage does not reach the end of its lifetime before the explicit `task` region completes its execution.

Execution Model Events

The *task-create* event occurs when a thread encounters a construct that causes a new task to be created. The event occurs after the task is initialized but before it begins execution or is deferred.

Tool Callbacks

A thread dispatches a registered **ompt_callback_task_create** callback for each occurrence of a *task-create* event in the context of the encountering task. This callback has the type signature **ompt_callback_task_create_t** and the *flags* argument indicates the task types shown in Table 2.7.

TABLE 2.7: ompt_callback_task_create callback flags evaluation

Operation	Evaluates to true
(*flags* & ompt_task_explicit)	Always in the dispatched callback
(*flags* & ompt_task_undeferred)	If the task is an undeferred task
(*flags* & ompt_task_final)	If the task is a final task
(*flags* & ompt_task_untied)	If the task is an untied task
(*flags* & ompt_task_mergeable)	If the task is a mergeable task
(*flags* & ompt_task_merged)	If the task is a merged task

Restrictions

Restrictions to the **task** construct are as follows:

- A program that branches into or out of a **task** region is non-conforming.
- A program must not depend on any ordering of the evaluations of the clauses of the **task** directive, or on any side effects of the evaluations of the clauses.
- At most one **if** clause can appear on the directive.
- At most one **final** clause can appear on the directive.
- At most one **priority** clause can appear on the directive.
- At most one **detach** clause can appear on the directive.
- If a **detach** clause appears on the directive, then a **mergeable** clause cannot appear on the same directive.

─────────────── C / C++ ───────────────

- A throw executed inside a **task** region must cause execution to resume within the same **task** region, and the same thread that threw the exception must catch it.

─────────────── C / C++ ───────────────

Cross References

- Task scheduling constraints, see Section 2.10.6 on page 149.
- `allocate` clause, see Section 2.11.4 on page 158.
- `if` clause, see Section 2.15 on page 220.
- `depend` clause, see Section 2.17.11 on page 255.
- Data-sharing attribute clauses, Section 2.19.4 on page 282.
- `default` clause, see Section 2.19.4.1 on page 282.
- `in_reduction` clause, see Section 2.19.5.6 on page 303.
- `omp_fulfill_event`, see Section 3.5.1 on page 396.
- `ompt_callback_task_create_t`, see Section 4.5.2.7 on page 467.

2.10.2 `taskloop` Construct

Summary

The `taskloop` construct specifies that the iterations of one or more associated loops will be executed in parallel using explicit tasks. The iterations are distributed across tasks generated by the construct and scheduled to be executed.

Syntax

─────────────────── C / C++ ───────────────────

The syntax of the `taskloop` construct is as follows:

```
#pragma omp taskloop [clause[[, ] clause] ...] new-line
    for-loops
```

where *clause* is one of the following:

```
if([ taskloop :] scalar-expression)
shared(list)
private(list)
firstprivate(list)
lastprivate(list)
reduction([default ,]reduction-identifier : list)
in_reduction(reduction-identifier : list)
```

```
default(shared | none)
grainsize(grain-size)
num_tasks(num-tasks)
collapse(n)
final(scalar-expr)
priority(priority-value)
untied
mergeable
nogroup
allocate([allocator :] list)
```

The **taskloop** directive places restrictions on the structure of all associated *for-loops*. Specifically, all associated *for-loops* must have *canonical loop form* (see Section 2.9.1 on page 95).

―――――――――――――――― C / C++ ――――――――――――――――
―――――――――――――――― Fortran ――――――――――――――――

The syntax of the **taskloop** construct is as follows:

```
!$omp taskloop [clause[[,] clause] ...]
    do-loops
[!$omp end taskloop]
```

where *clause* is one of the following:

```
if([ taskloop :] scalar-logical-expression)
shared(list)
private(list)
firstprivate(list)
lastprivate(list)
reduction([default ,]reduction-identifier : list)
in_reduction(reduction-identifier : list)
default(private | firstprivate | shared | none)
grainsize(grain-size)
num_tasks(num-tasks)
collapse(n)
final(scalar-logical-expr)
priority(priority-value)
```

CHAPTER 2. DIRECTIVES

```
untied
mergeable
nogroup
allocate([allocator :] list)
```

If an **end tasloop** directive is not specified, an **end tasloop** directive is assumed at the end of the *do-loops*.

The **tasloop** directive places restrictions on the structure of all associated *do-loops*. Specifically, all associated *do-loops* must have *canonical loop form* (see Section 2.9.1 on page 95).

───────────────────────── Fortran ─────────────────────────

Binding

The binding thread set of the **tasloop** region is the current team. A **tasloop** region binds to the innermost enclosing **parallel** region.

Description

The **tasloop** construct is a *task generating construct*. When a thread encounters a **tasloop** construct, the construct partitions the iterations of the associated loops into explicit tasks for parallel execution. The data environment of each generated task is created according to the data-sharing attribute clauses on the **tasloop** construct, per-data environment ICVs, and any defaults that apply. The order of the creation of the loop tasks is unspecified. Programs that rely on any execution order of the logical loop iterations are non-conforming.

By default, the **tasloop** construct executes as if it was enclosed in a **taskgroup** construct with no statements or directives outside of the **tasloop** construct. Thus, the **tasloop** construct creates an implicit **taskgroup** region. If the **nogroup** clause is present, no implicit **taskgroup** region is created.

If a **reduction** clause is present on the **tasloop** construct, the behavior is as if a **task_reduction** clause with the same reduction operator and list items was applied to the implicit **taskgroup** construct enclosing the **tasloop** construct. The **tasloop** construct executes as if each generated task was defined by a **task** construct on which an **in_reduction** clause with the same reduction operator and list items is present. Thus, the generated tasks are participants of the reduction defined by the **task_reduction** clause that was applied to the implicit **taskgroup** construct.

If an **in_reduction** clause is present on the **tasloop** construct, the behavior is as if each generated task was defined by a **task** construct on which an **in_reduction** clause with the same reduction operator and list items is present. Thus, the generated tasks are participants of a reduction previously defined by a reduction scoping clause.

If a `grainsize` clause is present on the `taskloop` construct, the number of logical loop iterations assigned to each generated task is greater than or equal to the minimum of the value of the *grain-size* expression and the number of logical loop iterations, but less than two times the value of the *grain-size* expression.

The parameter of the `grainsize` clause must be a positive integer expression. If `num_tasks` is specified, the `taskloop` construct creates as many tasks as the minimum of the *num-tasks* expression and the number of logical loop iterations. Each task must have at least one logical loop iteration. The parameter of the `num_tasks` clause must be a positive integer expression. If neither a `grainsize` nor `num_tasks` clause is present, the number of loop tasks generated and the number of logical loop iterations assigned to these tasks is implementation defined.

The `collapse` clause may be used to specify how many loops are associated with the `taskloop` construct. The parameter of the `collapse` clause must be a constant positive integer expression. If no `collapse` clause is present or its parameter is 1, the only loop that is associated with the `taskloop` construct is the one that immediately follows the `taskloop` directive. If a `collapse` clause is specified with a parameter value greater than 1 and more than one loop is associated with the `taskloop` construct, then the iterations of all associated loops are collapsed into one larger iteration space that is then divided according to the `grainsize` and `num_tasks` clauses. The sequential execution of the iterations in all associated loops determines the order of the iterations in the collapsed iteration space.

If more than one loop is associated with the `taskloop` construct then the number of times that any intervening code between any two associated loops will be executed is unspecified but will be at least once per iteration of the loop enclosing the intervening code and at most once per iteration of the innermost loop associated with the construct. If the iteration count of any loop that is associated with the `taskloop` construct is zero and that loop does not enclose intervening code, the behavior is unspecified.

A taskloop loop has logical iterations numbered 0,1,...,N-1 where N is the number of loop iterations, and the logical numbering denotes the sequence in which the iterations would be executed if the set of associated loop(s) were executed sequentially. At the beginning of each logical iteration, the loop iteration variable of each associated loop has the value that it would have if the set of the associated loop(s) were executed sequentially.

The iteration count for each associated loop is computed before entry to the outermost loop. If execution of any associated loop changes any of the values used to compute any of the iteration counts, then the behavior is unspecified.

The integer type (or kind, for Fortran) used to compute the iteration count for the collapsed loop is implementation defined.

When an `if` clause is present on a `taskloop` construct, and if the `if` clause expression evaluates to *false*, undeferred tasks are generated. The use of a variable in an `if` clause expression of a `taskloop` construct causes an implicit reference to the variable in all enclosing constructs.

When a `final` clause is present on a `taskloop` construct and the `final` clause expression evaluates to *true*, the generated tasks will be final tasks. The use of a variable in a `final` clause expression of a `taskloop` construct causes an implicit reference to the variable in all enclosing constructs.

When a `priority` clause is present on a `taskloop` construct, the generated tasks use the *priority-value* as if it was specified for each individual task. If the `priority` clause is not specified, tasks generated by the `taskloop` construct have the default task priority (zero).

If the `untied` clause is specified, all tasks generated by the `taskloop` construct are untied tasks.

When the `mergeable` clause is present on a `taskloop` construct, each generated task is a *mergeable task*.

──────────────── C++ ────────────────

For `firstprivate` variables of class type, the number of invocations of copy constructors to perform the initialization is implementation-defined.

──────────────── C++ ────────────────

Note – When storage is shared by a `taskloop` region, the programmer must ensure, by adding proper synchronization, that the storage does not reach the end of its lifetime before the `taskloop` region and its descendant tasks complete their execution.

Execution Model Events

The *taskloop-begin* event occurs after a task encounters a `taskloop` construct but before any other events that may trigger as a consequence of executing the `taskloop`. Specifically, a *taskloop-begin* event for a `taskloop` will precede the *taskgroup-begin* that occurs unless a `nogroup` clause is present. Regardless of whether an implicit taskgroup is present, a *taskloop-begin* will always precede any *task-create* events for generated tasks.

The *taskloop-end* event occurs after a `taskloop` region finishes execution but before resuming execution of the encountering task.

The *taskloop-iteration-begin* event occurs before an explicit task executes each iteration of a `taskloop`.

Tool Callbacks

A thread dispatches a registered **ompt_callback_work** callback for each occurrence of a *taskloop-begin* and *taskloop-end* event in that thread. The callback occurs in the context of the encountering task. The callback has type signature **ompt_callback_work_t**. The callback receives **ompt_scope_begin** or **ompt_scope_end** as its *endpoint* argument, as appropriate, and **ompt_work_taskloop** as its *wstype* argument.

A thread dispatches a registered **ompt_callback_dispatch** callback for each occurrence of a *taskloop-iteration-begin* event in that thread. The callback occurs in the context of the encountering task. The callback has type signature **ompt_callback_dispatch_t**.

Restrictions

The restrictions of the **taskloop** construct are as follows:

- A program that branches into or out of a **taskloop** region is non-conforming.
- No OpenMP directive may appear in the region between any associated loops.
- If a **collapse** clause is specified, exactly one loop must occur in the region at each nesting level up to the number of loops specified by the parameter of the **collapse** clause.
- If a **reduction** clause is present on the **taskloop** directive, the **nogroup** clause must not be specified.
- The same list item cannot appear in both a **reduction** and an **in_reduction** clause.
- At most one **grainsize** clause can appear on a **taskloop** directive.
- At most one **num_tasks** clause can appear on a **taskloop** directive.
- The **grainsize** clause and **num_tasks** clause are mutually exclusive and may not appear on the same **taskloop** directive.
- At most one **collapse** clause can appear on a **taskloop** directive.
- At most one **if** clause can appear on the directive.
- At most one **final** clause can appear on the directive.
- At most one **priority** clause can appear on the directive.

Cross References

- **task** construct, Section 2.10.1 on page 135.
- **if** clause, see Section 2.15 on page 220.
- **taskgroup** construct, Section 2.17.6 on page 232.
- Data-sharing attribute clauses, Section 2.19.4 on page 282.

- **default** clause, see Section 2.19.4.1 on page 282.
- **ompt_scope_begin** and **ompt_scope_end**, see Section 4.4.4.11 on page 443.
- **ompt_work_taskloop**, see Section 4.4.4.15 on page 445.
- **ompt_callback_work_t**, see Section 4.5.2.5 on page 464.
- **ompt_callback_dispatch_t**, see Section 4.5.2.6 on page 465.

2.10.3 `taskloop simd` Construct

Summary

The **taskloop simd** construct specifies a loop that can be executed concurrently using SIMD instructions and that those iterations will also be executed in parallel using explicit tasks. The **taskloop simd** construct is a composite construct.

Syntax

─────────────── C / C++ ───────────────

The syntax of the **taskloop simd** construct is as follows:

```
#pragma omp taskloop simd [clause[[,] clause] ...] new-line
    for-loops
```

where *clause* can be any of the clauses accepted by the **taskloop** or **simd** directives with identical meanings and restrictions.

─────────────── C / C++ ───────────────
─────────────── Fortran ───────────────

The syntax of the **taskloop simd** construct is as follows:

```
!$omp taskloop simd [clause[[,] clause] ...]
    do-loops
[!$omp end taskloop simd]
```

where *clause* can be any of the clauses accepted by the **taskloop** or **simd** directives with identical meanings and restrictions.

If an **end taskloop simd** directive is not specified, an **end taskloop simd** directive is assumed at the end of the *do-loops*.

─────────────── Fortran ───────────────

Binding

The binding thread set of the **taskloop simd** region is the current team. A **taskloop simd** region binds to the innermost enclosing parallel region.

Description

The **taskloop simd** construct will first distribute the iterations of the associated loop(s) across tasks in a manner consistent with any clauses that apply to the **taskloop** construct. The resulting tasks will then be converted to a SIMD loop in a manner consistent with any clauses that apply to the **simd** construct, except for the **collapse** clause. For the purposes of each task's conversion to a SIMD loop, the **collapse** clause is ignored and the effect of any **in_reduction** clause is as if a **reduction** clause with the same reduction operator and list items is present on the construct.

Execution Model Events

This composite construct generates the same events as the **taskloop** construct.

Tool Callbacks

This composite construct dispatches the same callbacks as the **taskloop** construct.

Restrictions

- The restrictions for the **taskloop** and **simd** constructs apply.
- The **conditional** modifier may not appear in a **lastprivate** clause.

Cross References

- **simd** construct, see Section 2.9.3.1 on page 110.
- **taskloop** construct, see Section 2.10.2 on page 140.
- Data-sharing attribute clauses, see Section 2.19.4 on page 282.

2.10.4 `taskyield` Construct

Summary

The **taskyield** construct specifies that the current task can be suspended in favor of execution of a different task. The **taskyield** construct is a stand-alone directive.

Syntax

---C / C++---

The syntax of the `taskyield` construct is as follows:

```
#pragma omp taskyield new-line
```

---C / C++---

---Fortran---

The syntax of the `taskyield` construct is as follows:

```
!$omp taskyield
```

---Fortran---

Binding

A `taskyield` region binds to the current task region. The binding thread set of the `taskyield` region is the current team.

Description

The `taskyield` region includes an explicit task scheduling point in the current task region.

Cross References

- Task scheduling, see Section 2.10.6 on page 149.

2.10.5 Initial Task

Execution Model Events

No events are associated with the implicit parallel region in each initial thread.

The *initial-thread-begin* event occurs in an initial thread after the OpenMP runtime invokes the tool initializer but before the initial thread begins to execute the first OpenMP region in the initial task.

The *initial-task-begin* event occurs after an *initial-thread-begin* event but before the first OpenMP region in the initial task begins to execute.

The *initial-task-end* event occurs before an *initial-thread-end* event but after the last OpenMP region in the initial task finishes to execute.

The *initial-thread-end* event occurs as the final event in an initial thread at the end of an initial task immediately prior to invocation of the tool finalizer.

Tool Callbacks

A thread dispatches a registered **ompt_callback_thread_begin** callback for the *initial-thread-begin* event in an initial thread. The callback occurs in the context of the initial thread. The callback has type signature **ompt_callback_thread_begin_t**. The callback receives **ompt_thread_initial** as its *thread_type* argument.

A thread dispatches a registered **ompt_callback_implicit_task** callback with **ompt_scope_begin** as its *endpoint* argument for each occurrence of an *initial-task-begin* in that thread. Similarly, a thread dispatches a registered **ompt_callback_implicit_task** callback with **ompt_scope_end** as its *endpoint* argument for each occurrence of an *initial-task-end* event in that thread. The callbacks occur in the context of the initial task and have type signature **ompt_callback_implicit_task_t**. In the dispatched callback, (*flag* **& ompt_task_initial**) always evaluates to *true*.

A thread dispatches a registered **ompt_callback_thread_end** callback for the *initial-thread-end* event in that thread. The callback occurs in the context of the thread. The callback has type signature **ompt_callback_thread_end_t**. The implicit parallel region does not dispatch a **ompt_callback_parallel_end** callback; however, the implicit parallel region can be finalized within this **ompt_callback_thread_end** callback.

Cross References

- **ompt_thread_initial**, see Section 4.4.4.10 on page 443.
- **ompt_task_initial**, see Section 4.4.4.18 on page 446.
- **ompt_callback_thread_begin_t**, see Section 4.5.2.1 on page 459.
- **ompt_callback_thread_end_t**, see Section 4.5.2.2 on page 460.
- **ompt_callback_parallel_begin_t**, see Section 4.5.2.3 on page 461.
- **ompt_callback_parallel_end_t**, see Section 4.5.2.4 on page 463.
- **ompt_callback_implicit_task_t**, see Section 4.5.2.11 on page 471.

2.10.6 Task Scheduling

Whenever a thread reaches a task scheduling point, the implementation may cause it to perform a task switch, beginning or resuming execution of a different task bound to the current team. Task scheduling points are implied at the following locations:

- during the generation of an explicit task;
- the point immediately following the generation of an explicit task;

- after the point of completion of the structured block associated with a task;
- in a **taskyield** region;
- in a **taskwait** region;
- at the end of a **taskgroup** region;
- in an implicit barrier region;
- in an explicit **barrier** region;
- during the generation of a **target** region;
- the point immediately following the generation of a **target** region;
- at the beginning and end of a **target data** region;
- in a **target update** region;
- in a **target enter data** region;
- in a **target exit data** region;
- in the **omp_target_memcpy** routine;
- in the **omp_target_memcpy_rect** routine;

When a thread encounters a task scheduling point it may do one of the following, subject to the *Task Scheduling Constraints* (below):

- begin execution of a tied task bound to the current team;
- resume any suspended task region, bound to the current team, to which it is tied;
- begin execution of an untied task bound to the current team; or
- resume any suspended untied task region bound to the current team.

If more than one of the above choices is available, it is unspecified as to which will be chosen.

Task Scheduling Constraints are as follows:

1. Scheduling of new tied tasks is constrained by the set of task regions that are currently tied to the thread and that are not suspended in a barrier region. If this set is empty, any new tied task may be scheduled. Otherwise, a new tied task may be scheduled only if it is a descendent task of every task in the set.
2. A dependent task shall not start its execution until its task dependences are fulfilled.
3. A task shall not be scheduled while any task with which it is mutually exclusive has been scheduled, but has not yet completed.

4. When an explicit task is generated by a construct containing an **if** clause for which the expression evaluated to *false*, and the previous constraints are already met, the task is executed immediately after generation of the task.

A program relying on any other assumption about task scheduling is non-conforming.

Note – Task scheduling points dynamically divide task regions into parts. Each part is executed uninterrupted from start to end. Different parts of the same task region are executed in the order in which they are encountered. In the absence of task synchronization constructs, the order in which a thread executes parts of different schedulable tasks is unspecified.

A program must behave correctly and consistently with all conceivable scheduling sequences that are compatible with the rules above.

For example, if **threadprivate** storage is accessed (explicitly in the source code or implicitly in calls to library routines) in one part of a task region, its value cannot be assumed to be preserved into the next part of the same task region if another schedulable task exists that modifies it.

As another example, if a lock acquire and release happen in different parts of a task region, no attempt should be made to acquire the same lock in any part of another task that the executing thread may schedule. Otherwise, a deadlock is possible. A similar situation can occur when a **critical** region spans multiple parts of a task and another schedulable task contains a **critical** region with the same name.

The use of threadprivate variables and the use of locks or critical sections in an explicit task with an **if** clause must take into account that when the **if** clause evaluates to *false*, the task is executed immediately, without regard to *Task Scheduling Constraint* 2.

Execution Model Events

The *task-schedule* event occurs in a thread when the thread switches tasks at a task scheduling point; no event occurs when switching to or from a merged task.

Tool Callbacks

A thread dispatches a registered **ompt_callback_task_schedule** callback for each occurrence of a *task-schedule* event in the context of the task that begins or resumes. This callback has the type signature **ompt_callback_task_schedule_t**. The argument *prior_task_status* is used to indicate the cause for suspending the prior task. This cause may be the completion of the prior task region, the encountering of a **taskyield** construct, or the encountering of an active cancellation point.

Cross References

- **ompt_callback_task_schedule_t**, see Section 4.5.2.10 on page 470.

2.11 Memory Management Directives

2.11.1 Memory Spaces

OpenMP memory spaces represent storage resources where variables can be stored and retrieved. Table 2.8 shows the list of predefined memory spaces. The selection of a given memory space expresses an intent to use storage with certain traits for the allocations. The actual storage resources that each memory space represents are implementation defined.

TABLE 2.8: Predefined Memory Spaces

Memory space name	Storage selection intent
omp_default_mem_space	Represents the system default storage.
omp_large_cap_mem_space	Represents storage with large capacity.
omp_const_mem_space	Represents storage optimized for variables with constant values. The result of writing to this storage is unspecified.
omp_high_bw_mem_space	Represents storage with high bandwidth.
omp_low_lat_mem_space	Represents storage with low latency.

Note – For variables allocated in the **omp_const_mem_space** memory space OpenMP supports initializing constant memory either by means of the **firstprivate** clause or through initialization with compile time constants for static and constant variables. Implementation-defined mechanisms to provide the constant value of these variables may also be supported.

Cross References

- omp_init_allocator routine, see Section 3.7.2 on page 409.

2.11.2 Memory Allocators

OpenMP memory allocators can be used by a program to make allocation requests. When a memory allocator receives a request to allocate storage of a certain size, an allocation of logically consecutive *memory* in the resources of its associated memory space of at least the size that was requested will be returned if possible. This allocation will not overlap with any other existing allocation from an OpenMP memory allocator.

The behavior of the allocation process can be affected by the allocator traits that the user specifies. Table 2.9 shows the allowed allocators traits, their possible values and the default value of each trait.

TABLE 2.9: Allocator Traits

Allocator trait	Allowed values	Default value
`sync_hint`	`contended`, `uncontended`, `serialized`, `private`	`contended`
`alignment`	A positive integer value that is a power of 2	1 byte
`access`	`all`, `cgroup`, `pteam`, `thread`	`all`
`pool_size`	Positive integer value	Implementation defined
`fallback`	`default_mem_fb`, `null_fb`, `abort_fb`, `allocator_fb`	`default_mem_fb`
`fb_data`	an allocator handle	(none)
`pinned`	`true`, `false`	`false`
`partition`	`environment`, `nearest`, `blocked`, `interleaved`	`environment`

The `sync_hint` trait describes the expected manner in which multiple threads may use the allocator. The values and their description are:

- `contended`: high contention is expected on the allocator; that is, many threads are expected to request allocations simultaneously.

- `uncontended`: low contention is expected on the allocator; that is, few threads are expected to request allocations simultaneously.

- `serialized`: only one thread at a time will request allocations with the allocator. Requesting two allocations simultaneously when specifying `serialized` results in unspecified behavior.

- `private`: the same thread will request allocations with the allocator every time. Requesting an allocation from different threads, simultaneously or not, when specifying `private` results in unspecified behavior.

Allocated memory will be byte aligned to at least the value specified for the `alignment` trait of the allocator. Some directives and API routines can specify additional requirements on alignment beyond those described in this section.

Memory allocated by allocators with the `access` trait defined to be `all` must be accessible by all threads in the device where the allocation was requested. Memory allocated by allocators with the `access` trait defined to be `cgroup` will be memory accessible by all threads in the same contention group as the thread that requested the allocation. Attempts to access the memory returned by an allocator with the **access** trait defined to be **cgroup** from a thread that is not part of the same contention group as the thread that allocated the memory result in unspecified behavior. Memory allocated by allocators with the **access** trait defined to be **pteam** will be memory accessible by all threads that bind to the same **parallel** region of the thread that requested the allocation. Attempts to access the memory returned by an allocator with the **access** trait defined to be **pteam** from a thread that does not bind to the same **parallel** region as the thread that allocated the memory result in unspecified behavior. Memory allocated by allocator with the **access** trait defined to be **thread** will be memory accessible by the *thread* that requested the allocation. Attempts to access the memory returned by an allocator with the **access** trait defined to be **thread** from a thread other than the one that allocated the memory result in unspecified behavior.

The total amount of storage in bytes that an allocator can use is limited by the **pool_size** trait. For allocators with the **access** trait defined to be **all**, this limit refers to allocations from all threads that access the allocator. For allocators with the **access** trait defined to be **cgroup**, this limit refers to allocations from threads that access the allocator from the same contention group. For allocators with the **access** trait defined to be **pteam**, this limit refers to allocations from threads that access the allocator from the same parallel team. For allocators with the **access** trait defined to be **thread**, this limit refers to allocations from each thread that access the allocator. Requests that would result in using more storage than **pool_size** will not be fulfilled by the allocator.

The **fallback** trait specifies how the allocator behaves when it cannot fulfill an allocation request. If the **fallback** trait is set to **null_fb**, the allocator returns the value zero if it fails to allocate the memory. If the **fallback** trait is set to **abort_fb**, program execution will be terminated if the allocation fails. If the **fallback** trait is set to **allocator_fb** then when an allocation fails the request will be delegated to the allocator specified in the **fb_data** trait. If the **fallback** trait is set to **default_mem_fb** then when an allocation fails another allocation will be tried in the **omp_default_mem_space** memory space, which assumes all allocator traits to be set to their default values except for **fallback** trait which will be set to **null_fb**.

Allocators with the **pinned** trait defined to be **true** ensure that their allocations remain in the same storage resource at the same location for their entire lifetime.

The **partition** trait describes the partitioning of allocated memory over the storage resources represented by the memory space associated with the allocator. The partitioning will be done in parts with a minimum size that is implementation defined. The values are:

- **environment**: the placement of allocated memory is determined by the execution environment.

- **nearest**: allocated memory is placed in the storage resource that is nearest to the thread that requests the allocation.

- **blocked**: allocated memory is partitioned into parts of approximately the same size with at most one part per storage resource.

- **interleaved**: allocated memory parts are distributed in a round-robin fashion across the storage resources.

Table 2.10 shows the list of predefined memory allocators and their associated memory spaces. The predefined memory allocators have default values for their allocator traits unless otherwise specified.

TABLE 2.10: Predefined Allocators

Allocator name	Associated memory space	Non-default trait values
omp_default_mem_alloc	omp_default_mem_space	(none)
omp_large_cap_mem_alloc	omp_large_cap_mem_space	(none)
omp_const_mem_alloc	omp_const_mem_space	(none)
omp_high_bw_mem_alloc	omp_high_bw_mem_space	(none)
omp_low_lat_mem_alloc	omp_low_lat_mem_space	(none)
omp_cgroup_mem_alloc	Implementation defined	access:cgroup
omp_pteam_mem_alloc	Implementation defined	access:pteam
omp_thread_mem_alloc	Implementation defined	access:thread

─────────── Fortran ───────────

If any operation of the base language causes a reallocation of an array that is allocated with a memory allocator then that memory allocator will be used to release the current memory and to allocate the new memory.

─────────── Fortran ───────────

Cross References

- `omp_init_allocator` routine, see Section 3.7.2 on page 409.
- `omp_destroy_allocator` routine, see Section 3.7.3 on page 410.
- `omp_set_default_allocator` routine, see Section 3.7.4 on page 411.
- `omp_get_default_allocator` routine, see Section 3.7.5 on page 412.
- `OMP_ALLOCATOR` environment variable, see Section 6.21 on page 618.

2.11.3 `allocate` Directive

Summary

The `allocate` directive specifies how a set of variables are allocated. The `allocate` directive is a declarative directive if it is not associated with an allocation statement.

Syntax

───────────────────── C / C++ ─────────────────────

The syntax of the `allocate` directive is as follows:

`#pragma omp allocate` (*list*) *[clause] new-line*

where *clause* is one of the following:

`allocator` (*allocator*)

where *allocator* is an expression of `omp_allocator_handle_t` type.

───────────────────── C / C++ ─────────────────────

───────────────────── Fortran ─────────────────────

The syntax of the `allocate` directive is as follows:

`!$omp allocate` (*list*) *[clause]*

or

`!$omp allocate[` (*list*) `]` *clause*
`[!$omp allocate` (*list*) *clause*
`[...]]`
   allocate statement

where *clause* is one of the following:

`allocator` (*allocator*)

where *allocator* is an integer expression of `omp_allocator_handle_kind` kind.

───────────────────── Fortran ─────────────────────

Description

If the directive is not associated with a statement, the storage for each *list item* that appears in the directive will be provided by an allocation through a memory allocator. If no clause is specified then the memory allocator specified by the *def-allocator-var* ICV will be used. If the **allocator** clause is specified, the memory allocator specified in the clause will be used. The allocation of each *list item* will be byte aligned to at least the alignment required by the base language for the type of that *list item*.

The scope of this allocation is that of the list item in the base language. At the end of the scope for a given list item the memory allocator used to allocate that list item deallocates the storage.

―――――――――――――― Fortran ――――――――――――――

If the directive is associated with an *allocate statement*, the same list items appearing in the directive list and the *allocate statement* list are allocated with the memory allocator of the directive. If no list items are specified then all variables listed in the *allocate statement* are allocated with the memory allocator of the directive.

―――――――――――――― Fortran ――――――――――――――

For allocations that arise from this directive the **null_fb** value of the fallback allocator trait will behave as if the **abort_fb** had been specified.

Restrictions

- A variable that is part of another variable (as an array or structure element) cannot appear in an **allocate** directive.

- The **allocate** directive must appear in the same scope as the declarations of each of its list items and must follow all such declarations.

- At most one **allocator** clause can appear on the **allocate** directive.

- **allocate** directives that appear in a **target** region must specify an **allocator** clause unless a **requires** directive with the **dynamic_allocators** clause is present in the same compilation unit.

―――――――――――――― C / C++ ――――――――――――――

- If a list item has a static storage type, the *allocator* expression in the **allocator** clause must be a constant expression that evaluates to one of the predefined memory allocator values.

- After a *list item* has been allocated, the scope that contains the **allocate** directive must not end abnormally other than through C++ exceptions, such as through a call to the **longjmp** function.

―――――――――――――― C / C++ ――――――――――――――

---------- Fortran ----------

- List items specified in the `allocate` directive must not have the **ALLOCATABLE** attribute unless the directive is associated with an *allocate statement*.
- List items specified in an `allocate` directive that is associated with an *allocate statement* must be variables that are allocated by the *allocate statement*.
- Multiple directives can only be associated with an *allocate statement* if list items are specified on each `allocate` directive.
- If a list item has the **SAVE** attribute, is a common block name, or is declared in the scope of a module, then only predefined memory allocator parameters can be used in the `allocator` clause.
- A type parameter inquiry cannot appear in an `allocate` directive.

---------- Fortran ----------

Cross References

- *def-allocator-var* ICV, see Section 2.5.1 on page 64.
- Memory allocators, see Section 2.11.2 on page 152.
- `omp_allocator_handle_t` and `omp_allocator_handle_kind`, see Section 3.7.1 on page 406.

2.11.4 allocate Clause

Summary

The `allocate` clause specifies the memory allocator to be used to obtain storage for private variables of a directive.

Syntax

The syntax of the `allocate` clause is as follows:

`allocate ([allocator:] list)`

―――――――――― C / C++ ――――――――――

where *allocator* is an expression of the **omp_allocator_handle_t** type.

―――――――――― C / C++ ――――――――――
―――――――――― Fortran ――――――――――

where *allocator* is an integer expression of the **omp_allocator_handle_kind** kind.

―――――――――― Fortran ――――――――――

Description

The storage for new list items that arise from list items that appear in the directive will be provided through a memory allocator. If an *allocator* is specified in the clause, that allocator will be used for allocations. For all directives except the **target** directive, if no *allocator* is specified in the clause then the memory allocator that is specified by the *def-allocator-var* ICV will be used for the list items that are specified in the **allocate** clause. The allocation of each *list item* will be byte aligned to at least the alignment required by the base language for the type of that *list item*.

For allocations that arise from this clause the **null_fb** value of the fallback allocator trait will behave as if the **abort_fb** had been specified.

Restrictions

- For any list item that is specified in the **allocate** clause on a directive, a data-sharing attribute clause that may create a private copy of that list item must be specified on the same directive.

- For **task**, **taskloop** or **target** directives, allocation requests to memory allocators with the trait **access** set to **thread** result in unspecified behavior.

- **allocate** clauses that appear on a **target** construct or on constructs in a **target** region must specify an *allocator* expression unless a **requires** directive with the **dynamic_allocators** clause is present in the same compilation unit.

Cross References

- *def-allocator-var* ICV, see Section 2.5.1 on page 64.
- Memory allocators, see Section 2.11.2 on page 152.
- **omp_allocator_handle_t** and **omp_allocator_handle_kind**, see Section 3.7.1 on page 406.

CHAPTER 2. DIRECTIVES   159

2.12 Device Directives

2.12.1 Device Initialization

Execution Model Events

The *device-initialize* event occurs in a thread that encounters the first `target`, `target data`, or `target enter data` construct or a device memory routine that is associated with a particular target device after the thread initiates initialization of OpenMP on the device and the device's OpenMP initialization, which may include device-side tool initialization, completes.

The *device-load* event for a code block for a target device occurs in some thread before any thread executes code from that code block on that target device.

The *device-unload* event for a target device occurs in some thread whenever a code block is unloaded from the device.

The *device-finalize* event for a target device that has been initialized occurs in some thread before an OpenMP implementation shuts down.

Tool Callbacks

A thread dispatches a registered `ompt_callback_device_initialize` callback for each occurrence of a *device-initialize* event in that thread. This callback has type signature `ompt_callback_device_initialize_t`.

A thread dispatches a registered `ompt_callback_device_load` callback for each occurrence of a *device-load* event in that thread. This callback has type signature `ompt_callback_device_load_t`.

A thread dispatches a registered `ompt_callback_device_unload` callback for each occurrence of a *device-unload* event in that thread. This callback has type signature `ompt_callback_device_unload_t`.

A thread dispatches a registered `ompt_callback_device_finalize` callback for each occurrence of a *device-finalize* event in that thread. This callback has type signature `ompt_callback_device_finalize_t`.

Restrictions

No thread may offload execution of an OpenMP construct to a device until a dispatched `ompt_callback_device_initialize` callback completes.

No thread may offload execution of an OpenMP construct to a device after a dispatched `ompt_callback_device_finalize` callback occurs.

Cross References

- `ompt_callback_device_load_t`, see Section 4.5.2.21 on page 484.
- `ompt_callback_device_unload_t`, see Section 4.5.2.22 on page 486.
- `ompt_callback_device_initialize_t`, see Section 4.5.2.19 on page 482.
- `ompt_callback_device_finalize_t`, see Section 4.5.2.20 on page 484.

2.12.2 `target data` Construct

Summary

Map variables to a device data environment for the extent of the region.

Syntax

──────────── C / C++ ────────────

The syntax of the `target data` construct is as follows:

```
#pragma omp target data clause[ [ [,] clause] ... ] new-line
    structured-block
```

where *clause* is one of the following:

> **if**([`target data` :] *scalar-expression*)
> **device**(*integer-expression*)
> **map**([[*map-type-modifier*[,] [*map-type-modifier*[,] ...] *map-type*:] *locator-list*)
> **use_device_ptr**(*ptr-list*)
> **use_device_addr**(*list*)

──────────── C / C++ ────────────

──────────── Fortran ────────────

The syntax of the `target data` construct is as follows:

```
!$omp target data clause[ [ [,] clause] ... ]
    structured-block
!$omp end target data
```

where *clause* is one of the following:

> **if** (*[* **target data** : *]* *scalar-logical-expression*)
> **device** (*scalar-integer-expression*)
> **map** (*[[map-type-modifier[,] [map-type-modifier[,] ...] map-type* : *] locator-list*)
> **use_device_ptr** (*ptr-list*)
> **use_device_addr** (*list*)

───────────────────────────── Fortran ─────────────────────────────

Binding

The binding task set for a **target data** region is the generating task. The **target data** region binds to the region of the generating task.

Description

When a **target data** construct is encountered, the encountering task executes the region. If there is no **device** clause, the default device is determined by the *default-device-var* ICV. When an **if** clause is present and the **if** clause expression evaluates to *false*, the device is the host. Variables are mapped for the extent of the region, according to any data-mapping attribute clauses, from the data environment of the encountering task to the device data environment.

Pointers that appear in a **use_device_ptr** clause are privatized and the device pointers to the corresponding list items in the device data environment are assigned into the private versions.

List items that appear in a **use_device_addr** clause have the address of the corresponding object in the device data environment inside the construct. For objects, any reference to the value of the object will be to the corresponding object on the device, while references to the address will result in a valid device address that points to that object. Array sections privatize the base of the array section and assign the private copy to the address of the corresponding array section in the device data environment.

If one or more of the **use_device_ptr** or **use_device_addr** clauses and one or more **map** clauses are present on the same construct, the address conversions of **use_device_addr** and **use_device_ptr** clauses will occur as if performed after all variables are mapped according to those **map** clauses.

Execution Model Events

The events associated with entering a target data region are the same events as associated with a target enter data construct, described in Section 2.12.3 on page 164.

The events associated with exiting a target data region are the same events as associated with a target exit data construct, described in Section 2.12.4 on page 166.

Tool Callbacks

The tool callbacks dispatched when entering a target data region are the same as the tool callbacks dispatched when encountering a target enter data construct, described in Section 2.12.3 on page 164.

The tool callbacks dispatched when exiting a target data region are the same as the tool callbacks dispatched when encountering a target exit data construct, described in Section 2.12.4 on page 166.

Restrictions

- A program must not depend on any ordering of the evaluations of the clauses of the **target data** directive, except as explicitly stated for **map** clauses relative to **use_device_ptr** and **use_device_addr** clauses, or on any side effects of the evaluations of the clauses.
- At most one **device** clause can appear on the directive. The **device** clause expression must evaluate to a non-negative integer value less than the value of **omp_get_num_devices()** or to the value of **omp_get_initial_device()**.
- At most one **if** clause can appear on the directive.
- A *map-type* in a **map** clause must be **to**, **from**, **tofrom** or **alloc**.
- At least one **map**, **use_device_addr** or **use_device_ptr** clause must appear on the directive.
- A list item in a **use_device_ptr** clause must hold the address of an object that has a corresponding list item in the device data environment.
- A list item in a **use_device_addr** clause must have a corresponding list item in the device data environment.
- A list item that specifies a given variable may not appear in more than one **use_device_ptr** clause.
- A reference to a list item in a **use_device_addr** clause must be to the address of the list item.

Cross References

- *default-device-var*, see Section 2.5 on page 63.
- **if** Clause, see Section 2.15 on page 220.
- **map** clause, see Section 2.19.7.1 on page 315.
- **omp_get_num_devices** routine, see Section 3.2.36 on page 371.
- **ompt_callback_target_t**, see Section 4.5.2.26 on page 490.

2.12.3 `target enter data` Construct

Summary

The `target enter data` directive specifies that variables are mapped to a device data environment. The `target enter data` directive is a stand-alone directive.

Syntax

―――――――――――――――――――――― C / C++ ――――――――――――――――――――――

The syntax of the `target enter data` construct is as follows:

`#pragma omp target enter data` *[clause[[,] clause]...] new-line*

where *clause* is one of the following:

> `if (`*[target enter data :] scalar-expression*`)`
> `device (`*integer-expression*`)`
> `map (`*[map-type-modifier[,] [map-type-modifier[,] ...] map-type : locator-list*`)`
> `depend (`*[depend-modifier,] dependence-type : locator-list*`)`
> `nowait`

―――――――――――――――――――――― C / C++ ――――――――――――――――――――――

―――――――――――――――――――――― Fortran ――――――――――――――――――――――

The syntax of the `target enter data` is as follows:

`!$omp target enter data` *[clause[[,] clause]...]*

where clause is one of the following:

> `if (`*[target enter data :] scalar-logical-expression*`)`
> `device (`*scalar-integer-expression*`)`
> `map (`*[map-type-modifier[,] [map-type-modifier[,] ...] map-type : locator-list*`)`
> `depend (`*[depend-modifier,] dependence-type : locator-list*`)`
> `nowait`

―――――――――――――――――――――― Fortran ――――――――――――――――――――――

Binding

The binding task set for a `target enter data` region is the generating task, which is the *target task* generated by the `target enter data` construct. The `target enter data` region binds to the corresponding *target task* region.

Description

When a **target enter data** construct is encountered, the list items are mapped to the device data environment according to the **map** clause semantics.

The **target enter data** construct is a task generating construct. The generated task is a *target task*. The generated task region encloses the **target enter data** region.

All clauses are evaluated when the **target enter data** construct is encountered. The data environment of the *target task* is created according to the data-sharing attribute clauses on the **target enter data** construct, per-data environment ICVs, and any default data-sharing attribute rules that apply to the **target enter data** construct. A variable that is mapped in the **target enter data** construct has a default data-sharing attribute of shared in the data environment of the *target task*.

Assignment operations associated with mapping a variable (see Section 2.19.7.1 on page 315) occur when the *target task* executes.

If the **nowait** clause is present, execution of the *target task* may be deferred. If the **nowait** clause is not present, the *target task* is an included task.

If a **depend** clause is present, it is associated with the *target task*.

If no **device** clause is present, the default device is determined by the *default-device-var* ICV.

When an **if** clause is present and the **if** clause expression evaluates to *false*, the device is the host.

Execution Model Events

Events associated with a *target task* are the same as for the **task** construct defined in Section 2.10.1 on page 135.

The *target-enter-data-begin* event occurs when a thread enters a **target enter data** region.

The *target-enter-data-end* event occurs when a thread exits a **target enter data** region.

Tool Callbacks

Callbacks associated with events for *target tasks* are the same as for the **task** construct defined in Section 2.10.1 on page 135; *(flags* **& ompt_task_target)** always evaluates to *true* in the dispatched callback.

A thread dispatches a registered **ompt_callback_target** callback with **ompt_scope_begin** as its *endpoint* argument and **ompt_target_enter_data** as its *kind* argument for each occurrence of a *target-enter-data-begin* event in that thread in the context of the target task on the host. Similarly, a thread dispatches a registered **ompt_callback_target** callback with **ompt_scope_end** as its *endpoint* argument and **ompt_target_enter_data** as its *kind* argument for each occurrence of a *target-enter-data-end* event in that thread in the context of the target task on the host. These callbacks have type signature **ompt_callback_target_t**.

Restrictions

- A program must not depend on any ordering of the evaluations of the clauses of the **target enter data** directive, or on any side effects of the evaluations of the clauses.
- At least one **map** clause must appear on the directive.
- At most one **device** clause can appear on the directive. The **device** clause expression must evaluate to a non-negative integer value less than the value of **omp_get_num_devices()** or to the value of **omp_get_initial_device()**.
- At most one **if** clause can appear on the directive.
- A *map-type* must be specified in all **map** clauses and must be either **to** or **alloc**.
- At most one **nowait** clause can appear on the directive.

Cross References

- *default-device-var*, see Section 2.5.1 on page 64.
- **task**, see Section 2.10.1 on page 135.
- **task scheduling constraints**, see Section 2.10.6 on page 149.
- **target data**, see Section 2.12.2 on page 161.
- **target exit data**, see Section 2.12.4 on page 166.
- **if** Clause, see Section 2.15 on page 220.
- map clause, see Section 2.19.7.1 on page 315.
- **omp_get_num_devices** routine, see Section 3.2.36 on page 371.
- **ompt_callback_target_t**, see Section 4.5.2.26 on page 490.

2.12.4 target exit data Construct

Summary

The **target exit data** directive specifies that list items are unmapped from a device data environment. The **target exit data** directive is a stand-alone directive.

Syntax

--- C / C++ ---

The syntax of the **target exit data** construct is as follows:

#pragma omp target exit data *[clause[[,] clause]...] new-line*

where *clause* is one of the following:

> **if**(*[* **target exit data** *:]* *scalar-expression*)
> **device**(*integer-expression*)
> **map**(*[map-type-modifier[,] [map-type-modifier[,] ...] map-type*: *locator-list*)
> **depend**(*[depend-modifier,] dependence-type* : *locator-list*)
> **nowait**

--- C / C++ ---

--- Fortran ---

The syntax of the **target exit data** is as follows:

!$omp target exit data *[clause[[,] clause]...]*

where clause is one of the following:

> **if**(*[* **target exit data** *:]* *scalar-logical-expression*)
> **device**(*scalar-integer-expression*)
> **map**(*[map-type-modifier[,] [map-type-modifier[,] ...] map-type*: *locator-list*)
> **depend**(*[depend-modifier,] dependence-type* : *locator-list*)
> **nowait**

--- Fortran ---

Binding

The binding task set for a **target exit data** region is the generating task, which is the *target task* generated by the **target exit data** construct. The **target exit data** region binds to the corresponding *target task* region.

Description

When a `target exit data` construct is encountered, the list items in the `map` clauses are unmapped from the device data environment according to the `map` clause semantics.

The `target exit data` construct is a task generating construct. The generated task is a *target task*. The generated task region encloses the `target exit data` region.

All clauses are evaluated when the `target exit data` construct is encountered. The data environment of the *target task* is created according to the data-sharing attribute clauses on the `target exit data` construct, per-data environment ICVs, and any default data-sharing attribute rules that apply to the `target exit data` construct. A variable that is mapped in the `target exit data` construct has a default data-sharing attribute of shared in the data environment of the *target task*.

Assignment operations associated with mapping a variable (see Section 2.19.7.1 on page 315) occur when the *target task* executes.

If the `nowait` clause is present, execution of the *target task* may be deferred. If the `nowait` clause is not present, the *target task* is an included task.

If a `depend` clause is present, it is associated with the *target task*.

If no `device` clause is present, the default device is determined by the *default-device-var* ICV.

When an `if` clause is present and the `if` clause expression evaluates to *false*, the device is the host.

Execution Model Events

Events associated with a *target task* are the same as for the `task` construct defined in Section 2.10.1 on page 135.

The *target-exit-data-begin* event occurs when a thread enters a `target exit data` region.

The *target-exit-data-end* event occurs when a thread exits a `target exit data` region.

Tool Callbacks

Callbacks associated with events for *target tasks* are the same as for the `task` construct defined in Section 2.10.1 on page 135; (*flags* `& ompt_task_target`) always evaluates to *true* in the dispatched callback.

A thread dispatches a registered `ompt_callback_target` callback with `ompt_scope_begin` as its *endpoint* argument and `ompt_target_exit_data` as its *kind* argument for each occurrence of a *target-exit-data-begin* event in that thread in the context of the target task on the host. Similarly, a thread dispatches a registered `ompt_callback_target` callback with `ompt_scope_end` as its *endpoint* argument and `ompt_target_exit_data` as its *kind* argument for each occurrence of a *target-exit-data-end* event in that thread in the context of the target task on the host. These callbacks have type signature `ompt_callback_target_t`.

Restrictions

- A program must not depend on any ordering of the evaluations of the clauses of the **target exit data** directive, or on any side effects of the evaluations of the clauses.
- At least one **map** clause must appear on the directive.
- At most one **device** clause can appear on the directive. The **device** clause expression must evaluate to a non-negative integer value less than the value of **omp_get_num_devices()** or to the value of **omp_get_initial_device()**.
- At most one **if** clause can appear on the directive.
- A *map-type* must be specified in all **map** clauses and must be either **from**, **release**, or **delete**.
- At most one **nowait** clause can appear on the directive.

Cross References

- *default-device-var*, see Section 2.5.1 on page 64.
- **task**, see Section 2.10.1 on page 135.
- **task scheduling constraints**, see Section 2.10.6 on page 149.
- **target data**, see Section 2.12.2 on page 161.
- **target enter data**, see Section 2.12.3 on page 164.
- **if** Clause, see Section 2.15 on page 220.
- **map** clause, see Section 2.19.7.1 on page 315.
- **omp_get_num_devices** routine, see Section 3.2.36 on page 371.
- **ompt_callback_target_t**, see Section 4.5.2.26 on page 490.

2.12.5 `target` Construct

Summary

Map variables to a device data environment and execute the construct on that device.

Syntax

─────────── C / C++ ───────────

The syntax of the `target` construct is as follows:

```
#pragma omp target [clause[ [, ] clause] ... ] new-line
    structured-block
```

where *clause* is one of the following:

> `if` ([`target` :] *scalar-expression*)
> `device` ([*device-modifier* :] *integer-expression*)
> `private` (*list*)
> `firstprivate` (*list*)
> `in_reduction` (*reduction-identifier* : *list*)
> `map` ([[*map-type-modifier*[,] [*map-type-modifier*[,] ...] *map-type* :] *locator-list*)
> `is_device_ptr` (*list*)
> `defaultmap` (*implicit-behavior*[:*variable-category*])
> `nowait`
> `depend` ([*depend-modifier*,] *dependence-type* : *locator-list*)
> `allocate` ([[*allocator* :] *list*)
> `uses_allocators` (*allocator*[(*allocator-traits-array*)]
>   [, *allocator*[(*allocator-traits-array*)] ...])

and where *device-modifier* is one of the following:

> `ancestor`
> `device_num`

and where *allocator* is an identifier of `omp_allocator_handle_t` type and *allocator-traits-array* is an identifier of `const omp_alloctrait_t *` type.

─────────── C / C++ ───────────

———————————— Fortran ————————————

The syntax of the **target** construct is as follows:

```
!$omp target [clause[ [,] clause] ... ]
    structured-block
!$omp end target
```

where *clause* is one of the following:

> **if** (*[* **target** :*]* scalar-logical-expression)
> **device** (*[* device-modifier :*]* scalar-integer-expression)
> **private** (*list*)
> **firstprivate** (*list*)
> **in_reduction** (*reduction-identifier* : *list*)
> **map** (*[[map-type-modifier[,] [map-type-modifier[,] ...] map-type:] locator-list*)
> **is_device_ptr** (*list*)
> **defaultmap** (*implicit-behavior[:variable-category]*)
> **nowait**
> **depend** (*[depend-modifier,] dependence-type : locator-list*)
> **allocate** (*[allocator:]list*)
> **uses_allocators** (*allocator[(allocator-traits-array)]*
>   *[, allocator[(allocator-traits-array)] ...]*)

and where *device-modifier* is one of the following:

> **ancestor**
> **device_num**

and where *allocator* is an integer expression of **omp_allocator_handle_kind** kind and *allocator-traits-array* is an array of **type(omp_alloctrait)** type.

———————————— Fortran ————————————

Binding

The binding task set for a **target** region is the generating task, which is the *target task* generated by the **target** construct. The **target** region binds to the corresponding *target task* region.

Description

The `target` construct provides a superset of the functionality provided by the `target data` directive, except for the `use_device_ptr` and `use_device_addr` clauses.

The functionality added to the `target` directive is the inclusion of an executable region to be executed by a device. That is, the `target` directive is an executable directive.

The `target` construct is a task generating construct. The generated task is a *target task*. The generated task region encloses the `target` region.

All clauses are evaluated when the `target` construct is encountered. The data environment of the *target task* is created according to the data-sharing attribute clauses on the `target` construct, per-data environment ICVs, and any default data-sharing attribute rules that apply to the `target` construct. If a variable or part of a variable is mapped by the `target` construct and does not appear as a list item in an `in_reduction` clause on the construct, the variable has a default data-sharing attribute of shared in the data environment of the *target task*.

Assignment operations associated with mapping a variable (see Section 2.19.7.1 on page 315) occur when the *target task* executes.

If a `device` clause in which the `device_num` *device-modifier* appears is present on the construct, the `device` clause expression specifies the device number of the target device. If *device-modifier* does not appear in the clause, the behavior of the clause is as if *device-modifier* is `device_num`.

If a `device` clause in which the `ancestor` *device-modifier* appears is present on the `target` construct and the `device` clause expression evaluates to 1, execution of the `target` region occurs on the parent device of the enclosing `target` region. If the `target` construct is not encountered in a `target` region, the current device is treated as the parent device. The encountering thread waits for completion of the `target` region on the parent device before resuming. For any list item that appears in a `map` clause on the same construct, if the corresponding list item exists in the device data environment of the parent device, it is treated as if it has a reference count of positive infinity.

If the `nowait` clause is present, execution of the *target task* may be deferred. If the `nowait` clause is not present, the *target task* is an included task.

If a `depend` clause is present, it is associated with the *target task*.

When an `if` clause is present and the `if` clause expression evaluates to *false*, the `target` region is executed by the host device in the host data environment.

The `is_device_ptr` clause is used to indicate that a list item is a device pointer already in the device data environment and that it should be used directly. Support for device pointers created outside of OpenMP, specifically outside of the `omp_target_alloc` routine and the `use_device_ptr` clause, is implementation defined.

If a function (C, C++, Fortran) or subroutine (Fortran) is referenced in a **target** construct then that function or subroutine is treated as if its name had appeared in a **to** clause on a **declare target** directive.

Each memory *allocator* specified in the **uses_allocators** clause will be made available in the **target** region. For each non-predefined allocator that is specified, a new allocator handle will be associated with an allocator that is created with the specified *traits* as if by a call to **omp_init_allocator** at the beginning of the **target** region. Each non-predefined allocator will be destroyed as if by a call to **omp_destroy_allocator** at the end of the **target** region.

---------- C / C++ ----------

If a list item in a **map** clause has a base pointer and it is a scalar variable with a predetermined data-sharing attribute of firstprivate (see Section 2.19.1.1 on page 270), then on entry to the **target** region:

- If the list item is not a zero-length array section, the corresponding private variable is initialized such that the corresponding list item in the device data environment can be accessed through the pointer in the **target** region.

- If the list item is a zero-length array section, the corresponding private variable is initialized such that the corresponding storage location of the array section can be referenced through the pointer in the **target** region. If the corresponding storage location is not present in the device data environment, the corresponding private variable is initialized to NULL.

---------- C / C++ ----------

Execution Model Events

Events associated with a *target task* are the same as for the **task** construct defined in Section 2.10.1 on page 135.

Events associated with the *initial task* that executes the **target** region are defined in Section 2.10.5 on page 148.

The *target-begin* event occurs when a thread enters a **target** region.

The *target-end* event occurs when a thread exits a **target** region.

The *target-submit* event occurs prior to creating an initial task on a target device for a **target** region.

Tool Callbacks

Callbacks associated with events for *target tasks* are the same as for the `task` construct defined in Section 2.10.1 on page 135; (*flags* `& ompt_task_target`) always evaluates to *true* in the dispatched callback.

A thread dispatches a registered `ompt_callback_target` callback with `ompt_scope_begin` as its *endpoint* argument and `ompt_target` as its *kind* argument for each occurrence of a *target-begin* event in that thread in the context of the target task on the host. Similarly, a thread dispatches a registered `ompt_callback_target` callback with `ompt_scope_end` as its *endpoint* argument and `ompt_target` as its *kind* argument for each occurrence of a *target-end* event in that thread in the context of the target task on the host. These callbacks have type signature `ompt_callback_target_t`.

A thread dispatches a registered `ompt_callback_target_submit` callback for each occurrence of a *target-submit* event in that thread. The callback has type signature `ompt_callback_target_submit_t`.

Restrictions

- If a `target update`, `target data`, `target enter data`, or `target exit data` construct is encountered during execution of a `target` region, the behavior is unspecified.
- The result of an `omp_set_default_device`, `omp_get_default_device`, or `omp_get_num_devices` routine called within a `target` region is unspecified.
- The effect of an access to a `threadprivate` variable in a target region is unspecified.
- If a list item in a `map` clause is a structure element, any other element of that structure that is referenced in the `target` construct must also appear as a list item in a `map` clause.
- A variable referenced in a `target` region but not the `target` construct that is not declared in the `target` region must appear in a `declare target` directive.
- At most one `defaultmap` clause for each category can appear on the directive.
- At most one `nowait` clause can appear on the directive.
- A *map-type* in a `map` clause must be `to`, `from`, `tofrom` or `alloc`.
- A list item that appears in an `is_device_ptr` clause must be a valid device pointer in the device data environment.
- At most one `device` clause can appear on the directive. The `device` clause expression must evaluate to a non-negative integer value less than the value of `omp_get_num_devices()` or to the value of `omp_get_initial_device()`.
- If a `device` clause in which the `ancestor` *device-modifier* appears is present on the construct, then the following restrictions apply:

- A **requires** directive with the **reverse_offload** clause must be specified;
- The **device** clause expression must evaluate to 1;
- Only the **device**, **firstprivate**, **private**, **defaultmap**, and **map** clauses may appear on the construct;
- No OpenMP constructs or calls to OpenMP API runtime routines are allowed inside the corresponding **target** region.

- Memory allocators that do not appear in a **uses_allocators** clause cannot appear as an allocator in an **allocate** clause or be used in the **target** region unless a **requires** directive with the **dynamic_allocators** clause is present in the same compilation unit.
- Memory allocators that appear in a **uses_allocators** clause cannot appear in other data-sharing attribute clauses or data-mapping attribute clauses in the same construct.
- Predefined allocators appearing in a **uses_allocators** clause cannot have *traits* specified.
- Non-predefined allocators appearing in a **uses_allocators** clause must have *traits* specified.
- Arrays that contain allocator traits that appear in a **uses_allocators** clause must be constant arrays, have constant values and be defined in the same scope as the construct in which the clause appears.
- Any IEEE floating-point exception status flag, halting mode, or rounding mode set prior to a **target** region is unspecified in the region.
- Any IEEE floating-point exception status flag, halting mode, or rounding mode set in a **target** region is unspecified upon exiting the region.

―――――――――――――― C / C++ ――――――――――――――
- An attached pointer must not be modified in a **target** region.
―――――――――――――― C / C++ ――――――――――――――

―――――――――――――― C ――――――――――――――
- A list item that appears in an **is_device_ptr** clause must have a type of pointer or array.
―――――――――――――― C ――――――――――――――

―――――――――――――― C++ ――――――――――――――
- A list item that appears in an **is_device_ptr** clause must have a type of pointer, array, reference to pointer or reference to array.
- The effect of invoking a virtual member function of an object on a device other than the device on which the object was constructed is implementation defined.
- A **throw** executed inside a **target** region must cause execution to resume within the same **target** region, and the same thread that threw the exception must catch it.
―――――――――――――― C++ ――――――――――――――

―――――――――――――――――――――― Fortran ――――――――――――――――――――――

- An attached pointer that is associated with a given pointer target must not become associated with a different pointer target in a **target** region.

- A list item that appears in an **is_device_ptr** clause must be a dummy argument that does not have the **ALLOCATABLE**, **POINTER** or **VALUE** attribute.

- If a list item in a **map** clause is an array section, and the array section is derived from a variable with a **POINTER** or **ALLOCATABLE** attribute then the behavior is unspecified if the corresponding list item's variable is modified in the region.

―――――――――――――――――――――― Fortran ――――――――――――――――――――――

Cross References

- *default-device-var*, see Section 2.5 on page 63.
- **task** construct, see Section 2.10.1 on page 135.
- **task** scheduling constraints, see Section 2.10.6 on page 149.
- Memory allocators, see Section 2.11.2 on page 152.
- **target data** construct, see Section 2.12.2 on page 161.
- **if** Clause, see Section 2.15 on page 220.
- **private** and **firstprivate** clauses, see Section 2.19.4 on page 282.
- Data-Mapping Attribute Rules and Clauses, see Section 2.19.7 on page 314.
- **omp_get_num_devices** routine, see Section 3.2.36 on page 371.
- **omp_alloctrait_t** and **omp_alloctrait** types, see Section 3.7.1 on page 406.
- **omp_set_default_allocator** routine, see Section 3.7.4 on page 411.
- **omp_get_default_allocator** routine, see Section 3.7.5 on page 412.
- **ompt_callback_target_t**, see Section 4.5.2.26 on page 490.
- **ompt_callback_target_submit_t**, Section 4.5.2.28 on page 494.

2.12.6 **target update** Construct

Summary

The **target update** directive makes the corresponding list items in the device data environment consistent with their original list items, according to the specified motion clauses. The **target update** construct is a stand-alone directive.

Syntax

---- C / C++ ----

The syntax of the `target update` construct is as follows:

`#pragma omp target update` *clause[[[,] clause] ...] new-line*

where *clause* is either *motion-clause* or one of the following:

> `if([ target update :]` *scalar-expression*`)`
> `device(`*integer-expression*`)`
> `nowait`
> `depend(`*[depend-modifier,] dependence-type : locator-list*`)`

and *motion-clause* is one of the following:

> `to([mapper(`*mapper-identifier*`) :]` *locator-list*`)`
> `from([mapper(`*mapper-identifier*`) :]` *locator-list*`)`

---- C / C++ ----

---- Fortran ----

The syntax of the `target update` construct is as follows:

`!$omp target update` *clause[[[,] clause] ...]*

where *clause* is either *motion-clause* or one of the following:

> `if([target update :]` *scalar-logical-expression*`)`
> `device(`*scalar-integer-expression*`)`
> `nowait`
> `depend(`*[depend-modifier,] dependence-type : locator-list*`)`

and *motion-clause* is one of the following:

> `to([mapper(`*mapper-identifier*`) :]` *locator-list*`)`
> `from([mapper(`*mapper-identifier*`) :]` *locator-list*`)`

---- Fortran ----

Binding

The binding task set for a `target update` region is the generating task, which is the *target task* generated by the `target update` construct. The `target update` region binds to the corresponding *target task* region.

CHAPTER 2. DIRECTIVES   177

Description

For each list item in a `to` or `from` clause there is a corresponding list item and an original list item. If the corresponding list item is not present in the device data environment then no assignment occurs to or from the original list item. Otherwise, each corresponding list item in the device data environment has an original list item in the current task's data environment. If a `mapper()` modifier appears in a `to` clause, each list item is replaced with the list items that the given mapper specifies are to be mapped with a `to` or `tofrom` map-type. If a `mapper()` modifier appears in a `from` clause, each list item is replaced with the list items that the given mapper specifies are to be mapped with a `from` or `tofrom` map-type.

For each list item in a `from` or a `to` clause:

- For each part of the list item that is an attached pointer:

----- C / C++ -----

  - On exit from the region that part of the original list item will have the value it had on entry to the region;

  - On exit from the region that part of the corresponding list item will have the value it had on entry to the region;

----- C / C++ -----

----- Fortran -----

  - On exit from the region that part of the original list item, if associated, will be associated with the same pointer target with which it was associated on entry to the region;

  - On exit from the region that part of the corresponding list item, if associated, will be associated with the same pointer target with which it was associated on entry to the region.

----- Fortran -----

- For each part of the list item that is not an attached pointer:

  - If the clause is `from`, the value of that part of the corresponding list item is assigned to that part of the original list item;

  - If the clause is `to`, the value of that part of the original list item is assigned to that part of the corresponding list item.

- To avoid data races:

  - Concurrent reads or updates of any part of the original list item must be synchronized with the update of the original list item that occurs as a result of the `from` clause;

  - Concurrent reads or updates of any part of the corresponding list item must be synchronized with the update of the corresponding list item that occurs as a result of the `to` clause.

----- C / C++ -----

The list items that appear in the `to` or `from` clauses may use shape-operators.

----- C / C++ -----

The list items that appear in the **to** or **from** clauses may include array sections with *stride* expressions.

The **target update** construct is a task generating construct. The generated task is a *target task*. The generated task region encloses the **target update** region.

All clauses are evaluated when the **target update** construct is encountered. The data environment of the *target task* is created according to the data-sharing attribute clauses on the **target update** construct, per-data environment ICVs, and any default data-sharing attribute rules that apply to the **target update** construct. A variable that is mapped in the **target update** construct has a default data-sharing attribute of **shared** in the data environment of the *target task*.

Assignment operations associated with mapping a variable (see Section 2.19.7.1 on page 315) occur when the *target task* executes.

If the **nowait** clause is present, execution of the *target task* may be deferred. If the **nowait** clause is not present, the *target task* is an included task.

If a **depend** clause is present, it is associated with the *target task*.

The device is specified in the **device** clause. If there is no **device** clause, the device is determined by the *default-device-var* ICV. When an **if** clause is present and the **if** clause expression evaluates to *false* then no assignments occur.

Execution Model Events

Events associated with a *target task* are the same as for the **task** construct defined in Section 2.10.1 on page 135.

The *target-update-begin* event occurs when a thread enters a **target update** region.

The *target-update-end* event occurs when a thread exits a **target update** region.

Tool Callbacks

Callbacks associated with events for *target tasks* are the same as for the **task** construct defined in Section 2.10.1 on page 135; *(flags* **& ompt_task_target)** always evaluates to *true* in the dispatched callback.

A thread dispatches a registered **ompt_callback_target** callback with **ompt_scope_begin** as its *endpoint* argument and **ompt_target_update** as its *kind* argument for each occurrence of a *target-update-begin* event in that thread in the context of the target task on the host. Similarly, a thread dispatches a registered **ompt_callback_target** callback with **ompt_scope_end** as its *endpoint* argument and **ompt_target_update** as its *kind* argument for each occurrence of a *target-update-end* event in that thread in the context of the target task on the host. These callbacks have type signature **ompt_callback_target_t**.

Restrictions

- A program must not depend on any ordering of the evaluations of the clauses of the **target update** directive, or on any side effects of the evaluations of the clauses.
- At least one *motion-clause* must be specified.
- A list item can only appear in a **to** or **from** clause, but not both.
- A list item in a **to** or **from** clause must have a mappable type.
- At most one **device** clause can appear on the directive. The **device** clause expression must evaluate to a non-negative integer value less than the value of **omp_get_num_devices()** or to the value of **omp_get_initial_device()**.
- At most one **if** clause can appear on the directive.
- At most one **nowait** clause can appear on the directive.

Cross References

- Array shaping, Section 2.1.4 on page 43
- Array sections, Section 2.1.5 on page 44
- *default-device-var*, see Section 2.5 on page 63.
- **task** construct, see Section 2.10.1 on page 135.
- **task** scheduling constraints, see Section 2.10.6 on page 149
- **target data**, see Section 2.12.2 on page 161.
- **if** Clause, see Section 2.15 on page 220.
- **omp_get_num_devices** routine, see Section 3.2.36 on page 371.
- **ompt_callback_task_create_t**, see Section 4.5.2.7 on page 467.
- **ompt_callback_target_t**, see Section 4.5.2.26 on page 490.

2.12.7 declare target Directive

Summary

The **declare target** directive specifies that variables, functions (C, C++ and Fortran), and subroutines (Fortran) are mapped to a device. The **declare target** directive is a declarative directive.

Syntax

---- C / C++ ----

The syntax of the **declare target** directive takes either of the following forms:

```
#pragma omp declare target new-line
    declaration-definition-seq
#pragma omp end declare target new-line
```

or

```
#pragma omp declare target (extended-list) new-line
```

or

```
#pragma omp declare target clause[ [,] clause ... ] new-line
```

where *clause* is one of the following:

> **to** (*extended-list*)
> **link** (*list*)
> **device_type** (host | nohost | any)

---- C / C++ ----

---- Fortran ----

The syntax of the **declare target** directive is as follows:

```
!$omp declare target (extended-list)
```

or

```
!$omp declare target [clause[ [,] clause] ... ]
```

where *clause* is one of the following:

> **to** (*extended-list*)
> **link** (*list*)
> **device_type** (host | nohost | any)

---- Fortran ----

Description

The **declare target** directive ensures that procedures and global variables can be executed or accessed on a device. Variables are mapped for all device executions, or for specific device executions through a **link** clause.

If an *extended-list* is present with no clause then the **to** clause is assumed.

The **device_type** clause specifies if a version of the procedure should be made available on host, device or both. If **host** is specified only a host version of the procedure is made available. If **nohost** is specified then only a device version of the procedure is made available. If **any** is specified then both device and host versions of the procedure are made available.

―――――――――――――――――――――― C / C++ ――――――――――――――――――――――

If a function appears in a **to** clause in the same translation unit in which the definition of the function occurs then a device-specific version of the function is created.

If a variable appears in a **to** clause in the same translation unit in which the definition of the variable occurs then the original list item is allocated a corresponding list item in the device data environment of all devices.

―――――――――――――――――――――― C / C++ ――――――――――――――――――――――
―――――――――――――――――――――― Fortran ――――――――――――――――――――――

If an internal procedure appears in a **to** clause then a device-specific version of the procedure is created.

If a variable that is host associated appears in a **to** clause then the original list item is allocated a corresponding list item in the device data environment of all devices.

―――――――――――――――――――――― Fortran ――――――――――――――――――――――

If a variable appears in a **to** clause then the corresponding list item in the device data environment of each device is initialized once, in the manner specified by the program, but at an unspecified point in the program prior to the first reference to that list item. The list item is never removed from those device data environments as if its reference count is initialized to positive infinity.

Including list items in a **link** clause supports compilation of functions called in a **target** region that refer to the list items. The list items are not mapped by the **declare target** directive. Instead, they are mapped according to the data mapping rules described in Section 2.19.7 on page 314.

―――――――――――――――――― C / C++ ――――――――――――――――――

If a function is referenced in a function that appears as a list item in a **to** clause on a
declare target directive then the name of the referenced function is treated as if it had
appeared in a **to** clause on a **declare target** directive.

If a variable with static storage duration or a function (except *lambda* for C++) is referenced in the
initializer expression list of a variable with static storage duration that appears as a list item in a **to**
clause on a **declare target** directive then the name of the referenced variable or function is
treated as if it had appeared in a **to** clause on a **declare target** directive.

The form of the **declare target** directive that has no clauses and requires a matching
end declare target directive defines an implicit *extended-list* to an implicit **to** clause. The
implicit *extended-list* consists of the variable names of any variable declarations at file or
namespace scope that appear between the two directives and of the function names of any function
declarations at file, namespace or class scope that appear between the two directives.

The *declaration-definition-seq* defined by a **declare target** directive and an
end declare target directive may contain **declare target** directives. If a
device_type clause is present on the contained **declare target** directive, then its argument
determines which versions are made available. If a list item appears both in an implicit and explicit
list, the explicit list determines which versions are made available.

―――――――――――――――――― C / C++ ――――――――――――――――――
―――――――――――――――――― Fortran ――――――――――――――――――

If a procedure is referenced in a procedure that appears as a list item in a **to** clause on a
declare target directive then the name of the procedure is treated as if it had appeared in a **to**
clause on a **declare target** directive.

If a **declare target** does not have any clauses then an implicit *extended-list* to an implicit **to**
clause of one item is formed from the name of the enclosing subroutine subprogram, function
subprogram or interface body to which it applies.

If a **declare target** directive has a **device_type** clause then any enclosed internal
procedures cannot contain any **declare target** directives. The enclosing **device_type**
clause implicitly applies to internal procedures.

―――――――――――――――――― Fortran ――――――――――――――――――

Restrictions

- A threadprivate variable cannot appear in a **declare target** directive.
- A variable declared in a **declare target** directive must have a mappable type.
- The same list item must not appear multiple times in clauses on the same directive.
- The same list item must not explicitly appear in both a **to** clause on one **declare target**
  directive and a **link** clause on another **declare target** directive.

―――――――――――――――――――――― C++ ――――――――――――――――――――――

- The function names of overloaded functions or template functions may only be specified within an implicit *extended-list*.

- If a *lambda declaration and definition* appears between a **declare target** directive and the matching **end declare target** directive, all variables that are captured by the *lambda* expression must also appear in a **to** clause.

―――――――――――――――――――――― C++ ――――――――――――――――――――――
―――――――――――――――――――――― Fortran ――――――――――――――――――――――

- If a list item is a procedure name, it must not be a generic name, procedure pointer or entry name.

- Any **declare target** directive with clauses must appear in a specification part of a subroutine subprogram, function subprogram, program or module.

- Any **declare target** directive without clauses must appear in a specification part of a subroutine subprogram, function subprogram or interface body to which it applies.

- If a **declare target** directive is specified in an interface block for a procedure, it must match a **declare target** directive in the definition of the procedure.

- If an external procedure is a type-bound procedure of a derived type and a **declare target** directive is specified in the definition of the external procedure, such a directive must appear in the interface block that is accessible to the derived type definition.

- If any procedure is declared via a procedure declaration statement that is not in the type-bound procedure part of a derived-type definition, any **declare target** with the procedure name must appear in the same specification part.

- A variable that is part of another variable (as an array, structure element or type parameter inquiry) cannot appear in a **declare target** directive.

- The **declare target** directive must appear in the declaration section of a scoping unit in which the common block or variable is declared.

- If a **declare target** directive that specifies a common block name appears in one program unit, then such a directive must also appear in every other program unit that contains a **COMMON** statement that specifies the same name, after the last such **COMMON** statement in the program unit.

- If a list item is declared with the **BIND** attribute, the corresponding C entities must also be specified in a **declare target** directive in the C program.

- A blank common block cannot appear in a **declare target** directive.

- A variable can only appear in a **declare target** directive in the scope in which it is declared. It must not be an element of a common block or appear in an **EQUIVALENCE** statement.

- A variable that appears in a **declare target** directive must be declared in the Fortran scope of a module or have the **SAVE** attribute, either explicitly or implicitly.

―――――――――――――――――――――― Fortran ――――――――――――――――――――――

Cross References

- **target data** construct, see Section 2.12.2 on page 161.
- **target** construct, see Section 2.12.5 on page 170.

2.13 Combined Constructs

Combined constructs are shortcuts for specifying one construct immediately nested inside another construct. The semantics of the combined constructs are identical to that of explicitly specifying the first construct containing one instance of the second construct and no other statements.

For combined constructs, tool callbacks are invoked as if the constructs were explicitly nested.

2.13.1 Parallel Worksharing-Loop Construct

Summary

The parallel worksharing-loop construct is a shortcut for specifying a **parallel** construct containing a worksharing-loop construct with one or more associated loops and no other statements.

Syntax

─────────── C / C++ ───────────

The syntax of the parallel worksharing-loop construct is as follows:

```
#pragma omp parallel for [clause[ [,] clause] ... ] new-line
    for-loops
```

where *clause* can be any of the clauses accepted by the **parallel** or **for** directives, except the **nowait** clause, with identical meanings and restrictions.

─────────── C / C++ ───────────

---- Fortran ----

The syntax of the parallel worksharing-loop construct is as follows:

```
!$omp parallel do [clause[ [,] clause] ... ]
    do-loops
[!$omp end parallel do]
```

where *clause* can be any of the clauses accepted by the **parallel** or **do** directives, with identical meanings and restrictions.

If an **end parallel do** directive is not specified, an **end parallel do** directive is assumed at the end of the *do-loops*. **nowait** may not be specified on an **end parallel do** directive.

---- Fortran ----

Description

The semantics are identical to explicitly specifying a **parallel** directive immediately followed by a worksharing-loop directive.

Restrictions

- The restrictions for the **parallel** construct and the worksharing-loop construct apply.

Cross References

- **parallel** construct, see Section 2.6 on page 74.
- Worksharing-loop construct, see Section 2.9.2 on page 101.
- Data attribute clauses, see Section 2.19.4 on page 282.

2.13.2 `parallel loop` Construct

Summary

The **parallel loop** construct is a shortcut for specifying a **parallel** construct containing a **loop** construct with one or more associated loops and no other statements.

Syntax

---C / C++---

The syntax of the **parallel loop** construct is as follows:

```
#pragma omp parallel loop [clause[ [,] clause] ... ] new-line
    for-loops
```

where *clause* can be any of the clauses accepted by the **parallel** or **loop** directives, with identical meanings and restrictions.

---C / C++---

---Fortran---

The syntax of the **parallel loop** construct is as follows:

```
!$omp parallel loop [clause[ [,] clause] ... ]
    do-loops
[!$omp end parallel loop]
```

where *clause* can be any of the clauses accepted by the **parallel** or **loop** directives, with identical meanings and restrictions.

If an **end parallel loop** directive is not specified, an **end parallel loop** directive is assumed at the end of the *do-loops*. **nowait** may not be specified on an **end parallel loop** directive.

---Fortran---

Description

The semantics are identical to explicitly specifying a **parallel** directive immediately followed by a **loop** directive.

Restrictions

- The restrictions for the **parallel** construct and the **loop** construct apply.

Cross References

- **parallel** construct, see Section 2.6 on page 74.
- **loop** construct, see Section 2.9.5 on page 128.
- Data attribute clauses, see Section 2.19.4 on page 282.

2.13.3 `parallel sections` Construct

Summary

The `parallel sections` construct is a shortcut for specifying a `parallel` construct containing a `sections` construct and no other statements.

Syntax

⎯⎯⎯⎯⎯⎯⎯⎯⎯⎯⎯⎯⎯⎯⎯⎯ C / C++ ⎯⎯⎯⎯⎯⎯⎯⎯⎯⎯⎯⎯⎯⎯⎯⎯

The syntax of the `parallel sections` construct is as follows:

```
#pragma omp parallel sections [clause[ [,] clause] ... ] new-line
    {
    [#pragma omp section new-line]
        structured-block
    [#pragma omp section new-line
        structured-block]
    ...
    }
```

where *clause* can be any of the clauses accepted by the `parallel` or `sections` directives, except the `nowait` clause, with identical meanings and restrictions.

⎯⎯⎯⎯⎯⎯⎯⎯⎯⎯⎯⎯⎯⎯⎯⎯ C / C++ ⎯⎯⎯⎯⎯⎯⎯⎯⎯⎯⎯⎯⎯⎯⎯⎯
⎯⎯⎯⎯⎯⎯⎯⎯⎯⎯⎯⎯⎯⎯⎯⎯ Fortran ⎯⎯⎯⎯⎯⎯⎯⎯⎯⎯⎯⎯⎯⎯⎯⎯

The syntax of the `parallel sections` construct is as follows:

```
!$omp parallel sections [clause[ [,] clause] ... ]
    [!$omp section]
        structured-block
    [!$omp section
        structured-block]
    ...
!$omp end parallel sections
```

where *clause* can be any of the clauses accepted by the `parallel` or `sections` directives, with identical meanings and restrictions.

The last section ends at the `end parallel sections` directive. `nowait` cannot be specified on an `end parallel sections` directive.

⎯⎯⎯⎯⎯⎯⎯⎯⎯⎯⎯⎯⎯⎯⎯⎯ Fortran ⎯⎯⎯⎯⎯⎯⎯⎯⎯⎯⎯⎯⎯⎯⎯⎯

Description

---- C / C++ ----

The semantics are identical to explicitly specifying a **parallel** directive immediately followed by a **sections** directive.

---- C / C++ ----

---- Fortran ----

The semantics are identical to explicitly specifying a **parallel** directive immediately followed by a **sections** directive, and an **end sections** directive immediately followed by an **end parallel** directive.

---- Fortran ----

Restrictions

The restrictions for the **parallel** construct and the **sections** construct apply.

Cross References

- **parallel** construct, see Section 2.6 on page 74.
- **sections** construct, see Section 2.8.1 on page 86.
- Data attribute clauses, see Section 2.19.4 on page 282.

---- Fortran ----

2.13.4 `parallel workshare` Construct

Summary

The **parallel workshare** construct is a shortcut for specifying a **parallel** construct containing a **workshare** construct and no other statements.

Syntax

The syntax of the **parallel workshare** construct is as follows:

```
!$omp parallel workshare [clause[ [,] clause] ... ]
    structured-block
!$omp end parallel workshare
```

where *clause* can be any of the clauses accepted by the **parallel** directive, with identical meanings and restrictions. **nowait** may not be specified on an **end parallel workshare** directive.

Description

The semantics are identical to explicitly specifying a `parallel` directive immediately followed by a `workshare` directive, and an `end workshare` directive immediately followed by an `end parallel` directive.

Restrictions

The restrictions for the `parallel` construct and the `workshare` construct apply.

Cross References

- `parallel` construct, see Section 2.6 on page 74.
- `workshare` construct, see Section 2.8.3 on page 92.
- Data attribute clauses, see Section 2.19.4 on page 282.

―――――――――――――― Fortran ――――――――――――――

2.13.5 Parallel Worksharing-Loop SIMD Construct

Summary

The parallel worksharing-loop SIMD construct is a shortcut for specifying a `parallel` construct containing a worksharing-loop SIMD construct and no other statements.

Syntax

―――――――――――――― C / C++ ――――――――――――――

The syntax of the parallel worksharing-loop SIMD construct is as follows:

```
#pragma omp parallel for simd [clause[ [,] clause] ... ] new-line
    for-loops
```

where *clause* can be any of the clauses accepted by the `parallel` or `for simd` directives, except the `nowait` clause, with identical meanings and restrictions.

―――――――――――――― C / C++ ――――――――――――――

Fortran

The syntax of the parallel worksharing-loop SIMD construct is as follows:

```
!$omp parallel do simd [clause[ [, ] clause] ... ]
    do-loops
[!$omp end parallel do simd]
```

where *clause* can be any of the clauses accepted by the **parallel** or **do simd** directives, with identical meanings and restrictions.

If an **end parallel do simd** directive is not specified, an **end parallel do simd** directive is assumed at the end of the *do-loops*. **nowait** may not be specified on an **end parallel do simd** directive.

Fortran

Description

The semantics of the parallel worksharing-loop SIMD construct are identical to explicitly specifying a **parallel** directive immediately followed by a worksharing-loop SIMD directive.

Restrictions

The restrictions for the **parallel** construct and the worksharing-loop SIMD construct apply.

Cross References

- **parallel** construct, see Section 2.6 on page 74.
- Worksharing-loop SIMD construct, see Section 2.9.3.2 on page 114.
- Data attribute clauses, see Section 2.19.4 on page 282.

2.13.6 parallel master Construct

Summary

The **parallel master** construct is a shortcut for specifying a **parallel** construct containing a **master** construct and no other statements.

Syntax

―――――――――――――――――――― C / C++ ――――――――――――――――――――

The syntax of the **parallel master** construct is as follows:

```
#pragma omp parallel master [clause[ [, ] clause] ... ] new-line
    structured-block
```

where *clause* can be any of the clauses accepted by the **parallel** or **master** directives, with identical meanings and restrictions.

―――――――――――――――――――― C / C++ ――――――――――――――――――――
―――――――――――――――――――― Fortran ――――――――――――――――――――

The syntax of the **parallel master** construct is as follows:

```
!$omp parallel master [clause[ [, ] clause] ... ]
    structured-block
!$omp end parallel master
```

where *clause* can be any of the clauses accepted by the **parallel** or **master** directives, with identical meanings and restrictions.

―――――――――――――――――――― Fortran ――――――――――――――――――――

Description

The semantics are identical to explicitly specifying a **parallel** directive immediately followed by a **master** directive.

Restrictions

The restrictions for the **parallel** construct and the **master** construct apply.

Cross References

- **parallel** construct, see Section 2.6 on page 74.
- **master** construct, see Section 2.16 on page 221.
- Data attribute clauses, see Section 2.19.4 on page 282.

2.13.7 `master taskloop` Construct

Summary

The **master taskloop** construct is a shortcut for specifying a **master** construct containing a **taskloop** construct and no other statements.

Syntax

---- C / C++ ----

The syntax of the **master taskloop** construct is as follows:

```
#pragma omp master taskloop [clause[ [,] clause] ... ] new-line
    for-loops
```

where *clause* can be any of the clauses accepted by the **master** or **taskloop** directives with identical meanings and restrictions.

---- C / C++ ----

---- Fortran ----

The syntax of the **master taskloop** construct is as follows:

```
!$omp master taskloop [clause[ [,] clause] ... ]
    do-loops
[!$omp end master taskloop]
```

where *clause* can be any of the clauses accepted by the **master** or **taskloop** directives with identical meanings and restrictions.

If an **end master taskloop** directive is not specified, an **end master taskloop** directive is assumed at the end of the *do-loops*.

---- Fortran ----

Description

The semantics are identical to explicitly specifying a **master** directive immediately followed by a **taskloop** directive.

Restrictions

The restrictions for the **master** and **taskloop** constructs apply.

Cross References

- **taskloop** construct, see Section 2.10.2 on page 140.
- **master** construct, see Section 2.16 on page 221.
- Data attribute clauses, see Section 2.19.4 on page 282.

2.13.8 `master taskloop simd` Construct

Summary

The **master taskloop simd** construct is a shortcut for specifying a **master** construct containing a **taskloop simd** construct and no other statements.

Syntax

─────────────── C / C++ ───────────────

The syntax of the **master taskloop simd** construct is as follows:

```
#pragma omp master taskloop simd [clause[ [, ] clause] ... ] new-line
    for-loops
```

where *clause* can be any of the clauses accepted by the **master** or **taskloop simd** directives with identical meanings and restrictions.

─────────────── C / C++ ───────────────

─────────────── Fortran ───────────────

The syntax of the **master taskloop simd** construct is as follows:

```
!$omp master taskloop simd [clause[ [, ] clause] ... ]
    do-loops
[!$omp end master taskloop simd]
```

where *clause* can be any of the clauses accepted by the **master** or **taskloop simd** directives with identical meanings and restrictions.

If an **end master taskloop simd** directive is not specified, an **end master taskloop simd** directive is assumed at the end of the *do-loops*.

─────────────── Fortran ───────────────

Description

The semantics are identical to explicitly specifying a **master** directive immediately followed by a **taskloop simd** directive.

Restrictions

The restrictions for the **master** and **taskloop simd** constructs apply.

Cross References

- **taskloop simd** construct, see Section 2.10.3 on page 146.
- **master** construct, see Section 2.16 on page 221.
- Data attribute clauses, see Section 2.19.4 on page 282.

2.13.9 parallel master taskloop Construct

Summary

The **parallel master taskloop** construct is a shortcut for specifying a **parallel** construct containing a **master taskloop** construct and no other statements.

Syntax

─────────────── C / C++ ───────────────

The syntax of the **parallel master taskloop** construct is as follows:

```
#pragma omp parallel master taskloop [clause[ [, ] clause] ... ] new-line
    for-loops
```

where *clause* can be any of the clauses accepted by the **parallel** or **master taskloop** directives, except the **in_reduction** clause, with identical meanings and restrictions.

─────────────── C / C++ ───────────────

─────────────── Fortran ───────────────

The syntax of the **parallel master taskloop** construct is as follows:

```
!$omp parallel master taskloop [clause[ [, ] clause] ... ]
    do-loops
[!$omp end parallel master taskloop]
```

where *clause* can be any of the clauses accepted by the **parallel** or **master taskloop** directives, except the **in_reduction** clause, with identical meanings and restrictions.

If an **end parallel master taskloop** directive is not specified, an **end parallel master taskloop** directive is assumed at the end of the *do-loops*.

─────────────── Fortran ───────────────

Description

The semantics are identical to explicitly specifying a **parallel** directive immediately followed by a **master taskloop** directive.

Restrictions

The restrictions for the `parallel` construct and the `master taskloop` construct apply.

Cross References

- `parallel` construct, see Section 2.6 on page 74.
- `master taskloop` construct, see Section 2.13.7 on page 192.
- Data attribute clauses, see Section 2.19.4 on page 282.

2.13.10 `parallel master taskloop simd` Construct

Summary

The `parallel master taskloop simd` construct is a shortcut for specifying a `parallel` construct containing a `master taskloop simd` construct and no other statements.

Syntax

―――――――――― C / C++ ――――――――――

The syntax of the `parallel master taskloop simd` construct is as follows:

> `#pragma omp parallel master taskloop simd` *[clause[[,] clause] ...] new-line*
>   *for-loops*

where *clause* can be any of the clauses accepted by the `parallel` or `master taskloop simd` directives, except the `in_reduction` clause, with identical meanings and restrictions.

―――――――――― C / C++ ――――――――――

―――――――――― Fortran ――――――――――

The syntax of the `parallel master taskloop simd` construct is as follows:

> `!$omp parallel master taskloop simd` *[clause[[,] clause] ...]*
>   *do-loops*
> *[!$omp end parallel master taskloop simd]*

where *clause* can be any of the clauses accepted by the `parallel` or `master taskloop simd` directives, except the `in_reduction` clause, with identical meanings and restrictions.

If an `end parallel master taskloop simd` directive is not specified, an `end parallel master taskloop simd` directive is assumed at the end of the *do-loops*.

―――――――――― Fortran ――――――――――

Description

The semantics are identical to explicitly specifying a **parallel** directive immediately followed by a **master taskloop simd** directive.

Restrictions

The restrictions for the **parallel** construct and the **master taskloop simd** construct apply.

Cross References

- **parallel** construct, see Section 2.6 on page 74.
- **master taskloop simd** construct, see Section 2.13.8 on page 194.
- Data attribute clauses, see Section 2.19.4 on page 282.

2.13.11 teams distribute Construct

Summary

The **teams distribute** construct is a shortcut for specifying a **teams** construct containing a **distribute** construct and no other statements.

Syntax

---- C / C++ ----

The syntax of the **teams distribute** construct is as follows:

```
#pragma omp teams distribute [clause[ [,] clause] ... ] new-line
    for-loops
```

where *clause* can be any of the clauses accepted by the **teams** or **distribute** directives with identical meanings and restrictions.

---- C / C++ ----

---------- Fortran ----------

The syntax of the **teams distribute** construct is as follows:

```
!$omp teams distribute [clause[ [, ] clause] ... ]
    do-loops
[!$omp end teams distribute]
```

where *clause* can be any of the clauses accepted by the **teams** or **distribute** directives with identical meanings and restrictions.

If an **end teams distribute** directive is not specified, an **end teams distribute** directive is assumed at the end of the *do-loops*.

---------- Fortran ----------

Description

The semantics are identical to explicitly specifying a **teams** directive immediately followed by a **distribute** directive.

Restrictions

The restrictions for the **teams** and **distribute** constructs apply.

Cross References

- **teams** construct, see Section 2.7 on page 82.
- **distribute** construct, see Section 2.9.4.1 on page 120.
- Data attribute clauses, see Section 2.19.4 on page 282.

2.13.12 teams distribute simd Construct

Summary

The **teams distribute simd** construct is a shortcut for specifying a **teams** construct containing a **distribute simd** construct and no other statements.

Syntax

―――――――― C / C++ ――――――――

The syntax of the **teams distribute simd** construct is as follows:

```
#pragma omp teams distribute simd [clause[ [,] clause] ... ] new-line
    for-loops
```

where *clause* can be any of the clauses accepted by the **teams** or **distribute simd** directives with identical meanings and restrictions.

―――――――― C / C++ ――――――――
―――――――― Fortran ――――――――

The syntax of the **teams distribute simd** construct is as follows:

```
!$omp teams distribute simd [clause[ [,] clause] ... ]
    do-loops
[!$omp end teams distribute simd]
```

where *clause* can be any of the clauses accepted by the **teams** or **distribute simd** directives with identical meanings and restrictions.

If an **end teams distribute simd** directive is not specified, an **end teams distribute simd** directive is assumed at the end of the *do-loops*.

―――――――― Fortran ――――――――

Description

The semantics are identical to explicitly specifying a **teams** directive immediately followed by a **distribute simd** directive.

Restrictions

The restrictions for the **teams** and **distribute simd** constructs apply.

Cross References

- **teams** construct, see Section 2.7 on page 82.
- **distribute simd** construct, see Section 2.9.4.2 on page 123.
- Data attribute clauses, see Section 2.19.4 on page 282.

2.13.13 Teams Distribute Parallel Worksharing-Loop Construct

Summary

The teams distribute parallel worksharing-loop construct is a shortcut for specifying a **teams** construct containing a distribute parallel worksharing-loop construct and no other statements.

Syntax

―――――――――――― C / C++ ――――――――――――

The syntax of the teams distribute parallel worksharing-loop construct is as follows:

```
#pragma omp teams distribute parallel for \
              [clause[ [, ] clause] ... ] new-line
    for-loops
```

where *clause* can be any of the clauses accepted by the **teams** or **distribute parallel for** directives with identical meanings and restrictions.

―――――――――――― C / C++ ――――――――――――
―――――――――――― Fortran ――――――――――――

The syntax of the teams distribute parallel worksharing-loop construct is as follows:

```
!$omp teams distribute parallel do [clause[ [, ] clause] ... ]
    do-loops
[ !$omp end teams distribute parallel do ]
```

where *clause* can be any of the clauses accepted by the **teams** or **distribute parallel do** directives with identical meanings and restrictions.

If an **end teams distribute parallel do** directive is not specified, an **end teams distribute parallel do** directive is assumed at the end of the *do-loops*.

―――――――――――― Fortran ――――――――――――

Description

The semantics are identical to explicitly specifying a **teams** directive immediately followed by a distribute parallel worksharing-loop directive.

Restrictions

The restrictions for the **teams** and distribute parallel worksharing-loop constructs apply.

Cross References

- **teams** construct, see Section 2.7 on page 82.
- Distribute parallel worksharing-loop construct, see Section 2.9.4.3 on page 125.
- Data attribute clauses, see Section 2.19.4 on page 282.

2.13.14 Teams Distribute Parallel Worksharing-Loop SIMD Construct

Summary

The teams distribute parallel worksharing-loop SIMD construct is a shortcut for specifying a **teams** construct containing a distribute parallel worksharing-loop SIMD construct and no other statements.

Syntax

―――――――――――――――― C / C++ ――――――――――――――――

The syntax of the teams distribute parallel worksharing-loop SIMD construct is as follows:

```
#pragma omp teams distribute parallel for simd \
            [clause[ [,] clause] ... ] new-line
    for-loops
```

where *clause* can be any of the clauses accepted by the **teams** or **distribute parallel for simd** directives with identical meanings and restrictions.

―――――――――――――――― C / C++ ――――――――――――――――
―――――――――――――――― Fortran ――――――――――――――――

The syntax of the teams distribute parallel worksharing-loop SIMD construct is as follows:

```
!$omp teams distribute parallel do simd [clause[ [,] clause] ... ]
    do-loops
[!$omp end teams distribute parallel do simd]
```

where *clause* can be any of the clauses accepted by the **teams** or **distribute parallel do simd** directives with identical meanings and restrictions.

If an **end teams distribute parallel do simd** directive is not specified, an **end teams distribute parallel do simd** directive is assumed at the end of the *do-loops*.

―――――――――――――――― Fortran ――――――――――――――――

Description

The semantics are identical to explicitly specifying a **teams** directive immediately followed by a distribute parallel worksharing-loop SIMD directive.

Restrictions

The restrictions for the **teams** and distribute parallel worksharing-loop SIMD constructs apply.

Cross References

- **teams** construct, see Section 2.7 on page 82.
- Distribute parallel worksharing-loop SIMD construct, see Section 2.9.4.4 on page 126.
- Data attribute clauses, see Section 2.19.4 on page 282.

2.13.15 `teams loop` Construct

Summary

The **teams loop** construct is a shortcut for specifying a **teams** construct containing a **loop** construct and no other statements.

Syntax

---------- C / C++ ----------

The syntax of the **teams loop** construct is as follows:

```
#pragma omp teams loop [clause[ [, ] clause] ... ] new-line
    for-loops
```

where *clause* can be any of the clauses accepted by the **teams** or **loop** directives with identical meanings and restrictions.

---------- C / C++ ----------

Fortran

The syntax of the **teams loop** construct is as follows:

```
!$omp teams loop [clause[ [,] clause] ... ]
    do-loops
[!$omp end teams loop]
```

where *clause* can be any of the clauses accepted by the **teams** or **loop** directives with identical meanings and restrictions.

If an **end teams loop** directive is not specified, an **end teams loop** directive is assumed at the end of the *do-loops*.

Fortran

Description

The semantics are identical to explicitly specifying a **teams** directive immediately followed by a **loop** directive.

Restrictions

The restrictions for the **teams** and **loop** constructs apply.

Cross References

- **teams** construct, see Section 2.7 on page 82.
- **loop** construct, see Section 2.9.5 on page 128.
- Data attribute clauses, see Section 2.19.4 on page 282.

2.13.16 target parallel Construct

Summary

The **target parallel** construct is a shortcut for specifying a **target** construct containing a **parallel** construct and no other statements.

Syntax

---C / C++---

The syntax of the **target parallel** construct is as follows:

```
#pragma omp target parallel [clause[ [, ] clause] ... ] new-line
    structured-block
```

where *clause* can be any of the clauses accepted by the **target** or **parallel** directives, except for **copyin**, with identical meanings and restrictions.

---C / C++---

---Fortran---

The syntax of the **target parallel** construct is as follows:

```
!$omp target parallel [clause[ [, ] clause] ... ]
    structured-block
!$omp end target parallel
```

where *clause* can be any of the clauses accepted by the **target** or **parallel** directives, except for **copyin**, with identical meanings and restrictions.

---Fortran---

Description

The semantics are identical to explicitly specifying a **target** directive immediately followed by a **parallel** directive.

Restrictions

The restrictions for the **target** and **parallel** constructs apply except for the following explicit modifications:

- If any **if** clause on the directive includes a *directive-name-modifier* then all **if** clauses on the directive must include a *directive-name-modifier*.
- At most one **if** clause without a *directive-name-modifier* can appear on the directive.
- At most one **if** clause with the **parallel** *directive-name-modifier* can appear on the directive.
- At most one **if** clause with the **target** *directive-name-modifier* can appear on the directive.

Cross References

- **parallel** construct, see Section 2.6 on page 74.
- **target** construct, see Section 2.12.5 on page 170.
- **if** Clause, see Section 2.15 on page 220.
- Data attribute clauses, see Section 2.19.4 on page 282.

2.13.17 Target Parallel Worksharing-Loop Construct

Summary

The target parallel worksharing-loop construct is a shortcut for specifying a **target** construct containing a parallel worksharing-loop construct and no other statements.

Syntax

─────────────────────── C / C++ ───────────────────────

The syntax of the target parallel worksharing-loop construct is as follows:

```
#pragma omp target parallel for [clause[ [, ] clause] ... ] new-line
    for-loops
```

where *clause* can be any of the clauses accepted by the **target** or **parallel for** directives, except for **copyin**, with identical meanings and restrictions.

─────────────────────── C / C++ ───────────────────────

─────────────────────── Fortran ───────────────────────

The syntax of the target parallel worksharing-loop construct is as follows:

```
!$omp target parallel do [clause[ [, ] clause] ... ]
    do-loops
[!$omp end target parallel do]
```

where *clause* can be any of the clauses accepted by the **target** or **parallel do** directives, except for **copyin**, with identical meanings and restrictions.

If an **end target parallel do** directive is not specified, an **end target parallel do** directive is assumed at the end of the *do-loops*.

─────────────────────── Fortran ───────────────────────

Description

The semantics are identical to explicitly specifying a `target` directive immediately followed by a parallel worksharing-loop directive.

Restrictions

The restrictions for the `target` and parallel worksharing-loop constructs apply except for the following explicit modifications:

- If any `if` clause on the directive includes a *directive-name-modifier* then all `if` clauses on the directive must include a *directive-name-modifier*.
- At most one `if` clause without a *directive-name-modifier* can appear on the directive.
- At most one `if` clause with the `parallel` *directive-name-modifier* can appear on the directive.
- At most one `if` clause with the `target` *directive-name-modifier* can appear on the directive.

Cross References

- `target` construct, see Section 2.12.5 on page 170.
- Parallel Worksharing-Loop construct, see Section 2.13.1 on page 185.
- `if` Clause, see Section 2.15 on page 220.
- Data attribute clauses, see Section 2.19.4 on page 282.

2.13.18 Target Parallel Worksharing-Loop SIMD Construct

Summary

The target parallel worksharing-loop SIMD construct is a shortcut for specifying a `target` construct containing a parallel worksharing-loop SIMD construct and no other statements.

Syntax

―――――― C / C++ ――――――

The syntax of the target parallel worksharing-loop SIMD construct is as follows:

```
#pragma omp target parallel for simd \
           [clause[[, ] clause] ... ] new-line
    for-loops
```

where *clause* can be any of the clauses accepted by the **target** or **parallel for simd** directives, except for **copyin**, with identical meanings and restrictions.

―――――― C / C++ ――――――

―――――― Fortran ――――――

The syntax of the target parallel worksharing-loop SIMD construct is as follows:

```
!$omp target parallel do simd [clause[ [, ] clause] ... ]
    do-loops
[!$omp end target parallel do simd]
```

where *clause* can be any of the clauses accepted by the **target** or **parallel do simd** directives, except for **copyin**, with identical meanings and restrictions.

If an **end target parallel do simd** directive is not specified, an **end target parallel do simd** directive is assumed at the end of the *do-loops*.

―――――― Fortran ――――――

Description

The semantics are identical to explicitly specifying a **target** directive immediately followed by a parallel worksharing-loop SIMD directive.

Restrictions

The restrictions for the **target** and parallel worksharing-loop SIMD constructs apply except for the following explicit modifications:

- If any **if** clause on the directive includes a *directive-name-modifier* then all **if** clauses on the directive must include a *directive-name-modifier*.
- At most one **if** clause without a *directive-name-modifier* can appear on the directive.
- At most one **if** clause with the **parallel** *directive-name-modifier* can appear on the directive.
- At most one **if** clause with the **target** *directive-name-modifier* can appear on the directive.

Cross References

- **target** construct, see Section 2.12.5 on page 170.
- Parallel worksharing-loop SIMD construct, see Section 2.13.5 on page 190.
- **if** Clause, see Section 2.15 on page 220.
- Data attribute clauses, see Section 2.19.4 on page 282.

2.13.19 `target parallel loop` Construct

Summary

The **target parallel loop** construct is a shortcut for specifying a **target** construct containing a **parallel loop** construct and no other statements.

Syntax

--- C / C++ ---

The syntax of the **target parallel loop** construct is as follows:

```
#pragma omp target parallel loop [clause[ [,] clause] ... ] new-line
    for-loops
```

where *clause* can be any of the clauses accepted by the **target** or **parallel loop** directives with identical meanings and restrictions.

--- C / C++ ---

--- Fortran ---

The syntax of the **target parallel loop** construct is as follows:

```
!$omp target parallel loop [clause[ [,] clause] ... ]
    do-loops
[!$omp end target parallel loop]
```

where *clause* can be any of the clauses accepted by the **teams** or **parallel loop** directives with identical meanings and restrictions.

If an **end target parallel loop** directive is not specified, an **end target parallel loop** directive is assumed at the end of the *do-loops*. **nowait** may not be specified on an **end target parallel loop** directive.

--- Fortran ---

Description

The semantics are identical to explicitly specifying a **target** directive immediately followed by a **parallel loop** directive.

Restrictions

The restrictions for the **target** and **parallel loop** constructs apply.

Cross References

- **target** construct, see Section 2.12.5 on page 170.
- **parallel loop** construct, see Section 2.13.2 on page 186.
- Data attribute clauses, see Section 2.19.4 on page 282.

2.13.20 `target simd` Construct

Summary

The **target simd** construct is a shortcut for specifying a **target** construct containing a **simd** construct and no other statements.

Syntax

--- C / C++ ---

The syntax of the **target simd** construct is as follows:

```
#pragma omp target simd [clause[ [,] clause] ... ] new-line
    for-loops
```

where *clause* can be any of the clauses accepted by the **target** or **simd** directives with identical meanings and restrictions.

--- C / C++ ---

―――――――――――――――――――――――― Fortran ――――――――――――――――――――――――

The syntax of the **target simd** construct is as follows:

```
!$omp target simd [clause[ [,] clause] ... ]
    do-loops
[!$omp end target simd]
```

where *clause* can be any of the clauses accepted by the **target** or **simd** directives with identical meanings and restrictions.

If an **end target simd** directive is not specified, an **end target simd** directive is assumed at the end of the *do-loops*.

―――――――――――――――――――――――― Fortran ――――――――――――――――――――――――

Description

The semantics are identical to explicitly specifying a **target** directive immediately followed by a **simd** directive.

Restrictions

The restrictions for the **target** and **simd** constructs apply.

Cross References

- **simd** construct, see Section 2.9.3.1 on page 110.
- **target** construct, see Section 2.12.5 on page 170.
- Data attribute clauses, see Section 2.19.4 on page 282.

2.13.21 target teams Construct

Summary

The **target teams** construct is a shortcut for specifying a **target** construct containing a **teams** construct and no other statements.

Syntax

───── C / C++ ─────

The syntax of the **target teams** construct is as follows:

#pragma omp target teams *[clause[[,] clause] ...] new-line*
    structured-block

where *clause* can be any of the clauses accepted by the **target** or **teams** directives with identical meanings and restrictions.

───── C / C++ ─────

───── Fortran ─────

The syntax of the **target teams** construct is as follows:

!$omp target teams *[clause[[,] clause] ...]*
    structured-block
!$omp end target teams

where *clause* can be any of the clauses accepted by the **target** or **teams** directives with identical meanings and restrictions.

───── Fortran ─────

Description

The semantics are identical to explicitly specifying a **target** directive immediately followed by a **teams** directive.

Restrictions

The restrictions for the **target** and **teams** constructs apply.

Cross References

- **teams** construct, see Section 2.7 on page 82.
- **target** construct, see Section 2.12.5 on page 170.
- Data attribute clauses, see Section 2.19.4 on page 282.

2.13.22 target teams distribute Construct

Summary

The **target teams distribute** construct is a shortcut for specifying a **target** construct containing a **teams distribute** construct and no other statements.

Syntax

---C / C++---

The syntax of the `target teams distribute` construct is as follows:

```
#pragma omp target teams distribute [clause[ [,] clause] ... ] new-line
    for-loops
```

where *clause* can be any of the clauses accepted by the `target` or `teams distribute` directives with identical meanings and restrictions.

---C / C++---

---Fortran---

The syntax of the `target teams distribute` construct is as follows:

```
!$omp target teams distribute [clause[ [,] clause] ... ]
    do-loops
[!$omp end target teams distribute]
```

where *clause* can be any of the clauses accepted by the `target` or `teams distribute` directives with identical meanings and restrictions.

If an `end target teams distribute` directive is not specified, an `end target teams distribute` directive is assumed at the end of the *do-loops*.

---Fortran---

Description

The semantics are identical to explicitly specifying a `target` directive immediately followed by a `teams distribute` directive.

Restrictions

The restrictions for the `target` and `teams distribute` constructs.

Cross References

- `target` construct, see Section 2.12.2 on page 161.
- `teams distribute` construct, see Section 2.13.11 on page 197.
- Data attribute clauses, see Section 2.19.4 on page 282.

2.13.23 `target teams distribute simd` Construct

Summary

The `target teams distribute simd` construct is a shortcut for specifying a `target` construct containing a `teams distribute simd` construct and no other statements.

Syntax

―――――――――――――――――― C / C++ ――――――――――――――――――

The syntax of the `target teams distribute simd` construct is as follows:

```
#pragma omp target teams distribute simd \
         [clause[ [, ] clause] ... ] new-line
    for-loops
```

where *clause* can be any of the clauses accepted by the `target` or `teams distribute simd` directives with identical meanings and restrictions.

―――――――――――――――――― C / C++ ――――――――――――――――――

―――――――――――――――――― Fortran ――――――――――――――――――

The syntax of the `target teams distribute simd` construct is as follows:

```
!$omp target teams distribute simd [clause[ [, ] clause] ... ]
    do-loops
[!$omp end target teams distribute simd]
```

where *clause* can be any of the clauses accepted by the `target` or `teams distribute simd` directives with identical meanings and restrictions.

If an `end target teams distribute simd` directive is not specified, an `end target teams distribute simd` directive is assumed at the end of the *do-loops*.

―――――――――――――――――― Fortran ――――――――――――――――――

Description

The semantics are identical to explicitly specifying a `target` directive immediately followed by a `teams distribute simd` directive.

Restrictions

The restrictions for the `target` and `teams distribute simd` constructs apply.

Cross References

- `target` construct, see Section 2.12.2 on page 161.
- `teams distribute simd` construct, see Section 2.13.12 on page 198.
- Data attribute clauses, see Section 2.19.4 on page 282.

2.13.24 `target teams loop` Construct

Summary

The `target teams loop` construct is a shortcut for specifying a `target` construct containing a `teams loop` construct and no other statements.

Syntax

―――――――――――――――― C / C++ ――――――――――――――――

The syntax of the `target teams loop` construct is as follows:

```
#pragma omp target teams loop [clause[ [,] clause] ... ] new-line
    for-loops
```

where *clause* can be any of the clauses accepted by the `target` or `teams loop` directives with identical meanings and restrictions.

―――――――――――――――― C / C++ ――――――――――――――――
―――――――――――――――― Fortran ――――――――――――――――

The syntax of the `target teams loop` construct is as follows:

```
!$omp target teams loop [clause[ [,] clause] ... ]
    do-loops
[!$omp end target teams loop]
```

where *clause* can be any of the clauses accepted by the `target` or `teams loop` directives with identical meanings and restrictions.

If an `end target teams loop` directive is not specified, an `end target teams loop` directive is assumed at the end of the *do-loops*.

―――――――――――――――― Fortran ――――――――――――――――

Description

The semantics are identical to explicitly specifying a `target` directive immediately followed by a `teams loop` directive.

Restrictions

The restrictions for the **target** and **teams loop** constructs.

Cross References

- **target** construct, see Section 2.12.5 on page 170.
- Teams loop construct, see Section 2.13.15 on page 202.
- Data attribute clauses, see Section 2.19.4 on page 282.

2.13.25 Target Teams Distribute Parallel Worksharing-Loop Construct

Summary

The target teams distribute parallel worksharing-loop construct is a shortcut for specifying a **target** construct containing a teams distribute parallel worksharing-loop construct and no other statements.

Syntax

―――――――――――――― C / C++ ――――――――――――――

The syntax of the target teams distribute parallel worksharing-loop construct is as follows:

```
#pragma omp target teams distribute parallel for \
           [clause[ [, ] clause] ... ] new-line
    for-loops
```

where *clause* can be any of the clauses accepted by the **target** or **teams distribute parallel for** directives with identical meanings and restrictions.

―――――――――――――― C / C++ ――――――――――――――
―――――――――――――― Fortran ――――――――――――――

The syntax of the target teams distribute parallel worksharing-loop construct is as follows:

```
!$omp target teams distribute parallel do [clause[ [, ] clause] ... ]
    do-loops
[!$omp end target teams distribute parallel do]
```

where *clause* can be any of the clauses accepted by the **target** or **teams distribute parallel do** directives with identical meanings and restrictions.

If an **end target teams distribute parallel do** directive is not specified, an **end target teams distribute parallel do** directive is assumed at the end of the *do-loops*.

―――――――――――――― Fortran ――――――――――――――

Description

The semantics are identical to explicitly specifying a `target` directive immediately followed by a teams distribute parallel worksharing-loop directive.

Restrictions

The restrictions for the `target` and teams distribute parallel worksharing-loop constructs apply except for the following explicit modifications:

- If any `if` clause on the directive includes a *directive-name-modifier* then all `if` clauses on the directive must include a *directive-name-modifier*.
- At most one `if` clause without a *directive-name-modifier* can appear on the directive.
- At most one `if` clause with the `parallel` *directive-name-modifier* can appear on the directive.
- At most one `if` clause with the `target` *directive-name-modifier* can appear on the directive.

Cross References

- `target` construct, see Section 2.12.5 on page 170.
- Teams distribute parallel worksharing-loop construct, see Section 2.13.13 on page 200.
- `if` Clause, see Section 2.15 on page 220.
- Data attribute clauses, see Section 2.19.4 on page 282.

2.13.26 Target Teams Distribute Parallel Worksharing-Loop SIMD Construct

Summary

The target teams distribute parallel worksharing-loop SIMD construct is a shortcut for specifying a `target` construct containing a teams distribute parallel worksharing-loop SIMD construct and no other statements.

Syntax

---- C / C++ ----

The syntax of the target teams distribute parallel worksharing-loop SIMD construct is as follows:

```
#pragma omp target teams distribute parallel for simd \
     [clause[ [, ] clause] ... ] new-line
   for-loops
```

where *clause* can be any of the clauses accepted by the **target** or **teams distribute parallel for simd** directives with identical meanings and restrictions.

---- C / C++ ----

---- Fortran ----

The syntax of the target teams distribute parallel worksharing-loop SIMD construct is as follows:

```
!$omp target teams distribute parallel do simd [clause[ [, ] clause] ... ]
   do-loops
[!$omp end target teams distribute parallel do simd]
```

where *clause* can be any of the clauses accepted by the **target** or **teams distribute parallel do simd** directives with identical meanings and restrictions.

If an **end target teams distribute parallel do simd** directive is not specified, an **end target teams distribute parallel do simd** directive is assumed at the end of the *do-loops*.

---- Fortran ----

Description

The semantics are identical to explicitly specifying a **target** directive immediately followed by a teams distribute parallel worksharing-loop SIMD directive.

Restrictions

The restrictions for the **target** and teams distribute parallel worksharing-loop SIMD constructs apply except for the following explicit modifications:

- If any **if** clause on the directive includes a *directive-name-modifier* then all **if** clauses on the directive must include a *directive-name-modifier*.
- At most one **if** clause without a *directive-name-modifier* can appear on the directive.
- At most one **if** clause with the **parallel** *directive-name-modifier* can appear on the directive.
- At most one **if** clause with the **target** *directive-name-modifier* can appear on the directive.

Cross References

- **target** construct, see Section 2.12.5 on page 170.
- Teams distribute parallel worksharing-loop SIMD construct, see Section 2.13.14 on page 201.
- **if** Clause, see Section 2.15 on page 220.
- Data attribute clauses, see Section 2.19.4 on page 282.

2.14 Clauses on Combined and Composite Constructs

This section specifies the handling of clauses on combined or composite constructs and the handling of implicit clauses from variables with predetermined data sharing if they are not predetermined only on a particular construct. Some clauses are permitted only on a single construct of the constructs that constitute the combined or composite construct, in which case the effect is as if the clause is applied to that specific construct. As detailed in this section, other clauses have the effect as if they are applied to one or more constituent constructs.

The **collapse** clause is applied once to the combined or composite construct.

The effect of the **private** clause is as if it is applied only to the innermost constituent construct that permits it.

The effect of the **firstprivate** clause is as if it is applied to one or more constructs as follows:

- To the **distribute** construct if it is among the constituent constructs;
- To the **teams** construct if it is among the constituent constructs and the **distribute** construct is not;
- To the worksharing-loop construct if it is among the constituent constructs;
- To the **taskloop** construct if it is among the constituent constructs;
- To the **parallel** construct if it is among the constituent constructs and the worksharing-loop construct or the **taskloop** construct is not;
- To the outermost constituent construct if not already applied to it by the above rules and the outermost constituent construct is not a **teams** construct, a **parallel** construct, a **master** construct, or a **target** construct; and
- To the **target** construct if it is among the constituent constructs and the same list item does not appear in a **lastprivate** or **map** clause.

If the **parallel** construct is among the constituent constructs and the effect is not as if the **firstprivate** clause is applied to it by the above rules, then the effect is as if the **shared** clause with the same list item is applied to the **parallel** construct. If the **teams** construct is among the constituent constructs and the effect is not as if the **firstprivate** clause is applied to it by the above rules, then the effect is as if the **shared** clause with the same list item is applied to the **teams** construct.

The effect of the **lastprivate** clause is as if it is applied to one or more constructs as follows:

- To the worksharing-loop construct if it is among the constituent constructs;
- To the **taskloop** construct if it is among the constituent constructs;
- To the **distribute** construct if it is among the constituent constructs; and
- To the innermost constituent construct that permits it unless it is a worksharing-loop or **distribute** construct.

If the **parallel** construct is among the constituent constructs and the list item is not also specified in the **firstprivate** clause, then the effect of the **lastprivate** clause is as if the **shared** clause with the same list item is applied to the **parallel** construct. If the **teams** construct is among the constituent constructs and the list item is not also specified in the **firstprivate** clause, then the effect of the **lastprivate** clause is as if the **shared** clause with the same list item is applied to the **teams** construct. If the **target** construct is among the constituent constructs and the list item is not specified in a **map** clause, the effect of the **lastprivate** clause is as if the same list item appears in a **map** clause with a *map-type* of **tofrom**.

The effect of the **shared**, **default**, **order**, or **allocate** clause is as if it is applied to all constituent constructs that permit the clause.

The effect of the **reduction** clause is as if it is applied to all constructs that permit the clause, except for the following constructs:

- The **parallel** construct, when combined with the **sections**, worksharing-loop, **loop**, or **taskloop** construct; and
- The **teams** construct, when combined with the **loop** construct.

For the **parallel** and **teams** constructs above, the effect of the **reduction** clause instead is as if each list item or, for any list item that is an array item, its corresponding base array or base pointer appears in a **shared** clause for the construct. If the **task** *reduction-modifier* is specified, the effect is as if it only modifies the behavior of the **reduction** clause on the innermost construct that constitutes the combined construct and that accepts the modifier (see Section 2.19.5.4 on page 300). If the **inscan** *reduction-modifier* is specified, the effect is as if it modifies the behavior of the **reduction** clause on all constructs of the combined construct to which the clause is applied and that accept the modifier. If a construct to which the **inscan** *reduction-modifier* is applied is combined with the **target** construct, the effect is as if the same list item also appears in a **map** clause with a *map-type* of **tofrom**.

The `in_reduction` clause is permitted on a single construct among those that constitute the combined or composite construct and the effect is as if the clause is applied to that construct, but if that construct is a `target` construct, the effect is also as if the same list item appears in a `map` clause with a *map-type* of `tofrom` and a *map-type-modifier* of `always`.

The effect of the `if` clause is described in Section 2.15 on page 220.

The effect of the `linear` clause is as if it is applied to the innermost constituent construct. Additionally, if the list item is not the iteration variable of a `simd` or worksharing-loop SIMD construct, the effect on the outer constituent constructs is as if the list item was specified in `firstprivate` and `lastprivate` clauses on the combined or composite construct, with the rules specified above applied. If a list item of the `linear` clause is the iteration variable of a `simd` or worksharing-loop SIMD construct and it is not declared in the construct, the effect on the outer constituent constructs is as if the list item was specified in a `lastprivate` clause on the combined or composite construct with the rules specified above applied.

The effect of the `nowait` clause is as if it is applied to the outermost constituent construct that permits it.

If the clauses have expressions on them, such as for various clauses where the argument of the clause is an expression, or *lower-bound*, *length*, or *stride* expressions inside array sections (or *subscript* and *stride* expressions in *subscript-triplet* for Fortran), or *linear-step* or *alignment* expressions, the expressions are evaluated immediately before the construct to which the clause has been split or duplicated per the above rules (therefore inside of the outer constituent constructs). However, the expressions inside the `num_teams` and `thread_limit` clauses are always evaluated before the outermost constituent construct.

The restriction that a list item may not appear in more than one data sharing clause with the exception of specifying a variable in both `firstprivate` and `lastprivate` clauses applies after the clauses are split or duplicated per the above rules.

2.15 `if` Clause

Summary

The semantics of an `if` clause are described in the section on the construct to which it applies. The `if` clause *directive-name-modifier* names the associated construct to which an expression applies, and is particularly useful for composite and combined constructs.

Syntax

――――――――――― C / C++ ―――――――――――

The syntax of the `if` clause is as follows:

`if ([ `*directive-name-modifier* `:] `*scalar-expression*`)`

――――――――――― C / C++ ―――――――――――
――――――――――― Fortran ―――――――――――

The syntax of the `if` clause is as follows:

`if ([ `*directive-name-modifier* `:] `*scalar-logical-expression*`)`

――――――――――― Fortran ―――――――――――

Description

The effect of the `if` clause depends on the construct to which it is applied. For combined or composite constructs, the `if` clause only applies to the semantics of the construct named in the *directive-name-modifier* if one is specified. If no *directive-name-modifier* is specified for a combined or composite construct then the `if` clause applies to all constructs to which an `if` clause can apply.

2.16 `master` Construct

Summary

The `master` construct specifies a structured block that is executed by the master thread of the team.

Syntax

――――――――――― C / C++ ―――――――――――

The syntax of the `master` construct is as follows:

```
#pragma omp master new-line
    structured-block
```

――――――――――― C / C++ ―――――――――――
――――――――――― Fortran ―――――――――――

The syntax of the `master` construct is as follows:

```
!$omp master
    structured-block
!$omp end master
```

――――――――――― Fortran ―――――――――――

Binding

The binding thread set for a **master** region is the current team. A **master** region binds to the innermost enclosing **parallel** region.

Description

Only the master thread of the team that executes the binding **parallel** region participates in the execution of the structured block of the **master** region. Other threads in the team do not execute the associated structured block. There is no implied barrier either on entry to, or exit from, the **master** construct.

Execution Model Events

The *master-begin* event occurs in the master thread of a team that encounters the **master** construct on entry to the master region.

The *master-end* event occurs in the master thread of a team that encounters the **master** construct on exit from the master region.

Tool Callbacks

A thread dispatches a registered **ompt_callback_master** callback with **ompt_scope_begin** as its *endpoint* argument for each occurrence of a *master-begin* event in that thread. Similarly, a thread dispatches a registered **ompt_callback_master** callback with **ompt_scope_end** as its *endpoint* argument for each occurrence of a *master-end* event in that thread. These callbacks occur in the context of the task executed by the master thread and have the type signature **ompt_callback_master_t**.

Restrictions

─────────────────────────── C++ ───────────────────────────

- A throw executed inside a **master** region must cause execution to resume within the same **master** region, and the same thread that threw the exception must catch it

─────────────────────────── C++ ───────────────────────────

Cross References

- **parallel** construct, see Section 2.6 on page 74.
- **ompt_scope_begin** and **ompt_scope_end**, see Section 4.4.4.11 on page 443.
- **ompt_callback_master_t**, see Section 4.5.2.12 on page 473.

2.17 Synchronization Constructs and Clauses

A synchronization construct orders the completion of code executed by different threads. This ordering is imposed by synchronizing flush operations that are executed as part of the region that corresponds to the construct.

Synchronization through the use of synchronizing flush operations and atomic operations is described in Section 1.4.4 on page 25 and Section 1.4.6 on page 28. Section 2.17.8.1 on page 246 defines the behavior of synchronizing flush operations that are implied at various other locations in an OpenMP program.

2.17.1 `critical` Construct

Summary

The `critical` construct restricts execution of the associated structured block to a single thread at a time.

Syntax

────────────────────── C / C++ ──────────────────────

The syntax of the `critical` construct is as follows:

```
#pragma omp critical [(name) [[,] hint(hint-expression)]] new-line
    structured-block
```

where *hint-expression* is an integer constant expression that evaluates to a valid synchronization hint (as described in Section 2.17.12 on page 260).

────────────────────── C / C++ ──────────────────────

────────────────────── Fortran ──────────────────────

The syntax of the `critical` construct is as follows:

```
!$omp critical [(name) [[,] hint(hint-expression)]]
    structured-block
!$omp end critical [(name)]
```

where *hint-expression* is a constant expression that evaluates to a scalar value with kind `omp_sync_hint_kind` and a value that is a valid synchronization hint (as described in Section 2.17.12 on page 260).

────────────────────── Fortran ──────────────────────

Binding

The binding thread set for a `critical` region is all threads in the contention group.

Description

The region that corresponds to a `critical` construct is executed as if only a single thread at a time among all threads in the contention group enters the region for execution, without regard to the team(s) to which the threads belong. An optional *name* may be used to identify the `critical` construct. All `critical` constructs without a name are considered to have the same unspecified name.

---------- C / C++ ----------

Identifiers used to identify a `critical` construct have external linkage and are in a name space that is separate from the name spaces used by labels, tags, members, and ordinary identifiers.

---------- C / C++ ----------

---------- Fortran ----------

The names of `critical` constructs are global entities of the program. If a name conflicts with any other entity, the behavior of the program is unspecified.

---------- Fortran ----------

The threads of a contention group execute the `critical` region as if only one thread of the contention group executes the `critical` region at a time. The `critical` construct enforces these execution semantics with respect to all `critical` constructs with the same name in all threads in the contention group.

If present, the `hint` clause gives the implementation additional information about the expected runtime properties of the `critical` region that can optionally be used to optimize the implementation. The presence of a `hint` clause does not affect the isolation guarantees provided by the `critical` construct. If no `hint` clause is specified, the effect is as if `hint(omp_sync_hint_none)` had been specified.

Execution Model Events

The *critical-acquiring* event occurs in a thread that encounters the `critical` construct on entry to the `critical` region before initiating synchronization for the region.

The *critical-acquired* event occurs in a thread that encounters the `critical` construct after it enters the region, but before it executes the structured block of the `critical` region.

The *critical-released* event occurs in a thread that encounters the `critical` construct after it completes any synchronization on exit from the `critical` region.

Tool Callbacks

A thread dispatches a registered **ompt_callback_mutex_acquire** callback for each occurrence of a *critical-acquiring* event in that thread. This callback has the type signature **ompt_callback_mutex_acquire_t**.

A thread dispatches a registered **ompt_callback_mutex_acquired** callback for each occurrence of a *critical-acquired* event in that thread. This callback has the type signature **ompt_callback_mutex_t**.

A thread dispatches a registered **ompt_callback_mutex_released** callback for each occurrence of a *critical-released* event in that thread. This callback has the type signature **ompt_callback_mutex_t**.

The callbacks occur in the task that encounters the critical construct. The callbacks should receive **ompt_mutex_critical** as their *kind* argument if practical, but a less specific kind is acceptable.

Restrictions

The following restrictions apply to the critical construct:

- Unless the effect is as if **hint(omp_sync_hint_none)** was specified, the **critical** construct must specify a name.
- If the **hint** clause is specified, each of the **critical** constructs with the same *name* must have a **hint** clause for which the *hint-expression* evaluates to the same value.

─────────────── C++ ───────────────

- A throw executed inside a **critical** region must cause execution to resume within the same **critical** region, and the same thread that threw the exception must catch it.

─────────────── C++ ───────────────

─────────────── Fortran ───────────────

- If a *name* is specified on a **critical** directive, the same *name* must also be specified on the **end critical** directive.
- If no *name* appears on the **critical** directive, no *name* can appear on the **end critical** directive.

─────────────── Fortran ───────────────

CHAPTER 2. DIRECTIVES

Cross References

- Synchronization Hints, see Section 2.17.12 on page 260.
- `ompt_mutex_critical`, see Section 4.4.4.16 on page 445.
- `ompt_callback_mutex_acquire_t`, see Section 4.5.2.14 on page 476.
- `ompt_callback_mutex_t`, see Section 4.5.2.15 on page 477.

2.17.2 `barrier` Construct

Summary

The `barrier` construct specifies an explicit barrier at the point at which the construct appears. The `barrier` construct is a stand-alone directive.

Syntax

------ C / C++ ------

The syntax of the `barrier` construct is as follows:

```
#pragma omp barrier new-line
```

------ C / C++ ------

------ Fortran ------

The syntax of the `barrier` construct is as follows:

```
!$omp barrier
```

------ Fortran ------

Binding

The binding thread set for a `barrier` region is the current team. A `barrier` region binds to the innermost enclosing `parallel` region.

Description

All threads of the team that is executing the binding `parallel` region must execute the `barrier` region and complete execution of all explicit tasks bound to this `parallel` region before any are allowed to continue execution beyond the barrier.

The `barrier` region includes an implicit task scheduling point in the current task region.

Execution Model Events

The *explicit-barrier-begin* event occurs in each thread that encounters the **barrier** construct on entry to the **barrier** region.

The *explicit-barrier-wait-begin* event occurs when a task begins an interval of active or passive waiting in a **barrier** region.

The *explicit-barrier-wait-end* event occurs when a task ends an interval of active or passive waiting and resumes execution in a **barrier** region.

The *explicit-barrier-end* event occurs in each thread that encounters the **barrier** construct after the barrier synchronization on exit from the **barrier** region.

A *cancellation* event occurs if cancellation is activated at an implicit cancellation point in a **barrier** region.

Tool Callbacks

A thread dispatches a registered **ompt_callback_sync_region** callback with **ompt_sync_region_barrier_explicit** — or **ompt_sync_region_barrier**, if the implementation cannot make a distinction — as its *kind* argument and **ompt_scope_begin** as its *endpoint* argument for each occurrence of an *explicit-barrier-begin* event in the task that encounters the **barrier** construct. Similarly, a thread dispatches a registered **ompt_callback_sync_region** callback with **ompt_sync_region_barrier_explicit** — or **ompt_sync_region_barrier**, if the implementation cannot make a distinction — as its *kind* argument and **ompt_scope_end** as its *endpoint* argument for each occurrence of an *explicit-barrier-end* event in the task that encounters the **barrier** construct. These callbacks occur in the task that encounters the **barrier** construct and have the type signature **ompt_callback_sync_region_t**.

A thread dispatches a registered **ompt_callback_sync_region_wait** callback with **ompt_sync_region_barrier_explicit** — or **ompt_sync_region_barrier**, if the implementation cannot make a distinction — as its *kind* argument and **ompt_scope_begin** as its *endpoint* argument for each occurrence of an *explicit-barrier-wait-begin* event. Similarly, a thread dispatches a registered **ompt_callback_sync_region_wait** callback with **ompt_sync_region_barrier_explicit** — or **ompt_sync_region_barrier**, if the implementation cannot make a distinction — as its *kind* argument and **ompt_scope_end** as its *endpoint* argument for each occurrence of an *explicit-barrier-wait-end* event. These callbacks occur in the context of the task that encountered the **barrier** construct and have type signature **ompt_callback_sync_region_t**.

A thread dispatches a registered **ompt_callback_cancel** callback with **ompt_cancel_detected** as its *flags* argument for each occurrence of a *cancellation* event in that thread. The callback occurs in the context of the encountering task. The callback has type signature **ompt_callback_cancel_t**.

Restrictions

The following restrictions apply to the `barrier` construct:

- Each `barrier` region must be encountered by all threads in a team or by none at all, unless cancellation has been requested for the innermost enclosing parallel region.
- The sequence of worksharing regions and `barrier` regions encountered must be the same for every thread in a team.

Cross References

- `ompt_scope_begin` and `ompt_scope_end`, see Section 4.4.4.11 on page 443.
- `ompt_sync_region_barrier`, see Section 4.4.4.13 on page 444.
- `ompt_callback_sync_region_t`, see Section 4.5.2.13 on page 474.
- `ompt_callback_cancel_t`, see Section 4.5.2.18 on page 481.

2.17.3 Implicit Barriers

This section describes the OMPT events and tool callbacks associated with implicit barriers, which occur at the end of various regions as defined in the description of the constructs to which they correspond. Implicit barriers are task scheduling points. For a description of task scheduling points, associated events, and tool callbacks, see Section 2.10.6 on page 149.

Execution Model Events

The *implicit-barrier-begin* event occurs in each implicit task at the beginning of an implicit barrier region.

The *implicit-barrier-wait-begin* event occurs when a task begins an interval of active or passive waiting in an implicit barrier region.

The *implicit-barrier-wait-end* event occurs when a task ends an interval of active or waiting and resumes execution of an implicit barrier region.

The *implicit-barrier-end* event occurs in each implicit task after the barrier synchronization on exit from an implicit barrier region.

A *cancellation* event occurs if cancellation is activated at an implicit cancellation point in an implicit barrier region.

Tool Callbacks

A thread dispatches a registered **ompt_callback_sync_region** callback with **ompt_sync_region_barrier_implicit** — or **ompt_sync_region_barrier**, if the implementation cannot make a distinction — as its *kind* argument and **ompt_scope_begin** as its *endpoint* argument for each occurrence of an *implicit-barrier-begin* event in that thread. Similarly, a thread dispatches a registered **ompt_callback_sync_region** callback with **ompt_sync_region_barrier_implicit** — or **ompt_sync_region_barrier**, if the implementation cannot make a distinction — as its *kind* argument and **ompt_scope_end** as its *endpoint* argument for each occurrence of an *implicit-barrier-end* event in that thread. These callbacks occur in the implicit task that executes the parallel region and have the type signature **ompt_callback_sync_region_t**.

A thread dispatches a registered **ompt_callback_sync_region_wait** callback with **ompt_sync_region_barrier_implicit** — or **ompt_sync_region_barrier**, if the implementation cannot make a distinction — as its *kind* argument and **ompt_scope_begin** as its *endpoint* argument for each occurrence of a *implicit-barrier-wait-begin* event in that thread. Similarly, a thread dispatches a registered **ompt_callback_sync_region_wait** callback with **ompt_sync_region_barrier_explicit** — or **ompt_sync_region_barrier**, if the implementation cannot make a distinction — as its *kind* argument and **ompt_scope_end** as its *endpoint* argument for each occurrence of an *implicit-barrier-wait-end* event in that thread. These callbacks occur in the implicit task that executes the parallel region and have type signature **ompt_callback_sync_region_t**.

A thread dispatches a registered **ompt_callback_cancel** callback with **ompt_cancel_detected** as its *flags* argument for each occurrence of a *cancellation* event in that thread. The callback occurs in the context of the encountering task. The callback has type signature **ompt_callback_cancel_t**.

Restrictions

If a thread is in the state **ompt_state_wait_barrier_implicit_parallel**, a call to **ompt_get_parallel_info** may return a pointer to a copy of the data object associated with the parallel region rather than a pointer to the associated data object itself. Writing to the data object returned by **omp_get_parallel_info** when a thread is in the **ompt_state_wait_barrier_implicit_parallel** results in unspecified behavior.

Cross References

- **ompt_scope_begin** and **ompt_scope_end**, see Section 4.4.4.11 on page 443.
- **ompt_sync_region_barrier**, see Section 4.4.4.13 on page 444
- **ompt_cancel_detected**, see Section 4.4.4.24 on page 450.
- **ompt_callback_sync_region_t**, see Section 4.5.2.13 on page 474.
- **ompt_callback_cancel_t**, see Section 4.5.2.18 on page 481.

2.17.4 Implementation-Specific Barriers

An OpenMP implementation can execute implementation-specific barriers that are not implied by the OpenMP specification; therefore, no *execution model events* are bound to these barriers. The implementation can handle these barriers like implicit barriers and dispatch all events as for implicit barriers. These callbacks are dispatched with `ompt_sync_region_barrier_implementation` — or `ompt_sync_region_barrier`, if the implementation cannot make a distinction — as the *kind* argument.

2.17.5 `taskwait` Construct

Summary

The `taskwait` construct specifies a wait on the completion of child tasks of the current task. The `taskwait` construct is a stand-alone directive.

Syntax

―――――――――――――――――――― C / C++ ――――――――――――――――――――

The syntax of the `taskwait` construct is as follows:

`#pragma omp taskwait` *[clause[[,] clause] ...] new-line*

where *clause* is one of the following:

depend (*[depend-modifier,]dependence-type* : *locator-list*)

―――――――――――――――――――― C / C++ ――――――――――――――――――――
―――――――――――――――――――― Fortran ――――――――――――――――――――

The syntax of the `taskwait` construct is as follows:

`!$omp taskwait` *[clause[[,] clause] ...]*

where *clause* is one of the following:

depend (*[depend-modifier,]dependence-type* : *locator-list*)

―――――――――――――――――――― Fortran ――――――――――――――――――――

Binding

The `taskwait` region binds to the current task region. The binding thread set of the `taskwait` region is the current team.

Description

If no **depend** clause is present on the **taskwait** construct, the current task region is suspended at an implicit task scheduling point associated with the construct. The current task region remains suspended until all child tasks that it generated before the **taskwait** region complete execution.

Otherwise, if one or more **depend** clauses are present on the **taskwait** construct, the behavior is as if these clauses were applied to a **task** construct with an empty associated structured block that generates a *mergeable* and *included task*. Thus, the current task region is suspended until the *predecessor tasks* of this task complete execution.

Execution Model Events

The *taskwait-begin* event occurs in each thread that encounters the **taskwait** construct on entry to the **taskwait** region.

The *taskwait-wait-begin* event occurs when a task begins an interval of active or passive waiting in a **taskwait** region.

The *taskwait-wait-end* event occurs when a task ends an interval of active or passive waiting and resumes execution in a **taskwait** region.

The *taskwait-end* event occurs in each thread that encounters the **taskwait** construct after the taskwait synchronization on exit from the **taskwait** region.

Tool Callbacks

A thread dispatches a registered **ompt_callback_sync_region** callback with **ompt_sync_region_taskwait** as its *kind* argument and **ompt_scope_begin** as its *endpoint* argument for each occurrence of a *taskwait-begin* event in the task that encounters the **taskwait** construct. Similarly, a thread dispatches a registered **ompt_callback_sync_region** callback with **ompt_sync_region_taskwait** as its *kind* argument and **ompt_scope_end** as its *endpoint* argument for each occurrence of a *taskwait-end* event in the task that encounters the **taskwait** construct. These callbacks occur in the task that encounters the **taskwait** construct and have the type signature **ompt_callback_sync_region_t**.

A thread dispatches a registered **ompt_callback_sync_region_wait** callback with **ompt_sync_region_taskwait** as its *kind* argument and **ompt_scope_begin** as its *endpoint* argument for each occurrence of a *taskwait-wait-begin* event. Similarly, a thread dispatches a registered **ompt_callback_sync_region_wait** callback with **ompt_sync_region_taskwait** as its *kind* argument and **ompt_scope_end** as its *endpoint* argument for each occurrence of a *taskwait-wait-end* event. These callbacks occur in the context of the task that encounters the **taskwait** construct and have type signature **ompt_callback_sync_region_t**.

Restrictions

The following restrictions apply to the **taskwait** construct:

- The **mutexinoutset** *dependence-type* may not appear in a **depend** clause on a **taskwait** construct.
- If the *dependence-type* of a **depend** clause is **depobj** then the dependence objects cannot represent dependences of the **mutexinoutset** dependence type.

Cross References

- **task** construct, see Section 2.10.1 on page 135.
- Task scheduling, see Section 2.10.6 on page 149.
- **depend** clause, see Section 2.17.11 on page 255.
- **ompt_scope_begin** and **ompt_scope_end**, see Section 4.4.4.11 on page 443.
- **ompt_sync_region_taskwait**, see Section 4.4.4.13 on page 444.
- **ompt_callback_sync_region_t**, see Section 4.5.2.13 on page 474.

2.17.6 `taskgroup` Construct

Summary

The **taskgroup** construct specifies a wait on completion of child tasks of the current task and their descendent tasks.

Syntax

―――――――――――― C / C++ ――――――――――――

The syntax of the **taskgroup** construct is as follows:

```
#pragma omp taskgroup [clause[[,] clause] ...] new-line
    structured-block
```

where *clause* is one of the following:

```
task_reduction(reduction-identifier : list)
allocate([allocator: ]list)
```

―――――――――――― C / C++ ――――――――――――

―――――――――――――――――― Fortran ――――――――――――――――――

The syntax of the **taskgroup** construct is as follows:

```
!$omp taskgroup [clause [ [ , ] clause] ...]
    structured-block
!$omp end taskgroup
```

where *clause* is one of the following:

> **task_reduction**(*reduction-identifier* : *list*)
> **allocate**([*allocator:*]*list*)

―――――――――――――――――― Fortran ――――――――――――――――――

Binding

The binding task set of a **taskgroup** region is all tasks of the current team that are generated in the region. A **taskgroup** region binds to the innermost enclosing **parallel** region.

Description

When a thread encounters a **taskgroup** construct, it starts executing the region. All child tasks generated in the **taskgroup** region and all of their descendants that bind to the same **parallel** region as the **taskgroup** region are part of the *taskgroup set* associated with the **taskgroup** region.

There is an implicit task scheduling point at the end of the **taskgroup** region. The current task is suspended at the task scheduling point until all tasks in the *taskgroup set* complete execution.

Execution Model Events

The *taskgroup-begin* event occurs in each thread that encounters the **taskgroup** construct on entry to the **taskgroup** region.

The *taskgroup-wait-begin* event occurs when a task begins an interval of active or passive waiting in a **taskgroup** region.

The *taskgroup-wait-end* event occurs when a task ends an interval of active or passive waiting and resumes execution in a **taskgroup** region.

The *taskgroup-end* event occurs in each thread that encounters the **taskgroup** construct after the taskgroup synchronization on exit from the **taskgroup** region.

Tool Callbacks

A thread dispatches a registered **ompt_callback_sync_region** callback with **ompt_sync_region_taskgroup** as its *kind* argument and **ompt_scope_begin** as its *endpoint* argument for each occurrence of a *taskgroup-begin* event in the task that encounters the **taskgroup** construct. Similarly, a thread dispatches a registered **ompt_callback_sync_region** callback with **ompt_sync_region_taskgroup** as its *kind* argument and **ompt_scope_end** as its *endpoint* argument for each occurrence of a *taskgroup-end* event in the task that encounters the **taskgroup** construct. These callbacks occur in the task that encounters the **taskgroup** construct and have the type signature **ompt_callback_sync_region_t**.

A thread dispatches a registered **ompt_callback_sync_region_wait** callback with **ompt_sync_region_taskgroup** as its *kind* argument and **ompt_scope_begin** as its *endpoint* argument for each occurrence of a *taskgroup-wait-begin* event. Similarly, a thread dispatches a registered **ompt_callback_sync_region_wait** callback with **ompt_sync_region_taskgroup** as its *kind* argument and **ompt_scope_end** as its *endpoint* argument for each occurrence of a *taskgroup-wait-end* event. These callbacks occur in the context of the task that encounters the **taskgroup** construct and have type signature **ompt_callback_sync_region_t**.

Cross References

- Task scheduling, see Section 2.10.6 on page 149.
- **task_reduction** Clause, see Section 2.19.5.5 on page 303.
- **ompt_scope_begin** and **ompt_scope_end**, see Section 4.4.4.11 on page 443.
- **ompt_sync_region_taskgroup**, see Section 4.4.4.13 on page 444.
- **ompt_callback_sync_region_t**, see Section 4.5.2.13 on page 474.

2.17.7 atomic Construct

Summary

The **atomic** construct ensures that a specific storage location is accessed atomically, rather than exposing it to the possibility of multiple, simultaneous reading and writing threads that may result in indeterminate values.

Syntax

In the following syntax, *atomic-clause* is a clause that indicates the semantics for which atomicity is enforced, *memory-order-clause* is a clause that indicates the memory ordering behavior of the construct and *clause* is a clause other than *atomic-clause*. Specifically, *atomic-clause* is one of the following:

> read
> write
> update
> capture

memory-order-clause is one of the following:

> seq_cst
> acq_rel
> release
> acquire
> relaxed

and *clause* is either *memory-order-clause* or one of the following:

> hint (*hint-expression*)

──────────── C / C++ ────────────

The syntax of the **atomic** construct takes one of the following forms:

> #pragma omp atomic *[clause[[,] clause] ...] [,]] atomic-clause*
>   *[[,] clause [[,] clause] ...]] new-line*
>   *expression-stmt*

or

> #pragma omp atomic *[clause[[,] clause] ...] new-line*
>   *expression-stmt*

or

> #pragma omp atomic *[clause[[,] clause] ...] [,]]* **capture**
>   *[[,] clause [[,] clause] ...]] new-line*
>   *structured-block*

where *expression-stmt* is an expression statement with one of the following forms:

- If *atomic-clause* is **read**:

> v = x;

---------- C/C++ (cont.) ----------

- If *atomic-clause* is **write**:

  $x = expr;$

- If *atomic-clause* is **update** or not present:

  $x\text{++};$
  $x\text{--};$
  $\text{++}x;$
  $\text{--}x;$
  $x \; binop\text{=} \; expr;$
  $x = x \; binop \; expr;$
  $x = expr \; binop \; x;$

- If *atomic-clause* is **capture**:

  $v = x\text{++};$
  $v = x\text{--};$
  $v = \text{++}x;$
  $v = \text{--}x;$
  $v = x \; binop\text{=} \; expr;$
  $v = x = x \; binop \; expr;$
  $v = x = expr \; binop \; x;$

  and where *structured-block* is a structured block with one of the following forms:

  { $v = x;\; x \; binop\text{=} \; expr;$ }
  { $x \; binop\text{=} \; expr;\; v = x;$ }
  { $v = x;\; x = x \; binop \; expr;$ }
  { $v = x;\; x = expr \; binop \; x;$ }
  { $x = x \; binop \; expr;\; v = x;$ }
  { $x = expr \; binop \; x;\; v = x;$ }
  { $v = x;\; x = expr;$ }
  { $v = x;\; x\text{++};$ }
  { $v = x;\; \text{++}x;$ }
  { $\text{++}x;\; v = x;$ }
  { $x\text{++};\; v = x;$ }
  { $v = x;\; x\text{--};$ }
  { $v = x;\; \text{--}x;$ }
  { $\text{--}x;\; v = x;$ }
  { $x\text{--};\; v = x;$ }

In the preceding expressions:

- *x* and *v* (as applicable) are both *l-value* expressions with scalar type.

- During the execution of an atomic region, multiple syntactic occurrences of *x* must designate the same storage location.

- Neither of *v* and *expr* (as applicable) may access the storage location designated by *x*.
- Neither of *x* and *expr* (as applicable) may access the storage location designated by *v*.
- *expr* is an expression with scalar type.
- *binop* is one of +, *, −, /, &, ^, |, <<, or >>.
- *binop*, *binop*=, ++, and −− are not overloaded operators.
- The expression *x binop expr* must be numerically equivalent to *x binop (expr)*. This requirement is satisfied if the operators in *expr* have precedence greater than *binop*, or by using parentheses around *expr* or subexpressions of *expr*.
- The expression *expr binop x* must be numerically equivalent to *(expr) binop x*. This requirement is satisfied if the operators in *expr* have precedence equal to or greater than *binop*, or by using parentheses around *expr* or subexpressions of *expr*.
- For forms that allow multiple occurrences of *x*, the number of times that *x* is evaluated is unspecified.
- *hint-expression* is a constant integer expression that evaluates to a valid synchronization hint.

―― C / C++ ――

―― Fortran ――

The syntax of the **atomic** construct takes any of the following forms:

```
!$omp atomic [clause[[,] clause] ... ] [,]] read [[,] clause [[,] clause] ... ]]
    capture-statement
[!$omp end atomic]
```

or

```
!$omp atomic [clause[[,] clause] ... ] [,]] write [[,] clause [[,] clause] ... ]]
    write-statement
[!$omp end atomic]
```

or

```
!$omp atomic [clause[[,] clause] ... ] [,]] update [[,] clause [[,] clause] ... ]]
    update-statement
[!$omp end atomic]
```

or

```
!$omp atomic [clause[[,] clause] ... ]
    update-statement
[!$omp end atomic]
```

or

▼ ------------------------------ Fortran (cont.) ------------------------------ ▼

```
!$omp atomic [clause[[,] clause] ... ] [,]] capture [[,] clause [[[,] clause] ... ]]
    update-statement
    capture-statement
!$omp end atomic
```

or

```
!$omp atomic [clause[[,] clause] ... ] [,]] capture [[,] clause [[[,] clause] ... ]]
    capture-statement
    update-statement
!$omp end atomic
```

or

```
!$omp atomic [clause[[,] clause] ... ] [,]] capture [[,] clause [[[,] clause] ... ]]
    capture-statement
    write-statement
!$omp end atomic
```

where *write-statement* has the following form (if *atomic-clause* is **capture** or **write**):

$x = expr$

where *capture-statement* has the following form (if *atomic-clause* is **capture** or **read**):

$v = x$

and where *update-statement* has one of the following forms (if *atomic-clause* is **update**, **capture**, or not present):

$x = x\ operator\ expr$

$x = expr\ operator\ x$

$x = intrinsic\_procedure\_name\ (x,\ expr\_list)$

$x = intrinsic\_procedure\_name\ (expr\_list,\ x)$

In the preceding statements:

- x and v (as applicable) are both scalar variables of intrinsic type.
- x must not have the **ALLOCATABLE** attribute.
- During the execution of an atomic region, multiple syntactic occurrences of x must designate the same storage location.
- None of v, *expr*, and *expr_list* (as applicable) may access the same storage location as x.

- None of *x*, *expr*, and *expr_list* (as applicable) may access the same storage location as *v*.
- *expr* is a scalar expression.
- *expr_list* is a comma-separated, non-empty list of scalar expressions. If *intrinsic_procedure_name* refers to **IAND**, **IOR**, or **IEOR**, exactly one expression must appear in *expr_list*.
- *intrinsic_procedure_name* is one of **MAX**, **MIN**, **IAND**, **IOR**, or **IEOR**.
- *operator* is one of **+**, *****, **−**, **/**, **.AND.**, **.OR.**, **.EQV.**, or **.NEQV.**.
- The expression *x operator expr* must be numerically equivalent to *x operator (expr)*. This requirement is satisfied if the operators in *expr* have precedence greater than *operator*, or by using parentheses around *expr* or subexpressions of *expr*.
- The expression *expr operator x* must be numerically equivalent to *(expr) operator x*. This requirement is satisfied if the operators in *expr* have precedence equal to or greater than *operator*, or by using parentheses around *expr* or subexpressions of *expr*.
- *intrinsic_procedure_name* must refer to the intrinsic procedure name and not to other program entities.
- *operator* must refer to the intrinsic operator and not to a user-defined operator.
- All assignments must be intrinsic assignments.
- For forms that allow multiple occurrences of *x*, the number of times that *x* is evaluated is unspecified.
- *hint-expression* is a constant expression that evaluates to a scalar value with kind **omp_sync_hint_kind** and a value that is a valid synchronization hint.

―――――――――――――――― Fortran ――――――――――――――――

Binding

If the size of *x* is 8, 16, 32, or 64 bits and *x* is aligned to a multiple of its size, the binding thread set for the **atomic** region is all threads on the device. Otherwise, the binding thread set for the **atomic** region is all threads in the contention group. **atomic** regions enforce exclusive access with respect to other **atomic** regions that access the same storage location *x* among all threads in the binding thread set without regard to the teams to which the threads belong.

Description

If *atomic-clause* is not present on the construct, the behavior is as if the **update** clause is specified.

The **atomic** construct with the **read** clause results in an atomic read of the location designated by *x* regardless of the native machine word size.

The **atomic** construct with the **write** clause results in an atomic write of the location designated by *x* regardless of the native machine word size.

The **atomic** construct with the **update** clause results in an atomic update of the location designated by *x* using the designated operator or intrinsic. Only the read and write of the location designated by *x* are performed mutually atomically. The evaluation of *expr* or *expr_list* need not be atomic with respect to the read or write of the location designated by *x*. No task scheduling points are allowed between the read and the write of the location designated by *x*.

The **atomic** construct with the **capture** clause results in an atomic captured update — an atomic update of the location designated by *x* using the designated operator or intrinsic while also capturing the original or final value of the location designated by *x* with respect to the atomic update. The original or final value of the location designated by *x* is written in the location designated by *v* based on the base language semantics of structured block or statements of the **atomic** construct. Only the read and write of the location designated by *x* are performed mutually atomically. Neither the evaluation of *expr* or *expr_list*, nor the write to the location designated by *v*, need be atomic with respect to the read or write of the location designated by *x*. No task scheduling points are allowed between the read and the write of the location designated by *x*.

The **atomic** construct may be used to enforce memory consistency between threads, based on the guarantees provided by Section 1.4.6 on page 28. A strong flush on the location designated by *x* is performed on entry to and exit from the atomic operation, ensuring that the set of all atomic operations in the program applied to the same location has a total completion order. If the **write**, **update**, or **capture** clause is specified and the **release**, **acq_rel**, or **seq_cst** clause is specified then the strong flush on entry to the atomic operation is also a release flush. If the **read** or **capture** clause is specified and the **acquire**, **acq_rel**, or **seq_cst** clause is specified then the strong flush on exit from the atomic operation is also an acquire flush. Therefore, if *memory-order-clause* is specified and is not **relaxed**, release and/or acquire flush operations are implied and permit synchronization between the threads without the use of explicit **flush** directives.

For all forms of the **atomic** construct, any combination of two or more of these **atomic** constructs enforces mutually exclusive access to the locations designated by *x* among threads in the binding thread set. To avoid data races, all accesses of the locations designated by *x* that could potentially occur in parallel must be protected with an **atomic** construct.

atomic regions do not guarantee exclusive access with respect to any accesses outside of **atomic** regions to the same storage location *x* even if those accesses occur during a **critical** or **ordered** region, while an OpenMP lock is owned by the executing task, or during the execution of a **reduction** clause.

However, other OpenMP synchronization can ensure the desired exclusive access. For example, a barrier that follows a series of atomic updates to *x* guarantees that subsequent accesses do not form a race with the atomic accesses.

A compliant implementation may enforce exclusive access between **atomic** regions that update different storage locations. The circumstances under which this occurs are implementation defined.

If the storage location designated by *x* is not size-aligned (that is, if the byte alignment of *x* is not a multiple of the size of *x*), then the behavior of the **atomic** region is implementation defined.

If present, the **hint** clause gives the implementation additional information about the expected properties of the atomic operation that can optionally be used to optimize the implementation. The presence of a **hint** clause does not affect the semantics of the **atomic** construct, and all hints may be ignored. If no **hint** clause is specified, the effect is as if
hint(omp_sync_hint_none) had been specified.

Execution Model Events

The *atomic-acquiring* event occurs in the thread that encounters the **atomic** construct on entry to the atomic region before initiating synchronization for the region.

The *atomic-acquired* event occurs in the thread that encounters the **atomic** construct after it enters the region, but before it executes the structured block of the **atomic** region.

The *atomic-released* event occurs in the thread that encounters the **atomic** construct after it completes any synchronization on exit from the **atomic** region.

Tool Callbacks

A thread dispatches a registered **ompt_callback_mutex_acquire** callback for each occurrence of an *atomic-acquiring* event in that thread. This callback has the type signature **ompt_callback_mutex_acquire_t**.

A thread dispatches a registered **ompt_callback_mutex_acquired** callback for each occurrence of an *atomic-acquired* event in that thread. This callback has the type signature **ompt_callback_mutex_t**.

A thread dispatches a registered **ompt_callback_mutex_released** callback with **ompt_mutex_atomic** as the *kind* argument if practical, although a less specific *kind* may be used, for each occurrence of an *atomic-released* event in that thread. This callback has the type signature **ompt_callback_mutex_t** and occurs in the task that encounters the atomic construct.

Restrictions

The following restrictions apply to the **atomic** construct:

- OpenMP constructs may not be encountered during execution of an **atomic** region.
- At most one *memory-order-clause* may appear on the construct.
- At most one **hint** clause may appear on the construct.
- If *atomic-clause* is **read** then *memory-order-clause* must not be **acq_rel** or **release**.

- If *atomic-clause* is **write** then *memory-order-clause* must not be **acq_rel** or **acquire**.
- If *atomic-clause* is **update** or not present then *memory-order-clause* must not be **acq_rel** or **acquire**.

―――――――――――――――― C / C++ ――――――――――――――――
- All atomic accesses to the storage locations designated by x throughout the program are required to have a compatible type.
―――――――――――――――― C / C++ ――――――――――――――――

―――――――――――――――― Fortran ――――――――――――――――
- All atomic accesses to the storage locations designated by x throughout the program are required to have the same type and type parameters.
―――――――――――――――― Fortran ――――――――――――――――

Cross References

- **critical** construct, see Section 2.17.1 on page 223.
- **barrier** construct, see Section 2.17.2 on page 226.
- **flush** construct, see Section 2.17.8 on page 242.
- **ordered** construct, see Section 2.17.9 on page 250.
- Synchronization Hints, see Section 2.17.12 on page 260.
- **reduction** clause, see Section 2.19.5.4 on page 300.
- lock routines, see Section 3.3 on page 381.
- **ompt_mutex_atomic**, see Section 4.4.4.16 on page 445.
- **ompt_callback_mutex_acquire_t**, see Section 4.5.2.14 on page 476.
- **ompt_callback_mutex_t**, see Section 4.5.2.15 on page 477.

2.17.8 flush Construct

Summary

The **flush** construct executes the OpenMP flush operation. This operation makes a thread's temporary view of memory consistent with memory and enforces an order on the memory operations of the variables explicitly specified or implied. See the memory model description in Section 1.4 on page 23 for more details. The **flush** construct is a stand-alone directive.

Syntax

--- C / C++ ---

The syntax of the **flush** construct is as follows:

#pragma omp flush *[memory-order-clause]* *[* **(***list***)** *] new-line*

where *memory-order-clause* is one of the following:

> acq_rel
> release
> acquire

--- C / C++ ---

--- Fortran ---

The syntax of the **flush** construct is as follows:

!$omp flush *[memory-order-clause]* *[* **(***list***)** *]*

where *memory-order-clause* is one of the following:

> acq_rel
> release
> acquire

--- Fortran ---

Binding

The binding thread set for a **flush** region is the encountering thread. Execution of a **flush** region affects the memory and the temporary view of memory of only the thread that executes the region. It does not affect the temporary view of other threads. Other threads must themselves execute a flush operation in order to be guaranteed to observe the effects of the flush operation of the encountering thread.

Description

If *memory-order-clause* is not specified then the **flush** construct results in a strong flush operation with the following behavior. A **flush** construct without a list, executed on a given thread, operates as if the whole thread-visible data state of the program, as defined by the base language, is flushed. A **flush** construct with a list applies the flush operation to the items in the list, and the flush operation does not complete until the operation is complete for all specified list items. An implementation may implement a **flush** with a list by ignoring the list, and treating it the same as a **flush** without a list.

If no list items are specified, the flush operation has the release and/or acquire flush properties:

- If *memory-order-clause* is not specified or is **acq_rel**, the flush operation is both a release flush and an acquire flush.
- If *memory-order-clause* is **release**, the flush operation is a release flush.
- If *memory-order-clause* is **acquire**, the flush operation is an acquire flush.

─────────────── C / C++ ───────────────

If a pointer is present in the list, the pointer itself is flushed, not the memory block to which the pointer refers.

─────────────── C / C++ ───────────────
─────────────── Fortran ───────────────

If the list item or a subobject of the list item has the **POINTER** attribute, the allocation or association status of the **POINTER** item is flushed, but the pointer target is not. If the list item is a Cray pointer, the pointer is flushed, but the object to which it points is not. If the list item is of type **C_PTR**, the variable is flushed, but the storage that corresponds to that address is not flushed. If the list item or the subobject of the list item has the **ALLOCATABLE** attribute and has an allocation status of allocated, the allocated variable is flushed; otherwise the allocation status is flushed.

─────────────── Fortran ───────────────

Note – Use of a **flush** construct with a list is extremely error prone and users are strongly discouraged from attempting it. The following examples illustrate the ordering properties of the flush operation. In the following incorrect pseudocode example, the programmer intends to prevent simultaneous execution of the protected section by the two threads, but the program does not work properly because it does not enforce the proper ordering of the operations on variables **a** and **b**. Any shared data accessed in the protected section is not guaranteed to be current or consistent during or after the protected section. The atomic notation in the pseudocode in the following two examples indicates that the accesses to **a** and **b** are atomic write and atomic read operations. Otherwise both examples would contain data races and automatically result in unspecified behavior. The *flush* operations are strong flushes that are applied to the specified flush lists

> *Incorrect example:*
>
> $$a = b = 0$$
>
> | thread 1 | thread 2 |
> |---|---|
> | `atomic(b = 1)` | `atomic(a = 1)` |
> | *flush*(b) | *flush*(a) |
> | *flush*(a) | *flush*(b) |
> | `atomic(tmp = a)` | `atomic(tmp = b)` |
> | `if (tmp == 0) then` | `if (tmp == 0) then` |
> | *protected section* | *protected section* |
> | `end if` | `end if` |

The problem with this example is that operations on variables **a** and **b** are not ordered with respect to each other. For instance, nothing prevents the compiler from moving the flush of **b** on thread 1 or the flush of **a** on thread 2 to a position completely after the protected section (assuming that the protected section on thread 1 does not reference **b** and the protected section on thread 2 does not reference **a**). If either re-ordering happens, both threads can simultaneously execute the protected section.

The following pseudocode example correctly ensures that the protected section is executed by not more than one of the two threads at any one time. Execution of the protected section by neither thread is considered correct in this example. This occurs if both flushes complete prior to either thread executing its `if` statement.

> *Correct example:*
>
> $$a = b = 0$$
>
> | thread 1 | thread 2 |
> |---|---|
> | `atomic(b = 1)` | `atomic(a = 1)` |
> | *flush*(a,b) | *flush*(a,b) |
> | `atomic(tmp = a)` | `atomic(tmp = b)` |
> | `if (tmp == 0) then` | `if (tmp == 0) then` |
> | *protected section* | *protected section* |
> | `end if` | `end if` |

The compiler is prohibited from moving the flush at all for either thread, ensuring that the respective assignment is complete and the data is flushed before the `if` statement is executed.

Execution Model Events

The *flush* event occurs in a thread that encounters the `flush` construct.

Tool Callbacks

A thread dispatches a registered `ompt_callback_flush` callback for each occurrence of a *flush* event in that thread. This callback has the type signature `ompt_callback_flush_t`.

Restrictions

The following restrictions apply to the `flush` construct:

- If *memory-order-clause* is `release`, `acquire`, or `acq_rel`, list items must not be specified on the `flush` directive.

Cross References

- `ompt_callback_flush_t`, see Section 4.5.2.17 on page 480.

2.17.8.1 Implicit Flushes

Flush operations implied when executing an `atomic` region are described in Section 2.17.7.

A `flush` region that corresponds to a `flush` directive with the `release` clause present is implied at the following locations:

- During a barrier region;
- At entry to a `parallel` region;
- At entry to a `teams` region;
- At exit from a `critical` region;
- During an `omp_unset_lock` region;
- During an `omp_unset_nest_lock` region;
- Immediately before every task scheduling point;

- At exit from the task region of each implicit task;
- At exit from an **ordered** region, if a **threads** clause or a **depend** clause with a **source** dependence type is present, or if no clauses are present; and
- During a **cancel** region, if the *cancel-var* ICV is *true*.

A **flush** region that corresponds to a **flush** directive with the **acquire** clause present is implied at the following locations:

- During a barrier region;
- At exit from a **teams** region;
- At entry to a **critical** region;
- If the region causes the lock to be set, during:
  - an **omp_set_lock** region;
  - an **omp_test_lock** region;
  - an **omp_set_nest_lock** region; and
  - an **omp_test_nest_lock** region;
- Immediately after every task scheduling point;
- At entry to the task region of each implicit task;
- At entry to an **ordered** region, if a **threads** clause or a **depend** clause with a **sink** dependence type is present, or if no clauses are present; and
- Immediately before a cancellation point, if the *cancel-var* ICV is *true* and cancellation has been activated.

Note – A **flush** region is not implied at the following locations:

- At entry to worksharing regions; and
- At entry to or exit from **master** regions.

The synchronization behavior of implicit flushes is as follows:

- When a thread executes an **atomic** region for which the corresponding construct has the **release**, **acq_rel**, or **seq_cst** clause and specifies an atomic operation that starts a given release sequence, the release flush that is performed on entry to the atomic operation synchronizes with an acquire flush that is performed by a different thread and has an associated atomic operation that reads a value written by a modification in the release sequence.

- When a thread executes an **atomic** region for which the corresponding construct has the **acquire**, **acq_rel**, or **seq_cst** clause and specifies an atomic operation that reads a value written by a given modification, a release flush that is performed by a different thread and has an associated release sequence that contains that modification synchronizes with the acquire flush that is performed on exit from the atomic operation.

- When a thread executes a **critical** region that has a given name, the behavior is as if the release flush performed on exit from the region synchronizes with the acquire flush performed on entry to the next **critical** region with the same name that is performed by a different thread, if it exists.

- When a thread team executes a **barrier** region, the behavior is as if the release flush performed by each thread within the region synchronizes with the acquire flush performed by all other threads within the region.

- When a thread executes a **taskwait** region that does not result in the creation of a dependent task, the behavior is as if each thread that executes a remaining child task performs a release flush upon completion of the child task that synchronizes with an acquire flush performed in the **taskwait** region.

- When a thread executes a **taskgroup** region, the behavior is as if each thread that executes a remaining descendant task performs a release flush upon completion of the descendant task that synchronizes with an acquire flush performed on exit from the **taskgroup** region.

- When a thread executes an **ordered** region that does not arise from a stand-alone **ordered** directive, the behavior is as if the release flush performed on exit from the region synchronizes with the acquire flush performed on entry to an **ordered** region encountered in the next logical iteration to be executed by a different thread, if it exists.

- When a thread executes an **ordered** region that arises from a stand-alone **ordered** directive, the behavior is as if the release flush performed in the **ordered** region from a given source iteration synchronizes with the acquire flush performed in all **ordered** regions executed by a different thread that are waiting for dependences on that iteration to be satisfied.

- When a thread team begins execution of a **parallel** region, the behavior is as if the release flush performed by the master thread on entry to the **parallel** region synchronizes with the acquire flush performed on entry to each implicit task that is assigned to a different thread.

- When an initial thread begins execution of a **target** region that is generated by a different thread from a target task, the behavior is as if the release flush performed by the generating thread in the target task synchronizes with the acquire flush performed by the initial thread on entry to its initial task region.

- When an initial thread completes execution of a **target** region that is generated by a different thread from a target task, the behavior is as if the release flush performed by the initial thread on exit from its initial task region synchronizes with the acquire flush performed by the generating thread in the target task.

- When a thread encounters a **teams** construct, the behavior is as if the release flush performed by the thread on entry to the **teams** region synchronizes with the acquire flush performed on entry to each initial task that is executed by a different initial thread that participates in the execution of the **teams** region.
- When a thread that encounters a **teams** construct reaches the end of the **teams** region, the behavior is as if the release flush performed by each different participating initial thread at exit from its initial task synchronizes with the acquire flush performed by the thread at exit from the **teams** region.
- When a task generates an explicit task that begins execution on a different thread, the behavior is as if the thread that is executing the generating task performs a release flush that synchronizes with the acquire flush performed by the thread that begins to execute the explicit task.
- When an undeferred task completes execution on a given thread that is different from the thread on which its generating task is suspended, the behavior is as if a release flush performed by the thread that completes execution of the undeferred task synchronizes with an acquire flush performed by the thread that resumes execution of the generating task.
- When a dependent task with one or more predecessor tasks begins execution on a given thread, the behavior is as if each release flush performed by a different thread on completion of a predecessor task synchronizes with the acquire flush performed by the thread that begins to execute the dependent task.
- When a task begins execution on a given thread and it is mutually exclusive with respect to another sibling task that is executed by a different thread, the behavior is as if each release flush performed on completion of the sibling task synchronizes with the acquire flush performed by the thread that begins to execute the task.
- When a thread executes a **cancel** region, the *cancel-var* ICV is *true*, and cancellation is not already activated for the specified region, the behavior is as if the release flush performed during the **cancel** region synchronizes with the acquire flush performed by a different thread immediately before a cancellation point in which that thread observes cancellation was activated for the region.
- When a thread executes an **omp_unset_lock** region that causes the specified lock to be unset, the behavior is as if a release flush is performed during the **omp_unset_lock** region that synchronizes with an acquire flush that is performed during the next **omp_set_lock** or **omp_test_lock** region to be executed by a different thread that causes the specified lock to be set.
- When a thread executes an **omp_unset_nest_lock** region that causes the specified nested lock to be unset, the behavior is as if a release flush is performed during the **omp_unset_nest_lock** region that synchronizes with an acquire flush that is performed during the next **omp_set_nest_lock** or **omp_test_nest_lock** region to be executed by a different thread that causes the specified nested lock to be set.

2.17.9 `ordered` Construct

Summary

The **ordered** construct either specifies a structured block in a worksharing-loop, **simd**, or worksharing-loop SIMD region that will be executed in the order of the loop iterations, or it is a stand-alone directive that specifies cross-iteration dependences in a doacross loop nest. The **ordered** construct sequentializes and orders the execution of **ordered** regions while allowing code outside the region to run in parallel.

Syntax

───────── C / C++ ─────────

The syntax of the **ordered** construct is as follows:

```
#pragma omp ordered [clause[ [,] clause] ] new-line
    structured-block
```

where *clause* is one of the following:

```
threads
simd
```

or

```
#pragma omp ordered clause [[[,] clause] ... ] new-line
```

where *clause* is one of the following:

```
depend(source)
depend(sink : vec)
```

───────── C / C++ ─────────
───────── Fortran ─────────

The syntax of the **ordered** construct is as follows:

```
!$omp ordered [clause[ [,] clause] ]
    structured-block
!$omp end ordered
```

where *clause* is one of the following:

```
threads
simd
```

or

```
!$omp ordered clause [[[,] clause] ... ]
```

where *clause* is one of the following:

```
depend(source)
depend(sink : vec)
```

───────────────────────────── Fortran ─────────────────────────────

If the **depend** clause is specified, the **ordered** construct is a stand-alone directive.

Binding

The binding thread set for an **ordered** region is the current team. An **ordered** region binds to the innermost enclosing **simd** or worksharing-loop SIMD region if the **simd** clause is present, and otherwise it binds to the innermost enclosing worksharing-loop region. **ordered** regions that bind to different regions execute independently of each other.

Description

If no clause is specified, the **ordered** construct behaves as if the **threads** clause had been specified. If the **threads** clause is specified, the threads in the team that is executing the worksharing-loop region execute **ordered** regions sequentially in the order of the loop iterations. If any **depend** clauses are specified then those clauses specify the order in which the threads in the team execute **ordered** regions. If the **simd** clause is specified, the **ordered** regions encountered by any thread will execute one at a time in the order of the loop iterations.

When the thread that is executing the first iteration of the loop encounters an **ordered** construct, it can enter the **ordered** region without waiting. When a thread that is executing any subsequent iteration encounters an **ordered** construct without a **depend** clause, it waits at the beginning of the **ordered** region until execution of all **ordered** regions belonging to all previous iterations has completed. When a thread that is executing any subsequent iteration encounters an **ordered** construct with one or more **depend(sink:***vec***)** clauses, it waits until its dependences on all valid iterations specified by the **depend** clauses are satisfied before it completes execution of the **ordered** region. A specific dependence is satisfied when a thread that is executing the corresponding iteration encounters an **ordered** construct with a **depend(source)** clause.

Execution Model Events

The *ordered-acquiring* event occurs in the task that encounters the **ordered** construct on entry to the ordered region before it initiates synchronization for the region.

The *ordered-acquired* event occurs in the task that encounters the **ordered** construct after it enters the region, but before it executes the structured block of the **ordered** region.

The *ordered-released* event occurs in the task that encounters the **ordered** construct after it completes any synchronization on exit from the **ordered** region.

The *doacross-sink* event occurs in the task that encounters a **ordered** construct for each **depend(sink:***vec***)** clause after the dependence is fulfilled.

The *doacross-source* event occurs in the task that encounters a **ordered** construct with a **depend(source:***vec***)** clause before signaling the dependence to be fulfilled.

Tool Callbacks

A thread dispatches a registered **ompt_callback_mutex_acquire** callback for each occurrence of an *ordered-acquiring* event in that thread. This callback has the type signature **ompt_callback_mutex_acquire_t**.

A thread dispatches a registered **ompt_callback_mutex_acquired** callback for each occurrence of an *ordered-acquired* event in that thread. This callback has the type signature **ompt_callback_mutex_t**.

A thread dispatches a registered **ompt_callback_mutex_released** callback with **ompt_mutex_ordered** as the *kind* argument if practical, although a less specific kind may be used, for each occurrence of an *ordered-released* event in that thread. This callback has the type signature **ompt_callback_mutex_t** and occurs in the task that encounters the atomic construct.

A thread dispatches a registered **ompt_callback_dependences** callback with all vector entries listed as **ompt_dependence_type_sink** in the *deps* argument for each occurrence of a *doacross-sink* event in that thread. A thread dispatches a registered **ompt_callback_dependences** callback with all vector entries listed as **ompt_dependence_type_source** in the *deps* argument for each occurrence of a *doacross-source* event in that thread. These callbacks have the type signature **ompt_callback_dependences_t**.

Restrictions

Restrictions to the **ordered** construct are as follows:

- At most one **threads** clause can appear on an **ordered** construct.
- At most one **simd** clause can appear on an **ordered** construct.
- At most one **depend(source)** clause can appear on an **ordered** construct.
- The construct corresponding to the binding region of an **ordered** region must not specify a **reduction** clause with the **inscan** modifier.
- Either **depend(sink:***vec***)** clauses or **depend(source)** clauses may appear on an **ordered** construct, but not both.

- The worksharing-loop or worksharing-loop SIMD region to which an **ordered** region corresponding to an **ordered** construct without a **depend** clause binds must have an **ordered** clause without the parameter specified on the corresponding worksharing-loop or worksharing-loop SIMD directive.
- The worksharing-loop region to which an **ordered** region corresponding to an **ordered** construct with any **depend** clauses binds must have an **ordered** clause with the parameter specified on the corresponding worksharing-loop directive.
- An **ordered** construct with the **depend** clause specified must be closely nested inside a worksharing-loop (or parallel worksharing-loop) construct.
- An **ordered** region corresponding to an **ordered** construct without the **simd** clause specified must be closely nested inside a loop region.
- An **ordered** region corresponding to an **ordered** construct with the **simd** clause specified must be closely nested inside a **simd** or worksharing-loop SIMD region.
- An **ordered** region corresponding to an **ordered** construct with both the **simd** and **threads** clauses must be closely nested inside a worksharing-loop SIMD region or must be closely nested inside a worksharing-loop and **simd** region.
- During execution of an iteration of a worksharing-loop or a loop nest within a worksharing-loop, **simd**, or worksharing-loop SIMD region, a thread must not execute more than one **ordered** region corresponding to an **ordered** construct without a **depend** clause.

──────── C++ ────────

- A throw executed inside a **ordered** region must cause execution to resume within the same **ordered** region, and the same thread that threw the exception must catch it.

──────── C++ ────────

Cross References

- worksharing-loop construct, see Section 2.9.2 on page 101.
- **simd** construct, see Section 2.9.3.1 on page 110.
- parallel Worksharing-loop construct, see Section 2.13.1 on page 185.
- **depend** Clause, see Section 2.17.11 on page 255
- **ompt_mutex_ordered**, see Section 4.4.4.16 on page 445.
- **ompt_callback_mutex_acquire_t**, see Section 4.5.2.14 on page 476.
- **ompt_callback_mutex_t**, see Section 4.5.2.15 on page 477.

2.17.10 Depend Objects

This section describes constructs that support OpenMP depend objects that can be used to supply user-computed dependences to **depend** clauses. OpenMP depend objects must be accessed only through the **depobj** construct or through the **depend** clause; programs that otherwise access OpenMP depend objects are non-conforming.

An OpenMP depend object can be in one of the following states: *uninitialized* or *initialized*. Initially OpenMP depend objects are in the *uninitialized* state.

2.17.10.1 depobj Construct

Summary

The **depobj** construct initializes, updates or destroys an OpenMP depend object. The **depobj** construct is a stand-alone directive.

Syntax

───────────── C / C++ ─────────────

The syntax of the **depobj** construct is as follows:

#pragma omp depobj(*depobj*)   *clause new-line*

where *depobj* is an lvalue expression of type **omp_depend_t**.

where *clause* is one of the following:

> **depend**(*dependence-type* : *locator*)
> **destroy**
> **update**(*dependence-type*)

───────────── C / C++ ─────────────
───────────── Fortran ─────────────

The syntax of the **depobj** construct is as follows:

!$omp depobj(*depobj*)   *clause*

where *depobj* is a scalar integer variable of the **omp_depend_kind** kind.

where *clause* is one of the following:

> **depend**(*dependence-type* : *locator*)
> **destroy**
> **update**(*dependence-type*)

───────────── Fortran ─────────────

Binding

The binding thread set for **depobj** regions is the encountering thread.

Description

A **depobj** construct with a **depend** clause present sets the state of *depobj* to initialized. The *depobj* is initialized to represent the dependence that the **depend** clause specifies.

A **depobj** construct with a **destroy** clause present changes the state of the *depobj* to uninitialized.

A **depobj** construct with an **update** clause present changes the dependence type of the dependence represented by *depobj* to the one specified by the *update* clause.

Restrictions

- A **depend** clause on a **depobj** construct must not have **source**, **sink** or **depobj** as *dependence-type*.
- A **depend** clause on a **depobj** construct can only specify one locator.
- The *depobj* of a **depobj** construct with the **depend** clause present must be in the uninitialized state.
- The *depobj* of a **depobj** construct with the **destroy** clause present must be in the initialized state.
- The *depobj* of a **depobj** construct with the **update** clause present must be in the initialized state.

Cross References

- **depend** clause, see Section 2.17.11 on page 255.

2.17.11 depend Clause

Summary

The **depend** clause enforces additional constraints on the scheduling of tasks or loop iterations. These constraints establish dependences only between sibling tasks or between loop iterations.

Syntax

The syntax of the **depend** clause is as follows:

depend (*[depend-modifier,] dependence-type* : *locator-list*)

where *dependence-type* is one of the following:

> `in`
> `out`
> `inout`
> `mutexinoutset`
> `depobj`

where *depend-modifier* is one of the following:

> `iterator` (*iterators-definition*)

or

depend (*dependence-type*)

where *dependence-type* is:

> `source`

or

depend (*dependence-type* : *vec*)

where *dependence-type* is:

> `sink`

and where *vec* is the iteration vector, which has the form:

$x_1 [\pm d_1], x_2 [\pm d_2], \ldots, x_n [\pm d_n]$

where n is the value specified by the **ordered** clause in the worksharing-loop directive, x_i denotes the loop iteration variable of the i-th nested loop associated with the worksharing-loop directive, and d_i is a constant non-negative integer.

Description

Task dependences are derived from the *dependence-type* of a **depend** clause and its list items when *dependence-type* is `in`, `out`, `inout`, or `mutexinoutset`. When the *dependence-type* is `depobj`, the task dependences are derived from the dependences represented by the depend objects specified in the **depend** clause as if the **depend** clauses of the **depobj** constructs were specified in the current construct.

For the **in** *dependence-type*, if the storage location of at least one of the list items is the same as the storage location of a list item appearing in a **depend** clause with an **out**, **inout**, or **mutexinoutset** *dependence-type* on a construct from which a sibling task was previously generated, then the generated task will be a dependent task of that sibling task.

For the **out** and **inout** *dependence-types*, if the storage location of at least one of the list items is the same as the storage location of a list item appearing in a **depend** clause with an **in**, **out**, **inout**, or **mutexinoutset** *dependence-type* on a construct from which a sibling task was previously generated, then the generated task will be a dependent task of that sibling task.

For the **mutexinoutset** *dependence-type*, if the storage location of at least one of the list items is the same as the storage location of a list item appearing in a **depend** clause with an **in**, **out**, or **inout** *dependence-type* on a construct from which a sibling task was previously generated, then the generated task will be a dependent task of that sibling task.

If a list item appearing in a **depend** clause with a **mutexinoutset** *dependence-type* on a task-generating construct has the same storage location as a list item appearing in a **depend** clause with a **mutexinoutset** *dependence-type* on a different task generating construct, and both constructs generate sibling tasks, the sibling tasks will be mutually exclusive tasks.

The list items that appear in the **depend** clause may reference iterators defined by an *iterators-definition* appearing on an **iterator** modifier.

The list items that appear in the **depend** clause may include array sections.

─────────── Fortran ───────────

If a list item has the **ALLOCATABLE** attribute and its allocation status is unallocated, the behavior is unspecified. If a list item has the **POINTER** attribute and its association status is disassociated or undefined, the behavior is unspecified.

─────────── Fortran ───────────
─────────── C / C++ ───────────

The list items that appear in a **depend** clause may use shape-operators.

─────────── C / C++ ───────────

Note – The enforced task dependence establishes a synchronization of memory accesses performed by a dependent task with respect to accesses performed by the predecessor tasks. However, it is the responsibility of the programmer to synchronize properly with respect to other concurrent accesses that occur outside of those tasks.

The **source** *dependence-type* specifies the satisfaction of cross-iteration dependences that arise from the current iteration.

The **sink** *dependence-type* specifies a cross-iteration dependence, where the iteration vector *vec* indicates the iteration that satisfies the dependence.

If the iteration vector *vec* does not occur in the iteration space, the **depend** clause is ignored. If all **depend** clauses on an **ordered** construct are ignored then the construct is ignored.

Note – An iteration vector *vec* that does not indicate a lexicographically earlier iteration may cause a deadlock.

Execution Model Events

The *task-dependences* event occurs in a thread that encounters a task generating construct or a **taskwait** construct with a **depend** clause immediately after the *task-create* event for the new task or the *taskwait-begin* event.

The *task-dependence* event indicates an unfulfilled dependence for the generated task. This event occurs in a thread that observes the unfulfilled dependence before it is satisfied.

Tool Callbacks

A thread dispatches the **ompt_callback_dependences** callback for each occurrence of the *task-dependences* event to announce its dependences with respect to the list items in the **depend** clause. This callback has type signature **ompt_callback_dependences_t**.

A thread dispatches the **ompt_callback_task_dependence** callback for a *task-dependence* event to report a dependence between a predecessor task (*src_task_data*) and a dependent task (*sink_task_data*). This callback has type signature **ompt_callback_task_dependence_t**.

Restrictions

Restrictions to the **depend** clause are as follows:

- List items used in **depend** clauses of the same task or sibling tasks must indicate identical storage locations or disjoint storage locations.
- List items used in **depend** clauses cannot be zero-length array sections.
- Array sections cannot be specified in **depend** clauses with the **depobj** dependence type.
- List items used in **depend** clauses with the **depobj** dependence type must be depend objects in the initialized state.

─────────────── C / C++ ───────────────

- List items used in **depend** clauses with the **depobj** dependence type must be expressions of the **omp_depend_t** type.
- List items used in **depend** clauses with the **in**, **out**, **inout** or **mutexinoutset** dependence types cannot be expressions of the **omp_depend_t** type.

─────────────── C / C++ ───────────────

---------- Fortran ----------

- A common block name cannot appear in a **depend** clause.

- List items used in **depend** clauses with the **depobj** dependence type must be integer expressions of the **omp_depend_kind** kind.

---------- Fortran ----------

- For a *vec* element of **sink** *dependence-type* of the form $x_i + d_i$ or $x_i - d_i$ if the loop iteration variable x_i has an integral or pointer type, the expression $x_i + d_i$ or $x_i - d_i$ for any value of the loop iteration variable x_i that can encounter the **ordered** construct must be computable without overflow in the type of the loop iteration variable.

---------- C++ ----------

- For a *vec* element of **sink** *dependence-type* of the form $x_i + d_i$ or $x_i - d_i$ if the loop iteration variable x_i is of a random access iterator type other than pointer type, the expression $(x_i - lb_i) + d_i$ or $(x_i - lb_i) - d_i$ for any value of the loop iteration variable x_i that can encounter the **ordered** construct must be computable without overflow in the type that would be used by *std::distance* applied to variables of the type of x_i.

---------- C++ ----------
---------- C / C++ ----------

- A bit-field cannot appear in a **depend** clause.

---------- C / C++ ----------

Cross References

- Array sections, see Section 2.1.5 on page 44.
- Iterators, see Section 2.1.6 on page 47.
- **task** construct, see Section 2.10.1 on page 135.
- Task scheduling constraints, see Section 2.10.6 on page 149.
- **target enter data** construct, see Section 2.12.3 on page 164.
- **target exit data** construct, see Section 2.12.4 on page 166.
- **target** construct, see Section 2.12.5 on page 170.
- **target update** construct, see Section 2.12.6 on page 176.
- **ordered** construct, see Section 2.17.9 on page 250.
- **depobj** construct, see Section 2.17.10.1 on page 254.
- **ompt_callback_dependences_t**, see Section 4.5.2.8 on page 468.
- **ompt_callback_task_dependence_t**, see Section 4.5.2.9 on page 470.

2.17.12 Synchronization Hints

Hints about the expected dynamic behavior or suggested implementation can be provided by the programmer to locks (by using the **omp_init_lock_with_hint** or **omp_init_nest_lock_with_hint** functions to initialize the lock), and to **atomic** and **critical** directives by using the **hint** clause. The effect of a hint does not change the semantics of the associated construct; if ignoring the hint changes the program semantics, the result is unspecified.

The C/C++ header file (**omp.h**) and the Fortran include file (**omp_lib.h**) and/or Fortran 90 module file (**omp_lib**) define the valid hint constants. The valid constants must include the following, which can be extended with implementation-defined values:

─────────── C / C++ ───────────
```
typedef enum omp_sync_hint_t {
  omp_sync_hint_none = 0x0,
  omp_lock_hint_none = omp_sync_hint_none,
  omp_sync_hint_uncontended = 0x1,
  omp_lock_hint_uncontended = omp_sync_hint_uncontended,
  omp_sync_hint_contended = 0x2,
  omp_lock_hint_contended = omp_sync_hint_contended,
  omp_sync_hint_nonspeculative = 0x4,
  omp_lock_hint_nonspeculative = omp_sync_hint_nonspeculative,
  omp_sync_hint_speculative = 0x8,
  omp_lock_hint_speculative = omp_sync_hint_speculative
} omp_sync_hint_t;

typedef omp_sync_hint_t omp_lock_hint_t;
```
─────────── C / C++ ───────────
─────────── Fortran ───────────
```
integer, parameter :: omp_lock_hint_kind = omp_sync_hint_kind

integer (kind=omp_sync_hint_kind), &
  parameter :: omp_sync_hint_none = &
                    int(Z'0', kind=omp_sync_hint_kind)
integer (kind=omp_lock_hint_kind), &
  parameter :: omp_lock_hint_none = omp_sync_hint_none
integer (kind=omp_sync_hint_kind), &
  parameter :: omp_sync_hint_uncontended = &
                    int(Z'1', kind=omp_sync_hint_kind)
integer (kind=omp_lock_hint_kind), &
  parameter :: omp_lock_hint_uncontended = &
                    omp_sync_hint_uncontended
integer (kind=omp_sync_hint_kind), &
```

```fortran
      parameter :: omp_sync_hint_contended = &
                   int(Z'2', kind=omp_sync_hint_kind)
integer (kind=omp_lock_hint_kind), &
   parameter :: omp_lock_hint_contended = &
                   omp_sync_hint_contended
integer (kind=omp_sync_hint_kind), &
   parameter :: omp_sync_hint_nonspeculative = &
                   int(Z'4', kind=omp_sync_hint_kind)
integer (kind=omp_lock_hint_kind), &
   parameter :: omp_lock_hint_nonspeculative = &
                   omp_sync_hint_nonspeculative
integer (kind=omp_sync_hint_kind), &
   parameter :: omp_sync_hint_speculative = &
                   int(Z'8', kind=omp_sync_hint_kind)
integer (kind=omp_lock_hint_kind), &
   parameter :: omp_lock_hint_speculative = &
                   omp_sync_hint_speculative
```

――――――――――――――――――――― Fortran ―――――――――――――――――――――

The hints can be combined by using the **+** or **|** operators in C/C++ or the **+** operator in Fortran. Combining **omp_sync_hint_none** with any other hint is equivalent to specifying the other hint.

The intended meaning of each hint is:

- **omp_sync_hint_uncontended**: low contention is expected in this operation, that is, few threads are expected to perform the operation simultaneously in a manner that requires synchronization;

- **omp_sync_hint_contended**: high contention is expected in this operation, that is, many threads are expected to perform the operation simultaneously in a manner that requires synchronization;

- **omp_sync_hint_speculative**: the programmer suggests that the operation should be implemented using speculative techniques such as transactional memory; and

- **omp_sync_hint_nonspeculative**: the programmer suggests that the operation should not be implemented using speculative techniques such as transactional memory.

Note – Future OpenMP specifications may add additional hints to the **omp_sync_hint_t** type and the **omp_sync_hint_kind** kind. Implementers are advised to add implementation-defined hints starting from the most significant bit of the **omp_sync_hint_t** type and **omp_sync_hint_kind** kind and to include the name of the implementation in the name of the added hint to avoid name conflicts with other OpenMP implementations.

The **omp_sync_hint_t** and **omp_lock_hint_t** enumeration types and the equivalent types in Fortran are synonyms for each other. The type **omp_lock_hint_t** has been deprecated.

Restrictions

Restrictions to the synchronization hints are as follows:

- The hints **omp_sync_hint_uncontended** and **omp_sync_hint_contended** cannot be combined.

- The hints **omp_sync_hint_nonspeculative** and **omp_sync_hint_speculative** cannot be combined.

The restrictions for combining multiple values of **omp_sync_hint** apply equally to the corresponding values of **omp_lock_hint**, and expressions that mix the two types.

Cross References

- **critical** construct, see Section 2.17.1 on page 223.

- **atomic** construct, see Section 2.17.7 on page 234

- **omp_init_lock_with_hint** and **omp_init_nest_lock_with_hint**, see Section 3.3.2 on page 385.

2.18 Cancellation Constructs

2.18.1 `cancel` Construct

Summary

The `cancel` construct activates cancellation of the innermost enclosing region of the type specified. The `cancel` construct is a stand-alone directive.

Syntax

───────────────── C / C++ ─────────────────

The syntax of the `cancel` construct is as follows:

`#pragma omp cancel` *construct-type-clause [[,] if-clause] new-line*

where *construct-type-clause* is one of the following:

> `parallel`
> `sections`
> `for`
> `taskgroup`

and *if-clause* is

> `if ([ cancel :]` *scalar-expression*`)`

───────────────── C / C++ ─────────────────
───────────────── Fortran ─────────────────

The syntax of the `cancel` construct is as follows:

`!$omp cancel` *construct-type-clause [[,] if-clause]*

where *construct-type-clause* is one of the following:

> `parallel`
> `sections`
> `do`
> `taskgroup`

and *if-clause* is

> `if ([ cancel :]` *scalar-logical-expression*`)`

───────────────── Fortran ─────────────────

Binding

The binding thread set of the **cancel** region is the current team. The binding region of the **cancel** region is the innermost enclosing region of the type corresponding to the *construct-type-clause* specified in the directive (that is, the innermost **parallel**, **sections**, worksharing-loop, or **taskgroup** region).

Description

The **cancel** construct activates cancellation of the binding region only if the *cancel-var* ICV is *true*, in which case the **cancel** construct causes the encountering task to continue execution at the end of the binding region if *construct-type-clause* is **parallel**, **for**, **do**, or **sections**. If the *cancel-var* ICV is *true* and *construct-type-clause* is **taskgroup**, the encountering task continues execution at the end of the current task region. If the *cancel-var* ICV is *false*, the **cancel** construct is ignored.

Threads check for active cancellation only at cancellation points that are implied at the following locations:

- **cancel** regions;
- **cancellation point** regions;
- **barrier** regions;
- implicit barriers regions.

When a thread reaches one of the above cancellation points and if the *cancel-var* ICV is *true*, then:

- If the thread is at a **cancel** or **cancellation point** region and *construct-type-clause* is **parallel**, **for**, **do**, or **sections**, the thread continues execution at the end of the canceled region if cancellation has been activated for the innermost enclosing region of the type specified.

- If the thread is at a **cancel** or **cancellation point** region and *construct-type-clause* is **taskgroup**, the encountering task checks for active cancellation of all of the *taskgroup sets* to which the encountering task belongs, and continues execution at the end of the current task region if cancellation has been activated for any of the *taskgroup sets*.

- If the encountering task is at a barrier region, the encountering task checks for active cancellation of the innermost enclosing **parallel** region. If cancellation has been activated, then the encountering task continues execution at the end of the canceled region.

Note – If one thread activates cancellation and another thread encounters a cancellation point, the order of execution between the two threads is non-deterministic. Whether the thread that encounters a cancellation point detects the activated cancellation depends on the underlying hardware and operating system.

When cancellation of tasks is activated through a **cancel** construct with the **taskgroup** *construct-type-clause*, the tasks that belong to the *taskgroup set* of the innermost enclosing **taskgroup** region will be canceled. The task that encountered that construct continues execution at the end of its task region, which implies completion of that task. Any task that belongs to the innermost enclosing **taskgroup** and has already begun execution must run to completion or until a cancellation point is reached. Upon reaching a cancellation point and if cancellation is active, the task continues execution at the end of its task region, which implies the task's completion. Any task that belongs to the innermost enclosing **taskgroup** and that has not begun execution may be discarded, which implies its completion.

When cancellation is active for a **parallel**, **sections**, or worksharing-loop region, each thread of the binding thread set resumes execution at the end of the canceled region if a cancellation point is encountered. If the canceled region is a **parallel** region, any tasks that have been created by a **task** or a **taskloop** construct and their descendent tasks are canceled according to the above **taskgroup** cancellation semantics. If the canceled region is a **sections**, or worksharing-loop region, no task cancellation occurs.

―――――――――――――――――― C++ ――――――――――――――――――

The usual C++ rules for object destruction are followed when cancellation is performed.

―――――――――――――――――― C++ ――――――――――――――――――

―――――――――――――――――― Fortran ――――――――――――――――――

All private objects or subobjects with **ALLOCATABLE** attribute that are allocated inside the canceled construct are deallocated.

―――――――――――――――――― Fortran ――――――――――――――――――

If the canceled construct contains a **reduction**, **task_reduction** or **lastprivate** clause, the final value of the list items that appeared in those clauses are undefined.

When an **if** clause is present on a **cancel** construct and the **if** expression evaluates to *false*, the **cancel** construct does not activate cancellation. The cancellation point associated with the **cancel** construct is always encountered regardless of the value of the **if** expression.

Note – The programmer is responsible for releasing locks and other synchronization data structures that might cause a deadlock when a **cancel** construct is encountered and blocked threads cannot be canceled. The programmer is also responsible for ensuring proper synchronizations to avoid deadlocks that might arise from cancellation of OpenMP regions that contain OpenMP synchronization constructs.

Execution Model Events

If a task encounters a **cancel** construct that will activate cancellation then a *cancel* event occurs.

A *discarded-task* event occurs for any discarded tasks.

Tool Callbacks

A thread dispatches a registered `ompt_callback_cancel` callback for each occurrence of a *cancel* event in the context of the encountering task. This callback has type signature `ompt_callback_cancel_t`; (*flags* `& ompt_cancel_activated`) always evaluates to *true* in the dispatched callback; (*flags* `& ompt_cancel_parallel`) evaluates to *true* in the dispatched callback if *construct-type-clause* is `parallel`; (*flags* `& ompt_cancel_sections`) evaluates to *true* in the dispatched callback if *construct-type-clause* is `sections`; (*flags* `& ompt_cancel_loop`) evaluates to *true* in the dispatched callback if *construct-type-clause* is `for` or `do`; and (*flags* `& ompt_cancel_taskgroup`) evaluates to *true* in the dispatched callback if *construct-type-clause* is `taskgroup`.

A thread dispatches a registered `ompt_callback_cancel` callback with the *ompt_data_t* associated with the discarded task as its *task_data* argument and `ompt_cancel_discarded_task` as its *flags* argument for each occurrence of a *discarded-task* event. The callback occurs in the context of the task that discards the task and has type signature `ompt_callback_cancel_t`.

Restrictions

The restrictions to the `cancel` construct are as follows:

- The behavior for concurrent cancellation of a region and a region nested within it is unspecified.
- If *construct-type-clause* is `taskgroup`, the `cancel` construct must be closely nested inside a `task` or a `taskloop` construct and the `cancel` region must be closely nested inside a `taskgroup` region. If *construct-type-clause* is `sections`, the `cancel` construct must be closely nested inside a `sections` or `section` construct. Otherwise, the `cancel` construct must be closely nested inside an OpenMP construct that matches the type specified in *construct-type-clause* of the `cancel` construct.
- A worksharing construct that is canceled must not have a `nowait` clause.
- A worksharing-loop construct that is canceled must not have an `ordered` clause.
- During execution of a construct that may be subject to cancellation, a thread must not encounter an orphaned cancellation point. That is, a cancellation point must only be encountered within that construct and must not be encountered elsewhere in its region.

Cross References

- *cancel-var* ICV, see Section 2.5.1 on page 64.
- `if` clause, see Section 2.15 on page 220.
- `cancellation point` construct, see Section 2.18.2 on page 267.

- `omp_get_cancellation` routine, see Section 3.2.9 on page 342.
- `omp_cancel_flag_t` enumeration type, see Section 4.4.4.24 on page 450.
- `ompt_callback_cancel_t`, see Section 4.5.2.18 on page 481.

2.18.2 cancellation point Construct

Summary

The `cancellation point` construct introduces a user-defined cancellation point at which implicit or explicit tasks check if cancellation of the innermost enclosing region of the type specified has been activated. The `cancellation point` construct is a stand-alone directive.

Syntax

─────────────── C / C++ ───────────────

The syntax of the `cancellation point` construct is as follows:

`#pragma omp cancellation point` *construct-type-clause new-line*

where *construct-type-clause* is one of the following:

> `parallel`
> `sections`
> `for`
> `taskgroup`

─────────────── C / C++ ───────────────

─────────────── Fortran ───────────────

The syntax of the `cancellation point` construct is as follows:

`!$omp cancellation point` *construct-type-clause*

where *construct-type-clause* is one of the following:

> `parallel`
> `sections`
> `do`
> `taskgroup`

─────────────── Fortran ───────────────

Binding

The binding thread set of the `cancellation point` construct is the current team. The binding region of the `cancellation point` region is the innermost enclosing region of the type corresponding to the *construct-type-clause* specified in the directive (that is, the innermost `parallel`, `sections`, worksharing-loop, or `taskgroup` region).

Description

This directive introduces a user-defined cancellation point at which an implicit or explicit task must check if cancellation of the innermost enclosing region of the type specified in the clause has been requested. This construct does not implement any synchronization between threads or tasks.

When an implicit or explicit task reaches a user-defined cancellation point and if the *cancel-var* ICV is *true*, then:

- If the *construct-type-clause* of the encountered `cancellation point` construct is `parallel`, `for`, `do`, or `sections`, the thread continues execution at the end of the canceled region if cancellation has been activated for the innermost enclosing region of the type specified.

- If the *construct-type-clause* of the encountered `cancellation point` construct is `taskgroup`, the encountering task checks for active cancellation of all *taskgroup sets* to which the encountering task belongs and continues execution at the end of the current task region if cancellation has been activated for any of them.

Execution Model Events

The *cancellation* event occurs if a task encounters a cancellation point and detected the activation of cancellation.

Tool Callbacks

A thread dispatches a registered `ompt_callback_cancel` callback for each occurrence of a *cancel* event in the context of the encountering task. This callback has type signature `ompt_callback_cancel_t`; (*flags* & `ompt_cancel_detected`) always evaluates to *true* in the dispatched callback; (*flags* & `ompt_cancel_parallel`) evaluates to *true* in the dispatched callback if *construct-type-clause* of the encountered `cancellation point` construct is `parallel`; (*flags* & `ompt_cancel_sections`) evaluates to *true* in the dispatched callback if *construct-type-clause* of the encountered `cancellation point` construct is `sections`; (*flags* & `ompt_cancel_loop`) evaluates to *true* in the dispatched callback if *construct-type-clause* of the encountered `cancellation point` construct is `for` or `do`; and (*flags* & `ompt_cancel_taskgroup`) evaluates to *true* in the dispatched callback if *construct-type-clause* of the encountered `cancellation point` construct is `taskgroup`.

Restrictions

- A `cancellation point` construct for which *construct-type-clause* is `taskgroup` must be closely nested inside a `task` or `taskloop` construct, and the `cancellation point` region must be closely nested inside a `taskgroup` region.

- A `cancellation point` construct for which *construct-type-clause* is `sections` must be closely nested inside a `sections` or `section` construct.

- A `cancellation point` construct for which *construct-type-clause* is neither `sections` nor `taskgroup` must be closely nested inside an OpenMP construct that matches the type specified in *construct-type-clause*.

Cross References

- *cancel-var* ICV, see Section 2.5.1 on page 64.
- `cancel` construct, see Section 2.18.1 on page 263.
- `omp_get_cancellation` routine, see Section 3.2.9 on page 342.
- `ompt_callback_cancel_t`, see Section 4.5.2.18 on page 481.

2.19 Data Environment

This section presents directives and clauses for controlling data environments.

2.19.1 Data-Sharing Attribute Rules

This section describes how the data-sharing attributes of variables referenced in data environments are determined. The following two cases are described separately:

- Section 2.19.1.1 on page 270 describes the data-sharing attribute rules for variables referenced in a construct.
- Section 2.19.1.2 on page 273 describes the data-sharing attribute rules for variables referenced in a region, but outside any construct.

2.19.1.1 Variables Referenced in a Construct

The data-sharing attributes of variables that are referenced in a construct can be *predetermined*, *explicitly determined*, or *implicitly determined*, according to the rules outlined in this section.

Specifying a variable in a data-sharing attribute clause, except for the **private** clause, or **copyprivate** clause of an enclosed construct causes an implicit reference to the variable in the enclosing construct. Specifying a variable in a **map** clause of an enclosed construct may cause an implicit reference to the variable in the enclosing construct. Such implicit references are also subject to the data-sharing attribute rules outlined in this section.

Certain variables and objects have *predetermined* data-sharing attributes as follows:

─────────────────── C / C++ ───────────────────

- Variables that appear in **threadprivate** directives are threadprivate.
- Variables with automatic storage duration that are declared in a scope inside the construct are private.
- Objects with dynamic storage duration are shared.
- Static data members are shared.
- The loop iteration variable(s) in the associated *for-loop(s)* of a **for**, **parallel for**, **taskloop**, or **distribute** construct is (are) private.
- The loop iteration variable in the associated *for-loop* of a **simd** construct with just one associated *for-loop* is linear with a *linear-step* that is the increment of the associated *for-loop*.
- The loop iteration variables in the associated *for-loops* of a **simd** construct with multiple associated *for-loops* are lastprivate.
- The loop iteration variable(s) in the associated *for-loop(s)* of a **loop** construct is (are) lastprivate.
- Variables with static storage duration that are declared in a scope inside the construct are shared.
- If a list item in a **map** clause on the **target** construct has a base pointer, and the base pointer is a scalar variable that does not appear in a **map** clause on the construct, the base pointer is firstprivate.
- If a list item in a **reduction** or **in_reduction** clause on a construct has a base pointer then the base pointer is private.

─────────────────── C / C++ ───────────────────
─────────────────── Fortran ───────────────────

- Variables and common blocks that appear in **threadprivate** directives are threadprivate.
- The loop iteration variable(s) in the associated *do-loop(s)* of a **do**, **parallel do**, **taskloop**, or **distribute** construct is (are) private.

- The loop iteration variable in the associated *do-loop* of a `simd` construct with just one associated *do-loop* is linear with a *linear-step* that is the increment of the associated *do-loop*.
- The loop iteration variables in the associated *do-loops* of a `simd` construct with multiple associated *do-loops* are lastprivate.
- The loop iteration variable(s) in the associated *do-loop(s)* of a `loop` construct is (are) lastprivate.
- A loop iteration variable for a sequential loop in a `parallel` or task generating construct is private in the innermost such construct that encloses the loop.
- Implied-do indices and `forall` indices are private.
- Cray pointees have the same data-sharing attribute as the storage with which their Cray pointers are associated.
- Assumed-size arrays are shared.
- An associate name preserves the association with the selector established at the **ASSOCIATE** or **SELECT TYPE** statement.

———————————— Fortran ————————————

Variables with predetermined data-sharing attributes may not be listed in data-sharing attribute clauses, except for the cases listed below. For these exceptions only, listing a predetermined variable in a data-sharing attribute clause is allowed and overrides the variable's predetermined data-sharing attributes.

———————————— C / C++ ————————————

- The loop iteration variable(s) in the associated *for-loop(s)* of a `for`, `parallel for`, `taskloop`, `distribute`, or `loop` construct may be listed in a `private` or `lastprivate` clause.
- The loop iteration variable in the associated *for-loop* of a `simd` construct with just one associated *for-loop* may be listed in a `private`, `lastprivate`, or `linear` clause with a *linear-step* that is the increment of the associated *for-loop*.
- The loop iteration variables in the associated *for-loops* of a `simd` construct with multiple associated *for-loops* may be listed in a `private` or `lastprivate` clause.
- Variables with `const`-qualified type with no mutable members may be listed in a `firstprivate` clause, even if they are static data members.

———————————— C / C++ ————————————

CHAPTER 2. DIRECTIVES   271

―――――――――――――――――――――― Fortran ――――――――――――――――――――――

- The loop iteration variable(s) in the associated *do-loop(s)* of a **do**, **parallel do**, **taskloop**, **distribute**, or **loop** construct may be listed in a **private** or **lastprivate** clause.

- The loop iteration variable in the associated *do-loop* of a **simd** construct with just one associated *do-loop* may be listed in a **private**, **lastprivate**, or **linear** clause with a *linear-step* that is the increment of the associated loop.

- The loop iteration variables in the associated *do-loops* of a **simd** construct with multiple associated *do-loops* may be listed in a **private** or **lastprivate** clause.

- Variables used as loop iteration variables in sequential loops in a **parallel** or task generating construct may be listed in data-sharing attribute clauses on the construct itself, and on enclosed constructs, subject to other restrictions.

- Assumed-size arrays may be listed in a **shared** clause.

―――――――――――――――――――――― Fortran ――――――――――――――――――――――

Additional restrictions on the variables that may appear in individual clauses are described with each clause in Section 2.19.4 on page 282.

Variables with *explicitly determined* data-sharing attributes are those that are referenced in a given construct and are listed in a data-sharing attribute clause on the construct.

Variables with *implicitly determined* data-sharing attributes are those that are referenced in a given construct, do not have predetermined data-sharing attributes, and are not listed in a data-sharing attribute clause on the construct.

Rules for variables with *implicitly determined* data-sharing attributes are as follows:

- In a **parallel**, **teams**, or task generating construct, the data-sharing attributes of these variables are determined by the **default** clause, if present (see Section 2.19.4.1 on page 282).

- In a **parallel** construct, if no **default** clause is present, these variables are shared.

- For constructs other than task generating constructs, if no **default** clause is present, these variables reference the variables with the same names that exist in the enclosing context.

- In a **target** construct, variables that are not mapped after applying data-mapping attribute rules (see Section 2.19.7 on page 314) are firstprivate.

―――――――――――――――――――――― C++ ――――――――――――――――――――――

- In an orphaned task generating construct, if no **default** clause is present, formal arguments passed by reference are firstprivate.

―――――――――――――――――――――― C++ ――――――――――――――――――――――

―――――――――――――――――――――― Fortran ――――――――――――――――――――――

- In an orphaned task generating construct, if no **default** clause is present, dummy arguments are firstprivate.

―――――――――――――――――――――― Fortran ――――――――――――――――――――――

- In a task generating construct, if no **default** clause is present, a variable for which the data-sharing attribute is not determined by the rules above and that in the enclosing context is determined to be shared by all implicit tasks bound to the current team is shared.

- In a task generating construct, if no **default** clause is present, a variable for which the data-sharing attribute is not determined by the rules above is firstprivate.

Additional restrictions on the variables for which data-sharing attributes cannot be implicitly determined in a task generating construct are described in Section 2.19.4.4 on page 286.

2.19.1.2 Variables Referenced in a Region but not in a Construct

The data-sharing attributes of variables that are referenced in a region, but not in a construct, are determined as follows:

―――――――――――― C / C++ ――――――――――――

- Variables with static storage duration that are declared in called routines in the region are shared.
- File-scope or namespace-scope variables referenced in called routines in the region are shared unless they appear in a **threadprivate** directive.
- Objects with dynamic storage duration are shared.
- Static data members are shared unless they appear in a **threadprivate** directive.
- In C++, formal arguments of called routines in the region that are passed by reference have the same data-sharing attributes as the associated actual arguments.
- Other variables declared in called routines in the region are private.

―――――――――――― C / C++ ――――――――――――
―――――――――――― Fortran ――――――――――――

- Local variables declared in called routines in the region and that have the **save** attribute, or that are data initialized, are shared unless they appear in a **threadprivate** directive.
- Variables belonging to common blocks, or accessed by host or use association, and referenced in called routines in the region are shared unless they appear in a **threadprivate** directive.
- Dummy arguments of called routines in the region that have the **VALUE** attribute are private.
- Dummy arguments of called routines in the region that do not have the **VALUE** attribute are private if the associated actual argument is not shared.
- Dummy arguments of called routines in the region that do not have the **VALUE** attribute are shared if the actual argument is shared and it is a scalar variable, structure, an array that is not a pointer or assumed-shape array, or a simply contiguous array section. Otherwise, the data-sharing attribute of the dummy argument is implementation-defined if the associated actual argument is shared.

- Cray pointees have the same data-sharing attribute as the storage with which their Cray pointers are associated.
- Implied-do indices, `forall` indices, and other local variables declared in called routines in the region are private.

―――――――――――――― Fortran ――――――――――――――

2.19.2 `threadprivate` Directive

Summary

The `threadprivate` directive specifies that variables are replicated, with each thread having its own copy. The `threadprivate` directive is a declarative directive.

Syntax

―――――――――――――― C / C++ ――――――――――――――

The syntax of the `threadprivate` directive is as follows:

`#pragma omp threadprivate(list)` *new-line*

where *list* is a comma-separated list of file-scope, namespace-scope, or static block-scope variables that do not have incomplete types.

―――――――――――――― C / C++ ――――――――――――――
―――――――――――――― Fortran ――――――――――――――

The syntax of the `threadprivate` directive is as follows:

`!$omp threadprivate(list)`

where *list* is a comma-separated list of named variables and named common blocks. Common block names must appear between slashes.

―――――――――――――― Fortran ――――――――――――――

Description

Each copy of a threadprivate variable is initialized once, in the manner specified by the program, but at an unspecified point in the program prior to the first reference to that copy. The storage of all copies of a threadprivate variable is freed according to how static variables are handled in the base language, but at an unspecified point in the program.

A program in which a thread references another thread's copy of a threadprivate variable is non-conforming.

The content of a threadprivate variable can change across a task scheduling point if the executing thread switches to another task that modifies the variable. For more details on task scheduling, see Section 1.3 on page 20 and Section 2.10 on page 135.

In **parallel** regions, references by the master thread will be to the copy of the variable in the thread that encountered the **parallel** region.

During a sequential part references will be to the initial thread's copy of the variable. The values of data in the initial thread's copy of a threadprivate variable are guaranteed to persist between any two consecutive references to the variable in the program provided that no **teams** construct that is not nested inside of a **target** construct is encountered between the references and that the initial thread is not nested inside of a **teams** region. For initial threads nested inside of a **teams** region, the values of data in the copies of a threadprivate variable of those initial threads are guaranteed to persist between any two consecutive references to the variable inside of that **teams** region.

The values of data in the threadprivate variables of threads that are not initial threads are guaranteed to persist between two consecutive active **parallel** regions only if all of the following conditions hold:

- Neither **parallel** region is nested inside another explicit **parallel** region;
- The number of threads used to execute both **parallel** regions is the same;
- The thread affinity policies used to execute both **parallel** regions are the same;
- The value of the *dyn-var* internal control variable in the enclosing task region is *false* at entry to both **parallel** regions; and
- No **teams** construct that is not nested inside of a **target** construct is encountered between both **parallel** regions.
- Neither the **omp_pause_resource** nor **omp_pause_resource_all** routine is called.

If these conditions all hold, and if a threadprivate variable is referenced in both regions, then threads with the same thread number in their respective regions will reference the same copy of that variable.

─────────── C / C++ ───────────

If the above conditions hold, the storage duration, lifetime, and value of a thread's copy of a threadprivate variable that does not appear in any **copyin** clause on the second region will be retained. Otherwise, the storage duration, lifetime, and value of a thread's copy of the variable in the second region is unspecified.

─────────── C / C++ ───────────

―――――――――――――――― Fortran ――――――――――――――――

If the above conditions hold, the definition, association, or allocation status of a thread's copy of a threadprivate variable or a variable in a threadprivate common block that is not affected by any **copyin** clause that appears on the second region (a variable is affected by a **copyin** clause if the variable appears in the **copyin** clause or it is in a common block that appears in the **copyin** clause) will be retained. Otherwise, the definition and association status of a thread's copy of the variable in the second region are undefined, and the allocation status of an allocatable variable will be implementation defined.

If a threadprivate variable or a variable in a threadprivate common block is not affected by any **copyin** clause that appears on the first **parallel** region in which it is referenced, the thread's copy of the variable inherits the declared type parameter and the default parameter values from the original variable. The variable or any subobject of the variable is initially defined or undefined according to the following rules:

- If it has the **ALLOCATABLE** attribute, each copy created will have an initial allocation status of unallocated;

- If it has the **POINTER** attribute:
  - If it has an initial association status of disassociated, either through explicit initialization or default initialization, each copy created will have an association status of disassociated;
  - Otherwise, each copy created will have an association status of undefined.

- If it does not have either the **POINTER** or the **ALLOCATABLE** attribute:
  - If it is initially defined, either through explicit initialization or default initialization, each copy created is so defined;
  - Otherwise, each copy created is undefined.

―――――――――――――――― Fortran ――――――――――――――――
―――――――――――――――― C / C++ ――――――――――――――――

The address of a threadprivate variable is not an address constant.

―――――――――――――――― C / C++ ――――――――――――――――
―――――――――――――――― C++ ――――――――――――――――

The order in which any constructors for different threadprivate variables of class type are called is unspecified. The order in which any destructors for different threadprivate variables of class type are called is unspecified.

―――――――――――――――― C++ ――――――――――――――――

Restrictions

The restrictions to the `threadprivate` directive are as follows:

- A threadprivate variable must not appear in any clause except the `copyin`, `copyprivate`, `schedule`, `num_threads`, `thread_limit`, and `if` clauses.
- A program in which an untied task accesses threadprivate storage is non-conforming.

―――――――――――――――― C / C++ ――――――――――――――――

- If the value of a variable referenced in an explicit initializer of a threadprivate variable is modified prior to the first reference to any instance of the threadprivate variable, then the behavior is unspecified.
- A variable that is part of another variable (as an array or structure element) cannot appear in a `threadprivate` clause unless it is a static data member of a C++ class.
- A `threadprivate` directive for file-scope variables must appear outside any definition or declaration, and must lexically precede all references to any of the variables in its list.
- A `threadprivate` directive for namespace-scope variables must appear outside any definition or declaration other than the namespace definition itself, and must lexically precede all references to any of the variables in its list.
- Each variable in the list of a `threadprivate` directive at file, namespace, or class scope must refer to a variable declaration at file, namespace, or class scope that lexically precedes the directive.
- A `threadprivate` directive for static block-scope variables must appear in the scope of the variable and not in a nested scope. The directive must lexically precede all references to any of the variables in its list.
- Each variable in the list of a `threadprivate` directive in block scope must refer to a variable declaration in the same scope that lexically precedes the directive. The variable declaration must use the static storage-class specifier.
- If a variable is specified in a `threadprivate` directive in one translation unit, it must be specified in a `threadprivate` directive in every translation unit in which it is declared.

―――――――――――――――― C / C++ ――――――――――――――――
―――――――――――――――― C++ ――――――――――――――――

- A `threadprivate` directive for static class member variables must appear in the class definition, in the same scope in which the member variables are declared, and must lexically precede all references to any of the variables in its list.
- A threadprivate variable must not have an incomplete type or a reference type.
- A threadprivate variable with class type must have:
  - An accessible, unambiguous default constructor in the case of default initialization without a given initializer;

– An accessible, unambiguous constructor that accepts the given argument in the case of direct initialization; and

– An accessible, unambiguous copy constructor in the case of copy initialization with an explicit initializer.

―――――――――――――――――― C++ ――――――――――――――――――

―――――――――――――――――― Fortran ――――――――――――――――――

- A variable that is part of another variable (as an array, structure element or type parameter inquiry) cannot appear in a `threadprivate` clause.

- The `threadprivate` directive must appear in the declaration section of a scoping unit in which the common block or variable is declared.

- If a `threadprivate` directive that specifies a common block name appears in one program unit, then such a directive must also appear in every other program unit that contains a `COMMON` statement that specifies the same name. It must appear after the last such `COMMON` statement in the program unit.

- If a threadprivate variable or a threadprivate common block is declared with the `BIND` attribute, the corresponding C entities must also be specified in a `threadprivate` directive in the C program.

- A blank common block cannot appear in a `threadprivate` directive.

- A variable can only appear in a `threadprivate` directive in the scope in which it is declared. It must not be an element of a common block or appear in an `EQUIVALENCE` statement.

- A variable that appears in a `threadprivate` directive must be declared in the scope of a module or have the `SAVE` attribute, either explicitly or implicitly.

―――――――――――――――――― Fortran ――――――――――――――――――

Cross References

- *dyn-var* ICV, see Section 2.5 on page 63.
- Number of threads used to execute a `parallel` region, see Section 2.6.1 on page 78.
- `copyin` clause, see Section 2.19.6.1 on page 310.

2.19.3 List Item Privatization

For any construct, a list item that appears in a data-sharing attribute clause, including a reduction clause, may be privatized. Each task that references a privatized list item in any statement in the construct receives at least one new list item if the construct has one or more associated loops, and otherwise each such task receives one new list item. Each SIMD lane used in a **simd** construct that references a privatized list item in any statement in the construct receives at least one new list item. Language-specific attributes for new list items are derived from the corresponding original list item. Inside the construct, all references to the original list item are replaced by references to a new list item received by the task or SIMD lane.

If the construct has one or more associated loops, within the same logical iteration of the loop(s) the same new list item replaces all references to the original list item. For any two logical iterations, if the references to the original list item are replaced by the same list item then the logical iterations must execute in some sequential order.

In the rest of the region, it is unspecified whether references are to a new list item or the original list item. Therefore, if an attempt is made to reference the original item, its value after the region is also unspecified. If a task or a SIMD lane does not reference a privatized list item, it is unspecified whether the task or SIMD lane receives a new list item.

The value and/or allocation status of the original list item will change only:

- If accessed and modified via pointer;
- If possibly accessed in the region but outside of the construct;
- As a side effect of directives or clauses; or

――――――――― Fortran ―――――――――

- If accessed and modified via construct association.

――――――――― Fortran ―――――――――

――――――――― C++ ―――――――――

If the construct is contained in a member function, it is unspecified anywhere in the region if accesses through the implicit **this** pointer refer to the new list item or the original list item.

――――――――― C++ ―――――――――

――――――――― C / C++ ―――――――――

A new list item of the same type, with automatic storage duration, is allocated for the construct. The storage and thus lifetime of these list items last until the block in which they are created exits. The size and alignment of the new list item are determined by the type of the variable. This allocation occurs once for each task generated by the construct and once for each SIMD lane used by the construct.

The new list item is initialized, or has an undefined initial value, as if it had been locally declared without an initializer.

――――――――― C / C++ ―――――――――

―――――――――――――――――― C++ ――――――――――――――――――

If the type of a list item is a reference to a type *T* then the type will be considered to be *T* for all purposes of this clause.

The order in which any default constructors for different private variables of class type are called is unspecified. The order in which any destructors for different private variables of class type are called is unspecified.

―――――――――――――――――― C++ ――――――――――――――――――

―――――――――――――――――― Fortran ――――――――――――――――――

If any statement of the construct references a list item, a new list item of the same type and type parameters is allocated. This allocation occurs once for each task generated by the construct and once for each SIMD lane used by the construct. The initial value of the new list item is undefined. The initial status of a private pointer is undefined.

For a list item or the subobject of a list item with the **ALLOCATABLE** attribute:

- If the allocation status is unallocated, the new list item or the subobject of the new list item will have an initial allocation status of unallocated;

- If the allocation status is allocated, the new list item or the subobject of the new list item will have an initial allocation status of allocated; and

- If the new list item or the subobject of the new list item is an array, its bounds will be the same as those of the original list item or the subobject of the original list item.

A privatized list item may be storage-associated with other variables when the data-sharing attribute clause is encountered. Storage association may exist because of constructs such as **EQUIVALENCE** or **COMMON**. If *A* is a variable that is privatized by a construct and *B* is a variable that is storage-associated with *A*, then:

- The contents, allocation, and association status of *B* are undefined on entry to the region;

- Any definition of *A*, or of its allocation or association status, causes the contents, allocation, and association status of *B* to become undefined; and

- Any definition of *B*, or of its allocation or association status, causes the contents, allocation, and association status of *A* to become undefined.

A privatized list item clause may be a selector of an **ASSOCIATE** or **SELECT TYPE** construct. If the construct association is established prior to a **parallel** region, the association between the associate name and the original list item will be retained in the region.

Finalization of a list item of a finalizable type or subobjects of a list item of a finalizable type occurs at the end of the region. The order in which any final subroutines for different variables of a finalizable type are called is unspecified.

―――――――――――――――――― Fortran ――――――――――――――――――

If a list item appears in both **firstprivate** and **lastprivate** clauses, the update required for the **lastprivate** clause occurs after all initializations for the **firstprivate** clause.

Restrictions

The following restrictions apply to any list item that is privatized unless otherwise stated for a given data-sharing attribute clause:

―――――――――――――― C ――――――――――――――

- A variable that is part of another variable (as an array or structure element) cannot be privatized.

―――――――――――――― C ――――――――――――――
―――――――――――――― C++ ――――――――――――――

- A variable that is part of another variable (as an array or structure element) cannot be privatized except if the data-sharing attribute clause is associated with a construct within a class non-static member function and the variable is an accessible data member of the object for which the non-static member function is invoked.
- A variable of class type (or array thereof) that is privatized requires an accessible, unambiguous default constructor for the class type.

―――――――――――――― C++ ――――――――――――――
―――――――――――――― C / C++ ――――――――――――――

- A variable that is privatized must not have a **const**-qualified type unless it is of class type with a **mutable** member. This restriction does not apply to the **firstprivate** clause.
- A variable that is privatized must not have an incomplete type or be a reference to an incomplete type.

―――――――――――――― C / C++ ――――――――――――――
―――――――――――――― Fortran ――――――――――――――

- A variable that is part of another variable (as an array or structure element) cannot be privatized.
- A variable that is privatized must either be definable, or an allocatable variable. This restriction does not apply to the **firstprivate** clause.
- Variables that appear in namelist statements, in variable format expressions, and in expressions for statement function definitions, may not be privatized.
- Pointers with the **INTENT(IN)** attribute may not be privatized. This restriction does not apply to the **firstprivate** clause.
- Assumed-size arrays may not be privatized in a **target**, **teams**, or **distribute** construct.

―――――――――――――― Fortran ――――――――――――――

2.19.4 Data-Sharing Attribute Clauses

Several constructs accept clauses that allow a user to control the data-sharing attributes of variables referenced in the construct. Not all of the clauses listed in this section are valid on all directives. The set of clauses that is valid on a particular directive is described with the directive.

Most of the clauses accept a comma-separated list of list items (see Section 2.1 on page 38). All list items that appear in a clause must be visible, according to the scoping rules of the base language. With the exception of the `default` clause, clauses may be repeated as needed. A list item may not appear in more than one clause on the same directive, except that it may be specified in both `firstprivate` and `lastprivate` clauses.

The reduction data-sharing attribute clauses are explained in Section 2.19.5 on page 293.

―――――――――――――――――― C++ ――――――――――――――――――

If a variable referenced in a data-sharing attribute clause has a type derived from a template, and the program does not otherwise reference that variable then any behavior related to that variable is unspecified.

―――――――――――――――――― C++ ――――――――――――――――――

―――――――――――――――――― Fortran ――――――――――――――――――

When a named common block appears in a `private`, `firstprivate`, `lastprivate`, or `shared` clause of a directive, none of its members may be declared in another data-sharing attribute clause in that directive. When individual members of a common block appear in a `private`, `firstprivate`, `lastprivate`, `reduction`, or `linear` clause of a directive, the storage of the specified variables is no longer Fortran associated with the storage of the common block itself.

―――――――――――――――――― Fortran ――――――――――――――――――

2.19.4.1 `default` Clause

Summary

The `default` clause explicitly determines the data-sharing attributes of variables that are referenced in a `parallel`, `teams`, or task generating construct and would otherwise be implicitly determined (see Section 2.19.1.1 on page 270).

Syntax

───────────── C / C++ ─────────────

The syntax of the **default** clause is as follows:

default(shared | none)

───────────── C / C++ ─────────────

───────────── Fortran ─────────────

The syntax of the **default** clause is as follows:

default(private | firstprivate | shared | none)

───────────── Fortran ─────────────

Description

The **default(shared)** clause causes all variables referenced in the construct that have implicitly determined data-sharing attributes to be shared.

───────────── Fortran ─────────────

The **default(firstprivate)** clause causes all variables in the construct that have implicitly determined data-sharing attributes to be firstprivate.

The **default(private)** clause causes all variables referenced in the construct that have implicitly determined data-sharing attributes to be private.

───────────── Fortran ─────────────

The **default(none)** clause requires that each variable that is referenced in the construct, and that does not have a predetermined data-sharing attribute, must have its data-sharing attribute explicitly determined by being listed in a data-sharing attribute clause.

Restrictions

The restrictions to the **default** clause are as follows:

- Only a single **default** clause may be specified on a **parallel**, **task**, **taskloop** or **teams** directive.

2.19.4.2 shared Clause

Summary

The **shared** clause declares one or more list items to be shared by tasks generated by a **parallel**, **teams**, or task generating construct.

CHAPTER 2. DIRECTIVES   283

Syntax

The syntax of the **shared** clause is as follows:

shared(*list*)

Description

All references to a list item within a task refer to the storage area of the original variable at the point the directive was encountered.

The programmer must ensure, by adding proper synchronization, that storage shared by an explicit task region does not reach the end of its lifetime before the explicit task region completes its execution.

───────────────────────────── Fortran ─────────────────────────────

The association status of a shared pointer becomes undefined upon entry to and exit from the **parallel**, **teams**, or task generating construct if it is associated with a target or a subobject of a target that appears as a privatized list item in a data-sharing attribute clause on the construct.

Note – Passing a shared variable to a procedure may result in the use of temporary storage in place of the actual argument when the corresponding dummy argument does not have the **VALUE** or **CONTIGUOUS** attribute and its data-sharing attribute is implementation-defined as per the rules in Section 2.19.1.2 on page 273. These conditions effectively result in references to, and definitions of, the temporary storage during the procedure reference. Furthermore, the value of the shared variable is copied into the intervening temporary storage before the procedure reference when the dummy argument does not have the **INTENT(OUT)** attribute, and is copied out of the temporary storage into the shared variable when the dummy argument does not have the **INTENT(IN)** attribute. Any references to (or definitions of) the shared storage that is associated with the dummy argument by any other task must be synchronized with the procedure reference to avoid possible data races.

───────────────────────────── Fortran ─────────────────────────────

Restrictions

The restrictions for the **shared** clause are as follows:

───────────────────────────── C ─────────────────────────────

- A variable that is part of another variable (as an array or structure element) cannot appear in a **shared** clause.

───────────────────────────── C ─────────────────────────────

─────────── C++ ───────────

- A variable that is part of another variable (as an array or structure element) cannot appear in a **shared** clause except if the **shared** clause is associated with a construct within a class non-static member function and the variable is an accessible data member of the object for which the non-static member function is invoked.

─────────── C++ ───────────

─────────── Fortran ───────────

- A variable that is part of another variable (as an array, structure element or type parameter inquiry) cannot appear in a **shared** clause.

─────────── Fortran ───────────

2.19.4.3 `private` Clause

Summary

The **private** clause declares one or more list items to be private to a task or to a SIMD lane.

Syntax

The syntax of the **private** clause is as follows:

private(*list*)

Description

The **private** clause specifies that its list items are to be privatized according to Section 2.19.3 on page 279. Each task or SIMD lane that references a list item in the construct receives only one new list item, unless the construct has one or more associated loops and the **order(concurrent)** clause is also present.

List items that appear in a **private**, **firstprivate**, or **reduction** clause in a **parallel** construct may also appear in a **private** clause in an enclosed **parallel**, worksharing, **loop**, **task**, **taskloop**, **simd**, or **target** construct.

List items that appear in a **private** or **firstprivate** clause in a **task** or **taskloop** construct may also appear in a **private** clause in an enclosed **parallel**, **loop**, **task**, **taskloop**, **simd**, or **target** construct.

List items that appear in a **private**, **firstprivate**, **lastprivate**, or **reduction** clause in a worksharing construct may also appear in a **private** clause in an enclosed **parallel**, **loop**, **task**, **simd**, or **target** construct.

List items that appear in a **private** clause on a **loop** construct may also appear in a **private** clause in an enclosed **loop**, **parallel**, or **simd** construct.

Restrictions

The restrictions to the `private` clause are as specified in Section 2.19.3.

Cross References

- List Item Privatization, see Section 2.19.3 on page 279.

2.19.4.4 `firstprivate` Clause

Summary

The `firstprivate` clause declares one or more list items to be private to a task, and initializes each of them with the value that the corresponding original item has when the construct is encountered.

Syntax

The syntax of the `firstprivate` clause is as follows:

`firstprivate(`*list*`)`

Description

The `firstprivate` clause provides a superset of the functionality provided by the `private` clause.

A list item that appears in a `firstprivate` clause is subject to the `private` clause semantics described in Section 2.19.4.3 on page 285, except as noted. In addition, the new list item is initialized from the original list item existing before the construct. The initialization of the new list item is done once for each task that references the list item in any statement in the construct. The initialization is done prior to the execution of the construct.

For a `firstprivate` clause on a `parallel`, `task`, `taskloop`, `target`, or `teams` construct, the initial value of the new list item is the value of the original list item that exists immediately prior to the construct in the task region where the construct is encountered unless otherwise specified. For a `firstprivate` clause on a worksharing construct, the initial value of the new list item for each implicit task of the threads that execute the worksharing construct is the value of the original list item that exists in the implicit task immediately prior to the point in time that the worksharing construct is encountered unless otherwise specified.

To avoid data races, concurrent updates of the original list item must be synchronized with the read of the original list item that occurs as a result of the `firstprivate` clause.

---- C / C++ ----

For variables of non-array type, the initialization occurs by copy assignment. For an array of elements of non-array type, each element is initialized as if by assignment from an element of the original array to the corresponding element of the new array.

---- C / C++ ----

---- C++ ----

For each variable of class type:

- If the **firstprivate** clause is not on a **target** construct then a copy constructor is invoked to perform the initialization; and

- If the **firstprivate** clause is on a **target** construct then it is unspecified how many copy constructors, if any, are invoked.

If copy constructors are called, the order in which copy constructors for different variables of class type are called is unspecified.

---- C++ ----

---- Fortran ----

If the original list item does not have the **POINTER** attribute, initialization of the new list items occurs as if by intrinsic assignment unless the list item has a type bound procedure as a defined assignment. If the original list item that does not have the **POINTER** attribute has the allocation status of unallocated, the new list items will have the same status.

If the original list item has the **POINTER** attribute, the new list items receive the same association status of the original list item as if by pointer assignment.

---- Fortran ----

Restrictions

The restrictions to the **firstprivate** clause are as follows:

- A list item that is private within a **parallel** region must not appear in a **firstprivate** clause on a worksharing construct if any of the worksharing regions arising from the worksharing construct ever bind to any of the **parallel** regions arising from the **parallel** construct.

- A list item that is private within a **teams** region must not appear in a **firstprivate** clause on a **distribute** construct if any of the **distribute** regions arising from the **distribute** construct ever bind to any of the **teams** regions arising from the **teams** construct.

- A list item that appears in a **reduction** clause of a **parallel** construct must not appear in a **firstprivate** clause on a worksharing, **task**, or **taskloop** construct if any of the worksharing or **task** regions arising from the worksharing, **task**, or **taskloop** construct ever bind to any of the **parallel** regions arising from the **parallel** construct.

- A list item that appears in a **reduction** clause of a **teams** construct must not appear in a **firstprivate** clause on a **distribute** construct if any of the **distribute** regions arising from the **distribute** construct ever bind to any of the **teams** regions arising from the **teams** construct.

- A list item that appears in a **reduction** clause of a worksharing construct must not appear in a **firstprivate** clause in a **task** construct encountered during execution of any of the worksharing regions arising from the worksharing construct.

―――――――――――――――――――― C++ ――――――――――――――――――――

- A variable of class type (or array thereof) that appears in a **firstprivate** clause requires an accessible, unambiguous copy constructor for the class type.

―――――――――――――――――――― C++ ――――――――――――――――――――
―――――――――――――――――――― C / C++ ――――――――――――――――――――

- If a list item in a **firstprivate** clause on a worksharing construct has a reference type then it must bind to the same object for all threads of the team.

―――――――――――――――――――― C / C++ ――――――――――――――――――――
―――――――――――――――――――― Fortran ――――――――――――――――――――

- If the list item is a polymorphic variable with the **ALLOCATABLE** attribute, the behavior is unspecified.

―――――――――――――――――――― Fortran ――――――――――――――――――――

2.19.4.5 `lastprivate` Clause

Summary

The `lastprivate` clause declares one or more list items to be private to an implicit task or to a SIMD lane, and causes the corresponding original list item to be updated after the end of the region.

Syntax

The syntax of the `lastprivate` clause is as follows:

lastprivate([*lastprivate-modifier*:] *list*)

where *lastprivate-modifier* is:

conditional

Description

The `lastprivate` clause provides a superset of the functionality provided by the `private` clause.

A list item that appears in a `lastprivate` clause is subject to the `private` clause semantics described in Section 2.19.4.3 on page 285. In addition, when a `lastprivate` clause without the `conditional` modifier appears on a directive, the value of each new list item from the sequentially last iteration of the associated loops, or the lexically last `section` construct, is assigned to the original list item. When the `conditional` modifier appears on the clause, if an assignment to a list item is encountered in the construct then the original list item is assigned the value that is assigned to the new list item in the sequentially last iteration or lexically last section in which such an assignment is encountered.

──────── C / C++ ────────

For an array of elements of non-array type, each element is assigned to the corresponding element of the original array.

──────── C / C++ ────────
──────── Fortran ────────

If the original list item does not have the `POINTER` attribute, its update occurs as if by intrinsic assignment unless it has a type bound procedure as a defined assignment.

If the original list item has the `POINTER` attribute, its update occurs as if by pointer assignment.

──────── Fortran ────────

When the `conditional` modifier does not appear on the `lastprivate` clause, list items that are not assigned a value by the sequentially last iteration of the loops, or by the lexically last `section` construct, have unspecified values after the construct. Unassigned subcomponents also have unspecified values after the construct.

If the `lastprivate` clause is used on a construct to which neither the `nowait` nor the `nogroup` clauses are applied, the original list item becomes defined at the end of the construct. To avoid data races, concurrent reads or updates of the original list item must be synchronized with the update of the original list item that occurs as a result of the `lastprivate` clause.

Otherwise, If the `lastprivate` clause is used on a construct to which the `nowait` or the `nogroup` clauses are applied, accesses to the original list item may create a data race. To avoid this data race, if an assignment to the original list item occurs then synchronization must be inserted to ensure that the assignment completes and the original list item is flushed to memory.

If a list item that appears in a `lastprivate` clause with the `conditional` modifier is modified in the region by an assignment outside the construct or not to the list item then the value assigned to the original list item is unspecified.

Restrictions

The restrictions to the `lastprivate` clause are as follows:

- A list item that is private within a `parallel` region, or that appears in the `reduction` clause of a `parallel` construct, must not appear in a `lastprivate` clause on a worksharing construct if any of the corresponding worksharing regions ever binds to any of the corresponding `parallel` regions.

- A list item that appears in a `lastprivate` clause with the `conditional` modifier must be a scalar variable.

─────────────────── C++ ───────────────────

- A variable of class type (or array thereof) that appears in a `lastprivate` clause requires an accessible, unambiguous default constructor for the class type, unless the list item is also specified in a `firstprivate` clause.

- A variable of class type (or array thereof) that appears in a `lastprivate` clause requires an accessible, unambiguous copy assignment operator for the class type. The order in which copy assignment operators for different variables of class type are called is unspecified.

─────────────────── C++ ───────────────────
─────────────────── C / C++ ───────────────────

- If a list item in a `lastprivate` clause on a worksharing construct has a reference type then it must bind to the same object for all threads of the team.

─────────────────── C / C++ ───────────────────
─────────────────── Fortran ───────────────────

- A variable that appears in a `lastprivate` clause must be definable.

- If the original list item has the `ALLOCATABLE` attribute, the corresponding list item whose value is assigned to the original list item must have an allocation status of allocated upon exit from the sequentially last iteration or lexically last `section` construct.

- If the list item is a polymorphic variable with the `ALLOCATABLE` attribute, the behavior is unspecified.

─────────────────── Fortran ───────────────────

2.19.4.6 `linear` Clause

Summary

The `linear` clause declares one or more list items to be private and to have a linear relationship with respect to the iteration space of a loop associated with the construct on which the clause appears.

Syntax

---------- C ----------

The syntax of the `linear` clause is as follows:

`linear` (*linear-list*[: *linear-step*])

where *linear-list* is one of the following

> *list*
> *modifier* (*list*)

where *modifier* is one of the following:

> `val`

---------- C ----------
---------- C++ ----------

The syntax of the `linear` clause is as follows:

`linear` (*linear-list*[: *linear-step*])

where *linear-list* is one of the following

> *list*
> *modifier* (*list*)

where *modifier* is one of the following:

> `ref`
> `val`
> `uval`

---------- C++ ----------
---------- Fortran ----------

The syntax of the `linear` clause is as follows:

`linear` (*linear-list*[: *linear-step*])

where *linear-list* is one of the following

> *list*
> *modifier* (*list*)

where *modifier* is one of the following:

```
ref
val
uval
```
———————————————— Fortran ————————————————

Description

The `linear` clause provides a superset of the functionality provided by the `private` clause. A list item that appears in a `linear` clause is subject to the `private` clause semantics described in Section 2.19.4.3 on page 285 except as noted. If *linear-step* is not specified, it is assumed to be 1.

When a `linear` clause is specified on a construct, the value of the new list item on each iteration of the associated loop(s) corresponds to the value of the original list item before entering the construct plus the logical number of the iteration times *linear-step*. The value corresponding to the sequentially last iteration of the associated loop(s) is assigned to the original list item.

When a `linear` clause is specified on a declarative directive, all list items must be formal parameters (or, in Fortran, dummy arguments) of a function that will be invoked concurrently on each SIMD lane. If no *modifier* is specified or the `val` or `uval` modifier is specified, the value of each list item on each lane corresponds to the value of the list item upon entry to the function plus the logical number of the lane times *linear-step*. If the `uval` modifier is specified, each invocation uses the same storage location for each SIMD lane; this storage location is updated with the final value of the logically last lane. If the `ref` modifier is specified, the storage location of each list item on each lane corresponds to an array at the storage location upon entry to the function indexed by the logical number of the lane times *linear-step*.

Restrictions

- The *linear-step* expression must be invariant during the execution of the region that corresponds to the construct. Otherwise, the execution results in unspecified behavior.

- Only a loop iteration variable of a loop that is associated with the construct may appear as a *list-item* in a `linear` clause if a `reduction` clause with the `inscan` modifier also appears on the construct.

———————————————— C ————————————————

- A *list-item* that appears in a `linear` clause must be of integral or pointer type.

———————————————— C ————————————————

―――――――――――――――――――― C++ ――――――――――――――――――――

- A *list-item* that appears in a `linear` clause without the `ref` modifier must be of integral or pointer type, or must be a reference to an integral or pointer type.

- The `ref` or `uval` modifier can only be used if the *list-item* is of a reference type.

- If a list item in a `linear` clause on a worksharing construct has a reference type then it must bind to the same object for all threads of the team.

- If the list item is of a reference type and the `ref` modifier is not specified and if any write to the list item occurs before any read of the list item then the result is unspecified.

―――――――――――――――――――― C++ ――――――――――――――――――――
―――――――――――――――――――― Fortran ――――――――――――――――――――

- A *list-item* that appears in a `linear` clause without the `ref` modifier must be of type `integer`.

- The `ref` or `uval` modifier can only be used if the *list-item* is a dummy argument without the `VALUE` attribute.

- Variables that have the `POINTER` attribute and Cray pointers may not appear in a `linear` clause.

- If the list item has the `ALLOCATABLE` attribute and the `ref` modifier is not specified, the allocation status of the list item in the sequentially last iteration must be allocated upon exit from that iteration.

- If the `ref` modifier is specified, variables with the `ALLOCATABLE` attribute, assumed-shape arrays and polymorphic variables may not appear in the `linear` clause.

- If the list item is a dummy argument without the `VALUE` attribute and the `ref` modifier is not specified and if any write to the list item occurs before any read of the list item then the result is unspecified.

- A common block name cannot appear in a `linear` clause.

―――――――――――――――――――― Fortran ――――――――――――――――――――

2.19.5 Reduction Clauses and Directives

The reduction clauses are data-sharing attribute clauses that can be used to perform some forms of recurrence calculations in parallel. Reduction clauses include reduction scoping clauses and reduction participating clauses. Reduction scoping clauses define the region in which a reduction is computed. Reduction participating clauses define the participants in the reduction. Reduction clauses specify a *reduction-identifier* and one or more list items.

2.19.5.1 Properties Common To All Reduction Clauses

Syntax

The syntax of a *reduction-identifier* is defined as follows:

─────────────────────────────── C ───────────────────────────────

A *reduction-identifier* is either an *identifier* or one of the following operators: +, -, *, &, |, ^, && and ||.

─────────────────────────────── C ───────────────────────────────

────────────────────────────── C++ ──────────────────────────────

A *reduction-identifier* is either an *id-expression* or one of the following operators: +, -, *, &, |, ^, && and ||.

────────────────────────────── C++ ──────────────────────────────

──────────────────────────── Fortran ────────────────────────────

A *reduction-identifier* is either a base language identifier, or a user-defined operator, or one of the following operators: +, -, *, .and., .or., .eqv., .neqv., or one of the following intrinsic procedure names: `max`, `min`, `iand`, `ior`, `ieor`.

──────────────────────────── Fortran ────────────────────────────

──────────────────────────── C / C++ ────────────────────────────

Table 2.11 lists each *reduction-identifier* that is implicitly declared at every scope for arithmetic types and its semantic initializer value. The actual initializer value is that value as expressed in the data type of the reduction list item.

TABLE 2.11: Implicitly Declared C/C++ *reduction-identifiers*

Identifier	Initializer	Combiner
+	omp_priv = 0	omp_out += omp_in
-	omp_priv = 0	omp_out += omp_in
*	omp_priv = 1	omp_out *= omp_in
&	omp_priv = ~ 0	omp_out &= omp_in
|	omp_priv = 0	omp_out |= omp_in
^	omp_priv = 0	omp_out ^= omp_in
&&	omp_priv = 1	omp_out = omp_in && omp_out

table continued on next page

table continued from previous page

Identifier	Initializer	Combiner
`||`	`omp_priv = 0`	`omp_out = omp_in || omp_out`
`max`	`omp_priv =` *Least representable number in the reduction list item type*	`omp_out = omp_in > omp_out ? omp_in : omp_out`
`min`	`omp_priv =` *Largest representable number in the reduction list item type*	`omp_out = omp_in < omp_out ? omp_in : omp_out`

▬▬▬▬▬ C / C++ ▬▬▬▬▬
▬▬▬▬▬ Fortran ▬▬▬▬▬

Table 2.12 lists each *reduction-identifier* that is implicitly declared for numeric and logical types and its semantic initializer value. The actual initializer value is that value as expressed in the data type of the reduction list item.

TABLE 2.12: Implicitly Declared Fortran *reduction-identifiers*

Identifier	Initializer	Combiner
`+`	`omp_priv = 0`	`omp_out = omp_in + omp_out`
`-`	`omp_priv = 0`	`omp_out = omp_in + omp_out`
`*`	`omp_priv = 1`	`omp_out = omp_in * omp_out`
`.and.`	`omp_priv = .true.`	`omp_out = omp_in .and. omp_out`
`.or.`	`omp_priv = .false.`	`omp_out = omp_in .or. omp_out`
`.eqv.`	`omp_priv = .true.`	`omp_out = omp_in .eqv. omp_out`
`.neqv.`	`omp_priv = .false.`	`omp_out = omp_in .neqv. omp_out`
`max`	`omp_priv =` *Least representable number in the reduction list item type*	`omp_out = max(omp_in, omp_out)`
`min`	`omp_priv =` *Largest representable number in the reduction list item type*	`omp_out = min(omp_in, omp_out)`

table continued on next page

table continued from previous page

Identifier	Initializer	Combiner
`iand`	`omp_priv =` *All bits on*	`omp_out = iand(omp_in, omp_out)`
`ior`	`omp_priv = 0`	`omp_out = ior(omp_in, omp_out)`
`ieor`	`omp_priv = 0`	`omp_out = ieor(omp_in, omp_out)`

——————————— Fortran ———————————

In the above tables, `omp_in` and `omp_out` correspond to two identifiers that refer to storage of the type of the list item. `omp_out` holds the final value of the combiner operation.

Any *reduction-identifier* that is defined with the **declare reduction** directive is also valid. In that case, the initializer and combiner of the *reduction-identifier* are specified by the *initializer-clause* and the *combiner* in the **declare reduction** directive.

Description

A reduction clause specifies a *reduction-identifier* and one or more list items.

The *reduction-identifier* specified in a reduction clause must match a previously declared *reduction-identifier* of the same name and type for each of the list items. This match is done by means of a name lookup in the base language.

The list items that appear in a reduction clause may include array sections.

——————————— C++ ———————————

If the type is a derived class, then any *reduction-identifier* that matches its base classes is also a match, if there is no specific match for the type.

If the *reduction-identifier* is not an *id-expression*, then it is implicitly converted to one by prepending the keyword operator (for example, **+** becomes *operator+*).

If the *reduction-identifier* is qualified then a qualified name lookup is used to find the declaration.

If the *reduction-identifier* is unqualified then an *argument-dependent name lookup* must be performed using the type of each list item.

——————————— C++ ———————————

If the list item is an array or array section, it will be treated as if a reduction clause would be applied to each separate element of the array section.

If the list item is an array section, the elements of any copy of the array section will be allocated contiguously.

―――――――――――――――――――― Fortran ――――――――――――――――――――

If the original list item has the **POINTER** attribute, any copies of the list item are associated with private targets.

―――――――――――――――――――― Fortran ――――――――――――――――――――

Any copies associated with the reduction are initialized with the initializer value of the *reduction-identifier*.

Any copies are combined using the combiner associated with the *reduction-identifier*.

Execution Model Events

The *reduction-begin* event occurs before a task begins to perform loads and stores that belong to the implementation of a reduction and the *reduction-end* event occurs after the task has completed loads and stores associated with the reduction. If a task participates in multiple reductions, each reduction may be bracketed by its own pair of *reduction-begin*/*reduction-end* events or multiple reductions may be bracketed by a single pair of events. The interval defined by a pair of *reduction-begin*/*reduction-end* events may not contain a task scheduling point.

Tool Callbacks

A thread dispatches a registered **ompt_callback_reduction** with **ompt_sync_region_reduction** in its *kind* argument and **ompt_scope_begin** as its *endpoint* argument for each occurrence of a *reduction-begin* event in that thread. Similarly, a thread dispatches a registered **ompt_callback_reduction** with **ompt_sync_region_reduction** in its *kind* argument and **ompt_scope_end** as its *endpoint* argument for each occurrence of a *reduction-end* event in that thread. These callbacks occur in the context of the task that performs the reduction and has the type signature **ompt_callback_sync_region_t**.

Restrictions

The restrictions common to reduction clauses are as follows:

- Any number of reduction clauses can be specified on the directive, but a list item (or any array element in an array section) can appear only once in reduction clauses for that directive.

- For a *reduction-identifier* declared with the **declare reduction** construct, the directive must appear before its use in a reduction clause.

- If a list item is an array section or an array element, its base expression must be a base language identifier.

- If a list item is an array section, it must specify contiguous storage and it cannot be a zero-length array section.

- If a list item is an array section or an array element, accesses to the elements of the array outside the specified array section or array element result in unspecified behavior.

---- C ----

- A variable that is part of another variable, with the exception of array elements, cannot appear in a reduction clause.

---- C ----

---- C++ ----

- A variable that is part of another variable, with the exception of array elements, cannot appear in a reduction clause except if the reduction clause is associated with a construct within a class non-static member function and the variable is an accessible data member of the object for which the non-static member function is invoked.

---- C++ ----

---- C / C++ ----

- The type of a list item that appears in a reduction clause must be valid for the *reduction-identifier*. For a **max** or **min** reduction in C, the type of the list item must be an allowed arithmetic data type: **char**, **int**, **float**, **double**, or **_Bool**, possibly modified with **long**, **short**, **signed**, or **unsigned**. For a **max** or **min** reduction in C++, the type of the list item must be an allowed arithmetic data type: **char**, **wchar_t**, **int**, **float**, **double**, or **bool**, possibly modified with **long**, **short**, **signed**, or **unsigned**.

- A list item that appears in a reduction clause must not be **const**-qualified.

- The *reduction-identifier* for any list item must be unambiguous and accessible.

---- C / C++ ----

---- Fortran ----

- A variable that is part of another variable, with the exception of array elements, cannot appear in a reduction clause.

- A type parameter inquiry cannot appear in a reduction clause.

- The type, type parameters and rank of a list item that appears in a reduction clause must be valid for the *combiner* and *initializer*.

- A list item that appears in a reduction clause must be definable.

- A procedure pointer may not appear in a reduction clause.

- A pointer with the **INTENT(IN)** attribute may not appear in the reduction clause.

- An original list item with the **POINTER** attribute or any pointer component of an original list item that is referenced in the *combiner* must be associated at entry to the construct that contains the reduction clause. Additionally, the list item or the pointer component of the list item must not be deallocated, allocated, or pointer assigned within the region.

- An original list item with the **ALLOCATABLE** attribute or any allocatable component of an original list item that corresponds to the special variable identifier in the *combiner* or the *initializer* must be in the allocated state at entry to the construct that contains the reduction clause. Additionally, the list item or the allocatable component of the list item must be neither deallocated nor allocated, explicitly or implicitly, within the region.
- If the *reduction-identifier* is defined in a **declare reduction** directive, the **declare reduction** directive must be in the same subprogram, or accessible by host or use association.
- If the *reduction-identifier* is a user-defined operator, the same explicit interface for that operator must be accessible as at the **declare reduction** directive.
- If the *reduction-identifier* is defined in a **declare reduction** directive, any subroutine or function referenced in the initializer clause or combiner expression must be an intrinsic function, or must have an explicit interface where the same explicit interface is accessible as at the **declare reduction** directive.

―――――― Fortran ――――――

Cross References

- **ompt_scope_begin** and **ompt_scope_end**, see Section 4.4.4.11 on page 443.
- **ompt_sync_region_reduction**, see Section 4.4.4.13 on page 444.
- **ompt_callback_sync_region_t**, see Section 4.5.2.13 on page 474.

2.19.5.2 Reduction Scoping Clauses

Reduction scoping clauses define the region in which a reduction is computed by tasks or SIMD lanes. All properties common to all reduction clauses, which are defined in Section 2.19.5.1 on page 294, apply to reduction scoping clauses.

The number of copies created for each list item and the time at which those copies are initialized are determined by the particular reduction scoping clause that appears on the construct.

The time at which the original list item contains the result of the reduction is determined by the particular reduction scoping clause.

The location in the OpenMP program at which values are combined and the order in which values are combined are unspecified. Therefore, when comparing sequential and parallel runs, or when comparing one parallel run to another (even if the number of threads used is the same), there is no guarantee that bitwise-identical results will be obtained or that side effects (such as floating-point exceptions) will be identical or take place at the same location in the OpenMP program.

To avoid data races, concurrent reads or updates of the original list item must be synchronized with the update of the original list item that occurs as a result of the reduction computation.

2.19.5.3 Reduction Participating Clauses

A reduction participating clause specifies a task or a SIMD lane as a participant in a reduction defined by a reduction scoping clause. All properties common to all reduction clauses, which are defined in Section 2.19.5.1 on page 294, apply to reduction participating clauses.

Accesses to the original list item may be replaced by accesses to copies of the original list item created by a region that corresponds to a construct with a reduction scoping clause.

In any case, the final value of the reduction must be determined as if all tasks or SIMD lanes that participate in the reduction are executed sequentially in some arbitrary order.

2.19.5.4 reduction Clause

Summary

The **reduction** clause specifies a *reduction-identifier* and one or more list items. For each list item, a private copy is created in each implicit task or SIMD lane and is initialized with the initializer value of the *reduction-identifier*. After the end of the region, the original list item is updated with the values of the private copies using the combiner associated with the *reduction-identifier*.

Syntax

reduction(*[reduction-modifier,*]*reduction-identifier* : *list*)

Where *reduction-identifier* is defined in Section 2.19.5.1 on page 294, and *reduction-modifier* is one of the following:

```
inscan
task
default
```

Description

The **reduction** clause is a reduction scoping clause and a reduction participating clause, as described in Section 2.19.5.2 on page 299 and Section 2.19.5.3 on page 300.

If *reduction-modifier* is not present or the **default** *reduction-modifier* is present, the behavior is as follows. For **parallel** and worksharing constructs, one or more private copies of each list item are created for each implicit task, as if the **private** clause had been used. For the **simd** construct, one or more private copies of each list item are created for each SIMD lane, as if the **private** clause had been used. For the **taskloop** construct, private copies are created according to the rules of the reduction scoping clauses. For the **teams** construct, one or more private copies of each list item are created for the initial task of each team in the league, as if the **private** clause had been used. For the **loop** construct, private copies are created and used in the construct according to the description and restrictions in Section 2.19.3 on page 279. At the end of a region that corresponds to a construct for which the **reduction** clause was specified, the original list item is updated by combining its original value with the final value of each of the private copies, using the combiner of the specified *reduction-identifier*.

If the **inscan** *reduction-modifier* is present, a scan computation is performed over updates to the list item performed in each logical iteration of the loop associated with the worksharing-loop, worksharing-loop SIMD, or **simd** construct (see Section 2.9.6 on page 132). The list items are privatized in the construct according to the description and restrictions in Section 2.19.3 on page 279. At the end of the region, each original list item is assigned the value of the private copy from the last logical iteration of the loops associated with the construct.

If the **task** *reduction-modifier* is present for a **parallel** or worksharing construct, then each list item is privatized according to the description and restrictions in Section 2.19.3 on page 279, and an unspecified number of additional private copies are created to support task reductions. Any copies associated with the reduction are initialized before they are accessed by the tasks that participate in the reduction, which include all implicit tasks in the corresponding region and all participating explicit tasks that specify an **in_reduction** clause (see Section 2.19.5.6 on page 303). After the end of the region, the original list item contains the result of the reduction.

If **nowait** is not specified for the construct, the reduction computation will be complete at the end of the construct; however, if the **reduction** clause is used on a construct to which **nowait** is also applied, accesses to the original list item will create a race and, thus, have unspecified effect unless synchronization ensures that they occur after all threads have executed all of their iterations or **section** constructs, and the reduction computation has completed and stored the computed value of that list item. This can most simply be ensured through a barrier synchronization.

Restrictions

The restrictions to the **reduction** clause are as follows:

- All restrictions common to all reduction clauses, which are listed in Section 2.19.5.1 on page 294, apply to this clause.
- A list item that appears in a **reduction** clause of a worksharing construct must be shared in the **parallel** region to which a corresponding worksharing region binds.
- If a list item that appears in a **reduction** clause of a worksharing construct or **loop** construct for which the corresponding region binds to a parallel region is an array section or an array element, all threads that participate in the reduction must specify the same storage location.
- A list item that appears in a **reduction** clause with the **inscan** *reduction-modifier* must appear as a list item in an **inclusive** or **exclusive** clause on a **scan** directive enclosed by the construct.

- A **reduction** clause without the **inscan** *reduction-modifier* may not appear on a construct on which a **reduction** clause with the **inscan** *reduction-modifier* appears.

- A **reduction** clause with the **task** *reduction-modifier* may only appear on a **parallel** construct, a worksharing construct or a combined or composite construct for which any of the aforementioned constructs is a constituent construct and **simd** or **loop** are not constituent constructs.

- A **reduction** clause with the **inscan** *reduction-modifier* may only appear on a worksharing-loop construct, a worksharing-loop SIMD construct, a **simd** construct, a parallel worksharing-loop construct or a parallel worksharing-loop SIMD construct.

- A list item that appears in a **reduction** clause of the innermost enclosing worksharing or **parallel** construct may not be accessed in an explicit task generated by a construct for which an **in_reduction** clause over the same list item does not appear.

- The **task** *reduction-modifier* may not appear in a **reduction** clause if the **nowait** clause is specified on the same construct.

─────────── C / C++ ───────────

- If a list item in a **reduction** clause on a worksharing construct or **loop** construct for which the corresponding region binds to a parallel region has a reference type then it must bind to the same object for all threads of the team.

- If a list item in a **reduction** clause on a worksharing construct or **loop** construct for which the corresponding region binds to a parallel region is an array section or an array element then the base pointer must point to the same variable for all threads of the team.

- A variable of class type (or array thereof) that appears in a **reduction** clause with the **inscan** *reduction-modifier* requires an accessible, unambiguous default constructor for the class type. The number of calls to the default constructor while performing the scan computation is unspecified.

- A variable of class type (or array thereof) that appears in a **reduction** clause with the **inscan** *reduction-modifier* requires an accessible, unambiguous copy assignment operator for the class type. The number of calls to the copy assignment operator while performing the scan computation is unspecified.

─────────── C / C++ ───────────

Cross References

- **scan** directive, see Section 2.9.6 on page 132.
- List Item Privatization, see Section 2.19.3 on page 279.
- **private** clause, see Section 2.19.4.3 on page 285.

2.19.5.5 `task_reduction` Clause

Summary

The `task_reduction` clause specifies a reduction among tasks.

Syntax

`task_reduction`(*reduction-identifier* : *list*)

Where *reduction-identifier* is defined in Section 2.19.5.1.

Description

The `task_reduction` clause is a reduction scoping clause, as described in 2.19.5.2.

For each list item, the number of copies is unspecified. Any copies associated with the reduction are initialized before they are accessed by the tasks participating in the reduction. After the end of the region, the original list item contains the result of the reduction.

Restrictions

The restrictions to the `task_reduction` clause are as follows:

- All restrictions common to all reduction clauses, which are listed in Section 2.19.5.1 on page 294, apply to this clause.

2.19.5.6 `in_reduction` Clause

Summary

The `in_reduction` clause specifies that a task participates in a reduction.

Syntax

`in_reduction`(*reduction-identifier* : *list*)

where *reduction-identifier* is defined in Section 2.19.5.1 on page 294.

Description

The `in_reduction` clause is a reduction participating clause, as described in Section 2.19.5.3 on page 300. For a given a list item, the `in_reduction` clause defines a task to be a participant in a task reduction that is defined by an enclosing region for a matching list item that appears in a `task_reduction` clause or a `reduction` clause with the `task` modifier, where either:

1. The matching list item has the same storage location as the list item in the `in_reduction` clause; or

2. A private copy, derived from the matching list item, that is used to perform the task reduction has the same storage location as the list item in the `in_reduction` clause.

For the `task` construct, the generated task becomes the participating task. For each list item, a private copy may be created as if the `private` clause had been used.

For the `target` construct, the target task becomes the participating task. For each list item, a private copy will be created in the data environment of the target task as if the `private` clause had been used, and this private copy will be implicitly mapped into the device data environment of the target device.

At the end of the task region, if a private copy was created its value is combined with a copy created by a reduction scoping clause or with the original list item.

Restrictions

The restrictions to the `in_reduction` clause are as follows:

- All restrictions common to all reduction clauses, which are listed in Section 2.19.5.1 on page 294, apply to this clause.

- A list item that appears in a `task_reduction` clause or a `reduction` clause with the `task` modifier that is specified on a construct that corresponds to a region in which the region of the participating task is closely nested must match each list item. The construct that corresponds to the innermost enclosing region that meets this condition must specify the same *reduction-identifier* for the matching list item as the `in_reduction` clause.

2.19.5.7 `declare reduction` Directive

Summary

The following section describes the directive for declaring user-defined reductions. The `declare reduction` directive declares a *reduction-identifier* that can be used in a `reduction` clause. The `declare reduction` directive is a declarative directive.

Syntax

---C---

`#pragma omp declare reduction`(*reduction-identifier* : *typename-list* : *combiner*) *[initializer-clause] new-line*

where:

- *reduction-identifier* is either a base language identifier or one of the following operators: `+`, `-`, `*`, `&`, `|`, `^`, `&&` and `||`
- *typename-list* is a list of type names
- *combiner* is an expression
- *initializer-clause* is `initializer`(*initializer-expr*) where *initializer-expr* is
  `omp_priv` = *initializer* or *function-name* (*argument-list*)

---C---

---C++---

`#pragma omp declare reduction`(*reduction-identifier* : *typename-list* : *combiner*) *[initializer-clause] new-line*

where:

- *reduction-identifier* is either an *id-expression* or one of the following operators: `+`, `-`, `*`, `&`, `|`, `^`, `&&` or `||`
- *typename-list* is a list of type names
- *combiner* is an expression
- *initializer-clause* is `initializer`(*initializer-expr*) where *initializer-expr* is
  `omp_priv` *initializer* or *function-name* (*argument-list*)

---C++---

---Fortran---

`!$omp declare reduction`(*reduction-identifier* : *type-list* : *combiner*)
[initializer-clause]

where:

- *reduction-identifier* is either a base language identifier, or a user-defined operator, or one of the following operators: `+`, `-`, `*`, `.and.`, `.or.`, `.eqv.`, `.neqv.`, or one of the following intrinsic procedure names: `max`, `min`, `iand`, `ior`, `ieor`.
- *type-list* is a list of type specifiers that must not be `CLASS(*)` and abstract type
- *combiner* is either an assignment statement or a subroutine name followed by an argument list
- *initializer-clause* is `initializer`(*initializer-expr*) , where *initializer-expr* is
  `omp_priv` = *expression* or *subroutine-name* (*argument-list*)

---Fortran---

Description

Custom reductions can be defined using the **declare reduction** directive; the *reduction-identifier* and the type identify the **declare reduction** directive. The *reduction-identifier* can later be used in a **reduction** clause that uses variables of the type or types specified in the **declare reduction** directive. If the directive applies to several types then it is considered as if there were multiple **declare reduction** directives, one for each type.

───────────────────────────── Fortran ─────────────────────────────

If a type with deferred or assumed length type parameter is specified in a **declare reduction** directive, the *reduction-identifier* of that directive can be used in a reduction clause with any variable of the same type and the same kind parameter, regardless of the length type Fortran parameters with which the variable is declared.

───────────────────────────── Fortran ─────────────────────────────

The visibility and accessibility of this declaration are the same as those of a variable declared at the same point in the program. The enclosing context of the *combiner* and of the *initializer-expr* is that of the **declare reduction** directive. The *combiner* and the *initializer-expr* must be correct in the base language as if they were the body of a function defined at the same point in the program.

───────────────────────────── Fortran ─────────────────────────────

If the *reduction-identifier* is the same as the name of a user-defined operator or an extended operator, or the same as a generic name that is one of the allowed intrinsic procedures, and if the operator or procedure name appears in an accessibility statement in the same module, the accessibility of the corresponding **declare reduction** directive is determined by the accessibility attribute of the statement.

If the *reduction-identifier* is the same as a generic name that is one of the allowed intrinsic procedures and is accessible, and if it has the same name as a derived type in the same module, the accessibility of the corresponding **declare reduction** directive is determined by the accessibility of the generic name according to the base language.

───────────────────────────── Fortran ─────────────────────────────
─────────────────────────────── C++ ───────────────────────────────

The **declare reduction** directive can also appear at points in the program at which a static data member could be declared. In this case, the visibility and accessibility of the declaration are the same as those of a static data member declared at the same point in the program.

─────────────────────────────── C++ ───────────────────────────────

The *combiner* specifies how partial results can be combined into a single value. The *combiner* can use the special variable identifiers **omp_in** and **omp_out** that are of the type of the variables that this *reduction-identifier* reduces. Each of them will denote one of the values to be combined before executing the *combiner*. The special **omp_out** identifier refers to the storage that holds the resulting combined value after executing the *combiner*.

The number of times that the *combiner* is executed, and the order of these executions, for any reduction clause is unspecified.

―――――― Fortran ――――――

If the *combiner* is a subroutine name with an argument list, the *combiner* is evaluated by calling the subroutine with the specified argument list.

If the *combiner* is an assignment statement, the *combiner* is evaluated by executing the assignment statement.

―――――― Fortran ――――――

As the *initializer-expr* value of a user-defined reduction is not known *a priori* the *initializer-clause* can be used to specify one. Then the contents of the *initializer-clause* will be used as the initializer for private copies of reduction list items where the **omp_priv** identifier will refer to the storage to be initialized. The special identifier **omp_orig** can also appear in the *initializer-clause* and it will refer to the storage of the original variable to be reduced.

The number of times that the *initializer-expr* is evaluated, and the order of these evaluations, is unspecified.

―――――― C / C++ ――――――

If the *initializer-expr* is a function name with an argument list, the *initializer-expr* is evaluated by calling the function with the specified argument list. Otherwise, the *initializer-expr* specifies how **omp_priv** is declared and initialized.

―――――― C / C++ ――――――

―――――― C ――――――

If no *initializer-clause* is specified, the private variables will be initialized following the rules for initialization of objects with static storage duration.

―――――― C ――――――

―――――― C++ ――――――

If no *initializer-expr* is specified, the private variables will be initialized following the rules for *default-initialization*.

―――――― C++ ――――――

―――――― Fortran ――――――

If the *initializer-expr* is a subroutine name with an argument list, the *initializer-expr* is evaluated by calling the subroutine with the specified argument list.

If the *initializer-expr* is an assignment statement, the *initializer-expr* is evaluated by executing the assignment statement.

If no *initializer-clause* is specified, the private variables will be initialized as follows.

- For **complex**, **real**, or **integer** types, the value 0 will be used.
- For **logical** types, the value **.false.** will be used.

- For derived types for which default initialization is specified, default initialization will be used.
- Otherwise, not specifying an *initializer-clause* results in unspecified behavior.

―――――――――――――――― Fortran ――――――――――――――――

―――――――――――――――― C / C++ ――――――――――――――――

If *reduction-identifier* is used in a **target** region then a **declare target** construct must be specified for any function that can be accessed through the *combiner* and *initializer-expr*.

―――――――――――――――― C / C++ ――――――――――――――――

―――――――――――――――― Fortran ――――――――――――――――

If *reduction-identifier* is used in a **target** region then a **declare target** construct must be specified for any function or subroutine that can be accessed through the *combiner* and *initializer-expr*.

―――――――――――――――― Fortran ――――――――――――――――

Restrictions

- The only variables allowed in the *combiner* are **omp_in** and **omp_out**.
- The only variables allowed in the *initializer-clause* are **omp_priv** and **omp_orig**.
- If the variable **omp_orig** is modified in the *initializer-clause*, the behavior is unspecified.
- If execution of the *combiner* or the *initializer-expr* results in the execution of an OpenMP construct or an OpenMP API call, then the behavior is unspecified.
- A *reduction-identifier* may not be re-declared in the current scope for the same type or for a type that is compatible according to the base language rules.
- At most one *initializer-clause* can be specified.
- The *typename-list* must not declare new types.

―――――――――――――――― C / C++ ――――――――――――――――

- A type name in a **declare reduction** directive cannot be a function type, an array type, a reference type, or a type qualified with **const**, **volatile** or **restrict**.

―――――――――――――――― C / C++ ――――――――――――――――

―――――――――――――――― C ――――――――――――――――

- If the *initializer-expr* is a function name with an argument list, then one of the arguments must be the address of **omp_priv**.

―――――――――――――――― C ――――――――――――――――

―――――――――――――――― C++ ――――――――――――――――

- If the *initializer-expr* is a function name with an argument list, then one of the arguments must be **omp_priv** or the address of **omp_priv**.

―――――――――――――――― C++ ――――――――――――――――

---- Fortran ----

- If the *initializer-expr* is a subroutine name with an argument list, then one of the arguments must be `omp_priv`.

- If the **declare reduction** directive appears in the specification part of a module and the corresponding reduction clause does not appear in the same module, the *reduction-identifier* must be the same as the name of a user-defined operator, one of the allowed operators that is extended or a generic name that is the same as the name of one of the allowed intrinsic procedures.

- If the **declare reduction** directive appears in the specification of a module, if the corresponding **reduction** clause does not appear in the same module, and if the *reduction-identifier* is the same as the name of a user-defined operator or an extended operator, or the same as a generic name that is the same as one of the allowed intrinsic procedures then the interface for that operator or the generic name must be defined in the specification of the same module, or must be accessible by use association.

- Any subroutine or function used in the **initializer** clause or *combiner* expression must be an intrinsic function, or must have an accessible interface.

- Any user-defined operator, defined assignment or extended operator used in the **initializer** clause or *combiner* expression must have an accessible interface.

- If any subroutine, function, user-defined operator, defined assignment or extended operator is used in the **initializer** clause or *combiner* expression, it must be accessible to the subprogram in which the corresponding **reduction** clause is specified.

- If the length type parameter is specified for a type, it must be a constant, a colon or an *.

- If a type with deferred or assumed length parameter is specified in a **declare reduction** directive, no other **declare reduction** directive with the same type, the same kind parameters and the same *reduction-identifier* is allowed in the same scope.

- Any subroutine used in the **initializer** clause or *combiner* expression must not have any alternate returns appear in the argument list.

---- Fortran ----

Cross References

- Properties Common To All Reduction Clauses, see Section 2.19.5.1 on page 294.

2.19.6 Data Copying Clauses

This section describes the **copyin** clause (allowed on the **parallel** construct and combined parallel worksharing constructs) and the **copyprivate** clause (allowed on the **single** construct).

These clauses support the copying of data values from private or threadprivate variables on one implicit task or thread to the corresponding variables on other implicit tasks or threads in the team.

The clauses accept a comma-separated list of list items (see Section 2.1 on page 38). All list items appearing in a clause must be visible, according to the scoping rules of the base language. Clauses may be repeated as needed, but a list item that specifies a given variable may not appear in more than one clause on the same directive.

―――――――――――――――――――――― Fortran ――――――――――――――――――――――

An associate name preserves the association with the selector established at the **ASSOCIATE** statement. A list item that appears in a data copying clause may be a selector of an **ASSOCIATE** construct. If the construct association is established prior to a parallel region, the association between the associate name and the original list item will be retained in the region.

―――――――――――――――――――――― Fortran ――――――――――――――――――――――

2.19.6.1 `copyin` Clause

Summary

The **copyin** clause provides a mechanism to copy the value of a threadprivate variable of the master thread to the threadprivate variable of each other member of the team that is executing the **parallel** region.

Syntax

The syntax of the **copyin** clause is as follows:

copyin (*list*)

Description

―――――――――――――――――――――― C / C++ ――――――――――――――――――――――

The copy is done after the team is formed and prior to the start of execution of the associated structured block. For variables of non-array type, the copy occurs by copy assignment. For an array of elements of non-array type, each element is copied as if by assignment from an element of the array of the master thread to the corresponding element of the array of the other thread.

―――――――――――――――――――――― C / C++ ――――――――――――――――――――――

―――――――――――――――――――――― C++ ――――――――――――――――――――――

For class types, the copy assignment operator is invoked. The order in which copy assignment operators for different variables of class type are called is unspecified.

―――――――――――――――――――――― C++ ――――――――――――――――――――――

---------- Fortran ----------

The copy is done, as if by assignment, after the team is formed and prior to the start of execution of the associated structured block.

On entry to any **parallel** region, each thread's copy of a variable that is affected by a **copyin** clause for the **parallel** region will acquire the type parameters, allocation, association, and definition status of the copy of the master thread, according to the following rules:

- If the original list item has the **POINTER** attribute, each copy receives the same association status as that of the copy of the master thread as if by pointer assignment.

- If the original list item does not have the **POINTER** attribute, each copy becomes defined with the value of the copy of the master thread as if by intrinsic assignment unless the list item has a type bound procedure as a defined assignment. If the original list item that does not have the **POINTER** attribute has the allocation status of unallocated, each copy will have the same status.

- If the original list item is unallocated or unassociated, the copy of the other thread inherits the declared type parameters and the default type parameter values from the original list item.

---------- Fortran ----------

Restrictions

The restrictions to the **copyin** clause are as follows:

---------- C / C++ ----------

- A list item that appears in a **copyin** clause must be threadprivate.

- A variable of class type (or array thereof) that appears in a **copyin** clause requires an accessible, unambiguous copy assignment operator for the class type.

---------- C / C++ ----------
---------- Fortran ----------

- A list item that appears in a **copyin** clause must be threadprivate. Named variables that appear in a threadprivate common block may be specified: it is not necessary to specify the whole common block.

- A common block name that appears in a **copyin** clause must be declared to be a common block in the same scoping unit in which the **copyin** clause appears.

- If the list item is a polymorphic variable with the **ALLOCATABLE** attribute, the behavior is unspecified.

---------- Fortran ----------

CHAPTER 2. DIRECTIVES

Cross References

- `parallel` construct, see Section 2.6 on page 74.
- `threadprivate` directive, see Section 2.19.2 on page 274.

2.19.6.2 `copyprivate` Clause

Summary

The `copyprivate` clause provides a mechanism to use a private variable to broadcast a value from the data environment of one implicit task to the data environments of the other implicit tasks that belong to the `parallel` region.

To avoid data races, concurrent reads or updates of the list item must be synchronized with the update of the list item that occurs as a result of the `copyprivate` clause.

Syntax

The syntax of the `copyprivate` clause is as follows:

> `copyprivate(list)`

Description

The effect of the `copyprivate` clause on the specified list items occurs after the execution of the structured block associated with the `single` construct (see Section 2.8.2 on page 89), and before any of the threads in the team have left the barrier at the end of the construct.

──────────── C / C++ ────────────

In all other implicit tasks that belong to the `parallel` region, each specified list item becomes defined with the value of the corresponding list item in the implicit task associated with the thread that executed the structured block. For variables of non-array type, the definition occurs by copy assignment. For an array of elements of non-array type, each element is copied by copy assignment from an element of the array in the data environment of the implicit task that is associated with the thread that executed the structured block to the corresponding element of the array in the data environment of the other implicit tasks

──────────── C / C++ ────────────
──────────── C++ ────────────

For class types, a copy assignment operator is invoked. The order in which copy assignment operators for different variables of class type are called is unspecified.

──────────── C++ ────────────

Fortran

If a list item does not have the **POINTER** attribute, then in all other implicit tasks that belong to the **parallel** region, the list item becomes defined as if by intrinsic assignment with the value of the corresponding list item in the implicit task that is associated with the thread that executed the structured block. If the list item has a type bound procedure as a defined assignment, the assignment is performed by the defined assignment.

If the list item has the **POINTER** attribute, then, in all other implicit tasks that belong to the **parallel** region, the list item receives, as if by pointer assignment, the same association status of the corresponding list item in the implicit task that is associated with the thread that executed the structured block.

The order in which any final subroutines for different variables of a finalizable type are called is unspecified.

Fortran

Note – The **copyprivate** clause is an alternative to using a shared variable for the value when providing such a shared variable would be difficult (for example, in a recursion requiring a different variable at each level).

Restrictions

The restrictions to the **copyprivate** clause are as follows:

- All list items that appear in the **copyprivate** clause must be either threadprivate or private in the enclosing context.

- A list item that appears in a **copyprivate** clause may not appear in a **private** or **firstprivate** clause on the **single** construct.

C++

- A variable of class type (or array thereof) that appears in a **copyprivate** clause requires an accessible unambiguous copy assignment operator for the class type.

C++

Fortran

- A common block that appears in a **copyprivate** clause must be threadprivate.

- Pointers with the **INTENT(IN)** attribute may not appear in the **copyprivate** clause.

- The list item with the **ALLOCATABLE** attribute must have the allocation status of allocated when the intrinsic assignment is performed.

- If the list item is a polymorphic variable with the **ALLOCATABLE** attribute, the behavior is unspecified.

Fortran

Cross References

- **parallel** construct, see Section 2.6 on page 74.
- **threadprivate** directive, see Section 2.19.2 on page 274.
- **private** clause, see Section 2.19.4.3 on page 285.

2.19.7 Data-Mapping Attribute Rules, Clauses, and Directives

This section describes how the data-mapping and data-sharing attributes of any variable referenced in a **target** region are determined. When specified, explicit data-sharing attributes, **map** or **is_device_ptr** clauses on **target** directives determine these attributes. Otherwise, the first matching rule from the following implicit data-mapping rules applies for variables referenced in a **target** construct that are not declared in the construct and do not appear in data-sharing attribute, **map** or **is_device_ptr** clauses.

- If a variable appears in a **to** or **link** clause on a **declare target** directive then it is treated as if it had appeared in a **map** clause with a *map-type* of **tofrom**.

- If a list item appears in a **reduction**, **lastprivate** or **linear** clause on a combined **target** construct then it is treated as if it also appears in a **map** clause with a *map-type* of **tofrom**.

- If a list item appears in an **in_reduction** clause on a **target** construct then it is treated as if it also appears in a **map** clause with a *map-type* of **tofrom** and a *map-type-modifier* of **always**.

- If a **defaultmap** clause is present for the category of the variable and specifies an implicit behavior other than **default**, the data-mapping attribute is determined by that clause.

──────────────────────────────── C++ ────────────────────────────────

- If the **target** construct is within a class non-static member function, and a variable is an accessible data member of the object for which the non-static data member function is invoked, the variable is treated as if the **this[:1]** expression had appeared in a **map** clause with a *map-type* of **tofrom**. Additionally, if the variable is of a type pointer or reference to pointer, it is also treated as if it has appeared in a **map** clause as a zero-length array section.

- If the **this** keyword is referenced inside a **target** construct within a class non-static member function, it is treated as if the **this[:1]** expression had appeared in a **map** clause with a *map-type* of **tofrom**.

──────────────────────────────── C++ ────────────────────────────────

―――――――――――――― C / C++ ――――――――――――――
- A variable that is of type pointer is treated as if it is the base pointer of a zero-length array section that appeared as a list item in a **map** clause.
―――――――――――――― C / C++ ――――――――――――――

―――――――――――――――― C++ ――――――――――――――――
- A variable that is of type reference to pointer is treated as if it had appeared in a **map** clause as a zero-length array section.
―――――――――――――――― C++ ――――――――――――――――
- If a variable is not a scalar then it is treated as if it had appeared in a **map** clause with a *map-type* of **tofrom**.

―――――――――――――― Fortran ――――――――――――――
- If a scalar variable has the **TARGET**, **ALLOCATABLE** or **POINTER** attribute then it is treated as if it has appeared in a **map** clause with a *map-type* of **tofrom**.
―――――――――――――― Fortran ――――――――――――――

- If none of the above rules applies then a scalar variable is not mapped, but instead has an implicit data-sharing attribute of mapped, but instead has an implicit data-sharing attribute of firstprivate (see Section 2.19.1.1 on page 270).

2.19.7.1 map Clause

Summary

The **map** clause specifies how an original list item is mapped from the current task's data environment to a corresponding list item in the device data environment of the device identified by the construct.

Syntax

The syntax of the map clause is as follows:

map (*[[map-type-modifier[,] [map-type-modifier[,] ...] map-type :] locator-list*)

where *map-type* is one of the following:

```
to
from
tofrom
alloc
release
delete
```

and *map-type-modifier* is one of the following:

> **always**
> **close**
> **mapper** (*mapper-identifier*)

Description

The list items that appear in a **map** clause may include array sections and structure elements.

The *map-type* and *map-type-modifier* specify the effect of the **map** clause, as described below.

For a given construct, the effect of a **map** clause with the **to**, **from**, or **tofrom** *map-type* is ordered before the effect of a **map** clause with the **alloc**, **release**, or **delete** *map-type*. If a mapper is specified for the type being mapped, or explicitly specified with the **mapper** *map-type-modifier*, then the effective **map-type** of a list item will be determined according to the rules of map-type decay.

If a mapper is specified for the type being mapped, or explicitly specified with the **mapper** *map-type-modifier*, then all map clauses that appear on the **declare mapper** directive are treated as though they appeared on the construct with the **map** clause. Array sections of a mapper type are mapped as normal, then each element in the array section is mapped according to the rules of the mapper.

───────────────── C / C++ ─────────────────

If a list item in a **map** clause is a variable of structure type then it is treated as if each structure element contained in the variable is a list item in the clause.

───────────────── C / C++ ─────────────────

───────────────── Fortran ─────────────────

If a list item in a **map** clause is a derived type variable then it is treated as if each component is a list item in the clause.

Each pointer component that is a list item that results from a mapped derived type variable is treated as if its association status is undefined, unless the pointer component appears as another list item or as the base pointer of another list item in a **map** clause on the same construct.

───────────────── Fortran ─────────────────

If a list item in a **map** clause is a structure element then all other structure elements of the containing structure variable form a *structure sibling list*. The **map** clause and the structure sibling list are associated with the same construct. If a corresponding list item of the structure sibling list item is present in the device data environment when the construct is encountered then:

- If the structure sibling list item does not appear in a **map** clause on the construct then:
  - If the construct is a **target**, **target data**, or **target enter data** construct then the structure sibling list item is treated as if it is a list item in a **map** clause on the construct with a *map-type* of **alloc**.
  - If the construct is **target exit data** construct, then the structure sibling list item is treated as if it is a list item in a **map** clause on the construct with a *map-type* of **release**.

---------- Fortran ----------

  - If the structure sibling list item is a pointer then it is treated as if its association status is undefined, unless it appears as the base pointer of another list item in a **map** clause on the same construct.

---------- Fortran ----------

- If the **map** clause in which the structure element appears as a list item has a *map-type* of **delete** and the structure sibling list item does not appear as a list item in a **map** clause on the construct with a *map-type* of **delete** then the structure sibling list item is treated as if it is a list item in a **map** clause on the construct with a *map-type* of **delete**.

If $item_1$ is a list item in a **map** clause, and $item_2$ is another list item in a **map** clause on the same construct that has a base pointer that is, or is part of, $item_1$, then:

- If the **map** clause(s) appear on a **target**, **target data**, or **target enter data** construct, then on entry to the corresponding region the effect of the **map** clause on $item_1$ is ordered to occur before the effect of the **map** clause on $item_2$.

- If the **map** clause(s) appear on a **target**, **target data**, or **target exit data** construct then on exit from the corresponding region the effect of the **map** clause on $item_2$ is ordered to occur before the effect of the **map** clause on $item_1$.

---------- Fortran ----------

If a list item in a **map** clause is an associated pointer and the pointer is not the base pointer of another list item in a **map** clause on the same construct, then it is treated as if its pointer target is implicitly mapped in the same clause. For the purposes of the **map** clause, the mapped pointer target is treated as if its base pointer is the associated pointer.

---------- Fortran ----------

If a list item in a **map** clause has a base pointer, and a pointer variable is present in the device data environment that corresponds to the base pointer when the effect of the **map** clause occurs, then if the corresponding pointer or the corresponding list item is created in the device data environment on entry to the construct, then:

---------- C / C++ ----------

1. The corresponding pointer variable is assigned an address such that the corresponding list item can be accessed through the pointer in a **target** region.

---------- C / C++ ----------

---------- Fortran ----------

1. The corresponding pointer variable is associated with a pointer target that has the same rank and bounds as the pointer target of the original pointer, such that the corresponding list item can be accessed through the pointer in a **target** region.

---------- Fortran ----------

2. The corresponding pointer variable becomes an attached pointer for the corresponding list item.

3. If the original base pointer and the corresponding attached pointer share storage, then the original list item and the corresponding list item must share storage.

---------- C++ ----------

If a *lambda* is mapped explicitly or implicitly, variables that are captured by the *lambda* behave as follows:

- the variables that are of pointer type are treated as if they had appeared in a **map** clause as zero-length array sections; and

- the variables that are of reference type are treated as if they had appeared in a **map** clause.

If a member variable is captured by a *lambda* in class scope, and the *lambda* is later mapped explicitly or implicitly with its full static type, the **this** pointer is treated as if it had appeared on a **map** clause.

---------- C++ ----------

The original and corresponding list items may share storage such that writes to either item by one task followed by a read or write of the other item by another task without intervening synchronization can result in data races.

If the **map** clause appears on a **target**, **target data**, or **target enter data** construct then on entry to the region the following sequence of steps occurs as if performed as a single atomic operation:

1. If a corresponding list item of the original list item is not present in the device data environment, then:

    a) A new list item with language-specific attributes is derived from the original list item and created in the device data environment;

    b) The new list item becomes the corresponding list item of the original list item in the device data environment;

    c) The corresponding list item has a reference count that is initialized to zero; and

    d) The value of the corresponding list item is undefined;

2. If the corresponding list item's reference count was not already incremented because of the effect of a **map** clause on the construct then:

    a) The corresponding list item's reference count is incremented by one;

3. If the corresponding list item's reference count is one or the **always** *map-type-modifier* is present, and if the *map-type* is **to** or **tofrom**, then:

─────────────── C / C++ ───────────────

a) For each part of the list item that is an attached pointer, that part of the corresponding list item will have the value that it had immediately prior to the effect of the **map** clause; and

─────────────── C / C++ ───────────────

─────────────── Fortran ───────────────

a) For each part of the list item that is an attached pointer, that part of the corresponding list item, if associated, will be associated with the same pointer target that it was associated with immediately prior to the effect of the **map** clause.

─────────────── Fortran ───────────────

b) For each part of the list item that is not an attached pointer, the value of that part of the original list item is assigned to that part of the corresponding list item.

Note – If the effect of the **map** clauses on a construct would assign the value of an original list item to a corresponding list item more than once, then an implementation is allowed to ignore additional assignments of the same value to the corresponding list item.

In all cases on entry to the region, concurrent reads or updates of any part of the corresponding list item must be synchronized with any update of the corresponding list item that occurs as a result of the **map** clause to avoid data races.

If the **map** clause appears on a **target**, **target data**, or **target exit data** construct and a corresponding list item of the original list item is not present in the device data environment on exit from the region then the list item is ignored. Alternatively, if the **map** clause appears on a **target**, **target data**, or **target exit data** construct and a corresponding list item of the original list item is present in the device data environment on exit from the region, then the following sequence of steps occurs as if performed as a single atomic operation:

1. If the *map-type* is not **delete** and the corresponding list item's reference count is finite and was not already decremented because of the effect of a **map** clause on the construct then:

   a) The corresponding list item's reference count is decremented by one;

2. If the *map-type* is **delete** and the corresponding list item's reference count is finite then:

   a) The corresponding list item's reference count is set to zero;

3. If the *map-type* is **from** or **tofrom** and if the corresponding list item's reference count is zero or the **always** *map-type-modifier* is present then:

---- C / C++ ----

a) For each part of the list item that is an attached pointer, that part of the original list item will have the value that it had immediately prior to the effect of the **map** clause;

---- C / C++ ----

---- Fortran ----

a) For each part of the list item that is an attached pointer, that part of the corresponding list item, if associated, will be associated with the same pointer target with which it was associated immediately prior to the effect of the **map** clause; and

---- Fortran ----

b) For each part of the list item that is not an attached pointer, the value of that part of the corresponding list item is assigned to that part of the original list item; and

4. If the corresponding list item's reference count is zero then the corresponding list item is removed from the device data environment.

Note – If the effect of the **map** clauses on a construct would assign the value of a corresponding list item to an original list item more than once, then an implementation is allowed to ignore additional assignments of the same value to the original list item.

In all cases on exit from the region, concurrent reads or updates of any part of the original list item must be synchronized with any update of the original list item that occurs as a result of the **map** clause to avoid data races.

If a single contiguous part of the original storage of a list item with an implicit data-mapping attribute has corresponding storage in the device data environment prior to a task encountering the construct that is associated with the **map** clause, only that part of the original storage will have corresponding storage in the device data environment as a result of the **map** clause.

If a list item with an implicit data-mapping attribute does not have any corresponding storage in the device data environment prior to a task encountering the construct associated with the **map** clause, and one or more contiguous parts of the original storage are either list items or base pointers to list items that are explicitly mapped on the construct, only those parts of the original storage will have corresponding storage in the device data environment as a result of the **map** clauses on the construct.

---- C / C++ ----

If a new list item is created then a new list item of the same type, with automatic storage duration, is allocated for the construct. The size and alignment of the new list item are determined by the static type of the variable. This allocation occurs if the region references the list item in any statement. Initialization and assignment of the new list item are through bitwise copy.

---- C / C++ ----

―――――――――――――――――――――― Fortran ――――――――――――――――――――――

If a new list item is created then a new list item of the same type, type parameter, and rank is allocated. The new list item inherits all default values for the type parameters from the original list item. The value of the new list item becomes that of the original list item in the map initialization and assignment.

If the allocation status of the original list item with the **ALLOCATABLE** attribute is changed in the host device data environment and the corresponding list item is already present in the device data environment, the allocation status of the corresponding list item is unspecified until a mapping operation is performed with a **map** clause on entry to a **target**, **target data**, or **target enter data** region.

―――――――――――――――――――――― Fortran ――――――――――――――――――――――

The *map-type* determines how the new list item is initialized.

If a *map-type* is not specified, the *map-type* defaults to **tofrom**.

The **close** *map-type-modifier* is a hint to the runtime to allocate memory close to the target device.

Execution Model Events

The *target-map* event occurs when a thread maps data to or from a target device.

The *target-data-op* event occurs when a thread initiates a data operation on a target device.

Tool Callbacks

A thread dispatches a registered **ompt_callback_target_map** callback for each occurrence of a *target-map* event in that thread. The callback occurs in the context of the target task and has type signature **ompt_callback_target_map_t**.

A thread dispatches a registered **ompt_callback_target_data_op** callback for each occurrence of a *target-data-op* event in that thread. The callback occurs in the context of the target task and has type signature **ompt_callback_target_data_op_t**.

Restrictions

The restrictions to the **map** clause are as follows:

- A list item cannot appear in both a **map** clause and a data-sharing attribute clause on the same construct unless the construct is a combined construct.

- Each of the *map-type-modifier* modifiers can appear at most once on the **map** clause.

―――――――――――――――――― C / C++ ――――――――――――――――――

- List items of the **map** clauses on the same construct must not share original storage unless they are the same lvalue expression or array section.

―――――――――――――――――― C / C++ ――――――――――――――――――

- If a list item is an array section, it must specify contiguous storage.

- If multiple list items are explicitly mapped on the same construct and have the same containing array or have base pointers that share original storage, and if any of the list items do not have corresponding list items that are present in the device data environment prior to a task encountering the construct, then the list items must refer to the same array elements of either the containing array or the implicit array of the base pointers.

- If any part of the original storage of a list item with an explicit data-mapping attribute has corresponding storage in the device data environment prior to a task encountering the construct associated with the **map** clause, all of the original storage must have corresponding storage in the device data environment prior to the task encountering the construct.

- If a list item is an element of a structure, and a different element of the structure has a corresponding list item in the device data environment prior to a task encountering the construct associated with the **map** clause, then the list item must also have a corresponding list item in the device data environment prior to the task encountering the construct.

- A list item must have a mappable type.

- **threadprivate** variables cannot appear in a **map** clause.

- If a **mapper** map-type-modifier is specified, its type must match the type of the list-items passed to that map clause.

- Memory spaces and memory allocators cannot appear as a list item in a **map** clause.

―――――――――――――――――― C++ ――――――――――――――――――

- If the type of a list item is a reference to a type T then the reference in the device data environment is initialized to refer to the object in the device data environment that corresponds to the object referenced by the list item. If mapping occurs, it occurs as though the object were mapped through a pointer with an array section of type T and length one.

- No type mapped through a reference can contain a reference to its own type, or any references to types that could produce a cycle of references.

- If the list item is a *lambda*, any pointers and references captured by the *lambda* must have the corresponding list item in the device data environment prior to the task encountering the construct.

―――――――――――――――――― C++ ――――――――――――――――――

―――――――――――――――――― C / C++ ――――――――――――――――――

- A list item cannot be a variable that is a member of a structure with a union type.
- A bit-field cannot appear in a **map** clause.
- A pointer that has a corresponding attached pointer must not be modified for the duration of the lifetime of the list item to which the corresponding pointer is attached in the device data environment.

―――――――――――――――――― C / C++ ――――――――――――――――――
―――――――――――――――――― Fortran ――――――――――――――――――

- List items of the **map** clauses on the same construct must not share original storage unless they are the same variable or array section.
- A pointer that has a corresponding attached pointer and is associated with a given pointer target must not become associated with a different pointer target for the duration of the lifetime of the list item to which the corresponding pointer is attached in the device data environment.
- If the allocation status of a list item or any subobject of the list item with the **ALLOCATABLE** attribute is unallocated upon entry to a **target** region, the list item or any subobject of the corresponding list item must be unallocated upon exit from the region.
- If the allocation status of a list item or any subobject of the list item with the **ALLOCATABLE** attribute is allocated upon entry to a **target** region, the allocation status of the corresponding list item or any subobject of the corresponding list item must not be changed and must not be reshaped in the region.
- If an array section is mapped and the size of the section is smaller than that of the whole array, the behavior of referencing the whole array in the **target** region is unspecified.
- A list item must not be a whole array of an assumed-size array.
- If the association status of a list item with the **POINTER** attribute is associated upon entry to a **target** region, the list item must be associated with the same pointer target upon exit from the region.
- If the association status of a list item with the **POINTER** attribute is disassociated upon entry to a **target** region, the list item must be disassociated upon exit from the region.
- If the association status of a list item with the **POINTER** attribute is undefined upon entry to a **target** region, the list item must be undefined upon exit from the region.
- If the association status of a list item with the **POINTER** attribute is disassociated or undefined on entry and if the list item is associated with a pointer target inside a **target** region, then the pointer association status must become disassociated before the end of the region.

―――――――――――――――――― Fortran ――――――――――――――――――

Cross References

- `ompt_callback_target_data_op_t`, see Section 4.5.2.25 on page 488.
- `ompt_callback_target_map_t`, see Section 4.5.2.27 on page 492.

2.19.7.2 `defaultmap` Clause

Summary

The `defaultmap` clause explicitly determines the data-mapping attributes of variables that are referenced in a `target` construct for which the data-mapping attributes would otherwise be implicitly determined (see Section 2.19.7 on page 314).

Syntax

The syntax of the `defaultmap` clause is as follows:

> `defaultmap(`*implicit-behavior*`[:`*variable-category*`])`

Where *implicit-behavior* is one of:

> `alloc`
> `to`
> `from`
> `tofrom`
> `firstprivate`
> `none`
> `default`

――――― C / C++ ―――――

and *variable-category* is one of:

> `scalar`
> `aggregate`
> `pointer`

――――― C / C++ ―――――

―――――――――――――――― Fortran ――――――――――――――――

and *variable-category* is one of:

> scalar
> aggregate
> allocatable
> pointer

―――――――――――――――― Fortran ――――――――――――――――

Description

The **defaultmap** clause sets the implicit data-mapping attribute for all variables referenced in the construct. If *variable-category* is specified, the effect of the **defaultmap** clause is as follows:

- If *variable-category* is **scalar**, all scalar variables of non-pointer type or all non-pointer non-allocatable scalar variables that have an implicitly determined data-mapping or data-sharing attribute will have a data-mapping or data-sharing attribute specified by *implicit-behavior*.

- If *variable-category* is **aggregate** or **allocatable**, all aggregate or allocatable variables that have an implicitly determined data-mapping or data-sharing attribute will have a data-mapping or data-sharing attribute specified by *implicit-behavior*.

- If *variable-category* is **pointer**, all variables of pointer type or with the POINTER attribute that have implicitly determined data-mapping or data-sharing attributes will have a data-mapping or data-sharing attribute specified by *implicit-behavior*. The zero-length array section and attachment that are otherwise applied to an implicitly mapped pointer are only provided for the **default** behavior.

If no *variable-category* is specified in the clause then *implicit-behavior* specifies the implicitly determined data-mapping or data-sharing attribute for all variables referenced in the construct. If *implicit-behavior* is **none**, each variable referenced in the construct that does not have a predetermined data-sharing attribute and does not appear in a **to** or **link** clause on a **declare target** directive must be listed in a data-mapping attribute clause, a data-sharing attribute clause (including a data-sharing attribute clause on a combined construct where **target** is one of the constituent constructs), or an **is_device_ptr** clause. If *implicit-behavior* is **default**, then the clause has no effect for the variables in the category specified by *variable-category*.

2.19.7.3 `declare mapper` Directive

Summary

The `declare mapper` directive declares a user-defined mapper for a given type, and may define a *mapper-identifier* that can be used in a `map` clause. The `declare mapper` directive is a declarative directive.

Syntax

―――――――――――――――― C / C++ ――――――――――――――――

The syntax of the `declare mapper` directive is as follows:

```
#pragma omp declare mapper ([mapper-identifier:]type var) \
        [clause[ [, ] clause] ... ] new-line
```

―――――――――――――――― C / C++ ――――――――――――――――
―――――――――――――――― Fortran ――――――――――――――――

The syntax of the `declare mapper` directive is as follows:

```
!$omp declare mapper ([mapper-identifier:] type :: var) &
        [clause[ [, ] clause] ... ]
```

―――――――――――――――― Fortran ――――――――――――――――

where:

- *mapper-identifier* is a base-language identifier or `default`
- *type* is a valid type in scope
- *var* is a valid base-language identifier
- *clause* is **map** (*[[map-type-modifier[,] [map-type-modifier[,] ...]] map-type :] list*) , where *map-type* is one of the following:
    - `alloc`
    - `to`
    - `from`
    - `tofrom`

    and where *map-type-modifier* is one of the following:
    - `always`
    - `close`

Description

User-defined mappers can be defined using the **declare mapper** directive. The type and the *mapper-identifier* uniquely identify the mapper for use in a **map** clause later in the program. If the *mapper-identifier* is not specified, then **default** is used. The visibility and accessibility of this declaration are the same as those of a variable declared at the same point in the program.

The variable declared by *var* is available for use in all **map** clauses on the directive, and no part of the variable to be mapped is mapped by default.

The default mapper for all types T, designated by the pre-defined *mapper-identifier* **default**, is as follows unless a user-defined mapper is specified for that type.

```
declare mapper(T v) map(tofrom: v)
```

Using the **default** *mapper-identifier* overrides the pre-defined default mapper for the given type, making it the default for all variables of *type*. All **map** clauses with this construct in scope that map a list item of *type* will use this mapper unless another is explicitly specified.

All **map** clauses on the directive are expanded into corresponding **map** clauses wherever this mapper is invoked, either by matching type or by being explicitly named in a **map** clause. A **map** clause with list item *var* maps *var* as though no mapper were specified.

----------------------------------- C++ -----------------------------------

The **declare mapper** directive can also appear at points in the program at which a static data member could be declared. In this case, the visibility and accessibility of the declaration are the same as those of a static data member declared at the same point in the program.

----------------------------------- C++ -----------------------------------

Restrictions

The restrictions to the **declare mapper** directive are as follows:

- No instance of *type* can be mapped as part of the mapper, either directly or indirectly through another type, except the instance passed as the list item. If a set of **declare mapper** directives results in a cyclic definition then the behavior is unspecified.

- The *type* must be of struct, union or class type in C and C++ or a non-intrinsic type in Fortran.

- The *type* must not declare a new type.

- At least one **map** clause that maps *var* or at least one element of *var* is required.

- List-items in **map** clauses on this construct may only refer to the declared variable *var* and entities that could be referenced by a procedure defined at the same location.

- Each *map-type-modifier* can appear at most once on the **map** clause.

- A *mapper-identifier* may not be redeclared in the current scope for the same type or for a type that is compatible according to the base language rules.

―――――――――――――――――――― Fortran ――――――――――――――――――――
- *type* must not be an abstract type.
―――――――――――――――――――― Fortran ――――――――――――――――――――

2.20 Nesting of Regions

This section describes a set of restrictions on the nesting of regions. The restrictions on nesting are as follows:

- A worksharing region may not be closely nested inside a worksharing, `loop`, `task`, `taskloop`, `critical`, `ordered`, `atomic`, or `master` region.
- A `barrier` region may not be closely nested inside a worksharing, `loop`, `task`, `taskloop`, `critical`, `ordered`, `atomic`, or `master` region.
- A `master` region may not be closely nested inside a worksharing, `loop`, `atomic`, `task`, or `taskloop` region.
- An `ordered` region corresponding to an `ordered` construct without any clause or with the `threads` or `depend` clause may not be closely nested inside a `critical`, `ordered`, `loop`, `atomic`, `task`, or `taskloop` region.
- An `ordered` region corresponding to an `ordered` construct without the `simd` clause specified must be closely nested inside a worksharing-loop region.
- An `ordered` region corresponding to an `ordered` construct with the `simd` clause specified must be closely nested inside a `simd` or worksharing-loop SIMD region.
- An `ordered` region corresponding to an `ordered` construct with both the `simd` and `threads` clauses must be closely nested inside a worksharing-loop SIMD region or closely nested inside a worksharing-loop and `simd` region.
- A `critical` region may not be nested (closely or otherwise) inside a `critical` region with the same name. This restriction is not sufficient to prevent deadlock.
- OpenMP constructs may not be encountered during execution of an `atomic` region.
- The only OpenMP constructs that can be encountered during execution of a `simd` (or worksharing-loop SIMD) region are the `atomic` construct, the `loop` construct, the `simd` construct and the `ordered` construct with the `simd` clause.

- If a **target update**, **target data**, **target enter data**, or **target exit data** construct is encountered during execution of a **target** region, the behavior is unspecified.

- If a **target** construct is encountered during execution of a **target** region and a **device** clause in which the **ancestor** *device-modifier* appears is not present on the construct, the behavior is unspecified.

- A **teams** region can only be strictly nested within the implicit parallel region or a **target** region. If a **teams** construct is nested within a **target** construct, that **target** construct must contain no statements, declarations or directives outside of the **teams** construct.

- **distribute**, **distribute simd**, distribute parallel worksharing-loop, distribute parallel worksharing-loop SIMD, **loop**, **parallel** regions, including any **parallel** regions arising from combined constructs, **omp_get_num_teams()** regions, and **omp_get_team_num()** regions are the only OpenMP regions that may be strictly nested inside the **teams** region.

- The region corresponding to the **distribute** construct must be strictly nested inside a **teams** region.

- If *construct-type-clause* is **taskgroup**, the **cancel** construct must be closely nested inside a **task** construct and the **cancel** region must be closely nested inside a **taskgroup** region. If *construct-type-clause* is **sections**, the **cancel** construct must be closely nested inside a **sections** or **section** construct. Otherwise, the **cancel** construct must be closely nested inside an OpenMP construct that matches the type specified in *construct-type-clause* of the **cancel** construct.

- A **cancellation point** construct for which *construct-type-clause* is **taskgroup** must be closely nested inside a **task** construct, and the **cancellation point** region must be closely nested inside a **taskgroup** region. A **cancellation point** construct for which *construct-type-clause* is **sections** must be closely nested inside a **sections** or **section** construct. Otherwise, a **cancellation point** construct must be closely nested inside an OpenMP construct that matches the type specified in *construct-type-clause*.

- The only constructs that may be nested inside a **loop** region are the **loop** construct, the **parallel** construct, the **simd** construct, and combined constructs for which the first construct is a **parallel** construct.

- A **loop** region may not contain calls to procedures that contain OpenMP directives or calls to the OpenMP Runtime API.

This page intentionally left blank

CHAPTER 3

Runtime Library Routines

This chapter describes the OpenMP API runtime library routines and queryable runtime states. In this chapter, *true* and *false* are used as generic terms to simplify the description of the routines.

―――――――――――――― C / C++ ――――――――――――――

true means a nonzero integer value and *false* means an integer value of zero.

―――――――――――――― C / C++ ――――――――――――――

―――――――――――――― Fortran ――――――――――――――

true means a logical value of `.TRUE.` and *false* means a logical value of `.FALSE.`.

―――――――――――――― Fortran ――――――――――――――

―――――――――――――― Fortran ――――――――――――――

Restrictions

The following restriction applies to all OpenMP runtime library routines:

- OpenMP runtime library routines may not be called from `PURE` or `ELEMENTAL` procedures.

―――――――――――――― Fortran ――――――――――――――

3.1 Runtime Library Definitions

For each base language, a compliant implementation must supply a set of definitions for the OpenMP API runtime library routines and the special data types of their parameters. The set of definitions must contain a declaration for each OpenMP API runtime library routine and variable and a definition of each required data type listed below. In addition, each set of definitions may specify other implementation specific values.

―――――――――――――――――――― C / C++ ――――――――――――――――――――

The library routines are external functions with "C" linkage.

Prototypes for the C/C++ runtime library routines described in this chapter shall be provided in a header file named **omp.h**. This file also defines the following:

- The type **omp_lock_t**;
- The type **omp_nest_lock_t**;
- The type **omp_sync_hint_t**;
- The type **omp_lock_hint_t** (deprecated);
- The type **omp_sched_t**;
- The type **omp_proc_bind_t**;
- The type **omp_control_tool_t**;
- The type **omp_control_tool_result_t**;
- The type **omp_depend_t**;
- The type **omp_memspace_handle_t**, which must be an implementation-defined enum type with an enumerator for at least each predefined memory space in Table 2.8 on page 152;
- The type **omp_allocator_handle_t**, which must be an implementation-defined enum type with at least the **omp_null_allocator** enumerator with the value zero and an enumerator for each predefined memory allocator in Table 2.10 on page 155;
- The type **omp_uintptr_t**, which is an unsigned integer type capable of holding a pointer on any device;
- The type **omp_pause_resource_t**; and
- The type **omp_event_handle_t**, which must be an implementation-defined enum type.

―――――――――――――――――――― C / C++ ――――――――――――――――――――

---- C++ ----

The **omp.h** header file also defines a class template that models the **Allocator** concept in the **omp::allocator** namespace for each predefined memory allocator in Table 2.10 on page 155 for which the name includes neither the **omp_** prefix nor the **_alloc** suffix.

---- C++ ----

---- Fortran ----

The OpenMP Fortran API runtime library routines are external procedures. The return values of these routines are of default kind, unless otherwise specified.

Interface declarations for the OpenMP Fortran runtime library routines described in this chapter shall be provided in the form of a Fortran **include** file named **omp_lib.h** or a Fortran 90 **module** named **omp_lib**. It is implementation defined whether the **include** file or the **module** file (or both) is provided.

These files also define the following:

- The **integer parameter** omp_lock_kind;
- The **integer parameter** omp_nest_lock_kind;
- The **integer parameter** omp_sync_hint_kind;
- The **integer parameter** omp_lock_hint_kind (deprecated);
- The **integer parameter** omp_sched_kind;
- The **integer parameter** omp_proc_bind_kind;
- The **integer parameter** omp_control_tool_kind;
- The **integer parameter** omp_control_tool_result_kind;
- The **integer parameter** omp_depend_kind;
- The **integer parameter** omp_memspace_handle_kind;
- The **integer parameter** omp_allocator_handle_kind;
- The **integer parameter** omp_alloctrait_key_kind;
- The **integer parameter** omp_alloctrait_val_kind;
- An **integer parameter** of kind **omp_memspace_handle_kind** for each predefined memory space in Table 2.8 on page 152;
- An **integer parameter** of kind **omp_allocator_handle_kind** for each predefined memory allocator in Table 2.10 on page 155;
- The **integer parameter** omp_pause_resource_kind;
- The **integer parameter** omp_event_handle_kind; and

- The **integer parameter openmp_version** with a value *yyyymm* where *yyyy* and *mm* are the year and month designations of the version of the OpenMP Fortran API that the implementation supports; this value matches that of the C preprocessor macro **_OPENMP**, when a macro preprocessor is supported (see Section 2.2 on page 49).

It is implementation defined whether any of the OpenMP runtime library routines that take an argument are extended with a generic interface so arguments of different **KIND** type can be accommodated.

─────────── Fortran ───────────

3.2 Execution Environment Routines

This section describes routines that affect and monitor threads, processors, and the parallel environment.

3.2.1 omp_set_num_threads

Summary

The **omp_set_num_threads** routine affects the number of threads to be used for subsequent parallel regions that do not specify a **num_threads** clause, by setting the value of the first element of the *nthreads-var* ICV of the current task.

Format

─────────── C / C++ ───────────
```
void omp_set_num_threads(int num_threads);
```
─────────── C / C++ ───────────

─────────── Fortran ───────────
```
subroutine omp_set_num_threads(num_threads)
integer num_threads
```
─────────── Fortran ───────────

Constraints on Arguments

The value of the argument passed to this routine must evaluate to a positive integer, or else the behavior of this routine is implementation defined.

Binding

The binding task set for an **omp_set_num_threads** region is the generating task.

Effect

The effect of this routine is to set the value of the first element of the *nthreads-var* ICV of the current task to the value specified in the argument.

Cross References

- *nthreads-var* ICV, see Section 2.5 on page 63.
- **parallel** construct and **num_threads** clause, see Section 2.6 on page 74.
- Determining the number of threads for a **parallel** region, see Section 2.6.1 on page 78.
- **omp_get_num_threads** routine, see Section 3.2.2 on page 335.
- **omp_get_max_threads** routine, see Section 3.2.3 on page 336.
- **OMP_NUM_THREADS** environment variable, see Section 6.2 on page 602.

3.2.2 omp_get_num_threads

Summary

The **omp_get_num_threads** routine returns the number of threads in the current team.

Format

―――――――――――― C / C++ ――――――――――――
```
int omp_get_num_threads(void);
```
―――――――――――― C / C++ ――――――――――――

―――――――――――― Fortran ――――――――――――
```
integer function omp_get_num_threads()
```
―――――――――――― Fortran ――――――――――――

Binding

The binding region for an **omp_get_num_threads** region is the innermost enclosing **parallel** region.

Effect

The `omp_get_num_threads` routine returns the number of threads in the team that is executing the `parallel` region to which the routine region binds. If called from the sequential part of a program, this routine returns 1.

Cross References

- *nthreads-var* ICV, see Section 2.5 on page 63.
- `parallel` construct and `num_threads` clause, see Section 2.6 on page 74.
- Determining the number of threads for a `parallel` region, see Section 2.6.1 on page 78.
- `omp_set_num_threads` routine, see Section 3.2.1 on page 334.
- `OMP_NUM_THREADS` environment variable, see Section 6.2 on page 602.

3.2.3 omp_get_max_threads

Summary

The `omp_get_max_threads` routine returns an upper bound on the number of threads that could be used to form a new team if a `parallel` construct without a `num_threads` clause were encountered after execution returns from this routine.

Format

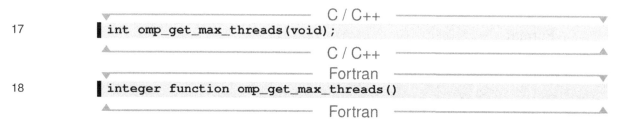

```
int omp_get_max_threads(void);
```

```
integer function omp_get_max_threads()
```

Binding

The binding task set for an `omp_get_max_threads` region is the generating task.

Effect

The value returned by **omp_get_max_threads** is the value of the first element of the *nthreads-var* ICV of the current task. This value is also an upper bound on the number of threads that could be used to form a new team if a parallel region without a **num_threads** clause were encountered after execution returns from this routine.

Note – The return value of the **omp_get_max_threads** routine can be used to allocate sufficient storage dynamically for all threads in the team formed at the subsequent active **parallel** region.

Cross References

- *nthreads-var* ICV, see Section 2.5 on page 63.
- **parallel** construct and **num_threads** clause, see Section 2.6 on page 74.
- Determining the number of threads for a **parallel** region, see Section 2.6.1 on page 78.
- **omp_set_num_threads** routine, see Section 3.2.1 on page 334.
- **omp_get_num_threads** routine, see Section 3.2.2 on page 335.
- **omp_get_thread_num** routine, see Section 3.2.4 on page 337.
- **OMP_NUM_THREADS** environment variable, see Section 6.2 on page 602.

3.2.4 omp_get_thread_num

Summary

The **omp_get_thread_num** routine returns the thread number, within the current team, of the calling thread.

Format

―――――――― C / C++ ――――――――
```
int omp_get_thread_num(void);
```
―――――――― C / C++ ――――――――

―――――――― Fortran ――――――――
```
integer function omp_get_thread_num()
```
―――――――― Fortran ――――――――

Binding

The binding thread set for an `omp_get_thread_num` region is the current team. The binding region for an `omp_get_thread_num` region is the innermost enclosing **parallel** region.

Effect

The `omp_get_thread_num` routine returns the thread number of the calling thread, within the team that is executing the **parallel** region to which the routine region binds. The thread number is an integer between 0 and one less than the value returned by `omp_get_num_threads`, inclusive. The thread number of the master thread of the team is 0. The routine returns 0 if it is called from the sequential part of a program.

Note – The thread number may change during the execution of an untied task. The value returned by `omp_get_thread_num` is not generally useful during the execution of such a task region.

Cross References

- *nthreads-var* ICV, see Section 2.5 on page 63.
- **parallel** construct and `num_threads` clause, see Section 2.6 on page 74.
- Determining the number of threads for a **parallel** region, see Section 2.6.1 on page 78.
- `omp_set_num_threads` routine, see Section 3.2.1 on page 334.
- `omp_get_num_threads` routine, see Section 3.2.2 on page 335.
- **OMP_NUM_THREADS** environment variable, see Section 6.2 on page 602.

3.2.5 omp_get_num_procs

Summary

The `omp_get_num_procs` routine returns the number of processors available to the device.

Format

─────────── C / C++ ───────────
```
int omp_get_num_procs(void);
```
─────────── C / C++ ───────────

─────────── Fortran ───────────
```
integer function omp_get_num_procs()
```
─────────── Fortran ───────────

Binding

The binding thread set for an **omp_get_num_procs** region is all threads on a device. The effect of executing this routine is not related to any specific region corresponding to any construct or API routine.

Effect

The **omp_get_num_procs** routine returns the number of processors that are available to the device at the time the routine is called. This value may change between the time that it is determined by the **omp_get_num_procs** routine and the time that it is read in the calling context due to system actions outside the control of the OpenMP implementation.

Cross References

- **omp_get_num_places** routine, see Section 3.2.24 on page 358.
- **omp_get_place_num_procs** routine, see Section 3.2.25 on page 359.
- **omp_get_place_proc_ids** routine, see Section 3.2.26 on page 360.
- **omp_get_place_num** routine, see Section 3.2.27 on page 362.

3.2.6 omp_in_parallel

Summary

The **omp_in_parallel** routine returns *true* if the *active-levels-var* ICV is greater than zero; otherwise, it returns *false*.

Format

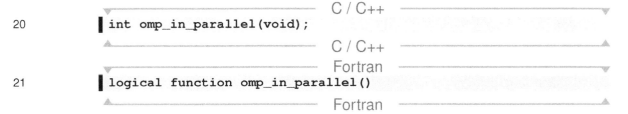

Binding

The binding task set for an **omp_in_parallel** region is the generating task.

Effect

The effect of the **omp_in_parallel** routine is to return *true* if the current task is enclosed by an active **parallel** region, and the **parallel** region is enclosed by the outermost initial task region on the device; otherwise it returns *false*.

Cross References

- *active-levels-var*, see Section 2.5 on page 63.
- **parallel** construct, see Section 2.6 on page 74.
- **omp_get_num_threads** routine, see Section 3.2.2 on page 335.
- **omp_get_active_level** routine, see Section 3.2.21 on page 355.

3.2.7 omp_set_dynamic

Summary

The **omp_set_dynamic** routine enables or disables dynamic adjustment of the number of threads available for the execution of subsequent **parallel** regions by setting the value of the *dyn-var* ICV.

Format

―――――――――――――――― C / C++ ――――――――――――――――
```
void omp_set_dynamic(int dynamic_threads);
```
―――――――――――――――― C / C++ ――――――――――――――――

―――――――――――――――― Fortran ――――――――――――――――
```
subroutine omp_set_dynamic(dynamic_threads)
logical dynamic_threads
```
―――――――――――――――― Fortran ――――――――――――――――

Binding

The binding task set for an **omp_set_dynamic** region is the generating task.

Effect

For implementations that support dynamic adjustment of the number of threads, if the argument to **omp_set_dynamic** evaluates to *true*, dynamic adjustment is enabled for the current task; otherwise, dynamic adjustment is disabled for the current task. For implementations that do not support dynamic adjustment of the number of threads, this routine has no effect: the value of *dyn-var* remains *false*.

Cross References

- *dyn-var* ICV, see Section 2.5 on page 63.
- Determining the number of threads for a **parallel** region, see Section 2.6.1 on page 78.
- **omp_get_num_threads** routine, see Section 3.2.2 on page 335.
- **omp_get_dynamic** routine, see Section 3.2.8 on page 341.
- **OMP_DYNAMIC** environment variable, see Section 6.3 on page 603.

3.2.8 omp_get_dynamic

Summary

The **omp_get_dynamic** routine returns the value of the *dyn-var* ICV, which determines whether dynamic adjustment of the number of threads is enabled or disabled.

Format

———————————————— C / C++ ————————————————
```
int omp_get_dynamic(void);
```
———————————————— C / C++ ————————————————

———————————————— Fortran ————————————————
```
logical function omp_get_dynamic()
```
———————————————— Fortran ————————————————

Binding

The binding task set for an **omp_get_dynamic** region is the generating task.

Effect

This routine returns *true* if dynamic adjustment of the number of threads is enabled for the current task; it returns *false*, otherwise. If an implementation does not support dynamic adjustment of the number of threads, then this routine always returns *false*.

Cross References

- *dyn-var* ICV, see Section 2.5 on page 63.
- Determining the number of threads for a **parallel** region, see Section 2.6.1 on page 78.
- **omp_set_dynamic** routine, see Section 3.2.7 on page 340.
- **OMP_DYNAMIC** environment variable, see Section 6.3 on page 603.

3.2.9 omp_get_cancellation

Summary

The **omp_get_cancellation** routine returns the value of the *cancel-var* ICV, which determines if cancellation is enabled or disabled.

Format

―――――――――――――― C / C++ ――――――――――――――
```
int omp_get_cancellation(void);
```
―――――――――――――― C / C++ ――――――――――――――

―――――――――――――― Fortran ――――――――――――――
```
logical function omp_get_cancellation()
```
―――――――――――――― Fortran ――――――――――――――

Binding

The binding task set for an **omp_get_cancellation** region is the whole program.

Effect

This routine returns *true* if cancellation is enabled. It returns *false* otherwise.

Cross References

- *cancel-var* ICV, see Section 2.5.1 on page 64.
- **cancel** construct, see Section 2.18.1 on page 263.
- **OMP_CANCELLATION** environment variable, see Section 6.11 on page 610.

3.2.10 omp_set_nested

Summary

The deprecated **omp_set_nested** routine enables or disables nested parallelism by setting the *max-active-levels-var* ICV.

Format

----------- C / C++ -----------
```
void omp_set_nested(int nested);
```
----------- C / C++ -----------

----------- Fortran -----------
```
subroutine omp_set_nested(nested)
logical nested
```
----------- Fortran -----------

Binding

The binding task set for an **omp_set_nested** region is the generating task.

Effect

If the argument to **omp_set_nested** evaluates to *true*, the value of the *max-active-levels-var* ICV is set to the number of active levels of parallelism that the implementation supports; otherwise, if the value of *max-active-levels-var* is greater than 1 then it is set to 1. This routine has been deprecated

Cross References

- *max-active-levels-var* ICV, see Section 2.5 on page 63.
- Determining the number of threads for a **parallel** region, see Section 2.6.1 on page 78.
- **omp_get_nested** routine, see Section 3.2.11 on page 344.
- **omp_set_max_active_levels** routine, see Section 3.2.16 on page 350.
- **omp_get_max_active_levels** routine, see Section 3.2.17 on page 351.
- **OMP_NESTED** environment variable, see Section 6.9 on page 609.

3.2.11 omp_get_nested

Summary

The deprecated **omp_get_nested** routine returns whether nested parallelism is enabled or disabled, according to the value of the *max-active-levels-var* ICV.

Format

―――――――――――――― C / C++ ――――――――――――――
```
int omp_get_nested(void);
```
―――――――――――――― C / C++ ――――――――――――――

―――――――――――――― Fortran ――――――――――――――
```
logical function omp_get_nested()
```
―――――――――――――― Fortran ――――――――――――――

Binding

The binding task set for an **omp_get_nested** region is the generating task.

Effect

This routine returns *true* if *max-active-levels-var* is greater than 1 for the current task; it returns *false*, otherwise. If an implementation does not support nested parallelism, this routine always returns *false*. This routine has been deprecated.

Cross References

- *max-active-levels-var* ICV, see Section 2.5 on page 63.
- Determining the number of threads for a **parallel** region, see Section 2.6.1 on page 78.
- **omp_set_nested** routine, see Section 3.2.10 on page 343.
- **omp_set_max_active_levels** routine, see Section 3.2.16 on page 350.
- **omp_get_max_active_levels** routine, see Section 3.2.17 on page 351.
- **OMP_NESTED** environment variable, see Section 6.9 on page 609.

3.2.12 omp_set_schedule

Summary

The **omp_set_schedule** routine affects the schedule that is applied when **runtime** is used as schedule kind, by setting the value of the *run-sched-var* ICV.

Format

─────────── C / C++ ───────────
```
void omp_set_schedule(omp_sched_t kind, int chunk_size);
```
─────────── C / C++ ───────────

─────────── Fortran ───────────
```
subroutine omp_set_schedule(kind, chunk_size)
integer (kind=omp_sched_kind) kind
integer chunk_size
```
─────────── Fortran ───────────

Constraints on Arguments

The first argument passed to this routine can be one of the valid OpenMP schedule kinds (except for **runtime**) or any implementation specific schedule. The C/C++ header file (**omp.h**) and the Fortran include file (**omp_lib.h**) and/or Fortran 90 module file (**omp_lib**) define the valid constants. The valid constants must include the following, which can be extended with implementation specific values:

––––––––––––––––––––––– C / C++ –––––––––––––––––––––––

```
typedef enum omp_sched_t {
  // schedule kinds
  omp_sched_static = 0x1,
  omp_sched_dynamic = 0x2,
  omp_sched_guided = 0x3,
  omp_sched_auto = 0x4,

  // schedule modifier
  omp_sched_monotonic = 0x80000000u
} omp_sched_t;
```

––––––––––––––––––––––– C / C++ –––––––––––––––––––––––

––––––––––––––––––––––– Fortran –––––––––––––––––––––––

```
! schedule kinds
integer(kind=omp_sched_kind), &
  parameter :: omp_sched_static = &
                  int(Z'1', kind=omp_sched_kind)
integer(kind=omp_sched_kind), &
  parameter :: omp_sched_dynamic = &
                  int(Z'2', kind=omp_sched_kind)
integer(kind=omp_sched_kind), &
  parameter :: omp_sched_guided = &
                  int(Z'3', kind=omp_sched_kind)
integer(kind=omp_sched_kind), &
  parameter :: omp_sched_auto = &
                  int(Z'4', kind=omp_sched_kind)

! schedule modifier
integer(kind=omp_sched_kind), &
  parameter :: omp_sched_monotonic = &
                  int(Z'80000000', kind=omp_sched_kind)
```

––––––––––––––––––––––– Fortran –––––––––––––––––––––––

Binding

The binding task set for an **omp_set_schedule** region is the generating task.

Effect

The effect of this routine is to set the value of the *run-sched-var* ICV of the current task to the values specified in the two arguments. The schedule is set to the schedule kind that is specified by the first argument *kind*. It can be any of the standard schedule kinds or any other implementation specific one. For the schedule kinds **static**, **dynamic**, and **guided** the *chunk_size* is set to the value of the second argument, or to the default *chunk_size* if the value of the second argument is less than 1; for the schedule kind **auto** the second argument has no meaning; for implementation specific schedule kinds, the values and associated meanings of the second argument are implementation defined.

Each of the schedule kinds can be combined with the **omp_sched_monotonic** modifier by using the + or | operators in C/C++ or the + operator in Fortran. If the schedule kind is combined with the **omp_sched_monotonic** modifier, the schedule is modified as if the **monotonic** schedule modifier was specified. Otherwise, the schedule modifier is **nonmonotonic**.

Cross References

- *run-sched-var* ICV, see Section 2.5 on page 63.
- Determining the schedule of a worksharing-loop, see Section 2.9.2.1 on page 109.
- **omp_set_schedule** routine, see Section 3.2.12 on page 345.
- **omp_get_schedule** routine, see Section 3.2.13 on page 347.
- **OMP_SCHEDULE** environment variable, see Section 6.1 on page 601.

3.2.13 omp_get_schedule

Summary

The **omp_get_schedule** routine returns the schedule that is applied when the runtime schedule is used.

Format

―――― C / C++ ――――
```
void omp_get_schedule(omp_sched_t *kind, int *chunk_size);
```
―――― C / C++ ――――

―――― Fortran ――――
```
subroutine omp_get_schedule(kind, chunk_size)
integer (kind=omp_sched_kind) kind
integer chunk_size
```
―――― Fortran ――――

Binding

The binding task set for an `omp_get_schedule` region is the generating task.

Effect

This routine returns the *run-sched-var* ICV in the task to which the routine binds. The first argument *kind* returns the schedule to be used. It can be any of the standard schedule kinds as defined in Section 3.2.12 on page 345, or any implementation specific schedule kind. The second argument *chunk_size* returns the chunk size to be used, or a value less than 1 if the default chunk size is to be used, if the returned schedule kind is `static`, `dynamic`, or `guided`. The value returned by the second argument is implementation defined for any other schedule kinds.

Cross References

- *run-sched-var* ICV, see Section 2.5 on page 63.
- Determining the schedule of a worksharing-loop, see Section 2.9.2.1 on page 109.
- `omp_set_schedule` routine, see Section 3.2.12 on page 345.
- `OMP_SCHEDULE` environment variable, see Section 6.1 on page 601.

3.2.14 omp_get_thread_limit

Summary

The `omp_get_thread_limit` routine returns the maximum number of OpenMP threads available to participate in the current contention group.

Format

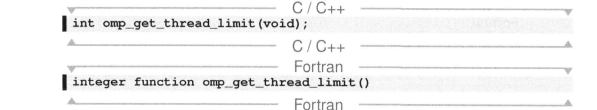

Binding

The binding thread set for an **omp_get_thread_limit** region is all threads on the device. The effect of executing this routine is not related to any specific region corresponding to any construct or API routine.

Effect

The **omp_get_thread_limit** routine returns the value of the *thread-limit-var* ICV.

Cross References

- *thread-limit-var* ICV, see Section 2.5 on page 63.
- **omp_get_num_threads** routine, see Section 3.2.2 on page 335.
- **OMP_THREAD_LIMIT** environment variable, see Section 6.10 on page 610.
- **OMP_NUM_THREADS** environment variable, see Section 6.2 on page 602.

3.2.15 omp_get_supported_active_levels

Summary

The **omp_get_supported_active_levels** routine returns the number of active levels of parallelism supported by the implementation.

Format

─────────────── C / C++ ───────────────
```
int omp_get_supported_active_levels(void);
```
─────────────── C / C++ ───────────────

─────────────── Fortran ───────────────
```
integer function omp_get_supported_active_levels()
```
─────────────── Fortran ───────────────

Binding

The binding task set for an **omp_get_supported_active_levels** region is the generating task.

Effect

The `omp_get_supported_active_levels` routine returns the number of active levels of parallelism supported by the implementation. The *max-active-levels-var* ICV may not have a value that is greater than this number. The value returned by the `omp_get_supported_active_levels` routine is implementation defined, but it must be greater than 0.

Cross References

- *max-active-levels-var* ICV, see Section 2.5 on page 63.
- `omp_get_max_active_levels` routine, see Section 3.2.17 on page 351.
- `omp_set_max_active_levels` routine, see Section 3.2.16 on page 350.

3.2.16 omp_set_max_active_levels

Summary

The `omp_set_max_active_levels` routine limits the number of nested active parallel regions on the device, by setting the *max-active-levels-var* ICV

Format

―――――――――――――――――― C / C++ ――――――――――――――――――
```
void omp_set_max_active_levels(int max_levels);
```
―――――――――――――――――― C / C++ ――――――――――――――――――

―――――――――――――――――― Fortran ――――――――――――――――――
```
subroutine omp_set_max_active_levels(max_levels)
integer max_levels
```
―――――――――――――――――― Fortran ――――――――――――――――――

Constraints on Arguments

The value of the argument passed to this routine must evaluate to a non-negative integer, otherwise the behavior of this routine is implementation defined.

Binding

When called from a sequential part of the program, the binding thread set for an `omp_set_max_active_levels` region is the encountering thread. When called from within any **parallel** or **teams** region, the binding thread set (and binding region, if required) for the `omp_set_max_active_levels` region is implementation defined.

Effect

The effect of this routine is to set the value of the *max-active-levels-var* ICV to the value specified in the argument.

If the number of active levels requested exceeds the number of active levels of parallelism supported by the implementation, the value of the *max-active-levels-var* ICV will be set to the number of active levels supported by the implementation.

This routine has the described effect only when called from a sequential part of the program. When called from within a **parallel** or **teams** region, the effect of this routine is implementation defined.

Cross References

- *max-active-levels-var* ICV, see Section 2.5 on page 63.
- **parallel** construct, see Section 2.6 on page 74.
- `omp_get_supported_active_levels` routine, see Section 3.2.15 on page 349.
- `omp_get_max_active_levels` routine, see Section 3.2.17 on page 351.
- **OMP_MAX_ACTIVE_LEVELS** environment variable, see Section 6.8 on page 608.

3.2.17 omp_get_max_active_levels

Summary

The `omp_get_max_active_levels` routine returns the value of the *max-active-levels-var* ICV, which determines the maximum number of nested active parallel regions on the device.

Format

––––––––––––––––––––––––––––– C / C++ –––––––––––––––––––––––––––––
```
int omp_get_max_active_levels(void);
```
––––––––––––––––––––––––––––– C / C++ –––––––––––––––––––––––––––––

––––––––––––––––––––––––––––– Fortran –––––––––––––––––––––––––––––
```
integer function omp_get_max_active_levels()
```
––––––––––––––––––––––––––––– Fortran –––––––––––––––––––––––––––––

Binding

When called from a sequential part of the program, the binding thread set for an `omp_get_max_active_levels` region is the encountering thread. When called from within any `parallel` or `teams` region, the binding thread set (and binding region, if required) for the `omp_get_max_active_levels` region is implementation defined.

Effect

The `omp_get_max_active_levels` routine returns the value of the *max-active-levels-var* ICV, which determines the maximum number of nested active parallel regions on the device.

Cross References

- *max-active-levels-var* ICV, see Section 2.5 on page 63.
- `parallel` construct, see Section 2.6 on page 74.
- `omp_get_supported_active_levels` routine, see Section 3.2.15 on page 349.
- `omp_set_max_active_levels` routine, see Section 3.2.16 on page 350.
- `OMP_MAX_ACTIVE_LEVELS` environment variable, see Section 6.8 on page 608.

3.2.18 omp_get_level

Summary

The `omp_get_level` routine returns the value of the *levels-var* ICV.

Format

───────────────── C / C++ ─────────────────
```
int omp_get_level(void);
```
───────────────── C / C++ ─────────────────

───────────────── Fortran ─────────────────
```
integer function omp_get_level()
```
───────────────── Fortran ─────────────────

Binding

The binding task set for an `omp_get_level` region is the generating task.

Effect

The effect of the **omp_get_level** routine is to return the number of nested **parallel** regions (whether active or inactive) that enclose the current task such that all of the **parallel** regions are enclosed by the outermost initial task region on the current device.

Cross References

- *levels-var* ICV, see Section 2.5 on page 63.
- **parallel** construct, see Section 2.6 on page 74.
- **omp_get_active_level** routine, see Section 3.2.21 on page 355.
- **OMP_MAX_ACTIVE_LEVELS** environment variable, see Section 6.8 on page 608.

3.2.19 omp_get_ancestor_thread_num

Summary

The **omp_get_ancestor_thread_num** routine returns, for a given nested level of the current thread, the thread number of the ancestor of the current thread.

Format

―――――――――――――― C / C++ ――――――――――――――
```
int omp_get_ancestor_thread_num(int level);
```
―――――――――――――― C / C++ ――――――――――――――

―――――――――――――― Fortran ――――――――――――――
```
integer function omp_get_ancestor_thread_num(level)
integer level
```
―――――――――――――― Fortran ――――――――――――――

Binding

The binding thread set for an **omp_get_ancestor_thread_num** region is the encountering thread. The binding region for an **omp_get_ancestor_thread_num** region is the innermost enclosing **parallel** region.

Effect

The **omp_get_ancestor_thread_num** routine returns the thread number of the ancestor at a given nest level of the current thread or the thread number of the current thread. If the requested nest level is outside the range of 0 and the nest level of the current thread, as returned by the **omp_get_level** routine, the routine returns -1.

Note – When the **omp_get_ancestor_thread_num** routine is called with a value of **level**=0, the routine always returns 0. If **level**=**omp_get_level()**, the routine has the same effect as the **omp_get_thread_num** routine.

Cross References

- **parallel** construct, see Section 2.6 on page 74.
- **omp_get_num_threads** routine, see Section 3.2.2 on page 335.
- **omp_get_thread_num** routine, see Section 3.2.4 on page 337.
- **omp_get_level** routine, see Section 3.2.18 on page 352.
- **omp_get_team_size** routine, see Section 3.2.20 on page 354.

3.2.20 omp_get_team_size

Summary

The **omp_get_team_size** routine returns, for a given nested level of the current thread, the size of the thread team to which the ancestor or the current thread belongs.

Format

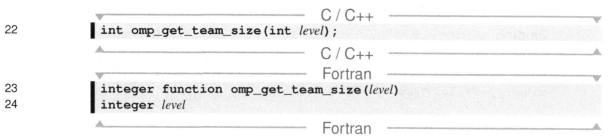

```
C / C++
int omp_get_team_size(int level);
C / C++
```

```
Fortran
integer function omp_get_team_size(level)
integer level
Fortran
```

Binding

The binding thread set for an `omp_get_team_size` region is the encountering thread. The binding region for an `omp_get_team_size` region is the innermost enclosing **parallel** region.

Effect

The `omp_get_team_size` routine returns the size of the thread team to which the ancestor or the current thread belongs. If the requested nested level is outside the range of 0 and the nested level of the current thread, as returned by the `omp_get_level` routine, the routine returns -1. Inactive parallel regions are regarded like active parallel regions executed with one thread.

Note – When the `omp_get_team_size` routine is called with a value of **level**=0, the routine always returns 1. If **level**=omp_get_level(), the routine has the same effect as the `omp_get_num_threads` routine.

Cross References

- `omp_get_num_threads` routine, see Section 3.2.2 on page 335.
- `omp_get_level` routine, see Section 3.2.18 on page 352.
- `omp_get_ancestor_thread_num` routine, see Section 3.2.19 on page 353.

3.2.21 omp_get_active_level

Summary

The `omp_get_active_level` routine returns the value of the *active-level-vars* ICV..

Format

―――――――――――――――― C / C++ ――――――――――――――――
```
int omp_get_active_level(void);
```
―――――――――――――――― C / C++ ――――――――――――――――
―――――――――――――――― Fortran ――――――――――――――――
```
integer function omp_get_active_level()
```
―――――――――――――――― Fortran ――――――――――――――――

Binding

The binding task set for the an `omp_get_active_level` region is the generating task.

Effect

The effect of the `omp_get_active_level` routine is to return the number of nested active **parallel** regions enclosing the current task such that all of the **parallel** regions are enclosed by the outermost initial task region on the current device.

Cross References

- *active-levels-var* ICV, see Section 2.5 on page 63.
- `omp_get_level` routine, see Section 3.2.18 on page 352.
- `omp_set_max_active_levels` routine, see Section 3.2.16 on page 350.
- `omp_get_max_active_levels` routine, see Section 3.2.17 on page 351.
- `OMP_MAX_ACTIVE_LEVELS` environment variable, see Section 6.8 on page 608.

3.2.22 omp_in_final

Summary

The `omp_in_final` routine returns *true* if the routine is executed in a final task region; otherwise, it returns *false*.

Format

―――――――――――――――――――――― C / C++ ――――――――――――――――――――――
```
int omp_in_final(void);
```
―――――――――――――――――――――― C / C++ ――――――――――――――――――――――

―――――――――――――――――――――― Fortran ――――――――――――――――――――――
```
logical function omp_in_final()
```
―――――――――――――――――――――― Fortran ――――――――――――――――――――――

Binding

The binding task set for an `omp_in_final` region is the generating task.

Effect

`omp_in_final` returns *true* if the enclosing task region is final. Otherwise, it returns *false*.

Cross References

- **task** construct, see Section 2.10.1 on page 135.

3.2.23 omp_get_proc_bind

Summary

The `omp_get_proc_bind` routine returns the thread affinity policy to be used for the subsequent nested **parallel** regions that do not specify a **proc_bind** clause.

Format

―――――――――――――― C / C++ ――――――――――――――
```
omp_proc_bind_t omp_get_proc_bind(void);
```
―――――――――――――― C / C++ ――――――――――――――

―――――――――――――― Fortran ――――――――――――――
```
integer (kind=omp_proc_bind_kind) function omp_get_proc_bind()
```
―――――――――――――― Fortran ――――――――――――――

Constraints on Arguments

The value returned by this routine must be one of the valid affinity policy kinds. The C/C++ header file (**omp.h**) and the Fortran include file (**omp_lib.h**) and/or Fortran 90 module file (**omp_lib**) define the valid constants. The valid constants must include the following:

―――――――――――――― C / C++ ――――――――――――――
```
typedef enum omp_proc_bind_t {
  omp_proc_bind_false = 0,
  omp_proc_bind_true = 1,
  omp_proc_bind_master = 2,
  omp_proc_bind_close = 3,
  omp_proc_bind_spread = 4
} omp_proc_bind_t;
```
―――――――――――――― C / C++ ――――――――――――――

```fortran
! Fortran
integer (kind=omp_proc_bind_kind), &
          parameter :: omp_proc_bind_false = 0
integer (kind=omp_proc_bind_kind), &
          parameter :: omp_proc_bind_true = 1
integer (kind=omp_proc_bind_kind), &
          parameter :: omp_proc_bind_master = 2
integer (kind=omp_proc_bind_kind), &
          parameter :: omp_proc_bind_close = 3
integer (kind=omp_proc_bind_kind), &
          parameter :: omp_proc_bind_spread = 4
! Fortran
```

Binding

The binding task set for an **omp_get_proc_bind** region is the generating task.

Effect

The effect of this routine is to return the value of the first element of the *bind-var* ICV of the current task. See Section 2.6.2 on page 80 for the rules that govern the thread affinity policy.

Cross References

- *bind-var* ICV, see Section 2.5 on page 63.
- Controlling OpenMP thread affinity, see Section 2.6.2 on page 80.
- **omp_get_num_places** routine, see Section 3.2.24 on page 358.
- **OMP_PROC_BIND** environment variable, see Section 6.4 on page 604.
- **OMP_PLACES** environment variable, see Section 6.5 on page 605.

3.2.24 omp_get_num_places

Summary

The **omp_get_num_places** routine returns the number of places available to the execution environment in the place list.

Format

```
C / C++
int omp_get_num_places(void);
C / C++
```

```
Fortran
integer function omp_get_num_places()
Fortran
```

Binding

The binding thread set for an **omp_get_num_places** region is all threads on a device. The effect of executing this routine is not related to any specific region corresponding to any construct or API routine.

Effect

The **omp_get_num_places** routine returns the number of places in the place list. This value is equivalent to the number of places in the *place-partition-var* ICV in the execution environment of the initial task.

Cross References

- *place-partition-var* ICV, see Section 2.5 on page 63.
- Controlling OpenMP thread affinity, see Section 2.6.2 on page 80.
- **omp_get_place_num** routine, see Section 3.2.27 on page 362.
- **OMP_PLACES** environment variable, see Section 6.5 on page 605.

3.2.25 omp_get_place_num_procs

Summary

The **omp_get_place_num_procs** routine returns the number of processors available to the execution environment in the specified place.

Format

```
C / C++
int omp_get_place_num_procs(int place_num);
C / C++
```

```
Fortran
integer function omp_get_place_num_procs(place_num)
    integer place_num
Fortran
```

Binding

The binding thread set for an `omp_get_place_num_procs` region is all threads on a device. The effect of executing this routine is not related to any specific region corresponding to any construct or API routine.

Effect

The `omp_get_place_num_procs` routine returns the number of processors associated with the place numbered *place_num*. The routine returns zero when *place_num* is negative, or is greater than or equal to the value returned by `omp_get_num_places()`.

Cross References

- *place-partition-var* ICV, see Section 2.5 on page 63.
- Controlling OpenMP thread affinity, see Section 2.6.2 on page 80.
- `omp_get_num_places` routine, see Section 3.2.24 on page 358.
- `omp_get_place_proc_ids` routine, see Section 3.2.26 on page 360.
- `OMP_PLACES` environment variable, see Section 6.5 on page 605.

3.2.26 omp_get_place_proc_ids

Summary

The `omp_get_place_proc_ids` routine returns the numerical identifiers of the processors available to the execution environment in the specified place.

Format

---C / C++---
```
void omp_get_place_proc_ids(int place_num, int *ids);
```
---C / C++---

---Fortran---
```
subroutine omp_get_place_proc_ids(place_num, ids)
integer place_num
integer ids(*)
```
---Fortran---

Binding

The binding thread set for an **omp_get_place_proc_ids** region is all threads on a device. The effect of executing this routine is not related to any specific region corresponding to any construct or API routine.

Effect

The **omp_get_place_proc_ids** routine returns the numerical identifiers of each processor associated with the place numbered *place_num*. The numerical identifiers are non-negative, and their meaning is implementation defined. The numerical identifiers are returned in the array *ids* and their order in the array is implementation defined. The array must be sufficiently large to contain **omp_get_place_num_procs**(*place_num*) integers; otherwise, the behavior is unspecified. The routine has no effect when *place_num* has a negative value, or a value greater than or equal to **omp_get_num_places()**.

Cross References

- *place-partition-var* ICV, see Section 2.5 on page 63.
- Controlling OpenMP thread affinity, see Section 2.6.2 on page 80.
- **omp_get_num_places** routine, see Section 3.2.24 on page 358.
- **omp_get_place_num_procs** routine, see Section 3.2.25 on page 359.
- **OMP_PLACES** environment variable, see Section 6.5 on page 605.

3.2.27 `omp_get_place_num`

Summary

The `omp_get_place_num` routine returns the place number of the place to which the encountering thread is bound.

Format

-- C / C++ --
```
int omp_get_place_num(void);
```
-- C / C++ --

-- Fortran --
```
integer function omp_get_place_num()
```
-- Fortran --

Binding

The binding thread set for an `omp_get_place_num` region is the encountering thread.

Effect

When the encountering thread is bound to a place, the `omp_get_place_num` routine returns the place number associated with the thread. The returned value is between 0 and one less than the value returned by `omp_get_num_places()`, inclusive. When the encountering thread is not bound to a place, the routine returns -1.

Cross References

- *place-partition-var* ICV, see Section 2.5 on page 63.
- Controlling OpenMP thread affinity, see Section 2.6.2 on page 80.
- `omp_get_num_places` routine, see Section 3.2.24 on page 358.
- `OMP_PLACES` environment variable, see Section 6.5 on page 605.

3.2.28 `omp_get_partition_num_places`

Summary

The `omp_get_partition_num_places` routine returns the number of places in the place partition of the innermost implicit task.

Format

---- C / C++ ----
```
int omp_get_partition_num_places(void);
```
---- C / C++ ----

---- Fortran ----
```
integer function omp_get_partition_num_places()
```
---- Fortran ----

Binding

The binding task set for an **omp_get_partition_num_places** region is the encountering implicit task.

Effect

The **omp_get_partition_num_places** routine returns the number of places in the *place-partition-var* ICV.

Cross References

- *place-partition-var* ICV, see Section 2.5 on page 63.
- Controlling OpenMP thread affinity, see Section 2.6.2 on page 80.
- **omp_get_num_places** routine, see Section 3.2.24 on page 358.
- **OMP_PLACES** environment variable, see Section 6.5 on page 605.

3.2.29 omp_get_partition_place_nums

Summary

The **omp_get_partition_place_nums** routine returns the list of place numbers corresponding to the places in the *place-partition-var* ICV of the innermost implicit task.

Format

―――――――――――――――― C / C++ ――――――――――――――――
```
void omp_get_partition_place_nums(int *place_nums);
```
―――――――――――――――― C / C++ ――――――――――――――――

―――――――――――――――― Fortran ――――――――――――――――
```
subroutine omp_get_partition_place_nums(place_nums)
integer place_nums(*)
```
―――――――――――――――― Fortran ――――――――――――――――

Binding

The binding task set for an `omp_get_partition_place_nums` region is the encountering implicit task.

Effect

The `omp_get_partition_place_nums` routine returns the list of place numbers that correspond to the places in the *place-partition-var* ICV of the innermost implicit task. The array must be sufficiently large to contain `omp_get_partition_num_places()` integers; otherwise, the behavior is unspecified.

Cross References

- *place-partition-var* ICV, see Section 2.5 on page 63.
- Controlling OpenMP thread affinity, see Section 2.6.2 on page 80.
- `omp_get_partition_num_places` routine, see Section 3.2.28 on page 362.
- `OMP_PLACES` environment variable, see Section 6.5 on page 605.

3.2.30 omp_set_affinity_format

Summary

The `omp_set_affinity_format` routine sets the affinity format to be used on the device by setting the value of the *affinity-format-var* ICV.

Format

―――――――――――― C / C++ ――――――――――――
```
void omp_set_affinity_format(const char *format);
```
―――――――――――― C / C++ ――――――――――――

―――――――――――― Fortran ――――――――――――
```
subroutine omp_set_affinity_format(format)
character(len=*),intent(in) :: format
```
―――――――――――― Fortran ――――――――――――

Binding

When called from a sequential part of the program, the binding thread set for an **omp_set_affinity_format** region is the encountering thread. When called from within any **parallel** or **teams** region, the binding thread set (and binding region, if required) for the **omp_set_affinity_format** region is implementation defined.

Effect

The effect of **omp_set_affinity_format** routine is to copy the character string specified by the *format* argument into the *affinity-format-var* ICV on the current device.

This routine has the described effect only when called from a sequential part of the program. When called from within a **parallel** or **teams** region, the effect of this routine is implementation defined.

Cross References

- Controlling OpenMP thread affinity, see Section 2.6.2 on page 80.
- **omp_get_affinity_format** routine, see Section 3.2.31 on page 366.
- **omp_display_affinity** routine, see Section 3.2.32 on page 367.
- **omp_capture_affinity** routine, see Section 3.2.33 on page 368.
- **OMP_DISPLAY_AFFINITY** environment variable, see Section 6.13 on page 612.
- **OMP_AFFINITY_FORMAT** environment variable, see Section 6.14 on page 613.

3.2.31 omp_get_affinity_format

Summary

The `omp_get_affinity_format` routine returns the value of the *affinity-format-var* ICV on the device.

Format

─────────── C / C++ ───────────
```
size_t omp_get_affinity_format(char *buffer, size_t size);
```
─────────── C / C++ ───────────

─────────── Fortran ───────────
```
integer function omp_get_affinity_format(buffer)
character(len=*),intent(out) :: buffer
```
─────────── Fortran ───────────

Binding

When called from a sequential part of the program, the binding thread set for an `omp_get_affinity_format` region is the encountering thread. When called from within any `parallel` or `teams` region, the binding thread set (and binding region, if required) for the `omp_get_affinity_format` region is implementation defined.

Effect

─────────── C / C++ ───────────
The `omp_get_affinity_format` routine returns the number of characters in the *affinity-format-var* ICV on the current device, excluding the terminating null byte (' \0 ') and if *size* is non-zero, writes the value of the *affinity-format-var* ICV on the current device to *buffer* followed by a null byte. If the return value is larger or equal to *size*, the affinity format specification is truncated, with the terminating null byte stored to *buffer*[*size*−1]. If *size* is zero, nothing is stored and *buffer* may be **NULL**.
─────────── C / C++ ───────────

─────────── Fortran ───────────
The `omp_get_affinity_format` routine returns the number of characters that are required to hold the *affinity-format-var* ICV on the current device and writes the value of the *affinity-format-var* ICV on the current device to *buffer*. If the return value is larger than **len**(*buffer*), the affinity format specification is truncated.
─────────── Fortran ───────────

If the *buffer* argument does not conform to the specified format then the result is implementation defined.

Cross References

- Controlling OpenMP thread affinity, see Section 2.6.2 on page 80.
- `omp_set_affinity_format` routine, see Section 3.2.30 on page 364.
- `omp_display_affinity` routine, see Section 3.2.32 on page 367.
- `omp_capture_affinity` routine, see Section 3.2.33 on page 368.
- `OMP_DISPLAY_AFFINITY` environment variable, see Section 6.13 on page 612.
- `OMP_AFFINITY_FORMAT` environment variable, see Section 6.14 on page 613.

3.2.32 omp_display_affinity

Summary

The `omp_display_affinity` routine prints the OpenMP thread affinity information using the format specification provided.

Format

―――――――――――――――――――― C / C++ ――――――――――――――――――――
```
void omp_display_affinity(const char *format);
```
―――――――――――――――――――― C / C++ ――――――――――――――――――――

―――――――――――――――――――― Fortran ――――――――――――――――――――
```
subroutine omp_display_affinity(format)
character(len=*),intent(in) :: format
```
―――――――――――――――――――― Fortran ――――――――――――――――――――

Binding

The binding thread set for an `omp_display_affinity` region is the encountering thread.

Effect

The `omp_display_affinity` routine prints the thread affinity information of the current thread in the format specified by the *format* argument, followed by a *new-line*. If the *format* is **NULL** (for C/C++) or a zero-length string (for Fortran and C/C++), the value of the *affinity-format-var* ICV is used. If the *format* argument does not conform to the specified format then the result is implementation defined.

Cross References

- Controlling OpenMP thread affinity, see Section 2.6.2 on page 80.
- `omp_set_affinity_format` routine, see Section 3.2.30 on page 364.
- `omp_get_affinity_format` routine, see Section 3.2.31 on page 366.
- `omp_capture_affinity` routine, see Section 3.2.33 on page 368.
- **OMP_DISPLAY_AFFINITY** environment variable, see Section 6.13 on page 612.
- **OMP_AFFINITY_FORMAT** environment variable, see Section 6.14 on page 613.

3.2.33 omp_capture_affinity

Summary

The `omp_capture_affinity` routine prints the OpenMP thread affinity information into a buffer using the format specification provided.

Format

─────────────── C / C++ ───────────────
```
size_t omp_capture_affinity(
    char *buffer,
    size_t size,
    const char *format
);
```
─────────────── C / C++ ───────────────

─────────────── Fortran ───────────────
```
integer function omp_capture_affinity(buffer, format)
character(len=*),intent(out) :: buffer
character(len=*),intent(in)  :: format
```
─────────────── Fortran ───────────────

Binding

The binding thread set for an `omp_capture_affinity` region is the encountering thread.

Effect

---------- C / C++ ----------

The **omp_capture_affinity** routine returns the number of characters in the entire thread affinity information string excluding the terminating null byte (' \0 ') and if *size* is non-zero, writes the thread affinity information of the current thread in the format specified by the *format* argument into the character string **buffer** followed by a null byte. If the return value is larger or equal to *size*, the thread affinity information string is truncated, with the terminating null byte stored to **buffer[size-1]**. If *size* is zero, nothing is stored and *buffer* may be **NULL**. If the *format* is **NULL** or a zero-length string, the value of the *affinity-format-var* ICV is used.

---------- C / C++ ----------

---------- Fortran ----------

The **omp_capture_affinity** routine returns the number of characters required to hold the entire thread affinity information string and prints the thread affinity information of the current thread into the character string **buffer** with the size of **len(*buffer*)** in the format specified by the *format* argument. If the *format* is a zero-length string, the value of the *affinity-format-var* ICV is used. If the return value is larger than **len(*buffer*)**, the thread affinity information string is truncated. If the *format* is a zero-length string, the value of the *affinity-format-var* ICV is used.

---------- Fortran ----------

If the *format* argument does not conform to the specified format then the result is implementation defined.

Cross References

- Controlling OpenMP thread affinity, see Section 2.6.2 on page 80.
- **omp_set_affinity_format** routine, see Section 3.2.30 on page 364.
- **omp_get_affinity_format** routine, see Section 3.2.31 on page 366.
- **omp_display_affinity** routine, see Section 3.2.32 on page 367.
- **OMP_DISPLAY_AFFINITY** environment variable, see Section 6.13 on page 612.
- **OMP_AFFINITY_FORMAT** environment variable, see Section 6.14 on page 613.

3.2.34 omp_set_default_device

Summary

The **omp_set_default_device** routine controls the default target device by assigning the value of the *default-device-var* ICV.

Format

―――――――――――――――― C / C++ ――――――――――――――――
```
void omp_set_default_device(int device_num);
```
―――――――――――――――― C / C++ ――――――――――――――――
―――――――――――――――― Fortran ――――――――――――――――
```
subroutine omp_set_default_device(device_num)
integer device_num
```
―――――――――――――――― Fortran ――――――――――――――――

Binding

The binding task set for an `omp_set_default_device` region is the generating task.

Effect

The effect of this routine is to set the value of the *default-device-var* ICV of the current task to the value specified in the argument. When called from within a `target` region the effect of this routine is unspecified.

Cross References

- *default-device-var*, see Section 2.5 on page 63.
- `target` construct, see Section 2.12.5 on page 170
- `omp_get_default_device`, see Section 3.2.35 on page 370.
- `OMP_DEFAULT_DEVICE` environment variable, see Section 6.15 on page 615

3.2.35 omp_get_default_device

Summary

The `omp_get_default_device` routine returns the default target device.

Format

―― C / C++ ――
```
int omp_get_default_device(void);
```
―― C / C++ ――

―― Fortran ――
```
integer function omp_get_default_device()
```
―― Fortran ――

Binding

The binding task set for an **omp_get_default_device** region is the generating task.

Effect

The **omp_get_default_device** routine returns the value of the *default-device-var* ICV of the current task. When called from within a **target** region the effect of this routine is unspecified.

Cross References

- *default-device-var*, see Section 2.5 on page 63.
- **target** construct, see Section 2.12.5 on page 170
- **omp_set_default_device**, see Section 3.2.34 on page 369.
- **OMP_DEFAULT_DEVICE** environment variable, see Section 6.15 on page 615.

3.2.36 omp_get_num_devices

Summary

The **omp_get_num_devices** routine returns the number of target devices.

Format

―― C / C++ ――
```
int omp_get_num_devices(void);
```
―― C / C++ ――

―― Fortran ――
```
integer function omp_get_num_devices()
```
―― Fortran ――

Binding

The binding task set for an **omp_get_num_devices** region is the generating task.

Effect

The **omp_get_num_devices** routine returns the number of available target devices. When called from within a **target** region the effect of this routine is unspecified.

Cross References

- **target** construct, see Section 2.12.5 on page 170
- **omp_get_default_device**, see Section 3.2.35 on page 370.
- **omp_get_device_num**, see Section 3.2.37 on page 372.

3.2.37 omp_get_device_num

Summary

The **omp_get_device_num** routine returns the device number of the device on which the calling thread is executing.

Format

```
int omp_get_device_num(void);
```
C / C++

```
integer function omp_get_device_num()
```
Fortran

Binding

The binding task set for an **omp_get_devices_num** region is the generating task.

Effect

The **omp_get_device_num** routine returns the device number of the device on which the calling thread is executing. When called on the host device, it will return the same value as the **omp_get_initial_device** routine.

Cross References

- **target** construct, see Section 2.12.5 on page 170
- **omp_get_default_device**, see Section 3.2.35 on page 370.
- **omp_get_num_devices**, see Section 3.2.36 on page 371.
- **omp_get_initial_device** routine, see Section 3.2.41 on page 376.

3.2.38 omp_get_num_teams

Summary

The **omp_get_num_teams** routine returns the number of initial teams in the current **teams** region.

Format

―――――――――――――――――― C / C++ ――――――――――――――――――
```
int omp_get_num_teams(void);
```
―――――――――――――――――― C / C++ ――――――――――――――――――
―――――――――――――――――― Fortran ――――――――――――――――――
```
integer function omp_get_num_teams()
```
―――――――――――――――――― Fortran ――――――――――――――――――

Binding

The binding task set for an **omp_get_num_teams** region is the generating task

Effect

The effect of this routine is to return the number of initial teams in the current **teams** region. The routine returns 1 if it is called from outside of a **teams** region.

Cross References

- **teams** construct, see Section 2.7 on page 82.
- **target** construct, see Section 2.12.5 on page 170.
- **omp_get_team_num** routine, see Section 3.2.39 on page 374.

3.2.39 omp_get_team_num

Summary

The `omp_get_team_num` routine returns the initial team number of the calling thread.

Format

─── C / C++ ───
```
int omp_get_team_num(void);
```
─── C / C++ ───

─── Fortran ───
```
integer function omp_get_team_num()
```
─── Fortran ───

Binding

The binding task set for an `omp_get_team_num` region is the generating task.

Effect

The `omp_get_team_num` routine returns the initial team number of the calling thread. The initial team number is an integer between 0 and one less than the value returned by `omp_get_num_teams()`, inclusive. The routine returns 0 if it is called outside of a `teams` region.

Cross References

- `teams` construct, see Section 2.7 on page 82.
- `target` construct, see Section 2.12.5 on page 170
- `omp_get_num_teams` routine, see Section 3.2.38 on page 373.

3.2.40 omp_is_initial_device

Summary

The **omp_is_initial_device** routine returns *true* if the current task is executing on the host device; otherwise, it returns *false*.

Format

---------- C / C++ ----------
```
int omp_is_initial_device(void);
```
---------- C / C++ ----------

---------- Fortran ----------
```
logical function omp_is_initial_device()
```
---------- Fortran ----------

Binding

The binding task set for an **omp_is_initial_device** region is the generating task.

Effect

The effect of this routine is to return *true* if the current task is executing on the host device; otherwise, it returns *false*.

Cross References

- **omp_get_get_initial_device** routine, see Section 3.2.41 on page 376.
- Device memory routines, see Section 3.6 on page 397.

3.2.41 omp_get_initial_device

Summary

The `omp_get_initial_device` routine returns a device number that represents the host device.

Format

―――――――――――――― C / C++ ――――――――――――――
```
int omp_get_initial_device(void);
```
―――――――――――――― C / C++ ――――――――――――――

―――――――――――――― Fortran ――――――――――――――
```
integer function omp_get_initial_device()
```
―――――――――――――― Fortran ――――――――――――――

Binding

The binding task set for an `omp_get_initial_device` region is the generating task.

Effect

The effect of this routine is to return the device number of the host device. The value of the device number is implementation defined. When called from within a `target` region the effect of this routine is unspecified.

Cross References

- `target` construct, see Section 2.12.5 on page 170.
- `omp_is_initial_device` routine, see Section 3.2.40 on page 375.
- Device memory routines, see Section 3.6 on page 397.

3.2.42 omp_get_max_task_priority

Summary
The `omp_get_max_task_priority` routine returns the maximum value that can be specified in the `priority` clause.

Format

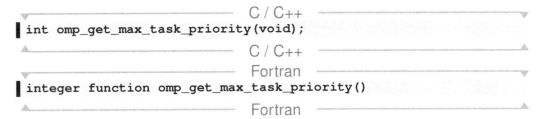

```
int omp_get_max_task_priority(void);
```

```
integer function omp_get_max_task_priority()
```

Binding
The binding thread set for an `omp_get_max_task_priority` region is all threads on the device. The effect of executing this routine is not related to any specific region that corresponds to any construct or API routine.

Effect
The `omp_get_max_task_priority` routine returns the value of the *max-task-priority-var* ICV, which determines the maximum value that can be specified in the `priority` clause.

Cross References
- *max-task-priority-var*, see Section 2.5 on page 63.
- `task` construct, see Section 2.10.1 on page 135.

3.2.43 omp_pause_resource

Summary

The `omp_pause_resource` routine allows the runtime to relinquish resources used by OpenMP on the specified device.

Format

```
C / C++
int omp_pause_resource(
  omp_pause_resource_t kind,
  int device_num
);
C / C++
```

```
Fortran
integer function omp_pause_resource(kind, device_num)
integer (kind=omp_pause_resource_kind) kind
integer device_num
Fortran
```

Constraints on Arguments

The first argument passed to this routine can be one of the valid OpenMP pause kind, or any implementation specific pause kind. The C/C++ header file (**omp.h**) and the Fortran include file (**omp_lib.h**) and/or Fortran 90 module file (**omp_lib**) define the valid constants. The valid constants must include the following, which can be extended with implementation specific values:

Format

```
C / C++
typedef enum omp_pause_resource_t {
  omp_pause_soft = 1,
  omp_pause_hard = 2
} omp_pause_resource_t;
C / C++
```

```
Fortran
integer (kind=omp_pause_resource_kind), parameter :: &
  omp_pause_soft = 1
integer (kind=omp_pause_resource_kind), parameter :: &
  omp_pause_hard = 2
Fortran
```

The second argument passed to this routine indicates the device that will be paused. The **device_num** parameter must be greater than or equal to zero and less than the result of **omp_get_num_devices()** or equal to the result of a call to **omp_get_initial_device()**.

Binding

The binding task set for an **omp_pause_resource** region is the whole program.

Effect

The **omp_pause_resource** routine allows the runtime to relinquish resources used by OpenMP on the specified device.

If successful, the **omp_pause_hard** value results in a hard pause for which the OpenMP state is not guaranteed to persist across the **omp_pause_resource** call. A hard pause may relinquish any data allocated by OpenMP on a given device, including data allocated by memory routines for that device as well as data present on the device as a result of a **declare target** or **target data** construct. A hard pause may also relinquish any data associated with a **threadprivate** directive. When relinquished and when applicable, base language appropriate deallocation/finalization is performed. When relinquished and when applicable, mapped data on a device will not be copied back from the device to the host.

If successful, the **omp_pause_soft** value results in a soft pause for which the OpenMP state is guaranteed to persist across the call, with the exception of any data associated with a **threadprivate** directive, which may be relinquished across the call. When relinquished and when applicable, base language appropriate deallocation/finalization is performed.

Note – A hard pause may relinquish more resources, but may resume processing OpenMP regions more slowly. A soft pause allows OpenMP regions to restart more quickly, but may relinquish fewer resources. An OpenMP implementation will reclaim resources as needed for OpenMP regions encountered after the **omp_pause_resource** region. Since a hard pause may unmap data on the specified device, appropriate data mapping is required before using data on the specified device after the **omp_pause_region** region.

The routine returns zero in case of success, and nonzero otherwise.

Tool Callbacks

If the tool is not allowed to interact with the specified device after encountering this call, then the runtime must call the tool finalizer for that device.

Restrictions

The `omp_pause_resource` routine has the following restrictions:

- The `omp_pause_resource` region may not be nested in any explicit OpenMP region.
- The routine may only be called when all explicit tasks have finalized execution. Calling the routine in any other circumstances may result in unspecified behavior.

Cross References

- `target` construct, see Section 2.12.5 on page 170
- `declare target` directive, see Section 2.12.7 on page 180
- `threadprivate` directives, see Section 2.19.2 on page 274.
- `omp_get_num_devices`, see Section 3.2.36 on page 371.
- `omp_get_get_initial_device` routine, see Section 3.2.41 on page 376.
- To pause resources on all devices at once, see Section 3.2.44 on page 380.

3.2.44 omp_pause_resource_all

Summary

The `omp_pause_resource_all` routine allows the runtime to relinquish resources used by OpenMP on all devices.

Format

─────────────── C / C++ ───────────────
```
int omp_pause_resource_all(omp_pause_resource_t kind);
```
─────────────── C / C++ ───────────────

─────────────── Fortran ───────────────
```
integer function omp_pause_resource_all(kind)
integer (kind=omp_pause_resource_kind) kind
```
─────────────── Fortran ───────────────

Binding

The binding task set for an `omp_pause_resource_all` region is the whole program.

Effect

The **omp_pause_resource_all** routine allows the runtime to relinquish resources used by OpenMP on all devices. It is equivalent to calling the **omp_pause_resource** routine once for each available device, including the host device.

The argument **kind** passed to this routine can be one of the valid OpenMP pause kind as defined in Section 3.2.43 on page 378, or any implementation specific pause kind.

Tool Callbacks

If the tool is not allowed to interact with a given device after encountering this call, then the runtime must call the tool finalizer for that device.

Restrictions

The **omp_pause_resource_all** routine has the following restrictions:

- The **omp_pause_resource_all** region may not be nested in any explicit OpenMP region.
- The routine may only be called when all explicit tasks have finalized execution. Calling the routine in any other circumstances may result in unspecified behavior.

Cross References

- **target** construct, see Section 2.12.5 on page 170
- **declare target** directive, see Section 2.12.7 on page 180
- **omp_get_num_devices**, see Section 3.2.36 on page 371.
- **omp_get_get_initial_device** routine, see Section 3.2.41 on page 376.
- To pause resources on a specific device only, see Section 3.2.43 on page 378.

3.3 Lock Routines

The OpenMP runtime library includes a set of general-purpose lock routines that can be used for synchronization. These general-purpose lock routines operate on OpenMP locks that are represented by OpenMP lock variables. OpenMP lock variables must be accessed only through the routines described in this section; programs that otherwise access OpenMP lock variables are non-conforming.

An OpenMP lock can be in one of the following states: *uninitialized*; *unlocked*; or *locked*. If a lock is in the *unlocked* state, a task can *set* the lock, which changes its state to *locked*. The task that sets the lock is then said to *own* the lock. A task that owns a lock can *unset* that lock, returning it to the *unlocked* state. A program in which a task unsets a lock that is owned by another task is non-conforming.

Two types of locks are supported: *simple locks* and *nestable locks*. A *nestable lock* can be set multiple times by the same task before being unset; a *simple lock* cannot be set if it is already owned by the task trying to set it. *Simple lock* variables are associated with *simple locks* and can only be passed to *simple lock* routines. *Nestable lock* variables are associated with *nestable locks* and can only be passed to *nestable lock* routines.

Each type of lock can also have a *synchronization hint* that contains information about the intended usage of the lock by the application code. The effect of the hint is implementation defined. An OpenMP implementation can use this hint to select a usage-specific lock, but hints do not change the mutual exclusion semantics of locks. A conforming implementation can safely ignore the hint.

Constraints on the state and ownership of the lock accessed by each of the lock routines are described with the routine. If these constraints are not met, the behavior of the routine is unspecified.

The OpenMP lock routines access a lock variable such that they always read and update the most current value of the lock variable. It is not necessary for an OpenMP program to include explicit **flush** directives to ensure that the lock variable's value is consistent among different tasks.

Binding

The binding thread set for all lock routine regions is all threads in the contention group. As a consequence, for each OpenMP lock, the lock routine effects relate to all tasks that call the routines, without regard to which teams the threads in the contention group that are executing the tasks belong.

Simple Lock Routines

―――――――――――――――――― C / C++ ――――――――――――――――――

The type **omp_lock_t** represents a simple lock. For the following routines, a simple lock variable must be of **omp_lock_t** type. All simple lock routines require an argument that is a pointer to a variable of type **omp_lock_t**.

―――――――――――――――――― C / C++ ――――――――――――――――――
―――――――――――――――――― Fortran ――――――――――――――――――

For the following routines, a simple lock variable must be an integer variable of **kind=omp_lock_kind**.

―――――――――――――――――― Fortran ――――――――――――――――――

The simple lock routines are as follows:

- The **omp_init_lock** routine initializes a simple lock;
- The **omp_init_lock_with_hint** routine initializes a simple lock and attaches a hint to it;
- The **omp_destroy_lock** routine uninitializes a simple lock;
- The **omp_set_lock** routine waits until a simple lock is available and then sets it;
- The **omp_unset_lock** routine unsets a simple lock; and
- The **omp_test_lock** routine tests a simple lock and sets it if it is available.

Nestable Lock Routines

―――――――――――――― C / C++ ――――――――――――――

The type **omp_nest_lock_t** represents a nestable lock. For the following routines, a nestable lock variable must be of **omp_nest_lock_t** type. All nestable lock routines require an argument that is a pointer to a variable of type **omp_nest_lock_t**.

―――――――――――――― C / C++ ――――――――――――――
―――――――――――――― Fortran ――――――――――――――

For the following routines, a nestable lock variable must be an integer variable of
kind=omp_nest_lock_kind.

―――――――――――――― Fortran ――――――――――――――

The nestable lock routines are as follows:

- The **omp_init_nest_lock** routine initializes a nestable lock;
- The **omp_init_nest_lock_with_hint** routine initializes a nestable lock and attaches a hint to it;
- The **omp_destroy_nest_lock** routine uninitializes a nestable lock;
- The **omp_set_nest_lock** routine waits until a nestable lock is available and then sets it;
- The **omp_unset_nest_lock** routine unsets a nestable lock; and
- The **omp_test_nest_lock** routine tests a nestable lock and sets it if it is available.

Restrictions

OpenMP lock routines have the following restriction:

- The use of the same OpenMP lock in different contention groups results in unspecified behavior.

3.3.1 `omp_init_lock` and `omp_init_nest_lock`

Summary

These routines initialize an OpenMP lock without a hint.

Format

---- C / C++ ----
```
void omp_init_lock(omp_lock_t *lock);
void omp_init_nest_lock(omp_nest_lock_t *lock);
```
---- C / C++ ----

---- Fortran ----
```
subroutine omp_init_lock(svar)
integer (kind=omp_lock_kind) svar

subroutine omp_init_nest_lock(nvar)
integer (kind=omp_nest_lock_kind) nvar
```
---- Fortran ----

Constraints on Arguments

A program that accesses a lock that is not in the uninitialized state through either routine is non-conforming.

Effect

The effect of these routines is to initialize the lock to the unlocked state; that is, no task owns the lock. In addition, the nesting count for a nestable lock is set to zero.

Execution Model Events

The *lock-init* event occurs in a thread that executes an `omp_init_lock` region after initialization of the lock, but before it finishes the region. The *nest-lock-init* event occurs in a thread that executes an `omp_init_nest_lock` region after initialization of the lock, but before it finishes the region.

Tool Callbacks

A thread dispatches a registered **ompt_callback_lock_init** callback with
omp_sync_hint_none as the *hint* argument and **ompt_mutex_lock** as the *kind* argument
for each occurrence of a *lock-init* event in that thread. Similarly, a thread dispatches a registered
ompt_callback_lock_init callback with **omp_sync_hint_none** as the *hint* argument
and **ompt_mutex_nest_lock** as the *kind* argument for each occurrence of a *nest-lock-init*
event in that thread. These callbacks have the type signature
ompt_callback_mutex_acquire_t and occur in the task that encounters the routine.

Cross References

- **ompt_callback_mutex_acquire_t**, see Section 4.5.2.14 on page 476.

3.3.2 omp_init_lock_with_hint and omp_init_nest_lock_with_hint

Summary

These routines initialize an OpenMP lock with a hint. The effect of the hint is
implementation-defined. The OpenMP implementation can ignore the hint without changing
program semantics.

Format

―――――――― C / C++ ――――――――
```
void omp_init_lock_with_hint(
    omp_lock_t *lock,
    omp_sync_hint_t hint
);
void omp_init_nest_lock_with_hint(
    omp_nest_lock_t *lock,
    omp_sync_hint_t hint
);
```
―――――――― C / C++ ――――――――

```fortran
! ─────────────────── Fortran ───────────────────
subroutine omp_init_lock_with_hint (svar, hint)
integer (kind=omp_lock_kind) svar
integer (kind=omp_sync_hint_kind) hint

subroutine omp_init_nest_lock_with_hint (nvar, hint)
integer (kind=omp_nest_lock_kind) nvar
integer (kind=omp_sync_hint_kind) hint
! ─────────────────── Fortran ───────────────────
```

Constraints on Arguments

A program that accesses a lock that is not in the uninitialized state through either routine is non-conforming.

The second argument passed to these routines (*hint*) is a hint as described in Section 2.17.12 on page 260.

Effect

The effect of these routines is to initialize the lock to the unlocked state and, optionally, to choose a specific lock implementation based on the hint. After initialization no task owns the lock. In addition, the nesting count for a nestable lock is set to zero.

Execution Model Events

The *lock-init* event occurs in a thread that executes an **omp_init_lock_with_hint** region after initialization of the lock, but before it finishes the region. The *nest-lock-init_with_hint* event occurs in a thread that executes an **omp_init_nest_lock** region after initialization of the lock, but before it finishes the region.

Tool Callbacks

A thread dispatches a registered **ompt_callback_lock_init** callback with the same value for its *hint* argument as the *hint* argument of the call to **omp_init_lock_with_hint** and **ompt_mutex_lock** as the *kind* argument for each occurrence of a *lock-init* event in that thread. Similarly, a thread dispatches a registered **ompt_callback_lock_init** callback with the same value for its *hint* argument as the *hint* argument of the call to **omp_init_nest_lock_with_hint** and **ompt_mutex_nest_lock** as the *kind* argument for each occurrence of a *nest-lock-init* event in that thread. These callbacks have the type signature **ompt_callback_mutex_acquire_t** and occur in the task that encounters the routine.

Cross References

- Synchronization Hints, see Section 2.17.12 on page 260.
- `ompt_callback_mutex_acquire_t`, see Section 4.5.2.14 on page 476.

3.3.3 omp_destroy_lock and omp_destroy_nest_lock

Summary

These routines ensure that the OpenMP lock is uninitialized.

Format

───────────────── C / C++ ─────────────────
```
void omp_destroy_lock(omp_lock_t *lock);
void omp_destroy_nest_lock(omp_nest_lock_t *lock);
```
───────────────── C / C++ ─────────────────

───────────────── Fortran ─────────────────
```
subroutine omp_destroy_lock(svar)
integer (kind=omp_lock_kind) svar

subroutine omp_destroy_nest_lock(nvar)
integer (kind=omp_nest_lock_kind) nvar
```
───────────────── Fortran ─────────────────

Constraints on Arguments

A program that accesses a lock that is not in the unlocked state through either routine is non-conforming.

Effect

The effect of these routines is to change the state of the lock to uninitialized.

Execution Model Events

The *lock-destroy* event occurs in a thread that executes an `omp_destroy_lock` region before it finishes the region. The *nest-lock-destroy_with_hint* event occurs in a thread that executes an `omp_destroy_nest_lock` region before it finishes the region.

Tool Callbacks

A thread dispatches a registered **ompt_callback_lock_destroy** callback with
ompt_mutex_lock as the *kind* argument for each occurrence of a *lock-destroy* event in that
thread. Similarly, a thread dispatches a registered **ompt_callback_lock_destroy** callback
with **ompt_mutex_nest_lock** as the *kind* argument for each occurrence of a *nest-lock-destroy*
event in that thread. These callbacks have the type signature
ompt_callback_mutex_acquire_t and occur in the task that encounters the routine.

Cross References

- **ompt_callback_mutex_t**, see Section 4.5.2.15 on page 477.

3.3.4 `omp_set_lock` and `omp_set_nest_lock`

Summary

These routines provide a means of setting an OpenMP lock. The calling task region behaves as if it
was suspended until the lock can be set by this task.

Format

―――――――――――――――――― C / C++ ――――――――――――――――――
```
void omp_set_lock(omp_lock_t *lock);
void omp_set_nest_lock(omp_nest_lock_t *lock);
```
―――――――――――――――――― C / C++ ――――――――――――――――――

―――――――――――――――――― Fortran ――――――――――――――――――
```
subroutine omp_set_lock(svar)
integer (kind=omp_lock_kind) svar

subroutine omp_set_nest_lock(nvar)
integer (kind=omp_nest_lock_kind) nvar
```
―――――――――――――――――― Fortran ――――――――――――――――――

Constraints on Arguments

A program that accesses a lock that is in the uninitialized state through either routine is
non-conforming. A simple lock accessed by **omp_set_lock** that is in the locked state must not
be owned by the task that contains the call or deadlock will result.

Effect

Each of these routines has an effect equivalent to suspension of the task that is executing the routine until the specified lock is available.

Note – The semantics of these routines is specified *as if* they serialize execution of the region guarded by the lock. However, implementations may implement them in other ways provided that the isolation properties are respected so that the actual execution delivers a result that could arise from some serialization.

A simple lock is available if it is unlocked. Ownership of the lock is granted to the task that executes the routine.

A nestable lock is available if it is unlocked or if it is already owned by the task that executes the routine. The task that executes the routine is granted, or retains, ownership of the lock, and the nesting count for the lock is incremented.

Execution Model Events

The *lock-acquire* event occurs in a thread that executes an **omp_set_lock** region before the associated lock is requested. The *nest-lock-acquire* event occurs in a thread that executes an **omp_set_nest_lock** region before the associated lock is requested.

The *lock-acquired* event occurs in a thread that executes an **omp_set_lock** region after it acquires the associated lock but before it finishes the region. The *nest-lock-acquired* event occurs in a thread that executes an **omp_set_nest_lock** region if the thread did not already own the lock, after it acquires the associated lock but before it finishes the region.

The *nest-lock-owned* event occurs in a thread when it already owns the lock and executes an **omp_set_nest_lock** region. The event occurs after the nesting count is incremented but before the thread finishes the region.

Tool Callbacks

A thread dispatches a registered **ompt_callback_mutex_acquire** callback for each occurrence of a *lock-acquire* or *nest-lock-acquire* event in that thread. This callback has the type signature **ompt_callback_mutex_acquire_t**.

A thread dispatches a registered **ompt_callback_mutex_acquired** callback for each occurrence of a *lock-acquired* or *nest-lock-acquired* event in that thread. This callback has the type signature **ompt_callback_mutex_t**.

A thread dispatches a registered **ompt_callback_nest_lock** callback with **ompt_scope_begin** as its *endpoint* argument for each occurrence of a *nest-lock-owned* event in that thread. This callback has the type signature **ompt_callback_nest_lock_t**.

The above callbacks occur in the task that encounters the lock function. The *kind* argument of these callbacks is `ompt_mutex_lock` when the events arise from an `omp_set_lock` region while it is `ompt_mutex_nest_lock` when the events arise from an `omp_set_nest_lock` region.

Cross References

- `ompt_callback_mutex_acquire_t`, see Section 4.5.2.14 on page 476.
- `ompt_callback_mutex_t`, see Section 4.5.2.15 on page 477.
- `ompt_callback_nest_lock_t`, see Section 4.5.2.16 on page 479.

3.3.5 `omp_unset_lock` and `omp_unset_nest_lock`

Summary

These routines provide the means of unsetting an OpenMP lock.

Format

―――― C / C++ ――――
```
void omp_unset_lock(omp_lock_t *lock);
void omp_unset_nest_lock(omp_nest_lock_t *lock);
```
―――― C / C++ ――――

―――― Fortran ――――
```
subroutine omp_unset_lock(svar)
integer (kind=omp_lock_kind) svar

subroutine omp_unset_nest_lock(nvar)
integer (kind=omp_nest_lock_kind) nvar
```
―――― Fortran ――――

Constraints on Arguments

A program that accesses a lock that is not in the locked state or that is not owned by the task that contains the call through either routine is non-conforming.

Effect

For a simple lock, the **omp_unset_lock** routine causes the lock to become unlocked.

For a nestable lock, the **omp_unset_nest_lock** routine decrements the nesting count, and causes the lock to become unlocked if the resulting nesting count is zero.

For either routine, if the lock becomes unlocked, and if one or more task regions were effectively suspended because the lock was unavailable, the effect is that one task is chosen and given ownership of the lock.

Execution Model Events

The *lock-release* event occurs in a thread that executes an **omp_unset_lock** region after it releases the associated lock but before it finishes the region. The *nest-lock-release* event occurs in a thread that executes an **omp_unset_nest_lock** region after it releases the associated lock but before it finishes the region.

The *nest-lock-held* event occurs in a thread that executes an **omp_unset_nest_lock** region before it finishes the region when the thread still owns the lock after the nesting count is decremented.

Tool Callbacks

A thread dispatches a registered **ompt_callback_mutex_released** callback with **ompt_mutex_lock** as the *kind* argument for each occurrence of a *lock-release* event in that thread. Similarly, a thread dispatches a registered **ompt_callback_mutex_released** callback with **ompt_mutex_nest_lock** as the *kind* argument for each occurrence of a *nest-lock-release* event in that thread. These callbacks have the type signature **ompt_callback_mutex_t** and occur in the task that encounters the routine.

A thread dispatches a registered **ompt_callback_nest_lock** callback with **ompt_scope_end** as its *endpoint* argument for each occurrence of a *nest-lock-held* event in that thread. This callback has the type signature **ompt_callback_nest_lock_t**.

Cross References

- **ompt_callback_mutex_t**, see Section 4.5.2.15 on page 477.
- **ompt_callback_nest_lock_t**, see Section 4.5.2.16 on page 479.

3.3.6 `omp_test_lock` and `omp_test_nest_lock`

Summary

These routines attempt to set an OpenMP lock but do not suspend execution of the task that executes the routine.

Format

―――――――――――――――― C / C++ ――――――――――――――――
```
int omp_test_lock(omp_lock_t *lock);
int omp_test_nest_lock(omp_nest_lock_t *lock);
```
―――――――――――――――― C / C++ ――――――――――――――――

―――――――――――――――― Fortran ――――――――――――――――
```
logical function omp_test_lock(svar)
integer (kind=omp_lock_kind) svar

integer function omp_test_nest_lock(nvar)
integer (kind=omp_nest_lock_kind) nvar
```
―――――――――――――――― Fortran ――――――――――――――――

Constraints on Arguments

A program that accesses a lock that is in the uninitialized state through either routine is non-conforming. The behavior is unspecified if a simple lock accessed by `omp_test_lock` is in the locked state and is owned by the task that contains the call.

Effect

These routines attempt to set a lock in the same manner as `omp_set_lock` and `omp_set_nest_lock`, except that they do not suspend execution of the task that executes the routine.

For a simple lock, the `omp_test_lock` routine returns *true* if the lock is successfully set; otherwise, it returns *false*.

For a nestable lock, the `omp_test_nest_lock` routine returns the new nesting count if the lock is successfully set; otherwise, it returns zero.

Execution Model Events

The *lock-test* event occurs in a thread that executes an **omp_test_lock** region before the associated lock is tested. The *nest-lock-test* event occurs in a thread that executes an **omp_test_nest_lock** region before the associated lock is tested.

The *lock-test-acquired* event occurs in a thread that executes an **omp_test_lock** region before it finishes the region if the associated lock was acquired. The *nest-lock-test-acquired* event occurs in a thread that executes an **omp_test_nest_lock** region before it finishes the region if the associated lock was acquired and the thread did not already own the lock.

The *nest-lock-owned* event occurs in a thread that executes an **omp_test_nest_lock** region before it finishes the region after the nesting count is incremented if the thread already owned the lock.

Tool Callbacks

A thread dispatches a registered **ompt_callback_mutex_acquire** callback for each occurrence of a *lock-test* or *nest-lock-test* event in that thread. This callback has the type signature **ompt_callback_mutex_acquire_t**.

A thread dispatches a registered **ompt_callback_mutex_acquired** callback for each occurrence of a *lock-test-acquired* or *nest-lock-test-acquired* event in that thread. This callback has the type signature **ompt_callback_mutex_t**.

A thread dispatches a registered **ompt_callback_nest_lock** callback with **ompt_scope_begin** as its *endpoint* argument for each occurrence of a *nest-lock-owned* event in that thread. This callback has the type signature **ompt_callback_nest_lock_t**.

The above callbacks occur in the task that encounters the lock function. The *kind* argument of these callbacks is **ompt_mutex_test_lock** when the events arise from an **omp_test_lock** region while it is **ompt_mutex_test_nest_lock** when the events arise from an **omp_test_nest_lock** region.

Cross References

- **ompt_callback_mutex_acquire_t**, see Section 4.5.2.14 on page 476.
- **ompt_callback_mutex_t**, see Section 4.5.2.15 on page 477.
- **ompt_callback_nest_lock_t**, see Section 4.5.2.16 on page 479.

3.4 Timing Routines

This section describes routines that support a portable wall clock timer.

3.4.1 `omp_get_wtime`

Summary

The `omp_get_wtime` routine returns elapsed wall clock time in seconds.

Format

―――――――――――――――――― C / C++ ――――――――――――――――――
```
double omp_get_wtime(void);
```
―――――――――――――――――― C / C++ ――――――――――――――――――

―――――――――――――――――― Fortran ――――――――――――――――――
```
double precision function omp_get_wtime()
```
―――――――――――――――――― Fortran ――――――――――――――――――

Binding

The binding thread set for an `omp_get_wtime` region is the encountering thread. The routine's return value is not guaranteed to be consistent across any set of threads.

Effect

The `omp_get_wtime` routine returns a value equal to the elapsed wall clock time in seconds since some *time-in-the-past*. The actual *time-in-the-past* is arbitrary, but it is guaranteed not to change during the execution of the application program. The time returned is a *per-thread time*, so it is not required to be globally consistent across all threads that participate in an application.

Note – The routine is anticipated to be used to measure elapsed times as shown in the following example:

C / C++

```
double start;
double end;
start = omp_get_wtime();
... work to be timed ...
end = omp_get_wtime();
printf("Work took %f seconds\n", end - start);
```

C / C++

Fortran

```
DOUBLE PRECISION START, END
START = omp_get_wtime()
... work to be timed ...
END = omp_get_wtime()
PRINT *, "Work took", END - START, "seconds"
```

Fortran

3.4.2 omp_get_wtick

Summary

The **omp_get_wtick** routine returns the precision of the timer used by **omp_get_wtime**.

Format

C / C++

```
double omp_get_wtick(void);
```

C / C++

Fortran

```
double precision function omp_get_wtick()
```

Fortran

Binding

The binding thread set for an **omp_get_wtick** region is the encountering thread. The routine's return value is not guaranteed to be consistent across any set of threads.

Effect

The `omp_get_wtick` routine returns a value equal to the number of seconds between successive clock ticks of the timer used by `omp_get_wtime`.

3.5 Event Routine

This section describes a routine that supports OpenMP event objects.

Binding

The binding thread set for all event routine regions is the encountering thread.

3.5.1 `omp_fulfill_event`

Summary

This routine fulfills and destroys an OpenMP event.

Format

―――――――――――――― C / C++ ――――――――――――――
```
void omp_fulfill_event(omp_event_handle_t event);
```
―――――――――――――― C / C++ ――――――――――――――

―――――――――――――― Fortran ――――――――――――――
```
subroutine omp_fulfill_event(event)
integer (kind=omp_event_handle_kind) event
```
―――――――――――――― Fortran ――――――――――――――

Constraints on Arguments

A program that calls this routine on an event that was already fulfilled is non-conforming. A program that calls this routine with an event handle that was not created by the `detach` clause is non-conforming.

Effect

The effect of this routine is to fulfill the event associated with the event handle argument. The effect of fulfilling the event will depend on how the event was created. The event is destroyed and cannot be accessed after calling this routine, and the event handle becomes unassociated with any event.

Execution Model Events

The *task-fulfill* event occurs in a thread that executes an **omp_fulfill_event** region before the event is fulfilled if the OpenMP event object was created by a **detach** clause on a task.

Tool Callbacks

A thread dispatches a registered **ompt_callback_task_schedule** callback with **NULL** as its *next_task_data* argument while the argument *prior_task_data* binds to the detached task for each occurrence of a *task-fulfill* event. If the *task-fulfill* event occurs before the detached task finished the execution of the associated *structured-block*, the callback has **ompt_task_early_fulfill** as its *prior_task_status* argument; otherwise the callback has **ompt_task_late_fulfill** as its *prior_task_status* argument. This callback has type signature **ompt_callback_task_schedule_t**.

Cross References

- **detach** clause, see Section 2.10.1 on page 135.
- **ompt_callback_task_schedule_t**, see Section 4.5.2.10 on page 470.

---------- C / C++ ----------

3.6 Device Memory Routines

This section describes routines that support allocation of memory and management of pointers in the data environments of target devices.

3.6.1 omp_target_alloc

Summary

The **omp_target_alloc** routine allocates memory in a device data environment.

------- C/C++ (cont.) -------

Format

```
void* omp_target_alloc(size_t size, int device_num);
```

Effect

The `omp_target_alloc` routine returns the device address of a storage location of *size* bytes. The storage location is dynamically allocated in the device data environment of the device specified by *device_num*, which must be greater than or equal to zero and less than the result of `omp_get_num_devices()` or the result of a call to `omp_get_initial_device()`. When called from within a `target` region the effect of this routine is unspecified.

The `omp_target_alloc` routine returns `NULL` if it cannot dynamically allocate the memory in the device data environment.

The device address returned by `omp_target_alloc` can be used in an `is_device_ptr` clause, Section 2.12.5 on page 170.

Unless `unified_address` clause appears on a `requires` directive in the compilation unit, pointer arithmetic is not supported on the device address returned by `omp_target_alloc`.

Freeing the storage returned by `omp_target_alloc` with any routine other than `omp_target_free` results in unspecified behavior.

Execution Model Events

The *target-data-allocation* event occurs when a thread allocates data on a target device.

Tool Callbacks

A thread invokes a registered `ompt_callback_target_data_op` callback for each occurrence of a *target-data-allocation* event in that thread. The callback occurs in the context of the target task and has type signature `ompt_callback_target_data_op_t`.

Cross References

- `target` construct, see Section 2.12.5 on page 170
- `omp_get_num_devices` routine, see Section 3.2.36 on page 371
- `omp_get_initial_device` routine, see Section 3.2.41 on page 376
- `omp_target_free` routine, see Section 3.6.2 on page 399
- `ompt_callback_target_data_op_t`, see Section 4.5.2.25 on page 488.

·------------------------ C/C++ (cont.) ----------------------·

3.6.2 omp_target_free

Summary

The `omp_target_free` routine frees the device memory allocated by the `omp_target_alloc` routine.

Format

```
void omp_target_free(void *device_ptr, int device_num);
```

Constraints on Arguments

A program that calls `omp_target_free` with a non-null pointer that does not have a value returned from `omp_target_alloc` is non-conforming. The *device_num* must be greater than or equal to zero and less than the result of `omp_get_num_devices()` or the result of a call to `omp_get_initial_device()`.

Effect

The `omp_target_free` routine frees the memory in the device data environment associated with *device_ptr*. If *device_ptr* is **NULL**, the operation is ignored.

Synchronization must be inserted to ensure that all accesses to *device_ptr* are completed before the call to `omp_target_free`.

When called from within a `target` region the effect of this routine is unspecified.

Execution Model Events

The *target-data-free* event occurs when a thread frees data on a target device.

Tool Callbacks

A thread invokes a registered `ompt_callback_target_data_op` callback for each occurrence of a *target-data-free* event in that thread. The callback occurs in the context of the target task and has type signature `ompt_callback_target_data_op_t`.

Cross References

- `target` construct, see Section 2.12.5 on page 170
- `omp_get_num_devices` routine, see Section 3.2.36 on page 371
- `omp_get_initial_device` routine, see Section 3.2.41 on page 376
- `omp_target_alloc` routine, see Section 3.6.1 on page 397
- `ompt_callback_target_data_op_t`, see Section 4.5.2.25 on page 488.

▼------------------------ C/C++ (cont.) ------------------------▼

3.6.3 `omp_target_is_present`

Summary

The `omp_target_is_present` routine tests whether a host pointer has corresponding storage on a given device.

Format

```
int omp_target_is_present(const void *ptr, int device_num);
```

Constraints on Arguments

The value of *ptr* must be a valid host pointer or **NULL**. The *device_num* must be greater than or equal to zero and less than the result of `omp_get_num_devices()` or the result of a call to `omp_get_initial_device()`.

Effect

This routine returns non-zero if the specified pointer would be found present on device *device_num* by a **map** clause; otherwise, it returns zero.

When called from within a `target` region the effect of this routine is unspecified.

Cross References

- `target` construct, see Section 2.12.5 on page 170.
- `map` clause, see Section 2.19.7.1 on page 315.
- `omp_get_num_devices` routine, see Section 3.2.36 on page 371
- `omp_get_initial_device` routine, see Section 3.2.41 on page 376

3.6.4 `omp_target_memcpy`

Summary

The `omp_target_memcpy` routine copies memory between any combination of host and device pointers.

----- C/C++ (cont.) -----

Format

```
int omp_target_memcpy(
  void *dst,
  const void *src,
  size_t length,
  size_t dst_offset,
  size_t src_offset,
  int dst_device_num,
  int src_device_num
);
```

Constraints on Arguments

Each device must be compatible with the device pointer specified on the same side of the copy. The *dst_device_num* and *src_device_num* must be greater than or equal to zero and less than the result of `omp_get_num_devices()` or equal to the result of a call to `omp_get_initial_device()`.

Effect

length bytes of memory at offset *src_offset* from *src* in the device data environment of device *src_device_num* are copied to *dst* starting at offset *dst_offset* in the device data environment of device *dst_device_num*. The return value is zero on success and non-zero on failure. The host device and host device data environment can be referenced with the device number returned by `omp_get_initial_device`. This routine contains a task scheduling point.

When called from within a `target` region the effect of this routine is unspecified.

Execution Model Events

The *target-data-op* event occurs when a thread transfers data on a target device.

Tool Callbacks

A thread invokes a registered `ompt_callback_target_data_op` callback for each occurrence of a *target-data-op* event in that thread. The callback occurs in the context of the target task and has type signature `ompt_callback_target_data_op_t`.

Cross References

- `target` construct, see Section 2.12.5 on page 170.
- `omp_get_initial_device` routine, see Section 3.2.41 on page 376
- `omp_target_alloc` routine, see Section 3.6.1 on page 397.
- `ompt_callback_target_data_op_t`, see Section 4.5.2.25 on page 488.

------- C/C++ (cont.) -------

3.6.5 omp_target_memcpy_rect

Summary

The `omp_target_memcpy_rect` routine copies a rectangular subvolume from a multi-dimensional array to another multi-dimensional array. The copies can use any combination of host and device pointers.

Format

```
int omp_target_memcpy_rect(
  void *dst,
  const void *src,
  size_t element_size,
  int num_dims,
  const size_t *volume,
  const size_t *dst_offsets,
  const size_t *src_offsets,
  const size_t *dst_dimensions,
  const size_t *src_dimensions,
  int dst_device_num,
  int src_device_num
);
```

Constraints on Arguments

The length of the offset and dimension arrays must be at least the value of *num_dims*. The `dst_device_num` and `src_device_num` must be greater than or equal to zero and less than the result of `omp_get_num_devices()` or equal to the result of a call to `omp_get_initial_device()`.

The value of *num_dims* must be between 1 and the implementation-defined limit, which must be at least three.

Effect

This routine copies a rectangular subvolume of *src*, in the device data environment of device *src_device_num*, to *dst*, in the device data environment of device *dst_device_num*. The volume is specified in terms of the size of an element, number of dimensions, and constant arrays of length *num_dims*. The maximum number of dimensions supported is at least three, support for higher dimensionality is implementation defined. The volume array specifies the length, in number of elements, to copy in each dimension from *src* to *dst*. The *dst_offsets* (*src_offsets*) parameter specifies number of elements from the origin of *dst* (*src*) in elements. The *dst_dimensions* (*src_dimensions*) parameter specifies the length of each dimension of *dst* (*src*)

---------- C/C++ (cont.) ----------

The routine returns zero if successful. If both *dst* and *src* are **NULL** pointers, the routine returns the number of dimensions supported by the implementation for the specified device numbers. The host device and host device data environment can be referenced with the device number returned by **omp_get_initial_device**. Otherwise, it returns a non-zero value. The routine contains a task scheduling point.

When called from within a **target** region the effect of this routine is unspecified.

Execution Model Events

The *target-data-op* event occurs when a thread transfers data on a target device.

Tool Callbacks

A thread invokes a registered **ompt_callback_target_data_op** callback for each occurrence of a *target-data-op* event in that thread. The callback occurs in the context of the target task and has type signature **ompt_callback_target_data_op_t**.

Cross References

- **target** construct, see Section 2.12.5 on page 170.
- **omp_get_initial_device** routine, see Section 3.2.41 on page 376
- **omp_target_alloc** routine, see Section 3.6.1 on page 397.
- **ompt_callback_target_data_op_t**, see Section 4.5.2.25 on page 488.

3.6.6 omp_target_associate_ptr

Summary

The **omp_target_associate_ptr** routine maps a device pointer, which may be returned from **omp_target_alloc** or implementation-defined runtime routines, to a host pointer.

▼------------------------ C/C++ (cont.) ------------------------▼

Format

```
int omp_target_associate_ptr(
  const void *host_ptr,
  const void *device_ptr,
  size_t size,
  size_t device_offset,
  int device_num
);
```

Constraints on Arguments

The value of *device_ptr* value must be a valid pointer to device memory for the device denoted by the value of *device_num*. The *device_num* argument must be greater than or equal to zero and less than the result of `omp_get_num_devices()` or equal to the result of a call to `omp_get_initial_device()`.

Effect

The `omp_target_associate_ptr` routine associates a device pointer in the device data environment of device *device_num* with a host pointer such that when the host pointer appears in a subsequent **map** clause, the associated device pointer is used as the target for data motion associated with that host pointer. The *device_offset* parameter specifies the offset into *device_ptr* that is used as the base address for the device side of the mapping. The reference count of the resulting mapping will be infinite. After being successfully associated, the buffer to which the device pointer points is invalidated and accessing data directly through the device pointer results in unspecified behavior. The pointer can be retrieved for other uses by disassociating it. When called from within a **target** region the effect of this routine is unspecified.

The routine returns zero if successful. Otherwise it returns a non-zero value.

Only one device buffer can be associated with a given host pointer value and device number pair. Attempting to associate a second buffer will return non-zero. Associating the same pair of pointers on the same device with the same offset has no effect and returns zero. Associating pointers that share underlying storage will result in unspecified behavior. The `omp_target_is_present` function can be used to test whether a given host pointer has a corresponding variable in the device data environment.

Execution Model Events

The *target-data-associate* event occurs when a thread associates data on a target device.

Tool Callbacks

A thread invokes a registered `ompt_callback_target_data_op` callback for each occurrence of a *target-data-associate* event in that thread. The callback occurs in the context of the target task and has type signature `ompt_callback_target_data_op_t`.

------- C/C++ (cont.) -------

Cross References

- **target** construct, see Section 2.12.5 on page 170.
- **map** clause, see Section 2.19.7.1 on page 315.
- **omp_target_alloc** routine, see Section 3.6.1 on page 397.
- **omp_target_disassociate_ptr** routine, see Section 3.6.6 on page 403
- **ompt_callback_target_data_op_t**, see Section 4.5.2.25 on page 488.

3.6.7 omp_target_disassociate_ptr

Summary

The **omp_target_disassociate_ptr** removes the associated pointer for a given device from a host pointer.

Format

```
int omp_target_disassociate_ptr(const void *ptr, int device_num);
```

Constraints on Arguments

The *device_num* must be greater than or equal to zero and less than the result of **omp_get_num_devices()** or equal to the result of a call to **omp_get_initial_device()**.

Effect

The **omp_target_disassociate_ptr** removes the associated device data on device *device_num* from the presence table for host pointer *ptr*. A call to this routine on a pointer that is not **NULL** and does not have associated data on the given device results in unspecified behavior. The reference count of the mapping is reduced to zero, regardless of its current value.

When called from within a **target** region the effect of this routine is unspecified.

The routine returns zero if successful. Otherwise it returns a non-zero value.

After a call to **omp_target_disassociate_ptr**, the contents of the device buffer are invalidated.

Execution Model Events

The *target-data-disassociate* event occurs when a thread disassociates data on a target device.

Tool Callbacks

A thread invokes a registered `ompt_callback_target_data_op` callback for each occurrence of a *target-data-disassociate* event in that thread. The callback occurs in the context of the target task and has type signature `ompt_callback_target_data_op_t`.

Cross References

- `target` construct, see Section 2.12.5 on page 170
- `omp_target_associate_ptr` routine, see Section 3.6.6 on page 403
- `ompt_callback_target_data_op_t`, see Section 4.5.2.25 on page 488.

―――― C / C++ ――――

3.7 Memory Management Routines

This section describes routines that support memory management on the current device.

Instances of memory management types must be accessed only through the routines described in this section; programs that otherwise access instances of these types are non-conforming.

3.7.1 Memory Management Types

The following type definitions are used by the memory management routines:

―――― C / C++ ――――
```
typedef enum omp_alloctrait_key_t {
  omp_atk_sync_hint = 1,
  omp_atk_alignment = 2,
  omp_atk_access = 3,
  omp_atk_pool_size = 4,
  omp_atk_fallback = 5,
  omp_atk_fb_data = 6,
  omp_atk_pinned = 7,
  omp_atk_partition = 8
} omp_alloctrait_key_t;

typedef enum omp_alloctrait_value_t {
```

```
  omp_atv_false = 0,
  omp_atv_true = 1,
  omp_atv_default = 2,
  omp_atv_contended = 3,
  omp_atv_uncontended = 4,
  omp_atv_sequential = 5,
  omp_atv_private = 6,
  omp_atv_all = 7,
  omp_atv_thread = 8,
  omp_atv_pteam = 9,
  omp_atv_cgroup = 10,
  omp_atv_default_mem_fb = 11,
  omp_atv_null_fb = 12,
  omp_atv_abort_fb = 13,
  omp_atv_allocator_fb = 14,
  omp_atv_environment = 15,
  omp_atv_nearest = 16,
  omp_atv_blocked = 17,
  omp_atv_interleaved = 18
} omp_alloctrait_value_t;

typedef struct omp_alloctrait_t {
  omp_alloctrait_key_t key;
  omp_uintptr_t value;
} omp_alloctrait_t;
```

──────────── C / C++ ────────────
──────────── Fortran ────────────

```
integer(kind=omp_alloctrait_key_kind), &
  parameter :: omp_atk_sync_hint = 1
integer(kind=omp_alloctrait_key_kind), &
  parameter :: omp_atk_alignment = 2
integer(kind=omp_alloctrait_key_kind), &
  parameter :: omp_atk_access = 3
integer(kind=omp_alloctrait_key_kind), &
  parameter :: omp_atk_pool_size = 4
integer(kind=omp_alloctrait_key_kind), &
  parameter :: omp_atk_fallback = 5
integer(kind=omp_alloctrait_key_kind), &
  parameter :: omp_atk_fb_data = 6
integer(kind=omp_alloctrait_key_kind), &
  parameter :: omp_atk_pinned = 7
integer(kind=omp_alloctrait_key_kind), &
```

---------------- Fortran (cont.) ----------------

```fortran
      parameter :: omp_atk_partition = 8

integer(kind=omp_alloctrait_val_kind), &
  parameter :: omp_atv_false = 0
integer(kind=omp_alloctrait_val_kind), &
  parameter :: omp_atv_true = 1
integer(kind=omp_alloctrait_val_kind), &
  parameter :: omp_atv_default = 2
integer(kind=omp_alloctrait_val_kind), &
  parameter :: omp_atv_contended = 3
integer(kind=omp_alloctrait_val_kind), &
  parameter :: omp_atv_uncontended = 4
integer(kind=omp_alloctrait_val_kind), &
  parameter :: omp_atv_sequential = 5
integer(kind=omp_alloctrait_val_kind), &
  parameter :: omp_atv_private = 6
integer(kind=omp_alloctrait_val_kind), &
  parameter :: omp_atv_all = 7
integer(kind=omp_alloctrait_val_kind), &
  parameter :: omp_atv_thread = 8
integer(kind=omp_alloctrait_val_kind), &
  parameter :: omp_atv_pteam = 9
integer(kind=omp_alloctrait_val_kind), &
  parameter :: omp_atv_cgroup = 10
integer(kind=omp_alloctratit_val_kind), &
  parameter :: omp_atv_default_mem_fb = 11
integer(kind=omp_alloctratit_val_kind), &
  parameter :: omp_atv_null_fb = 12
integer(kind=omp_alloctratit_val_kind), &
  parameter :: omp_atv_abort_fb = 13
integer(kind=omp_alloctratit_val_kind), &
  parameter :: omp_atv_allocator_fb = 14
integer(kind=omp_alloctrait_val_kind), &
  parameter :: omp_atv_environment = 15
integer(kind=omp_alloctrait_val_kind), &
  parameter :: omp_atv_nearest = 16
integer(kind=omp_alloctrait_val_kind), &
  parameter :: omp_atv_blocked = 17
integer(kind=omp_alloctrait_val_kind), &
  parameter :: omp_atv_interleaved = 18

type omp_alloctrait
  integer(kind=omp_alloctrait_key_kind) key
```

```fortran
    integer(kind=omp_alloctrait_val_kind) value
end type omp_alloctrait

integer(kind=omp_allocator_handle_kind), &
  parameter :: omp_null_allocator = 0
```
Fortran

3.7.2 omp_init_allocator

Summary

The `omp_init_allocator` routine initializes an allocator and associates it with a memory space.

Format

C / C++
```
omp_allocator_handle_t omp_init_allocator (
    omp_memspace_handle_t memspace,
    int ntraits,
    const omp_alloctrait_t traits[]
);
```
C / C++

Fortran
```fortran
integer(kind=omp_allocator_handle_kind) &
function omp_init_allocator ( memspace, ntraits, traits )
integer(kind=omp_memspace_handle_kind),intent(in) :: memspace
integer,intent(in) :: ntraits
type(omp_alloctrait),intent(in) :: traits(*)
```
Fortran

Constraints on Arguments

The *memspace* argument must be one of the predefined memory spaces defined in Table 2.8.

If the *ntraits* argument is greater than zero then the *traits* argument must specify at least that many traits. If it specifies fewer than *ntraits* traits the behavior is unspecified.

Unless a **requires** directive with the **dynamic_allocators** clause is present in the same compilation unit, using this routine in a **target** region results in unspecified behavior.

Binding

The binding thread set for an `omp_init_allocator` region is all threads on a device. The effect of executing this routine is not related to any specific region that corresponds to any construct or API routine.

Effect

The `omp_init_allocator` routine creates a new allocator that is associated with the *memspace* memory space and returns a handle to it. All allocations through the created allocator will behave according to the allocator traits specified in the *traits* argument. The number of traits in the *traits* argument is specified by the *ntraits* argument. Specifying the same allocator trait more than once results in unspecified behavior. The routine returns a handle for the created allocator. If the special `omp_atv_default` value is used for a given trait, then its value will be the default value specified in Table 2.9 for that given trait.

If *memspace* is `omp_default_mem_space` and the `traits` argument is an empty set this routine will always return a handle to an allocator. Otherwise if an allocator based on the requirements cannot be created then the special `omp_null_allocator` handle is returned.

The use of an allocator returned by this routine on a device other than the one on which it was created results in unspecified behavior.

Cross References

- Memory Spaces, see Section 2.11.1 on page 152.
- Memory Allocators, see Section 2.11.2 on page 152.

3.7.3 omp_destroy_allocator

Summary

The `omp_destroy_allocator` routine releases all resources used by the allocator handle.

Format

― C / C++ ―
```
void omp_destroy_allocator (omp_allocator_handle_t allocator);
```
― C / C++ ―

― Fortran ―
```
subroutine omp_destroy_allocator ( allocator )
integer(kind=omp_allocator_handle_kind),intent(in) :: allocator
```
― Fortran ―

Constraints on Arguments

The *allocator* argument must not represent a predefined memory allocator.

Unless a **requires** directive with the **dynamic_allocators** clause is present in the same compilation unit, using this routine in a **target** region results in unspecified behavior.

Binding

The binding thread set for an **omp_destroy_allocator** region is all threads on a device. The effect of executing this routine is not related to any specific region that corresponds to any construct or API routine.

Effect

The **omp_destroy_allocator** routine releases all resources used to implement the *allocator* handle. Accessing any memory allocated by the *allocator* after this call results in unspecified behavior.

If *allocator* is **omp_null_allocator** then this routine will have no effect.

Cross References

- Memory Allocators, see Section 2.11.2 on page 152.

3.7.4 omp_set_default_allocator

Summary

The **omp_set_default_allocator** routine sets the default memory allocator to be used by allocation calls, **allocate** directives and **allocate** clauses that do not specify an allocator.

Format

─────────────── C / C++ ───────────────
```
void omp_set_default_allocator (omp_allocator_handle_t allocator);
```
─────────────── C / C++ ───────────────

─────────────── Fortran ───────────────
```
subroutine omp_set_default_allocator ( allocator )
integer(kind=omp_allocator_handle_kind),intent(in) :: allocator
```
─────────────── Fortran ───────────────

Constraints on Arguments

The *allocator* argument must be a valid memory allocator handle.

Binding

The binding task set for an `omp_set_default_allocator` region is the binding implicit task.

Effect

The effect of this routine is to set the value of the *def-allocator-var* ICV of the binding implicit task to the value specified in the *allocator* argument.

Cross References

- *def-allocator-var* ICV, see Section 2.5 on page 63.
- Memory Allocators, see Section 2.11.2 on page 152.
- `omp_alloc` routine, see Section 3.7.6 on page 413.

3.7.5 omp_get_default_allocator

Summary

The `omp_get_default_allocator` routine returns a handle to the memory allocator to be used by allocation calls, `allocate` directives and `allocate` clauses that do not specify an allocator.

Format

─────────── C / C++ ───────────
```
omp_allocator_handle_t omp_get_default_allocator (void);
```
─────────── C / C++ ───────────

─────────── Fortran ───────────
```
integer(kind=omp_allocator_handle_kind) &
function omp_get_default_allocator ()
```
─────────── Fortran ───────────

Binding

The binding task set for an `omp_get_default_allocator` region is the binding implicit task.

Effect

The effect of this routine is to return the value of the *def-allocator-var* ICV of the binding implicit task.

Cross References

- *def-allocator-var* ICV, see Section 2.5 on page 63.
- Memory Allocators, see Section 2.11.2 on page 152.
- **omp_alloc** routine, see Section 3.7.6 on page 413.

―――――――――――――――――――――― C / C++ ――――――――――――――――――――――

3.7.6 omp_alloc

Summary

The **omp_alloc** routine requests a memory allocation from a memory allocator.

Format

―――――――――――――――――――――― C ――――――――――――――――――――――
```
void *omp_alloc (size_t size, omp_allocator_handle_t allocator);
```
―――――――――――――――――――――― C ――――――――――――――――――――――

―――――――――――――――――――――― C++ ――――――――――――――――――――――
```
void *omp_alloc(
    size_t size,
    omp_allocator_handle_t allocator=omp_null_allocator
);
```
―――――――――――――――――――――― C++ ――――――――――――――――――――――

Constraints on Arguments

Unless **dynamic_allocators** appears on a **requires** directive in the same compilation unit, **omp_alloc** invocations that appear in **target** regions must not pass **omp_null_allocator** as the *allocator* argument, which must be a constant expression that evaluates to one of the predefined memory allocator values.

----- C/C++ (cont.) -----

Effect

The **omp_alloc** routine requests a memory allocation of *size* bytes from the specified memory allocator. If the *allocator* argument is **omp_null_allocator** the memory allocator used by the routine will be the one specified by the *def-allocator-var* ICV of the binding implicit task. Upon success it returns a pointer to the allocated memory. Otherwise, the behavior specified by the **fallback** trait will be followed.

Allocated memory will be byte aligned to at least the alignment required by **malloc**.

Cross References

- Memory allocators, see Section 2.11.2 on page 152.

3.7.7 omp_free

Summary

The **omp_free** routine deallocates previously allocated memory.

Format

----- C -----
```
void omp_free (void *ptr, omp_allocator_handle_t allocator);
```
----- C -----

----- C++ -----
```
void omp_free(
   void *ptr,
   omp_allocator_handle_t allocator=omp_null_allocator
);
```
----- C++ -----

Effect

The **omp_free** routine deallocates the memory to which *ptr* points. The *ptr* argument must point to memory previously allocated with a memory allocator. If the *allocator* argument is specified it must be the memory allocator to which the allocation request was made. If the *allocator* argument is **omp_null_allocator** the implementation will determine that value automatically. Using **omp_free** on memory that was already deallocated or that was allocated by an allocator that has already been destroyed with **omp_destroy_allocator** results in unspecified behavior.

Cross References

- Memory allocators, see Section 2.11.2 on page 152.

―――――――――――――― C / C++ ――――――――――――――

3.8 Tool Control Routine

Summary

The `omp_control_tool` routine enables a program to pass commands to an active tool.

Format

―――――――――――――― C / C++ ――――――――――――――
```
int omp_control_tool(int command, int modifier, void *arg);
```
―――――――――――――― C / C++ ――――――――――――――

―――――――――――――― Fortran ――――――――――――――
```
integer function omp_control_tool(command, modifier)
integer (kind=omp_control_tool_kind) command
integer modifier
```
―――――――――――――― Fortran ――――――――――――――

Description

An OpenMP program may use `omp_control_tool` to pass commands to a tool. An application can use `omp_control_tool` to request that a tool starts or restarts data collection when a code region of interest is encountered, that a tool pauses data collection when leaving the region of interest, that a tool flushes any data that it has collected so far, or that a tool ends data collection. Additionally, `omp_control_tool` can be used to pass tool-specific commands to a particular tool.

The following types correspond to return values from `omp_control_tool`:

―――――――――――――― C / C++ ――――――――――――――
```
typedef enum omp_control_tool_result_t {
    omp_control_tool_notool = -2,
    omp_control_tool_nocallback = -1,
    omp_control_tool_success = 0,
    omp_control_tool_ignored = 1
} omp_control_tool_result_t;
```
―――――――――――――― C / C++ ――――――――――――――

---- Fortran ----
```fortran
integer (kind=omp_control_tool_result_kind), &
        parameter :: omp_control_tool_notool = -2
integer (kind=omp_control_tool_result_kind), &
        parameter :: omp_control_tool_nocallback = -1
integer (kind=omp_control_tool_result_kind), &
        parameter :: omp_control_tool_success = 0
integer (kind=omp_control_tool_result_kind), &
        parameter :: omp_control_tool_ignored = 1
```
---- Fortran ----

If the OMPT interface state is inactive, the OpenMP implementation returns `omp_control_tool_notool`. If the OMPT interface state is active, but no callback is registered for the *tool-control* event, the OpenMP implementation returns `omp_control_tool_nocallback`. An OpenMP implementation may return other implementation-defined negative values strictly smaller than -64; an application may assume that any negative return value indicates that a tool has not received the command. A return value of `omp_control_tool_success` indicates that the tool has performed the specified command. A return value of `omp_control_tool_ignored` indicates that the tool has ignored the specified command. A tool may return other positive values strictly greater than 64 that are tool-defined.

Constraints on Arguments

The following enumeration type defines four standard commands. Table 3.1 describes the actions that these commands request from a tool.

---- C / C++ ----
```c
typedef enum omp_control_tool_t {
  omp_control_tool_start = 1,
  omp_control_tool_pause = 2,
  omp_control_tool_flush = 3,
  omp_control_tool_end = 4
} omp_control_tool_t;
```
---- C / C++ ----

---- Fortran ----
```fortran
integer (kind=omp_control_tool_kind), &
        parameter :: omp_control_tool_start = 1
integer (kind=omp_control_tool_kind), &
        parameter :: omp_control_tool_pause = 2
integer (kind=omp_control_tool_kind), &
        parameter :: omp_control_tool_flush = 3
integer (kind=omp_control_tool_kind), &
        parameter :: omp_control_tool_end = 4
```
---- Fortran ----

Tool-specific values for *command* must be greater or equal to 64. Tools must ignore *command* values that they are not explicitly designed to handle. Other values accepted by a tool for *command*, and any values for *modifier* and *arg* are tool-defined.

TABLE 3.1: Standard Tool Control Commands

Command	Action
`omp_control_tool_start`	Start or restart monitoring if it is off. If monitoring is already on, this command is idempotent. If monitoring has already been turned off permanently, this command will have no effect.
`omp_control_tool_pause`	Temporarily turn monitoring off. If monitoring is already off, it is idempotent.
`omp_control_tool_flush`	Flush any data buffered by a tool. This command may be applied whether monitoring is on or off.
`omp_control_tool_end`	Turn monitoring off permanently; the tool finalizes itself and flushes all output.

Execution Model Events

The *tool-control* event occurs in the thread that encounters a call to `omp_control_tool` at a point inside its corresponding OpenMP region.

Tool Callbacks

A thread dispatches a registered `ompt_callback_control_tool` callback for each occurrence of a *tool-control* event. The callback executes in the context of the call that occurs in the user program and has type signature `ompt_callback_control_tool_t`. The callback may return any non-negative value, which will be returned to the application by the OpenMP implementation as the return value of the `omp_control_tool` call that triggered the callback.

Arguments passed to the callback are those passed by the user to `omp_control_tool`. If the call is made in Fortran, the tool will be passed `NULL` as the third argument to the callback. If any of the four standard commands is presented to a tool, the tool will ignore the *modifier* and *arg* argument values.

Cross References

- OMPT Interface, see Chapter 4 on page 419

- `ompt_callback_control_tool_t`, see Section 4.5.2.29 on page 495

This page intentionally left blank

CHAPTER 4

OMPT Interface

This chapter describes OMPT, which is an interface for *first-party* tools. *First-party* tools are linked or loaded directly into the OpenMP program. OMPT defines mechanisms to initialize a tool, to examine OpenMP state associated with an OpenMP thread, to interpret the call stack of an OpenMP thread, to receive notification about OpenMP *events*, to trace activity on OpenMP target devices, to assess implementation-dependent details of an OpenMP implementation (such as supported states and mutual exclusion implementations), and to control a tool from an OpenMP application.

4.1 OMPT Interfaces Definitions

─────────── C / C++ ───────────

A compliant implementation must supply a set of definitions for the OMPT runtime entry points, OMPT callback signatures, and the special data types of their parameters and return values. These definitions, which are listed throughout this chapter, and their associated declarations shall be provided in a header file named **omp-tools.h**. In addition, the set of definitions may specify other implementation-specific values.

The **ompt_start_tool** function is an external function with C linkage.

─────────── C / C++ ───────────

4.2 Activating a First-Party Tool

To activate a tool, an OpenMP implementation first determines whether the tool should be initialized. If so, the OpenMP implementation invokes the initializer of the tool, which enables the tool to prepare to monitor execution on the host. The tool may then also arrange to monitor computation that executes on target devices. This section explains how the tool and an OpenMP implementation interact to accomplish these tasks.

4.2.1 `ompt_start_tool`

Summary

In order to use the OMPT interface provided by an OpenMP implementation, a tool must implement the `ompt_start_tool` function, through which the OpenMP implementation initializes the tool.

Format

```c
ompt_start_tool_result_t *ompt_start_tool(
  unsigned int omp_version,
  const char *runtime_version
);
```

Description

For a tool to use the OMPT interface that an OpenMP implementation provides, the tool must define a globally-visible implementation of the function `ompt_start_tool`. The tool indicates that it will use the OMPT interface that an OpenMP implementation provides by returning a non-null pointer to an `ompt_start_tool_result_t` structure from the `ompt_start_tool` implementation that it provides. The `ompt_start_tool_result_t` structure contains pointers to tool initialization and finalization callbacks as well as a tool data word that an OpenMP implementation must pass by reference to these callbacks. A tool may return `NULL` from `ompt_start_tool` to indicate that it will not use the OMPT interface in a particular execution.

A tool may use the *omp_version* argument to determine if it is compatible with the OMPT interface that the OpenMP implementation provides.

Description of Arguments

The argument *omp_version* is the value of the **_OPENMP** version macro associated with the OpenMP API implementation. This value identifies the OpenMP API version that an OpenMP implementation supports, which specifies the version of the OMPT interface that it supports.

The argument *runtime_version* is a version string that unambiguously identifies the OpenMP implementation.

Constraints on Arguments

The argument *runtime_version* must be an immutable string that is defined for the lifetime of a program execution.

Effect

If a tool returns a non-null pointer to an **ompt_start_tool_result_t** structure, an OpenMP implementation will call the tool initializer specified by the *initialize* field in this structure before beginning execution of any OpenMP construct or completing execution of any environment routine invocation; the OpenMP implementation will call the tool finalizer specified by the *finalize* field in this structure when the OpenMP implementation shuts down.

Cross References

- **ompt_start_tool_result_t**, see Section 4.4.1 on page 433.

4.2.2 Determining Whether a First-Party Tool Should be Initialized

An OpenMP implementation examines the *tool-var* ICV as one of its first initialization steps. If the value of *tool-var* is *disabled*, the initialization continues without a check for the presence of a tool and the functionality of the OMPT interface will be unavailable as the program executes. In this case, the OMPT interface state remains *inactive*.

Otherwise, the OMPT interface state changes to *pending* and the OpenMP implementation activates any first-party tool that it finds. A tool can provide a definition of **ompt_start_tool** to an OpenMP implementation in three ways:

- By statically-linking its definition of **ompt_start_tool** into an OpenMP application;
- By introducing a dynamically-linked library that includes its definition of **ompt_start_tool** into the application's address space; or

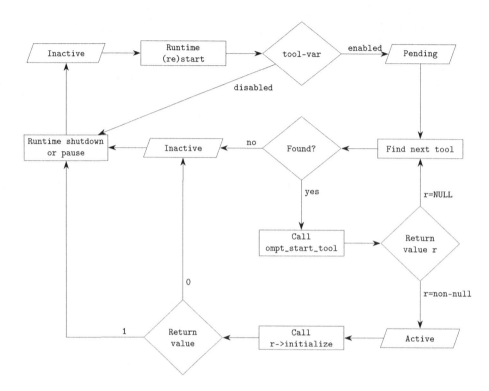

FIGURE 4.1: First-Party Tool Activation Flow Chart

- By providing, in the *tool-libraries-var* ICV, the name of a dynamically-linked library that is appropriate for the architecture and operating system used by the application and that includes a definition of **ompt_start_tool**.

If the value of *tool-var* is *enabled*, the OpenMP implementation must check if a tool has provided an implementation of **ompt_start_tool**. The OpenMP implementation first checks if a tool-provided implementation of **ompt_start_tool** is available in the address space, either statically-linked into the application or in a dynamically-linked library loaded in the address space. If multiple implementations of **ompt_start_tool** are available, the OpenMP implementation will use the first tool-provided implementation of **ompt_start_tool** that it finds.

If the implementation does not find a tool-provided implementation of **ompt_start_tool** in the address space, it consults the *tool-libraries-var* ICV, which contains a (possibly empty) list of dynamically-linked libraries. As described in detail in Section 6.19 on page 617, the libraries in *tool-libraries-var* are then searched for the first usable implementation of **ompt_start_tool** that one of the libraries in the list provides.

If the implementation finds a tool-provided definition of **ompt_start_tool**, it invokes that method; if a **NULL** pointer is returned, the OMPT interface state remains *pending* and the implementation continues to look for implementations of **ompt_start_tool**; otherwise a non-null pointer to an **ompt_start_tool_result_t** structure is returned, the OMPT interface state changes to *active* and the OpenMP implementation makes the OMPT interface available as the program executes. In this case, as the OpenMP implementation completes its initialization, it initializes the OMPT interface.

If no tool can be found, the OMPT interface state changes to *inactive*.

Cross References
- *tool-libraries-var* ICV, see Section 2.5 on page 63.
- *tool-var* ICV, see Section 2.5 on page 63.
- **ompt_start_tool** function, see Section 4.2.1 on page 420.
- **ompt_start_tool_result_t** type, see Section 4.4.1 on page 433.

4.2.3 Initializing a First-Party Tool

To initialize the OMPT interface, the OpenMP implementation invokes the tool initializer that is specified in the **ompt_start_tool_result_t** structure that is indicated by the non-null pointer that **ompt_start_tool** returns. The initializer is invoked prior to the occurrence of any OpenMP *event*.

A tool initializer, described in Section 4.5.1.1 on page 457, uses the function specified in its *lookup* argument to look up pointers to OMPT interface runtime entry points that the OpenMP implementation provides; this process is described in Section 4.2.3.1 on page 424. Typically, a tool initializer obtains a pointer to the **ompt_set_callback** runtime entry point with type signature **ompt_set_callback_t** and then uses this runtime entry point to register tool callbacks for OpenMP events, as described in Section 4.2.4 on page 425.

A tool initializer may use the **ompt_enumerate_states** runtime entry point, which has type signature **ompt_enumerate_states_t**, to determine the thread states that an OpenMP implementation employs. Similarly, it may use the **ompt_enumerate_mutex_impls** runtime entry point, which has type signature **ompt_enumerate_mutex_impls_t**, to determine the mutual exclusion implementations that the OpenMP implementation employs.

If a tool initializer returns a non-zero value, the OMPT interface state remains *active* for the execution; otherwise, the OMPT interface state changes to *inactive*.

Cross References

- `ompt_start_tool` function, see Section 4.2.1 on page 420.
- `ompt_start_tool_result_t` type, see Section 4.4.1 on page 433.
- `ompt_initialize_t` type, see Section 4.5.1.1 on page 457.
- `ompt_callback_thread_begin_t` type, see Section 4.5.2.1 on page 459.
- `ompt_enumerate_states_t` type, see Section 4.6.1.1 on page 498.
- `ompt_enumerate_mutex_impls_t` type, see Section 4.6.1.2 on page 499.
- `ompt_set_callback_t` type, see Section 4.6.1.3 on page 500.
- `ompt_function_lookup_t` type, see Section 4.6.3 on page 531.

4.2.3.1 Binding Entry Points in the OMPT Callback Interface

Functions that an OpenMP implementation provides to support the OMPT interface are not defined as global function symbols. Instead, they are defined as runtime entry points that a tool can only identify through the *lookup* function that is provided as an argument with type signature `ompt_function_lookup_t` to the tool initializer. A tool can use this function to obtain a pointer to each of the runtime entry points that an OpenMP implementation provides to support the OMPT interface. Once a tool has obtained a *lookup* function, it may employ it at any point in the future.

For each runtime entry point in the OMPT interface for the host device, Table 4.1 provides the string name by which it is known and its associated type signature. Implementations can provide additional implementation-specific names and corresponding entry points. Any names that begin with `ompt_` are reserved names.

During initialization, a tool should look up each runtime entry point in the OMPT interface by name and bind a pointer maintained by the tool that can later be used to invoke the entry point. The entry points described in Table 4.1 enable a tool to assess the thread states and mutual exclusion implementations that an OpenMP implementation supports, to register tool callbacks, to inspect registered callbacks, to introspect OpenMP state associated with threads, and to use tracing to monitor computations that execute on target devices.

Detailed information about each runtime entry point listed in Table 4.1 is included as part of the description of its type signature.

Cross References

- `ompt_enumerate_states_t` type, see Section 4.6.1.1 on page 498.
- `ompt_enumerate_mutex_impls_t` type, see Section 4.6.1.2 on page 499.

- **ompt_set_callback_t** type, see Section 4.6.1.3 on page 500.
- **ompt_get_callback_t** type, see Section 4.6.1.4 on page 502.
- **ompt_get_thread_data_t** type, see Section 4.6.1.5 on page 503.
- **ompt_get_num_procs_t** type, see Section 4.6.1.6 on page 503.
- **ompt_get_num_places_t** type, see Section 4.6.1.7 on page 504.
- **ompt_get_place_proc_ids_t** type, see Section 4.6.1.8 on page 505.
- **ompt_get_place_num_t** type, see Section 4.6.1.9 on page 506.
- **ompt_get_partition_place_nums_t** type, see Section 4.6.1.10 on page 507.
- **ompt_get_proc_id_t** type, see Section 4.6.1.11 on page 508.
- **ompt_get_state_t** type, see Section 4.6.1.12 on page 508.
- **ompt_get_parallel_info_t** type, see Section 4.6.1.13 on page 510.
- **ompt_get_task_info_t** type, see Section 4.6.1.14 on page 512.
- **ompt_get_task_memory_t** type, see Section 4.6.1.15 on page 514.
- **ompt_get_target_info_t** type, see Section 4.6.1.16 on page 515.
- **ompt_get_num_devices_t** type, see Section 4.6.1.17 on page 516.
- **ompt_get_unique_id_t** type, see Section 4.6.1.18 on page 517.
- **ompt_finalize_tool_t** type, see Section 4.6.1.19 on page 517.
- **ompt_function_lookup_t** type, see Section 4.6.3 on page 531.

4.2.4 Monitoring Activity on the Host with OMPT

To monitor the execution of an OpenMP program on the host device, a tool initializer must register to receive notification of events that occur as an OpenMP program executes. A tool can use the **ompt_set_callback** runtime entry point to register callbacks for OpenMP events. The return codes for **ompt_set_callback** use the **ompt_set_result_t** enumeration type. If the **ompt_set_callback** runtime entry point is called outside a tool initializer, registration of supported callbacks may fail with a return value of **ompt_set_error**.

All callbacks registered with **ompt_set_callback** or returned by **ompt_get_callback** use the dummy type signature **ompt_callback_t**.

Table 4.2 shows the valid registration return codes of the **ompt_set_callback** runtime entry point with specific values of its *event* argument. For callbacks for which **ompt_set_always** is

TABLE 4.1: OMPT Callback Interface Runtime Entry Point Names and Their Type Signatures

Entry Point String Name	Type signature
"ompt_enumerate_states"	ompt_enumerate_states_t
"ompt_enumerate_mutex_impls"	ompt_enumerate_mutex_impls_t
"ompt_set_callback"	ompt_set_callback_t
"ompt_get_callback"	ompt_get_callback_t
"ompt_get_thread_data"	ompt_get_thread_data_t
"ompt_get_num_places"	ompt_get_num_places_t
"ompt_get_place_proc_ids"	ompt_get_place_proc_ids_t
"ompt_get_place_num"	ompt_get_place_num_t
"ompt_get_partition_place_nums"	ompt_get_partition_place_nums_t
"ompt_get_proc_id"	ompt_get_proc_id_t
"ompt_get_state"	ompt_get_state_t
"ompt_get_parallel_info"	ompt_get_parallel_info_t
"ompt_get_task_info"	ompt_get_task_info_t
"ompt_get_task_memory"	ompt_get_task_memory_t
"ompt_get_num_devices"	ompt_get_num_devices_t
"ompt_get_num_procs"	ompt_get_num_procs_t
"ompt_get_target_info"	ompt_get_target_info_t
"ompt_get_unique_id"	ompt_get_unique_id_t
"ompt_finalize_tool"	ompt_finalize_tool_t

the only registration return code that is allowed, an OpenMP implementation must guarantee that the callback will be invoked every time that a runtime event that is associated with it occurs. Support for such callbacks is required in a minimal implementation of the OMPT interface. For callbacks for which the **ompt_set_callback** runtime entry may return values other than **ompt_set_always**, whether an OpenMP implementation invokes a registered callback never, sometimes, or always is implementation-defined. If registration for a callback allows a return code of **omp_set_never**, support for invoking such a callback may not be present in a minimal implementation of the OMPT interface. The return code from registering a callback indicates the implementation-defined level of support for the callback.

Two techniques reduce the size of the OMPT interface. First, in cases where events are naturally paired, for example, the beginning and end of a region, and the arguments needed by the callback at each endpoint are identical, a tool registers a single callback for the pair of events, with **ompt_scope_begin** or **ompt_scope_end** provided as an argument to identify for which endpoint the callback is invoked. Second, when a class of events is amenable to uniform treatment, OMPT provides a single callback for that class of events, for example, an **ompt_callback_sync_region_wait** callback is used for multiple kinds of synchronization regions, such as barrier, taskwait, and taskgroup regions. Some events, for example, **ompt_callback_sync_region_wait**, use both techniques.

Cross References

- **ompt_set_result_t** type, see Section 4.4.4.2 on page 438.
- **ompt_set_callback_t** type, see Section 4.6.1.3 on page 500.
- **ompt_get_callback_t** type, see Section 4.6.1.4 on page 502.

4.2.5 Tracing Activity on Target Devices with OMPT

A target device may or may not initialize a full OpenMP runtime system. Unless it does, it may not be possible to monitor activity on a device using a tool interface based on callbacks. To accommodate such cases, the OMPT interface defines a monitoring interface for tracing activity on target devices. Tracing activity on a target device involves the following steps:

- To prepare to trace activity on a target device, a tool must register for an **ompt_callback_device_initialize** callback. A tool may also register for an **ompt_callback_device_load** callback to be notified when code is loaded onto a target device or an **ompt_callback_device_unload** callback to be notified when code is unloaded from a target device. A tool may also optionally register an **ompt_callback_device_finalize** callback.

TABLE 4.2: Valid Return Codes of `ompt_set_callback` for Each Callback

Return code abbreviation	N	S/P	A
`ompt_callback_thread_begin`			*
`ompt_callback_thread_end`			*
`ompt_callback_parallel_begin`			*
`ompt_callback_parallel_end`			*
`ompt_callback_task_create`			*
`ompt_callback_task_schedule`			*
`ompt_callback_implicit_task`			*
`ompt_callback_target`			*
`ompt_callback_target_data_op`			*
`ompt_callback_target_submit`			*
`ompt_callback_control_tool`			*
`ompt_callback_device_initialize`			*
`ompt_callback_device_finalize`			*
`ompt_callback_device_load`			*
`ompt_callback_device_unload`			*
`ompt_callback_sync_region_wait`	*	*	*
`ompt_callback_mutex_released`	*	*	*
`ompt_callback_dependences`	*	*	*
`ompt_callback_task_dependence`	*	*	*
`ompt_callback_work`	*	*	*
`ompt_callback_master`	*	*	*
`ompt_callback_target_map`	*	*	*
`ompt_callback_sync_region`	*	*	*
`ompt_callback_reduction`	*	*	*
`ompt_callback_lock_init`	*	*	*
`ompt_callback_lock_destroy`	*	*	*
`ompt_callback_mutex_acquire`	*	*	*
`ompt_callback_mutex_acquired`	*	*	*
`ompt_callback_nest_lock`	*	*	*
`ompt_callback_flush`	*	*	*
`ompt_callback_cancel`	*	*	*
`ompt_callback_dispatch`	*	*	*

N = `ompt_set_never`
P = `ompt_set_sometimes_paired`
S = `ompt_set_sometimes`
A = `ompt_set_always`

- When an OpenMP implementation initializes a target device, the OpenMP implementation dispatches the device initialization callback of the tool on the host device. If the OpenMP implementation or target device does not support tracing, the OpenMP implementation passes **NULL** to the device initializer of the tool for its *lookup* argument; otherwise, the OpenMP implementation passes a pointer to a device-specific runtime entry point with type signature **ompt_function_lookup_t** to the device initializer of the tool.

- If a non-null *lookup* pointer is provided to the device initializer of the tool, the tool may use it to determine the runtime entry points in the tracing interface that are available for the device and may bind the returned function pointers to tool variables. Table 4.3 indicates the names of runtime entry points that may be available for a device; an implementations may provide additional implementation-defined names and corresponding entry points. The driver for the device provides the runtime entry points that enable a tool to control the trace collection interface of the device. The *native* trace format that the interface uses may be device specific and the available kinds of trace records are implementation-defined. Some devices may allow a tool to collect traces of records in a standard format known as OMPT trace records. Each OMPT trace record serves as a substitute for an OMPT callback that cannot be made on the device. The fields in each trace record type are defined in the description of the callback that the record represents. If this type of record is provided then the *lookup* function returns values for the runtime entry points **ompt_set_trace_ompt** and **ompt_get_record_ompt**, which support collecting and decoding OMPT traces. If the native tracing format for a device is the OMPT format then tracing can be controlled using the runtime entry points for native or OMPT tracing.

- The tool uses the **ompt_set_trace_native** and/or the **ompt_set_trace_ompt** runtime entry point to specify what types of events or activities to monitor on the device. The return codes for **ompt_set_trace_ompt** and **ompt_set_trace_native** use the **ompt_set_result_t** enumeration type. If the **ompt_set_trace_native** /or the **ompt_set_trace_ompt** runtime entry point is called outside a device initializer, registration of supported callbacks may fail with a return code of **ompt_set_error**.

- The tool initiates tracing on the device by invoking **ompt_start_trace**. Arguments to **ompt_start_trace** include two tool callbacks through which the OpenMP implementation can manage traces associated with the device. One allocates a buffer in which the device can deposit trace events. The second callback processes a buffer of trace events from the device.

- If the device requires a trace buffer, the OpenMP implementation invokes the tool-supplied callback function on the host device to request a new buffer.

- The OpenMP implementation monitors the execution of OpenMP constructs on the device and records a trace of events or activities into a trace buffer. If possible, device trace records are marked with a *host_op_id*—an identifier that associates device activities with the target operation that the host initiated to cause these activities. To correlate activities on the host with activities on a device, a tool can register a **ompt_callback_target_submit** callback. Before the host initiates each distinct activity associated with a structured block for a **target** construct on a device, the OpenMP implementation dispatches the **ompt_callback_target_submit** callback on the host in the thread that is executing the task that encounters the **target** construct.

TABLE 4.3: OMPT Tracing Interface Runtime Entry Point Names and Their Type Signatures

Entry Point String Name	Type Signature
"ompt_get_device_num_procs"	ompt_get_device_num_procs_t
"ompt_get_device_time"	ompt_get_device_time_t
"ompt_translate_time"	ompt_translate_time_t
"ompt_set_trace_ompt"	ompt_set_trace_ompt_t
"ompt_set_trace_native"	ompt_set_trace_native_t
"ompt_start_trace"	ompt_start_trace_t
"ompt_pause_trace"	ompt_pause_trace_t
"ompt_flush_trace"	ompt_flush_trace_t
"ompt_stop_trace"	ompt_stop_trace_t
"ompt_advance_buffer_cursor"	ompt_advance_buffer_cursor_t
"ompt_get_record_type"	ompt_get_record_type_t
"ompt_get_record_ompt"	ompt_get_record_ompt_t
"ompt_get_record_native"	ompt_get_record_native_t
"ompt_get_record_abstract"	ompt_get_record_abstract_t

Examples of activities that could cause an **ompt_callback_target_submit** callback to be dispatched include an explicit data copy between a host and target device or execution of a computation. This callback provides the tool with a pair of identifiers: one that identifies the target region and a second that uniquely identifies an activity associated with that region. These identifiers help the tool correlate activities on the target device with their target region.

- When appropriate, for example, when a trace buffer fills or needs to be flushed, the OpenMP implementation invokes the tool-supplied buffer completion callback to process a non-empty sequence of records in a trace buffer that is associated with the device.

- The tool-supplied buffer completion callback may return immediately, ignoring records in the trace buffer, or it may iterate through them using the **ompt_advance_buffer_cursor** entry point to inspect each record. A tool may use the **ompt_get_record_type** runtime entry point to inspect the type of the record at the current cursor position. Three runtime entry points (**ompt_get_record_ompt**, **ompt_get_record_native**, and **ompt_get_record_abstract**) allow tools to inspect the contents of some or all records in a trace buffer. The **ompt_get_record_native** runtime entry point uses the native trace format of the device. The **ompt_get_record_abstract** runtime entry point decodes the contents of a native trace record and summarizes them as an **ompt_record_abstract_t** record. The **ompt_get_record_ompt** runtime entry point can only be used to retrieve records in OMPT format.

- Once tracing has been started on a device, a tool may pause or resume tracing on the device at any time by invoking **ompt_pause_trace** with an appropriate flag value as an argument.

- A tool may invoke the **ompt_flush_trace** runtime entry point for a device at any time between device initialization and finalization to cause the device to flush pending trace records.

- At any time, a tool may use the **ompt_start_trace** runtime entry point to start tracing or the **ompt_stop_trace** runtime entry point to stop tracing on a device. When tracing is stopped on a device, the OpenMP implementation eventually gathers all trace records already collected on the device and presents them to the tool using the buffer completion callback.

- An OpenMP implementation can be shut down while device tracing is in progress.

- When an OpenMP implementation is shut down, it finalize each device. Device finalization occurs in three steps. First, the OpenMP implementation halts any tracing in progress for the device. Second, the OpenMP implementation flushes all trace records collected for the device and uses the buffer completion callback associated with that device to present them to the tool. Finally, the OpenMP implementation dispatches any **ompt_callback_device_finalize** callback registered for the device.

Restrictions

Tracing activity on devices has the following restriction:

- Implementation-defined names must not start with the prefix **ompt_**, which is reserved for the OpenMP specification.

Cross References

- `ompt_callback_device_initialize_t` callback type, see Section 4.5.2.19 on page 482.
- `ompt_callback_device_finalize_t` callback type, see Section 4.5.2.20 on page 484.
- `ompt_get_device_num_procs` runtime entry point, see Section 4.6.2.1 on page 518.
- `ompt_get_device_time` runtime entry point, see Section 4.6.2.2 on page 519.
- `ompt_translate_time` runtime entry point, see Section 4.6.2.3 on page 520.
- `ompt_set_trace_ompt` runtime entry point, see Section 4.6.2.4 on page 521.
- `ompt_set_trace_native` runtime entry point, see Section 4.6.2.5 on page 522.
- `ompt_start_trace` runtime entry point, see Section 4.6.2.6 on page 523.
- `ompt_pause_trace` runtime entry point, see Section 4.6.2.7 on page 524.
- `ompt_flush_trace` runtime entry point, see Section 4.6.2.8 on page 525.
- `ompt_stop_trace` runtime entry point, see Section 4.6.2.9 on page 526.
- `ompt_advance_buffer_cursor` runtime entry point, see Section 4.6.2.10 on page 527.
- `ompt_get_record_type` runtime entry point, see Section 4.6.2.11 on page 528.
- `ompt_get_record_ompt` runtime entry point, see Section 4.6.2.12 on page 529.
- `ompt_get_record_native` runtime entry point, see Section 4.6.2.13 on page 530.
- `ompt_get_record_abstract` runtime entry point, see Section 4.6.2.14 on page 531.

4.3 Finalizing a First-Party Tool

If the OMPT interface state is active, the tool finalizer, which has type signature `ompt_finalize_t` and is specified by the *finalize* field in the `ompt_start_tool_result_t` structure returned from the `ompt_start_tool` function, is called when the OpenMP implementation shuts down.

Cross References

- `ompt_finalize_t` callback type, see Section 4.5.1.2 on page 458

4.4 OMPT Data Types

The C/C++ header file (omp-tools.h) provides the definitions of the types that are specified throughout this subsection.

4.4.1 Tool Initialization and Finalization

Summary

A tool's implementation of **ompt_start_tool** returns a pointer to an **ompt_start_tool_result_t** structure, which contains pointers to the tool's initialization and finalization callbacks as well as an **ompt_data_t** object for use by the tool.

Format

```
C / C++
typedef struct ompt_start_tool_result_t {
  ompt_initialize_t initialize;
  ompt_finalize_t finalize;
  ompt_data_t tool_data;
} ompt_start_tool_result_t;
C / C++
```

Restrictions

The **ompt_start_tool_result_t** type has the following restriction:

- The *initialize* and *finalize* callback pointer values in an **ompt_start_tool_result_t** structure that **ompt_start_tool** returns must be non-null.

Cross References

- **ompt_start_tool** function, see Section 4.2.1 on page 420.
- **ompt_data_t** type, see Section 4.4.4.4 on page 440.
- **ompt_initialize_t** callback type, see Section 4.5.1.1 on page 457.
- **ompt_finalize_t** callback type, see Section 4.5.1.2 on page 458.

4.4.2 Callbacks

Summary

The `ompt_callbacks_t` enumeration type indicates the integer codes used to identify OpenMP callbacks when registering or querying them.

Format

C / C++
```
typedef enum ompt_callbacks_t {
    ompt_callback_thread_begin          = 1,
    ompt_callback_thread_end            = 2,
    ompt_callback_parallel_begin        = 3,
    ompt_callback_parallel_end          = 4,
    ompt_callback_task_create           = 5,
    ompt_callback_task_schedule         = 6,
    ompt_callback_implicit_task         = 7,
    ompt_callback_target                = 8,
    ompt_callback_target_data_op        = 9,
    ompt_callback_target_submit         = 10,
    ompt_callback_control_tool          = 11,
    ompt_callback_device_initialize     = 12,
    ompt_callback_device_finalize       = 13,
    ompt_callback_device_load           = 14,
    ompt_callback_device_unload         = 15,
    ompt_callback_sync_region_wait      = 16,
    ompt_callback_mutex_released        = 17,
    ompt_callback_dependences           = 18,
    ompt_callback_task_dependence       = 19,
    ompt_callback_work                  = 20,
    ompt_callback_master                = 21,
    ompt_callback_target_map            = 22,
    ompt_callback_sync_region           = 23,
    ompt_callback_lock_init             = 24,
    ompt_callback_lock_destroy          = 25,
    ompt_callback_mutex_acquire         = 26,
    ompt_callback_mutex_acquired        = 27,
    ompt_callback_nest_lock             = 28,
    ompt_callback_flush                 = 29,
    ompt_callback_cancel                = 30,
    ompt_callback_reduction             = 31,
    ompt_callback_dispatch              = 32
} ompt_callbacks_t;
```
C / C++

4.4.3 Tracing

OpenMP provides type definitions that support tracing with OMPT.

4.4.3.1 Record Type

Summary

The **ompt_record_t** enumeration type indicates the integer codes used to identify OpenMP trace record formats.

Format

―――――――――――――――――― C / C++ ――――――――――――――――――
```
typedef enum ompt_record_t {
  ompt_record_ompt          = 1,
  ompt_record_native        = 2,
  ompt_record_invalid       = 3
} ompt_record_t;
```
―――――――――――――――――― C / C++ ――――――――――――――――――

4.4.3.2 Native Record Kind

Summary

The **ompt_record_native_t** enumeration type indicates the integer codes used to identify OpenMP native trace record contents.

Format

―――――――――――――――――― C / C++ ――――――――――――――――――
```
typedef enum ompt_record_native_t {
  ompt_record_native_info  = 1,
  ompt_record_native_event = 2
} ompt_record_native_t;
```
―――――――――――――――――― C / C++ ――――――――――――――――――

4.4.3.3 Native Record Abstract Type

Summary

The `ompt_record_abstract_t` type provides an abstract trace record format that is used to summarize native device trace records.

Format

```c
typedef struct ompt_record_abstract_t {
    ompt_record_native_t rclass;
    const char *type;
    ompt_device_time_t start_time;
    ompt_device_time_t end_time;
    ompt_hwid_t hwid;
} ompt_record_abstract_t;
```

Description

An `ompt_record_abstract_t` record contains information that a tool can use to process a native record that it may not fully understand. The *rclass* field indicates that the record is informational or that it represents an event; this information can help a tool determine how to present the record. The record *type* field points to a statically-allocated, immutable character string that provides a meaningful name that a tool can use to describe the event to a user. The *start_time* and *end_time* fields are used to place an event in time. The times are relative to the device clock. If an event does not have an associated *start_time* (*end_time*), the value of the *start_time* (*end_time*) field is `ompt_time_none`. The hardware identifier field, *hwid*, indicates the location on the device where the event occurred. A *hwid* may represent a hardware abstraction such as a core or a hardware thread identifier. The meaning of a *hwid* value for a device is implementation defined. If no hardware abstraction is associated with the record then the value of *hwid* is `ompt_hwid_none`.

4.4.3.4 Record Type

Summary

The `ompt_record_ompt_t` type provides an standard complete trace record format.

Format

```
typedef struct ompt_record_ompt_t {
  ompt_callbacks_t type;
  ompt_device_time_t time;
  ompt_id_t thread_id;
  ompt_id_t target_id;
  union {
    ompt_record_thread_begin_t thread_begin;
    ompt_record_parallel_begin_t parallel_begin;
    ompt_record_parallel_end_t parallel_end;
    ompt_record_work_t work;
    ompt_record_dispatch_t dispatch;
    ompt_record_task_create_t task_create;
    ompt_record_dependences_t dependences;
    ompt_record_task_dependence_t task_dependence;
    ompt_record_task_schedule_t task_schedule;
    ompt_record_implicit_task_t implicit_task;
    ompt_record_master_t master;
    ompt_record_sync_region_t sync_region;
    ompt_record_mutex_acquire_t mutex_acquire;
    ompt_record_mutex_t mutex;
    ompt_record_nest_lock_t nest_lock;
    ompt_record_flush_t flush;
    ompt_record_cancel_t cancel;
    ompt_record_target_t target;
    ompt_record_target_data_op_t target_data_op;
    ompt_record_target_map_t target_map;
    ompt_record_target_kernel_t target_kernel;
    ompt_record_control_tool_t control_tool;
  } record;
} ompt_record_ompt_t;
```

Description

The field *type* specifies the type of record provided by this structure. According to the type, event specific information is stored in the matching *record* entry.

Restrictions

The **ompt_record_ompt_t** type has the following restriction:

- If *type* is set to **ompt_callback_thread_end_t** then the value of *record* is undefined.

4.4.4 Miscellaneous Type Definitions

This section describes miscellaneous types and enumerations used by the tool interface.

4.4.4.1 ompt_callback_t

Summary

Pointers to tool callback functions with different type signatures are passed to the **ompt_set_callback** runtime entry point and returned by the **ompt_get_callback** runtime entry point. For convenience, these runtime entry points expect all type signatures to be cast to a dummy type **ompt_callback_t**.

Format

```
C / C++
typedef void (*ompt_callback_t) (void);
C / C++
```

4.4.4.2 ompt_set_result_t

Summary

The **ompt_result_t** enumeration type corresponds to values that the **ompt_set_callback**, **ompt_set_trace_ompt** and **ompt_set_trace_native** runtime entry points return.

Format

```
C / C++
typedef enum ompt_set_result_t {
    ompt_set_error              = 0,
    ompt_set_never              = 1,
    ompt_set_impossible         = 2,
    ompt_set_sometimes          = 3,
    ompt_set_sometimes_paired   = 4,
    ompt_set_always             = 5
} ompt_set_result_t;
C / C++
```

Description

Values of **ompt_set_result_t**, may indicate several possible outcomes. The **omp_set_error** value indicates that the associated call failed. Otherwise, the value indicates when an event may occur and, when appropriate, *dispatching* a callback event leads to the invocation of the callback. The **ompt_set_never** value indicates that the event will never occur or that the callback will never be invoked at runtime. The **ompt_set_impossible** value indicates that the event may occur but that tracing of it is not possible. The **ompt_set_sometimes** value indicates that the event may occur and, for an implementation-defined subset of associated event occurrences, will be traced or the callback will be invoked at runtime. The **ompt_set_sometimes_paired** value indicates the same result as **ompt_set_sometimes** and, in addition, that a callback with an *endpoint* value of **ompt_scope_begin** will be invoked if and only if the same callback with an *endpoint* value of **ompt_scope_end** will also be invoked sometime in the future. The **ompt_set_always** value indicates that, whenever an associated event occurs, it will be traced or the callback will be invoked.

Cross References

- Monitoring activity on the host with OMPT, see Section 4.2.4 on page 425.
- Tracing activity on target devices with OMPT, see Section 4.2.5 on page 427.
- **ompt_set_callback** runtime entry point, see Section 4.6.1.3 on page 500.
- **ompt_set_trace_ompt** runtime entry point, see Section 4.6.2.4 on page 521.
- **ompt_set_trace_native** runtime entry point, see Section 4.6.2.5 on page 522.

4.4.4.3 ompt_id_t

Summary

The **ompt_id_t** type is used to provide various identifiers to tools.

Format

—————————————— C / C++ ——————————————
```
typedef uint64_t ompt_id_t;
```
—————————————— C / C++ ——————————————

Description

When tracing asynchronous activity on devices, identifiers enable tools to correlate target regions and operations that the host initiates with associated activities on a target device. In addition, OMPT provides identifiers to refer to parallel regions and tasks that execute on a device. These various identifiers are of type **ompt_id_t**.

ompt_id_none is defined as an instance of type **ompt_id_t** with the value 0.

Restrictions

The **ompt_id_t** type has the following restriction:

- Identifiers created on each device must be unique from the time an OpenMP implementation is initialized until it is shut down. Identifiers for each target region and target operation instance that the host device initiates must be unique over time on the host. Identifiers for parallel and task region instances that execute on a device must be unique over time within that device.

4.4.4.4 ompt_data_t

Summary

The **ompt_data_t** type represents data associated with threads and with parallel and task regions.

Format

```
C / C++
typedef union ompt_data_t {
    uint64_t value;
    void *ptr;
} ompt_data_t;
C / C++
```

Description

The **ompt_data_t** type represents data that is reserved for tool use and that is related to a thread or to a parallel or task region. When an OpenMP implementation creates a thread or an instance of a parallel or task region, it initializes the associated **ompt_data_t** object with the value **ompt_data_none**, which is an instance of the type with the data and pointer fields equal to 0.

4.4.4.5 ompt_device_t

Summary

The **ompt_device_t** opaque object type represents a device.

Format

```
typedef void ompt_device_t;
```

4.4.4.6 ompt_device_time_t

Summary

The **ompt_device_time_t** type represents raw device time values.

Format

```
typedef uint64_t ompt_device_time_t;
```

Description

The **ompt_device_time_t** opaque object type represents raw device time values.
ompt_time_none refers to an unknown or unspecified time and is defined as an instance of type
ompt_device_time_t with the value 0.

4.4.4.7 ompt_buffer_t

Summary

The **ompt_buffer_t** opaque object type is a handle for a target buffer.

Format

```
typedef void ompt_buffer_t;
```

4.4.4.8 ompt_buffer_cursor_t

Summary

The `ompt_buffer_cursor_t` opaque type is a handle for a position in a target buffer.

Format

```
C / C++
typedef uint64_t ompt_buffer_cursor_t;
C / C++
```

4.4.4.9 ompt_dependence_t

Summary

The `ompt_dependence_t` type represents a task dependence.

Format

```
C / C++
typedef struct ompt_dependence_t {
  ompt_data_t variable;
  ompt_dependence_type_t dependence_type;
} ompt_dependence_t;
C / C++
```

Description

The `ompt_dependence_t` type is a structure that holds information about a depend clause. For task dependences, the *variable* field points to the storage location of the dependence. For *doacross* dependences, the *variable* field contains the value of a vector element that describes the dependence. The *dependence_type* field indicates the type of the dependence.

Cross References

- `ompt_dependence_type_t` type, see Section 4.4.4.23 on page 450.

4.4.4.10 ompt_thread_t

Summary

The **ompt_thread_t** enumeration type defines the valid thread type values.

Format

```
C / C++
typedef enum ompt_thread_t {
  ompt_thread_initial                = 1,
  ompt_thread_worker                 = 2,
  ompt_thread_other                  = 3,
  ompt_thread_unknown                = 4
} ompt_thread_t;
C / C++
```

Description

Any *initial thread* has thread type **ompt_thread_initial**. All *OpenMP threads* that are not initial threads have thread type **ompt_thread_worker**. A thread that an OpenMP implementation uses but that does not execute user code has thread type **ompt_thread_other**. Any thread that is created outside an OpenMP implementation and that is not an *initial thread* has thread type **ompt_thread_unknown**.

4.4.4.11 ompt_scope_endpoint_t

Summary

The **ompt_scope_endpoint_t** enumeration type defines valid scope endpoint values.

Format

```
C / C++
typedef enum ompt_scope_endpoint_t {
  ompt_scope_begin                   = 1,
  ompt_scope_end                     = 2
} ompt_scope_endpoint_t;
C / C++
```

4.4.4.12 `ompt_dispatch_t`

Summary

The `ompt_dispatch_t` enumeration type defines the valid dispatch kind values.

Format

```c
typedef enum ompt_dispatch_t {
    ompt_dispatch_iteration          = 1,
    ompt_dispatch_section            = 2
} ompt_dispatch_t;
```

4.4.4.13 `ompt_sync_region_t`

Summary

The `ompt_sync_region_t` enumeration type defines the valid synchronization region kind values.

Format

```c
typedef enum ompt_sync_region_t {
    ompt_sync_region_barrier                  = 1,
    ompt_sync_region_barrier_implicit         = 2,
    ompt_sync_region_barrier_explicit         = 3,
    ompt_sync_region_barrier_implementation   = 4,
    ompt_sync_region_taskwait                 = 5,
    ompt_sync_region_taskgroup                = 6,
    ompt_sync_region_reduction                = 7
} ompt_sync_region_t;
```

4.4.4.14 `ompt_target_data_op_t`

Summary

The `ompt_target_data_op_t` enumeration type defines the valid target data operation values.

Format

```c
typedef enum ompt_target_data_op_t {
    ompt_target_data_alloc                 = 1,
    ompt_target_data_transfer_to_device    = 2,
    ompt_target_data_transfer_from_device  = 3,
    ompt_target_data_delete                = 4,
    ompt_target_data_associate             = 5,
    ompt_target_data_disassociate          = 6
} ompt_target_data_op_t;
```

4.4.4.15 ompt_work_t

Summary

The **ompt_work_t** enumeration type defines the valid work type values.

Format

```c
typedef enum ompt_work_t {
    ompt_work_loop            = 1,
    ompt_work_sections        = 2,
    ompt_work_single_executor = 3,
    ompt_work_single_other    = 4,
    ompt_work_workshare       = 5,
    ompt_work_distribute      = 6,
    ompt_work_taskloop        = 7
} ompt_work_t;
```

4.4.4.16 ompt_mutex_t

Summary

The **ompt_mutex_t** enumeration type defines the valid mutex kind values.

Format

```c
typedef enum ompt_mutex_t {
    ompt_mutex_lock              = 1,
    ompt_mutex_test_lock         = 2,
    ompt_mutex_nest_lock         = 3,
    ompt_mutex_test_nest_lock    = 4,
    ompt_mutex_critical          = 5,
    ompt_mutex_atomic            = 6,
    ompt_mutex_ordered           = 7
} ompt_mutex_t;
```

4.4.4.17 ompt_native_mon_flag_t

Summary

The `ompt_native_mon_flag_t` enumeration type defines the valid native monitoring flag values.

Format

```c
typedef enum ompt_native_mon_flag_t {
    ompt_native_data_motion_explicit    = 0x01,
    ompt_native_data_motion_implicit    = 0x02,
    ompt_native_kernel_invocation       = 0x04,
    ompt_native_kernel_execution        = 0x08,
    ompt_native_driver                  = 0x10,
    ompt_native_runtime                 = 0x20,
    ompt_native_overhead                = 0x40,
    ompt_native_idleness                = 0x80
} ompt_native_mon_flag_t;
```

4.4.4.18 ompt_task_flag_t

Summary

The `ompt_task_flag_t` enumeration type defines valid task types.

Format

```
typedef enum ompt_task_flag_t {
  ompt_task_initial              = 0x00000001,
  ompt_task_implicit             = 0x00000002,
  ompt_task_explicit             = 0x00000004,
  ompt_task_target               = 0x00000008,
  ompt_task_undeferred           = 0x08000000,
  ompt_task_untied               = 0x10000000,
  ompt_task_final                = 0x20000000,
  ompt_task_mergeable            = 0x40000000,
  ompt_task_merged               = 0x80000000
} ompt_task_flag_t;
```

Description

The **ompt_task_flag_t** enumeration type defines valid task type values. The least significant byte provides information about the general classification of the task. The other bits represent properties of the task.

4.4.4.19 ompt_task_status_t

Summary

The **ompt_task_status_t** enumeration type indicates the reason that a task was switched when it reached a task scheduling point.

Format

```
typedef enum ompt_task_status_t {
  ompt_task_complete       = 1,
  ompt_task_yield          = 2,
  ompt_task_cancel         = 3,
  ompt_task_detach         = 4,
  ompt_task_early_fulfill  = 5,
  ompt_task_late_fulfill   = 6,
  ompt_task_switch         = 7
} ompt_task_status_t;
```

Description

The value `ompt_task_complete` of the `ompt_task_status_t` type indicates that the task that encountered the task scheduling point completed execution of the associated *structured-block* and an associated *allow-completion-event* was fulfilled. The value `ompt_task_yield` indicates that the task encountered a `taskyield` construct. The value `ompt_task_cancel` indicates that the task was canceled when it encountered an active cancellation point. The value `ompt_task_detach` indicates that a task with `detach` clause completed execution of the associated *structured-block* and is waiting for an *allow-completion-event* to be fulfilled. The value `ompt_task_early_fulfill` indicates that the *allow-completion-event* of the task is fulfilled before the task completed execution of the associated structured-block. The value `ompt_task_late_fulfill` indicates that the *allow-completion-event* of the task is fulfilled after the task completed execution of the associated structured-block. The value `ompt_task_switch` is used for all other cases that a task was switched.

4.4.4.20 ompt_target_t

Summary

The `ompt_target_t` enumeration type defines the valid target type values.

Format

— C / C++ —
```
typedef enum ompt_target_t {
    ompt_target                    = 1,
    ompt_target_enter_data         = 2,
    ompt_target_exit_data          = 3,
    ompt_target_update             = 4
} ompt_target_t;
```
— C / C++ —

4.4.4.21 ompt_parallel_flag_t

Summary

The `ompt_parallel_flag_t` enumeration type defines valid invoker values.

Format

```
typedef enum ompt_parallel_flag_t {
  ompt_parallel_invoker_program = 0x00000001,
  ompt_parallel_invoker_runtime = 0x00000002,
  ompt_parallel_league          = 0x40000000,
  ompt_parallel_team            = 0x80000000
} ompt_parallel_flag_t;
```

Description

The `ompt_parallel_flag_t` enumeration type defines valid invoker values, which indicate how an outlined function is invoked.

The value `ompt_parallel_invoker_program` indicates that the outlined function associated with implicit tasks for the region is invoked directly by the application on the master thread for a parallel region.

The value `ompt_parallel_invoker_runtime` indicates that the outlined function associated with implicit tasks for the region is invoked by the runtime on the master thread for a parallel region.

The value `ompt_parallel_league` indicates that the callback is invoked due to the creation of a league of teams by a **teams** construct.

The value `ompt_parallel_team` indicates that the callback is invoked due to the creation of a team of threads by a **parallel** construct.

4.4.4.22 ompt_target_map_flag_t

Summary

The `ompt_target_map_flag_t` enumeration type defines the valid target map flag values.

Format

```
typedef enum ompt_target_map_flag_t {
    ompt_target_map_flag_to       = 0x01,
    ompt_target_map_flag_from     = 0x02,
    ompt_target_map_flag_alloc    = 0x04,
    ompt_target_map_flag_release  = 0x08,
    ompt_target_map_flag_delete   = 0x10,
    ompt_target_map_flag_implicit = 0x20
} ompt_target_map_flag_t;
```

4.4.4.23 ompt_dependence_type_t

Summary

The `ompt_dependence_type_t` enumeration type defines the valid task dependence type values.

Format

```
typedef enum ompt_dependence_type_t {
    ompt_dependence_type_in            = 1,
    ompt_dependence_type_out           = 2,
    ompt_dependence_type_inout         = 3,
    ompt_dependence_type_mutexinoutset = 4,
    ompt_dependence_type_source        = 5,
    ompt_dependence_type_sink          = 6
} ompt_dependence_type_t;
```

4.4.4.24 ompt_cancel_flag_t

Summary

The `ompt_cancel_flag_t` enumeration type defines the valid cancel flag values.

Format

```
C / C++
typedef enum ompt_cancel_flag_t {
    ompt_cancel_parallel       = 0x01,
    ompt_cancel_sections       = 0x02,
    ompt_cancel_loop           = 0x04,
    ompt_cancel_taskgroup      = 0x08,
    ompt_cancel_activated      = 0x10,
    ompt_cancel_detected       = 0x20,
    ompt_cancel_discarded_task = 0x40
} ompt_cancel_flag_t;
C / C++
```

4.4.4.25 ompt_hwid_t

Summary

The **ompt_hwid_t** opaque type is a handle for a hardware identifier for a target device.

Format

```
C / C++
typedef uint64_t ompt_hwid_t;
C / C++
```

Description

The **ompt_hwid_t** opaque type is a handle for a hardware identifier for a target device. **ompt_hwid_none** is an instance of the type that refers to an unknown or unspecified hardware identifier and that has the value 0. If no *hwid* is associated with an **ompt_record_abstract_t** then the value of *hwid* is **ompt_hwid_none**.

Cross References

- **ompt_record_abstract_t** type, see Section 4.4.3.3 on page 436.

4.4.4.26 ompt_state_t

Summary

If the OMPT interface is in the *active* state then an OpenMP implementation must maintain *thread state* information for each thread. The thread state maintained is an approximation of the instantaneous state of a thread.

Format

―――――――――――― C / C++ ――――――――――――

A thread state must be one of the values of the enumeration type **ompt_state_t** or an implementation-defined state value of 512 or higher.

```
typedef enum ompt_state_t {
  ompt_state_work_serial                       = 0x000,
  ompt_state_work_parallel                     = 0x001,
  ompt_state_work_reduction                    = 0x002,

  ompt_state_wait_barrier                      = 0x010,
  ompt_state_wait_barrier_implicit_parallel    = 0x011,
  ompt_state_wait_barrier_implicit_workshare   = 0x012,
  ompt_state_wait_barrier_implicit             = 0x013,
  ompt_state_wait_barrier_explicit             = 0x014,

  ompt_state_wait_taskwait                     = 0x020,
  ompt_state_wait_taskgroup                    = 0x021,

  ompt_state_wait_mutex                        = 0x040,
  ompt_state_wait_lock                         = 0x041,
  ompt_state_wait_critical                     = 0x042,
  ompt_state_wait_atomic                       = 0x043,
  ompt_state_wait_ordered                      = 0x044,

  ompt_state_wait_target                       = 0x080,
  ompt_state_wait_target_map                   = 0x081,
  ompt_state_wait_target_update                = 0x082,

  ompt_state_idle                              = 0x100,
  ompt_state_overhead                          = 0x101,
  ompt_state_undefined                         = 0x102
} ompt_state_t;
```

―――――――――――― C / C++ ――――――――――――

Description

A tool can query the OpenMP state of a thread at any time. If a tool queries the state of a thread that is not associated with OpenMP then the implementation reports the state as `ompt_state_undefined`.

The value `ompt_state_work_serial` indicates that the thread is executing code outside all **parallel** regions.

The value `ompt_state_work_parallel` indicates that the thread is executing code within the scope of a **parallel** region.

The value `ompt_state_work_reduction` indicates that the thread is combining partial reduction results from threads in its team. An OpenMP implementation may never report a thread in this state; a thread that is combining partial reduction results may have its state reported as `ompt_state_work_parallel` or `ompt_state_overhead`.

The value `ompt_state_wait_barrier` indicates that the thread is waiting at either an implicit or explicit barrier. An implementation may never report a thread in this state; instead, a thread may have its state reported as `ompt_state_wait_barrier_implicit` or `ompt_state_wait_barrier_explicit`, as appropriate.

The value `ompt_state_wait_barrier_implicit` indicates that the thread is waiting at an implicit barrier in a **parallel** region. An OpenMP implementation may report `ompt_state_wait_barrier` for implicit barriers.

The value `ompt_state_wait_barrier_implicit_parallel` indicates that the thread is waiting at an implicit barrier at the end of a **parallel** region. An OpenMP implementation may report `ompt_state_wait_barrier` or `ompt_state_wait_barrier_implicit` for these barriers.

The value `ompt_state_wait_barrier_implicit_workshare` indicates that the thread is waiting at an implicit barrier at the end of a worksharing construct. An OpenMP implementation may report `ompt_state_wait_barrier` or `ompt_state_wait_barrier_implicit` for these barriers.

The value `ompt_state_wait_barrier_explicit` indicates that the thread is waiting in a **barrier** region. An OpenMP implementation may report `ompt_state_wait_barrier` for these barriers.

The value `ompt_state_wait_taskwait` indicates that the thread is waiting at a **taskwait** construct.

The value `ompt_state_wait_taskgroup` indicates that the thread is waiting at the end of a **taskgroup** construct.

The value `ompt_state_wait_mutex` indicates that the thread is waiting for a mutex of an unspecified type.

The value `ompt_state_wait_lock` indicates that the thread is waiting for a lock or nestable lock.

The value `ompt_state_wait_critical` indicates that the thread is waiting to enter a **critical** region.

The value `ompt_state_wait_atomic` indicates that the thread is waiting to enter an **atomic** region.

The value `ompt_state_wait_ordered` indicates that the thread is waiting to enter an **ordered** region.

The value `ompt_state_wait_target` indicates that the thread is waiting for a **target** region to complete.

The value `ompt_state_wait_target_map` indicates that the thread is waiting for a target data mapping operation to complete. An implementation may report `ompt_state_wait_target` for **target data** constructs.

The value `ompt_state_wait_target_update` indicates that the thread is waiting for a **target update** operation to complete. An implementation may report `ompt_state_wait_target` for **target update** constructs.

The value `ompt_state_idle` indicates that the thread is idle, that is, it is not part of an OpenMP team.

The value `ompt_state_overhead` indicates that the thread is in the overhead state at any point while executing within the OpenMP runtime, except while waiting at a synchronization point.

The value `ompt_state_undefined` indicates that the native thread is not created by the OpenMP implementation.

4.4.4.27 ompt_frame_t

Summary

The `ompt_frame_t` type describes procedure frame information for an OpenMP task.

Format

C / C++

```
typedef struct ompt_frame_t {
  ompt_data_t exit_frame;
  ompt_data_t enter_frame;
  int exit_frame_flags;
  int enter_frame_flags;
} ompt_frame_t;
```

C / C++

Description

Each **ompt_frame_t** object is associated with the task to which the procedure frames belong. Each non-merged initial, implicit, explicit, or target task with one or more frames on the stack of a native thread has an associated **ompt_frame_t** object.

The *exit_frame* field of an **ompt_frame_t** object contains information to identify the first procedure frame executing the task region. The *exit_frame* for the **ompt_frame_t** object associated with the *initial task* that is not nested inside any OpenMP construct is **NULL**.

The *enter_frame* field of an **ompt_frame_t** object contains information to identify the latest still active procedure frame executing the task region before entering the OpenMP runtime implementation or before executing a different task. If a task with frames on the stack has not been suspended, the value of *enter_frame* for the **ompt_frame_t** object associated with the task may contain **NULL**.

For *exit_frame*, the *exit_frame_flags* and, for *enter_frame*, the *enter_frame_flags* field indicates that the provided frame information points to a runtime or an application frame address. The same fields also specify the kind of information that is provided to identify the frame, These fields are a disjunction of values in the **ompt_frame_flag_t** enumeration type.

The lifetime of an **ompt_frame_t** object begins when a task is created and ends when the task is destroyed. Tools should not assume that a frame structure remains at a constant location in memory throughout the lifetime of the task. A pointer to an **ompt_frame_t** object is passed to some callbacks; a pointer to the **ompt_frame_t** object of a task can also be retrieved by a tool at any time, including in a signal handler, by invoking the **ompt_get_task_info** runtime entry point (described in Section 4.6.1.14). A pointer to an **ompt_frame_t** object that a tool retrieved is valid as long as the tool does not pass back control to the OpenMP implementation.

Note – A monitoring tool that uses asynchronous sampling can observe values of *exit_frame* and *enter_frame* at inconvenient times. Tools must be prepared to handle **ompt_frame_t** objects observed just prior to when their field values will be set or cleared.

4.4.4.28 ompt_frame_flag_t

Summary

The **ompt_frame_flag_t** enumeration type defines valid frame information flags.

Format

```
typedef enum ompt_frame_flag_t {
    ompt_frame_runtime       = 0x00,
    ompt_frame_application   = 0x01,
    ompt_frame_cfa           = 0x10,
    ompt_frame_framepointer  = 0x20,
    ompt_frame_stackaddress  = 0x30
} ompt_frame_flag_t;
```

Description

The value **ompt_frame_runtime** of the **ompt_frame_flag_t** type indicates that a frame address is a procedure frame in the OpenMP runtime implementation. The value **ompt_frame_application** of the **ompt_frame_flag_t** type indicates that an exit frame address is a procedure frame in the OpenMP application.

Higher order bits indicate the kind of provided information that is unique for the particular frame pointer. The value **ompt_frame_cfa** indicates that a frame address specifies a *canonical frame address*. The value **ompt_frame_framepointer** indicates that a frame address provides the value of the frame pointer register. The value **ompt_frame_stackaddress** indicates that a frame address specifies a pointer address that is contained in the current stack frame.

4.4.4.29 ompt_wait_id_t

Summary

The **ompt_wait_id_t** type describes wait identifiers for an OpenMP thread.

Format

```
typedef uint64_t ompt_wait_id_t;
```

Description

Each thread maintains a *wait identifier* of type **ompt_wait_id_t**. When a task that a thread executes is waiting for mutual exclusion, the wait identifier of the thread indicates the reason that the thread is waiting. A wait identifier may represent a critical section *name*, a lock, a program variable accessed in an atomic region, or a synchronization object that is internal to an OpenMP implementation. When a thread is not in a wait state then the value of the wait identifier of the thread is undefined.

ompt_wait_id_none is defined as an instance of type **ompt_wait_id_t** with the value 0.

4.5 OMPT Tool Callback Signatures and Trace Records

The C/C++ header file (omp-tools.h) provides the definitions of the types that are specified throughout this subsection.

Restrictions

- Tool callbacks may not use OpenMP directives or call any runtime library routines described in Section 3.

4.5.1 Initialization and Finalization Callback Signature

4.5.1.1 ompt_initialize_t

Summary

A callback with type signature **ompt_initialize_t** initializes use of the OMPT interface.

Format

```
typedef int (*ompt_initialize_t) (
  ompt_function_lookup_t lookup,
  int initial_device_num,
  ompt_data_t *tool_data
);
```

Description

To use the OMPT interface, an implementation of **ompt_start_tool** must return a non-null pointer to an **ompt_start_tool_result_t** structure that contains a non-null pointer to a tool initializer with type signature **ompt_initialize_t**. An OpenMP implementation will call the initializer after fully initializing itself but before beginning execution of any OpenMP construct or completing execution of any environment routine invocation.

The initializer returns a non-zero value if it succeeds.

Description of Arguments

The *lookup* argument is a callback to an OpenMP runtime routine that must be used to obtain a pointer to each runtime entry point in the OMPT interface. The *initial_device_num* argument provides the value of **omp_get_initial_device()**. The *tool_data* argument is a pointer to the *tool_data* field in the **ompt_start_tool_result_t** structure that **ompt_start_tool** returned. The expected actions of an initializer are described in Section 4.2.3.

Cross References

- **omp_get_initial_device** routine, see Section 3.2.41 on page 376.
- **ompt_start_tool** function, see Section 4.2.1 on page 420.
- **ompt_start_tool_result_t** type, see Section 4.4.1 on page 433.
- **ompt_data_t** type, see Section 4.4.4.4 on page 440.
- **ompt_function_lookup_t** type, see Section 4.6.3 on page 531.

4.5.1.2 ompt_finalize_t

Summary

A tool implements a finalizer with the type signature **ompt_finalize_t** to finalize the tool's use of the OMPT interface.

Format

———————————————— C / C++ ————————————————
```
typedef void (*ompt_finalize_t) (
  ompt_data_t *tool_data
);
```
———————————————— C / C++ ————————————————

Description

To use the OMPT interface, an implementation of **ompt_start_tool** must return a non-null pointer to an **ompt_start_tool_result_t** structure that contains a non-null pointer to a tool finalizer with type signature **ompt_finalize_t**. An OpenMP implementation will call the tool finalizer after the last OMPT *event* as the OpenMP implementation shuts down.

Description of Arguments

The *tool_data* argument is a pointer to the *tool_data* field in the **ompt_start_tool_result_t** structure returned by **ompt_start_tool**.

Cross References

- **ompt_start_tool** function, see Section 4.2.1 on page 420.
- **ompt_start_tool_result_t** type, see Section 4.4.1 on page 433.
- **ompt_data_t** type, see Section 4.4.4.4 on page 440.

4.5.2 Event Callback Signatures and Trace Records

This section describes the signatures of tool callback functions that an OMPT tool may register and that are called during runtime of an OpenMP program. An implementation may also provide a trace of events per device. Along with the callbacks, the following defines standard trace records. For the trace records, tool data arguments are replaced by an ID, which must be initialized by the OpenMP implementation. Each of *parallel_id*, *task_id*, and *thread_id* must be unique per target region. Tool implementations of callbacks are not required to be *async signal safe*.

Cross References

- **ompt_id_t** type, see Section 4.4.4.3 on page 439.
- **ompt_data_t** type, see Section 4.4.4.4 on page 440.

4.5.2.1 ompt_callback_thread_begin_t

Summary

The **ompt_callback_thread_begin_t** type is used for callbacks that are dispatched when native threads are created.

Format

```
typedef void (*ompt_callback_thread_begin_t) (
  ompt_thread_t thread_type,
  ompt_data_t *thread_data
);
```

Trace Record

```
typedef struct ompt_record_thread_begin_t {
  ompt_thread_t thread_type;
} ompt_record_thread_begin_t;
```

Description of Arguments

The *thread_type* argument indicates the type of the new thread: initial, worker, or other. The binding of the *thread_data* argument is the new thread.

Cross References

- **parallel** construct, see Section 2.6 on page 74.
- **teams** construct, see Section 2.7 on page 82.
- Initial task, see Section 2.10.5 on page 148.
- `ompt_data_t` type, see Section 4.4.4.4 on page 440.
- `ompt_thread_t` type, see Section 4.4.4.10 on page 443.

4.5.2.2 ompt_callback_thread_end_t

Summary

The `ompt_callback_thread_end_t` type is used for callbacks that are dispatched when native threads are destroyed.

Format

```
typedef void (*ompt_callback_thread_end_t) (
  ompt_data_t *thread_data
);
```

Description of Arguments

The binding of the *thread_data* argument is the thread that will be destroyed.

Cross References

- **parallel** construct, see Section 2.6 on page 74.
- **teams** construct, see Section 2.7 on page 82.
- Initial task, see Section 2.10.5 on page 148.
- **ompt_record_ompt_t** type, see Section 4.4.3.4 on page 436.
- **ompt_data_t** type, see Section 4.4.4.4 on page 440.

4.5.2.3 ompt_callback_parallel_begin_t

Summary

The **ompt_callback_parallel_begin_t** type is used for callbacks that are dispatched when **parallel** and **teams** regions start.

Format

```
typedef void (*ompt_callback_parallel_begin_t) (
  ompt_data_t *encountering_task_data,
  const ompt_frame_t *encountering_task_frame,
  ompt_data_t *parallel_data,
  unsigned int requested_parallelism,
  int flags,
  const void *codeptr_ra
);
```

Trace Record

```
typedef struct ompt_record_parallel_begin_t {
    ompt_id_t encountering_task_id;
    ompt_id_t parallel_id;
    unsigned int requested_parallelism;
    int flags;
    const void *codeptr_ra;
} ompt_record_parallel_begin_t;
```

Description of Arguments

The binding of the *encountering_task_data* argument is the encountering task.

The *encountering_task_frame* argument points to the frame object that is associated with the encountering task.

The binding of the *parallel_data* argument is the **parallel** or **teams** region that is beginning.

The *requested_parallelism* argument indicates the number of threads or teams that the user requested.

The *flags* argument indicates whether the code for the region is inlined into the application or invoked by the runtime and also whether the region is a **parallel** or **teams** region. Valid values for *flags* are a disjunction of elements in the enum **ompt_parallel_flag_t**.

The *codeptr_ra* argument relates the implementation of an OpenMP region to its source code. If a runtime routine implements the region associated with a callback that has type signature **ompt_callback_parallel_begin_t** then *codeptr_ra* contains the return address of the call to that runtime routine. If the implementation the region is inlined then *codeptr_ra* contains the return address of the invocation of the callback. If attribution to source code is impossible or inappropriate, *codeptr_ra* may be **NULL**.

Cross References

- **parallel** construct, see Section 2.6 on page 74.
- **teams** construct, see Section 2.7 on page 82.
- **ompt_data_t** type, see Section 4.4.4.4 on page 440.
- **ompt_parallel_flag_t** type, see Section 4.4.4.21 on page 448.
- **ompt_frame_t** type, see Section 4.4.4.27 on page 454.

4.5.2.4 ompt_callback_parallel_end_t

Summary

The `ompt_callback_parallel_end_t` type is used for callbacks that are dispatched when **parallel** and **teams** regions ends.

Format

―――――――――――― C / C++ ――――――――――――
```
typedef void (*ompt_callback_parallel_end_t) (
  ompt_data_t *parallel_data,
  ompt_data_t *encountering_task_data,
  int flags,
  const void *codeptr_ra
);
```
―――――――――――― C / C++ ――――――――――――

Trace Record

―――――――――――― C / C++ ――――――――――――
```
typedef struct ompt_record_parallel_end_t {
  ompt_id_t parallel_id;
  ompt_id_t encountering_task_id;
  int flags;
  const void *codeptr_ra;
} ompt_record_parallel_end_t;
```
―――――――――――― C / C++ ――――――――――――

Description of Arguments

The binding of the *parallel_data* argument is the **parallel** or **teams** region that is ending.

The binding of the *encountering_task_data* argument is the encountering task.

The *flags* argument indicates whether the execution of the region is inlined into the application or invoked by the runtime and also whether it is a **parallel** or **teams** region. Values for *flags* are a disjunction of elements in the enum `ompt_parallel_flag_t`.

The *codeptr_ra* argument relates the implementation of an OpenMP region to its source code. If a runtime routine implements the region associated with a callback that has type signature `ompt_callback_parallel_end_t` then *codeptr_ra* contains the return address of the call to that runtime routine. If the implementation of the region is inlined then *codeptr_ra* contains the return address of the invocation of the callback. If attribution to source code is impossible or inappropriate, *codeptr_ra* may be **NULL**.

Cross References

- **parallel** construct, see Section 2.6 on page 74.
- **teams** construct, see Section 2.7 on page 82.
- ompt_data_t type, see Section 4.4.4.4 on page 440.
- ompt_parallel_flag_t type, see Section 4.4.4.21 on page 448.

4.5.2.5 ompt_callback_work_t

Summary

The ompt_callback_work_t type is used for callbacks that are dispatched when worksharing regions, loop-related regions, and **taskloop** regions begin and end.

Format

```
C / C++
typedef void (*ompt_callback_work_t) (
  ompt_work_t wstype,
  ompt_scope_endpoint_t endpoint,
  ompt_data_t *parallel_data,
  ompt_data_t *task_data,
  uint64_t count,
  const void *codeptr_ra
);
C / C++
```

Trace Record

```
C / C++
typedef struct ompt_record_work_t {
  ompt_work_t wstype;
  ompt_scope_endpoint_t endpoint;
  ompt_id_t parallel_id;
  ompt_id_t task_id;
  uint64_t count;
  const void *codeptr_ra;
} ompt_record_work_t;
C / C++
```

Description of Arguments

The *wstype* argument indicates the kind of region.

The *endpoint* argument indicates that the callback signals the beginning of a scope or the end of a scope.

The binding of the *parallel_data* argument is the current parallel region.

The binding of the *task_data* argument is the current task.

The *count* argument is a measure of the quantity of work involved in the construct. For a worksharing-loop construct, *count* represents the number of iterations of the loop. For a **taskloop** construct, *count* represents the number of iterations in the iteration space, which may be the result of collapsing several associated loops. For a **sections** construct, *count* represents the number of sections. For a **workshare** construct, *count* represents the units of work, as defined by the **workshare** construct. For a **single** construct, *count* is always 1. When the *endpoint* argument signals the end of a scope, a *count* value of 0 indicates that the actual *count* value is not available.

The *codeptr_ra* argument relates the implementation of an OpenMP region to its source code. If a runtime routine implements the region associated with a callback that has type signature **ompt_callback_work_t** then *codeptr_ra* contains the return address of the call to that runtime routine. If the implementation of the region is inlined then *codeptr_ra* contains the return address of the invocation of the callback. If attribution to source code is impossible or inappropriate, *codeptr_ra* may be **NULL**.

Cross References

- Worksharing constructs, see Section 2.8 on page 86 and Section 2.9.2 on page 101.
- Loop-related constructs, see Section 2.9 on page 95.
- **taskloop** construct, see Section 2.10.2 on page 140.
- **ompt_data_t** type, see Section 4.4.4.4 on page 440.
- **ompt_scope_endpoint_t** type, see Section 4.4.4.11 on page 443.
- **ompt_work_t** type, see Section 4.4.4.15 on page 445.

4.5.2.6 ompt_callback_dispatch_t

Summary

The **ompt_callback_dispatch_t** type is used for callbacks that are dispatched when a thread begins to execute a section or loop iteration.

Format

```c
typedef void (*ompt_callback_dispatch_t) (
  ompt_data_t *parallel_data,
  ompt_data_t *task_data,
  ompt_dispatch_t kind,
  ompt_data_t instance
);
```

Trace Record

```c
typedef struct ompt_record_dispatch_t {
  ompt_id_t parallel_id;
  ompt_id_t task_id;
  ompt_dispatch_t kind;
  ompt_data_t instance;
} ompt_record_dispatch_t;
```

Description of Arguments

The binding of the *parallel_data* argument is the current parallel region.

The binding of the *task_data* argument is the implicit task that executes the structured block of the parallel region.

The *kind* argument indicates whether a loop iteration or a section is being dispatched.

For a loop iteration, the *instance.value* argument contains the iteration variable value. For a structured block in the **sections** construct, *instance.ptr* contains a code address that identifies the structured block. In cases where a runtime routine implements the structured block associated with this callback, *instance.ptr* contains the return address of the call to the runtime routine. In cases where the implementation of the structured block is inlined, *instance.ptr* contains the return address of the invocation of this callback.

Cross References

- **sections** and **section** constructs, see Section 2.8.1 on page 86.
- Worksharing-loop construct, see Section 2.9.2 on page 101.
- **taskloop** construct, see Section 2.10.2 on page 140.
- **ompt_data_t** type, see Section 4.4.4.4 on page 440.
- **ompt_dispatch_t** type, see Section 4.4.4.12 on page 444.

4.5.2.7 ompt_callback_task_create_t

Summary

The **ompt_callback_task_create_t** type is used for callbacks that are dispatched when **task** regions or initial tasks are generated.

Format

```
C / C++
typedef void (*ompt_callback_task_create_t) (
  ompt_data_t *encountering_task_data,
  const ompt_frame_t *encountering_task_frame,
  ompt_data_t *new_task_data,
  int flags,
  int has_dependences,
  const void *codeptr_ra
);
C / C++
```

Trace Record

```
C / C++
typedef struct ompt_record_task_create_t {
  ompt_id_t encountering_task_id;
  ompt_id_t new_task_id;
  int flags;
  int has_dependences;
  const void *codeptr_ra;
} ompt_record_task_create_t;
C / C++
```

Description of Arguments

The binding of the *encountering_task_data* argument is the encountering task. This argument is **NULL** for an initial task.

The *encountering_task_frame* argument points to the frame object associated with the encountering task. This argument is **NULL** for an initial task.

The binding of the *new_task_data* argument is the generated task.

The *flags* argument indicates the kind of the task (initial, explicit, or target) that is generated. Values for *flags* are a disjunction of elements in the **ompt_task_flag_t** enumeration type.

The *has_dependences* argument is *true* if the generated task has dependences and *false* otherwise.

The *codeptr_ra* argument relates the implementation of an OpenMP region to its source code. If a runtime routine implements the region associated with a callback that has type signature **ompt_callback_task_create_t** then *codeptr_ra* contains the return address of the call to that runtime routine. If the implementation of the region is inlined then *codeptr_ra* contains the return address of the invocation of the callback. If attribution to source code is impossible or inappropriate, *codeptr_ra* may be **NULL**.

Cross References

- **task** construct, see Section 2.10.1 on page 135.
- Initial task, see Section 2.10.5 on page 148.
- **ompt_data_t** type, see Section 4.4.4.4 on page 440.
- **ompt_task_flag_t** type, see Section 4.4.4.18 on page 446.
- **ompt_frame_t** type, see Section 4.4.4.27 on page 454.

4.5.2.8 ompt_callback_dependences_t

Summary

The **ompt_callback_dependences_t** type is used for callbacks that are related to dependences and that are dispatched when new tasks are generated and when **ordered** constructs are encountered.

Format

```
typedef void (*ompt_callback_dependences_t) (
  ompt_data_t *task_data,
  const ompt_dependence_t *deps,
  int ndeps
);
```

Trace Record

```
typedef struct ompt_record_dependences_t {
  ompt_id_t task_id;
  ompt_dependence_t dep;
  int ndeps;
} ompt_record_dependences_t;
```

Description of Arguments

The binding of the *task_data* argument is the generated task.

The *deps* argument lists dependences of the new task or the dependence vector of the ordered construct.

The *ndeps* argument specifies the length of the list passed by the *deps* argument. The memory for *deps* is owned by the caller; the tool cannot rely on the data after the callback returns.

The performance monitor interface for tracing activity on target devices provides one record per dependence.

Cross References

- **ordered** construct, see Section 2.17.9 on page 250.
- **depend** clause, see Section 2.17.11 on page 255.
- **ompt_data_t** type, see Section 4.4.4.4 on page 440.
- **ompt_dependence_t** type, see Section 4.4.4.9 on page 442.

4.5.2.9 ompt_callback_task_dependence_t

Summary

The `ompt_callback_task_dependence_t` type is used for callbacks that are dispatched when unfulfilled task dependences are encountered.

Format

─────────── C / C++ ───────────
```
typedef void (*ompt_callback_task_dependence_t) (
  ompt_data_t *src_task_data,
  ompt_data_t *sink_task_data
);
```
─────────── C / C++ ───────────

Trace Record

─────────── C / C++ ───────────
```
typedef struct ompt_record_task_dependence_t {
  ompt_id_t src_task_id;
  ompt_id_t sink_task_id;
} ompt_record_task_dependence_t;
```
─────────── C / C++ ───────────

Description of Arguments

The binding of the *src_task_data* argument is a running task with an outgoing dependence.

The binding of the *sink_task_data* argument is a task with an unsatisfied incoming dependence.

Cross References

- **depend** clause, see Section 2.17.11 on page 255.
- `ompt_data_t` type, see Section 4.4.4.4 on page 440.

4.5.2.10 ompt_callback_task_schedule_t

Summary

The `ompt_callback_task_schedule_t` type is used for callbacks that are dispatched when task scheduling decisions are made.

Format

```
typedef void (*ompt_callback_task_schedule_t) (
  ompt_data_t *prior_task_data,
  ompt_task_status_t prior_task_status,
  ompt_data_t *next_task_data
);
```

Trace Record

```
typedef struct ompt_record_task_schedule_t {
  ompt_id_t prior_task_id;
  ompt_task_status_t prior_task_status;
  ompt_id_t next_task_id;
} ompt_record_task_schedule_t;
```

Description of Arguments

The *prior_task_status* argument indicates the status of the task that arrived at a task scheduling point.

The binding of the *prior_task_data* argument is the task that arrived at the scheduling point.

The binding of the *next_task_data* argument is the task that is resumed at the scheduling point. This argument is **NULL** if the callback is dispatched for a *task-fulfill* event.

Cross References

- Task scheduling, see Section 2.10.6 on page 149.
- `ompt_data_t` type, see Section 4.4.4.4 on page 440.
- `ompt_task_status_t` type, see Section 4.4.4.19 on page 447.

4.5.2.11 ompt_callback_implicit_task_t

Summary

The `ompt_callback_implicit_task_t` type is used for callbacks that are dispatched when initial tasks and implicit tasks are generated and completed.

Format

```
typedef void (*ompt_callback_implicit_task_t) (
  ompt_scope_endpoint_t endpoint,
  ompt_data_t *parallel_data,
  ompt_data_t *task_data,
  unsigned int actual_parallelism,
  unsigned int index,
  int flags
);
```

Trace Record

```
typedef struct ompt_record_implicit_task_t {
  ompt_scope_endpoint_t endpoint;
  ompt_id_t parallel_id;
  ompt_id_t task_id;
  unsigned int actual_parallelism;
  unsigned int index;
  int flags;
} ompt_record_implicit_task_t;
```

Description of Arguments

The *endpoint* argument indicates that the callback signals the beginning of a scope or the end of a scope.

The binding of the *parallel_data* argument is the current parallel region. For the *implicit-task-end* event, this argument is **NULL**.

The binding of the *task_data* argument is the implicit task that executes the structured block of the parallel region.

The *actual_parallelism* argument indicates the number of threads in the **parallel** region or the number of teams in the **teams** region. For initial tasks, that are not closely nested in a **teams** construct, this argument is **1**. For the *implicit-task-end* and the *initial-task-end* events, this argument is **0**.

The *index* argument indicates the thread number or team number of the calling thread, within the team or league that is executing the parallel or **teams** region to which the implicit task region binds. For initial tasks, that are not created by a **teams** construct, this argument is **1**.

The *flags* argument indicates the kind of the task (initial or implicit).

Cross References

- **parallel** construct, see Section 2.6 on page 74.
- **teams** construct, see Section 2.7 on page 82.
- ompt_data_t type, see Section 4.4.4.4 on page 440.
- ompt_scope_endpoint_t enumeration type, see Section 4.4.4.11 on page 443.

4.5.2.12 ompt_callback_master_t

Summary

The ompt_callback_master_t type is used for callbacks that are dispatched when **master** regions start and end.

Format

```
C / C++
typedef void (*ompt_callback_master_t) (
  ompt_scope_endpoint_t endpoint,
  ompt_data_t *parallel_data,
  ompt_data_t *task_data,
  const void *codeptr_ra
);
C / C++
```

Trace Record

```
C / C++
typedef struct ompt_record_master_t {
  ompt_scope_endpoint_t endpoint;
  ompt_id_t parallel_id;
  ompt_id_t task_id;
  const void *codeptr_ra;
} ompt_record_master_t;
C / C++
```

Description of Arguments

The *endpoint* argument indicates that the callback signals the beginning of a scope or the end of a scope.

The binding of the *parallel_data* argument is the current parallel region.

The binding of the *task_data* argument is the encountering task.

The *codeptr_ra* argument relates the implementation of an OpenMP region to its source code. If a runtime routine implements the region associated with a callback that has type signature **ompt_callback_master_t** then *codeptr_ra* contains the return address of the call to that runtime routine. If the implementation of the region is inlined then *codeptr_ra* contains the return address of the invocation of the callback. If attribution to source code is impossible or inappropriate, *codeptr_ra* may be **NULL**.

Cross References

- **master** construct, see Section 2.16 on page 221.
- **ompt_data_t** type, see Section 4.4.4.4 on page 440.
- **ompt_scope_endpoint_t** type, see Section 4.4.4.11 on page 443.

4.5.2.13 ompt_callback_sync_region_t

Summary

The **ompt_callback_sync_region_t** type is used for callbacks that are dispatched when barrier regions, **taskwait** regions, and **taskgroup** regions begin and end and when waiting begins and ends for them as well as for when reductions are performed.

Format

─────────── C / C++ ───────────
```
typedef void (*ompt_callback_sync_region_t) (
  ompt_sync_region_t kind,
  ompt_scope_endpoint_t endpoint,
  ompt_data_t *parallel_data,
  ompt_data_t *task_data,
  const void *codeptr_ra
);
```
─────────── C / C++ ───────────

Trace Record

```c
typedef struct ompt_record_sync_region_t {
    ompt_sync_region_t kind;
    ompt_scope_endpoint_t endpoint;
    ompt_id_t parallel_id;
    ompt_id_t task_id;
    const void *codeptr_ra;
} ompt_record_sync_region_t;
```

Description of Arguments

The *kind* argument indicates the kind of synchronization.

The *endpoint* argument indicates that the callback signals the beginning of a scope or the end of a scope.

The binding of the *parallel_data* argument is the current parallel region. For the *barrier-end* event at the end of a parallel region this argument is **NULL**.

The binding of the *task_data* argument is the current task.

The *codeptr_ra* argument relates the implementation of an OpenMP region to its source code. If a runtime routine implements the region associated with a callback that has type signature **ompt_callback_sync_region_t** then *codeptr_ra* contains the return address of the call to that runtime routine. If the implementation of the region is inlined then *codeptr_ra* contains the return address of the invocation of the callback. If attribution to source code is impossible or inappropriate, *codeptr_ra* may be **NULL**.

Cross References

- **barrier** construct, see Section 2.17.2 on page 226.
- Implicit barriers, see Section 2.17.3 on page 228.
- **taskwait** construct, see Section 2.17.5 on page 230.
- **taskgroup** construct, see Section 2.17.6 on page 232.
- Properties common to all reduction clauses, see Section 2.19.5.1 on page 294.
- **ompt_data_t** type, see Section 4.4.4.4 on page 440.
- **ompt_scope_endpoint_t** type, see Section 4.4.4.11 on page 443.
- **ompt_sync_region_t** type, see Section 4.4.4.13 on page 444.

4.5.2.14 ompt_callback_mutex_acquire_t

Summary

The `ompt_callback_mutex_acquire_t` type is used for callbacks that are dispatched when locks are initialized, acquired and tested and when `critical` regions, `atomic` regions, and `ordered` regions are begun.

Format

―――――――――――――――― C / C++ ――――――――――――――――
```
typedef void (*ompt_callback_mutex_acquire_t) (
    ompt_mutex_t kind,
    unsigned int hint,
    unsigned int impl,
    ompt_wait_id_t wait_id,
    const void *codeptr_ra
);
```
―――――――――――――――― C / C++ ――――――――――――――――

Trace Record

―――――――――――――――― C / C++ ――――――――――――――――
```
typedef struct ompt_record_mutex_acquire_t {
    ompt_mutex_t kind;
    unsigned int hint;
    unsigned int impl;
    ompt_wait_id_t wait_id;
    const void *codeptr_ra;
} ompt_record_mutex_acquire_t;
```
―――――――――――――――― C / C++ ――――――――――――――――

Description of Arguments

The *kind* argument indicates the kind of the lock involved.

The *hint* argument indicates the hint that was provided when initializing an implementation of mutual exclusion. If no hint is available when a thread initiates acquisition of mutual exclusion, the runtime may supply `omp_sync_hint_none` as the value for *hint*.

The *impl* argument indicates the mechanism chosen by the runtime to implement the mutual exclusion.

The *wait_id* argument indicates the object being awaited.

The *codeptr_ra* argument relates the implementation of an OpenMP region to its source code. If a runtime routine implements the region associated with a callback that has type signature **ompt_callback_mutex_acquire_t** then *codeptr_ra* contains the return address of the call to that runtime routine. If the implementation of the region is inlined then *codeptr_ra* contains the return address of the invocation of the callback. If attribution to source code is impossible or inappropriate, *codeptr_ra* may be **NULL**.

Cross References

- **critical** construct, see Section 2.17.1 on page 223.
- **atomic** construct, see Section 2.17.7 on page 234.
- **ordered** construct, see Section 2.17.9 on page 250.
- **omp_init_lock** and **omp_init_nest_lock** routines, see Section 3.3.1 on page 384.
- **ompt_mutex_t** type, see Section 4.4.4.16 on page 445.
- **ompt_wait_id_t** type, see Section 4.4.4.29 on page 456.

4.5.2.15 ompt_callback_mutex_t

Summary

The **ompt_callback_mutex_t** type is used for callbacks that indicate important synchronization events.

Format

```
C / C++
typedef void (*ompt_callback_mutex_t) (
  ompt_mutex_t kind,
  ompt_wait_id_t wait_id,
  const void *codeptr_ra
);
C / C++
```

Trace Record

```
C / C++
typedef struct ompt_record_mutex_t {
    ompt_mutex_t kind;
    ompt_wait_id_t wait_id;
    const void *codeptr_ra;
} ompt_record_mutex_t;
C / C++
```

Description of Arguments

The *kind* argument indicates the kind of mutual exclusion event.

The *wait_id* argument indicates the object being awaited.

The *codeptr_ra* argument relates the implementation of an OpenMP region to its source code. If a runtime routine implements the region associated with a callback that has type signature `ompt_callback_mutex_t` then *codeptr_ra* contains the return address of the call to that runtime routine. If the implementation of the region is inlined then *codeptr_ra* contains the return address of the invocation of the callback. If attribution to source code is impossible or inappropriate, *codeptr_ra* may be **NULL**.

Cross References

- `critical` construct, see Section 2.17.1 on page 223.
- `atomic` construct, see Section 2.17.7 on page 234.
- `ordered` construct, see Section 2.17.9 on page 250.
- `omp_destroy_lock` and `omp_destroy_nest_lock` routines, see Section 3.3.3 on page 387.
- `omp_set_lock` and `omp_set_nest_lock` routines, see Section 3.3.4 on page 388.
- `omp_unset_lock` and `omp_unset_nest_lock` routines, see Section 3.3.5 on page 390.
- `omp_test_lock` and `omp_test_nest_lock` routines, see Section 3.3.6 on page 392.
- `ompt_mutex_t` type, see Section 4.4.4.16 on page 445.
- `ompt_wait_id_t` type, see Section 4.4.4.29 on page 456.

4.5.2.16 ompt_callback_nest_lock_t

Summary

The **ompt_callback_nest_lock_t** type is used for callbacks that indicate that a thread that owns a nested lock has performed an action related to the lock but has not relinquished ownership of it.

Format

─────────── C / C++ ───────────
```
typedef void (*ompt_callback_nest_lock_t) (
  ompt_scope_endpoint_t endpoint,
  ompt_wait_id_t wait_id,
  const void *codeptr_ra
);
```
─────────── C / C++ ───────────

Trace Record

─────────── C / C++ ───────────
```
typedef struct ompt_record_nest_lock_t {
  ompt_scope_endpoint_t endpoint;
  ompt_wait_id_t wait_id;
  const void *codeptr_ra;
} ompt_record_nest_lock_t;
```
─────────── C / C++ ───────────

Description of Arguments

The *endpoint* argument indicates that the callback signals the beginning of a scope or the end of a scope.

The *wait_id* argument indicates the object being awaited.

The *codeptr_ra* argument relates the implementation of an OpenMP region to its source code. If a runtime routine implements the region associated with a callback that has type signature **ompt_callback_nest_lock_t** then *codeptr_ra* contains the return address of the call to that runtime routine. If the implementation of the region is inlined then *codeptr_ra* contains the return address of the invocation of the callback. If attribution to source code is impossible or inappropriate, *codeptr_ra* may be **NULL**.

Cross References

- `omp_set_nest_lock` routine, see Section 3.3.4 on page 388.
- `omp_unset_nest_lock` routine, see Section 3.3.5 on page 390.
- `omp_test_nest_lock` routine, see Section 3.3.6 on page 392.
- `ompt_scope_endpoint_t` type, see Section 4.4.4.11 on page 443.
- `ompt_wait_id_t` type, see Section 4.4.4.29 on page 456.

4.5.2.17 ompt_callback_flush_t

Summary

The `ompt_callback_flush_t` type is used for callbacks that are dispatched when **flush** constructs are encountered.

Format

―――――――――――――――――― C / C++ ――――――――――――――――――
```
typedef void (*ompt_callback_flush_t) (
  ompt_data_t *thread_data,
  const void *codeptr_ra
);
```
―――――――――――――――――― C / C++ ――――――――――――――――――

Trace Record

―――――――――――――――――― C / C++ ――――――――――――――――――
```
typedef struct ompt_record_flush_t {
  const void *codeptr_ra;
} ompt_record_flush_t;
```
―――――――――――――――――― C / C++ ――――――――――――――――――

Description of Arguments

The binding of the *thread_data* argument is the executing thread.

The *codeptr_ra* argument relates the implementation of an OpenMP region to its source code. If a runtime routine implements the region associated with a callback that has type signature `ompt_callback_flush_t` then *codeptr_ra* contains the return address of the call to that runtime routine. If the implementation of the region is inlined then *codeptr_ra* contains the return address of the invocation of the callback. If attribution to source code is impossible or inappropriate, *codeptr_ra* may be **NULL**.

Cross References

- `flush` construct, see Section 2.17.8 on page 242.
- `ompt_data_t` type, see Section 4.4.4.4 on page 440.

4.5.2.18 ompt_callback_cancel_t

Summary

The `ompt_callback_cancel_t` type is used for callbacks that are dispatched for *cancellation*, *cancel* and *discarded-task* events.

Format

─────── C / C++ ───────
```
typedef void (*ompt_callback_cancel_t) (
  ompt_data_t *task_data,
  int flags,
  const void *codeptr_ra
);
```
─────── C / C++ ───────

Trace Record

─────── C / C++ ───────
```
typedef struct ompt_record_cancel_t {
  ompt_id_t task_id;
  int flags;
  const void *codeptr_ra;
} ompt_record_cancel_t;
```
─────── C / C++ ───────

Description of Arguments

The binding of the *task_data* argument is the task that encounters a `cancel` construct, a `cancellation point` construct, or a construct defined as having an implicit cancellation point.

The *flags* argument, defined by the `ompt_cancel_flag_t` enumeration type, indicates whether cancellation is activated by the current task, or detected as being activated by another task. The construct that is being canceled is also described in the *flags* argument. When several constructs are detected as being concurrently canceled, each corresponding bit in the argument will be set.

The *codeptr_ra* argument relates the implementation of an OpenMP region to its source code. If a runtime routine implements the region associated with a callback that has type signature **ompt_callback_cancel_t** then *codeptr_ra* contains the return address of the call to that runtime routine. If the implementation of the region is inlined then *codeptr_ra* contains the return address of the invocation of the callback. If attribution to source code is impossible or inappropriate, *codeptr_ra* may be **NULL**.

Cross References

- **omp_cancel_flag_t** enumeration type, see Section 4.4.4.24 on page 450.

4.5.2.19 ompt_callback_device_initialize_t

Summary

The **ompt_callback_device_initialize_t** type is used for callbacks that initialize device tracing interfaces.

Format

```
C / C++
typedef void (*ompt_callback_device_initialize_t) (
  int device_num,
  const char *type,
  ompt_device_t *device,
  ompt_function_lookup_t lookup,
  const char *documentation
);
C / C++
```

Description

Registration of a callback with type signature **ompt_callback_device_initialize_t** for the **ompt_callback_device_initialize** event enables asynchronous collection of a trace for a device. The OpenMP implementation invokes this callback after OpenMP is initialized for the device but before execution of any OpenMP construct is started on the device.

Description of Arguments

The *device_num* argument identifies the logical device that is being initialized.

The *type* argument is a character string that indicates the type of the device. A device type string is a semicolon separated character string that includes at a minimum the vendor and model name of the device. These names may be followed by a semicolon-separated sequence of properties that describe the hardware or software of the device.

The *device* argument is a pointer to an opaque object that represents the target device instance. Functions in the device tracing interface use this pointer to identify the device that is being addressed.

The *lookup* argument points to a runtime callback that a tool must use to obtain pointers to runtime entry points in the device's OMPT tracing interface. If a device does not support tracing then *lookup* is **NULL**.

The *documentation* argument is a string that describes how to use any device-specific runtime entry points that can be obtained through the *lookup* argument. This documentation string may be a pointer to external documentation, or it may be inline descriptions that include names and type signatures for any device-specific interfaces that are available through the *lookup* argument along with descriptions of how to use these interface functions to control monitoring and analysis of device traces.

Constraints on Arguments

The *type* and *documentation* arguments must be immutable strings that are defined for the lifetime of a program execution.

Effect

A device initializer must fulfill several duties. First, the *type* argument should be used to determine if any special knowledge about the hardware and/or software of a device is employed. Second, the *lookup* argument should be used to look up pointers to runtime entry points in the OMPT tracing interface for the device. Finally, these runtime entry points should be used to set up tracing for the device.

Initialization of tracing for a target device is described in Section 4.2.5 on page 427.

Cross References

- **ompt_function_lookup_t** type, see Section 4.6.3 on page 531.

4.5.2.20 ompt_callback_device_finalize_t

Summary

The `ompt_callback_device_initialize_t` type is used for callbacks that finalize device tracing interfaces.

Format

```
C / C++
typedef void (*ompt_callback_device_finalize_t) (
  int device_num
);
C / C++
```

Description of Arguments

The *device_num* argument identifies the logical device that is being finalized.

Description

A registered callback with type signature `ompt_callback_device_finalize_t` is dispatched for a device immediately prior to finalizing the device. Prior to dispatching a finalization callback for a device on which tracing is active, the OpenMP implementation stops tracing on the device and synchronously flushes all trace records for the device that have not yet been reported. These trace records are flushed through one or more buffer completion callbacks with type signature `ompt_callback_buffer_complete_t` as needed prior to the dispatch of the callback with type signature `ompt_callback_device_finalize_t`.

Cross References

- `ompt_callback_buffer_complete_t` callback type, see Section 4.5.2.24 on page 487.

4.5.2.21 ompt_callback_device_load_t

Summary

The `ompt_callback_device_load_t` type is used for callbacks that the OpenMP runtime invokes to indicate that it has just loaded code onto the specified device.

Format

```
typedef void (*ompt_callback_device_load_t) (
  int device_num,
  const char *filename,
  int64_t offset_in_file,
  void *vma_in_file,
  size_t bytes,
  void *host_addr,
  void *device_addr,
  uint64_t module_id
);
```

Description of Arguments

The *device_num* argument specifies the device.

The *filename* argument indicates the name of a file in which the device code can be found. A NULL *filename* indicates that the code is not available in a file in the file system.

The *offset_in_file* argument indicates an offset into *filename* at which the code can be found. A value of -1 indicates that no offset is provided.

ompt_addr_none is defined as a pointer with the value ~0.

The *vma_in_file* argument indicates an virtual address in *filename* at which the code can be found. A value of **ompt_addr_none** indicates that a virtual address in the file is not available.

The *bytes* argument indicates the size of the device code object in bytes.

The *host_addr* argument indicates the address at which a copy of the device code is available in host memory. A value of **ompt_addr_none** indicates that a host code address is not available.

The *device_addr* argument indicates the address at which the device code has been loaded in device memory. A value of **ompt_addr_none** indicates that a device code address is not available.

The *module_id* argument is an identifier that is associated with the device code object.

Cross References

- Device directives, see Section 2.12 on page 160.

4.5.2.22 ompt_callback_device_unload_t

Summary

The `ompt_callback_device_unload_t` type is used for callbacks that the OpenMP runtime invokes to indicate that it is about to unload code from the specified device.

Format

```
C / C++
typedef void (*ompt_callback_device_unload_t) (
  int device_num,
  uint64_t module_id
);
C / C++
```

Description of Arguments

The *device_num* argument specifies the device.

The *module_id* argument is an identifier that is associated with the device code object.

Cross References

- Device directives, see Section 2.12 on page 160.

4.5.2.23 ompt_callback_buffer_request_t

Summary

The `ompt_callback_buffer_request_t` type is used for callbacks that are dispatched when a buffer to store event records for a device is requested.

Format

```
C / C++
typedef void (*ompt_callback_buffer_request_t) (
  int device_num,
  ompt_buffer_t **buffer,
  size_t *bytes
);
C / C++
```

Description

A callback with type signature **ompt_callback_buffer_request_t** requests a buffer to store trace records for the specified device. A buffer request callback may set *bytes* to 0 if it does not provide a buffer. If a callback sets *bytes* to 0, further recording of events for the device is disabled until the next invocation of **ompt_start_trace**. This action causes the device to drop future trace records until recording is restarted.

Description of Arguments

The *device_num* argument specifies the device.

The *buffer* argument points to a buffer where device events may be recorded. The *bytes* argument indicates the length of that buffer.

Cross References

- **ompt_buffer_t** type, see Section 4.4.4.7 on page 441.

4.5.2.24 ompt_callback_buffer_complete_t

Summary

The **ompt_callback_buffer_complete_t** type is used for callbacks that are dispatched when devices will not record any more trace records in an event buffer and all records written to the buffer are valid.

Format

―――――――――――――――――― C / C++ ――――――――――――――――――
```
typedef void (*ompt_callback_buffer_complete_t) (
  int device_num,
  ompt_buffer_t *buffer,
  size_t bytes,
  ompt_buffer_cursor_t begin,
  int buffer_owned
);
```
―――――――――――――――――― C / C++ ――――――――――――――――――

Description

A callback with type signature `ompt_callback_buffer_complete_t` provides a buffer that contains trace records for the specified device. Typically, a tool will iterate through the records in the buffer and process them.

The OpenMP implementation makes these callbacks on a thread that is not an OpenMP master or worker thread.

The callee may not delete the buffer if the *buffer_owned* argument is 0.

The buffer completion callback is not required to be *async signal safe*.

Description of Arguments

The *device_num* argument indicates the device which the buffer contains events.

The *buffer* argument is the address of a buffer that was previously allocated by a *buffer request* callback.

The *bytes* argument indicates the full size of the buffer.

The *begin* argument is an opaque cursor that indicates the position of the beginning of the first record in the buffer.

The *buffer_owned* argument is 1 if the data to which the buffer points can be deleted by the callback and 0 otherwise. If multiple devices accumulate trace events into a single buffer, this callback may be invoked with a pointer to one or more trace records in a shared buffer with *buffer_owned* = 0. In this case, the callback may not delete the buffer.

Cross References

- `ompt_buffer_t` type, see Section 4.4.4.7 on page 441.
- `ompt_buffer_cursor_t` type, see Section 4.4.4.8 on page 442.

4.5.2.25 `ompt_callback_target_data_op_t`

Summary

The `ompt_callback_target_data_op_t` type is used for callbacks that are dispatched when a thread maps data to a device.

Format

```
typedef void (*ompt_callback_target_data_op_t) (
    ompt_id_t target_id,
    ompt_id_t host_op_id,
    ompt_target_data_op_t optype,
    void *src_addr,
    int src_device_num,
    void *dest_addr,
    int dest_device_num,
    size_t bytes,
    const void *codeptr_ra
);
```

Trace Record

```
typedef struct ompt_record_target_data_op_t {
    ompt_id_t host_op_id;
    ompt_target_data_op_t optype;
    void *src_addr;
    int src_device_num;
    void *dest_addr;
    int dest_device_num;
    size_t bytes;
    ompt_device_time_t end_time;
    const void *codeptr_ra;
} ompt_record_target_data_op_t;
```

Description

A registered **ompt_callback_target_data_op** callback is dispatched when device memory is allocated or freed, as well as when data is copied to or from a device.

Note – An OpenMP implementation may aggregate program variables and data operations upon them. For instance, an OpenMP implementation may synthesize a composite to represent multiple scalars and then allocate, free, or copy this composite as a whole rather than performing data operations on each scalar individually. Thus, callbacks may not be dispatched as separate data operations on each variable.

Description of Arguments

The *host_op_id* argument is a unique identifier for a data operations on a target device.

The *optype* argument indicates the kind of data mapping.

The *src_addr* argument indicates the data address before the operation, where applicable.

The *src_device_num* argument indicates the source device number for the data operation, where applicable.

The *dest_addr* argument indicates the data address after the operation.

The *dest_device_num* argument indicates the destination device number for the data operation.

It is implementation defined whether in some operations *src_addr* or *dest_addr* may point to an intermediate buffer.

The *bytes* argument indicates the size of data.

The *codeptr_ra* argument relates the implementation of an OpenMP region to its source code. If a runtime routine implements the region associated with a callback that has type signature **ompt_callback_target_data_op_t** then *codeptr_ra* contains the return address of the call to that runtime routine. If the implementation of the region is inlined then *codeptr_ra* contains the return address of the invocation of the callback. If attribution to source code is impossible or inappropriate, *codeptr_ra* may be **NULL**.

Cross References

- **map** clause, see Section 2.19.7.1 on page 315.
- **ompt_id_t** type, see Section 4.4.4.3 on page 439.
- **ompt_target_data_op_t** type, see Section 4.4.4.14 on page 444.

4.5.2.26 ompt_callback_target_t

Summary

The **ompt_callback_target_t** type is used for callbacks that are dispatched when a thread begins to execute a device construct.

Format

```c
typedef void (*ompt_callback_target_t) (
    ompt_target_t kind,
    ompt_scope_endpoint_t endpoint,
    int device_num,
    ompt_data_t *task_data,
    ompt_id_t target_id,
    const void *codeptr_ra
);
```

Trace Record

```c
typedef struct ompt_record_target_t {
    ompt_target_t kind;
    ompt_scope_endpoint_t endpoint;
    int device_num;
    ompt_id_t task_id;
    ompt_id_t target_id;
    const void *codeptr_ra;
} ompt_record_target_t;
```

Description of Arguments

The *kind* argument indicates the kind of target region.

The *endpoint* argument indicates that the callback signals the beginning of a scope or the end of a scope.

The *device_num* argument indicates the id of the device that will execute the target region.

The binding of the *task_data* argument is the generating task.

The binding of the *target_id* argument is the target region.

The *codeptr_ra* argument relates the implementation of an OpenMP region to its source code. If a runtime routine implements the region associated with a callback that has type signature **ompt_callback_target_t** then *codeptr_ra* contains the return address of the call to that runtime routine. If the implementation of the region is inlined then *codeptr_ra* contains the return address of the invocation of the callback. If attribution to source code is impossible or inappropriate, *codeptr_ra* may be **NULL**.

Cross References

- **target data** construct, see Section 2.12.2 on page 161.
- **target enter data** construct, see Section 2.12.3 on page 164.
- **target exit data** construct, see Section 2.12.4 on page 166.
- **target** construct, see Section 2.12.5 on page 170.
- **target update** construct, see Section 2.12.6 on page 176.
- ompt_id_t type, see Section 4.4.4.3 on page 439.
- ompt_data_t type, see Section 4.4.4.4 on page 440.
- ompt_scope_endpoint_t type, see Section 4.4.4.11 on page 443.
- ompt_target_t type, see Section 4.4.4.20 on page 448.

4.5.2.27 ompt_callback_target_map_t

Summary

The ompt_callback_target_map_t type is used for callbacks that are dispatched to indicate data mapping relationships.

Format

```
C / C++
typedef void (*ompt_callback_target_map_t) (
    ompt_id_t target_id,
    unsigned int nitems,
    void **host_addr,
    void **device_addr,
    size_t *bytes,
    unsigned int *mapping_flags,
    const void *codeptr_ra
);
C / C++
```

Trace Record

```
typedef struct ompt_record_target_map_t {
  ompt_id_t target_id;
  unsigned int nitems;
  void **host_addr;
  void **device_addr;
  size_t *bytes;
  unsigned int *mapping_flags;
  const void *codeptr_ra;
} ompt_record_target_map_t;
```

Description

An instance of a **target**, **target data**, **target enter data**, or **target exit data** construct may contain one or more **map** clauses. An OpenMP implementation may report the set of mappings associated with **map** clauses for a construct with a single **ompt_callback_target_map** callback to report the effect of all mappings or multiple **ompt_callback_target_map** callbacks with each reporting a subset of the mappings. Furthermore, an OpenMP implementation may omit mappings that it determines are unnecessary. If an OpenMP implementation issues multiple **ompt_callback_target_map** callbacks, these callbacks may be interleaved with **ompt_callback_target_data_op** callbacks used to report data operations associated with the mappings.

Description of Arguments

The binding of the *target_id* argument is the target region.

The *nitems* argument indicates the number of data mappings that this callback reports.

The *host_addr* argument indicates an array of host data addresses.

The *device_addr* argument indicates an array of device data addresses.

The *bytes* argument indicates an array of size of data.

The *mapping_flags* argument indicates the kind of data mapping. Flags for a mapping include one or more values specified by the **ompt_target_map_flag_t** type.

The *codeptr_ra* argument relates the implementation of an OpenMP region to its source code. If a runtime routine implements the region associated with a callback that has type signature **ompt_callback_target_map_t** then *codeptr_ra* contains the return address of the call to that runtime routine. If the implementation of the region is inlined then *codeptr_ra* contains the return address of the invocation of the callback. If attribution to source code is impossible or inappropriate, *codeptr_ra* may be **NULL**.

Cross References

- **target data** construct, see Section 2.12.2 on page 161.
- **target enter data** construct, see Section 2.12.3 on page 164.
- **target exit data** construct, see Section 2.12.4 on page 166.
- **target** construct, see Section 2.12.5 on page 170.
- ompt_id_t type, see Section 4.4.4.3 on page 439.
- ompt_target_map_flag_t type, see Section 4.4.4.22 on page 449.
- ompt_callback_target_data_op_t callback type, see Section 4.5.2.25 on page 488.

4.5.2.28 ompt_callback_target_submit_t

Summary

The ompt_callback_target_submit_t type is used for callbacks that are dispatched when an initial task is created on a device.

Format

```
C / C++
typedef void (*ompt_callback_target_submit_t) (
  ompt_id_t target_id,
  ompt_id_t host_op_id,
  unsigned int requested_num_teams
);
C / C++
```

Trace Record

```
C / C++
typedef struct ompt_record_target_kernel_t {
  ompt_id_t host_op_id;
  unsigned int requested_num_teams;
  unsigned int granted_num_teams;
  ompt_device_time_t end_time;
} ompt_record_target_kernel_t;
C / C++
```

Description

A thread dispatches a registered `ompt_callback_target_submit` callback on the host when a target task creates an initial task on a target device.

Description of Arguments

The *target_id* argument is a unique identifier for the associated target region.

The *host_op_id* argument is a unique identifier for the initial task on the target device.

The *requested_num_teams* argument is the number of teams that the host requested to execute the kernel. The actual number of teams that execute the kernel may be smaller and generally will not be known until the kernel begins to execute on the device.

If `ompt_set_trace_ompt` has configured the device to trace kernel execution then the device will log a `ompt_record_target_kernel_t` record in a trace. The fields in the record are as follows:

- The *host_op_id* field contains a unique identifier that can be used to correlate a `ompt_record_target_kernel_t` record with its associated `ompt_callback_target_submit` callback on the host;
- The *requested_num_teams* field contains the number of teams that the host requested to execute the kernel;
- The *granted_num_teams* field contains the number of teams that the device actually used to execute the kernel;
- The time when the initial task began execution on the device is recorded in the *time* field of an enclosing `ompt_record_t` structure; and
- The time when the initial task completed execution on the device is recorded in the *end_time* field.

Cross References

- `target` construct, see Section 2.12.5 on page 170.
- `ompt_id_t` type, see Section 4.4.4.3 on page 439.

4.5.2.29 ompt_callback_control_tool_t

Summary

The `ompt_callback_control_tool_t` type is used for callbacks that dispatch *tool-control* events.

Format

```
typedef int (*ompt_callback_control_tool_t) (
  uint64_t command,
  uint64_t modifier,
  void *arg,
  const void *codeptr_ra
);
```

Trace Record

```
typedef struct ompt_record_control_tool_t {
  uint64_t command;
  uint64_t modifier;
  const void *codeptr_ra;
} ompt_record_control_tool_t;
```

Description

Callbacks with type signature `ompt_callback_control_tool_t` may return any non-negative value, which will be returned to the application as the return value of the `omp_control_tool` call that triggered the callback.

Description of Arguments

The *command* argument passes a command from an application to a tool. Standard values for *command* are defined by `omp_control_tool_t` in Section 3.8 on page 415.

The *modifier* argument passes a command modifier from an application to a tool.

The *command* and *modifier* arguments may have tool-specific values. Tools must ignore *command* values that they are not designed to handle.

The *arg* argument is a void pointer that enables a tool and an application to exchange arbitrary state. The *arg* argument may be **NULL**.

The *codeptr_ra* argument relates the implementation of an OpenMP region to its source code. If a runtime routine implements the region associated with a callback that has type signature `ompt_callback_control_tool_t` then *codeptr_ra* contains the return address of the call to that runtime routine. If the implementation of the region is inlined then *codeptr_ra* contains the return address of the invocation of the callback. If attribution to source code is impossible or inappropriate, *codeptr_ra* may be **NULL**.

Constraints on Arguments

Tool-specific values for *command* must be ≥ 64.

Cross References

- `omp_control_tool_t` enumeration type, see Section 3.8 on page 415.

4.6 OMPT Runtime Entry Points for Tools

OMPT supports two principal sets of runtime entry points for tools. One set of runtime entry points enables a tool to register callbacks for OpenMP events and to inspect the state of an OpenMP thread while executing in a tool callback or a signal handler. The second set of runtime entry points enables a tool to trace activities on a device. When directed by the tracing interface, an OpenMP implementation will trace activities on a device, collect buffers of trace records, and invoke callbacks on the host to process these records. OMPT runtime entry points should not be global symbols since tools cannot rely on the visibility of such symbols.

OMPT also supports runtime entry points for two classes of lookup routines. The first class of lookup routines contains a single member: a routine that returns runtime entry points in the OMPT callback interface. The second class of lookup routines includes a unique lookup routine for each kind of device that can return runtime entry points in a device's OMPT tracing interface.

The C/C++ header file (omp-tools.h) provides the definitions of the types that are specified throughout this subsection.

Restrictions

OMPT runtime entry points have the following restrictions:

- OMPT runtime entry points must not be called from a signal handler on a native thread before a *native-thread-begin* or after a *native-thread-end* event.
- OMPT device runtime entry points must not be called after a *device-finalize* event for that device.

4.6.1 Entry Points in the OMPT Callback Interface

Entry points in the OMPT callback interface enable a tool to register callbacks for OpenMP events and to inspect the state of an OpenMP thread while executing in a tool callback or a signal handler. Pointers to these runtime entry points are obtained through the lookup function that is provided through the OMPT initializer.

4.6.1.1 ompt_enumerate_states_t

Summary

The `ompt_enumerate_states_t` type is the type signature of the `ompt_enumerate_states` runtime entry point, which enumerates the thread states that an OpenMP implementation supports.

Format

─────────────── C / C++ ───────────────
```
typedef int (*ompt_enumerate_states_t) (
  int current_state,
  int *next_state,
  const char **next_state_name
);
```
─────────────── C / C++ ───────────────

Description

An OpenMP implementation may support only a subset of the states defined by the `ompt_state_t` enumeration type. An OpenMP implementation may also support implementation-specific states. The `ompt_enumerate_states` runtime entry point, which has type signature `ompt_enumerate_states_t`, enables a tool to enumerate the supported thread states.

When a supported thread state is passed as *current_state*, the runtime entry point assigns the next thread state in the enumeration to the variable passed by reference in *next_state* and assigns the name associated with that state to the character pointer passed by reference in *next_state_name*.

Whenever one or more states are left in the enumeration, the `ompt_enumerate_states` runtime entry point returns 1. When the last state in the enumeration is passed as *current_state*, `ompt_enumerate_states` returns 0, which indicates that the enumeration is complete.

Description of Arguments

The *current_state* argument must be a thread state that the OpenMP implementation supports. To begin enumerating the supported states, a tool should pass `ompt_state_undefined` as *current_state*. Subsequent invocations of `ompt_enumerate_states` should pass the value assigned to the variable passed by reference in *next_state* to the previous call.

The value `ompt_state_undefined` is reserved to indicate an invalid thread state. `ompt_state_undefined` is defined as an integer with the value 0.

The *next_state* argument is a pointer to an integer in which `ompt_enumerate_states` returns the value of the next state in the enumeration.

The *next_state_name* argument is a pointer to a character string pointer through which
ompt_enumerate_states returns a string that describes the next state.

Constraints on Arguments

Any string returned through the *next_state_name* argument must be immutable and defined for the
lifetime of a program execution.

Cross References

- **ompt_state_t** type, see Section 4.4.4.26 on page 452.

4.6.1.2 ompt_enumerate_mutex_impls_t

Summary

The **ompt_enumerate_mutex_impls_t** type is the type signature of the
ompt_enumerate_mutex_impls runtime entry point, which enumerates the kinds of mutual
exclusion implementations that an OpenMP implementation employs.

Format

―――――――――――――― C / C++ ――――――――――――――
```
typedef int (*ompt_enumerate_mutex_impls_t) (
    int current_impl,
    int *next_impl,
    const char **next_impl_name
);
```
―――――――――――――― C / C++ ――――――――――――――

Description

Mutual exclusion for locks, **critical** sections, and **atomic** regions may be implemented in
several ways. The **ompt_enumerate_mutex_impls** runtime entry point, which has type
signature **ompt_enumerate_mutex_impls_t**, enables a tool to enumerate the supported
mutual exclusion implementations.

When a supported mutex implementation is passed as *current_impl*, the runtime entry point assigns
the next mutex implementation in the enumeration to the variable passed by reference in *next_impl*
and assigns the name associated with that mutex implementation to the character pointer passed by
reference in *next_impl_name*.

Whenever one or more mutex implementations are left in the enumeration, the **ompt_enumerate_mutex_impls** runtime entry point returns 1. When the last mutex implementation in the enumeration is passed as *current_impl*, the runtime entry point returns 0, which indicates that the enumeration is complete.

Description of Arguments

The *current_impl* argument must be a mutex implementation that an OpenMP implementation supports. To begin enumerating the supported mutex implementations, a tool should pass **ompt_mutex_impl_none** as *current_impl*. Subsequent invocations of **ompt_enumerate_mutex_impls** should pass the value assigned to the variable passed in *next_impl* to the previous call.

The value **ompt_mutex_impl_none** is reserved to indicate an invalid mutex implementation. **ompt_mutex_impl_none** is defined as an integer with the value 0.

The *next_impl* argument is a pointer to an integer in which **ompt_enumerate_mutex_impls** returns the value of the next mutex implementation in the enumeration.

The *next_impl_name* argument is a pointer to a character string pointer in which **ompt_enumerate_mutex_impls** returns a string that describes the next mutex implementation.

Constraints on Arguments

Any string returned through the *next_impl_name* argument must be immutable and defined for the lifetime of a program execution.

Cross References

- **ompt_mutex_t** type, see Section 4.4.4.16 on page 445.

4.6.1.3 ompt_set_callback_t

Summary

The **ompt_set_callback_t** type is the type signature of the **ompt_set_callback** runtime entry point, which registers a pointer to a tool callback that an OpenMP implementation invokes when a host OpenMP event occurs.

Format

```
typedef ompt_set_result_t (*ompt_set_callback_t) (
    ompt_callbacks_t event,
    ompt_callback_t callback
);
```

Description

OpenMP implementations can use callbacks to indicate the occurrence of events during the execution of an OpenMP program. The **ompt_set_callback** runtime entry point, which has type signature **ompt_set_callback_t**, registers a callback for an OpenMP event on the current device, The return value of **ompt_set_callback** indicates the outcome of registering the callback.

Description of Arguments

The *event* argument indicates the event for which the callback is being registered.

The *callback* argument is a tool callback function. If *callback* is **NULL** then callbacks associated with *event* are disabled. If callbacks are successfully disabled then **ompt_set_always** is returned.

Constraints on Arguments

When a tool registers a callback for an event, the type signature for the callback must match the type signature appropriate for the event.

Restrictions

The **ompt_set_callback** runtime entry point has the following restriction:

- The entry point must not return **ompt_set_impossible**.

Cross References

- Monitoring activity on the host with OMPT, see Section 4.2.4 on page 425.
- **ompt_callbacks_t** enumeration type, see Section 4.4.2 on page 434.
- **ompt_callback_t** type, see Section 4.4.4.1 on page 438.
- **ompt_set_result_t** type, see Section 4.4.4.2 on page 438.
- **ompt_get_callback_t** host callback type signature, see Section 4.6.1.4 on page 502.

4.6.1.4 ompt_get_callback_t

Summary

The **ompt_get_callback_t** type is the type signature of the **ompt_get_callback** runtime entry point, which retrieves a pointer to a registered tool callback routine (if any) that an OpenMP implementation invokes when a host OpenMP event occurs.

Format

―――――――――――――――――――― C / C++ ――――――――――――――――――――
```
typedef int (*ompt_get_callback_t) (
  ompt_callbacks_t event,
  ompt_callback_t *callback
);
```
―――――――――――――――――――― C / C++ ――――――――――――――――――――

Description

The **ompt_get_callback** runtime entry point, which has type signature **ompt_get_callback_t**, retrieves a pointer to the tool callback that an OpenMP implementation may invoke when a host OpenMP event occurs. If a non-null tool callback is registered for the specified event, the pointer to the tool callback is assigned to the variable passed by reference in *callback* and **ompt_get_callback** returns 1; otherwise, it returns 0. If **ompt_get_callback** returns 0, the value of the variable passed by reference as *callback* is undefined.

Description of Arguments

The *event* argument indicates the event for which the callback would be invoked.

The *callback* argument returns a pointer to the callback associated with *event*.

Constraints on Arguments

The *callback* argument must be a reference to a variable of specified type.

Cross References

- **ompt_callbacks_t** enumeration type, see Section 4.4.2 on page 434.
- **ompt_callback_t** type, see Section 4.4.4.1 on page 438.
- **ompt_set_callback_t** type signature, see Section 4.6.1.3 on page 500.

4.6.1.5 ompt_get_thread_data_t

Summary

The **ompt_get_thread_data_t** type is the type signature of the **ompt_get_thread_data** runtime entry point, which returns the address of the thread data object for the current thread.

Format

───────── C / C++ ─────────
```
typedef ompt_data_t *(*ompt_get_thread_data_t) (void);
```
───────── C / C++ ─────────

Binding

The binding thread for the **ompt_get_thread_data** runtime entry point is the current thread.

Description

Each OpenMP thread can have an associated thread data object of type **ompt_data_t**. The **ompt_get_thread_data** runtime entry point, which has type signature **ompt_get_thread_data_t**, retrieves a pointer to the thread data object, if any, that is associated with the current thread. A tool may use a pointer to an OpenMP thread's data object that **ompt_get_thread_data** retrieves to inspect or to modify the value of the data object. When an OpenMP thread is created, its data object is initialized with value **ompt_data_none**.

This runtime entry point is *async signal safe*.

Cross References

- **ompt_data_t** type, see Section 4.4.4.4 on page 440.

4.6.1.6 ompt_get_num_procs_t

Summary

The **ompt_get_num_procs_t** type is the type signature of the **ompt_get_num_procs** runtime entry point, which returns the number of processors currently available to the execution environment on the host device.

Format

```
C / C++
typedef int (*ompt_get_num_procs_t) (void);
C / C++
```

Binding

The binding thread set for the **ompt_get_num_procs** runtime entry point is all threads on the host device.

Description

The **ompt_get_num_procs** runtime entry point, which has type signature **ompt_get_num_procs_t**, returns the number of processors that are available on the host device at the time the routine is called. This value may change between the time that it is determined and the time that it is read in the calling context due to system actions outside the control of the OpenMP implementation.

This runtime entry point is *async signal safe*.

4.6.1.7 ompt_get_num_places_t

Summary

The **ompt_get_num_places_t** type is the type signature of the **ompt_get_num_places** runtime entry point, which returns the number of places currently available to the execution environment in the place list.

Format

```
C / C++
typedef int (*ompt_get_num_places_t) (void);
C / C++
```

Binding

The binding thread set for the **ompt_get_num_places** runtime entry point is all threads on a device.

Description

The **ompt_get_num_places** runtime entry point, which has type signature **ompt_get_num_places_t**, returns the number of places in the place list. This value is equivalent to the number of places in the *place-partition-var* ICV in the execution environment of the initial task.

This runtime entry point is *async signal safe*.

Cross References

- *place-partition-var* ICV, see Section 2.5 on page 63.
- **OMP_PLACES** environment variable, see Section 6.5 on page 605.

4.6.1.8 ompt_get_place_proc_ids_t

Summary

The **ompt_get_place_procs_ids_t** type is the type signature of the **ompt_get_num_place_procs_ids** runtime entry point, which returns the numerical identifiers of the processors that are available to the execution environment in the specified place.

Format

```
C / C++
typedef int (*ompt_get_place_proc_ids_t) (
  int place_num,
  int ids_size,
  int *ids
);
C / C++
```

Binding

The binding thread set for the **ompt_get_place_proc_ids** runtime entry point is all threads on a device.

Description

The **ompt_get_place_proc_ids** runtime entry point, which has type signature **ompt_get_place_proc_ids_t**, returns the numerical identifiers of each processor that is associated with the specified place. These numerical identifiers are non-negative and their meaning is implementation defined.

Description of Arguments

The *place_num* argument specifies the place that is being queried.

The *ids* argument is an array in which the routine can return a vector of processor identifiers in the specified place.

The *ids_size* argument indicates the size of the result array that is specified by *ids*.

Effect

If the *ids* array of size *ids_size* is large enough to contain all identifiers then they are returned in *ids* and their order in the array is implementation defined. Otherwise, if the *ids* array is too small the values in *ids* when the function returns are unspecified. The routine always returns the number of numerical identifiers of the processors that are available to the execution environment in the specified place.

4.6.1.9 ompt_get_place_num_t

Summary

The `ompt_get_place_num_t` type is the type signature of the `ompt_get_place_num` runtime entry point, which returns the place number of the place to which the current thread is bound.

Format

C / C++
```
typedef int (*ompt_get_place_num_t) (void);
```
C / C++

Binding

The binding thread set of the `ompt_get_place_num` runtime entry point is the current thread.

Description

When the current thread is bound to a place, `ompt_get_place_num` returns the place number associated with the thread. The returned value is between 0 and one less than the value returned by `ompt_get_num_places`, inclusive. When the current thread is not bound to a place, the routine returns -1.

This runtime entry point is *async signal safe*.

4.6.1.10 ompt_get_partition_place_nums_t

Summary

The **ompt_get_partition_place_nums_t** type is the type signature of the **ompt_get_partition_place_nums** runtime entry point, which returns a list of place numbers that correspond to the places in the *place-partition-var* ICV of the innermost implicit task.

Format

C / C++
```
typedef int (*ompt_get_partition_place_nums_t) (
  int place_nums_size,
  int *place_nums
);
```
C / C++

Binding

The binding task set for the **ompt_get_partition_place_nums** runtime entry point is the current implicit task.

Description

The **ompt_get_partition_place_nums** runtime entry point, which has type signature **ompt_get_partition_place_nums_t**, returns a list of place numbers that correspond to the places in the *place-partition-var* ICV of the innermost implicit task.

This runtime entry point is *async signal safe*.

Description of Arguments

The *place_nums* argument is an array in which the routine can return a vector of place identifiers.

The *place_nums_size* argument indicates the size of the result array that the *place_nums* argument specifies.

Effect

If the *place_nums* array of size *place_nums_size* is large enough to contain all identifiers then they are returned in *place_nums* and their order in the array is implementation defined. Otherwise, if the *place_nums* array is too small, the values in *place_nums* when the function returns are unspecified. The routine always returns the number of places in the *place-partition-var* ICV of the innermost implicit task.

Cross References

- *place-partition-var* ICV, see Section 2.5 on page 63.
- `OMP_PLACES` environment variable, see Section 6.5 on page 605.

4.6.1.11 `ompt_get_proc_id_t`

Summary

The `ompt_get_proc_id_t` type is the type signature of the `ompt_get_proc_id` runtime entry point, which returns the numerical identifier of the processor of the current thread.

Format

———————————————— C / C++ ————————————————
```
typedef int (*ompt_get_proc_id_t) (void);
```
———————————————— C / C++ ————————————————

Binding

The binding thread set for the `ompt_get_proc_id` runtime entry point is the current thread.

Description

The `ompt_get_proc_id` runtime entry point, which has type signature `ompt_get_proc_id_t`, returns the numerical identifier of the processor of the current thread. A defined numerical identifier is non-negative and its meaning is implementation defined. A negative number indicates a failure to retrieve the numerical identifier.

This runtime entry point is *async signal safe*.

4.6.1.12 `ompt_get_state_t`

Summary

The `ompt_get_state_t` type is the type signature of the `ompt_get_state` runtime entry point, which returns the state and the wait identifier of the current thread.

Format

```
C / C++
typedef int (*ompt_get_state_t) (
  ompt_wait_id_t *wait_id
);
C / C++
```

Binding

The binding thread for the **ompt_get_state** runtime entry point is the current thread.

Description

Each OpenMP thread has an associated state and a wait identifier. If a thread's state indicates that the thread is waiting for mutual exclusion then its wait identifier contains an opaque handle that indicates the data object upon which the thread is waiting. The **ompt_get_state** runtime entry point, which has type signature **ompt_get_state_t**, retrieves the state and wait identifier of the current thread. The returned value may be any one of the states predefined by **ompt_state_t** or a value that represents any implementation specific state. The tool may obtain a string representation for each state with the **ompt_enumerate_states** function.

If the returned state indicates that the thread is waiting for a lock, nest lock, critical section, atomic region, or ordered region then the value of the thread's wait identifier is assigned to a non-null wait identifier passed as the *wait_id* argument.

This runtime entry point is *async signal safe*.

Description of Arguments

The *wait_id* argument is a pointer to an opaque handle that is available to receive the value of the thread's wait identifier. If *wait_id* is not **NULL** then the entry point assigns the value of the thread's wait identifier to the object to which *wait_id* points. If the returned state is not one of the specified wait states then the value of opaque object to which *wait_id* points is undefined after the call.

Constraints on Arguments

The argument passed to the entry point must be a reference to a variable of the specified type or **NULL**.

Cross References

- `ompt_state_t` type, see Section 4.4.4.26 on page 452.
- `ompt_wait_id_t` type, see Section 4.4.4.29 on page 456.
- `ompt_enumerate_states_t` type, see Section 4.6.1.1 on page 498.

4.6.1.13 `ompt_get_parallel_info_t`

Summary

The `ompt_get_parallel_info_t` type is the type signature of the `ompt_get_parallel_info` runtime entry point, which returns information about the parallel region, if any, at the specified ancestor level for the current execution context.

Format

—————————————————— C / C++ ——————————————————
```
typedef int (*ompt_get_parallel_info_t) (
    int ancestor_level,
    ompt_data_t **parallel_data,
    int *team_size
);
```
—————————————————— C / C++ ——————————————————

Description

During execution, an OpenMP program may employ nested parallel regions. The `ompt_get_parallel_info` runtime entry point known, which has type signature `ompt_get_parallel_info_t`, retrieves information, about the current parallel region and any enclosing parallel regions for the current execution context. The entry point returns 2 if there is a parallel region at the specified ancestor level and the information is available, 1 if there is a parallel region at the specified ancestor level but the information is currently unavailable, and 0 otherwise.

A tool may use the pointer to a parallel region's data object that it obtains from this runtime entry point to inspect or to modify the value of the data object. When a parallel region is created, its data object will be initialized with the value `ompt_data_none`.

This runtime entry point is *async signal safe*.

Between a *parallel-begin* event and an *implicit-task-begin* event, a call to `ompt_get_parallel_info(0,...)` may return information about the outer parallel team, the new parallel team or an inconsistent state.

If a thread is in the state `ompt_state_wait_barrier_implicit_parallel` then a call to `ompt_get_parallel_info` may return a pointer to a copy of the specified parallel region's *parallel_data* rather than a pointer to the data word for the region itself. This convention enables the master thread for a parallel region to free storage for the region immediately after the region ends, yet avoid having some other thread in the region's team potentially reference the region's *parallel_data* object after it has been freed.

Description of Arguments

The *ancestor_level* argument specifies the parallel region of interest by its ancestor level. Ancestor level 0 refers to the innermost parallel region; information about enclosing parallel regions may be obtained using larger values for *ancestor_level*.

The *parallel_data* argument returns the parallel data if the argument is not **NULL**.

The *team_size* argument returns the team size if the argument is not **NULL**.

Effect

If the runtime entry point returns 0 or 1, no argument is modified. Otherwise, `ompt_get_parallel_info` has the following effects:

- If a non-null value was passed for *parallel_data*, the value returned in *parallel_data* is a pointer to a data word that is associated with the parallel region at the specified level; and

- If a non-null value was passed for *team_size*, the value returned in the integer to which *team_size* point is the number of threads in the team that is associated with the parallel region.

Constraints on Arguments

While argument *ancestor_level* is passed by value, all other arguments to the entry point must be pointers to variables of the specified types or **NULL**.

Cross References

- **ompt_data_t** type, see Section 4.4.4.4 on page 440.

4.6.1.14 ompt_get_task_info_t

Summary

The `ompt_get_task_info_t` type is the type signature of the `ompt_get_task_info` runtime entry point, which returns information about the task, if any, at the specified ancestor level in the current execution context.

Format

```
typedef int (*ompt_get_task_info_t) (
  int ancestor_level,
  int *flags,
  ompt_data_t **task_data,
  ompt_frame_t **task_frame,
  ompt_data_t **parallel_data,
  int *thread_num
);
```

Description

During execution, an OpenMP thread may be executing an OpenMP task. Additionally, the thread's stack may contain procedure frames that are associated with suspended OpenMP tasks or OpenMP runtime system routines. To obtain information about any task on the current thread's stack, a tool uses the `ompt_get_task_info` runtime entry point, which has type signature `ompt_get_task_info_t`.

Ancestor level 0 refers to the active task; information about other tasks with associated frames present on the stack in the current execution context may be queried at higher ancestor levels.

The `ompt_get_task_info` runtime entry point returns 2 if there is a task region at the specified ancestor level and the information is available, 1 if there is a task region at the specified ancestor level but the information is currently unavailable, and 0 otherwise.

If a task exists at the specified ancestor level and the information is available then information is returned in the variables passed by reference to the entry point. If no task region exists at the specified ancestor level or the information is unavailable then the values of variables passed by reference to the entry point are undefined when `ompt_get_task_info` returns.

A tool may use a pointer to a data object for a task or parallel region that it obtains from `ompt_get_task_info` to inspect or to modify the value of the data object. When either a parallel region or a task region is created, its data object will be initialized with the value `ompt_data_none`.

This runtime entry point is *async signal safe*.

Description of Arguments

The *ancestor_level* argument specifies the task region of interest by its ancestor level. Ancestor level 0 refers to the active task; information about ancestor tasks found in the current execution context may be queried at higher ancestor levels.

The *flags* argument returns the task type if the argument is not **NULL**.

The *task_data* argument returns the task data if the argument is not **NULL**.

The *task_frame* argument returns the task frame pointer if the argument is not **NULL**.

The *parallel_data* argument returns the parallel data if the argument is not **NULL**.

The *thread_num* argument returns the thread number if the argument is not **NULL**.

Effect

If the runtime entry point returns 0 or 1, no argument is modified. Otherwise, `ompt_get_task_info` has the following effects:

- If a non-null value was passed for *flags* then the value returned in the integer to which *flags* points represents the type of the task at the specified level; possible task types include initial, implicit, explicit, and target tasks;

- If a non-null value was passed for *task_data* then the value that is returned in the object to which it points is a pointer to a data word that is associated with the task at the specified level;

- If a non-null value was passed for *task_frame* then the value that is returned in the object to which *task_frame* points is a pointer to the `ompt_frame_t` structure that is associated with the task at the specified level;

- If a non-null value was passed for *parallel_data* then the value that is returned in the object to which *parallel_data* points is a pointer to a data word that is associated with the parallel region that contains the task at the specified level or, if the task at the specified level is an initial task, **NULL**; and

- If a non-null value was passed for *thread_num* then the value that is returned in the object to which *thread_num* points indicates the number of the thread in the parallel region that is executing the task at the specified level.

Constraints on Arguments

While argument *ancestor_level* is passed by value, all other arguments to `ompt_get_task_info` must be pointers to variables of the specified types or **NULL**.

Cross References

- **ompt_data_t** type, see Section 4.4.4.4 on page 440.
- **ompt_task_flag_t** type, see Section 4.4.4.18 on page 446.
- **ompt_frame_t** type, see Section 4.4.4.27 on page 454.

4.6.1.15 ompt_get_task_memory_t

Summary

The **ompt_get_task_memory_t** type is the type signature of the **ompt_get_task_memory** runtime entry point, which returns information about memory ranges that are associated with the task.

Format

─────────────────────────── C / C++ ───────────────────────────
```
typedef int (*ompt_get_task_memory_t)(
  void **addr,
  size_t *size,
  int block
);
```
─────────────────────────── C / C++ ───────────────────────────

Description

During execution, an OpenMP thread may be executing an OpenMP task. The OpenMP implementation must preserve the data environment from the creation of the task for the execution of the task. The **ompt_get_task_memory** runtime entry point, which has type signature **ompt_get_task_memory_t**, provides information about the memory ranges used to store the data environment for the current task.

Multiple memory ranges may be used to store these data. The *block* argument supports iteration over these memory ranges.

The **ompt_get_task_memory** runtime entry point returns 1 if there are more memory ranges available, and 0 otherwise. If no memory is used for a task, *size* is set to 0. In this case, addr is unspecified.

This runtime entry point is *async signal safe*.

Description of Arguments

The *addr* argument is a pointer to a void pointer return value to provide the start address of a memory block.

The *size* argument is a pointer to a size type return value to provide the size of the memory block.

The *block* argument is an integer value to specify the memory block of interest.

4.6.1.16 ompt_get_target_info_t

Summary

The `ompt_get_target_info_t` type is the type signature of the `ompt_get_target_info` runtime entry point, which returns identifiers that specify a thread's current **target** region and target operation ID, if any.

Format

―――――――――――――――― C / C++ ――――――――――――――――
```
typedef int (*ompt_get_target_info_t) (
  uint64_t *device_num,
  ompt_id_t *target_id,
  ompt_id_t *host_op_id
);
```
―――――――――――――――― C / C++ ――――――――――――――――

Description

The `ompt_get_target_info` entry point, which has type signature `ompt_get_target_info_t`, returns 1 if the current thread is in a **target** region and 0 otherwise. If the entry point returns 0 then the values of the variables passed by reference as its arguments are undefined.

If the current thread is in a **target** region then `ompt_get_target_info` returns information about the current device, active **target** region, and active host operation, if any.

This runtime entry point is *async signal safe*.

Description of Arguments

The *device_num* argument returns the device number if the current thread is in a `target` region.

Th *target_id* argument returns the `target` region identifier if the current thread is in a `target` region.

If the current thread is in the process of initiating an operation on a target device (for example, copying data to or from an accelerator or launching a kernel) then *host_op_id* returns the identifier for the operation; otherwise, *host_op_id* returns `ompt_id_none`.

Constraints on Arguments

Arguments passed to the entry point must be valid references to variables of the specified types.

Cross References

- `ompt_id_t` type, see Section 4.4.4.3 on page 439.

4.6.1.17 `ompt_get_num_devices_t`

Summary

The `ompt_get_num_devices_t` type is the type signature of the `ompt_get_num_devices` runtime entry point, which returns the number of available devices.

Format

―――――――――――― C / C++ ――――――――――――
```
typedef int (*ompt_get_num_devices_t) (void);
```
―――――――――――― C / C++ ――――――――――――

Description

The `ompt_get_num_devices` runtime entry point, which has type signature `ompt_get_num_devices_t`, returns the number of devices available to an OpenMP program.

This runtime entry point is *async signal safe*.

4.6.1.18 ompt_get_unique_id_t

Summary

The `ompt_get_unique_id_t` type is the type signature of the `ompt_get_unique_id` runtime entry point, which returns a unique number.

Format

```
C / C++
typedef uint64_t (*ompt_get_unique_id_t) (void);
C / C++
```

Description

The `ompt_get_unique_id` runtime entry point, which has type signature `ompt_get_unique_id_t`, returns a number that is unique for the duration of an OpenMP program. Successive invocations may not result in consecutive or even increasing numbers.

This runtime entry point is *async signal safe*.

4.6.1.19 ompt_finalize_tool_t

Summary

The `ompt_finalize_tool_t` type is the type signature of the `ompt_finalize_tool` runtime entry point, which enables a tool to finalize itself.

Format

```
C / C++
typedef void (*ompt_finalize_tool_t) (void);
C / C++
```

Description

A tool may detect that the execution of an OpenMP program is ending before the OpenMP implementation does. To facilitate clean termination of the tool, the tool may invoke the `ompt_finalize_tool` runtime entry point, which has type signature `ompt_finalize_tool_t`. Upon completion of `ompt_finalize_tool`, no OMPT callbacks are dispatched.

Effect

The `ompt_finalize_tool` routine detaches the tool from the runtime, unregisters all callbacks and invalidates all OMPT entry points passed to the tool in the *lookup-function*. Upon completion of `ompt_finalize_tool`, no further callbacks will be issued on any thread.

Before the callbacks are unregistered, the OpenMP runtime should attempt to dispatch all outstanding registered callbacks as well as the callbacks that would be encountered during shutdown of the runtime, if possible in the current execution context.

4.6.2 Entry Points in the OMPT Device Tracing Interface

The runtime entry points with type signatures of the types that are specified in this section enable a tool to trace activities on a device.

4.6.2.1 ompt_get_device_num_procs_t

Summary

The `ompt_get_device_num_procs_t` type is the type signature of the `ompt_get_device_num_procs` runtime entry point, which returns the number of processors currently available to the execution environment on the specified device.

Format

─────────────────────── C / C++ ───────────────────────
```
typedef int (*ompt_get_device_num_procs_t) (
  ompt_device_t *device
);
```
─────────────────────── C / C++ ───────────────────────

Description

The `ompt_get_device_num_procs` runtime entry point, which has type signature `ompt_get_device_num_procs_t`, returns the number of processors that are available on the device at the time the routine is called. This value may change between the time that it is determined and the time that it is read in the calling context due to system actions outside the control of the OpenMP implementation.

Description of Arguments

The *device* argument is a pointer to an opaque object that represents the target device instance. The pointer to the device instance object is used by functions in the device tracing interface to identify the device being addressed.

Cross References

- ompt_device_t type, see Section 4.4.4.5 on page 441.

4.6.2.2 ompt_get_device_time_t

Summary

The ompt_get_device_time_t type is the type signature of the ompt_get_device_time runtime entry point, which returns the current time on the specified device.

Format

```
C / C++
typedef ompt_device_time_t (*ompt_get_device_time_t) (
    ompt_device_t *device
);
C / C++
```

Description

Host and target devices are typically distinct and run independently. If host and target devices are different hardware components, they may use different clock generators. For this reason, a common time base for ordering host-side and device-side events may not be available.

The ompt_get_device_time runtime entry point, which has type signature ompt_get_device_time_t, returns the current time on the specified device. A tool can use this information to align time stamps from different devices.

Description of Arguments

The *device* argument is a pointer to an opaque object that represents the target device instance. The pointer to the device instance object is used by functions in the device tracing interface to identify the device being addressed.

Cross References

- **ompt_device_t** type, see Section 4.4.4.5 on page 441.
- **ompt_device_time_t** type, see Section 4.4.4.6 on page 441.

4.6.2.3 ompt_translate_time_t

Summary

The **ompt_translate_time_t** type is the type signature of the **ompt_translate_time** runtime entry point, which translates a time value that is obtained from the specified device to a corresponding time value on the host device.

Format

```
C / C++
typedef double (*ompt_translate_time_t) (
  ompt_device_t *device,
  ompt_device_time_t time
);
C / C++
```

Description

The **ompt_translate_time** runtime entry point, which has type signature **ompt_translate_time_t**, translates a time value obtained from the specified device to a corresponding time value on the host device. The returned value for the host time has the same meaning as the value returned from **omp_get_wtime**.

Note – The accuracy of time translations may degrade if they are not performed promptly after a device time value is received and if either the host or device vary their clock speeds. Prompt translation of device times to host times is recommended.

Description of Arguments

The *device* argument is a pointer to an opaque object that represents the target device instance. The pointer to the device instance object is used by functions in the device tracing interface to identify the device being addressed.

The *time* argument is a time from the specified device.

Cross References

- **omp_get_wtime** routine, see Section 3.4.1 on page 394.
- **ompt_device_t** type, see Section 4.4.4.5 on page 441.
- **ompt_device_time_t** type, see Section 4.4.4.6 on page 441.

4.6.2.4 ompt_set_trace_ompt_t

Summary

The **ompt_set_trace_ompt_t** type is the type signature of the **ompt_set_trace_ompt** runtime entry point, which enables or disables the recording of trace records for one or more types of OMPT events.

Format

―――――――――――――――― C / C++ ――――――――――――――――
```
typedef ompt_set_result_t (*ompt_set_trace_ompt_t) (
  ompt_device_t *device,
  unsigned int enable,
  unsigned int etype
);
```
―――――――――――――――― C / C++ ――――――――――――――――

Description of Arguments

The *device* argument points to an opaque object that represents the target device instance. Functions in the device tracing interface use this pointer to identify the device that is being addressed.

The *etype* argument indicates the events to which the invocation of **ompt_set_trace_ompt** applies. If the value of *etype* is 0 then the invocation applies to all events. If *etype* is positive then it applies to the event in **ompt_callbacks_t** that matches that value.

The *enable* argument indicates whether tracing should be enabled or disabled for the event or events that the *etype* argument specifies. A positive value for *enable* indicates that recording should be enabled; a value of 0 for *enable* indicates that recording should be disabled.

Restrictions

The **ompt_set_trace_ompt** runtime entry point has the following restriction:

- The entry point must not return **ompt_set_sometimes_paired**.

Cross References

- Tracing activity on target devices with OMPT, see Section 4.2.5 on page 427.
- `ompt_callbacks_t` type, see Section 4.4.2 on page 434.
- `ompt_set_result_t` type, see Section 4.4.4.2 on page 438.
- `ompt_device_t` type, see Section 4.4.4.5 on page 441.

4.6.2.5 ompt_set_trace_native_t

Summary

The `ompt_set_trace_native_t` type is the type signature of the `ompt_set_trace_native` runtime entry point, which enables or disables the recording of native trace records for a device.

Format

```
typedef ompt_set_result_t (*ompt_set_trace_native_t) (
  ompt_device_t *device,
  int enable,
  int flags
);
```

Description

This interface is designed for use by a tool that cannot directly use native control functions for the device. If a tool can directly use the native control functions then it can invoke native control functions directly using pointers that the *lookup* function associated with the device provides and that are described in the *documentation* string that is provided to the device initializer callback.

Description of Arguments

The *device* argument points to an opaque object that represents the target device instance. Functions in the device tracing interface use this pointer to identify the device that is being addressed.

The *enable* argument indicates whether this invocation should enable or disable recording of events.

The *flags* argument specifies the kinds of native device monitoring to enable or to disable. Each kind of monitoring is specified by a flag bit. Flags can be composed by using logical `or` to combine enumeration values from type **ompt_native_mon_flag_t**.

To start, to pause, to flush, or to stop tracing for a specific target device associated with *device*, a tool invokes the **ompt_start_trace**, **ompt_pause_trace**, **ompt_flush_trace**, or **ompt_stop_trace** runtime entry point for the device.

Restrictions

The **ompt_set_trace_native** runtime entry point has the following restriction:

- The entry point must not return **ompt_set_sometimes_paired**.

Cross References

- Tracing activity on target devices with OMPT, see Section 4.2.5 on page 427.
- **ompt_set_result_t** type, see Section 4.4.4.2 on page 438.
- **ompt_device_t** type, see Section 4.4.4.5 on page 441.

4.6.2.6 ompt_start_trace_t

Summary

The **ompt_start_trace_t** type is the type signature of the **ompt_start_trace** runtime entry point, which starts tracing of activity on a specific device.

Format

```
typedef int (*ompt_start_trace_t) (
  ompt_device_t *device,
  ompt_callback_buffer_request_t request,
  ompt_callback_buffer_complete_t complete
);
```

Description

A device's `ompt_start_trace` runtime entry point, which has type signature
`ompt_start_trace_t`, initiates tracing on the device. Under normal operating conditions,
every event buffer provided to a device by a tool callback is returned to the tool before the OpenMP
runtime shuts down. If an exceptional condition terminates execution of an OpenMP program, the
OpenMP runtime may not return buffers provided to the device.

An invocation of `ompt_start_trace` returns 1 if the command succeeds and 0 otherwise.

Description of Arguments

The *device* argument points to an opaque object that represents the target device instance. Functions
in the device tracing interface use this pointer to identify the device that is being addressed.

The *request* argument specifies a tool callback that supplies a device with a buffer to deposit events.

The *complete* argument specifies a tool callback that is invoked by the OpenMP implementation to
empty a buffer that contains event records.

Cross References

- `ompt_device_t` type, see Section 4.4.4.5 on page 441.
- `ompt_callback_buffer_request_t` callback type, see Section 4.5.2.23 on page 486.
- `ompt_callback_buffer_complete_t` callback type, see Section 4.5.2.24 on page 487.

4.6.2.7 ompt_pause_trace_t

Summary

The `ompt_pause_trace_t` type is the type signature of the `ompt_pause_trace` runtime
entry point, which pauses or restarts activity tracing on a specific device.

Format

C / C++
```
typedef int (*ompt_pause_trace_t) (
  ompt_device_t *device,
  int begin_pause
);
```
C / C++

Description

A device's **ompt_pause_trace** runtime entry point, which has type signature **ompt_pause_trace_t**, pauses or resumes tracing on a device. An invocation of **ompt_pause_trace** returns 1 if the command succeeds and 0 otherwise. Redundant pause or resume commands are idempotent and will return the same value as the prior command.

Description of Arguments

The *device* argument points to an opaque object that represents the target device instance. Functions in the device tracing interface use this pointer to identify the device that is being addressed.

The *begin_pause* argument indicates whether to pause or to resume tracing. To resume tracing, zero should be supplied for *begin_pause*; To pause tracing, any other value should be supplied.

Cross References

- **ompt_device_t** type, see Section 4.4.4.5 on page 441.

4.6.2.8 ompt_flush_trace_t

Summary

The **ompt_flush_trace_t** type is the type signature of the **ompt_flush_trace** runtime entry point, which causes all pending trace records for the specified device to be delivered.

Format

―――――――――――――――― C / C++ ――――――――――――――――
```
typedef int (*ompt_flush_trace_t) (
  ompt_device_t *device
);
```
―――――――――――――――― C / C++ ――――――――――――――――

Description

A device's **ompt_flush_trace** runtime entry point, which has type signature **ompt_flush_trace_t**, causes the OpenMP implementation to issue a sequence of zero or more buffer completion callbacks to deliver all trace records that have been collected prior to the flush. An invocation of **ompt_flush_trace** returns 1 if the command succeeds and 0 otherwise.

Description of Arguments

The *device* argument points to an opaque object that represents the target device instance. Functions in the device tracing interface use this pointer to identify the device that is being addressed.

Cross References

- `ompt_device_t` type, see Section 4.4.4.5 on page 441.

4.6.2.9 ompt_stop_trace_t

Summary

The `ompt_stop_trace_t` type is the type signature of the `ompt_stop_trace` runtime entry point, which stops tracing for a device.

Format

```
C / C++
typedef int (*ompt_stop_trace_t) (
  ompt_device_t *device
);
C / C++
```

Description

A device's `ompt_stop_trace` runtime entry point, which has type signature `ompt_stop_trace_t`, halts tracing on the device and requests that any pending trace records are flushed. An invocation of `ompt_stop_trace` returns 1 if the command succeeds and 0 otherwise.

Description of Arguments

The *device* argument points to an opaque object that represents the target device instance. Functions in the device tracing interface use this pointer to identify the device that is being addressed.

Cross References

- `ompt_device_t` type, see Section 4.4.4.5 on page 441.

4.6.2.10 ompt_advance_buffer_cursor_t

Summary

The `ompt_advance_buffer_cursor_t` type is the type signature of the
`ompt_advance_buffer_cursor` runtime entry point, which advances a trace buffer cursor to
the next record.

Format

```
C / C++
typedef int (*ompt_advance_buffer_cursor_t) (
  ompt_device_t *device,
  ompt_buffer_t *buffer,
  size_t size,
  ompt_buffer_cursor_t current,
  ompt_buffer_cursor_t *next
);
C / C++
```

Description

A device's `ompt_advance_buffer_cursor` runtime entry point, which has type signature
`ompt_advance_buffer_cursor_t`, advances a trace buffer pointer to the next trace record.
An invocation of `ompt_advance_buffer_cursor` returns *true* if the advance is successful
and the next position in the buffer is valid.

Description of Arguments

The *device* argument points to an opaque object that represents the target device instance. Functions
in the device tracing interface use this pointer to identify the device that is being addressed.

The *buffer* argument indicates a trace buffer that is associated with the cursors.

The argument *size* indicates the size of *buffer* in bytes.

The *current* argument is an opaque buffer cursor.

The *next* argument returns the next value of an opaque buffer cursor.

Cross References

- `ompt_device_t` type, see Section 4.4.4.5 on page 441.
- `ompt_buffer_cursor_t` type, see Section 4.4.4.8 on page 442.

4.6.2.11 ompt_get_record_type_t

Summary

The `ompt_get_record_type_t` type is the type signature of the
`ompt_get_record_type` runtime entry point, which inspects the type of a trace record.

Format

```
C / C++
typedef ompt_record_t (*ompt_get_record_type_t) (
  ompt_buffer_t *buffer,
  ompt_buffer_cursor_t current
);
C / C++
```

Description

Trace records for a device may be in one of two forms: *native* record format, which may be device-specific, or *OMPT* record format, in which each trace record corresponds to an OpenMP *event* and most fields in the record structure are the arguments that would be passed to the OMPT callback for the event.

A device's `ompt_get_record_type` runtime entry point, which has type signature `ompt_get_record_type_t`, inspects the type of a trace record and indicates whether the record at the current position in the trace buffer is an OMPT record, a native record, or an invalid record. An invalid record type is returned if the cursor is out of bounds.

Description of Arguments

The *buffer* argument indicates a trace buffer.

The *current* argument is an opaque buffer cursor.

Cross References

- `ompt_record_t` type, see Section 4.4.3.1 on page 435.
- `ompt_buffer_t` type, see Section 4.4.4.7 on page 441.
- `ompt_buffer_cursor_t` type, see Section 4.4.4.8 on page 442.

4.6.2.12 ompt_get_record_ompt_t

Summary

The `ompt_get_record_ompt_t` type is the type signature of the `ompt_get_record_ompt` runtime entry point, which obtains a pointer to an OMPT trace record from a trace buffer associated with a device.

Format

C / C++

```
typedef ompt_record_ompt_t *(*ompt_get_record_ompt_t) (
  ompt_buffer_t *buffer,
  ompt_buffer_cursor_t current
);
```

C / C++

Description

A device's `ompt_get_record_ompt` runtime entry point, which has type signature `ompt_get_record_ompt_t`, returns a pointer that may point to a record in the trace buffer, or it may point to a record in thread local storage in which the information extracted from a record was assembled. The information available for an event depends upon its type.

The return value of the `ompt_record_ompt_t` type includes a field of a union type that can represent information for any OMPT event record type. Another call to the runtime entry point may overwrite the contents of the fields in a record returned by a prior invocation.

Description of Arguments

The *buffer* argument indicates a trace buffer.

The *current* argument is an opaque buffer cursor.

Cross References

- `ompt_record_ompt_t` type, see Section 4.4.3.4 on page 436.
- `ompt_device_t` type, see Section 4.4.4.5 on page 411.
- `ompt_buffer_cursor_t` type, see Section 4.4.4.8 on page 442.

4.6.2.13 `ompt_get_record_native_t`

Summary

The `ompt_get_record_native_t` type is the type signature of the `ompt_get_record_native` runtime entry point, which obtains a pointer to a native trace record from a trace buffer associated with a device.

Format

C / C++

```
typedef void *(*ompt_get_record_native_t) (
  ompt_buffer_t *buffer,
  ompt_buffer_cursor_t current,
  ompt_id_t *host_op_id
);
```

C / C++

Description

A device's `ompt_get_record_native` runtime entry point, which has type signature `ompt_get_record_native_t`, returns a pointer that may point may point into the specified trace buffer, or into thread local storage in which the information extracted from a trace record was assembled. The information available for a native event depends upon its type. If the function returns a non-null result, it will also set the object to which `host_op_id` points to a host-side identifier for the operation that is associated with the record. A subsequent call to `ompt_get_record_native` may overwrite the contents of the fields in a record returned by a prior invocation.

Description of Arguments

The *buffer* argument indicates a trace buffer.

The *current* argument is an opaque buffer cursor.

The *host_op_id* argument is a pointer to an identifier that is returned by the function. The entry point sets the identifier to which *host_op_id* points to the value of a host-side identifier for an operation on a target device that was created when the operation was initiated by the host.

Cross References

- `ompt_id_t` type, see Section 4.4.4.3 on page 439.
- `ompt_buffer_t` type, see Section 4.4.4.7 on page 441.
- `ompt_buffer_cursor_t` type, see Section 4.4.4.8 on page 442.

4.6.2.14 ompt_get_record_abstract_t

Summary

The `ompt_get_record_abstract_t` type is the type signature of the `ompt_get_record_abstract` runtime entry point, which summarizes the context of a native (device-specific) trace record.

Format

```
typedef ompt_record_abstract_t *
(*ompt_get_record_abstract_t) (
  void *native_record
);
```

Description

An OpenMP implementation may execute on a device that logs trace records in a native (device-specific) format that a tool cannot interpret directly. A device's `ompt_get_record_abstract` runtime entry point, which has type signature `ompt_get_record_abstract_t`, translates a native trace record into a standard form.

Description of Arguments

The *native_record* argument is a pointer to a native trace record.

Cross References

- `ompt_record_abstract_t` type, see Section 4.4.3.3 on page 436.

4.6.3 Lookup Entry Points: `ompt_function_lookup_t`

Summary

The `ompt_function_lookup_t` type is the type signature of the lookup runtime entry points that provide pointers to runtime entry points that are part of the OMPT interface.

Format

```
typedef void (*ompt_interface_fn_t) (void);

typedef ompt_interface_fn_t (*ompt_function_lookup_t) (
  const char *interface_function_name
);
```

Description

An OpenMP implementation provides a pointer to a lookup routine that provides pointers to OMPT runtime entry points. When the implementation invokes a tool initializer to configure the OMPT callback interface, it provides a lookup function that provides pointers to runtime entry points that implement routines that are part of the OMPT callback interface. Alternatively, when it invokes a tool initializer to configure the OMPT tracing interface for a device, it provides a lookup function that provides pointers to runtime entry points that implement tracing control routines appropriate for that device.

Description of Arguments

The *interface_function_name* argument is a C string that represents the name of a runtime entry point.

Cross References

- Tool initializer for a device's OMPT tracing interface, see Section 4.2.5 on page 427.
- Tool initializer for the OMPT callback interface, see Section 4.5.1.1 on page 457.
- Entry points in the OMPT callback interface, see Table 4.1 on page 426 for a list and Section 4.6.1 on page 497 for detailed definitions.
- Entry points in the OMPT tracing interface, see Table 4.3 on page 430 for a list and Section 4.6.2 on page 518 for detailed definitions.

CHAPTER 5

OMPD Interface

This chapter describes OMPD, which is an interface for *third-party* tools. *Third-party* tools exist in separate processes from the OpenMP program. To provide OMPD support, an OpenMP implementation must provide an OMPD library to be loaded by the *third-party* tool. An OpenMP implementation does not need to maintain any extra information to support OMPD inquiries from *third-party* tools *unless* it is explicitly instructed to do so.

OMPD allows *third-party tools* such as a debuggers to inspect the OpenMP state of a live program or core file in an implementation-agnostic manner. That is, a tool that uses OMPD should work with any conforming OpenMP implementation. An OpenMP implementor provides a library for OMPD that a third-party tool can dynamically load. Using the interface exported by the OMPD library, the external tool can inspect the OpenMP state of a program. In order to satisfy requests from the third-party tool, the OMPD library may need to read data from, or to find the addresses of symbols in the OpenMP program. The OMPD library provides this functionality through a callback interface that the third-party tool must instantiate for the OMPD library.

To use OMPD, the third-party tool loads the OMPD library. The OMPD library exports the API that is defined throughout this section and that the tool uses to determine OpenMP information about the OpenMP program. The OMPD library must look up the symbols and read data out of the program. It does not perform these operations directly, but instead it uses the callback interface that the tool exports to cause the tool to perform them.

The OMPD architecture insulates tools from the internal structure of the OpenMP runtime while the OMPD library is insulated from the details of how to access the OpenMP program. This decoupled design allows for flexibility in how the OpenMP program and tool are deployed, so that, for example, the tool and the OpenMP program are not required to execute on the same machine.

Generally the tool does not interact directly with the OpenMP runtime and, instead, interacts with it through the OMPD library. However, a few cases require the tool to access the OpenMP runtime directly. These cases fall into two broad categories. The first is during initialization, where the tool must look up symbols and read variables in the OpenMP runtime in order to identify the OMPD library that it should use, which is discussed in Section 5.2.2 on page 535 and Section 5.2.3 on page 536. The second category relates to arranging for the tool to be notified when certain events occur during the execution of the OpenMP program. For this purpose, the OpenMP implementation must define certain symbols in the runtime code, as is discussed in Section 5.6 on page 594. Each of these symbols corresponds to an event type. The runtime must ensure that control passes through the appropriate named location when events occur. If the tool requires notification of an event, it can plant a breakpoint at the matching location. The location can, but may not, be a function. It can, for example, simply be a label. However, the names of the locations must have external **C** linkage.

5.1 OMPD Interfaces Definitions

─────────────── C / C++ ───────────────

A compliant implementation must supply a set of definitions for the OMPD runtime entry points, OMPD tool callback signatures, OMPD tool interface routines, and the special data types of their parameters and return values. These definitions, which are listed throughout this chapter, and their associated declarations shall be provided in a header file named **omp-tools.h**. In addition, the set of definitions may specify other implementation-specific values.

The **ompd_dll_locations** function, all OMPD tool interface functions, and all OMPD runtime entry points are external functions with **C** linkage.

─────────────── C / C++ ───────────────

5.2 Activating an OMPD Tool

The tool and the OpenMP program exist as separate processes. Thus, coordination is required between the OpenMP runtime and the external tool for OMPD.

5.2.1 Enabling the Runtime for OMPD

In order to support third-party tools, the OpenMP runtime may need to collect and to maintain information that it might not otherwise. The OpenMP runtime collects whatever information is necessary to support OMPD if the environment variable **OMP_DEBUG** is set to *enabled*.

Cross References

- Activating an OMPT Tool, Section 4.2 on page 420
- **OMP_DEBUG**, Section 6.20 on page 617

5.2.2 ompd_dll_locations

Summary

The **ompd_dll_locations** global variable indicates the location of OMPD libraries that are compatible with the OpenMP implementation.

Format

```c
const char **ompd_dll_locations;
```

Description

An OpenMP runtime may have more than one OMPD library. The tool must be able to locate the right library to use for the OpenMP program that it is examining. The OpenMP runtime system must provide a public variable **ompd_dll_locations**, which is an **argv**-style vector of filename string pointers that provides the name(s) of any compatible OMPD library. This variable must have **C** linkage. The tool uses the name of the variable verbatim and, in particular, does not apply any name mangling before performing the look up.

The programming model or architecture of the tool and, thus, that of OMPD does not have to match that of the OpenMP program that is being examined. The tool must interpret the contents of **ompd_dll_locations** to find a suitable OMPD that matches its own architectural characteristics. On platforms that support different programming models (for example, 32-bit vs 64-bit), OpenMP implementations are encouraged to provide OMPD libraries for all models, and that can handle OpenMP programs of any model. Thus, for example, a 32-bit debugger that uses OMPD should be able to debug a 64-bit OpenMP program by loading a 32-bit OMPD implementation that can manage a 64-bit OpenMP runtime.

ompd_dll_locations points to a NULL-terminated vector of zero or more NULL-terminated pathname strings that do not have any filename conventions. This vector must be fully initialized *before* **ompd_dll_locations** is set to a non-null value, such that if a tool, such as a debugger, stops execution of the OpenMP program at any point at which **ompd_dll_locations** is non-null, then the vector of strings to which it points is valid and complete.

Cross References

- `ompd_dll_locations_valid`, see Section 5.2.3 on page 536

5.2.3 `ompd_dll_locations_valid`

Summary

The OpenMP runtime notifies third-party tools that `ompd_dll_locations` is valid by allowing execution to pass through a location that the symbol `ompd_dll_locations_valid` identifies.

Format

```C
void ompd_dll_locations_valid(void);
```

Description

Since `ompd_dll_locations` may not be a static variable, it may require runtime initialization. The OpenMP runtime notifies third-party tools that `ompd_dll_locations` is valid by having execution pass through a location that the symbol `ompd_dll_locations_valid` identifies. If `ompd_dll_locations` is NULL, a third-party tool can place a breakpoint at `ompd_dll_locations_valid` to be notified that `ompd_dll_locations` is initialized. In practice, the symbol `ompd_dll_locations_valid` may not be a function; instead, it may be a labeled machine instruction through which execution passes once the vector is valid.

5.3 OMPD Data Types

This section defines the OMPD types.

5.3.1 Size Type

Summary

The `ompd_size_t` type specifies the number of bytes in opaque data objects that are passed across the OMPD API.

Format

```
typedef uint64_t ompd_size_t;
```

5.3.2 Wait ID Type

Summary

This `ompd_wait_id_t` type identifies the object on which a thread.

Format

```
typedef uint64_t ompd_wait_id_t;
```

5.3.3 Basic Value Types

Summary

These definitions represent a word, address, and segment value types.

Format

```
typedef uint64_t ompd_addr_t;
typedef int64_t  ompd_word_t;
typedef uint64_t ompd_seg_t;
```

Description

The *ompd_addr_t* type represents an unsigned integer address in an OpenMP process. The *ompd_word_t* type represents a signed version of *ompd_addr_t* to hold a signed integer of the OpenMP process. The *ompd_seg_t* type represents an unsigned integer segment value.

5.3.4 Address Type

Summary

The **ompd_address_t** type is used to specify device addresses.

Format

─── C / C++ ───
```
typedef struct ompd_address_t {
  ompd_seg_t segment;
  ompd_addr_t address;
} ompd_address_t;
```
─── C / C++ ───

Description

The **ompd_address_t** type is a structure that OMPD uses to specify device addresses, which may or may not be segmented. For non-segmented architectures, **ompd_segment_none** is used in the *segment* field of **ompd_address_t**; it is an instance of the **ompd_seg_t** type that has the value 0.

5.3.5 Frame Information Type

Summary

The **ompd_frame_info_t** type is used to specify frame information.

Format

─── C / C++ ───
```
typedef struct ompd_frame_info_t {
  ompd_address_t frame_address;
  ompd_word_t frame_flag;
} ompd_frame_info_t;
```
─── C / C++ ───

Description

The **ompd_frame_info_t** type is a structure that OMPD uses to specify frame information. The *frame_address* field of **ompd_frame_info_t** identifies a frame. The *frame_flag* field of **ompd_frame_info_t** indicates what type of information is provided in *frame_address*. The values and meaning is the same as defined for the **ompt_frame_t** enumeration type.

Cross References

- **ompt_frame_t**, see Section 4.4.4.27 on page 454

5.3.6 System Device Identifiers

Summary

The **ompd_device_t** type provides information about OpenMP devices.

Format

─────────────── C / C++ ───────────────
```
typedef uint64_t ompd_device_t;
```
─────────────── C / C++ ───────────────

Description

Different OpenMP runtimes may utilize different underlying devices. The Device identifiers can vary in size and format and, thus, are not explicitly represented in OMPD. Instead, device identifiers are passed across the interface via the **ompd_device_t** type, which is a pointer to where the device identifier is stored, and the size of the device identifier in bytes. The OMPD library and a tool that uses it must agree on the format of the object that is passed. Each different kind of device identifier uses a unique unsigned 64-bit integer value.

Recommended values of **ompd_device_t** are defined in the **ompd-types.h** header file, which is available on http://www.openmp.org/.

5.3.7 Native Thread Identifiers

Summary

The **ompd_thread_id_t** type provides information about native threads.

Format

― C / C++ ―
```
typedef uint64_t ompd_thread_id_t;
```
― C / C++ ―

Description

Different OpenMP runtimes may use different native thread implementations. Native thread identifiers can vary in size and format and, thus, are not explicitly represented in the OMPD API. Instead, native thread identifiers are passed across the interface via the **ompd_thread_id_t** type, which is a pointer to where the native thread identifier is stored, and the size of the native thread identifier in bytes. The OMPD library and a tool that uses it must agree on the format of the object that is passed. Each different kind of native thread identifier uses a unique unsigned 64-bit integer value.

Recommended values of **ompd_thread_id_t** are defined in the **ompd-types.h** header file, which is available on http://www.openmp.org/.

5.3.8 OMPD Handle Types

Summary

OMPD handle types are opaque types.

Format

― C / C++ ―
```
typedef struct _ompd_aspace_handle ompd_address_space_handle_t;
typedef struct _ompd_thread_handle ompd_thread_handle_t;
typedef struct _ompd_parallel_handle ompd_parallel_handle_t;
typedef struct _ompd_task_handle ompd_task_handle_t;
```
― C / C++ ―

Description

OMPD uses handles for address spaces (**ompd_address_space_handle_t**), threads (**ompd_thread_handle_t**), parallel regions (**ompd_parallel_handle_t**), and tasks (**ompd_task_handle_t**). Each operation of the OMPD interface that applies to a particular address space, thread, parallel region, or task must explicitly specify a corresponding handle. A handle for an entity is constant while the entity itself is alive. Handles are defined by the OMPD library, and are opaque to the tool.

Defining externally visible type names in this way introduces type safety to the interface, and helps to catch instances where incorrect handles are passed by the tool to the OMPD library. The structures do not need to be defined; instead, the OMPD library must cast incoming (pointers to) handles to the appropriate internal, private types.

5.3.9 OMPD Scope Types

Summary

The **ompd_scope_t** type identifies OMPD scopes.

Format

```
C / C++
typedef enum ompd_scope_t {
  ompd_scope_global = 1,
  ompd_scope_address_space = 2,
  ompd_scope_thread = 3,
  ompd_scope_parallel = 4,
  ompd_scope_implicit_task = 5,
  ompd_scope_task = 6
} ompd_scope_t;
C / C++
```

Description

The **ompd_scope_t** type identifies OpenMP scopes, including those related to parallel regions and tasks. When used in an OMPD interface function call, the scope type and the ompd handle must match according to Table 5.1.

TABLE 5.1: Mapping of Scope Type and OMPD Handles

Scope types	Handles
ompd_scope_global	Address space handle for the host device
ompd_scope_address_space	Any address space handle
ompd_scope_thread	Any thread handle
ompd_scope_parallel	Any parallel handle
ompd_scope_implicit_task	Task handle for an implicit task
ompd_scope_task	Any task handle

5.3.10 ICV ID Type

Summary

The `ompd_icv_id_t` type identifies an OpenMP implementation ICV.

Format

C / C++
```
typedef uint64_t ompd_icv_id_t;
```
C / C++

The `ompd_icv_id_t` type identifies OpenMP implementation ICVs. `ompd_icv_undefined` is an instance of this type with the value 0.

5.3.11 Tool Context Types

Summary

A third-party tool uses contexts to uniquely identify abstractions. These contexts are opaque to the OMPD library and are defined as follows:

Format

C / C++
```
typedef struct _ompd_aspace_cont ompd_address_space_context_t;
typedef struct _ompd_thread_cont ompd_thread_context_t;
```
C / C++

5.3.12 Return Code Types

Summary

The `ompd_rc_t` type is the return code type of OMPD operations

Format

―――――――――――――――――― C / C++ ――――――――――――――――――
```
typedef enum ompd_rc_t {
  ompd_rc_ok = 0,
  ompd_rc_unavailable = 1,
  ompd_rc_stale_handle = 2,
  ompd_rc_bad_input = 3,
  ompd_rc_error = 4,
  ompd_rc_unsupported = 5,
  ompd_rc_needs_state_tracking = 6,
  ompd_rc_incompatible = 7,
  ompd_rc_device_read_error = 8,
  ompd_rc_device_write_error = 9,
  ompd_rc_nomem = 10,
} ompd_rc_t;
```
―――――――――――――――――― C / C++ ――――――――――――――――――

Description

The `ompd_rc_t` type is used for the return codes of OMPD operations. The return code types and their semantics are defined as follows:

- `ompd_rc_ok` is returned when the operation is successful;
- `ompd_rc_unavailable` is returned when information is not available for the specified context;
- `ompd_rc_stale_handle` is returned when the specified handle is no longer valid;
- `ompd_rc_bad_input` is returned when the input parameters (other than handle) are invalid;
- `ompd_rc_error` is returned when a fatal error occurred;
- `ompd_rc_unsupported` is returned when the requested operation is not supported;
- `ompd_rc_needs_state_tracking` is returned when the state tracking operation failed because state tracking is not currently enabled;
- `ompd_rc_device_read_error` is returned when a read operation failed on the device;
- `ompd_rc_device_write_error` is returned when a write operation failed on the device;

- **ompd_rc_incompatible** is returned when this OMPD library is incompatible with, or is not capable of handling, the OpenMP program; and

- **ompd_rc_nomem** is returned when a memory allocation fails.

5.3.13 Primitive Type Sizes

Summary

The **ompd_device_type_sizes_t** type provides the "sizeof" of primitive types in the OpenMP architecture address space.

Format

―――――――――――――― C / C++ ――――――――――――――
```
typedef struct ompd_device_type_sizes_t {
    uint8_t sizeof_char;
    uint8_t sizeof_short;
    uint8_t sizeof_int;
    uint8_t sizeof_long;
    uint8_t sizeof_long_long;
    uint8_t sizeof_pointer;
} ompd_device_type_sizes_t;
```
―――――――――――――― C / C++ ――――――――――――――

Description

The **ompd_device_type_sizes_t** type is used in operations through which the OMPD library can interrogate the tool about the "sizeof" of primitive types in the OpenMP architecture address space. The fields of **ompd_device_type_sizes_t** give the sizes of the eponymous basic types used by the OpenMP runtime. As the tool and the OMPD library, by definition, have the same architecture and programming model, the size of the fields can be given as **uint8_t**.

Cross References

- **ompd_callback_sizeof_fn_t**, see Section 5.4.2.2 on page 549

5.4 OMPD Tool Callback Interface

For the OMPD library to provide information about the internal state of the OpenMP runtime system in an OpenMP process or core file, it must have a means to extract information from the OpenMP process that the tool is debugging. The OpenMP process on which the tool is operating may be either a "live" process or a core file, and a thread may be either a "live" thread in an OpenMP process, or a thread in a core file. To enable the OMPD library to extract state information from an OpenMP process or core file, the tool must supply the OMPD library with callback functions to inquire about the size of primitive types in the device of the OpenMP process, to look up the addresses of symbols, and to read and to write memory in the device. The OMPD library uses these callbacks to implement its interface operations. The OMPD library only invokes the callback functions in direct response to calls made by the tool to the OMPD library.

5.4.1 Memory Management of OMPD Library

The OMPD library must not access the heap manager directly. Instead, if it needs heap memory it must use the memory allocation and deallocation callback functions that are described in this section, `ompd_callback_memory_alloc_fn_t` (see Section 5.4.1.1 on page 546) and `ompd_callback_memory_free_fn_t` (see Section 5.4.1.2 on page 546), which are provided by the tool to obtain and to release heap memory. This mechanism ensures that the library does not interfere with any custom memory management scheme that the tool may use.

If the OMPD library is implemented in C++, memory management operators like **new** and **delete** in all their variants, *must all* be overloaded and implemented in terms of the callbacks that the tool provides. The OMPD library must be coded so that any of its definitions of **new** or **delete** do not interfere with any that the tool defines.

In some cases, the OMPD library must allocate memory to return results to the tool. The tool then owns this memory and has the responsibility to release it. Thus, the OMPD library and the tool must use the same memory manager.

The OMPD library creates OMPD handles, which are opaque to the tool and may have a complex internal structure. The tool cannot determine if the handle pointers that the API returns correspond to discrete heap allocations. Thus, the tool must not simply deallocate a handle by passing an address that it receives from the OMPD library to its own memory manager. Instead, the API includes functions that the tool must use when it no longer needs a handle.

A tool creates contexts and passes them to the OMPD library. The OMPD library does not release contexts; instead the tool release them after it releases any handles that may reference the contexts.

5.4.1.1 ompd_callback_memory_alloc_fn_t

Summary

The ompd_callback_memory_alloc_fn_t type is the type signature of the callback routine that the tool provides to the OMPD library to allocate memory.

Format

```c
typedef ompd_rc_t (*ompd_callback_memory_alloc_fn_t) (
    ompd_size_t nbytes,
    void **ptr
);
```

Description

The ompd_callback_memory_alloc_fn_t type is the type signature of the memory allocation callback routine that the tool provides. The OMPD library may call the ompd_callback_memory_alloc_fn_t callback function to allocate memory.

Description of Arguments

The *nbytes* argument is the size in bytes of the block of memory to allocate.

The address of the newly allocated block of memory is returned in the location to which the *ptr* argument points. The newly allocated block is suitably aligned for any type of variable, and is not guaranteed to be zeroed.

Cross References

- ompd_size_t, see Section 5.3.1 on page 536.
- ompd_rc_t, see Section 5.3.12 on page 543.

5.4.1.2 ompd_callback_memory_free_fn_t

Summary

The ompd_callback_memory_free_fn_t type is the type signature of the callback routine that the tool provides to the OMPD library to deallocate memory.

Format

```c
typedef ompd_rc_t (*ompd_callback_memory_free_fn_t) (
  void *ptr
);
```

Description

The `ompd_callback_memory_free_fn_t` type is the type signature of the memory deallocation callback routine that the tool provides. The OMPD library may call the `ompd_callback_memory_free_fn_t` callback function to deallocate memory that was obtained from a prior call to the `ompd_callback_memory_alloc_fn_t` callback function.

Description of Arguments

The *ptr* argument is the address of the block to be deallocated.

Cross References

- `ompd_rc_t`, see Section 5.3.12 on page 543.
- `ompd_callback_memory_alloc_fn_t`, see Section 5.4.1.1 on page 546.
- `ompd_callbacks_t`, see Section 5.4.6 on page 556.

5.4.2 Context Management and Navigation

Summary

The tool provides the OMPD library with callbacks to manage and to navigate context relationships.

5.4.2.1 ompd_callback_get_thread_context_for_thread_id_fn_t

Summary

The `ompd_callback_get_thread_context_for_thread_id_fn_t` is the type signature of the callback routine that the tool provides to the OMPD library to map a thread identifier to a tool thread context.

Format

```c
typedef ompd_rc_t
(*ompd_callback_get_thread_context_for_thread_id_fn_t) (
    ompd_address_space_context_t *address_space_context,
    ompd_thread_id_t kind,
    ompd_size_t sizeof_thread_id,
    const void *thread_id,
    ompd_thread_context_t **thread_context
);
```

Description

The `ompd_callback_get_thread_context_for_thread_id_fn_t` is the type signature of the context mapping callback routine that the tool provides. This callback maps a thread identifier to a tool thread context. The thread identifier is within the address space that *address_space_context* identifies. The OMPD library can use the thread context, for example, to access thread local storage.

Description of Arguments

The *address_space_context* argument is an opaque handle that the tool provides to reference an address space. The *kind*, *sizeof_thread_id*, and *thread_id* arguments represent a native thread identifier. On return, the *thread_context* argument provides an opaque handle that maps a native thread identifier to a tool thread context.

Restrictions

Routines that use `ompd_callback_get_thread_context_for_thread_id_fn_t` have the following restriction:

- The provided *thread_context* must be valid until the OMPD library returns from the OMPD tool interface routine.

Cross References

- `ompd_size_t`, see Section 5.3.1 on page 536.
- `ompd_thread_id_t`, see Section 5.3.7 on page 539.
- `ompd_address_space_context_t`, see Section 5.3.11 on page 542.
- `ompd_thread_context_t`, see Section 5.3.11 on page 542.
- `ompd_rc_t`, see Section 5.3.12 on page 543.

5.4.2.2 ompd_callback_sizeof_fn_t

Summary

The `ompd_callback_sizeof_fn_t` type is the type signature of the callback routine that the tool provides to the OMPD library to determine the sizes of the primitive types in an address space.

Format

```c
typedef ompd_rc_t (*ompd_callback_sizeof_fn_t) (
  ompd_address_space_context_t *address_space_context,
  ompd_device_type_sizes_t *sizes
);
```

Description

The `ompd_callback_sizeof_fn_t` is the type signature of the type-size query callback routine that the tool provides. This callback provides the sizes of the basic primitive types for a given address space.

Description of Arguments

The callback returns the sizes of the basic primitive types used by the address space context that the *address_space_context* argument specifies in the location to which the *sizes* argument points.

Cross References

- `ompd_address_space_context_t`, see Section 5.3.11 on page 542.
- `ompd_rc_t`, see Section 5.3.12 on page 543.
- `ompd_device_type_sizes_t`, see Section 5.3.13 on page 544.
- `ompd_callbacks_t`, see Section 5.4.6 on page 556.

5.4.3 Accessing Memory in the OpenMP Program or Runtime

The OMPD library may need to read from or to write to the OpenMP program. It cannot do this directly. Instead the OMPD library must use callbacks that the tool provides so that the tool performs the operation.

5.4.3.1 ompd_callback_symbol_addr_fn_t

Summary

The `ompd_callback_symbol_addr_fn_t` type is the type signature of the callback that the tool provides to look up the addresses of symbols in an OpenMP program.

Format

```c
typedef ompd_rc_t (*ompd_callback_symbol_addr_fn_t) (
  ompd_address_space_context_t *address_space_context,
  ompd_thread_context_t *thread_context,
  const char *symbol_name,
  ompd_address_t *symbol_addr,
  const char *file_name
);
```

Description

The `ompd_callback_symbol_addr_fn_t` is the type signature of the symbol-address query callback routine that the tool provides. This callback looks up addresses of symbols within a specified address space.

Description of Arguments

This callback looks up the symbol provided in the *symbol_name* argument.

The *address_space_context* argument is the tool's representation of the address space of the process, core file, or device.

The *thread_context* argument is NULL for global memory access. If *thread_context* is not NULL, *thread_context* gives the thread specific context for the symbol lookup, for the purpose of calculating thread local storage addresses. If *thread_context* is non-null then the thread to which *thread_context* refers must be associated with either the process or the device that corresponds to the *address_space_context* argument.

The tool uses the *symbol_name* argument that the OMPD library supplies verbatim. In particular, no name mangling, demangling or other transformations are performed prior to the lookup. The *symbol_name* parameter must correspond to a statically allocated symbol within the specified address space. The symbol can correspond to any type of object, such as a variable, thread local storage variable, function, or untyped label. The symbol can have a local, global, or weak binding.

The *file_name* argument is an optional input parameter that indicates the name of the shared library in which the symbol is defined, and is intended to help the third party tool disambiguate symbols that are defined multiple times across the executable or shared library files. The shared library name may not be an exact match for the name seen by the tool. If *file_name* is NULL then the tool first tries to find the symbol in the executable file, and, if the symbol is not found, the tool tries to find the symbol in the shared libraries in the order in which the shared libraries are loaded into the address space. If *file_name* is non-null then the tool first tries to find the symbol in the libraries that match the name in the *file_name* argument and, if the symbol is not found, the tool then uses the same procedure as when *file_name* is NULL.

The callback does not support finding symbols that are dynamically allocated on the call stack, or statically allocated symbols that are defined within the scope of a function or subroutine.

The callback returns the symbol's address in the location to which *symbol_addr* points.

Restrictions

Routines that use the **ompd_callback_symbol_addr_fn_t** type have the following restrictions:

- The *address_space_context* argument must be non-null.
- The symbol that the *symbol_name* argument specifies must be defined.

Cross References

- **ompd_address_t**, see Section 5.3.4 on page 538.
- **ompd_address_space_context_t**, see Section 5.3.11 on page 542.
- **ompd_thread_context_t**, see Section 5.3.11 on page 542.
- **ompd_rc_t**, see Section 5.3.12 on page 543.
- **ompd_callbacks_t**, see Section 5.4.6 on page 556.

5.4.3.2 ompd_callback_memory_read_fn_t

Summary

The **ompd_callback_memory_read_fn_t** type is the type signature of the callback that the tool provides to read data from an OpenMP program.

Format

```c
typedef ompd_rc_t (*ompd_callback_memory_read_fn_t) (
    ompd_address_space_context_t *address_space_context,
    ompd_thread_context_t *thread_context,
    const ompd_address_t *addr,
    ompd_size_t nbytes,
    void *buffer
);
```

Description

The `ompd_callback_memory_read_fn_t` is the type signature of the read callback routines that the tool provides.

The `read_memory` callback copies a block of data from *addr* within the address space to the tool *buffer*.

The `read_string` callback copies a string to which *addr* points, including the terminating null byte ('\0'), to the tool *buffer*. At most *nbytes* bytes are copied. If a null byte is not among the first *nbytes* bytes, the string placed in *buffer* is not null-terminated.

Description of Arguments

The address from which the data are to be read from the OpenMP program specified by *address_space_context* is given by *addr*. while *nbytes* gives the number of bytes to be transferred. The *thread_context* argument is optional for global memory access, and in this case should be NULL. If it is non-null, *thread_context* identifies the thread specific context for the memory access for the purpose of accessing thread local storage.

The data are returned through *buffer*, which is allocated and owned by the OMPD library. The contents of the buffer are unstructured, raw bytes. The OMPD library must arrange for any transformations such as byte-swapping that may be necessary (see Section 5.4.4 on page 554) to interpret the data.

Cross References

- `ompd_size_t`, see Section 5.3.1 on page 536.
- `ompd_address_t`, see Section 5.3.4 on page 538.
- `ompd_address_space_context_t`, see Section 5.3.11 on page 542.
- `ompd_thread_context_t`, see Section 5.3.11 on page 542.
- `ompd_rc_t`, see Section 5.3.12 on page 543.
- `ompd_callback_device_host_fn_t`, see Section 5.4.4 on page 554.
- `ompd_callbacks_t`, see Section 5.4.6 on page 556.

5.4.3.3 ompd_callback_memory_write_fn_t

Summary

The `ompd_callback_memory_write_fn_t` type is the type signature of the callback that the tool provides to write data to an OpenMP program.

Format

```c
typedef ompd_rc_t (*ompd_callback_memory_write_fn_t) (
    ompd_address_space_context_t *address_space_context,
    ompd_thread_context_t *thread_context,
    const ompd_address_t *addr,
    ompd_size_t nbytes,
    const void *buffer
);
```

Description

The `ompd_callback_memory_write_fn_t` is the type signature of the write callback routine that the tool provides. The OMPD library may call this callback to have the tool write a block of data to a location within an address space from a provided buffer.

Description of Arguments

The address to which the data are to be written in the OpenMP program that *address_space_context* specifies is given by *addr*. The *nbytes* argument is the number of bytes to be transferred. The *thread_context* argument is optional for global memory access, and, in this case, should be NULL. If it is non-null then *thread_context* identifies the thread-specific context for the memory access for the purpose of accessing thread local storage.

The data to be written are passed through *buffer*, which is allocated and owned by the OMPD library. The contents of the buffer are unstructured, raw bytes. The OMPD library must arrange for any transformations such as byte-swapping that may be necessary (see Section 5.4.4 on page 554) to render the data into a form that is compatible with the OpenMP runtime.

Cross References

- `ompd_size_t`, see Section 5.3.1 on page 536.
- `ompd_address_t`, see Section 5.3.4 on page 538.
- `ompd_address_space_context_t`, see Section 5.3.11 on page 542.
- `ompd_thread_context_t`, see Section 5.3.11 on page 542.
- `ompd_rc_t`, see Section 5.3.12 on page 543.
- `ompd_callback_device_host_fn_t`, see Section 5.4.4 on page 554.
- `ompd_callbacks_t`, see Section 5.4.6 on page 556.

5.4.4 Data Format Conversion: `ompd_callback_device_host_fn_t`

Summary

The `ompd_callback_device_host_fn_t` type is the type signature of the callback that the tool provides to convert data between the formats that the tool and the OMPD library use and that the OpenMP program uses.

Format

```c
typedef ompd_rc_t (*ompd_callback_device_host_fn_t) (
    ompd_address_space_context_t *address_space_context,
    const void *input,
    ompd_size_t unit_size,
    ompd_size_t count,
    void *output
);
```

Description

The architecture and/or programming-model of the tool and the OMPD library may be different from that of the OpenMP program that is being examined. Thus, the conventions for representing data may differ. The callback interface includes operations to convert between the conventions, such as the byte order (endianness), that the tool and OMPD library use and the one that the OpenMP program uses. The callback with the **ompd_callback_device_host_fn_t** type signature convert data between formats

Description of Arguments

The *address_space_context* argument specifies the OpenMP address space that is associated with the data. The *input* argument is the source buffer and the *output* argument is the destination buffer. The *unit_size* argument is the size of each of the elements to be converted. The *count* argument is the number of elements to be transformed.

The OMPD library allocates and owns the input and output buffers. It must ensure that the buffers have the correct size, and are eventually deallocated when they are no longer needed.

Cross References

- **ompd_size_t**, see Section 5.3.1 on page 536.
- **ompd_address_space_context_t**, see Section 5.3.11 on page 542.
- **ompd_rc_t**, see Section 5.3.12 on page 543.
- **ompd_callbacks_t**, see Section 5.4.6 on page 556.

5.4.5 Output: `ompd_callback_print_string_fn_t`

Summary

The `ompd_callback_print_string_fn_t` type is the type signature of the callback that tool provides so that the OMPD library can emit output.

Format

```c
typedef ompd_rc_t (*ompd_callback_print_string_fn_t) (
  const char *string,
  int category
);
```

Description

The OMPD library may call the `ompd_callback_print_string_fn_t` callback function to emit output, such as logging or debug information. The tool may set the `ompd_callback_print_string_fn_t` callback function to NULL to prevent the OMPD library from emitting output; the OMPD may not write to file descriptors that it did not open.

Description of Arguments

The *string* argument is the null-terminated string to be printed. No conversion or formatting is performed on the string.

The *category* argument is the implementation-defined category of the string to be printed.

Cross References

- `ompd_rc_t`, see Section 5.3.12 on page 543.
- `ompd_callbacks_t`, see Section 5.4.6 on page 556.

5.4.6 The Callback Interface

Summary

All OMPD library interactions with the OpenMP program must be through a set of callbacks that the tool provides. These callbacks must also be used for allocating or releasing resources, such as memory, that the library needs.

Format

```
typedef struct ompd_callbacks_t {
    ompd_callback_memory_alloc_fn_t alloc_memory;
    ompd_callback_memory_free_fn_t free_memory;
    ompd_callback_print_string_fn_t print_string;
    ompd_callback_sizeof_fn_t sizeof_type;
    ompd_callback_symbol_addr_fn_t symbol_addr_lookup;
    ompd_callback_memory_read_fn_t read_memory;
    ompd_callback_memory_write_fn_t write_memory;
    ompd_callback_memory_read_fn_t read_string;
    ompd_callback_device_host_fn_t device_to_host;
    ompd_callback_device_host_fn_t host_to_device;
    ompd_callback_get_thread_context_for_thread_id_fn_t
        get_thread_context_for_thread_id;
} ompd_callbacks_t;
```

Description

The set of callbacks that the OMPD library must use is collected in the **ompd_callbacks_t** record structure. An instance of this type is passed to the OMPD library as a parameter to **ompd_initialize** (see Section 5.5.1.1 on page 558). Each field points to a function that the OMPD library must use to interact with the OpenMP program or for memory operations.

The *alloc_memory* and *free_memory* fields are pointers to functions the OMPD library uses to allocate and to release dynamic memory.

print_string points to a function that prints a string.

The architectures or programming models of the OMPD library and third party tool may be different from that of the OpenMP program that is being examined. *sizeof_type* points to function that allows the OMPD library to determine the sizes of the basic integer and pointer types that the OpenMP program uses. Because of the differences in architecture or programming model, the conventions for representing data in the OMPD library and the OpenMP program may be different. The *device_to_host* field points to a function that translates data from the conventions that the OpenMP program uses to those that the tool and OMPD library use. The reverse operation is performed by the function to which the *host_to_device* field points.

The *symbol_addr_lookup* field points to a callback that the OMPD library can use to find the address of a global or thread local storage symbol. The *read_memory*, *read_string*, and *write_memory* fields are pointers to functions for reading from and writing to global memory or thread local storage in the OpenMP program.

The *get_thread_context_for_thread_id* field is a pointer to a function that the OMPD library can use to obtain a thread context that corresponds to a native thread identifier.

Cross References

- `ompd_callback_memory_alloc_fn_t`, see Section 5.4.1.1 on page 546.
- `ompd_callback_memory_free_fn_t`, see Section 5.4.1.2 on page 546.
- `ompd_callback_get_thread_context_for_thread_id_fn_t`, see Section 5.4.2.1 on page 547.
- `ompd_callback_sizeof_fn_t`, see Section 5.4.2.2 on page 549.
- `ompd_callback_symbol_addr_fn_t`, see Section 5.4.3.1 on page 550.
- `ompd_callback_memory_read_fn_t`, see Section 5.4.3.2 on page 551.
- `ompd_callback_memory_write_fn_t`, see Section 5.4.3.3 on page 553.
- `ompd_callback_device_host_fn_t`, see Section 5.4.4 on page 554.
- `ompd_callback_print_string_fn_t`, see Section 5.4.5 on page 556

5.5 OMPD Tool Interface Routines

5.5.1 Per OMPD Library Initialization and Finalization

The OMPD library must be initialized exactly once after it is loaded, and finalized exactly once before it is unloaded. Per OpenMP process or core file initialization and finalization are also required.

Once loaded, the tool can determine the version of the OMPD API that the library supports by calling **ompd_get_api_version** (see Section 5.5.1.2 on page 559). If the tool supports the version that **ompd_get_api_version** returns, the tool starts the initialization by calling **ompd_initialize** (see Section 5.5.1.1 on page 558) using the version of the OMPD API that the library supports. If the tool does not support the version that **ompd_get_api_version** returns, it may attempt to call **ompd_initialize** with a different version.

5.5.1.1 ompd_initialize

Summary

The **ompd_initialize** function initializes the OMPD library.

Format

```c
ompd_rc_t ompd_initialize(
    ompd_word_t api_version,
    const ompd_callbacks_t *callbacks
);
```

Description

A tool that uses OMPD calls **ompd_initialize** to initialize each OMPD library that it loads. More than one library may be present in a third-party tool, such as a debugger, because the tool may control multiple devices, which may use different runtime systems that require different OMPD libraries. This initialization must be performed exactly once before the tool can begin to operate on an OpenMP process or core file.

Description of Arguments

The *api_version* argument is the OMPD API version that the tool requests to use. The tool may call **ompd_get_api_version** to obtain the latest version that the OMPD library supports.

The tool provides the OMPD library with a set of callback functions in the *callbacks* input argument which enables the OMPD library to allocate and to deallocate memory in the tool's address space, to lookup the sizes of basic primitive types in the device, to lookup symbols in the device, and to read and to write memory in the device.

Cross References

- **ompd_rc_t** type, see Section 5.3.12 on page 543.
- **ompd_callbacks_t** type, see Section 5.4.6 on page 556.
- **ompd_get_api_version** call, see Section 5.5.1.2 on page 559.

5.5.1.2 ompd_get_api_version

Summary

The **ompd_get_api_version** function returns the OMPD API version.

Format

```c
ompd_rc_t ompd_get_api_version(ompd_word_t *version);
```

Description

The tool may call the `ompd_get_api_version` function to obtain the latest OMPD API version number of the OMPD library.

Description of Arguments

The latest version number is returned into the location to which the *version* argument points.

Cross References

- `ompd_rc_t` type, see Section 5.3.12 on page 543.

5.5.1.3 ompd_get_version_string

Summary

The `ompd_get_version_string` function returns a descriptive string for the OMPD API version.

Format

```c
ompd_rc_t ompd_get_version_string(const char **string);
```

Description

The tool may call this function to obtain a pointer to a descriptive version string of the OMPD API version.

Description of Arguments

A pointer to a descriptive version string is placed into the location to which *string* output argument points. The OMPD library owns the string that the OMPD library returns; the tool must not modify or release this string. The string remains valid for as long as the library is loaded. The **ompd_get_version_string** function may be called before **ompd_initialize** (see Section 5.5.1.1 on page 558). Accordingly, the OMPD library must not use heap or stack memory for the string.

The signatures of **ompd_get_api_version** (see Section 5.5.1.2 on page 559) and **ompd_get_version_string** are guaranteed not to change in future versions of the API. In contrast, the type definitions and prototypes in the rest of the API do not carry the same guarantee. Therefore a tool that uses OMPD should check the version of the API of the loaded OMPD library before it calls any other function of the API.

Cross References

- **ompd_rc_t** type, see Section 5.3.12 on page 543.

5.5.1.4 ompd_finalize

Summary

When the tool is finished with the OMPD library it should call **ompd_finalize** before it unloads the library.

Format

```c
ompd_rc_t ompd_finalize(void);
```

Description

The call to **ompd_finalize** must be the last OMPD call that the tool makes before it unloads the library. This call allows the OMPD library to free any resources that it may be holding.

The OMPD library may implement a *finalizer* section, which executes as the library is unloaded and therefore after the call to **ompd_finalize**. During finalization, the OMPD library may use the callbacks that the tool earlier provided after the call to **ompd_initialize**.

Cross References

- **ompd_rc_t** type, see Section 5.3.12 on page 543.

5.5.2 Per OpenMP Process Initialization and Finalization

5.5.2.1 ompd_process_initialize

Summary

A tool calls **ompd_process_initialize** to obtain an address space handle when it initializes a session on a live process or core file.

Format

```c
ompd_rc_t ompd_process_initialize(
    ompd_address_space_context_t *context,
    ompd_address_space_handle_t **handle
);
```

Description

A tool calls **ompd_process_initialize** to obtain an address space handle when it initializes a session on a live process or core file. On return from **ompd_process_initialize**, the tool owns the address space handle, which it must release with **ompd_rel_address_space_handle**. The initialization function must be called before any OMPD operations are performed on the OpenMP process. This call allows the OMPD library to confirm that it can handle the OpenMP process or core file that the *context* identifies. Incompatibility is signaled by a return value of **ompd_rc_incompatible**.

Description of Arguments

The *context* argument is an opaque handle that the tool provides to address an address space. On return, the *handle* argument provides an opaque handle to the tool for this address space, which the tool must release when it is no longer needed.

Cross References

- `ompd_address_space_handle_t` type, see Section 5.3.8 on page 540.
- `ompd_address_space_context_t` type, see Section 5.3.11 on page 542.
- `ompd_rc_t` type, see Section 5.3.12 on page 543.
- `ompd_rel_address_space_handle` type, see Section 5.5.2.3 on page 564.

5.5.2.2 ompd_device_initialize

Summary

A tool calls **ompd_device_initialize** to obtain an address space handle for a device that has at least one active target region.

Format

```c
ompd_rc_t ompd_device_initialize(
    ompd_address_space_handle_t *process_handle,
    ompd_address_space_context_t *device_context,
    ompd_device_t kind,
    ompd_size_t sizeof_id,
    void *id,
    ompd_address_space_handle_t **device_handle
);
```

Description

A tool calls **ompd_device_initialize** to obtain an address space handle for a device that has at least one active target region. On return from **ompd_device_initialize**, the tool owns the address space handle.

Description of Arguments

The *process_handle* argument is an opaque handle that the tool provides to reference the address space of the OpenMP process. The *device_context* argument is an opaque handle that the tool provides to reference a device address space. The *kind*, *sizeof_id*, and *id* arguments represent a device identifier. On return the *device_handle* argument provides an opaque handle to the tool for this address space.

Cross References

- `ompd_size_t` type, see Section 5.3.1 on page 536.
- `ompd_device_t` type, see Section 5.3.6 on page 539.
- `ompd_address_space_handle_t` type, see Section 5.3.8 on page 540.
- `ompd_address_space_context_t` type, see Section 5.3.11 on page 542.
- `ompd_rc_t` type, see Section 5.3.12 on page 543.

5.5.2.3 ompd_rel_address_space_handle

Summary

A tool calls `ompd_rel_address_space_handle` to release an address space handle.

Format

```c
ompd_rc_t ompd_rel_address_space_handle(
    ompd_address_space_handle_t *handle
);
```

Description

When the tool is finished with the OpenMP process address space handle it should call `ompd_rel_address_space_handle` to release the handle, which allows the OMPD library to release any resources that it has related to the address space.

Description of Arguments

The *handle* argument is an opaque handle for the address space to be released.

Restrictions

The `ompd_rel_address_space_handle` has the following restriction:

- An address space context must not be used after the corresponding address space handle is released.

Cross References

- `ompd_address_space_handle_t` type, see Section 5.3.8 on page 540.
- `ompd_rc_t` type, see Section 5.3.12 on page 543.

5.5.3 Thread and Signal Safety

The OMPD library does not need to be reentrant. The tool must ensure that only one thread enters the OMPD library at a time. The OMPD library must not install signal handlers or otherwise interfere with the tool's signal configuration.

5.5.4 Address Space Information

5.5.4.1 ompd_get_omp_version

Summary

The tool may call the **ompd_get_omp_version** function to obtain the version of the OpenMP API that is associated with an address space.

Format

```c
ompd_rc_t ompd_get_omp_version(
    ompd_address_space_handle_t *address_space,
    ompd_word_t *omp_version
);
```

Description

The tool may call the **ompd_get_omp_version** function to obtain the version of the OpenMP API that is associated with the address space.

Description of Arguments

The *address_space* argument is an opaque handle that the tool provides to reference the address space of the OpenMP process or device.

Upon return, the *omp_version* argument contains the version of the OpenMP runtime in the `_OPENMP` version macro format.

Cross References

- `ompd_address_space_handle_t` type, see Section 5.3.8 on page 540.
- `ompd_rc_t` type, see Section 5.3.12 on page 543.

5.5.4.2 `ompd_get_omp_version_string`

Summary

The `ompd_get_omp_version_string` function returns a descriptive string for the OpenMP API version that is associated with an address space.

Format

```c
ompd_rc_t ompd_get_omp_version_string(
  ompd_address_space_handle_t *address_space,
  const char **string
);
```

Description

After initialization, the tool may call the `ompd_get_omp_version_string` function to obtain the version of the OpenMP API that is associated with an address space.

Description of Arguments

The *address_space* argument is an opaque handle that the tool provides to reference the address space of the OpenMP process or device. A pointer to a descriptive version string is placed into the location to which the *string* output argument points. After returning from the call, the tool owns the string. The OMPD library must use the memory allocation callback that the tool provides to allocate the string storage. The tool is responsible for releasing the memory.

Cross References

- `ompd_address_space_handle_t` type, see Section 5.3.8 on page 540.
- `ompd_rc_t` type, see Section 5.3.12 on page 543.

5.5.5 Thread Handles

5.5.5.1 ompd_get_thread_in_parallel

Summary

The `ompd_get_thread_in_parallel` function enables a tool to obtain handles for OpenMP threads that are associated with a parallel region.

Format

```c
ompd_rc_t ompd_get_thread_in_parallel(
    ompd_parallel_handle_t *parallel_handle,
    int thread_num,
    ompd_thread_handle_t **thread_handle
);
```

Description

A successful invocation of `ompd_get_thread_in_parallel` returns a pointer to a thread handle in the location to which `thread_handle` points. This call yields meaningful results only if all OpenMP threads in the parallel region are stopped.

Description of Arguments

The *parallel_handle* argument is an opaque handle for a parallel region and selects the parallel region on which to operate. The *thread_num* argument selects the thread of the team to be returned. On return, the *thread_handle* argument is an opaque handle for the selected thread.

Restrictions

The `ompd_get_thread_in_parallel` function has the following restriction:

- The value of *thread_num* must be a non-negative integer smaller than the team size that was provided as the *ompd-team-size-var* from `ompd_get_icv_from_scope`.

Cross References

- `ompd_parallel_handle_t` type, see Section 5.3.8 on page 540.
- `ompd_thread_handle_t` type, see Section 5.3.8 on page 540.
- `ompd_rc_t` type, see Section 5.3.12 on page 543.
- `ompd_get_icv_from_scope` call, see Section 5.5.9.2 on page 590.

5.5.5.2 ompd_get_thread_handle

Summary

The `ompd_get_thread_handle` function maps a native thread to an OMPD thread handle.

Format

```c
ompd_rc_t ompd_get_thread_handle(
    ompd_address_space_handle_t *handle,
    ompd_thread_id_t kind,
    ompd_size_t sizeof_thread_id,
    const void *thread_id,
    ompd_thread_handle_t **thread_handle
);
```

Description

The `ompd_get_thread_handle` function determines if the native thread identifier to which *thread_id* points represents an OpenMP thread. If so, the function returns `ompd_rc_ok` and the location to which *thread_handle* points is set to the thread handle for the OpenMP thread.

Description of Arguments

The *handle* argument is an opaque handle that the tool provides to reference an address space. The *kind*, *sizeof_thread_id*, and *thread_id* arguments represent a native thread identifier. On return, the *thread_handle* argument provides an opaque handle to the thread within the provided address space.

The native thread identifier to which *thread_id* points is guaranteed to be valid for the duration of the call. If the OMPD library must retain the native thread identifier, it must copy it.

Cross References

- `ompd_size_t` type, see Section 5.3.1 on page 536.
- `ompd_thread_id_t` type, see Section 5.3.7 on page 539.
- `ompd_address_space_handle_t` type, see Section 5.3.8 on page 540.
- `ompd_thread_handle_t` type, see Section 5.3.8 on page 540.
- `ompd_rc_t` type, see Section 5.3.12 on page 543.

5.5.5.3 ompd_rel_thread_handle

Summary

The `ompd_rel_thread_handle` function releases a thread handle.

Format

```c
ompd_rc_t ompd_rel_thread_handle(
    ompd_thread_handle_t *thread_handle
);
```

Description

Thread handles are opaque to tools, which therefore cannot release them directly. Instead, when the tool is finished with a thread handle it must pass it to `ompd_rel_thread_handle` for disposal.

Description of Arguments

The *thread_handle* argument is an opaque handle for a thread to be released.

Cross References

- `ompd_thread_handle_t` type, see Section 5.3.8 on page 540.
- `ompd_rc_t` type, see Section 5.3.12 on page 543.

5.5.5.4 ompd_thread_handle_compare

Summary

The `ompd_thread_handle_compare` function allows tools to compare two thread handles.

Format

```c
ompd_rc_t ompd_thread_handle_compare(
  ompd_thread_handle_t *thread_handle_1,
  ompd_thread_handle_t *thread_handle_2,
  int *cmp_value
);
```

Description

The internal structure of thread handles is opaque to a tool. While the tool can easily compare pointers to thread handles, it cannot determine whether handles of two different addresses refer to the same underlying thread. The `ompd_thread_handle_compare` function compares thread handles.

On success, `ompd_thread_handle_compare` returns in the location to which *cmp_value* points a signed integer value that indicates how the underlying threads compare: a value less than, equal to, or greater than 0 indicates that the thread corresponding to *thread_handle_1* is, respectively, less than, equal to, or greater than that corresponding to *thread_handle_2*.

Description of Arguments

The *thread_handle_1* and *thread_handle_2* arguments are opaque handles for threads. On return the *cmp_value* argument is set to a signed integer value.

Cross References

- `ompd_thread_handle_t` type, see Section 5.3.8 on page 540.
- `ompd_rc_t` type, see Section 5.3.12 on page 543.

5.5.5.5 ompd_get_thread_id

Summary

The `ompd_get_thread_id` maps an OMPD thread handle to a native thread.

Format

```c
ompd_rc_t ompd_get_thread_id(
    ompd_thread_handle_t *thread_handle,
    ompd_thread_id_t kind,
    ompd_size_t sizeof_thread_id,
    void *thread_id
);
```

Description

The `ompd_get_thread_id` function maps an OMPD thread handle to a native thread identifier.

Description of Arguments

The *thread_handle* argument is an opaque thread handle. The *kind* argument represents the native thread identifier. The *sizeof_thread_id* argument represents the size of the native thread identifier. On return, the *thread_id* argument is a buffer that represents a native thread identifier.

Cross References

- `ompd_size_t` type, see Section 5.3.1 on page 536.
- `ompd_thread_id_t` type, see Section 5.3.7 on page 539.
- `ompd_thread_handle_t` type, see Section 5.3.8 on page 540.
- `ompd_rc_t` type, see Section 5.3.12 on page 543.

5.5.6 Parallel Region Handles

5.5.6.1 ompd_get_curr_parallel_handle

Summary

The `ompd_get_curr_parallel_handle` function obtains a pointer to the parallel handle for an OpenMP thread's current parallel region.

Format

```c
ompd_rc_t ompd_get_curr_parallel_handle(
    ompd_thread_handle_t *thread_handle,
    ompd_parallel_handle_t **parallel_handle
);
```

Description

The `ompd_get_curr_parallel_handle` function enables the tool to obtain a pointer to the parallel handle for the current parallel region that is associated with an OpenMP thread. This call is meaningful only if the associated thread is stopped. The parallel handle must be released by calling `ompd_rel_parallel_handle`.

Description of Arguments

The *thread_handle* argument is an opaque handle for a thread and selects the thread on which to operate. On return, the *parallel_handle* argument is set to a handle for the parallel region that the associated thread is currently executing, if any.

Cross References

- `ompd_thread_handle_t` type, see Section 5.3.8 on page 540.
- `ompd_parallel_handle_t` type, see Section 5.3.8 on page 540.
- `ompd_rc_t` type, see Section 5.3.12 on page 543.
- `ompd_rel_parallel_handle` call, see Section 5.5.6.4 on page 574.

5.5.6.2 ompd_get_enclosing_parallel_handle

Summary

The `ompd_get_enclosing_parallel_handle` function obtains a pointer to the parallel handle for an enclosing parallel region.

Format

```c
ompd_rc_t ompd_get_enclosing_parallel_handle(
    ompd_parallel_handle_t *parallel_handle,
    ompd_parallel_handle_t **enclosing_parallel_handle
);
```

Description

The `ompd_get_enclosing_parallel_handle` function enables a tool to obtain a pointer to the parallel handle for the parallel region that encloses the parallel region that `parallel_handle` specifies. This call is meaningful only if at least one thread in the parallel region is stopped. A pointer to the parallel handle for the enclosing region is returned in the location to which *enclosing_parallel_handle* points. After the call, the tool owns the handle; the tool must release the handle with `ompd_rel_parallel_handle` when it is no longer required.

Description of Arguments

The *parallel_handle* argument is an opaque handle for a parallel region that selects the parallel region on which to operate. On return, the *enclosing_parallel_handle* argument is set to a handle for the parallel region that encloses the selected parallel region.

Cross References

- `ompd_parallel_handle_t` type, see Section 5.3.8 on page 540.
- `ompd_rc_t` type, see Section 5.3.12 on page 543.
- `ompd_rel_parallel_handle` call, see Section 5.5.6.4 on page 574.

5.5.6.3 ompd_get_task_parallel_handle

Summary

The `ompd_get_task_parallel_handle` function obtains a pointer to the parallel handle for the parallel region that encloses a task region.

Format

```c
ompd_rc_t ompd_get_task_parallel_handle(
    ompd_task_handle_t *task_handle,
    ompd_parallel_handle_t **task_parallel_handle
);
```

Description

The `ompd_get_task_parallel_handle` function enables a tool to obtain a pointer to the parallel handle for the parallel region that encloses the task region that *task_handle* specifies. This call is meaningful only if at least one thread in the parallel region is stopped. A pointer to the parallel regions handle is returned in the location to which *task_parallel_handle* points. The tool owns that parallel handle, which it must release with `ompd_rel_parallel_handle`.

Description of Arguments

The *task_handle* argument is an opaque handle that selects the task on which to operate. On return, the *parallel_handle* argument is set to a handle for the parallel region that encloses the selected task.

Cross References

- `ompd_task_handle_t` type, see Section 5.3.8 on page 540.
- `ompd_parallel_handle_t` type, see Section 5.3.8 on page 540.
- `ompd_rc_t` type, see Section 5.3.12 on page 543.
- `ompd_rel_parallel_handle` call, see Section 5.5.6.4 on page 574.

5.5.6.4 ompd_rel_parallel_handle

Summary

The `ompd_rel_parallel_handle` function releases a parallel region handle.

Format

```c
ompd_rc_t ompd_rel_parallel_handle(
    ompd_parallel_handle_t *parallel_handle
);
```

Description

Parallel region handles are opaque so tools cannot release them directly. Instead, a tool must pass a parallel region handle to the `ompd_rel_parallel_handle` function for disposal when finished with it.

Description of Arguments

The *parallel_handle* argument is an opaque handle to be released.

Cross References

- `ompd_parallel_handle_t` type, see Section 5.3.8 on page 540.
- `ompd_rc_t` type, see Section 5.3.12 on page 543.

5.5.6.5 ompd_parallel_handle_compare

Summary

The `ompd_parallel_handle_compare` function compares two parallel region handles.

Format

```c
ompd_rc_t ompd_parallel_handle_compare(
  ompd_parallel_handle_t *parallel_handle_1,
  ompd_parallel_handle_t *parallel_handle_2,
  int *cmp_value
);
```

Description

The internal structure of parallel region handles is opaque to tools. While tools can easily compare pointers to parallel region handles, they cannot determine whether handles at two different addresses refer to the same underlying parallel region and, instead must use the `ompd_parallel_handle_compare` function.

On success, `ompd_parallel_handle_compare` returns a signed integer value in the location to which *cmp_value* points that indicates how the underlying parallel regions compare. A value less than, equal to, or greater than 0 indicates that the region corresponding to *parallel_handle_1* is, respectively, less than, equal to, or greater than that corresponding to *parallel_handle_2*. This function is provided since the means by which parallel region handles are ordered is implementation defined.

Description of Arguments

The *parallel_handle_1* and *parallel_handle_2* arguments are opaque handles that correspond to parallel regions. On return the *cmp_value* argument points to a signed integer value that indicates how the underlying parallel regions compare.

Cross References

- `ompd_parallel_handle_t` type, see Section 5.3.8 on page 540.
- `ompd_rc_t` type, see Section 5.3.12 on page 543.

5.5.7 Task Handles

5.5.7.1 ompd_get_curr_task_handle

Summary

The `ompd_get_curr_task_handle` function obtains a pointer to the task handle for the current task region that is associated with an OpenMP thread.

Format

```C
ompd_rc_t ompd_get_curr_task_handle(
  ompd_thread_handle_t *thread_handle,
  ompd_task_handle_t **task_handle
);
```

Description

The `ompd_get_curr_task_handle` function obtains a pointer to the task handle for the current task region that is associated with an OpenMP thread. This call is meaningful only if the thread for which the handle is provided is stopped. The task handle must be released with `ompd_rel_task_handle`.

Description of Arguments

The *thread_handle* argument is an opaque handle that selects the thread on which to operate. On return, the *task_handle* argument points to a location that points to a handle for the task that the thread is currently executing.

Cross References

- `ompd_thread_handle_t` type, see Section 5.3.8 on page 540.
- `ompd_task_handle_t` type, see Section 5.3.8 on page 540.
- `ompd_rc_t` type, see Section 5.3.12 on page 543.
- `ompd_rel_task_handle` call, see Section 5.5.7.5 on page 580.

5.5.7.2 `ompd_get_generating_task_handle`

Summary

The `ompd_get_generating_task_handle` function obtains a pointer to the task handle of the generating task region.

Format

```c
ompd_rc_t ompd_get_generating_task_handle(
  ompd_task_handle_t *task_handle,
  ompd_task_handle_t **generating_task_handle
);
```

Description

The `ompd_get_generating_task_handle` function obtains a pointer to the task handle for the task that encountered the OpenMP task construct that generated the task represented by *task_handle*. The generating task is the OpenMP task that was active when the task specified by *task_handle* was created. This call is meaningful only if the thread that is executing the task that *task_handle* specifies is stopped. The generating task handle must be released with `ompd_rel_task_handle`.

Description of Arguments

The *task_handle* argument is an opaque handle that selects the task on which to operate. On return, the *generating_task_handle* argument points to a location that points to a handle for the generating task.

Cross References

- `ompd_task_handle_t` type, see Section 5.3.8 on page 540.
- `ompd_rc_t` type, see Section 5.3.12 on page 543.
- `ompd_rel_task_handle` call, see Section 5.5.7.5 on page 580.

5.5.7.3 ompd_get_scheduling_task_handle

Summary

The `ompd_get_scheduling_task_handle` function obtains a task handle for the task that was active at a task scheduling point.

Format

```c
ompd_rc_t ompd_get_scheduling_task_handle(
    ompd_task_handle_t *task_handle,
    ompd_task_handle_t **scheduling_task_handle
);
```

Description

The `ompd_get_scheduling_task_handle` function obtains a task handle for the task that was active when the task that *task_handle* represents was scheduled. This call is meaningful only if the thread that is executing the task that *task_handle* specifies is stopped. The scheduling task handle must be released with `ompd_rel_task_handle`.

Description of Arguments

The *task_handle* argument is an opaque handle for a task and selects the task on which to operate. On return, the *scheduling_task_handle* argument points to a location that points to a handle for the task that is still on the stack of execution on the same thread and was deferred in favor of executing the selected task.

Cross References

- `ompd_task_handle_t` type, see Section 5.3.8 on page 540.
- `ompd_rc_t` type, see Section 5.3.12 on page 543.
- `ompd_rel_task_handle` call, see Section 5.5.7.5 on page 580.

5.5.7.4 ompd_get_task_in_parallel

Summary
The **ompd_get_task_in_parallel** function obtains handles for the implicit tasks that are associated with a parallel region.

Format
```c
ompd_rc_t ompd_get_task_in_parallel(
  ompd_parallel_handle_t *parallel_handle,
  int thread_num,
  ompd_task_handle_t **task_handle
);
```

Description
The **ompd_get_task_in_parallel** function obtains handles for the implicit tasks that are associated with a parallel region. A successful invocation of **ompd_get_task_in_parallel** returns a pointer to a task handle in the location to which *task_handle* points. This call yields meaningful results only if all OpenMP threads in the parallel region are stopped.

Description of Arguments
The *parallel_handle* argument is an opaque handle that selects the parallel region on which to operate. The *thread_num* argument selects the implicit task of the team that is returned. The selected implicit task would return *thread_num* from a call of the **omp_get_thread_num()** routine. On return, the *task_handle* argument points to a location that points to an opaque handle for the selected implicit task.

Restrictions
The following restriction applies to the **ompd_get_task_in_parallel** function:

- The value of *thread_num* must be a non-negative integer that is smaller than the size of the team size that is the value of the *ompd-team-size-var* that **ompd_get_icv_from_scope** returns.

Cross References

- `ompd_parallel_handle_t` type, see Section 5.3.8 on page 540.
- `ompd_task_handle_t` type, see Section 5.3.8 on page 540.
- `ompd_rc_t` type, see Section 5.3.12 on page 543.
- `ompd_get_icv_from_scope` call, see Section 5.5.9.2 on page 590.

5.5.7.5 ompd_rel_task_handle

Summary

This `ompd_rel_task_handle` function releases a task handle.

Format

```C
ompd_rc_t ompd_rel_task_handle(
    ompd_task_handle_t *task_handle
);
```

Description

Task handles are opaque so tools cannot release them directly. Instead, when a tool is finished with a task handle it must use the `ompd_rel_task_handle` function to release it.

Description of Arguments

The *task_handle* argument is an opaque task handle to be released.

Cross References

- `ompd_task_handle_t` type, see Section 5.3.8 on page 540.
- `ompd_rc_t` type, see Section 5.3.12 on page 543.

5.5.7.6 ompd_task_handle_compare

Summary

The `ompd_task_handle_compare` function compares task handles.

Format

```c
ompd_rc_t ompd_task_handle_compare(
    ompd_task_handle_t *task_handle_1,
    ompd_task_handle_t *task_handle_2,
    int *cmp_value
);
```

Description

The internal structure of task handles is opaque so tools cannot directly determine if handles at two different addresses refer to the same underlying task. The **ompd_task_handle_compare** function compares task handles. After a successful call to **ompd_task_handle_compare**, the value of the location to which *cmp_value* points is a signed integer that indicates how the underlying tasks compare: a value less than, equal to, or greater than 0 indicates that the task that corresponds to *task_handle_1* is, respectively, less than, equal to, or greater than the task that corresponds to *task_handle_2*. The means by which task handles are ordered is implementation defined.

Description of Arguments

The *task_handle_1* and *task_handle_2* arguments are opaque handles that correspond to tasks. On return, the *cmp_value* argument points to a location in which a signed integer value indicates how the underlying tasks compare.

Cross References

- **ompd_task_handle_t** type, see Section 5.3.8 on page 540.
- **ompd_rc_t** type, see Section 5.3.12 on page 543.

5.5.7.7 ompd_get_task_function

Summary

This **ompd_get_task_function** function returns the entry point of the code that corresponds to the body of a task.

Format

```C
ompd_rc_t ompd_get_task_function (
    ompd_task_handle_t *task_handle,
    ompd_address_t *entry_point
);
```

Description

The `ompd_get_task_function` function returns the entry point of the code that corresponds to the body of code that the task executes.

Description of Arguments

The *task_handle* argument is an opaque handle that selects the task on which to operate. On return, the *entry_point* argument is set to an address that describes the beginning of application code that executes the task region.

Cross References

- `ompd_address_t` type, see Section 5.3.4 on page 538.
- `ompd_task_handle_t` type, see Section 5.3.8 on page 540.
- `ompd_rc_t` type, see Section 5.3.12 on page 543.

5.5.7.8 ompd_get_task_frame

Summary

The `ompd_get_task_frame` function extracts the frame pointers of a task.

Format

```C
ompd_rc_t ompd_get_task_frame (
    ompd_task_handle_t *task_handle,
    ompd_frame_info_t *exit_frame,
    ompd_frame_info_t *enter_frame
);
```

Description

An OpenMP implementation maintains an **ompt_frame_t** object for every implicit or explicit task. The **ompd_get_task_frame** function extracts the *enter_frame* and *exit_frame* fields of the **ompt_frame_t** object of the task that *task_handle* identifies.

Description of Arguments

The *task_handle* argument specifies an OpenMP task. On return, the *exit_frame* argument points to an **ompd_frame_info_t** object that has the frame information with the same semantics as the *exit_frame* field in the **ompt_frame_t** object that is associated with the specified task. On return, the *enter_frame* argument points to an **ompd_frame_info_t** object that has the frame information with the same semantics as the *enter_frame* field in the **ompt_frame_t** object that is associated with the specified task.

Cross References

- **ompt_frame_t** type, see Section 4.4.4.27 on page 454.
- **ompd_address_t** type, see Section 5.3.4 on page 538.
- **ompd_frame_info_t** type, see Section 5.3.5 on page 538.
- **ompd_task_handle_t** type, see Section 5.3.8 on page 540.
- **ompd_rc_t** type, see Section 5.3.12 on page 543.

5.5.7.9 ompd_enumerate_states

Summary

The **ompd_enumerate_states** function enumerates thread states that an OpenMP implementation supports.

Format

```C
ompd_rc_t ompd_enumerate_states (
  ompd_address_space_handle_t *address_space_handle,
  ompd_word_t current_state,
  ompd_word_t *next_state,
  const char **next_state_name,
  ompd_word_t *more_enums
);
```

Description

An OpenMP implementation may support only a subset of the states that the `ompt_state_t` enumeration type defines. In addition, an OpenMP implementation may support implementation-specific states. The `ompd_enumerate_states` call enables a tool to enumerate the thread states that an OpenMP implementation supports.

When the *current_state* argument is a thread state that an OpenMP implementation supports, the call assigns the value and string name of the next thread state in the enumeration to the locations to which the *next_state* and *next_state_name* arguments point.

On return, the third-party tool owns the *next_state_name* string. The OMPD library allocates storage for the string with the memory allocation callback that the tool provides. The tool is responsible for releasing the memory.

On return, the location to which the *more_enums* argument points has the value 1 whenever one or more states are left in the enumeration. On return, the location to which the *more_enums* argument points has the value 0 when *current_state* is the last state in the enumeration.

Description of Arguments

The *address_space_handle* argument identifies the address space. The *current_state* argument must be a thread state that the OpenMP implementation supports. To begin enumerating the supported states, a tool should pass `ompt_state_undefined` as the value of *current_state*. Subsequent calls to `ompd_enumerate_states` by the tool should pass the value that the call returned in the *next_state* argument. On return, the *next_state* argument points to an integer with the value of the next state in the enumeration. On return, the *next_state_name* argument points to a character string that describes the next state. On return, the *more_enums* argument points to an integer with a value of 1 when more states are left to enumerate and a value of 0 when no more states are left.

Constraints on Arguments

Any string that is returned through the *next_state_name* argument must be immutable and defined for the lifetime of program execution.

Cross References

- `ompt_state_t` type, see Section 4.4.4.26 on page 452.
- `ompd_address_space_handle_t` type, see Section 5.3.8 on page 540.
- `ompd_rc_t` type, see Section 5.3.12 on page 543.

5.5.7.10 ompd_get_state

Summary

The **ompd_get_state** function obtains the state of a thread.

Format

```c
ompd_rc_t ompd_get_state (
    ompd_thread_handle_t *thread_handle,
    ompd_word_t *state,
    ompt_wait_id_t *wait_id
);
```

Description

The **ompd_get_state** function returns the state of an OpenMP thread.

Description of Arguments

The *thread_handle* argument identifies the thread. The *state* argument represents the state of that thread as represented by a value that **ompd_enumerate_states** returns. On return, if the *wait_id* argument is non-null then it points to a handle that corresponds to the *wait_id* wait identifier of the thread. If the thread state is not one of the specified wait states, the value to which *wait_id* points is undefined.

Cross References

- **ompd_wait_id_t** type, see Section 5.3.2 on page 537.
- **ompd_thread_handle_t** type, see Section 5.3.8 on page 540.
- **ompd_rc_t** type, see Section 5.3.12 on page 543.
- **ompd_enumerate_states** call, see Section 5.5.7.9 on page 583.

5.5.8 Display Control Variables

5.5.8.1 `ompd_get_display_control_vars`

Summary

The `ompd_get_display_control_vars` function returns a list of name/value pairs for OpenMP control variables.

Format

```c
ompd_rc_t ompd_get_display_control_vars (
  ompd_address_space_handle_t *address_space_handle,
  const char * const **control_vars
);
```

Description

The `ompd_get_display_control_vars` function returns a NULL-terminated vector of NULL-terminated strings of name/value pairs of control variables that have user controllable settings and are important to the operation or performance of an OpenMP runtime system. The control variables that this interface exposes include all OpenMP environment variables, settings that may come from vendor or platform-specific environment variables, and other settings that affect the operation or functioning of an OpenMP runtime.

The format of the strings is `name=a string`.

On return, the third-party tool owns the vector and the strings. The OMP library must satisfy the termination constraints; it may use static or dynamic memory for the vector and/or the strings and is unconstrained in how it arranges them in memory. If it uses dynamic memory then the OMPD library must use the allocate callback that the tool provides to `ompd_initialize`. The tool must use `ompd_rel_display_control_vars()` to release the vector and the strings.

Description of Arguments

The *address_space_handle* argument identifies the address space. On return, the *control_vars* argument points to the vector of display control variables.

Cross References

- `ompd_address_space_handle_t` type, see Section 5.3.8 on page 540.
- `ompd_rc_t` type, see Section 5.3.12 on page 543.
- `ompd_initialize` call, see Section 5.5.1.1 on page 558.
- `ompd_rel_display_control_vars` type, see Section 5.5.8.2 on page 587.

5.5.8.2 ompd_rel_display_control_vars

Summary

The `ompd_rel_display_control_vars` releases a list of name/value pairs of OpenMP control variables previously acquired with `ompd_get_display_control_vars`.

Format

```C
ompd_rc_t ompd_rel_display_control_vars (
    const char * const **control_vars
);
```

Description

The third-party tool owns the vector and strings that `ompd_get_display_control_vars` returns. The tool must call `ompd_rel_display_control_vars` to release the vector and the strings.

Description of Arguments

The *control_vars* argument is the vector of display control variables to be released.

Cross References

- `ompd_rc_t` type, see Section 5.3.12 on page 543.
- `ompd_get_display_control_vars` call, see Section 5.5.8.1 on page 586.

5.5.9 Accessing Scope-Specific Information

5.5.9.1 `ompd_enumerate_icvs`

Summary

The `ompd_enumerate_icvs` function enumerates ICVs.

Format

```c
ompd_rc_t ompd_enumerate_icvs (
  ompd_address_space_handle_t *handle,
  ompd_icv_id_t current,
  ompd_icv_id_t *next_id,
  const char **next_icv_name,
  ompd_scope_t *next_scope,
  int *more
);
```

Description

In addition to the ICVs listed in Table 2.1, an OpenMP implementation must support the OMPD specific ICVs listed in Table 5.2. An OpenMP implementation may support additional implementation specific variables. An implementation may store ICVs in a different scope than Table 2.3 indicates. The `ompd_enumerate_icvs` function enables a tool to enumerate the ICVs that an OpenMP implementation supports and their related scopes.

When the *current* argument is set to the identifier of a supported ICV, `ompd_enumerate_icvs` assigns the value, string name, and scope of the next ICV in the enumeration to the locations to which the *next_id*, *next_icv_name*, and *next_scope* arguments point. On return, the third-party tool owns the *next_icv_name* string. The OMPD library uses the memory allocation callback that the tool provides to allocate the string storage; the tool is responsible for releasing the memory.

On return, the location to which the *more* argument points has the value of 1 whenever one or more ICV are left in the enumeration. on return, that location has the value 0 when *current* is the last ICV in the enumeration.

Description of Arguments

The *address_space_handle* argument identifies the address space. The *current* argument must be an ICV that the OpenMP implementation supports. To begin enumerating the ICVs, a tool should pass **ompd_icv_undefined** as the value of *current*. Subsequent calls to **ompd_enumerate_icvs** should pass the value returned by the call in the *next_id* output argument. On return, the *next_id* argument points to an integer with the value of the ID of the next ICV in the enumeration. On return, the *next_icv* argument points to a character string with the name of the next ICV. On return, the *next_scope* argument points to the scope enum value of the scope of the next ICV. On return, the *more_enums* argument points to an integer with the value of 1 when more ICVs are left to enumerate and the value of 0 when no more ICVs are left.

Constraints on Arguments

Any string that *next_icv* returns must be immutable and defined for the lifetime of a program execution.

TABLE 5.2: OMPD-specific ICVs

Variable	Scope	Meaning
ompd-num-procs-var	device	return value of **omp_get_num_procs()** when executed on this device
ompd-thread-num-var	task	return value of **omp_get_thread_num()** when executed in this task
ompd-final-var	task	return value of **omp_in_final()** when executed in this task
ompd-implicit-var	task	the task is an implicit task
ompd-team-size-var	team	return value of **omp_get_num_threads()** when executed in this team

Cross References

- **ompd_address_space_handle_t** type, see Section 5.3.8 on page 540.
- **ompd_scope_t** type, see Section 5.3.9 on page 541.
- **ompd_icv_id_t** type, see Section 5.3.10 on page 542.
- **ompd_rc_t** type, see Section 5.3.12 on page 543.

5.5.9.2 ompd_get_icv_from_scope

Summary

The `ompd_get_icv_from_scope` function returns the value of an ICV.

Format

```c
ompd_rc_t ompd_get_icv_from_scope (
    void *handle,
    ompd_scope_t scope,
    ompd_icv_id_t icv_id,
    ompd_word_t *icv_value
);
```

Description

The `ompd_get_icv_from_scope` function provides access to the ICVs that `ompd_enumerate_icvs` identifies.

Description of Arguments

The *handle* argument provides an OpenMP scope handle. The *scope* argument specifies the kind of scope provided in *handle*. The *icv_id* argument specifies the ID of the requested ICV. On return, the *icv_value* argument points to a location with the value of the requested ICV.

Constraints on Arguments

If the ICV cannot be represented by an integer type value then the function returns `ompd_rc_incompatible`.

The provided *handle* must match the *scope* as defined in Section 5.3.10 on page 542.

The provided *scope* must match the scope for *icv_id* as requested by `ompd_enumerate_icvs`.

Cross References

- `ompd_address_space_handle_t` type, see Section 5.3.8 on page 540.
- `ompd_thread_handle_t` type, see Section 5.3.8 on page 540.
- `ompd_parallel_handle_t` type, see Section 5.3.8 on page 540.
- `ompd_task_handle_t` type, see Section 5.3.8 on page 540.
- `ompd_scope_t` type, see Section 5.3.9 on page 541.
- `ompd_icv_id_t` type, see Section 5.3.10 on page 542.
- `ompd_rc_t` type, see Section 5.3.12 on page 543.
- `ompd_enumerate_icvs`, see Section 5.5.9.1 on page 588.

5.5.9.3 ompd_get_icv_string_from_scope

Summary

The `ompd_get_icv_string_from_scope` function returns the value of an ICV.

Format

```c
ompd_rc_t ompd_get_icv_string_from_scope (
    void *handle,
    ompd_scope_t scope,
    ompd_icv_id_t icv_id,
    const char **icv_string
);
```

Description

The `ompd_get_icv_string_from_scope` function provides access to the ICVs that `ompd_enumerate_icvs` identifies.

Description of Arguments

The *handle* argument provides an OpenMP scope handle. The *scope* argument specifies the kind of scope provided in *handle*. The *icv_id* argument specifies the ID of the requested ICV. On return, the *icv_string* argument points to a string representation of the requested ICV.

On return, the third-party tool owns the *icv_string* string. The OMPD library allocates the string storage with the memory allocation callback that the tool provides. The tool is responsible for releasing the memory.

Constraints on Arguments

The provided *handle* must match the *scope* as defined in Section 5.3.10 on page 542.

The provided *scope* must match the scope for *icv_id* as requested by `ompd_enumerate_icvs`.

Cross References

- `ompd_address_space_handle_t` type, see Section 5.3.8 on page 540.
- `ompd_thread_handle_t` type, see Section 5.3.8 on page 540.
- `ompd_parallel_handle_t` type, see Section 5.3.8 on page 540.
- `ompd_task_handle_t` type, see Section 5.3.8 on page 540.
- `ompd_scope_t` type, see Section 5.3.9 on page 541.
- `ompd_icv_id_t` type, see Section 5.3.10 on page 542.
- `ompd_rc_t` type, see Section 5.3.12 on page 543.
- `ompd_enumerate_icvs`, see Section 5.5.9.1 on page 588.

5.5.9.4 ompd_get_tool_data

Summary

The `ompd_get_tool_data` function provides access to the OMPT data variable stored for each OpenMP scope.

Format

```c
ompd_rc_t ompd_get_tool_data(
    void* handle,
    ompd_scope_t scope,
    ompd_word_t *value,
    ompd_address_t *ptr
);
```

Description

The **ompd_get_tool_data** function provides access to the OMPT tool data stored for each scope. If the runtime library does not support OMPT then the function returns **ompd_rc_unsupported**.

Description of Arguments

The *handle* argument provides an OpenMP scope handle. The *scope* argument specifies the kind of scope provided in *handle*. On return, the *value* argument points to the *value* field of the **ompt_data_t** union stored for the selected scope. On return, the *ptr* argument points to the *ptr* field of the **ompt_data_t** union stored for the selected scope.

Cross References

- **ompt_data_t** type, see Section 4.4.4.4 on page 440.
- **ompd_address_space_handle_t** type, see Section 5.3.8 on page 540.
- **ompd_thread_handle_t** type, see Section 5.3.8 on page 540.
- **ompd_parallel_handle_t** type, see Section 5.3.8 on page 540.
- **ompd_task_handle_t** type, see Section 5.3.8 on page 540.
- **ompd_scope_t** type, see Section 5.3.9 on page 541.
- **ompd_rc_t** type, see Section 5.3.12 on page 543.

5.6 Runtime Entry Points for OMPD

The OpenMP implementation must define several entry point symbols through which execution must pass when particular events occur *and* data collection for OMPD is enabled. A tool can enable notification of an event by setting a breakpoint at the address of the entry point symbol.

Entry point symbols have external C linkage and do not require demangling or other transformations to look up their names to obtain the address in the OpenMP program. While each entry point symbol conceptually has a function type signature, it may not be a function. It may be a labeled location

5.6.1 Beginning Parallel Regions

Summary

Before starting the execution of an OpenMP parallel region, the implementation executes **ompd_bp_parallel_begin**.

Format

```C
void ompd_bp_parallel_begin(void);
```

Description

The OpenMP implementation must execute **ompd_bp_parallel_begin** at every *parallel-begin* event. At the point that the implementation reaches **ompd_bp_parallel_begin**, the binding for **ompd_get_curr_parallel_handle** is the parallel region that is beginning and the binding for **ompd_get_curr_task_handle** is the task that encountered the **parallel** construct.

Cross References

- **parallel** construct, see Section 2.6 on page 74.
- **ompd_get_curr_parallel_handle**, see Section 5.5.6.1 on page 571.
- **ompd_get_curr_task_handle**, see Section 5.5.7.1 on page 576.

5.6.2 Ending Parallel Regions

Summary
After finishing the execution of an OpenMP parallel region, the implementation executes **ompd_bp_parallel_end**.

Format
```c
void ompd_bp_parallel_end(void);
```

Description
The OpenMP implementation must execute **ompd_bp_parallel_end** at every *parallel-end* event. At the point that the implementation reaches **ompd_bp_parallel_end**, the binding for **ompd_get_curr_parallel_handle** is the **parallel** region that is ending and the binding for **ompd_get_curr_task_handle** is the task that encountered the **parallel** construct. After execution of **ompd_bp_parallel_end**, any *parallel_handle* that was acquired for the **parallel** region is invalid and should be released.

Cross References
- **parallel** construct, see Section 2.6 on page 74.
- **ompd_get_curr_parallel_handle**, see Section 5.5.6.1 on page 571.
- **ompd_rel_parallel_handle**, see Section 5.5.6.4 on page 574.
- **ompd_get_curr_task_handle**, see Section 5.5.7.1 on page 576.

5.6.3 Beginning Task Regions

Summary
Before starting the execution of an OpenMP task region, the implementation executes **ompd_bp_task_begin**.

Format

```C
void ompd_bp_task_begin(void);
```

Description

The OpenMP implementation must execute **ompd_bp_task_begin** immediately before starting execution of a *structured-block* that is associated with a non-merged task. At the point that the implementation reaches **ompd_bp_task_begin**, the binding for **ompd_get_curr_task_handle** is the task that is scheduled to execute.

Cross References

- **ompd_get_curr_task_handle**, see Section 5.5.7.1 on page 576.

5.6.4 Ending Task Regions

Summary

After finishing the execution of an OpenMP task region, the implementation executes **ompd_bp_task_end**.

Format

```C
void ompd_bp_task_end(void);
```

Description

The OpenMP implementation must execute **ompd_bp_task_end** immediately after completion of a *structured-block* that is associated with a non-merged task. At the point that the implementation reaches **ompd_bp_task_end**, the binding for **ompd_get_curr_task_handle** is the task that finished execution. After execution of **ompd_bp_task_end**, any *task_handle* that was acquired for the task region is invalid and should be released.

Cross References

- `ompd_get_curr_task_handle`, see Section 5.5.7.1 on page 576.
- `ompd_rel_task_handle`, see Section 5.5.7.5 on page 580.

5.6.5 Beginning OpenMP Threads

Summary

When starting an OpenMP thread, the implementation executes **ompd_bp_thread_begin**.

Format

```c
void ompd_bp_thread_begin(void);
```

Description

The OpenMP implementation must execute **ompd_bp_thread_begin** at every *native-thread-begin* and *initial-thread-begin* event. This execution occurs before the thread starts the execution of any OpenMP region.

Cross References

- `parallel` construct, see Section 2.6 on page 74.
- Initial task, see Section 2.10.5 on page 148.

5.6.6 Ending OpenMP Threads

Summary

When terminating an OpenMP thread, the implementation executes **ompd_bp_thread_end**.

Format

```c
void ompd_bp_thread_end(void);
```

Description

The OpenMP implementation must execute **ompd_bp_thread_end** at every *native-thread-end* and the *initial-thread-end* event. This execution occurs after the thread completes the execution of all OpenMP regions. After executing **ompd_bp_thread_end**, any *thread_handle* that was acquired for this thread is invalid and should be released.

Cross References

- **parallel** construct, see Section 2.6 on page 74.
- Initial task, see Section 2.10.5 on page 148.
- **ompd_rel_thread_handle**, see Section 5.5.5.3 on page 569.

5.6.7 Initializing OpenMP Devices

Summary

The OpenMP implementation must execute **ompd_bp_device_begin** at every *device-initialize* event.

Format

```C
void ompd_bp_device_begin(void);
```

Description

When initializing a device for execution of a **target** region, the implementation must execute **ompd_bp_device_begin**. This execution occurs before the work associated with any OpenMP region executes on the device.

Cross References

- Device Initialization, see Section 2.12.1 on page 160.

5.6.8 Finalizing OpenMP Devices

Summary
When terminating an OpenMP thread, the implementation executes **ompd_bp_device_end**.

Format
```c
void ompd_bp_device_end(void);
```

Description
The OpenMP implementation must execute **ompd_bp_device_end** at every *device-finalize* event. This execution occurs after the thread executes all OpenMP regions. After execution of **ompd_bp_device_end**, any *address_space_handle* that was acquired for this device is invalid and should be released.

Cross References
- Device Initialization, see Section 2.12.1 on page 160.
- **ompd_rel_address_space_handle**, see Section 5.5.2.3 on page 564.

This page intentionally left blank

CHAPTER 6

Environment Variables

This chapter describes the OpenMP environment variables that specify the settings of the ICVs that affect the execution of OpenMP programs (see Section 2.5 on page 63). The names of the environment variables must be upper case. The values assigned to the environment variables are case insensitive and may have leading and trailing white space. Modifications to the environment variables after the program has started, even if modified by the program itself, are ignored by the OpenMP implementation. However, the settings of some of the ICVs can be modified during the execution of the OpenMP program by the use of the appropriate directive clauses or OpenMP API routines.

The following examples demonstrate how the OpenMP environment variables can be set in different environments:

- csh-like shells:

```
setenv OMP_SCHEDULE "dynamic"
```

- bash-like shells:

```
export OMP_SCHEDULE="dynamic"
```

- Windows Command Line:

```
set OMP_SCHEDULE=dynamic
```

6.1 OMP_SCHEDULE

The **OMP_SCHEDULE** environment variable controls the schedule kind and chunk size of all loop directives that have the schedule kind **runtime**, by setting the value of the *run-sched-var* ICV.

The value of this environment variable takes the form:

[modifier:]kind[, chunk]

where

- *modifier* is one of **monotonic** or **nonmonotonic**;
- *kind* is one of **static**, **dynamic**, **guided**, or **auto**;
- *chunk* is an optional positive integer that specifies the chunk size.

If the *modifier* is not present, the *modifier* is set to **monotonic** if *kind* is **static**; for any other *kind* it is set to **nonmonotonic**.

If *chunk* is present, white space may be on either side of the ",". See Section 2.9.2 on page 101 for a detailed description of the schedule kinds.

The behavior of the program is implementation defined if the value of **OMP_SCHEDULE** does not conform to the above format.

Implementation specific schedules cannot be specified in **OMP_SCHEDULE**. They can only be specified by calling **omp_set_schedule**, described in Section 3.2.12 on page 345.

Examples:
```
setenv OMP_SCHEDULE "guided,4"
setenv OMP_SCHEDULE "dynamic"
setenv OMP_SCHEDULE "nonmonotonic:dynamic,4"
```

Cross References

- *run-sched-var* ICV, see Section 2.5 on page 63.
- Worksharing-Loop construct, see Section 2.9.2 on page 101.
- Parallel worksharing-loop construct, see Section 2.13.1 on page 185.
- **omp_set_schedule** routine, see Section 3.2.12 on page 345.
- **omp_get_schedule** routine, see Section 3.2.13 on page 347.

6.2 OMP_NUM_THREADS

The **OMP_NUM_THREADS** environment variable sets the number of threads to use for **parallel** regions by setting the initial value of the *nthreads-var* ICV. See Section 2.5 on page 63 for a comprehensive set of rules about the interaction between the **OMP_NUM_THREADS** environment variable, the **num_threads** clause, the **omp_set_num_threads** library routine and dynamic adjustment of threads, and Section 2.6.1 on page 78 for a complete algorithm that describes how the number of threads for a `parallel` region is determined.

The value of this environment variable must be a list of positive integer values. The values of the list set the number of threads to use for `parallel` regions at the corresponding nested levels.

The behavior of the program is implementation defined if any value of the list specified in the `OMP_NUM_THREADS` environment variable leads to a number of threads that is greater than an implementation can support, or if any value is not a positive integer.

Example:
```
setenv OMP_NUM_THREADS 4,3,2
```

Cross References

- *nthreads-var* ICV, see Section 2.5 on page 63.
- `num_threads` clause, see Section 2.6 on page 74.
- `omp_set_num_threads` routine, see Section 3.2.1 on page 334.
- `omp_get_num_threads` routine, see Section 3.2.2 on page 335.
- `omp_get_max_threads` routine, see Section 3.2.3 on page 336.
- `omp_get_team_size` routine, see Section 3.2.20 on page 354.

6.3 OMP_DYNAMIC

The `OMP_DYNAMIC` environment variable controls dynamic adjustment of the number of threads to use for executing `parallel` regions by setting the initial value of the *dyn-var* ICV.

The value of this environment variable must be one of the following:

`true | false`

If the environment variable is set to `true`, the OpenMP implementation may adjust the number of threads to use for executing `parallel` regions in order to optimize the use of system resources. If the environment variable is set to `false`, the dynamic adjustment of the number of threads is disabled. The behavior of the program is implementation defined if the value of `OMP_DYNAMIC` is neither `true` nor `false`.

Example:
```
setenv OMP_DYNAMIC true
```

Cross References

- *dyn-var* ICV, see Section 2.5 on page 63.
- `omp_set_dynamic` routine, see Section 3.2.7 on page 340.
- `omp_get_dynamic` routine, see Section 3.2.8 on page 341.

6.4 OMP_PROC_BIND

The `OMP_PROC_BIND` environment variable sets the initial value of the *bind-var* ICV. The value of this environment variable is either **true**, **false**, or a comma separated list of **master**, **close**, or **spread**. The values of the list set the thread affinity policy to be used for parallel regions at the corresponding nested level.

If the environment variable is set to **false**, the execution environment may move OpenMP threads between OpenMP places, thread affinity is disabled, and `proc_bind` clauses on `parallel` constructs are ignored.

Otherwise, the execution environment should not move OpenMP threads between OpenMP places, thread affinity is enabled, and the initial thread is bound to the first place in the OpenMP place list prior to the first active parallel region.

The behavior of the program is implementation defined if the value in the `OMP_PROC_BIND` environment variable is not **true**, **false**, or a comma separated list of **master**, **close**, or **spread**. The behavior is also implementation defined if an initial thread cannot be bound to the first place in the OpenMP place list.

Examples:
```
setenv OMP_PROC_BIND false
setenv OMP_PROC_BIND "spread, spread, close"
```

Cross References

- *bind-var* ICV, see Section 2.5 on page 63.
- `proc_bind` clause, see Section 2.6.2 on page 80.
- `omp_get_proc_bind` routine, see Section 3.2.23 on page 357.

6.5 OMP_PLACES

A list of places can be specified in the **OMP_PLACES** environment variable. The *place-partition-var* ICV obtains its initial value from the **OMP_PLACES** value, and makes the list available to the execution environment. The value of **OMP_PLACES** can be one of two types of values: either an abstract name that describes a set of places or an explicit list of places described by non-negative numbers.

The **OMP_PLACES** environment variable can be defined using an explicit ordered list of comma-separated places. A place is defined by an unordered set of comma-separated non-negative numbers enclosed by braces. The meaning of the numbers and how the numbering is done are implementation defined. Generally, the numbers represent the smallest unit of execution exposed by the execution environment, typically a hardware thread.

Intervals may also be used to define places. Intervals can be specified using the *<lower-bound>* : *<length>* : *<stride>* notation to represent the following list of numbers: "*<lower-bound>*, *<lower-bound>* + *<stride>*, ..., *<lower-bound>* + (*<length>* - 1)**<stride>*." When *<stride>* is omitted, a unit stride is assumed. Intervals can specify numbers within a place as well as sequences of places.

An exclusion operator "!" can also be used to exclude the number or place immediately following the operator.

Alternatively, the abstract names listed in Table 6.1 should be understood by the execution and runtime environment. The precise definitions of the abstract names are implementation defined. An implementation may also add abstract names as appropriate for the target platform.

TABLE 6.1: Defined Abstract Names for **OMP_PLACES**

Abstract Name	Meaning
threads	Each place corresponds to a single hardware thread on the target machine.
cores	Each place corresponds to a single core (having one or more hardware threads) on the target machine.
sockets	Each place corresponds to a single socket (consisting of one or more cores) on the target machine.

The abstract name may be appended by a positive number in parentheses to denote the length of the place list to be created, that is *abstract_name(num-places)*. When requesting fewer places than available on the system, the determination of which resources of type *abstract_name* are to be included in the place list is implementation defined. When requesting more resources than available, the length of the place list is implementation defined.

The behavior of the program is implementation defined when the execution environment cannot map a numerical value (either explicitly defined or implicitly derived from an interval) within the

`OMP_PLACES` list to a processor on the target platform, or if it maps to an unavailable processor. The behavior is also implementation defined when the `OMP_PLACES` environment variable is defined using an abstract name.

The following grammar describes the values accepted for the `OMP_PLACES` environment variable.

$$
\begin{aligned}
\langle\text{list}\rangle &\models \langle\text{p-list}\rangle \mid \langle\text{aname}\rangle \\
\langle\text{p-list}\rangle &\models \langle\text{p-interval}\rangle \mid \langle\text{p-list}\rangle,\langle\text{p-interval}\rangle \\
\langle\text{p-interval}\rangle &\models \langle\text{place}\rangle:\langle\text{len}\rangle:\langle\text{stride}\rangle \mid \langle\text{place}\rangle:\langle\text{len}\rangle \mid \langle\text{place}\rangle \mid !\langle\text{place}\rangle \\
\langle\text{place}\rangle &\models \{\langle\text{res-list}\rangle\} \\
\langle\text{res-list}\rangle &\models \langle\text{res-interval}\rangle \mid \langle\text{res-list}\rangle,\langle\text{res-interval}\rangle \\
\langle\text{res-interval}\rangle &\models \langle\text{res}\rangle:\langle\text{num-places}\rangle:\langle\text{stride}\rangle \mid \langle\text{res}\rangle:\langle\text{num-places}\rangle \mid \langle\text{res}\rangle \mid !\langle\text{res}\rangle \\
\langle\text{aname}\rangle &\models \langle\text{word}\rangle(\langle\text{num-places}\rangle) \mid \langle\text{word}\rangle \\
\langle\text{word}\rangle &\models \text{sockets} \mid \text{cores} \mid \text{threads} \mid \text{<implementation-defined abstract name>} \\
\langle\text{res}\rangle &\models \textit{non-negative integer} \\
\langle\text{num-places}\rangle &\models \textit{positive integer} \\
\langle\text{stride}\rangle &\models \textit{integer} \\
\langle\text{len}\rangle &\models \textit{positive integer}
\end{aligned}
$$

Examples:
```
setenv OMP_PLACES threads
setenv OMP_PLACES "threads(4)"
setenv OMP_PLACES
   "{0,1,2,3},{4,5,6,7},{8,9,10,11},{12,13,14,15}"
setenv OMP_PLACES "{0:4},{4:4},{8:4},{12:4}"
setenv OMP_PLACES "{0:4}:4:4"
```

where each of the last three definitions corresponds to the same 4 places including the smallest units of execution exposed by the execution environment numbered, in turn, 0 to 3, 4 to 7, 8 to 11, and 12 to 15.

Cross References

- *place-partition-var*, see Section 2.5 on page 63.
- Controlling OpenMP thread affinity, see Section 2.6.2 on page 80.
- `omp_get_num_places` routine, see Section 3.2.24 on page 358.
- `omp_get_place_num_procs` routine, see Section 3.2.25 on page 359.

- `omp_get_place_proc_ids` routine, see Section 3.2.26 on page 360.
- `omp_get_place_num` routine, see Section 3.2.27 on page 362.
- `omp_get_partition_num_places` routine, see Section 3.2.28 on page 362.
- `omp_get_partition_place_nums` routine, see Section 3.2.29 on page 363.

6.6 OMP_STACKSIZE

The **OMP_STACKSIZE** environment variable controls the size of the stack for threads created by the OpenMP implementation, by setting the value of the *stacksize-var* ICV. The environment variable does not control the size of the stack for an initial thread.

The value of this environment variable takes the form:

size | *size*B | *size*K | *size*M | *size*G

where:

- *size* is a positive integer that specifies the size of the stack for threads that are created by the OpenMP implementation.
- **B**, **K**, **M**, and **G** are letters that specify whether the given size is in Bytes, Kilobytes (1024 Bytes), Megabytes (1024 Kilobytes), or Gigabytes (1024 Megabytes), respectively. If one of these letters is present, there may be white space between *size* and the letter.

If only *size* is specified and none of **B**, **K**, **M**, or **G** is specified, then *size* is assumed to be in Kilobytes.

The behavior of the program is implementation defined if **OMP_STACKSIZE** does not conform to the above format, or if the implementation cannot provide a stack with the requested size.

Examples:
```
setenv OMP_STACKSIZE 2000500B
setenv OMP_STACKSIZE "3000 k "
setenv OMP_STACKSIZE 10M
setenv OMP_STACKSIZE " 10 M "
setenv OMP_STACKSIZE "20 m "
setenv OMP_STACKSIZE " 1G"
setenv OMP_STACKSIZE 20000
```

Cross References

- *stacksize-var* ICV, see Section 2.5 on page 63.

6.7 OMP_WAIT_POLICY

The `OMP_WAIT_POLICY` environment variable provides a hint to an OpenMP implementation about the desired behavior of waiting threads by setting the *wait-policy-var* ICV. A compliant OpenMP implementation may or may not abide by the setting of the environment variable.

The value of this environment variable must be one of the following:

`ACTIVE | PASSIVE`

The `ACTIVE` value specifies that waiting threads should mostly be active, consuming processor cycles, while waiting. An OpenMP implementation may, for example, make waiting threads spin.

The `PASSIVE` value specifies that waiting threads should mostly be passive, not consuming processor cycles, while waiting. For example, an OpenMP implementation may make waiting threads yield the processor to other threads or go to sleep.

The details of the `ACTIVE` and `PASSIVE` behaviors are implementation defined.

The behavior of the program is implementation defined if the value of `OMP_WAIT_POLICY` is neither `ACTIVE` nor `PASSIVE`.

Examples:
```
setenv OMP_WAIT_POLICY ACTIVE
setenv OMP_WAIT_POLICY active
setenv OMP_WAIT_POLICY PASSIVE
setenv OMP_WAIT_POLICY passive
```

Cross References

- *wait-policy-var* ICV, see Section 2.5 on page 63.

6.8 OMP_MAX_ACTIVE_LEVELS

The `OMP_MAX_ACTIVE_LEVELS` environment variable controls the maximum number of nested active `parallel` regions by setting the initial value of the *max-active-levels-var* ICV.

The value of this environment variable must be a non-negative integer. The behavior of the program is implementation defined if the requested value of `OMP_MAX_ACTIVE_LEVELS` is greater than the maximum number of nested active parallel levels an implementation can support, or if the value is not a non-negative integer.

Cross References

- *max-active-levels-var* ICV, see Section 2.5 on page 63.
- `omp_set_max_active_levels` routine, see Section 3.2.16 on page 350.
- `omp_get_max_active_levels` routine, see Section 3.2.17 on page 351.

6.9 OMP_NESTED

The `OMP_NESTED` environment variable controls nested parallelism by setting the initial value of the *max-active-levels-var* ICV. If the environment variable is set to `true`, the initial value of *max-active-levels-var* is set to the number of active levels of parallelism supported by the implementation. If the environment variable is set to `false`, the initial value of *max-active-levels-var* is set to 1. The behavior of the program is implementation defined if the value of `OMP_NESTED` is neither `true` nor `false`.

If both the `OMP_NESTED` and `OMP_MAX_ACTIVE_LEVELS` environment variables are set, the value of `OMP_NESTED` is `false`, and the value of `OMP_MAX_ACTIVE_LEVELS` is greater than 1, the behavior is implementation defined. Otherwise, if both environment variables are set then the `OMP_NESTED` environment variable has no effect.

The `OMP_NESTED` environment variable has been deprecated.

Example:
```
setenv OMP_NESTED false
```

Cross References

- *max-active-levels-var* ICV, see Section 2.5 on page 63.
- `omp_set_nested` routine, see Section 3.2.10 on page 343.
- `omp_get_team_size` routine, see Section 3.2.20 on page 354.
- `OMP_MAX_ACTIVE_LEVELS` environment variable, see Section 6.8 on page 608.

6.10 OMP_THREAD_LIMIT

The `OMP_THREAD_LIMIT` environment variable sets the maximum number of OpenMP threads to use in a contention group by setting the *thread-limit-var* ICV.

The value of this environment variable must be a positive integer. The behavior of the program is implementation defined if the requested value of `OMP_THREAD_LIMIT` is greater than the number of threads an implementation can support, or if the value is not a positive integer.

Cross References
- *thread-limit-var* ICV, see Section 2.5 on page 63.
- `omp_get_thread_limit` routine, see Section 3.2.14 on page 348.

6.11 OMP_CANCELLATION

The `OMP_CANCELLATION` environment variable sets the initial value of the *cancel-var* ICV.

The value of this environment variable must be one of the following:

`true | false`

If set to `true`, the effects of the `cancel` construct and of cancellation points are enabled and cancellation is activated. If set to `false`, cancellation is disabled and the `cancel` construct and cancellation points are effectively ignored. The behavior of the program is implementation defined if `OMP_CANCELLATION` is set to neither `true` nor `false`.

Cross References
- *cancel-var*, see Section 2.5.1 on page 64.
- `cancel` construct, see Section 2.18.1 on page 263.
- `cancellation point` construct, see Section 2.18.2 on page 267.
- `omp_get_cancellation` routine, see Section 3.2.9 on page 342.

6.12 OMP_DISPLAY_ENV

The **OMP_DISPLAY_ENV** environment variable instructs the runtime to display the OpenMP version number and the value of the ICVs associated with the environment variables described in Chapter 6, as *name = value* pairs. The runtime displays this information once, after processing the environment variables and before any user calls to change the ICV values by runtime routines defined in Chapter 3.

The value of the **OMP_DISPLAY_ENV** environment variable may be set to one of these values:

TRUE | FALSE | VERBOSE

The **TRUE** value instructs the runtime to display the OpenMP version number defined by the **_OPENMP** version macro (or the **openmp_version** Fortran parameter) value and the initial ICV values for the environment variables listed in Chapter 6. The **VERBOSE** value indicates that the runtime may also display the values of runtime variables that may be modified by vendor-specific environment variables. The runtime does not display any information when the **OMP_DISPLAY_ENV** environment variable is **FALSE** or undefined. For all values of the environment variable other than **TRUE**, **FALSE**, and **VERBOSE**, the displayed information is unspecified.

The display begins with "OPENMP DISPLAY ENVIRONMENT BEGIN", followed by the **_OPENMP** version macro (or the **openmp_version** Fortran parameter) value and ICV values, in the format *NAME* '=' *VALUE*. *NAME* corresponds to the macro or environment variable name, optionally prepended by a bracketed *device-type*. *VALUE* corresponds to the value of the macro or ICV associated with this environment variable. Values are enclosed in single quotes. The display is terminated with "OPENMP DISPLAY ENVIRONMENT END".

For the **OMP_NESTED** environment variable, the printed value is *true* if the *max-active-levels-var* ICV is initialized to a value greater than 1; otherwise the printed value is *false*.

Example:

```
% setenv OMP_DISPLAY_ENV TRUE
```

The above example causes an OpenMP implementation to generate output of the following form:

```
OPENMP DISPLAY ENVIRONMENT BEGIN
   _OPENMP='201811'
  [host] OMP_SCHEDULE='GUIDED,4'
  [host] OMP_NUM_THREADS='4,3,2'
  [device] OMP_NUM_THREADS='2'
  [host,device] OMP_DYNAMIC='TRUE'
  [host] OMP_PLACES='{0:4},{4:4},{8:4},{12:4}'
  ...
OPENMP DISPLAY ENVIRONMENT END
```

6.13 OMP_DISPLAY_AFFINITY

The `OMP_DISPLAY_AFFINITY` environment variable instructs the runtime to display formatted affinity information for all OpenMP threads in the parallel region upon entering the first parallel region and when any change occurs in the information accessible by the format specifiers listed in Table 6.2. If affinity of any thread in a parallel region changes then thread affinity information for all threads in that region is displayed. If the thread affinity for each respective parallel region at each nesting level has already been displayed and the thread affinity has not changed, then the information is not displayed again. There is no specific order in displaying thread affinity information for all threads in the same parallel region.

The value of the `OMP_DISPLAY_AFFINITY` environment variable may be set to one of these values:

`TRUE | FALSE`

The `TRUE` value instructs the runtime to display the OpenMP thread affinity information, and uses the format setting defined in the *affinity-format-var* ICV.

The runtime does not display the OpenMP thread affinity information when the value of the `OMP_DISPLAY_AFFINITY` environment variable is `FALSE` or undefined. For all values of the environment variable other than `TRUE` or `FALSE`, the display action is implementation defined.

Example:

```
setenv OMP_DISPLAY_AFFINITY TRUE
```

The above example causes an OpenMP implementation to display OpenMP thread affinity information during execution of the program, in a format given by the *affinity-format-var* ICV. The following is a sample output:

```
nesting_level=    1,    thread_num=    0,    thread_affinity=    0,1
nesting_level=    1,    thread_num=    1,    thread_affinity=    2,3
```

Cross References

- Controlling OpenMP thread affinity, see Section 2.6.2 on page 80.
- `omp_set_affinity_format` routine, see Section 3.2.30 on page 364.
- `omp_get_affinity_format` routine, see Section 3.2.31 on page 366.
- `omp_display_affinity` routine, see Section 3.2.32 on page 367.
- `omp_capture_affinity` routine, see Section 3.2.33 on page 368.
- `OMP_AFFINITY_FORMAT` environment variable, see Section 6.14 on page 613.

6.14 OMP_AFFINITY_FORMAT

The **OMP_AFFINITY_FORMAT** environment variable sets the initial value of the *affinity-format-var* ICV which defines the format when displaying OpenMP thread affinity information.

The value of this environment variable is a character string that may contain as substrings one or more field specifiers, in addition to other characters. The format of each field specifier is

%[[0].] *size*] *type*

where an individual field specifier must contain the percent symbol (%) and a type. The type can be a single character short name or its corresponding long name delimited with curly braces, such as %n or %{thread_num}. A literal percent is specified as %%. Field specifiers can be provided in any order.

The **0** modifier indicates whether or not to add leading zeros to the output, following any indication of sign or base. The **.** modifier indicates the output should be right justified when *size* is specified. By default, output is left justified. The minimum field length is *size*, which is a decimal digit string with a non-zero first digit. If no *size* is specified, the actual length needed to print the field will be used. If the **0** modifier is used with *type* of **A**, **{thread_affinity}**, **H**, **{host}**, or a type that is not printed as a number, the result is unspecified. Any other characters in the format string that are not part of a field specifier will be included literally in the output.

TABLE 6.2: Available Field Types for Formatting OpenMP Thread Affinity Information

Short Name	Long Name	Meaning
t	team_num	The value returned by omp_get_team_num().
T	num_teams	The value returned by omp_get_num_teams().
L	nesting_level	The value returned by omp_get_level().
n	thread_num	The value returned by omp_get_thread_num().
N	num_threads	The value returned by omp_get_num_threads().
a	ancestor_tnum	The value returned by omp_get_ancestor_thread_num(*level*), where *level* is omp_get_level() minus 1.

table continued on next page

table continued from previous page

Short Name	Long Name	Meaning
H	host	The name for the host machine on which the OpenMP program is running.
P	process_id	The process identifier used by the implementation.
i	native_thread_id	The native thread identifier used by the implementation.
A	thread_affinity	The list of numerical identifiers, in the format of a comma-separated list of integers or integer ranges, that represent processors on which a thread may execute, subject to OpenMP thread affinity control and/or other external affinity mechanisms.

Implementations may define additional field types. If an implementation does not have information for a field type, "undefined" is printed for this field when displaying the OpenMP thread affinity information.

Example:

```
setenv OMP_AFFINITY_FORMAT
        "Thread Affinity: %0.3L %.8n %.15{thread_affinity} %.12H"
```

The above example causes an OpenMP implementation to display OpenMP thread affinity information in the following form:

```
Thread Affinity: 001        0       0-1,16-17       nid003
Thread Affinity: 001        1       2-3,18-19       nid003
```

Cross References

- Controlling OpenMP thread affinity, see Section 2.6.2 on page 80.
- omp_set_affinity_format routine, see Section 3.2.30 on page 364.
- omp_get_affinity_format routine, see Section 3.2.31 on page 366.
- omp_display_affinity routine, see Section 3.2.32 on page 367.
- omp_capture_affinity routine, see Section 3.2.33 on page 368.
- OMP_DISPLAY_AFFINITY environment variable, see Section 6.13 on page 612.

6.15 OMP_DEFAULT_DEVICE

The **OMP_DEFAULT_DEVICE** environment variable sets the device number to use in device constructs by setting the initial value of the *default-device-var* ICV.

The value of this environment variable must be a non-negative integer value.

Cross References

- *default-device-var* ICV, see Section 2.5 on page 63.
- device directives, Section 2.12 on page 160.

6.16 OMP_MAX_TASK_PRIORITY

The **OMP_MAX_TASK_PRIORITY** environment variable controls the use of task priorities by setting the initial value of the *max-task-priority-var* ICV. The value of this environment variable must be a non-negative integer.

Example:
```
% setenv OMP_MAX_TASK_PRIORITY 20
```

Cross References

- *max-task-priority-var* ICV, see Section 2.5 on page 63.
- Tasking Constructs, see Section 2.10 on page 135.
- **omp_get_max_task_priority** routine, see Section 3.2.42 on page 377.

6.17 OMP_TARGET_OFFLOAD

The **OMP_TARGET_OFFLOAD** environment variable sets the initial value of the *target-offload-var* ICV. The value of the **OMP_TARGET_OFFLOAD** environment variable must be one of the following:

MANDATORY | DISABLED | DEFAULT

The **MANDATORY** value specifies that program execution is terminated if a device construct or device memory routine is encountered and the device is not available or is not supported by the implementation. Support for the **DISABLED** value is implementation defined. If an implementation supports it, the behavior is as if the only device is the host device.

The **DEFAULT** value specifies the default behavior as described in Section 1.3 on page 20.

Example:

```
% setenv OMP_TARGET_OFFLOAD MANDATORY
```

Cross References

- *target-offload-var* ICV, see Section 2.5 on page 63.
- Device Directives, see Section 2.12 on page 160.
- Device Memory Routines, see Section 3.6 on page 397.

6.18 OMP_TOOL

The `OMP_TOOL` environment variable sets the *tool-var* ICV, which controls whether an OpenMP runtime will try to register a first party tool.

The value of this environment variable must be one of the following:

```
enabled | disabled
```

If `OMP_TOOL` is set to any value other than `enabled` or `disabled`, the behavior is unspecified.
If `OMP_TOOL` is not defined, the default value for *tool-var* is `enabled`.

Example:

```
% setenv OMP_TOOL enabled
```

Cross References

- *tool-var* ICV, see Section 2.5 on page 63.
- OMPT Interface, see Chapter 4 on page 419.

6.19 OMP_TOOL_LIBRARIES

The **OMP_TOOL_LIBRARIES** environment variable sets the *tool-libraries-var* ICV to a list of tool libraries that are considered for use on a device on which an OpenMP implementation is being initialized. The value of this environment variable must be a list of names of dynamically-loadable libraries, separated by an implementation specific, platform typical separator.

If the *tool-var* ICV is not enabled, the value of *tool-libraries-var* is ignored. Otherwise, if **ompt_start_tool** is not visible in the address space on a device where OpenMP is being initialized or if **ompt_start_tool** returns **NULL**, an OpenMP implementation will consider libraries in the *tool-libraries-var* list in a left to right order. The OpenMP implementation will search the list for a library that meets two criteria: it can be dynamically loaded on the current device and it defines the symbol **ompt_start_tool**. If an OpenMP implementation finds a suitable library, no further libraries in the list will be considered.

Example:

```
% setenv OMP_TOOL_LIBRARIES libtoolXY64.so:/usr/local/lib/
    libtoolXY32.so
```

Cross References

- *tool-libraries-var* ICV, see Section 2.5 on page 63.
- OMPT Interface, see Chapter 4 on page 419.
- **ompt_start_tool** routine, see Section 4.2.1 on page 420.

6.20 OMP_DEBUG

The **OMP_DEBUG** environment variable sets the *debug-var* ICV, which controls whether an OpenMP runtime collects information that an OMPD library may need to support a tool.

The value of this environment variable must be one of the following:

enabled | disabled

If **OMP_DEBUG** is set to any value other than **enabled** or **disabled** then the behavior is implementation defined.

Example:

```
% setenv OMP_DEBUG enabled
```

Cross References

- *debug-var* ICV, see Section 2.5 on page 63.
- OMPD Interface, see Chapter 5 on page 533.
- Enabling the Runtime for OMPD, see Section 5.2.1 on page 534.

6.21 OMP_ALLOCATOR

OMP_ALLOCATOR sets the *def-allocator-var* ICV that specifies the default allocator for allocation calls, directives and clauses that do not specify an allocator. The value of this environment variable is a predefined allocator from Table 2.10 on page 155. The value of this environment variable is not case sensitive.

Cross References

- *def-allocator-var* ICV, see Section 2.5 on page 63.
- Memory allocators, see Section 2.11.2 on page 152.
- **omp_set_default_allocator** routine, see Section 3.7.4 on page 411.
- **omp_get_default_allocator** routine, see Section 3.7.5 on page 412.

APPENDIX A

OpenMP Implementation-Defined Behaviors

This appendix summarizes the behaviors that are described as implementation defined in this API. Each behavior is cross-referenced back to its description in the main specification. An implementation is required to define and to document its behavior in these cases.

- **Processor**: a hardware unit that is implementation defined (see Section 1.2.1 on page 2).
- **Device**: an implementation defined logical execution engine (see Section 1.2.1 on page 2).
- **Device address**: reference to an address in a *device data environment* (see Section 1.2.6 on page 12).
- **Memory model**: the minimum size at which a memory update may also read and write back adjacent variables that are part of another variable (as array or structure elements) is implementation defined but is no larger than required by the base language (see Section 1.4.1 on page 23).
- **requires directive**: support of requirements is implementation defined. All implementation-defined requirements should begin with **ext_** (see Section 2.4 on page 60).
- **Requires directive**: Support for any feature specified by a requirement clause on a **requires** directive is implementation defined (see Section 2.4 on page 60).
- **Internal control variables**: the initial values of *dyn-var*, *nthreads-var*, *run-sched-var*, *def-sched-var*, *bind-var*, *stacksize-var*, *wait-policy-var*, *thread-limit-var*, *max-active-levels-var*, *place-partition-var*, *affinity-format-var*, *default-device-var* and *def-allocator-var* are implementation defined. The method for initializing a target device's internal control variable is implementation defined (see Section 2.5.2 on page 66).
- **OpenMP context**: the accepted *isa-name* values for the *isa* trait, the accepted *arch-name* values for the *arch* trait, and the accepted *extension-name* values for the *extension* trait are implementation defined (see Section 2.3.1 on page 51).

- **declare variant directive**: whether, for some specific OpenMP context, the prototype of the variant should differ from that of the base function, and if so how it should differ, is implementation defined (see Section 2.3.5 on page 58).

- **Dynamic adjustment of threads**: providing the ability to adjust the number of threads dynamically is implementation defined. Implementations are allowed to deliver fewer threads (but at least one) than indicated in Algorithm 2.1 even if dynamic adjustment is disabled (see Section 2.6.1 on page 78).

- **Thread affinity**: For the **close** thread affinity policy, if $T > P$ and P does not divide T evenly, the exact number of threads in a particular place is implementation defined. For the **spread** thread affinity, if $T > P$ and P does not divide T evenly, the exact number of threads in a particular subpartition is implementation defined. The determination of whether the affinity request can be fulfilled is implementation defined. If not, the mapping of threads in the team to places is implementation defined (see Section 2.6.2 on page 80).

- **teams construct**: the number of teams that are created is implementation defined but less than or equal to the value of the **num_teams** clause if specified. The maximum number of threads that participate in the contention group that each team initiates is implementation defined but less than or equal to the value of the **thread_limit** clause if specified. The assignment of the initial threads to places and the values of the *place-partition-var* and *default-device-var* ICVs for each initial thread are implementation defined (see Section 2.7 on page 82).

- **sections construct**: the method of scheduling the structured blocks among threads in the team is implementation defined (see Section 2.8.1 on page 86).

- **single construct**: the method of choosing a thread to execute the structured block is implementation defined (see Section 2.8.2 on page 89)

- **Worksharing-Loop directive**: the integer type (or kind, for Fortran) used to compute the iteration count of a collapsed loop is implementation defined. The effect of the **schedule(runtime)** clause when the *run-sched-var* ICV is set to **auto** is implementation defined. The value of *simd_width* for the **simd** schedule modifier is implementation defined (see Section 2.9.2 on page 101).

- **simd construct**: the integer type (or kind, for Fortran) used to compute the iteration count for the collapsed loop is implementation defined. The number of iterations that are executed concurrently at any given time is implementation defined. If the *alignment* parameter is not specified in the **aligned** clause, the default alignments for the SIMD instructions are implementation defined (see Section 2.9.3.1 on page 110).

- **declare simd directive**: if the parameter of the **simdlen** clause is not a constant positive integer expression, the number of concurrent arguments for the function is implementation defined. If the *alignment* parameter of the **aligned** clause is not specified, the default alignments for SIMD instructions are implementation defined (see Section 2.9.3.3 on page 116).

- **distribute construct**: the integer type (or kind, for Fortran) used to compute the iteration count for the collapsed loop is implementation defined. If no **dist_schedule** clause is specified then the schedule for the `distribute` construct is implementation defined (see Section 2.9.4.1 on page 120).

- **`taskloop` construct**: The number of loop iterations assigned to a task created from a `taskloop` construct is implementation defined, unless the `grainsize` or `num_tasks` clause is specified. The integer type (or kind, for Fortran) used to compute the iteration count for the collapsed loop is implementation defined (see Section 2.10.2 on page 140).

---------- C++ ----------

- **`taskloop` construct**: For `firstprivate` variables of class type, the number of invocations of copy constructors to perform the initialization is implementation defined (see Section 2.10.2 on page 140).

---------- C++ ----------

- **Memory spaces**: The actual storage resource that each memory space defined in Table 2.8 on page 152 represents is implementation defined.

- **Memory allocators**: The minimum partitioning size for partitioning of allocated memory over the storage resources is implementation defined (see Section 2.11.2 on page 152). The default value for the `pool_size` allocator trait is implementation defined (see Table 2.9 on page 153). The associated memory space for each of the predefined `omp_cgroup_mem_alloc`, `omp_pteam_mem_alloc` and `omp_thread_mem_alloc` allocators is implementation defined (see Table 2.10 on page 155).

- **`is_device_ptr` clause**: Support for pointers created outside of the OpenMP device data management routines is implementation defined (see Section 2.12.5 on page 170).

- **`target` construct**: the effect of invoking a virtual member function of an object on a device other than the device on which the object was constructed is implementation defined (see Section 2.12.5 on page 170).

- **`atomic` construct**: a compliant implementation may enforce exclusive access between `atomic` regions that update different storage locations. The circumstances under which this occurs are implementation defined. If the storage location designated by x is not size-aligned (that is, if the byte alignment of x is not a multiple of the size of x), then the behavior of the atomic region is implementation defined (see Section 2.17.7 on page 234).

---------- Fortran ----------

- **Data-sharing attributes**: The data-sharing attributes of dummy arguments without the `VALUE` attribute are implementation-defined if the associated actual argument is shared, except for the conditions specified (see Section 2.19.1.2 on page 273).

- **`threadprivate` directive**: if the conditions for values of data in the threadprivate objects of threads (other than an initial thread) to persist between two consecutive active parallel regions do not all hold, the allocation status of an allocatable variable in the second region is implementation defined (see Section 2.19.2 on page 274).

- **Runtime library definitions**: it is implementation defined whether the include file `omp_lib.h` or the module `omp_lib` (or both) is provided. It is implementation defined whether any of the OpenMP runtime library routines that take an argument are extended with a generic interface so arguments of different **KIND** type can be accommodated (see Section 3.1 on page 332).

---------- Fortran ----------

- `omp_set_num_threads` routine: if the argument is not a positive integer the behavior is implementation defined (see Section 3.2.1 on page 334).

- `omp_set_schedule` routine: for implementation specific schedule kinds, the values and associated meanings of the second argument are implementation defined (see Section 3.2.12 on page 345).

- `omp_get_supported_active_levels` routine: the number of active levels of parallelism supported by the implementation is implementation defined, but must be greater than 0 (see Section 3.2.15 on page 349).

- `omp_set_max_active_levels` routine: when called from within any explicit **parallel** region the binding thread set (and binding region, if required) for the `omp_set_max_active_levels` region is implementation defined and the behavior is implementation defined. If the argument is not a non-negative integer then the behavior is implementation defined (see Section 3.2.16 on page 350).

- `omp_get_max_active_levels` routine: when called from within any explicit **parallel** region the binding thread set (and binding region, if required) for the `omp_get_max_active_levels` region is implementation defined (see Section 3.2.17 on page 351).

- `omp_get_place_proc_ids` routine: the meaning of the non-negative numerical identifiers returned by the `omp_get_place_proc_ids` routine is implementation defined. The order of the numerical identifiers returned in the array *ids* is implementation defined (see Section 3.2.26 on page 360).

- `omp_set_affinity_format` routine: when called from within any explicit **parallel** region, the binding thread set (and binding region, if required) for the `omp_set_affinity_format` region is implementation defined and the behavior is implementation defined. If the argument does not conform to the specified format then the result is implementation defined (see Section 3.2.30 on page 364).

- `omp_get_affinity_format` routine: when called from within any explicit **parallel** region the binding thread set (and binding region, if required) for the `omp_get_affinity_format` region is implementation defined (see Section 3.2.31 on page 366).

- `omp_display_affinity` routine: if the argument does not conform to the specified format then the result is implementation defined (see Section 3.2.32 on page 367).

- **omp_capture_affinity routine**: if the *format* argument does not conform to the specified format then the result is implementation defined (see Section 3.2.33 on page 368).
- **omp_get_initial_device routine**: the value of the device number of the host device is implementation defined (see Section 3.2.41 on page 376).
- **omp_target_memcpy_rect routine**: the maximum number of dimensions supported is implementation defined, but must be at least three (see Section 3.6.5 on page 402).
- **ompt_callback_sync_region_wait, ompt_callback_mutex_released, ompt_callback_dependences, ompt_callback_task_dependence, ompt_callback_work, ompt_callback_master, ompt_callback_target_map, ompt_callback_sync_region, ompt_callback_lock_init, ompt_callback_lock_destroy, ompt_callback_mutex_acquire, ompt_callback_mutex_acquired, ompt_callback_nest_lock, ompt_callback_flush, ompt_callback_cancel** and **ompt_callback_dispatch tool callbacks**: if a tool attempts to register a callback with the string name using the runtime entry point **ompt_set_callback**, it is implementation defined whether the registered callback may never or sometimes invoke this callback for the associated events (see Table 4.2 on page 428)
- **Device tracing**: Whether a target device supports tracing or not is implementation defined; if a target device does not support tracing, a **NULL** may be supplied for the *lookup* function to a tool's device initializer (see Section 4.2.5 on page 427).
- **ompt_set_trace_ompt** and **ompt_buffer_get_record_ompt runtime entry points**: it is implementation defined whether a device-specific tracing interface will define this runtime entry point, indicating that it can collect traces in OMPT format. The kinds of trace records available for a device is implementation defined (see Section 4.2.5 on page 427).
- **ompt_callback_target_data_op_t callback type**: it is implementation defined whether in some operations *src_addr* or *dest_addr* might point to an intermediate buffer (see Section 4.5.2.25 on page 488).
- **ompt_set_callback_t entry point type**: the subset of the associated event in which the callback is invoked is implementation defined (see Section 4.6.1.3 on page 500).
- **ompt_get_place_proc_ids_t entry point type**: the meaning of the numerical identifiers returned is implementation defined. The order of *ids* returned in the array is implementation defined (see Section 4.6.1.8 on page 505).
- **ompt_get_partition_place_nums_t entry point type**: the order of the identifiers returned in the array *place_nums* is implementation defined (see Section 4.6.1.10 on page 507).
- **ompt_get_proc_id_t entry point type**: the meaning of the numerical identifier returned is implementation defined (see Section 4.6.1.11 on page 508).
- **ompd_callback_print_string_fn_t callback function**: the value of *catergory* is implementation defined (see Section 5.4.5 on page 556).

- **ompd_parallel_handle_compare operation**: the means by which parallel region handles are ordered is implementation defined (see Section 5.5.6.5 on page 575).

- **ompd_task_handle_compare operation**: the means by which task handles are ordered is implementation defined (see Section 5.5.7.6 on page 580).

- **OMPT thread states**: The set of OMPT thread states supported is implementation defined (see Section 4.4.4.26 on page 452).

- **OMP_SCHEDULE environment variable**: if the value does not conform to the specified format then the result is implementation defined (see Section 6.1 on page 601).

- **OMP_NUM_THREADS environment variable**: if any value of the list specified leads to a number of threads that is greater than the implementation can support, or if any value is not a positive integer, then the result is implementation defined (see Section 6.2 on page 602).

- **OMP_DYNAMIC environment variable**: if the value is neither **true** nor **false** the behavior is implementation defined (see Section 6.3 on page 603).

- **OMP_PROC_BIND environment variable**: if the value is not **true**, **false**, or a comma separated list of **master**, **close**, or **spread**, the behavior is implementation defined. The behavior is also implementation defined if an initial thread cannot be bound to the first place in the OpenMP place list (see Section 6.4 on page 604).

- **OMP_PLACES environment variable**: the meaning of the numbers specified in the environment variable and how the numbering is done are implementation defined. The precise definitions of the abstract names are implementation defined. An implementation may add implementation-defined abstract names as appropriate for the target platform. When creating a place list of n elements by appending the number *n* to an abstract name, the determination of which resources to include in the place list is implementation defined. When requesting more resources than available, the length of the place list is also implementation defined. The behavior of the program is implementation defined when the execution environment cannot map a numerical value (either explicitly defined or implicitly derived from an interval) within the **OMP_PLACES** list to a processor on the target platform, or if it maps to an unavailable processor. The behavior is also implementation defined when the **OMP_PLACES** environment variable is defined using an abstract name (see Section 6.5 on page 605).

- **OMP_STACKSIZE environment variable**: if the value does not conform to the specified format or the implementation cannot provide a stack of the specified size then the behavior is implementation defined (see Section 6.6 on page 607).

- **OMP_WAIT_POLICY environment variable**: the details of the **ACTIVE** and **PASSIVE** behaviors are implementation defined (see Section 6.7 on page 608).

- **OMP_MAX_ACTIVE_LEVELS environment variable**: if the value is not a non-negative integer or is greater than the number of parallel levels an implementation can support then the behavior is implementation defined (see Section 6.8 on page 608).

- **OMP_NESTED environment variable**: if the value is neither `true` nor `false` the behavior is implementation defined (see Section 6.9 on page 609).
- **Conflicting OMP_NESTED and OMP_MAX_ACTIVE_LEVELS environment variables**: if both environment variables are set, the value of `OMP_NESTED` is `false`, and the value of `OMP_MAX_ACTIVE_LEVELS` is greater than 1, the behavior is implementation defined (see Section 6.9 on page 609).
- **OMP_THREAD_LIMIT environment variable**: if the requested value is greater than the number of threads an implementation can support, or if the value is not a positive integer, the behavior of the program is implementation defined (see Section 6.10 on page 610).
- **OMP_DISPLAY_AFFINITY environment variable**: for all values of the environment variables other than `TRUE` or `FALSE`, the display action is implementation defined (see Section 6.13 on page 612).
- **OMP_AFFINITY_FORMAT environment variable**: if the value does not conform to the specified format then the result is implementation defined (see Section 6.14 on page 613).
- **OMP_TARGET_OFFLOAD environment variable**: the support of `disabled` is implementation defined (see Section 6.17 on page 615).
- **OMP_DEBUG environment variable**: if the value is neither `disabled` nor `enabled` the behavior is implementation defined (see Section 6.20 on page 617).

This page intentionally left blank

APPENDIX B

Features History

This appendix summarizes the major changes between OpenMP API versions since version 2.5.

B.1 Deprecated Features

The following features have been deprecated in Version 5.0.

- The *nest-var* ICV, the **OMP_NESTED** environment variable, and the **omp_set_nested** and **omp_get_nested** routines were deprecated.
- Lock hints were renamed to synchronization hints. The following lock hint type and constants were deprecated:
  - the C/C++ type **omp_lock_hint_t** and the Fortran kind **omp_lock_hint_kind**;
  - the constants **omp_lock_hint_none**, **omp_lock_hint_uncontended**, **omp_lock_hint_contended**, **omp_lock_hint_nonspeculative**, and **omp_lock_hint_speculative**.

B.2 Version 4.5 to 5.0 Differences

- The memory model was extended to distinguish different types of flush operations according to specified flush properties (see Section 1.4.4 on page 25) and to define a happens before order based on synchronizing flush operations (see Section 1.4.5 on page 27).

- Various changes throughout the specification were made to provide initial support of C11, C++11, C++14, C++17 and Fortran 2008 (see Section 1.7 on page 31).

- Fortran 2003 is now fully supported (see Section 1.7 on page 31).

- The **requires** directive (see Section 2.4 on page 60) was added to support applications that require implementation-specific features.

- The *target-offload-var* internal control variable (see Section 2.5 on page 63) and the **OMP_TARGET_OFFLOAD** environment variable (see Section 6.17 on page 615) were added to support runtime control of the execution of device constructs.

- Control over whether nested parallelism is enabled or disabled was integrated into the *max-active-levels-var* internal control variable (see Section 2.5.2 on page 66), the default value of which is now implementation defined, unless determined according to the values of the **OMP_NUM_THREADS** (see Section 6.2 on page 602) or **OMP_PROC_BIND** (see Section 6.4 on page 604) environment variables.

- Support for array shaping (see Section 2.1.4 on page 43) and for array sections with non-unit strides in C and C++ (see Section 2.1.5 on page 44) was added to facilitate specification of discontiguous storage and the **target update** construct (see Section 2.12.6 on page 176) and the **depend** clause (see Section 2.17.11 on page 255) were extended to allow the use of shape-operators (see Section 2.1.4 on page 43).

- Iterators (see Section 2.1.6 on page 47) were added to support expressions in a list that expand to multiple expressions.

- The **metadirective** directive (see Section 2.3.4 on page 56) and **declare variant** directive (see Section 2.3.5 on page 58) were added to support selection of directive variants and declared function variants at a callsite, respectively, based on compile-time traits of the enclosing context.

- The **teams** construct (see Section 2.7 on page 82) was extended to support execution on the host device without an enclosing **target** construct (see Section 2.12.5 on page 170).

- The canonical loop form was defined for Fortran and, for all base languages, extended to permit non-rectangular loop nests (see Section 2.9.1 on page 95).

- The *relational-op* in the *canonical loop form* for C/C++ was extended to include **!=** (see Section 2.9.1 on page 95).

- The default loop schedule modifier for worksharing-loop constructs without the **static** schedule and the **ordered** clause was changed to **nonmonotonic** (see Section 2.9.2 on page 101).

- The collapse of associated loops that are imperfectly nested loops was defined for the worksharing-loop (see Section 2.9.2 on page 101), **simd** (see Section 2.9.3.1 on page 110), **taskloop** (see Section 2.10.2 on page 140) and **distribute** (see Section 2.9.4.2 on page 123) constructs.

- The **simd** construct (see Section 2.9.3.1 on page 110) was extended to accept the **if**, **nontemporal** and **order(concurrent)** clauses and to allow the use of **atomic** constructs within it.
- The **loop** construct and the **order(concurrent)** clause were added to support compiler optimization and parallelization of loops for which iterations may execute in any order, including concurrently (see Section 2.9.5 on page 128).
- The **scan** directive (see Section 2.9.6 on page 132) and the **inscan** modifier for the **reduction** clause (see Section 2.19.5.4 on page 300) were added to support inclusive and exclusive scan computations.
- To support task reductions, the **task** (see Section 2.10.1 on page 135) and **target** (see Section 2.12.5 on page 170) constructs were extended to accept the **in_reduction** clause (see Section 2.19.5.6 on page 303), the **taskgroup** construct (see Section 2.17.6 on page 232) was extended to accept the **task_reduction** clause Section 2.19.5.5 on page 303), and the **task** modifier was added to the **reduction** clause (see Section 2.19.5.4 on page 300).
- The **affinity** clause was added to the **task** construct (see Section 2.10.1 on page 135) to support hints that indicate data affinity of explicit tasks.
- The **detach** clause for the **task** construct (see Section 2.10.1 on page 135) and the **omp_fulfill_event** runtime routine (see Section 3.5.1 on page 396) were added to support execution of detachable tasks.
- To support taskloop reductions, the **taskloop** (see Section 2.10.2 on page 140) and **taskloop simd** (see Section 2.10.3 on page 146) constructs were extended to accept the **reduction** (see Section 2.19.5.4 on page 300) and **in_reduction** (see Section 2.19.5.6 on page 303) clauses.
- The **taskloop** construct (see Section 2.10.2 on page 140) was added to the list of constructs that can be canceled by the **cancel** construct (see Section 2.18.1 on page 263)).
- To support mutually exclusive inout sets, a **mutexinoutset** *dependence-type* was added to the **depend** clause (see Section 2.10.6 on page 149 and Section 2.17.11 on page 255).
- Predefined memory spaces (see Section 2.11.1 on page 152), predefined memory allocators and allocator traits (see Section 2.11.2 on page 152) and directives, clauses (see Section 2.11 on page 152 and API routines (see Section 3.7 on page 406) to use them were added to support different kinds of memories.
- The semantics of the **use_device_ptr** clause for pointer variables was clarified and the **use_device_addr** clause for using the device address of non-pointer variables inside the **target data** construct was added (see Section 2.12.2 on page 161).
- To support reverse offload, the **ancestor** modifier was added to the **device** clause for **target** constructs (see Section 2.12.5 on page 170).

- To reduce programmer effort implicit declare target directives for some functions (C, C++, Fortran) and subroutines (Fortran) were added (see Section 2.12.5 on page 170 and Section 2.12.7 on page 180).

- The **target update** construct (see Section 2.12.6 on page 176) was modified to allow array sections that specify discontiguous storage.

- The **to** and **from** clauses on the **target update** construct (see Section 2.12.6 on page 176), the **depend** clause on task generating constructs (see Section 2.17.11 on page 255), and the **map** clause (see Section 2.19.7.1 on page 315) were extended to allow any lvalue expression as a list item for C/C++.

- Support for nested **declare target** directives was added (see Section 2.12.7 on page 180).

- New combined constructs **master taskloop** (see Section 2.13.7 on page 192), **parallel master** (see Section 2.13.6 on page 191), **parallel master taskloop** (see Section 2.13.9 on page 195), **master taskloop simd** (see Section 2.13.8 on page 194), **parallel master taskloop simd** (see Section 2.13.10 on page 196) were added.

- The **depend** clause was added to the **taskwait** construct (see Section 2.17.5 on page 230).

- To support acquire and release semantics with weak memory ordering, the **acq_rel**, **acquire**, and **release** clauses were added to the **atomic** construct (see Section 2.17.7 on page 234) and **flush** construct (see Section 2.17.8 on page 242), and the memory ordering semantics of implicit flushes on various constructs and runtime routines were clarified (see Section 2.17.8.1 on page 246).

- The **atomic** construct was extended with the **hint** clause (see Section 2.17.7 on page 234).

- The **depend** clause (see Section 2.17.11 on page 255) was extended to support iterators and to support depend objects that can be created with the new **depobj** construct.

- Lock hints were renamed to synchronization hints, and the old names were deprecated (see Section 2.17.12 on page 260).

- To support conditional assignment to lastprivate variables, the **conditional** modifier was added to the **lastprivate** clause (see Section 2.19.4.5 on page 288).

- The description of the **map** clause was modified to clarify the mapping order when multiple *map-types* are specified for a variable or structure members of a variable on the same construct. The **close** *map-type-modifier* was added as a hint for the runtime to allocate memory close to the target device (see Section 2.19.7.1 on page 315).

- The capability to map C/C++ pointer variables and to assign the address of device memory that is mapped by an array section to them was added. Support for mapping of Fortran pointer and allocatable variables, including pointer and allocatable components of variables, was added (see Section 2.19.7.1 on page 315).

- The **defaultmap** clause (see Section 2.19.7.2 on page 324) was extended to allow selecting the data-mapping or data-sharing attributes for any of the scalar, aggregate, pointer or allocatable classes on a per-region basis. Additionally it accepts the **none** parameter to support the requirement that all variables referenced in the construct must be explicitly mapped or privatized.

- The **declare mapper** directive was added to support mapping of data types with direct and indirect members (see Section 2.19.7.3 on page 326).

- The **omp_set_nested** (see Section 3.2.10 on page 343) and **omp_get_nested** (see Section 3.2.11 on page 344) routines and the **OMP_NESTED** environment variable (see Section 6.9 on page 609) were deprecated.

- The **omp_get_supported_active_levels** routine was added to query the number of active levels of parallelism supported by the implementation (see Section 3.2.15 on page 349).

- Runtime routines **omp_set_affinity_format** (see Section 3.2.30 on page 364), **omp_get_affinity_format** (see Section 3.2.31 on page 366), **omp_set_affinity** (see Section 3.2.32 on page 367), and **omp_capture_affinity** (see Section 3.2.33 on page 368) and environment variables **OMP_DISPLAY_AFFINITY** (see Section 6.13 on page 612) and **OMP_AFFINITY_FORMAT** (see Section 6.14 on page 613) were added to provide OpenMP runtime thread affinity information.

- The **omp_get_device_num** runtime routine (see Section 3.2.37 on page 372) was added to support determination of the device on which a thread is executing.

- The **omp_pause_resource** and **omp_pause_resource_all** runtime routines were added to allow the runtime to relinquish resources used by OpenMP (see Section 3.2.43 on page 378 and Section 3.2.44 on page 380).

- Support for a first-party tool interface (see Section 4 on page 419) was added.

- Support for a third-party tool interface (see Section 5 on page 533) was added.

- Support for controlling offloading behavior with the **OMP_TARGET_OFFLOAD** environment variable was added (see Section 6.17 on page 615).

- Stubs for Runtime Library Routines (previously Appendix A) were moved to a separate document.

- Interface Declarations (previously Appendix B) were moved to a separate document.

B.3 Version 4.0 to 4.5 Differences

- Support for several features of Fortran 2003 was added (see Section 1.7 on page 31 for features that are still not supported).

- A parameter was added to the **ordered** clause of the worksharing-loop construct (see Section 2.9.2 on page 101) and clauses were added to the **ordered** construct (see

Section 2.17.9 on page 250) to support doacross loop nests and use of the **simd** construct on loops with loop-carried backward dependences.

- The **linear** clause was added to the worksharing-loop construct (see Section 2.9.2 on page 101).

- The **simdlen** clause was added to the **simd** construct (see Section 2.9.3.1 on page 110) to support specification of the exact number of iterations desired per SIMD chunk.

- The **priority** clause was added to the **task** construct (see Section 2.10.1 on page 135) to support hints that specify the relative execution priority of explicit tasks. The **omp_get_max_task_priority** routine was added to return the maximum supported priority value (see Section 3.2.42 on page 377) and the **OMP_MAX_TASK_PRIORITY** environment variable was added to control the maximum priority value allowed (see Section 6.16 on page 615).

- Taskloop constructs (see Section 2.10.2 on page 140 and Section 2.10.3 on page 146) were added to support nestable parallel loops that create OpenMP tasks.

- To support interaction with native device implementations, the **use_device_ptr** clause was added to the **target data** construct (see Section 2.12.2 on page 161) and the **is_device_ptr** clause was added to the **target** construct (see Section 2.12.5 on page 170).

- The **nowait** and **depend** clauses were added to the **target** construct (see Section 2.12.5 on page 170) to improve support for asynchronous execution of **target** regions.

- The **private**, **firstprivate** and **defaultmap** clauses were added to the **target** construct (see Section 2.12.5 on page 170).

- The **declare target** directive was extended to allow mapping of global variables to be deferred to specific device executions and to allow an *extended-list* to be specified in C/C++ (see Section 2.12.7 on page 180).

- To support unstructured data mapping for devices, the **target enter data** (see Section 2.12.3 on page 164) and **target exit data** (see Section 2.12.4 on page 166) constructs were added and the **map** clause (see Section 2.19.7.1 on page 315) was updated.

- To support a more complete set of device construct shortcuts, the **target parallel** (see Section 2.13.16 on page 203), target parallel worksharing-loop (see Section 2.13.17 on page 205), target parallel worksharing-loop SIMD (see Section 2.13.18 on page 206), and **target simd** (see Section 2.13.20 on page 209), combined constructs were added.

- The **if** clause was extended to take a *directive-name-modifier* that allows it to apply to combined constructs (see Section 2.15 on page 220).

- The **hint** clause was adddded to the **critical** construct (see Section 2.17.1 on page 223).

- The **source** and **sink** dependence types were added to the **depend** clause (see Section 2.17.11 on page 255) to support doacross loop nests.

- The implicit data-sharing attribute for scalar variables in **target** regions was changed to **firstprivate** (see Section 2.19.1.1 on page 270).
- Use of some C++ reference types was allowed in some data sharing attribute clauses (see Section 2.19.4 on page 282).
- Semantics for reductions on C/C++ array sections were added and restrictions on the use of arrays and pointers in reductions were removed (see Section 2.19.5.4 on page 300).
- The **ref**, **val**, and **uval** modifiers were added to the **linear** clause (see Section 2.19.4.6 on page 290).
- Support was added to the map clauses to handle structure elements (see Section 2.19.7.1 on page 315).
- Query functions for OpenMP thread affinity were added (see Section 3.2.24 on page 358 to Section 3.2.29 on page 363).
- The lock API was extended with lock routines that support storing a hint with a lock to select a desired lock implementation for a lock's intended usage by the application code (see Section 3.3.2 on page 385).
- Device memory routines were added to allow explicit allocation, deallocation, memory transfers and memory associations (see Section 3.6 on page 397).
- C/C++ Grammar (previously Appendix B) was moved to a separate document.

B.4 Version 3.1 to 4.0 Differences

- Various changes throughout the specification were made to provide initial support of Fortran 2003 (see Section 1.7 on page 31).
- C/C++ array syntax was extended to support array sections (see Section 2.1.5 on page 44).
- The **proc_bind** clause (see Section 2.6.2 on page 80), the **OMP_PLACES** environment variable (see Section 6.5 on page 605), and the **omp_get_proc_bind** runtime routine (see Section 3.2.23 on page 357) were added to support thread affinity policies.
- SIMD directives were added to support SIMD parallelism (see Section 2.9.3 on page 110).
- Implementation defined task scheduling points for untied tasks were removed (see Section 2.10.6 on page 149).
- Device directives (see Section 2.12 on page 160), the **OMP_DEFAULT_DEVICE** environment variable (see Section 6.15 on page 615), and the **omp_set_default_device**, **omp_get_default_device**, **omp_get_num_devices**, **omp_get_num_teams**,

`omp_get_team_num`, and `omp_is_initial_device` routines were added to support execution on devices.

- The `taskgroup` construct (see Section 2.17.6 on page 232) was added to support more flexible deep task synchronization.

- The `atomic` construct (see Section 2.17.7 on page 234) was extended to support atomic swap with the `capture` clause, to allow new atomic update and capture forms, and to support sequentially consistent atomic operations with a new `seq_cst` clause.

- The `depend` clause (see Section 2.17.11 on page 255) was added to support task dependences.

- The `cancel` construct (see Section 2.18.1 on page 263), the `cancellation point` construct (see Section 2.18.2 on page 267), the `omp_get_cancellation` runtime routine (see Section 3.2.9 on page 342) and the `OMP_CANCELLATION` environment variable (see Section 6.11 on page 610) were added to support the concept of cancellation.

- The `reduction` clause (see Section 2.19.5.4 on page 300) was extended and the `declare reduction` construct (see Section 2.19.5.7 on page 304) was added to support user defined reductions.

- The `OMP_DISPLAY_ENV` environment variable (see Section 6.12 on page 611) was added to display the value of ICVs associated with the OpenMP environment variables.

- Examples (previously Appendix A) were moved to a separate document.

B.5 Version 3.0 to 3.1 Differences

- The *bind-var* ICV has been added, which controls whether or not threads are bound to processors (see Section 2.5.1 on page 64). The value of this ICV can be set with the `OMP_PROC_BIND` environment variable (see Section 6.4 on page 604).

- The *nthreads-var* ICV has been modified to be a list of the number of threads to use at each nested parallel region level and the algorithm for determining the number of threads used in a parallel region has been modified to handle a list (see Section 2.6.1 on page 78).

- The `final` and `mergeable` clauses (see Section 2.10.1 on page 135) were added to the `task` construct to support optimization of task data environments.

- The `taskyield` construct (see Section 2.10.4 on page 147) was added to allow user-defined task scheduling points.

- The `atomic` construct (see Section 2.17.7 on page 234) was extended to include `read`, `write`, and `capture` forms, and an `update` clause was added to apply the already existing form of the `atomic` construct.

- Data environment restrictions were changed to allow **intent(in)** and **const**-qualified types for the **firstprivate** clause (see Section 2.19.4.4 on page 286).
- Data environment restrictions were changed to allow Fortran pointers in **firstprivate** (see Section 2.19.4.4 on page 286) and **lastprivate** (see Section 2.19.4.5 on page 288).
- New reduction operators **min** and **max** were added for C and C++ (see Section 2.19.5 on page 293).
- The nesting restrictions in Section 2.20 on page 328 were clarified to disallow closely-nested OpenMP regions within an **atomic** region. This allows an **atomic** region to be consistently defined with other OpenMP regions so that they include all code in the atomic construct.
- The **omp_in_final** runtime library routine (see Section 3.2.22 on page 356) was added to support specialization of final task regions.
- Descriptions of examples (previously Appendix A) were expanded and clarified.
- Replaced incorrect use of **omp_integer_kind** in Fortran interfaces with **selected_int_kind(8)**.

B.6 Version 2.5 to 3.0 Differences

- The definition of active **parallel** region has been changed: in Version 3.0 a **parallel** region is active if it is executed by a team consisting of more than one thread (see Section 1.2.2 on page 2).
- The concept of tasks has been added to the OpenMP execution model (see Section 1.2.5 on page 10 and Section 1.3 on page 20).
- The OpenMP memory model now covers atomicity of memory accesses (see Section 1.4.1 on page 23). The description of the behavior of **volatile** in terms of **flush** was removed.
- In Version 2.5, there was a single copy of the *nest-var*, *dyn-var*, *nthreads-var* and *run-sched-var* internal control variables (ICVs) for the whole program. In Version 3.0, there is one copy of these ICVs per task (see Section 2.5 on page 63). As a result, the **omp_set_num_threads**, **omp_set_nested** and **omp_set_dynamic** runtime library routines now have specified effects when called from inside a **parallel** region (see Section 3.2.1 on page 334, Section 3.2.7 on page 340 and Section 3.2.10 on page 343).
- The *thread-limit-var* ICV has been added, which controls the maximum number of threads participating in the OpenMP program. The value of this ICV can be set with the **OMP_THREAD_LIMIT** environment variable and retrieved with the **omp_get_thread_limit** runtime library routine (see Section 2.5.1 on page 64, Section 3.2.14 on page 348 and Section 6.10 on page 610).

- The *max-active-levels-var* ICV has been added, which controls the number of nested active **parallel** regions. The value of this ICV can be set with the **OMP_MAX_ACTIVE_LEVELS** environment variable and the **omp_set_max_active_levels** runtime library routine, and it can be retrieved with the **omp_get_max_active_levels** runtime library routine (see Section 2.5.1 on page 64, Section 3.2.16 on page 350, Section 3.2.17 on page 351 and Section 6.8 on page 608).

- The *stacksize-var* ICV has been added, which controls the stack size for threads that the OpenMP implementation creates. The value of this ICV can be set with the **OMP_STACKSIZE** environment variable (see Section 2.5.1 on page 64 and Section 6.6 on page 607).

- The *wait-policy-var* ICV has been added, which controls the desired behavior of waiting threads. The value of this ICV can be set with the **OMP_WAIT_POLICY** environment variable (see Section 2.5.1 on page 64 and Section 6.7 on page 608).

- The rules for determining the number of threads used in a **parallel** region have been modified (see Section 2.6.1 on page 78).

- In Version 3.0, the assignment of iterations to threads in a loop construct with a **static** schedule kind is deterministic (see Section 2.9.2 on page 101).

- In Version 3.0, a loop construct may be associated with more than one perfectly nested loop. The number of associated loops is controlled by the **collapse** clause (see Section 2.9.2 on page 101).

- Random access iterators, and variables of unsigned integer type, may now be used as loop iterators in loops associated with a loop construct (see Section 2.9.2 on page 101).

- The schedule kind **auto** has been added, which gives the implementation the freedom to choose any possible mapping of iterations in a loop construct to threads in the team (see Section 2.9.2 on page 101).

- The **task** construct (see Section 2.10 on page 135) has been added, which provides a mechanism for creating tasks explicitly.

- The **taskwait** construct (see Section 2.17.5 on page 230) has been added, which causes a task to wait for all its child tasks to complete.

- Fortran assumed-size arrays now have predetermined data-sharing attributes (see Section 2.19.1.1 on page 270).

- In Version 3.0, static class members variables may appear in a **threadprivate** directive (see Section 2.19.2 on page 274).

- Version 3.0 makes clear where, and with which arguments, constructors and destructors of private and threadprivate class type variables are called (see Section 2.19.2 on page 274, Section 2.19.4.3 on page 285, Section 2.19.4.4 on page 286, Section 2.19.6.1 on page 310 and Section 2.19.6.2 on page 312).

- In Version 3.0, Fortran allocatable arrays may appear in **private**, **firstprivate**, **lastprivate**, **reduction**, **copyin** and **copyprivate** clauses (see Section 2.19.2 on page 274, Section 2.19.4.3 on page 285, Section 2.19.4.4 on page 286, Section 2.19.4.5 on page 288, Section 2.19.5.4 on page 300, Section 2.19.6.1 on page 310 and Section 2.19.6.2 on page 312).

- In Fortran, **firstprivate** is now permitted as an argument to the **default** clause (see Section 2.19.4.1 on page 282).

- For list items in the **private** clause, implementations are no longer permitted to use the storage of the original list item to hold the new list item on the master thread. If no attempt is made to reference the original list item inside the **parallel** region, its value is well defined on exit from the **parallel** region (see Section 2.19.4.3 on page 285).

- The runtime library routines **omp_set_schedule** and **omp_get_schedule** have been added; these routines respectively set and retrieve the value of the *run-sched-var* ICV (see Section 3.2.12 on page 345 and Section 3.2.13 on page 347).

- The **omp_get_level** runtime library routine has been added, which returns the number of nested **parallel** regions enclosing the task that contains the call (see Section 3.2.18 on page 352).

- The **omp_get_ancestor_thread_num** runtime library routine has been added, which returns, for a given nested level of the current thread, the thread number of the ancestor (see Section 3.2.19 on page 353).

- The **omp_get_team_size** runtime library routine has been added, which returns, for a given nested level of the current thread, the size of the thread team to which the ancestor belongs (see Section 3.2.20 on page 354).

- The **omp_get_active_level** runtime library routine has been added, which returns the number of nested active **parallel** regions enclosing the task that contains the call (see Section 3.2.21 on page 355).

- In Version 3.0, locks are owned by tasks, not by threads (see Section 3.3 on page 381).

This page intentionally left blank

Index

Symbols
`_OPENMP` macro, 49, 611–613

A
acquire flush, 27
affinity, 80
`allocate`, 156, 158
array sections, 44
array shaping, 43
`atomic`, 234
`atomic` construct, 621
attribute clauses, 282
attributes, data-mapping, 314
attributes, data-sharing, 269
`auto`, 105

B
`barrier`, 226
barrier, implicit, 228

C
`cancel`, 263
cancellation constructs, 263
    `cancel`, 263
    `cancellation point`, 267
`cancellation point`, 267
canonical loop form, 95
`capture`, `atomic`, 234
clauses
    `allocate`, 158
    attribute data-sharing, 282
    `collapse`, 101, 102
    `copyin`, 310
    `copyprivate`, 312
    data copying, 309
    data-sharing, 282
    `default`, 282
    `defaultmap`, 324
    `depend`, 255
    `firstprivate`, 286
    `hint`, 260
    `if` Clause, 220
    `in_reduction`, 303
    `lastprivate`, 288
    `linear`, 290
    `map`, 315
    `private`, 285
    `reduction`, 300
    `schedule`, 103
    `shared`, 283
    `task_reduction`, 303
combined constructs, 185
    `master taskloop`, 192
    `master taskloop simd`, 194
    `parallel loop`, 186
    `parallel master`, 191
    `parallel master taskloop`, 195
    `parallel master taskloop simd`, 196
    `parallel sections`, 188
    `parallel workshare`, 189

parallel worksharing-loop
    construct, 185
parallel worksharing-loop SIMD
    construct, 190
target parallel, 203
target parallel loop, 208
target parallel worksharing-loop
    construct, 205
target parallel worksharing-loop SIMD
    construct, 206
target simd, 209
target teams, 210
target teams distribute, 211
target teams distribute parallel
    worksharing-loop construct, 215
target teams distribute parallel
    worksharing-loop SIMD
    construct, 216
target teams distribute simd,
    213
target teams loop construct, 214
teams distribute, 197
teams distribute parallel
    worksharing-loop construct, 200
teams distribute parallel
    worksharing-loop SIMD
    construct, 201
teams distribute simd, 198
teams loop, 202
compilation sentinels, 50
compliance, 31
conditional compilation, 49
constructs
    atomic, 234
    barrier, 226
    cancel, 263
    cancellation constructs, 263
    cancellation point, 267
    combined constructs, 185
    critical, 223
    declare mapper, 326
    declare target, 180
    depobj, 254

device constructs, 160
distribute, 120
distribute parallel do, 125
distribute parallel do simd,
    126
distribute parallel for, 125
distribute parallel for simd,
    126
distribute parallel worksharing-loop
    construct, 125
distribute parallel worksharing-loop
    SIMD construct, 126
distribute simd, 123
do *Fortran*, 101
flush, 242
for, *C/C++*, 101
loop, 128
master, 221
master taskloop, 192
master taskloop simd, 194
ordered, 250
parallel, 74
parallel do *Fortran*, 185
parallel for *C/C++*, 185
parallel loop, 186
parallel master, 191
parallel master taskloop, 195
parallel master taskloop simd,
    196
parallel sections, 188
parallel workshare, 189
parallel worksharing-loop
    construct, 185
parallel worksharing-loop SIMD
    construct, 190
sections, 86
simd, 110
single, 89
target, 170
target data, 161
target enter data, 164
target exit data, 166
target parallel, 203

`target parallel do`, 205
`target parallel do simd`, 206
`target parallel for`, 205
`target parallel for simd`, 206
`target parallel loop`, 208
target parallel worksharing-loop construct, 205
target parallel worksharing-loop SIMD construct, 206
`target simd`, 209
`target teams`, 210
`target teams distribute`, 211
target teams distribute parallel worksharing-loop construct, 215
target teams distribute parallel worksharing-loop SIMD construct, 216
`target teams distribute simd`, 213
`target teams loop`, 214
`target update`, 176
`task`, 135
`taskgroup`, 232
tasking constructs, 135
`taskloop`, 140
`taskloop simd`, 146
`taskwait`, 230
`taskyield`, 147
`teams`, 82
`teams distribute`, 197
teams distribute parallel worksharing-loop construct, 200
teams distribute parallel worksharing-loop SIMD construct, 201
`teams distribute simd`, 198
`teams loop`, 202
`workshare`, 92
worksharing, 86
worksharing-loop construct, 101
worksharing-loop SIMD construct, 114
controlling OpenMP thread affinity, 80
`copyin`, 310

`copyprivate`, 312
`critical`, 223

D

data copying clauses, 309
data environment, 269
data terminology, 12
data-mapping rules and clauses, 314
data-sharing attribute clauses, 282
data-sharing attribute rules, 269
`declare mapper`, 326
`declare reduction`, 304
`declare simd`, 116
`declare target`, 180
`declare variant`, 58
`default`, 282
`defaultmap`, 324
`depend`, 255
depend object, 254
`depobj`, 254
deprecated features, 627
device constructs
    `declare mapper`, 326
    `declare target`, 180
    device constructs, 160
    `distribute`, 120
    distribute parallel worksharing-loop construct, 125
    distribute parallel worksharing-loop SIMD construct, 126
    `distribute simd`, 123
    `target`, 170
    `target update`, 176
    `teams`, 82
device data environments, 24, 164, 166
device directives, 160
device memory routines, 397
directive format, 38
directives, 37
    `allocate`, 156
    `declare mapper`, 326
    `declare reduction`, 304
    `declare simd`, 116
    `declare target`, 180

`declare variant`, 58
memory management directives, 152
`metadirective`, 56
`requires`, 60
`scan` Directive, 132
`threadprivate`, 274
variant directives, 51
`distribute`, 120
distribute parallel worksharing-loop construct, 125
distribute parallel worksharing-loop SIMD construct, 126
`distribute simd`, 123
`do`, *Fortran*, 101
`do simd`, 114
`dynamic`, 105
dynamic thread adjustment, 620

E
environment variables, 601
    `OMP_AFFINITY_FORMAT`, 613
    `OMP_ALLOCATOR`, 618
    `OMP_CANCELLATION`, 610
    `OMP_DEBUG`, 617
    `OMP_DEFAULT_DEVICE`, 615
    `OMP_DISPLAY_AFFINITY`, 612
    `OMP_DISPLAY_ENV`, 611
    `OMP_DYNAMIC`, 603
    `OMP_MAX_ACTIVE_LEVELS`, 608
    `OMP_MAX_TASK_PRIORITY`, 615
    `OMP_NESTED`, 609
    `OMP_NUM_THREADS`, 602
    `OMP_PLACES`, 605
    `OMP_PROC_BIND`, 604
    `OMP_SCHEDULE`, 601
    `OMP_STACKSIZE`, 607
    `OMP_TARGET_OFFLOAD`, 615
    `OMP_THREAD_LIMIT`, 610
    `OMP_TOOL`, 616
    `OMP_TOOL_LIBRARIES`, 617
    `OMP_WAIT_POLICY`, 608
event, 396
event callback registration, 425
event callback signatures, 459
event routines, 396
execution environment routines, 334
execution model, 20

F
features history, 627
`firstprivate`, 286
fixed source form conditional compilation sentinels, 50
fixed source form directives, 41
`flush`, 242
flush operation, 25
flush synchronization, 27
flush-set, 25
`for`, *C/C++*, 101
`for simd`, 114
frames, 454
free source form conditional compilation sentinel, 50
free source form directives, 41

G
glossary, 2
`guided`, 105

H
happens before, 27
header files, 332
history of features, 627

I
ICVs (internal control variables), 63
`if` Clause, 220
implementation, 619
implementation terminology, 16
implicit barrier, 228
implicit flushes, 246
`in_reduction`, 303
include files, 332
internal control variables, 619
internal control variables (ICVs), 63
introduction, 1
iterators, 47

L

lastprivate, 288
linear, 290
list item privatization, 279
lock routines, 381
loop, 128
loop terminology, 8

M

map, 315
master, 221
master taskloop, 192
master taskloop simd, 194
memory allocators, 152
memory management, 152
memory management directives
    memory management directives, 152
memory management routines, 406
memory model, 23
memory spaces, 152
metadirective, 56
modifying and retrieving ICV values, 68
modifying ICVs, 66

N

nesting of regions, 328
normative references, 31

O

OMP_AFFINITY_FORMAT, 613
omp_alloc, 413
OMP_ALLOCATOR, 618
OMP_CANCELLATION, 610
omp_capture_affinity, 368
OMP_DEBUG, 617
OMP_DEFAULT_DEVICE, 615
omp_destroy_allocator, 410
omp_destroy_lock, 387
omp_destroy_nest_lock, 387
OMP_DISPLAY_AFFINITY, 612
omp_display_affinity, 367
OMP_DISPLAY_ENV, 611
OMP_DYNAMIC, 603
omp_free, 414
omp_fulfill_event, 396
omp_get_active_level, 355
omp_get_affinity_format, 366
omp_get_ancestor_thread_num, 353
omp_get_cancellation, 342
omp_get_default_allocator, 412
omp_get_default_device, 370
omp_get_device_num, 372
omp_get_dynamic, 341
omp_get_initial_device, 376
omp_get_level, 352
omp_get_max_active_levels, 351
omp_get_max_task_priority, 377
omp_get_max_threads, 336
omp_get_nested, 344
omp_get_num_devices, 371
omp_get_num_places, 358
omp_get_num_procs, 338
omp_get_num_teams, 373
omp_get_num_threads, 335
omp_get_partition_num_places, 362
omp_get_partition_place_nums, 363
omp_get_place_num, 362
omp_get_place_num_procs, 359
omp_get_place_proc_ids, 360
omp_get_proc_bind, 357
omp_get_schedule, 347
omp_get_supported_active
        _levels, 349
omp_get_team_num, 374
omp_get_team_size, 354
omp_get_thread_limit, 348
omp_get_thread_num, 337
omp_get_wtick, 395
omp_get_wtime, 394
omp_in_final, 356
omp_in_parallel, 339
omp_init_allocator, 409
omp_init_lock, 384, 385
omp_init_nest_lock, 384, 385
omp_is_initial_device, 375

OMP_MAX_ACTIVE_LEVELS, 608
OMP_MAX_TASK_PRIORITY, 615
OMP_NESTED, 609
OMP_NUM_THREADS, 602
omp_pause_resource, 378
omp_pause_resource_all, 380
OMP_PLACES, 605
OMP_PROC_BIND, 604
OMP_SCHEDULE, 601
omp_set_affinity_format, 364
omp_set_default_allocator, 411
omp_set_default_device, 369
omp_set_dynamic, 340
omp_set_lock, 388
omp_set_max_active_levels, 350
omp_set_nest_lock, 388
omp_set_nested, 343
omp_set_num_threads, 334
omp_set_schedule, 345
OMP_STACKSIZE, 607
omp_target_alloc, 397
omp_target_associate_ptr, 403
omp_target_disassociate_ptr, 405
omp_target_free, 399
omp_target_is_present, 400
omp_target_memcpy, 400
omp_target_memcpy_rect, 402
OMP_TARGET_OFFLOAD, 615
omp_test_lock, 392
omp_test_nest_lock, 392
OMP_THREAD_LIMIT, 610
OMP_TOOL, 616
OMP_TOOL_LIBRARIES, 617
omp_unset_lock, 390
omp_unset_nest_lock, 390
OMP_WAIT_POLICY, 608
ompd_bp_device_begin, 598
ompd_bp_device_end, 599
ompd_bp_parallel_begin, 594
ompd_bp_parallel_end, 595
ompd_bp_task_begin, 595
ompd_bp_task_end, 596
ompd_bp_thread_begin, 597

ompd_bp_thread_end, 597
ompd_callback_device_host
    _fn_t, 554
ompd_callback_get_thread
    _context_for_thread_id
    _fn_t, 547
ompd_callback_memory_alloc
    _fn_t, 546
ompd_callback_memory_free
    _fn_t, 546
ompd_callback_memory_read
    _fn_t, 551
ompd_callback_memory_write
    _fn_t, 553
ompd_callback_print_string
    _fn_t, 556
ompd_callback_sizeof_fn_t, 549
ompd_callback_symbol_addr
    _fn_t, 550
ompd_callbacks_t, 556
ompd_dll_locations_valid, 536
ompd_dll_locations, 535
ompt_callback_buffer
    _complete_t, 487
ompt_callback_buffer
    _request_t, 486
ompt_callback_cancel_t, 481
ompt_callback_control
    _tool_t, 495
ompt_callback_dependences_t, 468
ompt_callback_dispatch_t, 465
ompt_callback_device
    _finalize_t, 484
ompt_callback_device
    _initialize_t, 482
ompt_callback_flush_t, 480
ompt_callback_implicit
    _task_t, 471
ompt_callback_master_t, 473
ompt_callback_mutex
    _acquire_t, 476
ompt_callback_mutex_t, 477
ompt_callback_nest_lock_t, 479

`ompt_callback_parallel_begin_t`, 461
`ompt_callback_parallel_end_t`, 463
`ompt_callback_sync_region_t`, 474
`ompt_callback_device_load_t`, 484
`ompt_callback_device_unload_t`, 486
`ompt_callback_target_data_op_t`, 488
`ompt_callback_target_map_t`, 492
`ompt_callback_target_submit_t`, 494
`ompt_callback_target_t`, 490
`ompt_callback_task_create_t`, 467
`ompt_callback_task_dependence_t`, 470
`ompt_callback_task_schedule_t`, 470
`ompt_callback_thread_begin_t`, 459
`ompt_callback_thread_end_t`, 460
`ompt_callback_work_t`, 464
OpenMP compliance, 31
`ordered`, 250

P
`parallel`, 74
`parallel loop`, 186
`parallel master construct`, 191
`parallel master taskloop`, 195
`parallel master taskloop simd`, 196
`parallel sections`, 188
`parallel workshare`, 189
parallel worksharing-loop construct, 185
parallel worksharing-loop SIMD construct, 190
`private`, 285

R
`read, atomic`, 234
`reduction`, 300
reduction clauses, 293
release flush, 27

`requires`, 60
`runtime`, 105
runtime library definitions, 332
runtime library routines, 331

S
`scan` Directive, 132
scheduling, 149
`sections`, 86
`shared`, 283
`simd`, 110
SIMD Directives, 110
Simple Lock Routines, 382
`single`, 89
stand-alone directives, 42
`static`, 104
strong flush, 25
synchronization constructs, 223
synchronization constructs and clauses, 223
synchronization hints, 260
synchronization terminology, 9

T
`target`, 170
`target data`, 161
target memory routines, 397
`target parallel`, 203
`target parallel loop`, 208
target parallel worksharing-loop construct construct, 205
target parallel worksharing-loop SIMD construct, 206
`target simd`, 209
`target teams`, 210
`target teams distribute`, 211
target teams distribute parallel worksharing-loop construct, 215
target teams distribute parallel worksharing-loop SIMD construct, 216
`target teams distribute simd`, 213
`target teams loop`, 214
`target update`, 176
`task`, 135

Index 645

task scheduling, 149
task_reduction, 303
taskgroup, 232
tasking constructs, 135
tasking terminology, 10
taskloop, 140
taskloop simd, 146
taskwait, 230
taskyield, 147
teams, 82
teams distribute, 197
teams distribute parallel worksharing-loop
 construct, 200
teams distribute parallel worksharing-loop
 SIMD construct, 201
teams distribute simd, 198
teams loop, 202
thread affinity, 80
threadprivate, 274
timer, 394
timing routines, 394
tool control, 415
tool initialization, 423
tool interfaces definitions, 419, 534
tools header files, 419, 534
tracing device activity, 427

U
update, atomic, 234

V
variables, environment, 601
variant directives, 51

W
wait identifier, 456
wall clock timer, 394
workshare, 92
worksharing
 constructs, 86
  parallel, 185
  scheduling, 109
worksharing constructs, 86
worksharing-loop construct, 101

worksharing-loop SIMD construct, 114
write, atomic, 234

Made in the USA
Las Vegas, NV
16 November 2021